AN EXEGETICAL SUMMARY OF
2 CORINTHIANS

AN EXEGETICAL SUMMARY OF 2 CORINTHIANS

Second Edition

David Abernathy

SIL International

Second Edition
© 2007, 2008 by SIL International

Library of Congress Catalog Card Number: 2008923532
ISBN: 978-155671-206-7

Printed in the United States of America

All Rights Reserved
No part of this publication may be reproduced, stored in a retrieval system, or transmitted in any form or by any means without the express permission of SIL International. However, brief excerpts, generally understood to be within the limits of fair use, may be quoted without written permission.

Copies of this and other publications
of SIL International may be obtained from

International Academic Bookstore
SIL International
7500 West Camp Wisdom Road
Dallas, TX 75236-5699, USA

Voice: 972-708-7404
Fax: 972-708-7363
academic_books@sil.org
www.ethnologue.com

In memory of John David West, linguist, translator, friend.

"But we have this treasure in jars of clay to show that this all-surpassing power is from God and not from us." (2 Cor. 4:7)

PREFACE

Exegesis is concerned with the interpretation of a text. Exegesis of the New Testament involves determining the meaning of the Greek text. Translators must be especially careful and thorough in their exegesis of the New Testament in order to accurately communicate its message in the vocabulary, grammar, and literary devices of another language. Questions occurring to translators as they study the Greek text are answered by summarizing how scholars have interpreted the text. This is information that should be considered by translators as they make their own exegetical decisions regarding the message they will communicate in their translations.

The Semi-Literal Translation

As a basis for discussion, a semi-literal translation of the Greek text is given so that the reasons for different interpretations can best be seen. When one Greek word is translated into English by several words, these words are joined by hyphens. There are a few times when clarity requires that a string of words joined by hyphens have a separate word, such as "not" (μή), inserted in their midst. In this case, the separate word is surrounded by spaces between the hyphens. When alternate translations of a Greek word are given, these are separated by slashes.

The Text

Variations in the Greek text are noted under the heading TEXT. The base text for the summary is the text of the fourth revised edition of *The Greek New Testament,* published by the United Bible Societies, which has the same text as the twenty-sixth edition of the *Novum Testamentum Graece* (Nestle-Aland). The versions that follow different variations are listed without evaluating their choices.

The Lexicon

The meaning of a key word in context is the first question to be answered. Words marked with a raised letter in the semi-literal translation are treated separately under the heading LEXICON. First, the lexicon form of the Greek word is given. Within the parentheses following the Greek word is the location number where, in the author's judgment, this word is defined in the *Greek-English Lexicon of the New Testament Based on Semantic Domains* (Louw and Nida 1988). When a semantic domain includes a translation of the particular verse being treated, **LN** in bold type indicates that specific translation. If the specific reference for the verse is listed in *A Greek-English Lexicon of the New Testament and Other Early Christian Literature* (Bauer, Arndt, Gingrich, and Danker 1979), the outline location and page number is given. Then English equivalents of the Greek word are given to show how it is translated by commentators who offer their own translations of the whole text and, after a semicolon, all the versions in the list of abbreviations for translations. When reference is made to "all versions," it refers to only the versions in the list of translations. Sometimes further comments are made about the meaning of the word or the significance of a verb's tense, voice, or mood.

The Questions

Under the heading QUESTION, a question is asked that comes from examining the Greek text under consideration. Typical questions concern the identity of an implied actor or object of an event word, the antecedent of a pronominal reference, the connection indicated by a relational word, the meaning of a genitive construction, the meaning of figurative language, the function of a rhetorical question, the identification of an ambiguity, and the presence of implied information that is needed to understand the passage correctly. Background information is also considered for a proper understanding of a passage. Although not all implied information and background information is made explicit in a translation, it is important to consider it so that the translation will not be stated in such a way that prevents a reader from arriving at the proper interpretation. The question is answered with a summary of what commentators have said. If there are contrasting differences of opinion, the different interpretations are numbered and the commentaries that support each are listed. Differences that are not treated by many of the commentaries often are not numbered, but are introduced with a contrastive 'Or' at the beginning of the sentence. No attempt has been made to select which interpretation is best.

In listing support for various statements of interpretation, the author is often faced with the difficult task of matching the different terminologies used in commentaries with the terminology he has adopted. Sometimes he can only infer the position of a commentary from incidental remarks. This book, then, includes the author's interpretation of the views taken in the various commentaries. General statements are followed by specific statements, which indicate the author's understanding of the pertinent relationships, actors, events, and objects implied by that interpretation.

The Use of This Book

This book does not replace the commentaries that it summarizes. Commentaries contain much more information about the meaning of words and passages. They often contain arguments for the interpretations that are taken and they may have important discussions about the discourse features of the text. In addition, they have information about the historical, geographical, and cultural setting. Translators will want to refer to at least four commentaries as they exegete a passage. However, since no one commentary contains all the answers translators need, this book will be a valuable supplement. It makes more sources of exegetical help available than most translators have access to. Even if they had all the books available, few would have the time to search through all of them for the answers.

When many commentaries are studied, it soon becomes apparent that they frequently disagree in their interpretations. That is the reason why so many answers in this book are divided into two or more interpretations. The reader's initial reaction may be that all of these different interpretations complicate exegesis rather than help it. However, before translating a passage, a translator needs to know exactly where there is a problem of interpretation and what the exegetical options are.

ABBREVIATIONS

COMMENTARIES AND REFERENCE BOOKS

AB   Furnish, Victor Paul. *2 Corinthians.* The Anchor Bible, edited by W. F. Albright and D. N. Freedman. Garden City, N.Y.: Doubleday, 1984.

BAGD   Bauer, Walter. *A Greek–English Lexicon of the New Testament and Other Early Christian Literature.* Translated and adapted from the 5th ed., 1958 by William F. Arndt and F. Wilbur Gingrich. 2d English ed. revised and augmented by F. Wilbur Gingrich and Frederick W. Danker. Chicago: University of Chicago Press, 1979.

Car   Carson, D. A. *From Triumphalism to Maturity: An Exposition of 2 Corinthians 10–13.* Grand Rapids: Baker, 1984.

EBC   Harris, Murray J. *2 Corinthians.* In the Expositor's Bible Commentary, edited by Frank E. Gaebelein. Vol. 10. Grand Rapids: Zondervan, 1976.

EGT   Bernard, J. H. *The Second Epistle to the Corinthians.* In the Expositor's Greek Testament, edited by W. Robertson Nicoll. Vol. 3. 1900. Reprint. Grand Rapids: Eerdmans, 1967.

He   Héring, Jean. *The Second Epistle of Saint Paul to the Corinthians.* Translated by A. W. Heathcote and P. J. Allcock. London: Epworth Press, 1967.

HNTC   Barrett, C. K. *A Commentary on the Second Epistle to the Corinthians.* Harper's New Testament Commentaries, edited by Henry Chadwick. New York: Harper & Row, 1973.

Ho   Hodge, Charles. *An Exposition of the Second Epistle to the Corinthians.* Thornapple Commentaries. 1859. Reprint. Grand Rapids: Baker, 1980.

ICC1   Plummer, Alfred. *A Critical and Exegetical Commentary on the Second Epistle of St Paul to the Corinthians.* The International Critical Commentary, edited by S. R. Driver, A. Plummer, and C. A. Briggs. 1915. Reprint. Edinburgh: T. & T. Clark, 1970.

ICC2   Thrall, Margaret E. *A Critical and Exegetical Commentary on the Second Epistle of St Paul to the Corinthians.* Vol. 1. The International Critical Commentary, edited by J. A. Emerton, C. E. B. Cranfield, and G. N. Stanton. Edinburgh: T. & T. Clark, 1994.

LN   Louw, Johannes P., and Eugene A. Nida. *Greek–English Lexicon of the New Testament Based on Semantic Domains.* New York: United Bible Societies, 1988.

Lns   Lenski, R. C. H. *The Interpretation of St. Paul's First and Second Epistles to the Corinthians.* Minneapolis: Augsburg, 1963.

My   Meyer, Heinrich August Wilhelm. *Critical and Exegetical Handbook to the Epistles to the Corinthians.* Translated from the 5th ed. by D. Douglas Bannerman. Revised and edited by William P. Dickson. Meyer's Commentary on the New Testament. New York: Funk & Wagnalls, 1890.

NAC   Garland, David E. *2 Corinthians.* New American Commentary. Nashville: Broadman and Holman, 1999.

NCBC   Bruce, F. F. *1 and 2 Corinthians.* New Century Bible Commentary, edited by M. Black. Grand Rapids: Eerdmans, 1971.

NIC1   Hughes, Philip Edgcumbe. *Paul's Second Epistle to the Corinthians.* The New International Commentary on the New Testament, edited by F. F. Bruce. Grand Rapids: Eerdmans, 1962.

NIC2   Barnett, Paul. *The Second Epist0le to the Corinthians.* The New International Commentary on the New Testament, edited by Gordon D. Fee. Grand Rapids: Eerdmans, 1997.

NTC   Kistemaker, Simon J. *Exposition of the Second Epistle to Corinthians.* New Testament Commentary. Grand Rapids: Baker, 1997.

SP   Lambrecht, Jan. *Second Corinthians.* Sacra Pagina Series, vol. 8, edited by Daniel J. Harrington. Collegeville, Minnesota: The Liturgical Press, 1999.

TG   Bratcher, Robert G. *A Translator's Guide to Paul's Second Letter to the Corinthians.* Helps for Translators. London: United Bible Societies, 1983.

TH   Omanson, Roger L. and John Ellington. *A Handbook on Paul's Second Letter to the Corinthians.* Helps for Translators. London: United Bible Societies, 1996.

TNTC   Kruse, Colin. *The Second Epistle of Paul to the Corinthians.* The Tyndale New Testament Commentaries. Grand Rapids: Eerdmans, 1987.

WBC   Martin, Ralph P. *2 Corinthians.* Word Biblical Commentary, vol. 40. Waco, Texas: Word, 1986.

JOURNAL ARTICLES

Aber NEO   Abernathy, David. 2001. Paul's thorn in the flesh: A messenger of Satan? *Neotestamentica* 35/1-2 (2001), 69-79.

Aber NOT1   Abernathy, David. 2000. Exegetical problems in 2 Corinthians 3. *Notes On Translation,* 14/4: 44-56.

Aber NOT2   Abernathy, David. 2001. Paul's ministry of reconciliation: Exegeting and translating 2 Corinthians 5:11-6:2. *Notes On Translation,* 14/4: 44-56.

Dumbrell   Dumbrell, William J. 1986. Paul's use of Exodus 34 in 2 Corinthians 3. In *God Who Is Rich In Mercy: Essays Presented to Dr. D. B. Knox.* Ed. Peter O'Brien and David G. Peterson. Homebush West NSW Australia: Lancer.

Dunn	Dunn, J. D. G. 1970. 2 Cor. 3: The Lord is the Spirit. *Journal of Theological Studies.* 21:309–20.
Hafemann	Hafemann, S. J. 1992. The Glory and the Veil of Moses in 2 Cor. 3:7–14: An Example of Paul's Contextual Exegesis of the OT – A proposal. *Horizons in Biblical Theology,* 14/1:31–49.
Hanson	Hanson, A. T. 1980. The Midrash in 2 Corinthians 3: A Reconsideration. *Journal for the Study of the New Testament* 9:2–28.
Kim	Kim, Seyoon. 1997. 2 Cor. 5:11–21 and the Origin of Paul's Concept of 'Reconciliation'. *Novum Testamentum,* 39:360–84.
Lambrecht	Lambrecht, Jan. 1983. Transformation in 2 Cor. 3:18. *Biblica 64,* 2:243–354.
Provence	Provence, Thomas E. 1982. Who is Sufficient for These Things? An exegesis of 2 Corinthians 2:15–3:18. *Novum Testamentum XXIV,* 1:54–81.
Van Unnik	Van Unnik, W.C. 1973. 'With unveiled face': An exegesis of 2 Corinthians 3:12–18. In *Sparsa collecta: The collected essays of W. C. Van Unnik,* part 1. *Novum Testamentum,* suppl. 29, 192–210. Leiden: E. J. Brill. (Originally published in 1964 in *Novum Testamentum* 6:153–69.)
Westerholm	Westerholm, Stephen. 1984. Letter and Spirit: The Foundation of Pauline Ethics. *New Testament Studies,* 30:229–248.
Wong	Wong, Emily. 1985. The Lord is the Spirit. *Ephemerides Theological Lovanienses* 61:1:48–72.

OTHERS

Danker	Danker, Fredrick W. Exegesis of 2 Corinthians 5:14–21. In *Interpreting 2 Corinthians 5:14–21: An Exercise in Hermeneutics* (105–28), ed. Jack P. Lewis. Lewiston NY: Edwin Mellen Press. 1989.
Lewis	Lewis, Jack P. Exegesis of 2 Corinthians 5:14–21 (129–42). In *Interpreting 2 Corinthians 5:14–21: An Exercise in Hermeneutics,* ed. Jack P. Lewis. Lewiston NY: Edwin Mellen Press, 1989.
Marshall	Marshall, I. Howard. The Meaning of reconciliation. In *Unity and Diversity in New Testament Theology: Essays in Honor of George E. Ladd,* (117–32), ed. Robert A. Guelich. Grand Rapids: Eerdmans, 1978.
Mead	Mead, Richard T. Exegesis of 2 Corinthians 5:14–21. In *Interpreting 2 Corinthians 5:14–21: An Exercise in Hermeneutics* (143–62), ed. Jack P. Lewis. Lewiston NY: Edwin Mellen Press. 1989.

Murphy-O'Connor Murphy-O'Connor, Jerome. *The Theology of the Second Letter to the Corinthians.* New York: Cambridge University Press, 1991.
Stagg Stagg, Frank. Exegesis of 2 Corinthians 5:14–21. In *Interpreting 2 Corinthians 5:14–21: An Exercise in Hermeneutics* (163–92), ed. Jack P. Lewis. Lewiston NY: Edwin Mellen Press. 1989.

GREEK TEXT AND TRANSLATIONS

GNT   The Greek New Testament. Edited by B. Aland, K Aland, J. Karavidopoulos, C. Martini, and B. Metzger. 4th ed. London, New York: United Bible Societies, 1993.
CEV   The Holy Bible, Contemporary English Version. New York: American Bible Society, 1995.
KJV   The Holy Bible. Authorized (or King James) Version. 1611.
NAB   The New American Bible. Camden, New Jersey: Thomas Nelson, 1971.
NIV   The Holy Bible, New International Version. Grand Rapids: Zondervan, 1984.
NJB   The New Jerusalem Bible. Garden City, New York: Doubleday, 1985.
NLT   The Holy Bible, New Living Translation. Wheaton, Ill.: Tyndale House Publishers, 1996.
NRSV The Holy Bible: New Revised Standard Version. New York: Oxford University Press, 1989.
REB   The Revised English Bible. Oxford: Oxford University Press and Cambridge University Press, 1989.
TEV   Good News Bible, Today's English Version. 2d ed. New York: American Bible Society, 1992.
TNT   The Translator's New Testament. London: British and Foreign Bible Society, 1973.

GRAMMATICAL TERMS

act.	active	opt.	optative
fut.	future	pass.	passive
impera.	imperative	perf.	perfect
indic.	indicative	pres.	present
infin.	infinitive	subj.	subjunctive
mid.	middle		

BACKGROUND AND OVERVIEW OF 2 CORINTHIANS

Paul's eighteen month ministry in Corinth began during the time when Gallio was proconsul, which tells us that he was there from mid to late 50 to early 52. He then ministered in Ephesus for three years, from 52 to 55, and toward the end of that period and while still at Ephesus wrote canonical 1 Corinthians. In that letter he references an earlier letter he had written after having left Corinth (1 Cor 5:9). Then in 2 Corinthians he refers to a "sorrowful letter" (2 Cor 2:3), one which he wrote in lieu of making another "painful visit," apparently referring to a visit he had made after having written canonical 1 Corinthians and during which confrontation and unresolved conflict prompted him to leave in order to avoid worsening his relationship with the Corinthian church. Titus was the bearer of that letter. Then Paul wrote canonical 2 Corinthians, and probably in late 56, and a short time later went on to Corinth, where he spent the winter of 56/57. If this scenario is accurate, we have at least three visits and four epistles to Corinth in the space of about six and a half years. Of these four epistles only two have survived.

Not all scholars agree with the scenario represented here. Some would equate the sorrowful letter with canonical 1 Corinthians, and others would equate it with chapters 10-13 of canonical 2 Corinthians. Some scholars see 2 Corinthians as a composite of separate letters consisting of chapters 8 and 9 as one letter, 10-13 as another, and possibly 2:14-7:2 as a fragment of another inserted into the present text. A few see 6:14-7:2 as a non-Pauline insertion. Generally conservative scholars, and even some others, are able to explain perceived differences between those chapters or sections as being transitions within an integrated whole, based on vocabulary and themes common to all sections as well as textual evidence itself, which supports unity. The most serious challenge to the integrity of canonical 2 Corinthians comes from the sudden change of tone from the chapters 1-9 to chapters 10-13. While there is a change of tone between the two sections, it has been accounted for in various ways, including the possibility that Paul received fresh news from Corinth of troubles in that church. However the internal evidence is viewed, the textual evidence is decidedly in favor of the unity of the entire epistle, and no manuscript evidence indicates that the letter ever existed in any form other than as we have it now.

Judging from what Paul does and does not say in his epistle to the Romans, which was written from Corinth in early 57, it is assumed that 2 Corinthians probably had the effect Paul desired, since he gives no indication of continuing conflict or difficulty in that setting at that time. The fact that the epistle was preserved by the church is also evidence that it was well received on their part.

While 2 Corinthians was written to deal with problems in the church, and bears the marks of the strain of the extreme emotion under which Paul wrote it as evidenced by the numerous passages which are grammatically difficult and convoluted, it also contains unique theological treasures found nowhere else. His digressions on the new covenant, on the resurrection body, on the relation of weakness and suffering to glory and successful ministry, and on the theology of ministry itself are developed here as nowhere else in his writings. It also reveals Paul's personal struggles to an extent and depth not shown in any other epistle.

EXEGETICAL SUMMARY OF 2 CORINTHIANS

DISCOURSE UNIT: 1:1–9:15 [TNTC]. Paul's response to a crisis resolved.

DISCOURSE UNIT: 1:1–7:16 [EBC, EGT]. Paul's explanation of his conduct and apostolic ministry [EBC], the obedience of the Corinthians to the instructions of the first epistle [EGT].

DISCOURSE UNIT: 1:1–11 [AB, EBC, HNTC, ICC1, ICC2, NIC2, NTC, TG, TH; NJB]. The topic is the introduction [EBC, HNTC, NIC2, NTC, TG, TH], the letter opening [AB], epistolary introduction [ICC1], prescript and introductory blessing [ICC2], address and greetings, thanksgiving [NJB].

DISCOURSE UNIT: 1:1–2 [AB, EBC, HNTC, ICC1, NIC2, NTC, TNTC, WBC; NAB, NLT, NRSV]. The topic is the address [AB, HNTC, NTC, WBC], the salutation [EBC, NIC2; NRSV], the apostolic salutation [ICC1], the greeting [TNTC], greeting to the church [NAB], greetings from Paul [NLT]. This epistle opens with a format typical of correspondence of that day, A to B, and greetings or a blessing [EGT, ICC2, NIC2, TG, TNTC, WBC]. This format is like the address on an envelope [NTC]. The author is named in the nominative case, recipients in the dative case, and greetings again in the nominative [Lns]. Paul also customarily adds any co-sender, in this case Timothy [TG].

1:1 **Paul, an apostle**[a] **of Christ Jesus**

TEXT—Instead of Χριστοῦ Ἰησοῦ 'Christ Jesus', some manuscripts have Ἰησοῦ Χριστοῦ 'Jesus Christ'. GNT does not mention this alternative. Only CEV, KJV, and NAB read 'Jesus Christ'.

LEXICON—a. ἀπόστολος (LN 53.74) (BAGD 3. p. 99): 'apostle' [AB, BAGD, HNTC, ICC2, LN, Lns, NTC, WBC; all versions], 'special messenger' [LN].

QUESTION—What is meant by ἀπόστολος 'apostle'?

The term apostle means a special representative [ICC1], an authorized representative or ambassador who can speak and act for another [NTC, TG]. An apostle is a divinely appointed emissary who speaks with the authority of God himself as did the OT prophets [NIC1]. An apostle is God's servant set apart and commissioned for ministry [WBC]. An apostle was primarily a missionary, commissioned by an encounter with Christ [ICC2]. Paul is an emissary of Christ [TNTC], and by using the term 'apostle' was making a claim of equality with the twelve chosen by Christ [EBC]. As an ambassador who represents his superior, Paul is accountable to Christ for his care of the Corinthians [Lns].

QUESTION—How are the nouns related in the genitive construction ἀπόστολος Χριστοῦ Ἰησοῦ 'apostle of Christ Jesus'?

It means that Christ Jesus is the author or source of Paul's office [HNTC], and Paul's authority is derived from Christ [NIC2]. Paul is appointed, commissioned, and sent by Christ [NTC]. It means that Paul's apostolate is inseparably associated with the person and work of Jesus Christ [NIC1]. An apostle of Christ Jesus would refer only to those who have been commissioned by means of an encounter with the risen Christ [ICC2].

QUESTION—What is indicated by the order of the names 'Christ Jesus' in this verse? (The names are listed in the opposite order 'Jesus Christ', by CEV, KJV, NAB.)
1. The order Christ Jesus emphasizes the title 'Christ' and this refers to his messianic office [ICC2, NIC2].
2. There is no difference in meaning between 'Christ Jesus' and 'Jesus Christ' [AB] and in this combination 'Christ' is a proper name, not a title [TG].

by[a] the will[b] of God

LEXICON—a. διά with genitive object (LN 89.76) (BAGD A.III.1.d. p. 180): 'by' [AB, BAGD, ICC2, LN, WBC; all versions], 'through' [BAGD, HNTC, LN, Lns, NTC], 'by means of' [BAGD, LN]. The phrase διὰ θελήματος θεοῦ 'by the will of God' is translated 'chosen by God' [CEV], 'appointed by God' [NLT].
b. θέλημα (LN 30.59) (BAGD 2.b. p 354): 'will' [AB, BAGD, HNTC, ICC2, LN, Lns, NTC, WBC; all versions except CEV, NLT], 'intent, purpose, plan' [LN]. This noun is also translated as a passive verb: 'to be chosen' [CEV], 'to be appointed' [NLT].

QUESTION—What relationship is indicated by διά 'by'?
It indicates that the will of God is the reason Paul became an apostle [AB, Lns, NIC1, NTC, TNTC, WBC], and by which his ministry is directed [AB]. Paul's apostleship is by divine decree [ICC1], it comes from divine initiative and not human initiative [AB, HNTC, ICC1, ICC2, Lns, NIC1, NIC2]. It indicates that God is the agent of the choosing and the source of Paul's authority over the Corinthians [EBC, He, HNTC]. God commissioned Paul by means of the revelation of Christ at his conversion [EBC, He].

and Timothy the brother,[a]

LEXICON—a. ἀδελφός (LN 11.23) (BAGD 2. p. 16): 'brother' [AB, BAGD, HNTC, ICC2, Lns, WBC; all versions except CEV, REB], 'follower' [CEV], 'colleague' [REB], 'brother Christian' [HNTC], 'fellow believer, Christian brother' [LN]. The definite article with this noun is variously represented as 'the' [Lns], 'our' [KJV, NIV, NJB, NLT, NRSV, REB, TEV], 'his' [AB, ICC2, WBC; NAB, TNT].

QUESTION—With respect to whom does Paul use the term 'brother' of Timothy?
1. It is an inclusive term, referring to his relationship with Paul and to the Corinthians [He, ICC1, ICC2, Lns, NIC1, NTC, TG; CEV]: Timothy, our brother.
2. It refers to Timothy's relationship with Paul [HNTC, ICC2; NAB], or his status as Paul's co-worker [AB; REB] or Paul's envoy [WBC]: Timothy, my brother.

QUESTION—Does the inclusion of Timothy's name in this introduction imply that he was a co-author of the letter?
1. Paul is the author of the letter, and Timothy is a co-sender, but not a co-author [AB, Ho, ICC1, ICC2, NIC1, NTC, WBC]. Paul included Timothy's name in order to strengthen his relationship to the Corinthian church [NTC]. Timothy's name is included to strengthen the fraternal appeal of the letter by his agreement with its contents, and because he had helped to found the church and had recently been to Corinth [Lns]. The inclusion of Timothy's name gives it a second witness, much like a copy to the file in contemporary practice [AB]. His name is mentioned because he was present when the letter was written [ICC2, NIC2] and may have discussed its contents with Paul [ICC2].
2. Paul and Timothy are identified as co-authors [TG].

to the church[a] of God being[b] in Corinth
LEXICON—a. ἐκκλησία (LN 11.32) (BAGD 4.b, 4.e.α. p. 241): 'church' [AB, BAGD, HNTC, ICC2, LN, Lns, NTC, WBC; all versions], 'congregation' [BAGD, LN].
b. pres. act. participle of εἰμί 'to be'. This participle is translated so as to identify the church: 'which is' [AB, ICC2, Lns; KJV], 'that is' [HNTC, NTC, WBC; NAB, NRSV]. It is left untranslated by CEV, NIV, NJB, NLT, REB, TEV, TNT.
QUESTION—How are the nouns related in the genitive construction τῇ ἐκκλησίᾳ τοῦ θεοῦ 'the church of God'?
The construction indicates possession: the church belonging to God [EBC, HNTC, ICC1, LN, Lns, NIC1, TG, TNTC]. The church belongs to God, who brought it into being, and not to any apostle or sect [NIC1]. The genitive indicates possession and special relationship to God [TNTC]. It belongs to God and everything about it relates to God who is its creator, protector, ruler, and comforter [Lns]. The genitive construction 'of God' reminds us that the church is an eschatological reality that will ultimately be manifested as the people of God [NIC2]. The genitive reminds them that the creator of the world is the founder of their congregation [ICC1]. The term 'of God' indicates that the believers were viewed as a continuation and extension of God's chosen people of the OT [NTC].
QUESTION—Is the term 'church' used in a local sense or its universal sense?
It refers to the particular congregation, not the universal church [ICC1, ICC2]. It is the plenary assembly of all the local Christians, not just the various house meetings [BAGD (4.b. p. 241), NIC2]. The church in Corinth is a local expression of the universal church [BAGD (4.e.α. p. 241), EBC, NIC1, NIC2, NTC, WBC].
QUESTION—What was the location and importance of Corinth in the Graeco-Roman world?
Corinth was situated on the isthmus between northern Greece and the Peloponnesus with two harbors very close by, which made it a central hub of

commerce and travel in the ancient world. It became the leading commercial center of southern Greece and also hosted the biennial Isthmian games which attracted large crowds. Corinth had been a Greek city until its destruction by Rome in 146 BC. It was rebuilt as a Roman colony in 44 BC by order of Julius Caesar and became the capital of the Roman province of Achaia. Its reputation for licentiousness was based primarily on the earlier history of the Greek Corinth with its temples to Apollo and Aphrodite, but the later Roman city had its own reputation for immorality as well [NIC2, WBC].

with[a] all the saints[b] being in all Achaia:
LEXICON—a. σύν (LN 89.107): 'with' [HNTC, ICC2, LN, Lns, NTC; KJV], 'together with' [LN; NIV, REB], 'and' [WBC; CEV, NAB, NJB, NLT, TEV, TNT], 'including' [AB; NRSV].
   b. ἅγιος (LN 11.27) (BAGD 2.d.β p. 10): The plural form is translated 'saints' [AB, BAGD, HNTC, Lns, NTC, WBC; KJV, NIV, NRSV], 'God's people' [LN; CEV, REB, TEV, TNT], 'God's holy people' [NJB], 'the holy people' [ICC2], 'holy ones' [NAB], 'Christians' [NLT]. This adjective, which normally means 'holy' in the singular, is used as a substantive 'saints' when occurring in the plural [LN]. The plural is virtually synonymous with the word 'church' [HNTC, NIC2, TG].
QUESTION—What relationship is indicated by σύν 'with'?
   It was also intended for the churches in Athens and Cenchrea [EBC, NTC; and probably WBC; CEV, NAB, NJB, NLT, TEV, TNT, which translate it as 'and']. It was directed to every church that had been founded throughout the province [NTC]. The term 'with' is used instead of 'and' to indicate that not all topics addressed apply to all in Achaia, only certain ones such as the collection for the poor [Lns]. The letter is primarily intended for the people of Corinth, but also extended to neighbors in a secondary sense [AB, EGT, Lns]. It was intended to include other believers outside of Corinth who would be aware of and affected by what was happening in Corinth [ICC2]. It was intended for the Corinthians and for other believers in the province who were connected to the Corinthian church [Ho, My].
QUESTION—In what way were the Corinthians 'saints'?
   All believers are called saints because they are called of God to be his special possession [TNTC]. They were called saints because they were God's people [EBC, TG], holy by virtue of their calling to be set apart for God [ICC1]. They were saints by virtue of a dual separation, being separated from evil and also to God and to his service [NIC2, WBC]. They are saints by being chosen and called by God and set apart to serve him [HNTC]. They are saints by being sanctified and made right with God through Jesus Christ [Lns, NTC]. The church is made up of all who are regenerated and sanctified by the Holy Spirit because they belong to Christ [NIC1]. The focus is on the relationship to God and not a state of holiness [LN].

QUESTION—What geographical area is being referred to here?
1. It is the entire Roman province of Achaia (Greece), of which Corinth was the capital [EGT, He, Ho, My, NIC1, NTC, TG]. It is the larger district around Corinth, including Athens, possibly all of Greece [ICC1, Lns].
2. It is a smaller area reflecting the earlier designation of a smaller territory on the northern coast of the Peloponnese [WBC]. It is the city of Corinth and adjacent districts but not the whole Roman province of Achaia [AB, HNTC, ICC2, TNTC]. It does not include Athens [AB, ICC2, TNTC, WBC].

1:2 Grace^a to you and peace^b from God our father and (from the) Lord Jesus Christ.

LEXICON—a. χάρις (LN 88.66) (BAGD 2.c. p. 877): 'grace' [AB, BAGD, HNTC, ICC2, LN, Lns, NTC, WBC; all versions except CEV], 'kindness' [LN], 'divine favor' [BAGD]. This noun is also translated as a verbal phrase: 'to be kind to' [CEV]. 'Grace' means favor, gracious assistance, and God's saving activity coming because of God's undeserved love prior to any activity on the part of man [ICC2]. It is God's care or love demonstrated by his ongoing acts of love, help, and provision [TNTC].
  b. εἰρήνη (LN 22.42, 25.248) (BAGD 2. p. 227): 'peace' [AB, HNTC, ICC2, LN (22.42, 25.248), Lns, NTC, WBC; all versions], 'freedom from worry' [LN (25.248)], 'tranquility' [LN (22.42)]. Paul has modified the customary Greek epistolary greeting χαίρειν to χάρις and then coupled it with the typical Hebrew greeting *shalom*, meaning 'welfare and health' [BAGD]. Paul is then wishing spiritual and material prosperity to his readers [NTC]. This peace comes as a result of grace [Ho, ICC1, ICC2, Lns]. Peace comes as a fruit of reconciliation and of God's redemption [HNTC].

QUESTION—Is there an implied verb in this verse?
  An implied optative verb is supplied: 'may it be (yours)' [TNT], 'may (God) give' [REB, TEV]. An implied indicative verb 'pray' is supplied along with a subjunctive verb in a dependent clause: 'I pray that he will be kind (to you)' [CEV]. An implied indicative verb is supplied: 'I wish you' [HNTC].

QUESTION—What is implied here about the relationship between God the Father and Jesus Christ?
  The fact that they are linked together as a single source of blessing by the use of the one preposition ἀπό 'from' indicates their equal status [EGT, ICC1, ICC2, Lns, NIC1, NIC2, WBC]. They are represented as beings of the same order [HNTC, ICC2]. The use of the title κύριος 'Lord' is an assertion of Christ's divinity [ICC1, Lns, NIC1, NIC2].

QUESTION—Is 'our' inclusive or exclusive?
  It is inclusive [TH].

DISCOURSE UNIT: 1:3–11 [AB, HNTC, ICC1, TNTC, WBC; CEV, NAB, NIV, NLT, NRSV, TEV]. The topic is blessing [AB], thanksgiving [HNTC, TNTC], the past experience of Paul reviewed [WBC], preamble of thanksgiving and hope [ICC1], the God of all comfort [NIV], God offers comfort to all [NLT], Paul gives thanks [CEV], Paul gives thanks to God [TEV], Paul's thanksgiving after affliction [NRSV].

DISCOURSE UNIT: 1:3–7 [EBC, NIC2, NTC, WBC]. The topic is gratitude for divine comfort [EBC], benediction [NIC2], distress and comfort [NTC], praise and encouragements [WBC].

1:3 Blessed[a] (is/be) the God and Father of our Lord Jesus Christ

LEXICON—a. εὐλογητός (LN 33.362) (BAGD p. 322): 'blessed' [AB, BAGD, HNTC, ICC2, Lns, NTC, WBC; KJV, NJB, NRSV], 'praised' [BAGD, LN; NAB]. This adjective is also translated as a noun: 'praise' [NIV, NLT, REB, TNT]; as a verb: 'to give thanks to' [TEV], 'to praise' [CEV]. Since there is no verb in the main clause of this sentence, one must be supplied in English translation: a subjunctive 'may he be blessed/may praise be to him' [ICC2, Lns, WBC; KJV, NAB, NIV, NJB, NRSV, REB, TNT]; or an indicative: 'he is blessed' [AB, HNTC]; or an imperative: 'praise/give thanks to' [CEV, TEV]. In the NT this word is used only with reference to God and expresses gratitude and adoration [Ho].

QUESTION—How are the nouns related in the genitive construction ὁ θεὸς καὶ πατὴρ τοῦ κυρίου ἡμῶν Ἰησοῦ Χριστοῦ 'the God and Father of our Lord Jesus Christ'?

    1. The words 'of the Lord Jesus Christ' are to be taken both with 'God' and with 'Father' [EGT, He, ICC1, ICC2, Lns, NIC1, NIC2, NTC, TG, WBC; NIV, NJB, NLT, NRSV, REB, TEV, TNT]: Blessed be God, who is both God and Father of the Lord Jesus Christ. With reference to Jesus' human nature since the incarnation, God was Jesus' God, but with reference to Jesus' eternal nature as deity, he was Jesus' father [Lns, NTC].

    2. The words 'of the Lord Jesus Christ' refer only to Father [AB, HNTC, My, TH; CEV, KJV, NAB]: Blessed be God, who is the Father of the Lord Jesus Christ.

the Father/father[a] of mercies[b] and God of all comfort[c]

LEXICON—a. πατήρ (LN 10.14) (BAGD 3.c.β. p. 636): 'Father' [AB, BAGD, HNTC, ICC2, LN, Lns, NTC, WBC; all versions except NLT], 'source' [NLT].

    b. οἰκτιρμός (LN 88.80, 88.81) (BAGD p. 561): 'mercy' [AB, BAGD, HNTC, ICC2, LN (88.80), WBC; KJV, NAB, NLT, NRSV], 'compassion' [BAGD, Lns, NTC; NIV], 'tender compassion' [LN (88.80)]. This plural noun is translated in the singular [ICC2; NIV, NLT] and in the plural [AB, HNTC, Lns, WBC; KJV, NAB, NRSV]. It is also translated as an adjective: 'merciful' [BAGD, LN (88.81); CEV, NJB, TEV, TNT], 'all-merciful' [REB].

    c. παράκλησις (LN 25.150) (BAGD 3. p. 618): 'comfort' [AB, BAGD, HNTC, ICC2, NTC; CEV, KJV, NIV, TNT], 'comforting' [Lns], 'consolation' [BAGD; NAB, NRSV, REB], 'encouragement' [LN, WBC;

NJB], 'help' [TEV]. This noun is also translated as a verb: 'to comfort' [NLT].

QUESTION—How are the nouns related in the genitive construction ὁ πατὴρ τῶν οἰκτιρμῶν 'the Father of mercies'?

The plural noun οἰκτιρμός in the genitive case is attributive and functions to modify 'Father' [BAGD, He, ICC1, LN (88.81), My, NIC1, TG; CEV, NJB, REB, TEV, TNT]: 'the merciful Father'. It is a way of saying 'most merciful', that is, one who is characterized by mercy [Ho], whose constant attitude is mercy [TG]. The genitive construction qualifies him as the Father who shows mercy [ICC1]. It indicates that God is the source or fount of all mercy [EGT, ICC2, NIC2, WBC]. It means that he is merciful as well as the source of all mercy [WBC], that he is the one from whom merciful acts proceed [EGT]. He is the epitome of mercy [HNTC] and full of compassion [ICC1]. The genitive indicates that God possesses mercy and therefore acts accordingly [Lns].

QUESTION—What is the function of the plural 'mercies'?
1. It is an Semitic idiomatic plural [HNTC, ICC1, ICC2, Lns, NIC1, NTC, TG]. It has a singular meaning, 'mercy' [ICC1, ICC2, Lns, NTC, TG; NIV, NLT].
2. It refers to multiple expressions of mercy [EGT, TNTC].

QUESTION—How are the nouns related in the genitive construction θεὸς πάσης παρακλήσεως 'God of all encouragement'?

God is the source of comfort [NIC2], the source of every incident of comforting [HNTC], the source of all consolation [ICC1, NIC1]. He is the God from who every consolation proceeds [EGT], the author of all consolation [Ho]. It is parallel to 'the Father of mercies' and means the God who gives all comfort [TG]. The genitive indicates what God gives, which is comfort [AB]. This genitive construction shows the effect that results from the mercy that God possesses [Lns, My]: the God who has mercy gives comfort.

1:4 **the-one-comforting[a] us in all[b] our affliction[c]**

LEXICON—a. pres. act. participle of παρακαλέω (LN 25.150) (BAGD 4. p. 617): 'to comfort' [AB, BAGD, HNTC, ICC2, Lns, NTC; CEV, KJV, NAB, NIV, NLT, TNT], 'to encourage' [BAGD, LN, WBC], 'to console' [LN; NRSV, REB], 'to help' [TEV], 'to support' [NJB], 'to cheer up' [BAGD]. This word is used in the sense of standing beside someone for the purpose of helping through a severe testing. The participle is in the timeless present tense, showing ongoing encouragement in all kinds of affliction [ICC1, NIC1]. This comfort came in the form of encouragement and strengthening grace in the midst of afflictions [TNTC]. This word appears four times in this verse, first in the participial form, then in the infinitive form, then as a noun (see also 1:3) and finally as a passive verb.

b. πᾶς (LN 59.23) (BAGD 1.c.β. p. 631): 'all' [BAGD, HNTC, ICC2, Lns, NTC, WBC; all versions except CEV, NJB], 'every' [LN; NJB], 'every one' [AB], not explicit [CEV].

c. θλῖψις (LN 22.2) (BAGD 1. p 362): 'affliction' [BAGD, HNTC, ICC2, Lns, NTC; NRSV], 'afflictions' [AB; NAB], 'hardship' [NJB], 'tribulation' [BAGD; KJV], 'trouble' [LN; CEV], 'troubles' [NIV, NLT, REB, TEV, TNT], 'trial' [WBC].

QUESTION—Who is included in the first person plural pronouns 'us, our, we' of this verse?

1. It is an epistolary plural and Paul is referring to himself [Ho, NIC2]. Paul contrasts himself with 'you' in 1:6–7, 11 [NIC2].
2. It is an exclusive plural: Paul is referring to himself and his colleagues in ministry, but not the Corinthians [HNTC, ICC2, My, TNTC]. It primarily refers to Paul, but refers to others as well [HNTC, My, NTC]. He is referring to himself and all missionaries, possibly all who suffer [ICC1]. It refers to anyone such as Paul and Timothy who does missionary work [TG].
3. It is inclusive plural and Paul is referring to himself as well as the Corinthians [AB, NTC, WBC]. Paul includes himself, Timothy, and the Corinthians [NTC]. Paul is referring to himself, the Corinthians, and all Christians who experience hostility because of the gospel [WBC]. This reference is inclusive, but the discussion of affliction in 1:5 is that which comes to him and his colleagues, not the Corinthians [AB].

so-as[a] to-enable[b] us to-comfort those in any[c] affliction

LEXICON—a. εἰς (LN 89.48, 89.57): 'so as' [Lns], 'so that' [AB, ICC2, WBC; all versions except KJV, NAB], 'that' [KJV], 'to the end that' [HNTC], 'in order to, for the purpose of' [LN (89.57)], 'and thus (enables us)' [NAB], 'with the result that, so that as a result' [LN (89.48)], not explicit [NTC].

b. pres. pass. (deponent = act.) infin. of δύναμαι (LN 74.5): 'to enable' [Lns, NTC; NAB], 'to be able' [AB, HNTC, ICC2, LN; KJV, NJB, NLT, NRSV, REB, TEV, TNT], 'can' [LN, WBC; CEV, NIV].

c. πᾶς (LN 59.24) (BAGD 1.a.γ. p. 631):'any' [AB, HNTC, ICC2, LN, NTC, WBC; KJV, NIV, NRSV, REB], 'every' [BAGD, Lns; NJB], 'any and every' [BAGD], 'all kinds' [TEV], not explicit [CEV, NAB, NLT].

QUESTION—What relationship is indicated by εἰς 'so as to'?

1. It indicates God's purpose in comforting us [AB, EGT, HNTC, Ho, ICC1, My, NIC1, NIC2, NTC].
2. It indicates the result of God comforting us [ICC2, TH, WBC; NAB]. Purpose and result merge when God is the agent [ICC2].

with/through[a] the comfort[b] by which we ourselves[c] are-comforted[d] by God.

LEXICON—a. διά with genitive object (LN 89.76): 'with' [NAB, NIV, NRSV, TNT], 'through' [AB, HNTC, ICC2, LN, NTC], 'by' [LN, WBC; KJV]

'by means of' [LN, Lns], 'because of' [NJB], 'using' [TEV], not explicit [CEV, NLT, REB].
b. παράκλησις: 'comfort'. See this word at 1:3.
c. αὐτός (LN 92.37): '(we) ourselves' [AB, HNTC, ICC2, Lns, NTC, WBC; all versions except CEV, NAB, NLT], '-self, -selves' [LN], not explicit [CEV, NAB, NLT].
d. pres. pass. indic. of παρακαλέω: 'to be comforted' [AB, HNTC, ICC2, Lns, NTC; KJV], 'to receive comfort' [NIV, TNT], 'to receive consolation' [NAB, REB], 'to be consoled' [NRSV], 'to receive help' [TEV], 'to receive encouragement' [NJB], 'to be encouraged' [WBC], not explicit [CEV]. This passive verb is also translated as an active verb with God as the subject and 'us' as the object: 'God has given us comfort' [NLT]. The verb is translated as a present tense: 'we are (comforted)' [ICC2, WBC; KJV, NRSV, REB]; as a present progressive: 'we receive (comfort)/we are being (comforted)' [HNTC, LN; NJB]; as a perfect tense: 'we have received (comfort)/have been (comforted)' [AB; NAB, NIV, NLT, TEV, TNT].

1:5 For^a just-as^b the sufferings^c of-Christ abound^d to us,
LEXICON—a. ὅτι (LN 89.33): 'for' [AB, HNTC, LN, WBC; KJV, NIV, NJB, NRSV, TNT], 'because' [ICC2, LN, NTC], 'seeing that' [Lns], 'you can be sure that' [NLT], not explicit [CEV, NAB, REB, TEV].
b. καθώς (LN 64.14) (BAGD 1. p. 391): 'just as' [AB, BAGD, ICC2, LN, NTC, WBC; NIV, NJB], 'as' [HNTC, Lns; KJV, NAB], not explicit [CEV]. The construction καθώς...οὕτως 'just as...so' is translated 'the more (this), the more (that)' [NLT].
c. πάθημα (LN 24.78) (BAGD 1. p. 602): 'suffering' [AB, BAGD, HNTC, ICC2, LN, Lns, NTC, WBC; all versions]. The phrase 'the sufferings of Christ' is also translated as a verb phrase: 'to suffer for Christ' [NLT].
d. pres. act. indic. of περισσεύω (LN **59.52**) (BAGD 1.a. β. p. 650): 'to abound' [**LN**, Lns; KJV], 'to be in abundance' [LN; NRSV], 'to be abundant' [NTC], 'to be present in abundance' [AB, BAGD], 'to share abundantly in' [BAGD], 'to overflow' [HNTC, WBC; NJB], 'to flow over' [NIV], 'to be overflowing' [AB], 'to exceed all measure and extend to (us)' [REB]. The phrase 'abound to us' is translated 'we share in the terrible (sufferings of Christ)' [CEV], 'we have shared much (in the sufferings of Christ)' [NAB], 'we have a share (in Christ's) many (sufferings)' [TEV], 'the flood (of Christ's sufferings) has overwhelmed us' [TNT], 'the more (we suffer)' [NLT].
QUESTION—What relationship is indicated by ὅτι 'for'?
 1. It indicates the reason for the previous verse [EBC, Ho, ICC2, NIC2]: God enables us to comfort others with the comfort we have received because the comfort of God overflows to us.
 2. It clarifies and explains the previous verse [AB, NTC]. It explains the affliction of 1:4 by referring to what Paul and others suffer as

representatives of Christ [NTC]. It clarifies how God's comfort of 1:4 is received, which is that as Christ's representatives share his suffering, he causes his comfort to flow through them into the lives of others who are suffering as well [AB].
3. It indicates that all of 1:5–7 is the grounds for the blessing and praise of 1:3–4 [Lns]: God is to be blessed for his mercy and comfort, ὅτι 'seeing that' he makes comfort abound where suffering abounds.

QUESTION—What are the 'sufferings of Christ' that Paul experienced?
1. They are sufferings that Christians endure for Christ [NTC, WBC; NLT].
2. They are the sufferings that Christ endured [AB, He, Lns, My, NIC2; CEV, NAB, NIV, REB, TEV, TNT]. Just as Christ suffered in his ministry, so Paul suffered in his ministry [NIC2]. Paul shares in what Christ suffered [CEV, NAB, TEV]. Christ's sufferings also overwhelm Paul [TNT].

so[a] also through[b] Christ our comfort[c] abounds[d]
LEXICON—a. οὕτω (LN 61.9) (BAGD 1.a. p. 597): 'so' [AB, BAGD, HNTC, ICC2, LN, Lns, NTC, WBC; all versions except CEV, NLT], not explicit [CEV]. The construction καθὼς...οὕτως 'just as...so' is also translated 'the more (this), the more (that)' [NLT].
b. διά with genitive object (LN 90.4): 'through' [AB, HNTC, ICC2, LN, Lns, NTC, WBC; all versions except CEV, KJV], 'by' [LN; KJV], not explicit [CEV]. Christ gives the comfort [CEV]. Christ is the intermediary through who God comforts us [TH].
c. παράκλησις: 'comfort' [AB, ICC2, NTC; NIV, NLT, TNT], 'comforting' [HNTC, Lns], 'wonderful comfort' [CEV], 'encouragement' [WBC; NJB], 'consolation' [KJV, NAB, NRSV, REB], 'God's great help' [TEV].
d. pres. act. indic. of περισσεύω: 'to abound' [Lns; KJV], 'to be abundant' [NTC; NRSV], 'to be abundantly available' [ICC2], 'to share abundantly' [NAB], 'to overflow' [HNTC, WBC; NIV, NJB], 'to be overflowing' [AB], not explicit [CEV]. The phrase 'encouragement abounds' is also translated 'God will shower us with his comfort' [NLT], 'our consolation has no limit' [REB], 'we share in God's great help' [TEV].

QUESTION—What relationship is indicated by the genitive ἡμῶν 'our'?
1. It is possessive, 'of us, our' [AB, EGT, He, HNTC, ICC2, Lns, NIC2; KJV, NIV, NRSV, REB]: our comfort abounds. It is implied that 'our comfort' abounds or overflows 'to you' that is, to the Corinthians [HNTC, ICC1].
2. It is objective, 'to us' [Lns, NTC]: God's comfort abounds to us.

1:6 If[a] we-are-being-afflicted,[b] (it is) for your comfort[c] and salvation;[d] if[a] we-are-being-comforted,[e] (it is) for your comfort[f]
TEXT—There is a considerable amount of variation among manuscripts in the order of words in 1:6–7. There is little difference in meaning except for the addition of the words καὶ σωτηρία 'and salvation' after the second occurrence of παράκλησις 'comfort'. This reading is followed by KJV only.

LEXICON—a. εἴτε...εἴτε (**LN** 89.69) (BAGD VI.13.a. p. 220): 'if...if' [BAGD, HNTC, LN, NTC, WBC; NIV, NJB, NRSV, REB, TEV, TNT], 'and if...whilst if' [ICC2], 'if...and when' [NAB], 'when...when' [AB; NLT], 'whether...or' [BAGD, LN], 'whether...whether' [Lns; KJV], not explicit [CEV]. This word is used to describe a condition that really exists, not a hypothetical one [AB, ICC1, Lns, NIC2, NTC, TG, TH, WBC; NLT].
  b. pres. pass. indic. of θλίβω (LN **22.15**) (BAGD 3. p. 362): 'to be afflicted' [AB, BAGD, HNTC, ICC2, Lns, NTC; KJV, NAB, NRSV, TNT], 'to be distressed' [NIV], 'to be oppressed' [BAGD], 'to face trials' [WBC], 'to be troubled' [LN], 'to suffer hardship' [**LN**], 'to suffer' [CEV, TEV], 'to have hardships to undergo' [NJB], 'to be weighed down with troubles' [NLT], 'to have distress as one's lot' [REB].
  c. παράκλησις: 'comfort' [AB, ICC2, NTC; NIV], 'comforting' [HNTC, Lns], 'encouragement' [WBC; NAB, NJB], 'consolation' [KJV, NRSV, REB], 'benefit' [NLT], 'help' [TEV]. This noun is also translated as a verbal phrase: 'that you may be comforted' [TNT], 'the hope that you will be comforted' [CEV].
  d. σωτηρία (LN 21.26) (BAGD 2. p. 801): 'salvation' [AB, BAGD, HNTC, ICC2, LN, Lns, NTC, WBC; all versions except CEV, TNT]. This noun is also translated as a verb: 'to be saved' [CEV, TNT].
  e. pres. pass. indic. of παρακαλέω: 'to be comforted' [AB, HNTC, ICC2, Lns, NTC; CEV, KJV, NIV, NLT, TNT], 'to be encouraged' [WBC], 'to receive encouragement' [NJB], 'to be consoled' [NAB, NRSV], 'to have consolation as one's lot' [REB], 'to be helped' [TEV]. See this word also at 1:4.
  f. παράκλησις: 'comfort' [AB, ICC2, NTC; NIV], 'comforting' [HNTC, Lns], 'encouragement' [WBC; NJB, NLT], 'consolation' [KJV, NAB, NRSV, REB], This noun is also translated as a verb: 'to be comforted' [CEV], 'to be helped' [TEV]; or as a verb phrase: 'that God may comfort you' [TNT].

QUESTION—What is meant by σωτηρία 'salvation' in this context?
  It is spiritual well-being and health [ICC1, TG, TH, WBC], protection from evil [WBC], and preservation in trial [EBC]. It adds an eschatological dimension to the benefit they receive from Paul's ministry [SP]. It is God's eschatological action in history in which he has established a new covenant which gives life to people through the gospel [NIC2]. It refers to the ultimate restoration of man's status of divine glory when Christ returns, and for which the process has already been set in motion by the gospel [ICC2]. It is that eschatological hope which believers have of being delivered from God's wrath on judgment day [AB]. It means being saved by God from sin and judgment [Lns]. It refers to Christ leading sinners to himself through Paul's ministry [NTC]. Salvation refers to the eternal weight of glory produced by suffering [Ho].

QUESTION—In what way would Paul's affliction be for the comfort and salvation of the Corinthians?

Affliction and opposition was the context within which Paul brought the message of salvation to unbelievers [AB, ICC2]. Through his preaching ministry, which was carried out in affliction, the Corinthians could share in the comfort of the hope of final eschatological salvation [TNTC]. Since it is through much tribulation that we enter the kingdom and have final salvation, leaders who endure set an example whereby believers are enabled to endure to the end and so be saved [Lns]. By his own affliction Paul was equipped to administer God's encouragement to help them endure trial [EBC]. Paul's experience of consolation in suffering enabled him to comfort others [ICC1]. Paul became an example of appropriating the Lord's support in difficulty [NTC]. In his affliction Paul mediated comfort to them either in person or by letter [NIC2].

the (comfort) producing[a] in (you) an-endurance[b] of-the same sufferings[c] which we also suffer.[d]

LEXICON—a. pres. mid. participle of ἐνεργέω (LN 13.9, 42.3, 42.4) (BAGD 1.b. p. 265): 'to produce' [Lns, WBC; NIV], 'to effect' [NTC], 'to result in, to bring about' [LN (13.9)], 'to help to bring (strength)' [REB], 'to enable' [NJB], 'to experience' [NRSV], 'to cause to function, to grant the ability to do' [LN (42.4)], 'to be effective' [BAGD], 'to be effectual' [KJV], 'to operate' [BAGD], 'to be operative' [ICC2], 'to work' [BAGD, LN (42.3), Lns], 'to take effect' [HNTC], 'to express itself' [AB], 'to be given (the strength to endure)' [TEV], not explicit [CEV, NAB, NLT, TNT]. This middle participle is identical in form to the passive participle, so some commentators view it as a divine passive with God as the implied agent [ICC1, NIC2, WBC].

b. ὑπομονή (LN 25.174) (BAGD 1. p. 846): 'endurance' [AB, BAGD, HNTC, ICC2, LN, Lns, NTC], 'enduring' [KJV], 'patience' [BAGD], 'patient endurance' [NIV], 'strength to face with fortitude' [REB], 'strength to endure with patience' [TEV], 'perseverance, steadfastness' [BAGD]. This noun is also translated in conjunction with the preposition ἐν 'in' as a verb phrase 'as you remain steadfast' [WBC], 'as you patiently endure' [CEV], 'you can patiently endure' [NLT], 'when you patiently endure' [NRSV], 'that you may endure patiently' [NAB], 'to bear with perseverance' [NJB], 'when you are steadfast under' [TNT].

c. πάθημα (LN 24.78) (BAGD 1. p. 602): 'suffering' [AB, BAGD, HNTC, ICC2, LN, Lns, NTC, WBC; all versions except NLT], 'things we suffer' [NLT]. This plural noun 'sufferings' is also translated in the singular 'suffering' [CEV].

d. pres. act. indic. of πάσχω (LN **24.78**) (BAGD 3.b. p. 634): 'to suffer' [AB, HNTC, ICC2, LN, Lns, NTC, WBC; KJV, NIV, NLT, NRSV, TNT], 'to endure suffering' [BAGD], 'to endure' [BAGD; NAB, REB, TEV], not explicit [CEV, NJB].

QUESTION—What relationship is indicated by ἐν 'in'?
1. It is instrumental [NIC2]: it is for your comfort, which is energized by endurance.
2. It indicates the condition in which the action occurs [AB, EGT, HNTC, Ho, ICC1, Lns, WBC; CEV, NRSV, TNT]: it is for your comfort, which works or takes effect as you endure.
3. It indicates result [He, ICC2, My, NTC, SP, TG; NAB, NIV, NJB, NLT, REB, TEV]: it is for your comfort, which produces the ability to endure.

QUESTION—In what way did the Corinthians experience the same sufferings as Paul's?

They experienced opposition from both Judaism and heathendom, just as Paul did [EGT]. They experienced the sufferings of Christ in general which come to God's people from forces hostile to God [NIC2, WBC], and which for them occurred specifically in the clash with the licentiousness and paganism around them [NIC2, TNTC]. They experienced the same general sufferings that all Christians experienced [Lns, My], possibly also including the pain of the unruly members who were causing trouble to the church [Lns]. They suffer because of their loyalty to Christ [TH]. They were the same only in the sense that they were afflictions, and came as a consequence of the decision to be true to Christ [NTC]. He is referring to the Jewish criticism of Paul and his message which was also directed toward the Corinthian believers [ICC2]. They were the same in kind, and arising out of devotion to Christ [ICC1]. Paul is telling them that an apostle is no different from ordinary Christians, to whom God sends suffering and comfort, death and resurrection. The apostle is simply the one in whom this common pattern is seen in sharp focus [HNTC]. Their suffering is for being Christians, as well as a sympathy with Paul in all that he suffered [Ho].

1:7 And[a] our hope[b] for[c] you (is) firm[d] knowing[e] that

LEXICON—a. καί (LN 91.1): 'and' [AB, HNTC, ICC2, Lns, NTC, WBC; KJV, NIV, REB, TNT], 'so' [NJB, TEV], not explicit [CEV, NAB, NLT, NRSV]. Καί can be a marker of transition which is often best left untranslated [LN].
b. ἐλπίς (LN 25.59) (BAGD 1. p. 253): 'hope' [AB, BAGD, HNTC, ICC2, LN, Lns, NTC, WBC; all versions except CEV, NLT]. The phrase 'our hope for you is firm' is translated 'you never disappoint us' [CEV], 'we are confident' [NLT].
c. ὑπέρ (LN **90.24**): 'for' [AB, HNTC, ICC2, Lns, NTC, WBC; NAB, NIV, NJB, NRSV, REB, TNT], 'concerning, about' [LN], 'of' [LN; KJV], 'in' [TEV], not explicit [CEV, NLT].
d. βέβαιος (LN **31.90**) (BAGD 2. p. 138): 'firm' [ICC2, Lns; NAB, NIV], 'firmly grounded' [WBC; REB], 'firmly based' [TNT], 'secure' [HNTC; NJB], 'certain' [AB], 'steadfast' [NTC; KJV], 'unshaken' [NRSV], 'never shaken' [TEV], not explicit [CEV, NLT]. The phrase 'our hope for you is

firm' is translated 'we are able to rely on our hope for you' [LN]. This is a commercial term that means 'secure and guaranteed' [NIC2, WBC].
   e. perf. act. participle of οἶδα (LN 28.1): 'to know' [AB, HNTC, ICC2, LN, NTC, WBC; all versions except NJB, NLT], 'to see' [Lns], not explicit [NLT]. The phrase 'knowing that' is translated 'in the knowledge that' [NJB]. This participle is also translated as a present indicative verb with a causal meaning: 'because we know' [AB, HNTC, WBC; NAB, NIV, TNT], 'since we know' [ICC2], 'for we know' [NRSV, REB].
QUESTION—What is Paul's hope?
His hope is that the Corinthians will endure in their trials [AB, WBC], that they will continue in faith [NIC2, TH], and bear up under the pressures that come to them because they are Christians [NTC]. His hope is that the God of all comfort will comfort them [Lns]. His confidence is that they will respond to his admonitions [NIC1]. His hope is his expectation that the Corinthians will share in the consolations [SP].
QUESTION—What relationship is indicated by ὑπέρ 'for'?
   1. It indicates a hope for or concerning the Corinthians about their situation [AB, He, HNTC, ICC2, Lns, My, NIC2, WBC; NAB, NIV, NJB, NRSV, REB, TNT].
   2. It indicates a confidence in the Corinthians themselves [NIC1, TG, TH; CEV, TEV].

as[a] you-are sharers[b] of the sufferings, so[c] also of the comfort.
LEXICON—a. ὡς (LN 64.12) (BAGD II.1. p. 897): 'as' [HNTC, ICC2, LN, Lns, NTC, WBC; KJV, NLT, NRSV, TNT], 'just as' [NAB, NIV, TEV], 'if' [REB], not explicit [AB; CEV, NJB].
   b. κοινωνός (LN 34.6) (BAGD 1.b.α. p. 439): 'sharer' [BAGD, NTC], 'partner' [AB, BAGD, LN], 'participant' [ICC2], 'partaker' [Lns; KJV], not explicit [CEV]. The phrase 'you are sharers' is translated as a verb: 'to share' [HNTC, WBC; all versions except CEV, KJV].
   c. οὕτως (BAGD II.1. p. 897): 'so' [BAGD, HNTC, ICC2, Lns, NTC, WBC; KJV, NAB, NIV, NRSV, TNT], 'just as' [AB], 'no less than' [NJB], not explicit [CEV, NLT, REB, TEV].
QUESTION—What is the tense of the implied verb 'to be' in the second half of this sentence?
   1. The implied verb refers to a present condition [AB, EGT, He, HNTC, ICC1, ICC2, NIC2, TG, TNTC, WBC; NIV, NJB, NRSV, REB, TEV, TNT]: so also you are sharers of the comfort.
   2. The implied verb refers to a future condition [Ho, TH; CEV, KJV, NAB, NLT]: so also you will be sharers of the comfort.

DISCOURSE UNIT: 1:8–11 [EBC, NIC2, NTC, WBC]. The topic is deliverance from a deadly peril [EBC], escape from Asia [NIC2], deliverance and gratitude [NTC], Paul's trial in Asia [WBC].

2 CORINTHIANS 1:8

1:8 For[a] we- do-not -want you to-be-ignorant,[b] brothers,[c] about our affliction[d] having-happened[e] in Asia,

LEXICON—a. γάρ (LN 91.1) (BAGD 1.b. p. 152): 'for' [AB, BAGD, HNTC, ICC2, Lns, NTC], 'so' [NJB], not explicit [CEV, NAB, NIV, NLT, NRSV, TEV, TNT]. This enclitic particle is also translated 'in saying this' [REB].

b. pres. act. infin. of ἀγνοέω (LN 28.13) (BAGD 1. p. 11): 'to be ignorant' [AB, BAGD, ICC2, LN, Lns, NTC; KJV], 'to not know' [BAGD, HNTC, LN], 'to be unaware' [LN; NRSV], 'to be uninformed' [NIV], 'to be left in the dark' [NAB]. The statement 'we do not want you to be ignorant' is translated 'we want you to know' [WBC; TNT], 'I want you to know' [CEV], 'we want you to be quite certain' [NJB], 'I think you ought to know' [NLT], 'we should like you to know' [REB], 'we want to remind you' [TEV].

c. ἀδελφός (LN 11.23): 'brother' [HNTC, ICC2, Lns, NTC, WBC; KJV, NAB, NIV, NJB, TNT], 'fellow believer, Christian brother' [LN]. The plural noun is translated 'friends' [TEV], 'my friends' [CEV, REB], 'dear friends' [NLT], 'brothers and sisters' [AB; NRSV]. The plural form is used inclusively here to refer to both male and female [AB, NIC2, NTC, TG, TH, TNTC; NRSV; and probably CEV, NLT, REB, TEV]. See this word also at 1:1.

d. θλῖψις (LN 22.2) (BAGD 1. p 362): 'affliction' [AB, BAGD, HNTC, ICC2, NTC, WBC; NRSV], 'trouble' [LN; KJV, NAB, NLT, REB, TEV, TNT], 'distress' [Lns], 'hardships' [NIV, NJB], 'hard time' [CEV]. See this word also at 1:4.

e. aorist mid. (deponent = act.) participle of γίνομαι (LN 13.107): 'to happen' [HNTC, LN; TNT], 'to occur' [LN, Lns], 'to take place' [AB, ICC2]. The phrase 'our affliction having happened' is translated 'what a hard time we had' [CEV], 'the trouble we had' [NAB, TEV] 'the hardships we suffered' [NIV], 'the hardships we underwent' [NJB], 'the trouble we went through' [NLT], 'the affliction we experienced' [NRSV], 'the affliction we endured' [NTC], 'the trouble that came upon us' [REB], 'our trouble that came to us' [KJV], 'the affliction that came to us' [WBC].

QUESTION—What relationship is indicated by γάρ 'for'?

It joins 1:7 to 1:8 by giving a personal example [NTC]. It joins this passage with the benediction begun in 1:3 [Lns, NIC2], and moves from a general statement about all their afflictions to the particular affliction in Asia [EGT, NIC2, TNTC]. Paul uses γάρ to introduce a new paragraph that explains and amplifies his feelings about what had been discussed in the previous one [Lns]. It connects his general statement about suffering in 1:7 with more specific comments about suffering in 1:8–10 [TH].

QUESTION—To whom does 'we' refer?
1. This is an editorial 'we', referring to Paul [CEV, NLT]: I do not want you to be ignorant. The rest of the verse and paragraph reverts back to 'we' and changes to singular once more at 1:13 'I write' [CEV, NLT].
2 This is translated in the plural form [all translations except CEV, NLT].
QUESTION—What region is he referring to as Asia?
He is referring to Ephesus [EGT, NIC2, TNTC], probably in reference to the riot there [NIC2]. It refers to some outlying part of the province outside of Ephesus [EBC]. It is western Asia Minor (modern Turkey) [AB, Ho, TG, TH].

that we-were-burdened[a] excessively[b] beyond[c] (our) strength[d] to-the-point-of[e] us despairing[f] even[g] of-living;[h]

LEXICON—a. aorist pass. indic. of βαρέω (LN 22.18) (BAGD p. 133): 'to be burdened' [AB, BAGD, LN, NTC; TNT], 'to be weighed down' [BAGD, HNTC, ICC2], 'to be weighted down' [Lns], 'to be under pressure' [WBC; NIV, NJB], 'to be pressed' [KJV]. The phrase 'we were burdened exceedingly beyond our power' is translated 'we were crushed beyond our strength' [NAB], 'we were crushed and completely overwhelmed' [NLT], 'we were so utterly, unbearably crushed' [NRSV], 'the burden of it was far to heavy for us to bear' [REB], 'the burdens laid upon us were so great and so heavy' [TEV], 'our sufferings were so horrible' [CEV]. This word is used to describe a ship that is too heavily laden [He, HNTC, NIC2, WBC] or a wearied beast of burden that sinks under a load that is too great [Ho].

b. ὑπερβολή (LN 78.33) (BAGD p. 840): 'excessively' [ICC2; TNT], 'excess' [BAGD], 'beyond measure' [BAGD, HNTC], 'utterly' [BAGD], 'far more, much greater, to a far greater degree' [LN], 'exceedingly' [AB, Lns, NTC], 'out of measure' [KJV], not explicit [NAB]. This word is part of the expression καθ' ὑπερβολὴν, which is also translated as an adjective: 'extreme' [WBC], 'horrible' [CEV], 'great' [NIV], 'extraordinary' [NJB].

c. ὑπέρ (LN 78.29) (BAGD 2. p. 839): 'beyond' [AB, BAGD, HNTC, ICC2, LN, Lns, NTC, WBC; NAB, NIV, NJB, TNT], 'above' [KJV], 'more than' [LN], not explicit [CEV, NLT, NRSV]. The phrase 'excessively beyond our power' is also translated 'far too heavy for us to bear' [REB], 'so great and so heavy' [TEV].

d. δύναμις (LN 74.1) (BAGD 2. p. 208): 'strength' [AB, HNTC, ICC2, NTC; KJV, NAB, TNT], 'ability' [BAGD, LN, Lns], 'ability to endure' [NIV], 'powers of endurance' [NJB], 'power to cope' [WBC], not explicit [CEV, NLT, NRSV, REB, TEV].

e. ὥστε (LN 89.52) (BAGD 2.a.β. p. 900): 'so that' [BAGD, ICC2, LN, Lns, NTC, WBC; NIV, NJB, TNT], 'that' [AB; CEV, NRSV, REB, TEV], 'insomuch that' [KJV], 'with the result that' [HNTC], 'to the point of' [NAB], not explicit [NLT].

f. aorist pass. (deponent = act.) infin. of ἐξαπορέω (LN **25.237**) (BAGD p. 273): 'to despair' [AB, BAGD, HNTC, ICC2, NTC, WBC; KJV, NAB, NIV, NRSV, REB, TNT], 'to be in utter despair, to despair completely' [LN], 'to get to despair' [Lns], 'to give up all hope' [NJB]. The phrase 'despairing even of living' is translated 'we thought we would never live through it' [NLT], 'we gave up all hope of staying alive' [TEV], 'death seemed certain' [CEV]. This verb means to be utterly at a loss [Ho, NIC1], beset on every side [Ho] with no way of exit [EBC].

g. καί: 'even' [AB, HNTC, ICC2, Lns, NTC, WBC; KJV, NAB, NIV, NJB, REB], not explicit [CEV, NLT, NRSV, TEV, TNT].

h. pres. act. infin. of ζάω (LN 23.88) (BAGD 1.a.α. p. 336): 'to live' [BAGD, LN], 'to live through' [NLT], not explicit [CEV]. This infinitive is also translated as a noun: 'life' [HNTC, NTC; KJV, NAB, NIV, REB, TNT], 'life itself' [WBC; NRSV], 'survival' [AB]; or as a verbal noun 'surviving' [NJB], 'living' [ICC2], 'living on' [Lns], 'staying alive' [TEV].

QUESTION—What does καθ' ὑπερβολήν 'excessively' modify?

1. It modifies the preceding verb ἐβαρήθημεν 'we were burdened' [AB, EGT, He, HNTC, Ho, ICC2, SP, TH, WBC; KJV]: we were excessively burdened, beyond our strength.
2. It modifies the following phrase ὑπὲρ δύναμιν 'beyond (our) strength' [Lns, My, NTC; TNT]: we were burdened excessively beyond our strength.

1:9 Indeed/but^a we ourselves have-had^b the sentence^c of death within ourselves

LEXICON—a. ἀλλά (LN 91.2): 'indeed' [AB, WBC; NRSV, REB, TNT], 'in fact' [NJB], 'yes' [HNTC], 'yea' [Lns], 'but' [ICC2; KJV, TEV], 'however' [NTC], not explicit [NAB]. Some versions divide this verse into two sentences with ἀλλά used as a marker of transition to introduce the first sentence: 'in fact' [CEV, NLT], 'indeed' [NIV]; and as a contrastive conjunction to introduce the second: 'but' [CEV, NIV, NLT].

b. perf. act. indic. of ἔχω (LN 90.65) (BAGD I.2.j. p. 333): 'to have' [ICC2, Lns, NTC; KJV], 'to have within oneself' [BAGD], 'to receive' [AB, HNTC, WBC], 'to carry' [NJB]. The phrase 'we have had the sentence of death within ourselves' is viewed as a subjective experience and translated 'we felt sure that we were going to die' [CEV], 'we were left to feel like men condemned to death' [NAB], 'in our hearts we felt the sentence of death' [NIV], 'we expected to die' [NLT], 'we felt that we had received the sentence of death' [NRSV], 'we felt in our hearts that we had received a death sentence' [REB], 'we felt that the death sentence had been passed on us' [TEV]. It is also viewed as a present subjective reality 'we have in ourselves the sentence of death' [NTC].

c. ἀπόκριμα (LN **56.26**) (BAGD p. 93): 'sentence' [AB, HNTC, NTC, WBC; KJV, NIV, NJB, NRSV, REB, TEV, TNT], 'verdict' [ICC2, LN,

Lns], 'official report, decision' [BAGD], not explicit [CEV, NAB, NLT]. This word could refer to an answer given by God to Paul in response to prayer [NTC], or Paul's own conclusion about the hopelessness of his situation [Lns, TNTC].

QUESTION—What relationship is indicated by ἀλλά 'indeed/but'?
1. It confirms and intensifies what he has just said about despair for life by what follows regarding the sentence of death [AB, ICC1, TNTC, WBC; NJB, NRSV, REB, TNT]: indeed. It reinforces what he has just said in the previous verse [SP].
2. It contrasts 'trust in God who raises the dead' with 'despair for life' in 1:8 [ICC2]. It contrasts the 'hope' that he has spoken of in 1:7 with the despair mentioned in 1:8 [TH]. It contrasts 'sentence of death' in 1:9 with 'despair for life' in 1:8 [HNTC, Ho, NIC2], and

QUESTION—What meaning does the perfect tense of ἐσχήκαμεν 'have had' express in this sentence?
1. The perfect tense is used to convey an aorist meaning of an event in time past [AB, EGT, ICC2, WBC].
2. The perfect tense is used in its normal sense of an event in time past that has an ongoing effect [EBC, He, HNTC, My, NIC1, NIC2]. The aorist tense of ἔχω 'to have' is rarely used to express the normal constative aorist sense 'possessed, had' but usually conveys the ingressive sense 'got, received' [HNTC, NIC1]. Though not carried out, the sentence remains in force [HNTC]. The event, though past, was very vivid in Paul's mind and was still affecting him [Lns, NTC]. Paul has accepted the inevitability of his death [He].

so-that[a] we-should- not -be ones-having-trusted[b] in ourselves but in God the-one-raising[c] the dead.

LEXICON—a. ἵνα (LN 89.59): 'so that' [AB, ICC2, LN, NTC; NAB, NJB, NRSV], 'in order that' [LN, Lns; TNT], 'that' [HNTC, WBC; KJV], 'this happened that' [NIV], 'this happened so that' [TEV], 'this was meant to teach us' [REB], 'as a result' [NLT], 'this made us' [CEV].

b. perf. act. participle of πείθω (LN **31.82**) (BAGD 2.a. p. 639): 'to trust in' [BAGD, HNTC, ICC2, LN, NTC, WBC; CEV, KJV, NAB, NJB], 'to rely on' [AB, **LN**; NIV, NLT, NRSV, TEV, TNT], 'to place reliance on' [REB], 'to depend on' [LN], 'to place confidence in/on' [BAGD, Lns]. The perfect tense of the participle is translated as indicating the interruption of an existing condition or process: 'we should trust no more in ourselves' [HNTC], 'we should trust no longer in ourselves' [WBC], 'stop trusting in ourselves and start trusting in God' [CEV].

c. pres. act. participle of ἐγείρω (LN 23.94): 'to raise' [AB, HNTC, ICC2, NTC, WBC; all versions except CEV, NLT], 'to raise up' [Lns], 'to raise to life' [LN; CEV], 'to be able to raise' [NLT]. This participle is timeless, expressing the fact that raising the dead is a permanent attribute of God [ICC1, NIC1].

QUESTION—What relationship is indicated by ἵνα 'so that'?
1. It expresses purpose [AB, HNTC, Ho, ICC1, ICC2, Lns, NTC, TG, TH, TNTC, WBC; KJV, NAB, NIV, NJB, NRSV, REB, TEV, TNT]: this happened in order that we might learn to trust in God.
2. It expresses result [CEV, NLT]: this caused us to trust in God.

QUESTION—What is indicated by the use of the negated present subjunctive μὴ ὦμεν 'we should not be' with the perfect participle πεποιθότες 'ones having trusted'?
1. It indicates the discontinuation of an existing condition or process [HNTC, ICC1, WBC; CEV]: 'that we should stop trusting in ourselves'.
2. It has a present tense meaning [Ho, ICC2, NTC, TG, TNTC; all versions except CEV]: 'that we not rely on ourselves but on God'.
3. The participle is a periphrastic perfect indicating the beginning of an activity that continues, and the subjunctive makes it future in reference [Lns]: 'that we not get to placing confidence in ourselves'.

1:10 who delivered^a us from^b so-great^c a death,^d

TEXT—Instead of the singular τηλικούτου θανάτου 'so great a death', some manuscripts have the plural τηλικούτων θανάτων 'such great perils of death'. GNT selects the singular reading 'so great a death' with a B rating, indicating that the text is almost certain. The plural reading is taken by AB, ICC2; TEV, TNT.

LEXICON—a. aorist mid. (deponent = act.) indic. of ῥύομαι (LN 21.23) (BAGD p. 737): 'to deliver' [BAGD, ICC2, LN, Lns, NTC; KJV, NIV, NLT, REB, TNT], 'to save' [BAGD; CEV, NJB, TEV], 'to rescue' [AB, BAGD, LN, NTC, WBC; NAB, NRSV].

b. ἐκ (LN 89.121): 'from' [AB, HNTC, ICC2, LN, NTC, WBC; all versions], 'out of' [Lns].

c. τηλικοῦτος (LN 78.36): 'so great' [LN, Lns; KJV], 'such severe' [AB], 'so threatening' [HNTC], 'so menacing' [WBC], 'such immense' [ICC2], 'such terrible' [TEV, TNT], 'such' [NTC; NIV, NJB, REB, TEV], 'so' [NRSV], not explicit [CEV, NAB, NLT].

d. θάνατος (LN 23.117) (BAGD 1.c. p. 351): 'death' [HNTC, Lns, WBC; KJV, NJB], 'danger of death' [BAGD, LN; NAB, TEV], 'risk of death' [TNT], 'threat of death' [AB; CEV], 'mortal peril' [ICC2; REB], 'deadly peril' [NIV, NRSV], 'mortal danger' [NTC; NLT].

and will-deliver^a us, in^b whom we-have-hoped^c that also he-will-deliver still^d,

TEXT—Instead of ῥύσεται 'will deliver', some manuscripts have ῥύεται 'does deliver'. GNT selects the reading 'will deliver' with a B rating, indicating that the text is almost certain. The reading 'does deliver' is taken by KJV.

TEXT—The word ὅτι 'that' does not occur in some manuscripts. It is included by GNT with a C rating, indicating difficulty in deciding whether or not to place it in the text. It is omitted or not translated by AB, HNTC, NAB, REB.

36   2 CORINTHIANS 1:10

LEXICON—a. future mid. (deponent = act.) indic. of ῥύομαι (LN 21.23) (BAGD p. 737): 'to deliver' [BAGD, ICC2, LN, Lns; KJV, NIV, NLT, REB, TNT], 'to save' [BAGD; NJB, TEV], 'to rescue' [AB, BAGD, HNTC, LN, NTC, WBC; NRSV], not explicit [CEV, NAB]. This word is translated as 'rescue' in its first occurrence in this sentence and as 'deliver' in its final occurrence [HNTC; NAB].
  b. εἰς (LN 90.23): 'in' [HNTC, ICC2, LN, Lns, NTC; KJV, NAB, TEV], 'on' [AB, WBC; NIV, NJB, NRSV, REB, TNT], not explicit [CEV, NLT].
  c. perf. act. indic. of ἐλπίζω (LN 25.59) (BAGD 3. p. 252): 'to hope' [LN, Lns], 'to set one's hope' [HNTC, WBC; NIV, NRSV, TNT], 'to place one's hope' [ICC2, LN; TEV], 'to put one's hope' [BAGD, ICC2, NTC; NAB], 'to set one's hope firmly' [AB], 'to fix one's hope' [REB], 'to be sure' [CEV], 'to trust' [KJV], 'to rely on' [NJB], 'to be confident' [NLT].
  d. ἔτι (LN 67.128): 'still' [ICC2, LN, Lns], 'yet' [HNTC, LN; KJV], 'yet again' [WBC], 'again' [NTC; NRSV, TEV], 'again and again' [CEV], 'even further' [TNT], not explicit [NJB]. This adverb used in conjunction with the future tense of ῥύσεται 'he will deliver' is also translated as a verbal phrase: 'to continue to (deliver)' [AB; NIV, NLT, REB], 'to never cease to (deliver)' [NAB].

QUESTION—Does the clause καὶ ἔτι ῥύσεται 'he will also deliver still' go with what precedes it as a conclusion or with what follows in 1:11?
  The decision about whether to accept ὅτι 'that' as part of the text will affect how this clause is seen in relation to its context. Those that view this clause as connected to what follows all omit ὅτι.
  1. It is connected to what precedes it [ICC2, Lns, My, WBC; all versions except REB]: 'we have set our hope that he will still deliver'.
  2. It is connected to what follows it [AB, HNTC, NTC; REB]: 'he will continue to deliver us as you help in prayer'.

1:11 **you also joining-in-helping^a by^b prayer^c for^d us,**

LEXICON—a. pres. act. participle of συνυπουργέω (LN 35.5) (BAGD p. 793): 'to join in helping' [BAGD, LN, Lns; NRSV], 'to help' [AB, NTC; CEV, NAB, NIV, NLT, TEV, TNT], 'to help together' [KJV], 'to cooperate with' [BAGD], 'to cooperate' [HNTC, ICC2; REB], 'to work with' [WBC]. The phrase 'you also joining in helping by prayer for us' is translated 'your prayer for us will contribute to this' [NJB]. The present participle indicates that the act of helping is continuous [NTC].
  b. There is no lexical entry for the preposition 'by' in the Greek text, the dative case being used to express the relation between δέησις 'prayer' and the participle. This instrumental dative is translated 'by' [HNTC, ICC2, WBC; CEV, KJV, NIV, NLT, NRSV, REB, TNT], 'by means of' [TEV], 'with' [AB, Lns; NAB], 'through' [NTC], not explicit [NJB].
  c. δέησις (LN 33.171) (BAGD p. 172): 'prayer' [AB, BAGD, HNTC, ICC2, LN, NTC, WBC; KJV, NAB, NIV, NJB, NRSV, TEV], 'praying' [CEV,

NLT, REB, TNT], 'petition' [Lns]. This singular noun is also translated by the plural 'prayers' [ICC1, NTC; NAB, NIV, NRSV, TEV].
  d. ὑπέρ (LN 90.36) (BAGD 1.a.δ. p. 838): 'for' [AB, BAGD, LN, NTC; CEV, KJV, NJB, NLT, REB, TEV, TNT], 'for the sake of' [BAGD, LN], 'in behalf of' [BAGD, Lns], 'on behalf of' [HNTC, ICC2, LN], not explicit [WBC; NAB, NIV, NRSV].

QUESTION—What is this clause connected with?
  1. It is connected with what precedes it [AB, HNTC, ICC1, NIC2, NTC, WBC; NIV, NLT, REB, TEV, TNT]: 'he will deliver us as you join in helping by prayer for us'.
  2. It is connected with what follows it [He, HNTC, Lns; CEV, KJV, NAB, NJB]: 'As you join in helping by your prayer for us many will glorify God'.
  3. It forms a transition between what precedes and what follows [ICC2; NRSV]: 'he will rescue us again, as you also pray for us, and as a result many will glorify God'.

QUESTION—What does the genitive absolute συνυπουργούντων καὶ ὑμῶν 'you also joining in helping' connote?
  It refers to an attendant circumstance [He, ICC1, ICC2, Lns, My, NIC2, NTC, TG; NIV, NJB, NRSV, REB, TEV]: 'as you help'. It is also an implicit request for prayer [ICC1]. It is conditional [AB, EBC, HNTC, WBC; NLT, TNT]: 'if you help'. It is an implied imperative 'you must help' [NAB], or an explicit request 'please help us' [CEV].

QUESTION—Whom would they be joining in helping or cooperating with by their prayer?
  1. They would be helping Paul and Timothy [EBC, He, HNTC, ICC2, Lns, My, NTC, SP, WBC; CEV, NAB, NIV, TEV, TNT].
  2. They would be cooperating with each other in prayer for Paul and Timothy [NIC1, NIC2] or with other churches [Ho].
  3. They would be cooperating with God [ICC1].

QUESTION—What relationship is indicated by ὑπέρ ἡμῶν 'for us'?
  1. It is connected with 'helping' and indicates the object of the verb [EGT, He, HNTC, ICC1, Lns, My, NIC2, WBC; NAB, NIV, NRSV]: 'joining in helping us'.
  2. It is connected with prayer and indicates whom the prayers benefit [AB, Ho, ICC2; KJV, NJB, NLT, REB]: 'prayer for us'.
  3. It is connected with both the verb and the prayer [NTC; CEV, TEV, TNT]: 'you help us by your prayer for us'.

so-that[a] from[b] many persons[c] the blessing[d] for us through[e] many may-be-thanked-for[f] in our behalf.

LEXICON—a. ἵνα (LN 89.59, 89.49): 'so that' [AB, ICC2, LN (89.59); NAB, NJB, NRSV], 'that' [KJV], 'in order to' [LN (89.59)], 'in order that' [HNTC, Lns], 'then' [NTC, WBC; CEV, NIV, REB, TNT], 'as a result' [LN (89.49); NLT], 'so it will be that' [TEV].

b. ἐκ (LN 90.16) (BAGD 3.e.α. p. 235): 'from' [AB, HNTC, LN, NTC, WBC], 'as (coming) from' [Lns], 'by' [BAGD, LN; NJB], 'by the means of' [KJV], 'by the agency of' [ICC2], not explicit [CEV, NAB, NIV, NLT, NRSV, REB, TEV, TNT].

c. πρόσωπον (LN **9.9**) (BAGD 1.e.2. p. 721): 'people' [AB, HNTC, LN, NTC, WBC; CEV, REB, TNT], 'person' [BAGD, LN, Lns; KJV], 'figures' [ICC2], not explicit [NAB, NIV, NJB, NLT, NRSV].

d. χάρισμα (LN 57.103) (BAGD 1. p. 879): 'blessing' [NTC; CEV, NRSV], 'gift' [LN; KJV, NAB], 'gracious gift' [BAGD, LN, Lns, WBC], 'gracious benefit' [AB], 'gracious favor' [NIV, REB], 'God's favor' [NJB], 'gift of grace' [HNTC], 'act of grace' [ICC2; TNT], not explicit [NLT]. This noun is also translated as a verb: 'to bless' [TEV].

e. διά with genitive object (LN 90.4, 90.8) (BAGD A.III.2.b.α. p. 180): 'through' [AB, BAGD, LN (90.4); NAB, NRSV], 'through the agency of' [HNTC], 'through the help of' [WBC], 'by' [ICC2, LN; KJV], 'by means of' [LN (90.8), Lns], 'in answer to' [NIV], 'as the result of' [NJB], 'from' [NTC], not explicit [CEV, TEV, TNT]. The prepositional phrase διὰ πολλῶν 'through many' is used to indicate means with reference to prayer, or agency with reference to people who pray: 'in answer to all these prayers' [CEV], 'through the prayers of so many' [NAB], 'in answer to the prayers of many' [NIV], 'as a result of the prayers of so many' [NJB], 'so many people's prayers have been answered' [NLT], 'through the prayers of many' [NRSV], 'with so many people praying' [REB], 'many prayers for us will be answered' [TEV].

f. aorist pass. subj. of εὐχαριστέω (LN 33.349) (BAGD 2. p. 328): 'to be thanked for' (indicating the object for which thanks is given, not the subject to whom it is given) [BAGD, LN]. The passive subjunctive form of this verb is translated 'that thanks may be rendered' [AB, HNTC, WBC; KJV], 'that thanks may be given' [NJB], 'thanks may be expressed' [NTC], 'to be the subject of thanksgiving' [ICC2], 'to get to receive thanks' [Lns], 'that (God) may be thanked' [NAB]. This verb is also translated in the active voice 'to give thanks' [CEV, NIV, NLT, NRSV, REB], 'to raise the voice in thanksgiving' [TEV], 'thanksgiving will rise' [TNT].

QUESTION—What relationship is indicated by ἵνα 'so that'?
1. It indicates the purpose Paul had in asking them to help by praying for him [AB, EGT, He, HNTC, Ho, ICC2, Lns, My, NIC2, TNTC; KJV, NAB, NJB, NRSV].
2. It indicates the result of their helping by praying for Paul [ICC1, NTC, TG, WBC; CEV, NIV, NLT, REB, TEV, TNT].

QUESTION—What is meant by ἐκ πολλῶν προσώπων 'from many persons'?
The primary meaning of πρόσωπον is 'face' [BAGD (1.a. p. 720), LN (8.18)].
1. The word πρόσωπον, literally 'face', is figurative and refers to the whole person [He, HNTC, Lns, My, NIC1, NTC, TG, WBC]: from many people

thanksgiving will be offered. Although translating the word as 'persons', some comment that it speaks of people whose faces are lifted to God in prayer or thanksgiving [HNTC, LN, NTC, TNTC].
2. It is used literally and refers to faces turned upward in thanksgiving [EGT, Ho, ICC1]: from many (uplifted) faces thanksgiving will be offered.
3. It refers to actors in a stage drama, each with a separate part to play [ICC2].

QUESTION—What is the τὸ εἰς ἡμᾶς χάρισμα 'the blessing for us'?
1. It is rescue or deliverance [AB, HNTC, Ho, ICC1, ICC2, Lns, My, NIC1, NIC2, NTC, TNTC, WBC].
  1.1 It is a deliverance that has already occurred [ICC1, NTC].
  1.2 It is a deliverance that will occur in the future as an answer to prayer [AB, ICC2, Lns].
  1.3 It is an on-going deliverance that Paul experiences [NIC2].
2. It is the prayers being offered for Paul [He].

QUESTION—What does διὰ πολλῶν 'through many' refer to?
The adjective πολλῶν could be either neuter, referring to many prayers, or masculine, referring to many persons.
1. It refers to persons as agents: 'through many persons'.
  1.1 They are agents of the blessing, through their prayers [He, HNTC, Ho, Lns, My, NIC1, NTC, WBC; NAB, NIV, NJB, NLT, NRSV]: 'the blessing that comes through many persons'. If this meaning is taken, the sense of the sentence is that God may be thanked by many people because of the blessing that comes through the prayers of many people.
  1.2 They are agents of the thanksgiving [AB, EGT, ICC1, ICC2, TNTC; KJV, REB, TNT]: 'thanks will be given through many persons'. If this meaning is taken, then both ἐκ πολλῶν 'from many people' and διὰ πολλῶν 'through many people' have essentially the same meaning and function, both indicating who it is that is thanking God. Then the sense of the sentence would be that from many people God may be thanked through many people, and the second phrase, διὰ πολλῶν would be somewhat redundant.
2. It refers to prayers as means of the blessing [NIC2; CEV, TEV]: 'the blessing through many prayers'.

QUESTION—What is the subject of the passive verb εὐχαριστηθῇ 'to be thanked for'?
This verb is translated as an active verb by CEV, NIV, NLT, NRSV, REB, TEV. For those who translate it as passive the subject varies: 'thanks (is given)' [AB, HNTC, WBC; KJV, NJB]; 'the act of grace (is given thanks for)' [ICC2]; 'the gracious gift (is given thanks for)' [Lns]; 'God (is thanked)' [NAB].

QUESTION—To what does ὑπὲρ ἡμῶν 'for us' refer?
1. It refers to thanksgiving 'on our behalf' [AB, EGT, HNTC, Ho, ICC1, ICC2, Lns, My, NIC1, NTC, TNTC, WBC; KJV, NAB, NIV, NJB, NRSV, REB, TEV].

2. It refers to prayer 'on our behalf' [He, NIC2, TG; NLT].

DISCOURSE UNIT: 1:12–7:16 [ICC1, NTC, TG, TH, TNTC]. The topic is a review of his recent relations with the Corinthians [ICC1], apostolic ministry [NTC], Paul and the church at Corinth [TG, TH], the body of the response [TNTC].

DISCOURSE UNIT: 1:12–2:17 [ICC1; REB]. The topic is Paul's conduct with regard to his promised visit and the great offender [ICC1], Paul's concern for the church at Corinth [REB].

DISCOURSE UNIT: 1:12–2:13 [AB, EBC, HNTC, ICC2]. The topic is assurances of concern [AB], Paul's conduct explained [EBC], Paul's plans for Corinth, and their working out in the past [HNTC], self-defense [ICC2].

DISCOURSE UNIT: 1:12–2:11 [NTC; NJB]. The topic is Paul's travel plans [NTC], why Paul changed his plans [NJB].

DISCOURSE UNIT: 1:12–2:4 [ICC1, TH, TNTC; CEV, NAB, NIV, NLT, NRSV, TEV]. The topic is the postponement of his intended visit [ICC1; NRSV], Paul's change of plans [TNTC; CEV, NIV, NLT, TEV], Paul's sincerity [NAB], an explanation of Paul's past actions [TH].

DISCOURSE UNIT: 1:12–24 [ICC2]. The topic is introduction; failure to visit.

DISCOURSE UNIT: 1:12–22 [HNTC]. The topic is Paul's boasting; behind Paul's plans lies the fulfillment of God's plan in Christ.

DISCOURSE UNIT: 1:12–14 [AB, EBC, NIC2, WBC]. The topic is the introduction [AB], characteristics of Paul's conduct [EBC], a preliminary defense [NIC2], transition to the letter's first theme [WBC].

1:12 For[a] our boasting[b] is this, the testimony[c] of our conscience[d]

LEXICON—a. γάρ (LN 91.1) (BAGD 4. p. 152): 'for' [HNTC, ICC2, Lns, NTC; KJV], 'indeed' [BAGD; NRSV], 'now' [AB; NIV], not explicit [WBC; CEV, NAB, NJB, NLT, REB, TEV, TNT].

b. καύχησις (LN **33.371**) (BAGD 2. p. 426): 'boasting' [HNTC, NTC], 'boast' [ICC2; NAB, NIV, NRSV], 'object or reason for boasting' [BAGD], 'what one boasts about' [LN], 'glorying' [Lns], 'rejoicing' [KJV], 'confidence' [WBC; NLT]. This noun is also translated as an adjective: '(to be) proud' [AB; CEV, NJB, REB, TEV, TNT].

c. μαρτύριον (LN 33.264) (BAGD 1.b. p. 494): 'testimony' [AB, BAGD, HNTC, ICC2, Lns, NTC, WBC; KJV, NAB, NRSV, TNT]. 'The testimony of our conscience' is translated 'our conscience testifies' [NIV], 'our conscience shows us' [REB], 'our conscience assures us' [TEV], 'we can say...with a clear conscience' [NLT], 'our conscientious conviction' [NJB]. The whole clause is translated 'we can be proud of our clear conscience' [CEV].

d. συνείδησις (LN 26.13) (BAGD 2. p. 786): 'conscience' [AB, BAGD, HNTC, ICC2, LN, Lns, NTC, WBC; all versions except NJB]. This noun is also translated as an adjective: 'conscientious (conviction)' [NJB]. Conscience is the moral faculty of critical self-evaluation or judgment [AB, NTC], the ability to evaluate one's own behavior in an objective way in the light of whatever standards or criteria a person perceives to be highest [ICC2, TNTC], the ability to detach from oneself and view one's own actions and character independently [HNTC].

QUESTION—What relationship is indicated by γάρ 'for'?
1. It introduces grounds for Paul's request for prayer [Ho, ICC1, ICC2, Lns, NIC1]. He can freely ask their prayer because of his blameless conduct with them and ministry to them [Ho, ICC1, ICC2, My, NIC1], and because he has suffered for their sakes [NIC1]. Paul and Timothy count on their prayers because they value the Corinthians and the Corinthians value them [Lns].
2. It introduces a new section [AB, NIC2, TH]. It corresponds to the typical Semitic letter salutation 'and now' [AB]. It introduces the main material to be dealt with, Paul's chief concern [NIC2].

QUESTION—Is the phrase 'the testimony of our conscience' parallel to 'our boasting is this' and restating the same thought, or does it represent the object of their boasting?
1. It represents the object of their boasting [AB, EGT, He, HNTC, Ho, ICC1, ICC2, NIC2, NTC, TG, WBC; CEV, NIV, NJB, REB, TEV, TNT]. That is, their boast is the testimony of their conscience, which is that they have conducted themselves in simplicity and sincerity.
2. It is parallel and explanatory of 'boasting' [Lns, My; NAB, NLT, NRSV]. That is, their boast, which is also the testimony of their conscience, is that they have conducted themselves in simplicity and sincerity.

that in[a] simplicity[b] and sincerity[c] of God,

TEXT—Instead of ἁπλότητι 'simplicity', some manuscripts have ἁγιότητι 'holiness'. GNT selects the reading 'simplicity' with a B rating, indicating that the text is almost certain. The reading 'holiness' is taken by ICC2, Lns; NAB, NIV, NJB, and REB.

LEXICON—a. ἐν (LN 89.84): 'in' [HNTC, LN, Lns; KJV, NIV], 'with' [AB, ICC2, NTC, WBC; NJB, NRSV, TNT], 'by' [REB, TEV], 'from' [NAB], not explicit [CEV, NLT].

b. ἁπλότης (LN 88.44) (BAGD 1. p. 85): 'simplicity' [BAGD, NTC; KJV], 'sincerity' [BAGD, LN], 'frankness' [BAGD; NRSV, TEV, TNT], 'honesty' [WBC], 'purity of motive' [LN]. This noun is also translated as an adverb: 'honestly' [CEV]; as an adjective: 'honest' [NLT]. Those that accept the variant ἁγιότητι translate it as a noun: 'holiness' [NAB, NIV]; or as an adjective: 'devout' [REB]. The phrase 'holiness and sincerity' is translated 'unalloyed holiness' [NJB]. Paul is asserting that he has acted with singleness of purpose and not irresolutely [NIC2].

c. εἰλικρίνεια (LN 88.42) (BAGD p. 222): 'sincerity' [AB, BAGD, HNTC, ICC2, LN, Lns, NTC, WBC; KJV, NIV, NRSV, REB, TEV, TNT], 'candor' [NAB], 'purity of motives' [BAGD, LN]. This noun is also translated as an adjective: 'sincere' [NLT], 'unalloyed' [NJB]; as an adverb: 'sincerely' [CEV]. Paul is asserting that he has acted with sincerity, not craftily [NIC2].

QUESTION—How are the nouns related in the genitive construction ἐν ἁπλότητι καὶ εἰλικρινείᾳ τοῦ θεοῦ 'in simplicity and sincerity of God'?
1. The words 'of God' indicate that God is the source or author of the qualities: they are from God [EGT, He, HNTC, ICC1, My, NIC1, NIC2; NAB, NIV, NJB, TEV, TNT].
2. The words τοῦ θεοῦ are objective, meaning 'to God'; Paul's undivided attention and purity of motive in ministry were in the presence of God [NTC].
3. The words 'of God' are adjectival, meaning 'godly' [AB, ICC2; KJV, NRSV, REB], or that they are like those of God [Lns, NIC2, WBC]. It represents those qualities which God expects and demands [TG].

QUESTION—Does the genitive τοῦ θεοῦ 'of God' apply to both nouns that precede it or only to εἰλικρίνεια 'sincerity'?
1. It applies to both nouns that precede it [He, HNTC, ICC1, ICC2, Lns, My, NTC, WBC; NAB, NIV, NJB, TEV, TNT].
2. It applies only to εἰλικρίνεια 'sincerity' [AB; KJV, NRSV, REB].

not in[a] fleshly[b] wisdom[c] but in (the) grace[d] of God,

LEXICON—a. ἐν (LN 89.84): 'in' [HNTC, LN, Lns], 'with' [NTC, WBC; KJV], 'by' [AB; NRSV, REB, TEV, TNT], 'actuated by' [ICC2], 'guided by' [CEV], 'prompted by' [NAB], 'according to' [NIV], 'relying on' [NJB], 'depending on' [NLT].
b. σαρκικός (LN **26.8**) (BAGD 3. p. 743): 'fleshly' [HNTC, Lns; KJV], 'human' [LN; NJB, TEV, TNT], 'debased human' [NAB], 'ordinary' [AB], 'worldly' [ICC2, NTC, WBC; NIV, REB], 'of this world' [CEV], 'earthly' [NLT, NRSV]. This word connotes that which belongs to the realm of the flesh as opposed to the spirit [BAGD], the human and finite as opposed to the divine [AB, Ho], or that which contrasts with moral integrity [ICC2]. It represents, not a part of man or a phase of his existence, but the whole of man wrongly directed with his mind not set on God [HNTC].
c. σοφία (LN 32.32) (BAGD 1. p. 759): 'wisdom' [AB, BAGD, HNTC, ICC2, LN, Lns, NTC, WBC; all versions except NJB], 'reasoning' [NJB]. This is the natural wisdom of this world which stands in contrast to God's wisdom [BAGD], and which seeks its own selfish ends through devious means [Lns].
d. χάρις (LN 88.66) (BAGD 4. p. 878): 'grace' [AB, HNTC, ICC2, LN, Lns, NTC, WBC; KJV, NIV, NJB, NLT, NRSV, REB, TNT], 'the power of (God's) grace' [TEV], 'wonderful kindness' [CEV], 'goodness'

[NAB]. In this passage this word refers to the exceptional effects produced by the grace of God [BAGD]. See this word also at 1:2.

QUESTION—What is meant by the phrase ἐν χάριτι θεοῦ 'in the grace of God'?

The word 'grace' is a synonym for divine power [ICC2, Lns, WBC]. Grace is the power of God's love in action that helps Paul do the will of God [TG]. It is God's power at work enabling his ministry [EGT, TNTC]. It is the gracious influence of God's spirit [Ho]. It is the source of integrity and selflessness that marked Paul's ministry [NIC1]. It is set in contrast to self-interest, expediency or corruption [Ho], unprincipled dealing or reliance on human ability alone [ICC1]. Paul's good behavior is due to God's goodness to him [TH].

QUESTION—How is ἐν 'in' used in this context?

In all three places it refers to the element within which Paul's life has moved [ICC1, My]. It means 'in union with and in connection with' [Lns]. It indicates cause [HNTC, TH].

we-conducted-ourselves[a] in the world,[b] and especially[c] toward[d] you.

LEXICON—a. aorist pass. indic. of ἀναστρέφω (LN 41.3) (BAGD 2.b.δ. p. 61): 'to conduct oneself' [AB, BAGD, LN, Lns, NTC; NIV], 'to live' [LN; CEV], 'to behave' [HNTC, ICC2, WBC; NJB, NRSV, TNT], 'to have one's conversation' [KJV]. This verb is also translated by a clause: 'in our behavior we have always acted' [NAB], 'we have been (honest and sincere) in all our dealings' [NLT], 'our conduct has been governed' [REB], 'our relations with you have been ruled' [TEV].

b. κόσμος (LN 9.23) (BAGD 5.a. p. 446): 'world' [AB, HNTC, ICC2, Lns, NTC, WBC; KJV, NIV, NRSV, TEV], 'mankind' [BAGD], 'people of the world' [LN], not explicit [CEV]. The phrase ἐν τῷ κόσμῳ 'in the world' is translated 'toward all' [NAB], 'towards everyone' [NJB, NLT], 'with others' [REB], 'among men' [TNT], 'in this world' [NTC].

c. περισσοτέρως (LN 78.31) (BAGD 2. p. 651): 'especially' [BAGD, HNTC, ICC2, Lns, NTC; CEV, NAB, NIV, NJB, NLT, TEV, TNT], 'all the more' [AB, LN; NRSV], 'more particularly' [WBC], 'more abundantly' [KJV], 'above all' [REB].

d. πρός with accusative object (LN 89.112) (BAGD III. 7. p. 711): 'toward' [Lns, NTC; KJV, NAB, NLT, NRSV], 'towards' [NJB, TNT], 'with' [AB, BAGD, LN; CEV], 'before' [LN], 'in relation to' [HNTC], 'in our relationship with' [ICC2], 'in our relations with' [NIV, TEV], 'in our dealings with' [WBC; REB].

QUESTION—What is meant by the use of the first person plural in this verse?

Paul is referring to himself [TG, WBC]. Paul is speaking primarily of himself, but others are in mind too [AB, HNTC, LN].

QUESTION—What is meant by ἐν τῷ κόσμῳ 'in the world'?

Paul is referring to activities and relationships with people other than the Corinthians Christians [TG] or to his daily life among people [TH]. Paul is referring to his conduct in all places at all times [NIC1], wherever he ministers [TNTC], among men in general [Ho, Lns], among profane humanity [My], and among the everyday matters of people, events, and places [AB]. It is a reference to Paul's ministry of bringing the gospel to all people in all nations [NTC, WBC].

QUESTION—What does Paul mean by saying περισσοτέρως πρὸς ὑμᾶς 'and especially toward you'?

Paul was especially careful during his time in Corinth to be above reproach and avoid any appearance of wrong that might discredit his ministry [ICC2, NTC, TNTC]. Since Paul spent so much time in Corinth the people there had much more opportunity to see the evidence of the integrity of Paul's ministry [EGT, Ho, ICC1, NIC1].

1:13 For[a] we-write[b] to-you nothing other than what you-read[c] and understand;[d]

LEXICON—a. γάρ (LN 89.23) (BAGD 1.b., e. p. 152): 'for' [BAGD, HNTC, ICC2, LN, Lns, NTC; KJV, NIV, NRSV], 'now' [AB, WBC], not explicit [CEV, NAB, NJB, REB, TEV, TNT].

b. pres. act. indic. of γράφω (LN 33.61) (BAGD 2.d. p. 167): 'to write' [AB, HNTC, ICC2, LN, Lns, NTC, WBC; CEV, KJV, NAB, NIV, NJB, NRSV, TEV], 'to write to someone' [BAGD]. This verb is also translated as a substantive: 'our writing' [NJB], 'my letters' [NLT], 'our letters' [REB], 'these words' [TNT].

c. pres. act. indic. of ἀναγινώσκω (LN 33.68) (BAGD 1. p. 51): 'to read' [BAGD, HNTC, ICC2, LN, Lns, WBC; KJV, TNT]. This word is also translated as reflecting the ability to read with understanding: '(what) you can read' [HNTC; NRSV, REB, TEV], '(nothing/anything) you cannot read' [CEV, NAB, NIV]; 'nothing that you cannot read clearly' [NJB], 'nothing between the lines' [NLT].

d. pres. act. indic. of ἐπιγινώσκω (LN **32.16**) (BAGD 2.d. p. 291): 'to understand' [BAGD, LN, Lns, NTC; all versions except KJV], 'to know' [BAGD], 'to recognize' [HNTC, WBC], 'to accord recognition' [ICC2], 'to acknowledge' [KJV]. This word, which is frequently used by Paul, is an intensive compound meaning 'to know with certainty', and refers to the firsthand knowledge of his character that the Corinthians had [NIC1]. It would mean to accept and implement what was read [AB, NIC2].

QUESTION—What relationship is indicated by γάρ 'for'?

It indicates the grounds for Paul's assertions of honesty and integrity in 1:12 by specific reference to the clarity of his letters [HNTC, Ho, ICC1, ICC2, Lns, NIC1, NIC2, TH]. It continues his general defense [TNTC, WBC].

QUESTION—What written communication is Paul referring to when he says 'we write'?

It refers to all his letters to the Corinthians [AB, EBC, He, HNTC, Ho, ICC1, ICC2, NIC2, TH, WBC]. It refers to his letters to them as well as to letters to other churches [NTC].

2 CORINTHIANS 1:13

and[a] I-hope that you-will-understand[b] fully/to the end,[c]

LEXICON—a. δέ (LN 89.94): 'and' [AB, HNTC, ICC2, LN, Lns, NTC, WBC; KJV, NIV, NJB], 'but' [REB, TEV], not explicit [CEV, NAB, NLT, NRSV, TNT].

b. fut. mid. (deponent = act.) indic. of ἐπιγινώσκω. The future tense is translated as a completion of a process that is occurring partially: 'you will understand completely' [AB; CEV], 'you will come to understand us completely' [TEV], 'you will recognize fully' [ICC2, WBC], 'you will fully understand' [NTC; NJB, NLT, TNT], 'you will come to understand fully' [NIV, REB], 'you will come to know us well' [NAB]. It is also translated as a continuation of a present state: 'you will go on recognizing' [HNTC], 'you will continue to understand' [Lns].

c. τέλος (LN **78.47**) (BAGD 1.d.β. p. 812): 'fully' [ICC2, NTC, WBC; NIV, NJB, NLT, REB], 'fully and finally' [TNT], 'completely' [AB, LN; CEV, TEV], 'well' [NAB]. The prepositional phrase ἕως τέλους is also translated in a temporal sense '(to/until the) end' [BAGD, HNTC, Lns; KJV, NRSV].

QUESTION—Why does Paul shift to the first person 'I hope'

Paul speaks for himself in this matter as opposed to his statement 'we write' where he includes the co-author [Lns]. It expresses his intensity of personal feelings in this matter [AB, NIC2]. It is purely stylistic [ICC2].

QUESTION—What does he hope that they will understand?

1. He hopes that they will understand that he is their boast and they are his [AB, HNTC, Ho, ICC2, Lns, My, NTC, TNTC, WBC; KJV, NIV, NJB, NRSV, REB].
2. He hopes that they will come to know and understand him personally [He, NIC2; NAB, NLT, TEV, TNT].
3. He hopes that they will understand that what he writes is what he means [ICC1; CEV].

QUESTION—What is meant by ἕως τέλους 'fully/until the end'?

1. It indicates degree, 'fully' and is in contrast with ἀπό μέρους 'in part' (1:14) [ICC2, LN, NIC1, NTC, WBC; CEV, NAB, NIV, NJB, NLT, REB, TEV, TNT].
2. It is temporal, 'until the end' [BAGD, EGT, HNTC, Ho, ICC1, Lns, My; KJV, NRSV]. It means until the end of your lives [Ho, ICC1, Lns], or the end of the world or the day of the Lord Jesus [EGT, Ho, ICC1, My].
3. It may be a double entendre, with both meanings [NIC2].

1:14 just-as indeed[a] you-understood us in part,[b]

LEXICON—a. καί (LN 89.93): 'indeed' [HNTC, ICC2, NTC], 'also' [LN, Lns; KJV], not explicit [AB, WBC; CEV, NAB, NIV, NJB, NLT, NRSV, REB, TEV, TNT].

b. μέρος (LN **63.15**) (BAGD 1.c. p. 506): 'in part' [BAGD, HNTC, LN, Lns, NTC; KJV, NIV, NRSV, TEV, TNT], 'partially' [AB, ICC2, WBC; NJB], 'partly' [CEV], 'to a certain degree' [NAB], 'in some measure'

[REB]. The phrase 'you understood us in part' is translated 'you don't fully understand us now' [NLT]. This noun is used idiomatically in the prepositional phrase ἀπό μέρους.

QUESTION—What is meant by ἐπέγνωτε ἡμᾶς 'you understood us'?

1. They understood Paul himself and his associates [NIC2], and had a right estimate of him [ICC1]. They knew them [NAB]. They understood his motives [EBC, He, Lns, TG], his actions [NIC2, TG], his communications [Lns], his intentions [EBC, He]. They partly understood Paul's story and now he will fill in more details [WBC].
2. They accorded recognition or acknowledged them [ICC2, WBC; KJV], and recognized Paul's authority [ICC2].
3. They understood that Paul was their cause for glorying [AB, HNTC, ICC1, Lns, My, TNTC]. 'That we are your subjects for glorying' further explains 'us' [Lns].

QUESTION—What is meant by ἀπό μέρους 'in part'?

1. It means a partial or incomplete understanding [He, HNTC, ICC2, NIC2, NTC, TNTC, WBC; CEV, NAB, NJB, NLT, REB, TEV, TNT]. They only partially understood the truths he preached to them [Lns].
2. It means that only some of the Corinthians understood Paul [EGT, Ho, ICC1, My, NIC1]. 'In part' can have both meanings, because some of them understood him more than others, but none fully appreciated him [ICC1, NIC1].

that we-are your boast[a] just-as[b] also you (are) ours

LEXICON—a. καύχημα (LN **33.371**) (BAGD 1. p. 426): 'boast' [AB, BAGD, NTC; NAB, NRSV], 'object of boasting' [BAGD], 'boasting' [HNTC], 'what one boasts about' [LN], 'cause for pride' [ICC2], 'subjects of glorying' [Lns], 'rejoicing' [KJV], 'confidence' [WBC]. The phrase 'we are your boast' is translated 'you can boast of us' [NIV], 'you can be proud of us' [CEV, NJB, TEV], 'you will be proud of us' [NLT], 'you have cause to be proud of us' [TNT], 'you have reason to be proud of us' [REB]. This word is used metonymously as grounds for boasting [He, HNTC, Ho, ICC2].

b. καθάπερ (LN 64.15) (BAGD p. 387): 'just as' [BAGD, HNTC, ICC2, LN; NIV], 'as' [BAGD, Lns, WBC; CEV, NJB, TEV], 'inasmuch as' [NTC], 'even as' [AB; KJV, NRSV], 'as much as' [REB, TNT], 'in the same way' [NLT], not explicit [NAB].

QUESTION—What relationship is indicated by ὅτι 'that'.

1. It indicates discourse content, 'that' [AB, EGT, HNTC, Ho, ICC1, ICC2, Lns, NTC, WBC; KJV, NAB, NIV, NJB, NRSV, REB, TNT].
   1.1 Paul is saying that he hopes the Corinthians will understand that he and they are one another's cause for boasting [AB, EGT, HNTC, Ho, ICC2, Lns, My, NTC, WBC; KJV, NAB, NIV, NJB, NRSV, REB, TNT].
   1.2 Paul is saying that the Corinthians have understood that they have good cause to boast in him [ICC1].

2. It means 'because' and indicates grounds for a statement already made [He, NIC2]: because they are one another's boast, Paul therefore hopes that they will understand him.
3. It indicates a result or consequence, 'then' [TG; CEV, NLT], 'so that' [TEV]. Paul hopes that they will understand him, so that on the day of the Lord Jesus the Corinthians will be as proud of him as he is of them.

QUESTION—What is the difference between καύχεσις 'boasting' (1:12) and καύχημα 'boast'?

Καύχεσις is the verbal idea of the act of boasting whereas καύχημα is the concrete expression of it, the boast itself [EGT, ICC1, Lns, NIC2]. Paul's boasting represents a confidence or justifiable pride as opposed to self-glorification [NIC2], and by it he glorifies God for what God has produced in him [Lns]. This boasting represents a confidence that comes from what God has done and enabled one to do [TNTC]. The two words are synonymous and refer to the act of boasting [NTC].

QUESTION—How is καθάπερ 'just as' used in this clause?

It shows mutuality in that just as Paul is (or will be) their boast so also they are his boast [EGT, HNTC, ICC1, My, NIC1, NIC2; NAB, NIV, NRSV]. It effectively puts them on the same level with Paul himself [EGT, HNTC, ICC1, NIC1]. Paul is their boast in the same way or manner that the Corinthians are Paul's boast [Lns; NLT]. The Corinthians can be proud of Paul to the same degree that Paul is proud of them [CEV, NJB, REB, TEV, TNT].

in^a the day of our Lord Jesus.

TEXT—The word ἡμῶν 'our' does not occur in some manuscripts. It is included by GNT with a C rating, indicating difficulty in deciding whether or not to place it in the text. It is omitted or not translated by WBC, KJV, NIV, NRSV, TNT.

LEXICON—a. ἐν (LN 67.33): 'in' [HNTC, NTC; KJV, NIV, TEV, TNT], 'on' [AB, ICC2; NAB, NRSV, REB], 'when, at the time of' [LN], 'in connection with' [Lns], 'in the light of' [WBC]. The phrase 'in the day of our Lord Jesus' is translated 'when our Lord Jesus returns' [CEV], 'when our Lord Jesus comes back again' [NLT], 'when the day of our Lord Jesus comes' [NJB].

QUESTION—Why does he say 'in the day of our Lord Jesus'?

He means that the coming of the Lord must be kept in mind and everything viewed in light of that [Lns, NIC1, NTC, WBC]. Paul sees himself as already involved in that future event [NTC]. It means that Paul wants them to acknowledge him until that time, that is, unto the end [EGT, HNTC]. That is the time when the Corinthians will feel the pride in him that he now feels in them [TNTC; REB, TNT] or that they will recognize fully that he is their boast [ICC2]. The fact that they will be one another's glory in that day is the grounds for his wish that they understand him now [He]. Paul is saying that they are one another's boasting both now and then [Ho]. The day of the Lord

Jesus is when Paul will glory in the Corinthians and when the value and fruit of his ministry will finally be shown [ICC1]. If the Corinthians come to understand Paul completely then they will rejoice in him on the final day just as he will in them [TG; CEV, NLT, TEV]. Paul hopes that how the Corinthians know and understand him here and now will be in conformity to how he will be shown to be in the day of final vindication [NIC2]. It is an appeal to the final time of judgment and vindication that will show everyone's motives for what they are [WBC].

DISCOURSE UNIT: 1:15–2:13 [WBC]. The topic is Paul's self-defense of his travel plans.

DISCOURSE UNIT: 1:15–2:11 [NIC2]. The topic is a defense of changed travel plans.

DISCOURSE UNIT: 1:15–2:4 [TNTC]. The topic is a defense of changed travel plans.

DISCOURSE UNIT: 1:15–2:2 [AB]. The topic is a cancelled visit.

DISCOURSE UNIT: 1:15–22 [EBC]. The topic is the charge of fickleness answered.

1:15 And in this confidence[a] I-was-planning[b] first[c] to-come to you,
LEXICON—a. πεποίθησις (LN 31.82) (BAGD 1. p. 643): 'confidence' [BAGD, HNTC, ICC2, LN, Lns, NTC; KJV], 'assurance' [NJB]. The phrase 'in this confidence' is translated 'on the ground of this confidence' [WBC], 'because of this confidence' [NTC], 'I was confident' [AB; NIV, TNT], 'I felt so confident' [REB], 'I was so sure' [CEV, NLT, TEV], 'since I was so sure' [NRSV], 'confident as I am' [NAB]. Of the six occurrences of this word in the NT, four are in this epistle, this being the first [NTC].

b. imperf. mid. or pass. (deponent = act.) indic. of βούλομαι (LN **30.56**) (BAGD 2.a.β. p. 146): 'to plan' [**LN**, NTC; CEV, NIV, TNT], 'to make plans' [TEV], 'to decide' [HNTC, Lns], 'to intend' [ICC2, LN, WBC; REB], 'to mean' [NJB], 'to be minded' [KJV], 'to want' [AB; NAB, NLT, NRSV]. The imperfect tense conveys the idea that the plan was not carried out [Lns].

c. πρότερος (LN 60.47, 67.18) (BAGD 1.b.α. p. 722): 'first' [AB, LN (60.47), NTC, WBC; CEV, NAB, NIV, NJB, NRSV, TNT], 'first of all' [REB], 'at first' [HNTC; TEV], 'formerly' [BAGD, LN (67.18), Lns], 'earlier' [BAGD], 'previously' [ICC2], 'before' [KJV], not explicit [NLT].

QUESTION—What is the confidence to which he is referring?
It is his confidence in their readiness to receive him [WBC], or that he was their pride and they trusted him as their apostle [NIC2]. The confidence is his boast of personal integrity and of the mutual respect that he and the Corinthians had for one another [NTC]. He was confident concerning them

and their relationship with each other [HNTC], of their mutual trust and respect [ICC1, ICC2], of their mutual pride in one another [Ho, TNTC]. He was confident that they would acknowledge his sincerity [EGT], or understand his intentions [TG, TH], that they would understand and appreciate why he had changed his plans [Lns]. Paul's confidence is that they would know him fully and would boast in him as he did in them [My]. Paul's confidence is the assurance of his conscience which is the content of all of 1:12–14 [He]. He is speaking of their mutual confidence in one another [SP].

QUESTION—What does the switch to the first person singular signify?
1. There is no intended contrast between singulars and plurals, it is purely stylistic [ICC2].
2. He is answering for the changed plans that put his apostolic credibility and integrity into question [AB].

QUESTION—What does πρότερον 'first' go with?
1. It goes with ἐλθεῖν πρὸς ὑμᾶς 'to come to you' and means that Paul was planning to go to Corinth first before going to Macedonia [AB, EGT, He, HNTC, ICC1, My, NIC2, NTC, TH, WBC; CEV, NAB, NIV, NJB, NRSV, REB]. The word 'first' is paired with 'second', which follows [AB].
2. It goes with ἐβουλόμην 'I was planning' and means that his initial or previous plan had been to visit Corinth and then go to Macedonia [ICC2, Lns, TG; TEV, TNT].

QUESTION—What was Paul's plan, and what did he actually do?
1. Paul's original plan, outlined in 1 Corinthians 16:5–7, was to go to Macedonia and then spend time in Corinth. For some reason he then changed his mind and decided to go briefly to Corinth first, and then return after visiting Macedonia [AB, EGT, He, HNTC, NIC2, NTC, TNTC, WBC].
    1.1 What actually came about was that he had a brief and unpleasant visit to Corinth, probably went to Macedonia, and then went directly to Ephesus, avoiding a second trip to Corinth because of the opposition he had encountered; later he went to Macedonia where he wrote this letter [NIC2, NTC, WBC].
    1.2 Alternatively, he made these plans and followed the above itinerary except that he skipped the planned trip to Macedonia and went directly back to Ephesus after the difficult visit in Corinth [EBC, He, SP]. At this point he reverted to the first plan, which was to go from Ephesus to Macedonia and then Corinth, which he did do with the exception of a stop in Troas before visiting Macedonia [EBC].
    1.3 While Paul was in Corinth dealing with problems he devised the plan in 1:15–16 that he would return to Corinth from Ephesus, visit Macedonia, and then return to Corinth after they would have had time to make the collection. However, after he returned to Ephesus he sent this letter in place of the first visit to Corinth, and went on to Macedonia and subsequently to Corinth [AB].

2. Paul's first plan was that outlined in 2 Corinthians 1:15–16, which was to go to Corinth, visit Macedonia, and then return to Corinth. 1 Corinthians 16:5–7 represents the revised plan, whereby he would go first to Macedonia and then to Corinth. Paul was in the process of completing that visit to Macedonia when he wrote 2 Corinthians [Lns, My, NIC1].

so-that[a] you-might-have[b] a second benefit,[c]
LEXICON—a. ἵνα (LN 89.59): 'so that' [ICC2, LN, NTC, WBC; NAB, NIV, NJB, NRSV], 'that' [HNTC, LN; KJV], 'so' [AB], 'in order that' [Lns; TEV, TNT], 'in this way (you would)' [CEV], not explicit [NLT, REB].
  b. aorist act. subj. of ἔχω (LN 90.65): 'to have' [AB, ICC2, LN, WBC; CEV, KJV, NRSV], 'to get' [HNTC], 'to get to have' [Lns], 'to receive' [NTC]. The phrase 'so that you might have a second benefit' is translated 'that you might benefit twice' [NIV], 'that a double grace might be yours' [NAB], 'so that you would benefit doubly' [NJB], 'to give you a double blessing' [NLT], 'and give you the benefit of a double visit' [REB], 'in order that you might be blessed twice' [TEV], 'I wanted to give you a double favor' [TNT].
  c. χάρις (LN 57.103) (BAGD 3.a. p. 877): 'benefit' [AB, ICC2; KJV], 'blessing' [NTC; CEV, NLT], 'kindness' [HNTC], 'proof of goodwill' [BAGD], 'grace' [Lns; NAB], 'favor' [NRSV, TNT], 'gift' [LN], 'opportunity to do a favor' [WBC], 'visit' [REB]. This noun is also translated as a verb: 'to benefit' [NIV, NJB], 'to be blessed' [TEV]. See this word also at 8:4, 6, 19.
QUESTION—What would be the 'second benefit'?
  1. It refers to benefit to the Corinthians which would come from Paul's two visits to Corinth—before and after his Macedonia trip [AB, HNTC, Ho, ICC1, ICC2, NIC1, NIC2, TG, TH, TNTC].
    1.1 The Corinthians would have two opportunities to enjoy the favor or benefit of Paul's company [AB, Ho, ICC1, NIC1, TG]. It would be a second occasion for Paul to demonstrate his own kindness and goodwill toward the Corinthians [HNTC].
    1.2 There would be two occasions of spiritual benefit as Paul ministers God's grace to the Corinthians [AB, Ho, ICC2, My, NIC2, TNTC].
    1.3 Paul would have two opportunities of showing his own favor and goodwill to them through his visits [ICC2].
  2. It refers to the benefit they would receive from the blessing of Paul's ministry among them the second time. The first grace would have been Paul's initial stay of 18 months when he first evangelized them [Lns].
  3. The word χάρις refers not to benefit received but benefit given; that is, the Corinthians would have the opportunity to give or contribute to ministry [NTC, WBC]. It is a second opportunity to contribute to the collection [WBC]. It is the opportunity to help Paul twice; once on his trip to Macedonia and once again on his trip to Judea [NTC].

4. In this context the word χάρις means rejoicing; Paul's second visit would give the Corinthians a second opportunity for rejoicing [He].

1:16 and to-pass-through^a through^b you into Macedonia and again from Macedonia to-come to you

LEXICON—a. aorist act. infin. of διέρχομαι (LN 15.17) (BAGD 1.b.α. p. 194): 'to pass through' [AB], 'to go through' [BAGD], 'to go on through' [Lns], 'to go on' [HNTC], 'to go on to' [LN], 'to travel through' [ICC2], 'to pass' [KJV]. The phrase δι' ὑμῶν διελθεῖν 'to pass through you' is translated 'to visit you on the way' [NTC], 'to visit you on my way' [NAB, NIV, NJB, NRSV, REB, TEV], 'visiting you on my way' [TNT], 'to stop and see you on my way' [NLT], 'a visit from me...on my way' [CEV], 'having been with you, to go my way' [WBC].

b. διά with genitive object (LN 84.29): 'through' [LN, Lns], 'by way of' [HNTC], 'by' [KJV], 'with your assistance' [ICC2], 'having been with' [WBC], not explicit [AB, NTC; CEV, NAB, NIV, NJB, NRSV, REB, TEV, TNT].

QUESTION—What relationship is indicated by the first καί 'and'?

1. It is epexegetic of the previous verse in that it explains what the two benefits would be [AB, He, Lns, My, NIC2, NTC]: I was planning to come so you could have a second benefit; that is, I was wanting to pass through, etc.
2. It connects the four infinitives representing the four stages of Paul's travel to the one verb ἐβουλόμην 'I was planning' [ICC2]: I was planning to come so you could have a second benefit, and to pass through...and to come again...and to be sent on.

QUESTION—What relationship is indicated by διά 'through'?

1. It represents spatial extension through an area [AB, He, ICC1, NIC2, NTC, WBC]: Paul will travel through Corinth on the way to Macedonia.
2. It represents agency [ICC2]: Paul hopes to have the help of the Corinthians in his journey to Macedonia.

and to-be-sent-on^a by^b you into Judea.

LEXICON—a. aorist pass. infin. of προπέμπω (LN 15.72) (BAGD 2. p. 709): 'to be helped on one's journey/way' [BAGD, LN, WBC], 'to be sent on one's way' [AB, BAGD, HNTC, ICC2, LN], 'to be sent on forward' [Lns], 'to be sent forth' [NTC], 'to be sent on' [CEV], 'to be brought on one's way' [KJV]. The phrase ὑφ' ὑμῶν προπεμφθῆναι 'to be sent on by you' is translated 'that I might receive your help on my journey' [NAB], 'to have you send me on my way' [NIV], 'you could set me on my way' [NJB], 'you could send me on my way' [NLT], 'to have you send me on' [NRSV], 'you could have sent me on my way' [REB], 'to get help from you on my trip' [TEV], 'I wanted you to help me on my way' [TNT].

b. ὑπό (LN 90.1): 'by' [HNTC, LN, Lns, NTC], 'by your help' [AB], 'by your agency' [ICC2], 'with your support' [WBC], 'of you' [KJV], not explicit [CEV, NAB, NIV, NJB, NLT, NRSV, REB, TEV, TNT].

QUESTION—What does he mean by ὑφ' ὑμῶν προπεμφθῆναι 'to be sent on by you'?

He wants to be helped by the Corinthians [ICC1, TH]. He wants them to see him off in safety [EGT]. It means that he wants to have them escort him as traveling companions [NIC1]. He wants delegates to go to Judea to take the money that was collected [He]. Paul is looking for hospitality and letters of recommendation, but not financial help [NIC2]. It means to provide escorts for the journey or to furnish with the means of traveling [Ho]. It means to outfit a traveler and accompany him at least part of the way [Lns]. He wants them to help with the expense of his travel [ICC2, TG]. He is looking for provision for the journey and escorts [AB]. He is wanting them to provide for everything he would need for the trip, including money, food, beverage, clothing, and escorts [NTC].

1:17 Therefore[a] planning[b] this, then[c] surely-not[d] did-I-act[e] with-fickleness?[f]

LEXICON—a. οὖν (LN 89.50): 'therefore' [LN], 'when therefore' [KJV], 'so, consequently' [LN], 'then' [AB, HNTC, LN], 'so then' [ICC2, LN], 'now' [Lns], not explicit [NTC, WBC; CEV, NAB, NIV, NJB, NLT, NRSV, REB, TEV, TNT].

b. pres. mid. or pass. (deponent = act.) participle of βούλομαι (LN 30.56) (BAGD 2.a.α. p. 146): 'to plan' [LN; NIV, TEV], 'to make plans' [NAB], 'to purpose' [LN], 'to intend' [LN], 'to decide' [Lns], 'to make a decision' [HNTC], 'to form an intention' [ICC2], 'to have an intention' [WBC], 'to be minded' [KJV], 'to desire' [BAGD], 'to want' [AB; NRSV], not explicit [CEV, NLT, TNT]. The phrase 'therefore planning this' is translated 'since that was my purpose' [NJB], 'that was my intention' [REB].

c. ἄρα (LN 89.46) (BAGD 2. p. 103): 'then' [LN, NTC], 'so' [LN], 'really' [AB]. This word is used to draw an inference from what precedes it [BAGD, HNTC, Lns, NIC1, NIC2, NTC], possibly signaling what some in Corinth were thinking or even claiming, and which he must now refute [AB]. Here it adds liveliness to Paul's question [BAGD, ICC2]. This word is not translated explicitly in the English versions and most commentaries, but is implicit in the rhetorical question.

d. μήτι (LN 69.16): 'surely not' [ICC2]. In Greek this emphatic particle is used to indicate that the rhetorical question expects a negative answer [LN]. It is translated in conjunction with ἄρα or οὖν...(μήτι) ἄρα as 'did I really...?' [AB], 'do you think...?' [HNTC; CEV, NJB], 'do you suppose...?' [NAB], 'surely I was not...?' [WBC], 'did I...?' [ICC2, NTC; KJV, NIV, REB], 'was I...?' [Lns], 'hadn't I...?' [NLT], 'do I...?' [NRSV, TEV], 'have I...?' [TNT].

e. aorist mid. (deponent = act.) indic. of χράομαι (LN 41.4) (BAGD 2. p. 884): 'to act' [BAGD, HNTC, ICC2], 'to behave toward' [LN]. The phrase 'to act with fickleness' is translated 'to be fickle' [WBC], 'to appear fickle' [TEV], 'to use fickleness' [Lns], 'to use lightness' [KJV], 'to not be able to make up one's mind' [CEV], 'to have not made up one's mind' [NLT], 'to be irresponsible' [TNT], 'to act irresponsibly' [AB], 'to act insincerely' [NAB], 'to do something lightly' [NTC; NIV], 'to change one's mind lightly' [NJB, REB], 'to vacillate' [NRSV].

f. ἐλαφρία (LN **88.99**) (BAGD p. 248): 'fickleness' [BAGD, HNTC, LN, Lns], 'a light-minded way' [ICC2], 'lightness' [KJV]. This word, which is used nowhere else in the NT, may indicate that Paul was accused not so much of fickleness in changing his plans, but of changing his plans in an 'off-hand' manner [TNTC] or of not even caring about keeping his promises to begin with [ICC1].

QUESTION—What is the significance of the definite article τῇ with τῇ ἐλαφρίᾳ 'fickleness'?

1. It refers to a specific fickleness, which some in Corinth have charged him with, and of which charge he is aware [EBC, HNTC, ICC2, NIC2, NTC, SP, TH, WBC]: 'the fickleness (that you accuse me of)'.
2. It is normal with abstract nouns and would not be translated with a definite article in English [EGT, Lns, My].

QUESTION—What is the basis of the accusation from which he is defending himself?

There were people who opposed Paul and who used his change of plans as a pretext for accusing him of being unpredictable and insincere [He, Lns, NIC1, WBC]. The Corinthians had an underlying resentment of the Macedonian churches because Paul accepted financial support from Macedonia but not from Corinth [AB, NIC2], and they were jealous because of Paul's praise of the Macedonians and the time he spent with them [AB]. They objected to his canceling visits that he had announced [HNTC].

Or the-things-which I-plan,[a] do I-plan according-to the flesh,[b] so-that with me there-would-be[c] the 'yes, yes' and the 'no, no'?

LEXICON—a. pres. mid. or pass. (deponent = act.) indic. of βουλεύομαι (LN 30.56) (BAGD 2. p. 145): 'to plan' [LN], 'to make plans' [AB, HNTC, WBC; NIV, NRSV, TEV], 'to frame plans' [REB], 'to intend' [LN], 'to form an intention' [ICC2], 'to purpose' [LN; KJV], 'to resolve' [BAGD], 'to decide' [BAGD], 'to decide on' [Lns], 'to make decisions' [TNT], 'to want to do something' [NTC], not explicit [CEV, NLT]. The phrase 'the things which I plan' is translated 'my plans' [NAB, NJB]. The present tense of the verb indicates that Paul is talking about his habitual patterns of character or decision-making [Ho, ICC1, ICC2].

b. σάρξ (LN 26.7) (BAGD 7. p. 744): 'flesh' [BAGD, HNTC; KJV], 'human nature' [LN]. The phrase κατὰ σάρκα 'according to the flesh' is translated as 'opportunistically' [AB], 'in a worldly fashion' [ICC2], 'in a worldly manner' [NIV], 'in a fleshly way' [Lns], 'as the world does' [NTC], 'on a human level' [WBC; TNT], 'simply to please others' [CEV], 'determined by self-interest' [NAB], 'based on ordinary human promptings' [NJB], 'like people of the world' [NLT], 'according to ordinary human standards' [NRSV], 'as a worldly man might' [REB], 'from selfish motives' [TEV].

    c. pres. act. subj. of εἰμί: 'to be'. The clause 'so that with me there would be the yes, yes and the no, no' is translated 'so it seems I am saying yes, yes and no no' [AB], 'so as to say at the same time, Yes, yes and No, no' [HNTC], 'so that, in my case, there is (simultaneously) the "Yes, yes" and the "No, no"' [ICC2], 'so that I say first "Yes, yes" and then "No, no"' [NTC], 'that there should be on my part a vacillating attitude, saying "Yes" and "No" in the same breath' [WBC], 'do I seem like someone who says "Yes" or "No"' [CEV], 'that with me there should be yea, yea, and nay, nay' [KJV], 'that I change my mind from one minute to the next' [NAB], 'so that in the same breath I say, "Yes, yes" and "No, no"' [NIV], 'I have in my mind Yes, yes at the same time as No, no' [NJB], 'am I like people who say yes when they really mean no' [NLT], 'ready to say "Yes, yes" and "No, no" at the same time' [NRSV, TEV], 'first saying "Yes, yes" and then "No, no"' [REB], 'saying "yes" and "no" at the same time' [TNT].

QUESTION—What is the answer anticipated by this rhetorical question?
    This rhetorical question also expects a 'no' answer [He, ICC2, My, NIC1, NIC2, NTC, TH, TNTC].

QUESTION—What difference is there between βούλομαι 'to plan' in the first sentence of this verse, and βουλεύομαι 'to plan' which occurs twice in the second sentence?
    1. They are used synonymously [He, ICC2, LN, Lns, TG, WBC; NAB, NIV, NJB, TEV]. They may be used synonymously but in this verse the two verbs are used to make a slight distinction in meaning, βούλομαι referring to making a decision and βουλεύομαι being used for the making of plans [HNTC].
    2. They are distinct, with βούλομαι referring to what is wanted or desired and βουλεύομαι to what is decided or planned [AB, BAGD, ICC1, NTC; NRSV].

QUESTION—What does Paul mean by κατὰ σάρκα 'according to the flesh'?
    It refers to the lower nature which is guided by expediency [AB, ICC1], and not by internal principles such as reason or spirit [ICC1]. It refers to that which is according to a person's own desires or corrupt human nature instead of according to the leading of the Spirit [He, Ho, ICC2, NIC2, NTC, WBC]. It is that which is opposed to the Spirit of God [NIC1]. It means being ready to go back on his promises if it suits him [TNTC], having a low commitment to keeping one's word [ICC1], being capricious because his principles are changeable [EGT], acting on impulse [EBC], or being selfishly expedient and therefore inconsistent [ICC2]. It means being self-centered [EBC,

HNTC, Lns] as opposed to being concerned for others or directed by God [HNTC], to be unprincipled and acting from unworthy or selfish motives [TG].

QUESTION—What relationship is indicated by ἵνα?

It expresses a result clause, indicating the consequence or result of acting according to the flesh [AB, He, HNTC, Ho, ICC1, Lns, My, NIC1, NTC, WBC], or of acting according to the flesh and fickleness [Lns]. It is epexegetic, explaining what it means to act according to the flesh, namely, my words would be yes, yes, and no, no [NIC2].

QUESTION—What is the function of the repetition of 'yes' and 'no'?

It is intensive, giving emphasis [Ho, ICC1, My, NIC1]. It shows that he is quoting specific accusations from Corinth [EBC]. It reflects Jesus' teaching which is recorded in Matthew 5:37 with its Semitic pattern of doubling for emphasis, and means 'again and again yes, and again and again no' [NTC].

QUESTION—Is there any significance in the use of the definite article in the phrase τὸ ναὶ ναὶ καὶ τὸ οὒ οὒ 'the yes, yes and the no, no'?

1. It indicates that Paul is quoting a specific charge of the Corinthians [NIC2, WBC].
2. It does not represent a quote, but merely marks them as nouns which Paul himself is saying [Lns].
3. It marks them as well known solemn formulas of denial or assertion [My].

QUESTION—What does he mean by the statement 'that with me there would be the "yes, yes" and the "no, no"'?

It means that he would be saying two conflicting things at the same time [EBC, He, HNTC, Ho, ICC2, Lns, My, TG, TH; NIV, NJB, NRSV, TEV, TNT], or about the same subject [Ho], or that he would change unpredictably [EBC, NTC, TG; NAB, REB]. It means that he is unreliable [HNTC], that he does not mean what he says when he says it [ICC2; NLT], or that he reserves the right to break his promises if he wants to [ICC1]. He is dishonest, and says yes when he really means no [NIC2, WBC]. It means that Paul is a flatterer, saying yes when others say yes, and no when others say no [AB], or who says yes or no just to please others [CEV].

1:18 But[a] God (is) faithful[b] that[c] our word[d] to you is not yes and no.

LEXICON—a. δέ (LN 89.124): 'but' [LN, Lns], 'but as surely as' [NTC; NIV], 'as surely as' [NJB, NLT, NRSV, TEV], 'but as certain as' [WBC], 'but as' [CEV], 'as' [AB, ICC2; NAB, TNT], not explicit [HNTC; CEV, REB].

b. πιστός (LN 31.87) (BAGD 1.a.β. p. 664): 'faithful' [AB, BAGD, ICC2, LN, Lns, NTC; NIV, NRSV], 'trustworthy' [BAGD, LN, WBC; NJB], 'true' [KJV, NLT]. This adjective is also translated as a verb phrase: '(God) can be trusted' [CEV], '(God) is to be trusted' [HNTC; REB, TNT], '(God) keeps his word' [NAB], '(God) speaks the truth' [TEV].

c. ὅτι (LN 90.21) (BAGD 1.b.α. p. 588): 'that' [BAGD, LN, Lns]. This word is not translated by the English versions and by most commentators, who take it as indicating the content of that which Paul swears by God's faithfulness is true, namely, that Paul's word was not equivocal. This relation is translated 'God can be trusted, and so can I, when I say' [CEV], 'as God is faithful, our word to you' [AB, ICC2], 'as surely as God is faithful, our word/message to you' [NTC; NIV, NRSV], 'as God is true, our word' [KJV], 'God is to be trusted, and he will bear witness that our word to you' [HNTC], 'but faithful is God in respect to this that our word' [Lns], 'but as certain as God is trustworthy, our message to you' [WBC], 'as surely as God is trustworthy, what we say' [NJB], 'as God keeps his word, I declare that my word' [NAB], 'God is to be trusted, and therefore what we tell you' [REB], 'as surely as God is true, I am not that sort of person' [NLT], 'as surely as God speaks the truth, my promise to you' [TEV], 'as God is to be trusted, our word to you' [TNT].

d. λόγος (LN 33.98) (BAGD 1.a.β. p. 477): 'word' [AB, BAGD, HNTC, ICC2, LN, Lns, NTC; KJV, NAB, NRSV, TNT], 'message' [BAGD, LN, WBC; NIV], 'instruction, teaching' [BAGD], 'what we say' [NJB], 'what we tell you' [REB], 'when I say' [CEV], 'my promise' [TEV], not explicit [NLT].

QUESTION—What does he mean by 'but God is faithful'?

1. It is an oath formula whereby Paul asserts the truth of what he has said [AB, EBC, EGT, He, HNTC, Ho, ICC2, NIC2, NTC, TG, TNTC]: 'but as God is faithful, our word to you is true'.
2. It is an assertion or confession of God's essential faithfulness and truthfulness, though not an oath, intended to lend credence to Paul's communications [ICC1, Lns, My]. Paul's reliability rests on God's faithfulness [ICC1].
3. He calls God, who is trustworthy, as witness to his integrity [HNTC, TH].

QUESTION—In what sense does he use the term λόγος 'word'?

1. It refers both to the gospel message that he preached as well as to other communications such as his travel plans [AB, EBC, EGT, HNTC, ICC2, Lns, NIC2, NTC]. It refers in general to all he says [He, TG, TNTC].
2. It refers to the gospel message [Ho, ICC1, My].
3. It refers to his personal statements such as those concerning his travel plans [TNTC].

QUESTION—What is the intent of Paul's argument?

1. It is an argument from the greater to the lesser: God is faithful and so are we; the gospel we preached was valid, and so is our promise [AB, ICC2, NIC2, NTC]. He is arguing for his own credibility as well as for the validity of his ministry [NIC2].
2. He is defending not just his own integrity, but that of the gospel, as they both rise or fall together [Ho, ICC1, WBC]. He wants the Corinthians to be confident in the gospel message that he had preached to them, even if they lack confidence in him personally [Ho, ICC1].

1:19 For^a the son of-God Jesus Christ the-one preached^b by us among you, by me and Silas^c and Timothy,

LEXICON—a. γάρ (LN 89.23): 'for' [AB, HNTC, ICC2, LN, Lns, NTC, WBC; KJV, NIV, NRSV, TEV], 'because' [LN; NLT], 'this is because' [CEV], not explicit [NAB, NJB, REB, TNT].

  b. aorist pass. participle of κηρύσσω (LN 33.256) (BAGD 2.b.β. p. 431): 'to be preached' [AB, BAGD, LN, Lns, NTC; KJV, NAB, NIV, NLT, TEV], 'to be proclaimed' [BAGD, HNTC, ICC2, WBC; NJB, NRSV, REB, TNT]. The phrase 'the one preached by us among you' is translated 'he is the one that Silas, Timothy, and I told you about' [CEV].

  c. Σιλουανός (LN 93.339, 93.340) (BAGD p. 750): 'Silvanus' [AB, BAGD, HNTC, ICC2, LN, Lns, NTC, WBC; KJV, NAB, NJB, NRSV, REB, TNT], 'Silas' [BAGD, LN; CEV, NIV, NLT, TEV]. Silvanus is the same as Silas [AB, EBC, EGT, HNTC, ICC1, ICC2, Lns, NIC1, NIC2, NTC, TG, TNTC]. His Jewish name would have been Saul, Silas would be the Aramaic form, and Silvanus the Latinized form [AB, BAGD, NTC].

QUESTION—What relationship is indicated by γάρ 'for'?

It introduces an explanation of what is said in 1:18 [EBC, NTC]. It indicates the grounds for his claim to reliability in the previous verse: his preaching is true for Christ is true [Ho, WBC]. It is a connective between the statement in the previous verse that God is faithful and the assertion in this verse that Jesus Christ was not ambiguous [NIC2].

QUESTION—What is the significance of the phrase ὁ τοῦ θεοῦ γὰρ υἱὸς Ἰησοῦς Χριστός 'for the son of God Jesus Christ'?

In the Greek text 'God' comes before 'son' and 'Jesus Christ', and this word order places the emphasis on God [EGT, ICC1, ICC2, My, NTC], since Jesus is this faithful God's son [ICC1]. 'Son of God' is a messianic title [ICC2], and also implies likeness of character to God [ICC2, NTC]. It stresses Jesus' divinity [AB, NTC], and his filial relationship to God [NTC]. This is the only place in the NT where Paul use the phrase 'Jesus Christ the Son of God' [NIC2, NTC].

QUESTION—What does it mean for Christ to be preached?

The message about Christ is preached [NIC2, TG]. Christ is the content of the message [ICC2] and the essence of the message [EBC]. Christ is the object and sum of Paul's preaching [EGT], the subject or theme of the preaching [NTC].

QUESTION—Why does he mention Silas and Timothy?

He does this so that there will be the 'two or three' corroborating witnesses as required by OT law to confirm testimony, which in this case is Paul's testimony concerning the gospel message [AB, EBC, ICC2, NIC2, NTC]. Paul's mention of himself first emphasizes his own role [AB, TH].

was not yes and no but^a has-always-been^b yes in him.

LEXICON—a. ἀλλά (LN 89.124): 'but' [LN, Lns, NTC; NIV, NRSV, TNT], 'on the contrary' [HNTC, ICC2, LN; TEV], 'instead' [LN], 'rather' [AB, WBC], not explicit [CEV, NAB, NJB, NLT, REB]

b. perf. act. indic. of γίνομαι (LN 13.48): 'to become' [LN]. The perfect tense of this verb indicates an ongoing and continuing state [AB, EBC, EGT, HNTC, Ho, ICC1, ICC2, Lns, NIC1, NIC2, NTC, TG, WBC]. This verb is sometimes used in its aorist and perfect tense forms in place of the verb εἰμί 'to be', which lacks those tenses. The phrase 'has always been yes in him' is translated 'in him it has been an enduring "Yes"' [AB], 'in him a final Yes has been pronounced' [HNTC], '"Yes" has come about in him' [ICC2], 'has been yea in him' [Lns], 'in him it continues to be Yes' [NTC], 'the "Yes" has always been a reality in him' [WBC], '(the Son of God) is always "Yes"' [CEV], 'in him was yea' [KJV], 'he was never anything but "yes"' [NAB], 'in him it has always been "Yes"' [NIV], 'his nature is all Yes' [NJB], 'he is the divine Yes' [NLT], 'in him it is always "Yes"' [NRSV], 'with him it is always Yes' [REB], 'he is God's "Yes"' [TEV], 'God's "Yes" is in him' [TNT].

QUESTION—What does 'yes in him' mean?

Jesus Christ is the affirmation of God's truth and the affirmation and fulfillment of God's promises [My, WBC]. He is the embodiment of the truth [AB], the personification of God's truth [NTC]. He is the climax and summation of God's revelation of himself [EBC]. The 'yes' that is pronounced is an affirmation of God's plans [HNTC]. Christ fully represents God's will and purpose and is the guarantee of God's promises [TG]. God's promises are confirmed and achieved through Christ [He]. God's purpose of reconciling lost people to himself was expressed deliberately and unambiguously through his son, who came as God's everlasting and unretracted 'yes' [NIC2].

1:20 **For^a as-many^b promises^c of God (as there are), in him (is) the yes;**

LEXICON—a. γάρ (LN 89.23): 'for' [HNTC, ICC2, LN, Lns, NTC; KJV, NIV, NLT, NRSV, REB, TEV], not explicit [AB, WBC; CEV, NAB, NJB, TNT].

b. ὅσος (LN 59.7): 'as many as' [LN], 'as many as there are' [ICC2, NTC], 'however many' [HNTC, Lns], 'no matter how many' [NIV], 'every one' [NRSV], 'whatever' [NAB], 'all' [AB, WBC; CEV, NJB, NLT, REB, TEV, TNT].

c. ἐπαγγελία (LN 33.288) (BAGD 2.a. p. 280): 'promise' [AB, BAGD, HNTC, ICC2, LN, Lns, NTC, WBC; all versions].

QUESTION—What relationship is indicated by γάρ 'for'?

It introduces a further amplification of the statement that God is faithful [NIC2].

QUESTION—What promises is he talking about?
These promises are all the OT promises [NTC, WBC]. It refers to those of the OT, especially the covenant promises to Abraham [NIC1, NIC2]. They are all God's purposes announced in the OT [HNTC]. They are all the promises concerning the messiah [Ho], the messianic salvation [ICC2], or the messianic age [TNTC]. It refers to God's promises about the coming of the messiah which he made to the Jews, and through the Jews to all mankind [ICC1].

QUESTION—What does it mean that he is 'the yes'?
It indicates the fulfillment of all God's promises in Christ [EBC, He, Ho, ICC1, Lns, NIC2, NTC, TNTC; NAB, NLT]. Christ is the climax and summation of God's revelation of himself [EBC]. He confirms all God's promises [Ho], and proves that God keeps his promises [TG]. He affirms God's promises because he is the living word of God [NIC1]. Christ affirmed the diving promises by fulfilling them and affirmed the will of God by obedience [ICC2]. Christ says 'yes' to all God's promises [CEV]. God says 'yes' to all his own promises through Christ [TNT]. In Christ the fulfillment of God's promises are an ongoing event in the life of the believer [AB]. The guarantee of the fulfillment of the promises of the OT is given in Christ [My].

therefore[a] also through[b] him the amen[c] to God for[d] glory[e] through us.

TEXT—Instead of δι' αὐτοῦ 'through him', some manuscripts have ἐν αὐτῷ 'in him'. GNT does not mention this alternative. Only KJV reads 'in him'.

LEXICON—a. διό (LN 89.47) (BAGD p. 198): 'therefore' [BAGD, ICC2, LN; NAB, NJB], 'wherefore' [Lns, NTC], 'for this reason' [HNTC, LN; NRSV], 'hence' [AB], 'that is why' [WBC; CEV, NLT, REB, TEV, TNT], 'and so' [NIV], not explicit [KJV].
   b. διά with genitive object (LN 90.4) (BAGD A.III.2.b.γ. p. 180): 'through' [AB, BAGD, HNTC, ICC2, LN, Lns, NTC, WBC; all versions except CEV, KJV]. (KJV follows the variant reading ἐν αὐτῷ 'in him', which renders this phrase being parallel to the phrase before it, 'in him are yea, and in him amen'). This sentence is translated 'That's why we have Christ to say "Amen" for us to the glory of God' [CEV].
   c. αμήν (LN 72.6) (BAGD 3. p. 46): 'amen' [AB, BAGD, HNTC, ICC2, Lns, NTC, WBC; all versions], 'truly, indeed' [LN].
   d. πρός with accusative object (LN 89.60) (BAGD III.3.c. p. 710): 'for' [BAGD, Lns, NTC, WBC], 'for the purpose of' [BAGD, LN], 'to (the/his glory)' [HNTC; CEV, NIV, NRSV, TEV], 'unto (the glory)' [KJV]. The two prepositional phrases 'to God for glory' are translated as a single verbal phrase: 'when we worship' [NAB], 'when we give glory' [NLT, REB], 'to give praise' [NJB], 'to glorify God' [TNT], '(the amen) glorifies God' [AB].

e. δόξα (LN 33.357): 'glory' [HNTC, ICC2, Lns, NTC, WBC; all versions except NAB, NJB, TNT], 'praise' [LN; NJB]. This noun is also translated as a verb: 'to glorify (God)' [AB; TNT], 'to worship' [NAB].

QUESTION—What relationship is indicated by δι' αὐτοῦ 'through him'?
1. It is through Christ that we offer worship [EBC; NAB, NLT, REB]. Through Christ we say 'amen' to God, which glorifies him [HNTC, ICC2, NTC; NIV, NJB, NRSV, TEV, TNT]. It is in his name that we say 'amen' when we pray or worship [NIC1, TG, TH], or invoke all the promises of God which Christ fulfills [NIC1]. We can respond in faith to God because his promises are fulfilled in Christ [My].
2. It is through Christ that the promises are 'amen' to God, that is, they are fulfilled [Lns].
3. Christ is the one who says 'amen' for us [CEV], or who also says the 'amen' to God, along with believers [TNTC].

QUESTION—What does 'amen to God' mean?
1. 'Amen' is a response to God in worship [EBC, EGT, HNTC, ICC1, ICC2, WBC], in obedience [HNTC], and in submission to God's purposes in the whole of life [ICC2]. During worship the Corinthian congregation would say 'amen' to affirm Christ as the sign of God's faithfulness [AB] or say 'amen' to the doxology that is offered in response to the fulfillment of God's promises [EGT]. Believers would say 'amen' to affirm confidence in God and his purposes [EBC, NIC1], to affirm what God reveals [NIC2], and to acknowledge their agreement and commitment [EBC]. The 'amen' means that people assent to and experience the truth of God's promises [Ho]. 'Amen' is a pledge of faithfulness in response to God as well as a commitment to believe his promises [He]. 'Amen' is a synonym for 'yes' [EGT, Ho, NTC], and people glorify God by responding 'amen' to God's 'yes' in Christ [HNTC, NTC, WBC]. In corporate prayer people agree to and affirm what is said by saying 'amen' [NIC1, TG], or express assurance that their prayer is heard [My].
2. It means that Christ is the 'amen' to God's promises because through him the promises are made true, that is, they are fulfilled [Lns].

QUESTION—What is meant by the phrase τὸ ἀμὴν τῷ θεῷ πρὸς δόξαν 'the amen to God for glory'?
1. Πρὸς δόξαν 'for glory' states the purpose or result of the 'amen'. Believers glorify God by saying 'amen' [AB, EBC, EGT, HNTC, Ho, ICC1, My, NTC, TNTC, WBC; NIV, NJB, NRSV, TEV, TNT]. Or, when Christ says the 'amen' for believers it glorifies God [CEV].
2. Πρὸς δόξαν 'for glory' states the context of worship within which the 'amen' is expressed. When believers worship or give glory to God they say 'amen' [TG; NAB, NLT, REB].
3. Πρὸς δόξαν indicates the glory God receives through believers who submit their lives to God as a result of apostolic ministry. Through bringing people to faith who will ultimately say 'amen' or 'yes' to God's purposes for their lives, Paul and his co-workers glorify God [ICC2].

4. Πρὸς δόξαν refers to the glory God receives through the ministry of Christ and the apostles. Christ glorifies God through being the 'amen' or fulfillment of his promises, and Paul and his co-workers glorify God through preaching the fulfilled promises, bringing people to faith who will ultimately glorify God [Lns].

QUESTION—Is the 'us' in this clause inclusive or exclusive, and what relationship is indicated by δι' ἡμῶν 'through us'?

1. It is inclusive [AB, EBC, EGT, He, HNTC, NIC1, NIC2, NTC, TG, TH, TNTC, WBC; NAB]. It refers to the 'amen' spoken by Christians in corporate worship [AB, EBC, EGT, HNTC, NIC2, WBC; NAB], or corporate prayer [NIC1, TG]. The phrase δι' ἡμῶν 'through us' really means 'we say', that is, we say 'amen' to God [NTC; NRSV].
2. It is exclusive, referring to Paul and his co-workers, through whom men are brought to faith [Ho, ICC1, ICC2, Lns]. Those who are brought to faith through the apostolic ministry will then glorify God in worship [ICC1], by saying 'amen' to God's promises fulfilled through Christ [Ho], or by saying 'amen' to God's purposes for their lives [ICC2].

1:21 **Now[a] the one-establishing[b] us with you in/into[c] Christ and having-anointed[d] us (is) God,**

LEXICON—a. δέ (LN 89.124, 89.94): 'now' [NTC, WBC; KJV, NIV], 'and' [HNTC, ICC2, LN (89.94); CEV, REB], 'but' [LN (89.124); NRSV], 'moreover' [Lns], not explicit [AB; NAB, NJB, NLT, TEV, TNT].

b. pres. act. participle of βεβαιόω (LN 31.91) (BAGD 2. p. 138): 'to establish' [BAGD; KJV, NRSV], 'to firmly establish' [NAB], 'to establish in belief' [LN], 'to strengthen' [BAGD; TNT], 'to make to stand firm' [NIV], 'to give the ability to stand firm' [NLT], 'to make firm' [Lns], 'to confirm' [AB, NTC, WBC], 'to guarantee' [HNTC], 'to secure' [ICC2], 'to make it possible to stand firmly' [CEV], 'to give a sure place' [NJB], 'to belong to Christ, guaranteed as his' [REB], 'to make sure of (life in union with Christ)' [TEV]. The present participle shows that the action is ongoing [AB, EBC, ICC1, Lns, NIC1, NIC2, NTC]. See the adjectival form of this word at 1:7.

c. εἰς (LN 83.3): 'in' [AB, LN, NTC; KJV, NAB, NIV, NJB, NRSV, TNT], 'in our relationship to' [ICC2, WBC], 'in union with' [TEV], 'for' [HNTC, Lns; NLT], '(to belong) to' [REB], 'with' [CEV].

d. aorist act. participle χρίω (LN 37.107) (BAGD 4. p. 887): 'to anoint' [AB, BAGD, ICC2, LN, Lns, NTC, WBC; KJV, NAB, NIV, NJB, NRSV, REB, TNT], 'to make to share (his) anointing' [HNTC], 'to appoint' [LN], 'to choose' [CEV], 'to commission' [NLT], 'to set apart' [TEV]. The use of the aorist points to one specific event [AB].

QUESTION—In what sense are they established?

This is a legal and commercial term [EBC, HNTC, NIC2, NTC, WBC]. It means that God guarantees the covenant he has made with his people by means of his promises which are like a legally certified security [NTC]. It means that God guarantees and upholds their relationship with Christ and they will ultimately have all the blessings he has promised [NIC2]. God confers the privilege of becoming a partaker of Christ himself and confirms the relationship [WBC]. Believers are placed into a stable but growing union with Christ [NIC1]. God is the one who produces stability and strengthens believers in their faith [EBC]. God is the one who calls them into the messianic community and keeps them in that relationship [ICC2]. He causes them to stand firm and persevere in Christ with unshakable constancy [Ho]. God confirms them for Christ by incorporating them into the body of Christ [AB]. God confirms the gospel by fulfilling its promises and guarantees that those who believe belong to Christ [HNTC]. It means being rooted and grounded ever more solidly in Christ [Lns]. He continues to establish those whom he has set apart for himself once for all [ICC1]. It means that God has established Paul as trustworthy [TNTC]. God assures Paul and the believers that their union with Christ is firm [TH].

QUESTION—Is the ἡμᾶς 'us' in χρίσας ἡμᾶς 'having-anointed us' inclusive or exclusive?

    1. It is inclusive, referring to Paul and his co-workers as well as the Corinthians [AB, EBC, EGT, HNTC, Ho, ICC1, ICC2, Lns, NIC2, NTC; REB].

    2. It is exclusive, referring only to Paul and his co-workers [NIC1, TG, TNTC, WBC]. The passage is apologetic, in defense of Paul's ministry [NIC1, TNTC, WBC].

QUESTION—What does the verb χρίω 'anoint' mean in this passage?

There is a play on words between Χριστός 'Christ' or 'Anointed One' and χρίω 'anoint' [HNTC, NIC1, NTC, WBC].

    1. Christ is the anointed One and believers are anointed ones, the anointing referring to the gift of the Holy Spirit [NTC]. They are made like Christ, the anointed one, as kings and priests under him [Lns]. The believers are anointed to future royal privileges as they reign with the messianic king [ICC2]. They share Christ's vocation and mission [HNTC], and are commissioned, consecrated and enabled for divine service [EBC, Ho]. To be anointed means to be chosen or set apart [CEV, TEV] or commissioned [NLT].

    2. It means that the apostles are chosen and commissioned as ministers [TG, TNTC], appointed and empowered for their ministry [NIC1], and set apart for the apostolic office [My, WBC].

QUESTION—What relationship is indicated by εἰς Χριστόν 'in/into Christ'?

It means they are established with reference to Christ [Ho], or established for Christ [Lns], or with relation to Christ such that they are faithful to him [My]. It means that the believers had been placed into the body of Christ [AB]. With reference to the participle βεβαιῶν 'establishing', which is a commercial term, it means that believers are placed into Christ's account [HNTC]. It indicates that the believer is a partaker of Christ himself [WBC]. The preposition εἰς combined with the present participle βεβαιῶν represents a progressive and intensifying experience of being put into Christ [NIC1, NIC2]. It refers to being placed into the messianic community and kept in that relation [ICC2]. It means that they are established in that relationship [ICC1]. It means that the new life a believer has depends entirely on Christ [TH].

QUESTION—What relationship is indicated by the position of Θεός 'God' at the end of this clause that has no finite verb?

Θεός 'God' is the predicate of this sentence, and the verb 'to be' is implied. [AB, HNTC, ICC1, ICC2, Lns, NTC, WBC; KJV, NIV, NJB, NLT, NRSV, TEV, TNT]. Its position at the end of the sentence makes it emphatic [EBC, Lns]. Its position at the end of the sentence divides it from the next, indicating that the relationship between the participles of the two sentences are parallel, the two in the second explaining the two in the first [NTC].

1:22 the-one also having-sealed[a] us and having-given[b] us the earnest[c] of the Spirit in our hearts.[d]

LEXICON—a. aorist mid. participle of σφραγίζω (LN 33.484) (BAGD 2.b. p. 796): 'to seal' [AB, HNTC, ICC2, LN, Lns, NTC; CEV, KJV, NAB], 'to mark' [LN], 'to mark with a seal' [BAGD; NJB], 'to set his seal upon' [WBC], 'to set his seal on' [REB], 'to set his seal of ownership on' [NIV], 'to put his seal of ownership on' [TNT], 'to place his mark of ownership on' [TEV], 'to put his seal on' [NRSV], 'to identify as his own' [NLT]. The actions of sealing and giving the earnest of the spirit are combined and translated as a purpose clause: 'to show that we belong only to him' [CEV]. The middle voice is used to indicate that God sealed them for himself [ICC1, Lns].

b. δίδωμι aorist act. participle of δίδωμι (LN 57.71) (BAGD 1.b.β. p. 193): 'to give' [AB, BAGD, ICC2, LN, Lns, NTC; KJV, NJB, REB, TEV, TNT], 'to grant' [BAGD], 'to put' [HNTC; CEV, NIV, NRSV], 'to place' [NLT], 'to impart' [WBC], 'to deposit' [NAB].

c. ἀρραβών (LN 57.170) (BAGD p. 109): 'earnest' [KJV], 'first installment' [BAGD, HNTC, LN, NTC; NRSV], 'first installment of everything he will give us' [NLT], 'pledge' [LN, Lns, WBC; NJB], 'pledge of what is to come' [REB], 'installment and pledge of what is to come' [TNT], 'guarantee' [LN], 'guarantee of all he has in store for us' [TEV], 'deposit' [BAGD, ICC2], 'a deposit guaranteeing what is to come' [NIV], 'down payment' [AB, BAGD, LN], 'first payment' [NAB], not explicit [CEV].

d. καρδία (LN 26.3) (BAGD 1.b.θ. p. 404): 'heart' [AB, BAGD, HNTC, ICC2, LN, Lns, NTC; all versions except REB], 'to dwell in our hearts' [REB], not explicit [WBC]. It refers to the soul or spirit, the inner spiritual experience [TG]. It is figurative for the entire person [NTC, WBC]. It represents the innermost part of a person, the center of reason, will and moral choice [TH].

QUESTION—What is the meaning of the sealing?

It refers to a marking that indicates ownership [AB, EBC, HNTC, Ho, ICC1, ICC2, Lns, NTC, TG, TH, WBC]; believers are marked as being God's very own property [AB, Ho, ICC1; CEV, NIV, NLT, TEV, TNT] or as belonging to the chosen people [ICC2]. It attests value [ICC1], or authenticates genuineness of faith [EBC, HNTC, Ho, NIC1, NTC]. It means to endow with the Holy Spirit [AB, TNTC], who marks every believer [TNTC]. It indicates a guarantee of the status of the believer for the last day [EBC, HNTC, NIC1], secures them from apostasy [Ho], and protects them from harm [NTC]. It authenticates the ministry and message of Paul and his coworkers [TNTC]. The sealing is a stamping of the character of God on the personality to restore the image of God lost in the fall [NIC1].

QUESTION—Is the 'us' inclusive or exclusive?
1. It is inclusive [AB, EBC, EGT, HNTC, Ho, ICC1, ICC2, Lns, NIC2, NTC, TG].
2. It is exclusive [NIC1, TNTC, WBC].

QUESTION—What is meant by the term ἀρραβών 'earnest'?

The earnest is the first installment or down payment in token of what is yet to come [AB, EGT, Ho, Lns, NIC2, NTC, TH, WBC; NLT, NRSV, REB, TEV, TNT]. The giving of the Spirit is a guarantee for all other blessings to be received later [TG; NIV] or that he will fully redeem his people [TH]; it attests to the future glorified life [NIC1], eternal life [ICC1], full participation in the blessing of the age to come [TNTC], of the future messianic salvation [My], of full and final salvation [Ho, ICC2], of eschatological blessing and life centered on God [HNTC]. In defining the term ἀρραβών 'earnest' as a first deposit in token of more of the same to be given later, none of the commentators understood this to mean that only a portion of the Spirit had given now, in anticipation of the fullness of the Spirit to be received later.

QUESTION—How are the nouns related in the genitive construction 'earnest of the spirit'?

The nouns are appositional: the Spirit is the earnest [AB, EBC, He, HNTC, Ho, ICC1, ICC2, Lns, My, NIC1, NIC2, NTC, SP, TG, WBC; NAB, NIV, NJB, NLT, NRSV, REB, TEV, TNT]. In mentioning the 'earnest of the spirit' Paul completes a trinitarian statement: the one who establishes believers in Christ is God, who also gives the Spirit as an earnest [AB, He, HNTC, ICC1, Lns, NIC1, NIC2, NTC, WBC].

QUESTION—What is the relationship of the two participles 'establishing' and 'having anointed' in 1:21 with the two participles 'having sealed' and 'having given' in 1:22?

The first participle is present active, the second aorist active, the third aorist middle, and the fourth aorist active (all in the indicative mood). In each of the two verses the initial participle has the definite article and is paired with the inarticular participle that follows by means of the conjunction καί 'and'. (The verb 'to be' must be supplied, since there is no main verb.)

The structure is as follows: 'the one doing this and having done that (is) God, also the one having done this and having done that'.

1. The two verses are balanced and parallel [AB, NTC]. The two participles in 1:22 explain and strengthen the two in 1:21, and the two verses together relate the whole process of relationship with God through conversion, faith, baptism, and the presence of the Holy Spirit [NTC]. The two sets of participles are appositional and are balanced in that each pair has a single article. The two in 1:22 add to those of 1:21 to further emphasize and elaborate on the saving acts of God in the lives of the Corinthians [AB].
2. The last three participles (all aorists) are related in meaning, as apart from the first, and are to be taken together.
   2.1 All three aorist participles relate to the work of the Holy Spirit [He, HNTC, ICC1, NIC1, NIC2, WBC] or to the giving of the Holy Spirit and the entry into the Christian life [HNTC]. 'Giving the Holy Spirit' is epexegetical of and synonymous with 'sealing'; that is, sealing is the giving of the Holy Spirit [EBC, He, Ho, Lns, NIC2, WBC]. The words 'anoint' and 'seal' refer to the granting of charismatic gifts by the Holy Spirit [He]. The Holy Spirit is the anointing [ICC1] as well as the sealing and the earnest [ICC1, NIC2].
   2.2 All three participles relate to the work of the Holy Spirit, the last two flowing from and explaining χρισάς 'having anointed'. Having been anointed, they were thereby sealed by the anointing in that they were given the Holy Spirit [NIC2].
   2.3 The three aorist participles are exclusive and not related to the first participle, which is inclusive. The anointing and sealing refer to Paul's being commissioned and set apart by the Holy Spirit for ministry [WBC].
   2.4 The first participle points to an ongoing act of establishing, and the other three recall what occurred in baptism [SP].

QUESTION—At what point in time did the action of these three aorist participles occur?

Anointing, sealing, and the giving of the Holy Spirit took place in response to the preaching of Paul [NIC2], at baptism [Lns], or at conversion and baptism [EBC]. Baptism was the occasion of sealing [EGT, ICC2], and of the gift of the Holy Spirit [EGT]. Anointing, sealing, and giving the Holy Spirit are the ongoing evidence of the action of the first verb, that God establishes or confirms believers in their union with Christ [Ho]. These three participles refer to the whole complex of entry into the Christian life: conversion, faith, baptism and receiving the Holy Spirit [HNTC].

QUESTION—What is the point of Paul's digression in these five verses?

1. It is primarily apologetic. Paul is introducing evidence to validate his ministry and to demonstrate that he and his group were men approved by God [WBC]. Paul is saying that since God can be trusted in matters of ultimate importance, those whom he appoints as ministers can be trusted in matters of less importance [AB]. This passage is all part of his defense

against the charge of levity [EBC]. Paul is defending himself with the argument that, as Christ is the embodiment of reality, those who are in Christ are also reliable [ICC2]. He is saying that a minister of Christ, who is the eternal affirmation of God's promises, cannot be insincere [ICC1]. Paul is affirming his integrity by saying that all that God has done to attest him means that he cannot be lacking in sincerity in making his plans [NIC1]. Paul wants to show that his integrity and the truth of the gospel rest on God's work [TNTC]. Paul is defending not only himself, but also his co-workers and even those in Corinth who were loyal to him. He does this by attesting to the faithfulness and confirming work of God and Christ, and of the instruments of his grace [Lns].
 2. It is hortatory. Paul is endeavoring to show that believers are indebted to God for their faith and that God will cause them to endure [Ho]. Paul is encouraging them to continue as faithful believers [NIC2].

DISCOURSE UNIT: 1:23-2:13 [HNTC]. The topic is that Paul's plans may change but his purpose remains.

DISCOURSE UNIT: 1:23-2:11 [WBC]. The topic is Paul's travel plans explained and his earlier letter justified.

DISCOURSE UNIT: 1:23-2:4 [EBC]. The topic is a canceled painful visit.

1:23 But[a] I-call-upon[b] God (as) witness[c] against[d] my soul,[e]
LEXICON—a. δέ (LN 89.94, 89.124): 'but' [ICC2, LN (89.124); NRSV], 'and' [LN (89.94), NTC], 'now' [Lns; NLT], 'moreover' [KJV], not explicit [AB, HNTC, WBC; CEV, NAB, NIV, NJB, REB, TEV, TNT].
 b. pres. mid. indic. of ἐπικαλέω (LN **33.176**) (BAGD 2.a.α. p. 294): 'to call upon' [LN, WBC; NLT, TNT], 'to call on' [NAB, NJB, NRSV], 'to call' [ICC2, NTC; KJV, NIV, TEV], 'to call upon someone as a witness' [BAGD], 'to invoke' [HNTC], 'to appeal to' [Lns; REB], 'to summon' [AB].
 c. μάρτυς (LN 33.270) (BAGD 2.a. p. 494): 'witness' [AB, BAGD, HNTC, ICC2, LN, Lns, NTC, WBC; all versions except KJV], 'for a record' [KJV].
 d. ἐπί (LN 90.34) (BAGD III.1.b.ε. p. 289): 'against' [AB, HNTC, ICC2, LN, NTC, WBC; NRSV], 'on behalf of' [Lns], 'upon' [KJV], 'by' [NJB], 'on, for, toward' [BAGD], not explicit [CEV, NAB, NIV, NLT, REB, TEV, TNT].
 e. ψυχή (LN 23.88) (BAGD 1.c., f. p. 893, 894): 'soul' [BAGD, HNTC, ICC2, Lns, NTC; KJV], 'life' [LN], 'me' [AB, NTC, WBC; NRSV], not explicit [CEV, NAB, NIV, TNT]. The phrase 'against my soul' is translated 'by my life' [NJB], 'that I am telling the truth' [NLT], 'he knows my heart' [TEV], 'and stake my life on it' [REB].
QUESTION—What relationship is indicated by δέ 'but'?
 1. It is adversative [EGT, ICC2; NRSV]: 'but'. It marks a contrast with what his opponents may say [EGT]. It marks a return to his own particular

circumstance in contrast to what he has just been saying about God [ICC2].
2. It is transitional [Lns, NTC, TH; NLT]: 'now' [Lns; NLT], 'and' [NTC]. It is resumptive [AB]: 'now then'. It is additive [KJV]: 'moreover'. It marks the relation between Paul and what has been said about God [ICC1]: I call the God I have just described as my witness.

QUESTION—Why does he use the pronoun ἐγώ 'I', which is unnecessary with a first person singular inflected verb and normally is not used?

The first person singular pronoun ἐγώ gives additional emphasis [AB, HNTC, ICC1, ICC2, Lns, My, NTC]: 'I for my part' [He, Lns], 'for myself' [ICC2]. Ἐγώ distinguishes Paul from his co-workers [NTC]. Ἐγώ δέ marks a return to his own particular circumstance, in contrast to what he has just been saying about God [ICC2]. It is used not for contrast with God or the Corinthians but to emphasize that he is referring to his own thoughts [Lns].

QUESTION—What does ἐπί 'against' indicate?
1. He is using an oath to attest to his truthfulness by calling a curse upon himself with God as judge and witness against him if he is lying [AB, EBC, EGT, He, HNTC, ICC1, ICC2, NIC1, NIC2, NTC, TG, TH, TNTC, WBC].
2. He calls God as witness against him if he is lying, and as witness for him to attest to the truthfulness of what he says [EBC, Ho].
3. He is not using an oath, but calls God to witness on behalf of his soul to support its testimony because only God knows what happens in the soul [Lns].

that sparing^a you I-came not-again^b to Corinth.

LEXICON—a. pres. mid. or pass. (deponent = act.) participle of φείδομαι (LN 22.28) (BAGD 1. p. 854): 'to spare' [AB, BAGD, HNTC, ICC2, LN, Lns, NTC, WBC; KJV, NIV, NJB, NRSV, TEV, TNT], 'to spare from a severe rebuke' [NLT], 'to prevent trouble happening to someone' [LN], 'to keep from being hard on' [CEV], 'out of consideration for' [NAB, REB]. In the NT the future participle, which expresses intention for the future, is rarely used, and the present participle is used instead for this function [ICC2].
b. οὐκέτι (LN 67.130) (BAGD 1. p. 592): '(did) not (come) again' [HNTC, Lns, NTC, WBC; NAB, NJB, NRSV], 'not (coming) again' [TNT], 'did not return' [NIV, NLT], 'did not after all return' [REB], 'when I did not (come)' [AB], 'no longer' [BAGD, ICC2, LN], 'not as yet' [KJV], 'I stayed away' [CEV], 'I decided not to go' [TEV].

QUESTION—What was Paul sparing the Corinthians from?

He wanted to spare them as well as himself from a mutually painful visit like the previous one [EBC, EGT]. He wanted to give them time to repent and change so that he would not have to exercise discipline [AB, Ho, Lns, NIC1]. He did not want to have to exercise his authority to correct behavior or error [ICC2]. He wanted to avoid disciplinary action [My, NIC2, TNTC].

He wanted to avoid upsetting them or causing any more trouble [TG, TH]. He did not want to cause them sadness [He].

QUESTION—What does οὐκέτι mean here?

1. It means 'not again' [AB, EGT, He, HNTC, ICC1, ICC2, Lns, My, NIC2, NTC, WBC; NAB, NIV, NJB, NLT, NRSV, REB, TNT]: Paul was avoiding an unpleasant second trip.
2. It means 'not yet' [NIC1; KJV]: Paul postponed his planned trip.
3. It can mean 'not again' as well as 'not yet', because the trip that Paul postponed ('not yet') was a return visit ('not again') [EBC, Ho].

1:24 Not that we-lord-it-over[a] your faith[b] but we-are co-workers[c] for your joy;[d]

LEXICON—a. pres. act. indic. of κυριεύω (LN 37.50) (BAGD 1. p. 458): 'to lord it over' [BAGD, NTC; NIV, NJB, NRSV], 'to be lord over' [HNTC], 'to domineer' [AB; NAB], 'to rule' [BAGD, LN], 'to control' [BAGD], 'to exercise control over' [ICC2], 'to have control over' [REB], 'to exercise lordship over' [Lns], 'to rule over' [WBC], 'to reign over' [LN], 'to have dominion over' [KJV]. The phrase 'to lord it over your faith' is translated 'to tell you exactly how to put your faith into practice' [NLT], 'to be bosses who tell you what to believe' [CEV], 'to dictate to you what you must believe' [TEV], 'to tell you what you must believe' [TNT].

b. πίστις (LN 31.102) (BAGD 2.d.α. p. 663): 'faith' [AB, BAGD, HNTC, ICC2, Lns, NTC, WBC; KJV, NAB, NIV, NJB, NLT, NRSV, REB], 'Christian faith' [LN], 'what to believe' [CEV], 'what you must believe' [TEV, TNT].

c. συνεργός (LN 42.44) (BAGD p. 787): 'co-worker' [AB, Lns], 'fellow worker' [BAGD, ICC2, LN, NTC], 'helper' [KJV], 'workers with you' [NRSV]. This noun is also translated as a verbal phrase: 'we are working with you' [BAGD, WBC; CEV, REB, TEV, TNT], 'we work with you' [NIV], 'we work together with you' [HNTC], 'we want to work together with you' [NLT], 'I prefer to work with you' [NAB], 'we want to work with you' [NJB].

d. χαρά (LN 25.123) (BAGD 1. p. 875): 'joy' [AB, BAGD, HNTC, ICC2, LN, Lns, NTC, WBC; KJV, NIV, NJB, NLT, NRSV], 'happiness' [NAB, REB, TEV, TNT], 'great happiness' [LN]. The phrase 'for your joy' is translated 'to make you glad' [CEV].

QUESTION—What relationship is indicated by οὐχ ὅτι 'not that'?

This introduces 1:24 as a parenthetical digression given to clarify 1:23 and eliminate a possible misunderstanding [EBC, EGT, He, HNTC, Ho, ICC1, ICC2, Lns, My, NIC1, NIC2, TH, TNTC]. Οὐχ ὅτι 'not that' is an ellipsis for οὐ λέγω τοῦτο ὅτι 'I don't say this because' [ICC1], or 'οὐ λέγω ὅτι 'I am not saying that' [Ho, ICC2]. 1:24 provides the basis for 1:23, because οὐχ ὅτι 'not that' gives the rationale for the previous verse, that their desire is the Corinthians' joy and standing by faith [WBC].

2 CORINTHIANS 1:24

QUESTION—What does he mean by 'we don't lord it over your faith'?

It means that Paul does not tell them what they should believe [ICC1, TG, TH; CEV, TEV, TNT]. It means that Paul has authority in matters of discipline but not in matters of faith, which is subject to God alone since it rests on the testimony of God through the Scripture [Ho]. It means that Paul does not domineer and control their faith [AB, He, ICC1, ICC2; NAB, REB]. It means that the church and not Paul has primary authority in matters of discipline [WBC]. It means that those who minister are to be helpers and not lords over men's consciences [HNTC]. It means that he serves them and does not dominate them by causing them unnecessary pain [EBC]. It means that he will not be tyrannical nor exercise authority to serve his own ends instead of their needs [AB]. Paul disavows any form of hierarchy in the church and refuses to dispense faith or add any requirement to faith or practice that is contrary to or goes beyond the Lord's word [Lns]. It means that the faith of the Corinthians was to be subject to the word of God and not the rule of men, since they are primarily responsible for examining and testing the validity of their own faith. Paul's authority is limited to correcting error and disorder and punishing misconduct [NIC1]. It means that the believers' faith and standing before God is their own, resting on God's power [TNTC]. No one may exercise authority over the spiritual relationship between the individual and God [NTC]. The Corinthians must accept the responsibility for standing by faith in their relationship with God [NIC2]. The content and expression of their faith was to be shaped by his teaching and exhortation and not by way of his command [My].

QUESTION—How are the nouns related in the genitive construction 'co-workers for your joy'?

The genitive is objective, indicating that the purpose or result of the work is joy and spiritual benefit in the life of the Corinthian believers [AB, EBC, EGT, He, HNTC, Ho, ICC1, ICC2, Lns, My, NIC1, NIC2, NTC, TG, TH, WBC; CEV, NAB, NIV, NJB, NLT, NRSV, REB, TEV, TNT].

QUESTION—Who is working together with whom as 'co-workers'?

1. Paul, Silas, and Timothy are the co-workers, working for the benefit of the Corinthians [AB, ICC2, Lns, NIC2, NTC, SP].
2. Paul, Silas, and Timothy are co-workers with the Corinthians themselves [EBC, EGT, He, HNTC, Ho, ICC1, My, NIC1, TG, TH, TNTC, WBC; CEV, NAB, NIV, NJB, NLT, NRSV, REB, TEV, TNT]. The concept of a relationship with them is intended to counterbalance the idea of being lords over them [HNTC].

for[a] in/by[b] the faith you-stand-firm.[c]

LEXICON—a. γάρ (LN 89.23): 'for' [HNTC, ICC2, LN, Lns, NTC; KJV, NJB, REB], 'because' [AB, WBC; CEV, NIV, NRSV], not explicit [NAB, NLT, TEV, TNT].

b. There is no lexical entry in the Greek text for the preposition 'in/by', the relationship being indicated by the use of the dative τῇ πίστει 'in/by faith'. This is translated 'in' [AB; NJB, NLT, NRSV, TEV], 'in respect of' [ICC2], 'as regards' [Lns; NAB], 'by' [HNTC, NTC, WBC; KJV, NIV, REB], not explicit [CEV, TNT].

   c. perf. act. indic. of ἵστημι (LN 13.29) (BAGD II.2.c.β. p. 382): 'to stand firm' [AB, ICC2, NTC, WBC; NAB, NIV, NLT, NRSV, TEV], 'to stand' [BAGD, HNTC, Lns; KJV, REB], 'to be strong' [CEV], 'to continue steadfastly, to firmly remain' [LN]. This verb is also translated by the verbal clause 'your faith is firm' [TNT], 'your stand in the faith is firm' [NJB]. The perfect tense of this verb is viewed as having present tense meaning [AB, EGT, He, HNTC, Ho, ICC1, ICC2, Lns, NIC1, NTC, TG, WBC; all versions].

QUESTION—What relationship is indicated by the dative τῇ πιστει: 'in/by the faith'?

   1. It is local [AB, ICC1, NIC1, TG; NJB, NLT, NRSV, TEV]: 'in faith'; or referential [He, Ho, ICC2, Lns, My; CEV, NAB, TNT]: 'with regard to faith/the faith'. The contrast is between someone lording it over them and their being firm in faith: the Corinthians were firm in their faith, which is why he did not have to tell them what to believe [TG; TEV, TNT], or why he had no wish to lord it over them [ICC1; NAB, NJB].

   2. It is instrumental [EGT, HNTC, NIC2, NTC, WBC; KJV, NIV, REB]: 'by faith'. The contrast is between being strong by faith or by another's domination [EGT, NTC].

QUESTION—What is meant by τῇ πιστει 'the faith'?

   1. It is subjective, 'faith' [AB, HNTC, Ho, ICC1, ICC2, NIC1, NIC2, NTC, WBC; CEV, KJV, NAB, NIV, NLT, REB, TNT].

   2. It is objective, 'the faith', that is, the Christian faith [Lns, My; NJB, NRSV, TEV].

DISCOURSE UNIT: 2:1–13 [ICC2]. The topic is the reason for the painful letter; its aftermath; further proof of Paul's concern for the Corinthians.

2:1 **For[a] I-decided[b] this in-myself not to-come to you again in grief.[c]**

TEXT—Instead of γάρ 'for', some manuscripts have δέ 'but'. GNT selects the reading 'for' with a C rating, indicating difficulty in deciding which variant to place in the text. The reading δέ is taken by HNTC, Lns, WBC; KJV, NAB, and translated 'but' [HNTC; KJV], 'moreover' [Lns], 'so' [WBC], 'however' [NAB].

LEXICON—a. γάρ (LN 89.23): 'for' [ICC2, LN], 'and' [AB], 'so' [NTC; NIV, NLT, REB, TEV], 'then' [NJB], not explicit [CEV, TNT].

   b. aorist act. indic. of κρίνω (LN 30.75) (BAGD 3. p. 451): 'to decide' [BAGD, LN, NTC, WBC; CEV, NAB, TEV], 'to make a decision' [ICC2], 'to make up one's mind' [AB, LN, NTC; NIV, NJB, NRSV, REB, TEV], 'to come to a judgment' [Lns], 'to determine' [KJV], 'to say to oneself' [NLT]. The phrase ἔκρινα ἐμαυτῷ τοῦτο 'I decided this in myself' is translated 'I had made up my mind about this' [AB], 'I made up my mind to do this' [HNTC], 'in my own mind I made this decision'

[ICC2], 'I came to this judgment as regards myself' [Lns]; 'I determined this with myself' [KJV], 'I said to myself' [NLT]. Ἐμαυτῷ τοῦτο 'this in myself' is not translated by NTC, WBC; CEV, NAB, NIV, NJB, NRSV, REB, TEV, TNT. The aorist tense of this verb 'I decided' stands in contrast to the imperfect of ἐβουλόμην 'I was planning' of 1:15 in that the planning was tentative, but the decision was a carefully weighed judgment [AB, NIC1].

c. λύπη (LN 25.273) (BAGD p. 482): 'grief' [BAGD, Lns], 'sorrow' [BAGD, HNTC, ICC2, LN], 'pain' [BAGD], 'heaviness' [KJV]. The phrase 'to come to you again in sorrow' is translated 'to pay you another sorrowful visit' [AB, NTC], 'to pay you another painful visit' [WBC; TNT], 'to make another painful visit' [NIV, NRSV], 'to make you a visit occasioning sorrow' [ICC2], 'to go back to you in grief' [Lns], 'to make my next visit with you so painful' [CEV], 'to visit you again in painful circumstances' [NAB], 'my next visit would not be a painful one' [NJB, REB], '(to) make them unhappy with another painful visit' [NLT], 'to come to you again to make you sad' [TEV].

QUESTION—What relationship is indicated by γάρ 'for'?

It introduces an explanation about why he did not return to Corinth (1:23) [AB, ICC1, ICC2, NIC2, NTC, TG, TH].

QUESTION—Does πάλιν 'again' modify 'to come' or 'in grief'?

1. It modifies 'in grief' [AB, EBC, EGT, He, HNTC, Ho, ICC2, My, NIC1, NIC2, NTC, TG, TH, WBC; NAB, NIV, NLT, NRSV, REB, TNT]: not to come to you in grief again. Paul does not want to have another painful visit like the previous one.
2. It modifies 'to come' [Lns; NJB]: not to come again to you in grief. When Paul visits again he does not want his visit to be painful.

QUESTION—What is meant by ἐν λύπῃ πρὸς ὑμᾶς ἐλθεῖν 'to come to you in grief'?

1. It means to bring or cause grief or sorrow to the Corinthians [AB, He, Ho, ICC1, ICC2, My, WBC; NLT, TEV], reflecting the Aramaic 'ata b^e 'to come in' meaning to bring or cause [AB, He, WBC]. Paul is concerned that he not only would cause sorrow, but likely experience it himself as well if he caused it to them [EBC, ICC1, ICC2, TH].
2. Coming in grief would refer to Paul's own state of mind, his personal sorrow at the condition of the church [Lns].

2:2 For if I grieve[a] you, then who (is) the-one-cheering[b] me but the one-being-grieved by me?

LEXICON—a. pres. act. indic. λυπέω (LN 25.275) (BAGD 1. p. 481): 'to grieve' [AB, Lns, NTC; NIV, TNT], 'to cause sorrow' [HNTC, ICC2, WBC], 'to cause distress' [NJB], 'to cause pain' [NAB, NRSV, REB], 'to make sad' [LN; TEV], 'to cause pain and make sad' [NLT], 'to make to feel bad' [CEV], 'to make sorry' [KJV], 'to irritate, offend, vex' [BAGD].

b. pres. act. participle of εὐφραίνω (LN **25.131**) (BAGD 1. p. 327): 'to cheer (up)' [AB, BAGD, **LN**, NTC, WBC; CEV, REB, TEV, TNT], 'to make glad' [BAGD, LN, Lns; KJV, NIV, NLT, NRSV], 'to make happy' [HNTC], 'to make happy again' [NAB], 'to gladden' [BAGD, ICC2]. The phrase 'the one cheering me up' is translated 'my only possible source of joy' [NJB].

QUESTION—What function does the personal pronoun ἔγω 'I' perform in this sentence?

It is used for emphasis [AB, ICC1, ICC2, Lns, NIC2, TH].
1. Used with καί 'then' it makes τίς 'who' emphatic in contrast with 'I' [ICC1]; if *I* grieve you, then *who* will cheer me?
2. The contrast is between the words ἔγω 'I' and ὑμᾶς 'you', which emphasize the interpersonal relationship between Paul and the Corinthians [ICC2, Lns, NIC2].
3. Paul is contrasting the fact that he should be a co-worker for their joy, instead of one who brings them grief [AB].
4. The contrast is between Paul and others who were not as intimate with them as he was [My].

QUESTION—What relationship is indicated by καί 'then'?

This conjunction, which is normally translated 'and', is used here to introduce the apodosis or conclusion of a conditional clause [AB, EBC, EGT, He, HNTC, ICC1, ICC2, Lns, NIC1, NIC2, NTC, TG, WBC]. It strengthens the logical link between the two clauses [ICC2]: if this be true, then how could that? It accepts the protasis (the 'if' statement) and introduces the conclusion as a paradox [ICC1]. See LN 91.15.

QUESTION—What relationship is indicated by εἰ μή 'but' (literally 'if not')?
1. It indicates exception [AB, HNTC, ICC1, ICC2, Lns, NIC2, NTC]: 'but' [KJV, NAB, NIV, NRSV], 'except' [CEV, REB], 'only' [TEV].
2. A question mark should be placed after 'sorrow' and εἰ μή 'certainly not' would begin the next sentence [He, WBC]. The sentence would then express sarcasm: 'who is there to cheer me? Certainly not the one whom I made sorrowful!'

QUESTION—Who is ὁ λυπούμενος 'the one being grieved by me'?
1. This singular participle refers to the representative Corinthian, the whole community being spoken of an individual [AB, EBC, HNTC, Ho, ICC1, ICC2, Lns, My, NIC1, NIC2, NTC, TG, TH]. He generalizes to be more gentle and polite [Lns].
2. This participle refers to an individual who actively opposed Paul and was causing the trouble that Paul is referring to [He, TNTC, WBC]. The individual offender who opposed Paul was also the incestuous man mention in 1 Corinthians 5 [TNTC].

QUESTION—Is the 'if...then' conditional clause a contrary-to-fact situation or was it something that actually occurred?
   1. It is hypothetical, referring to what would have been the case had Paul made the visit as planned [AB, EBC, EGT, HNTC, Ho, ICC1, ICC2, NIC1, NIC2, TG].
   2. It states an actual fact [Lns, NTC, WBC]. It refers to the previous visit in which he had grieved them [NTC]. It refers to his previous letter in which he had grieved them [Lns, WBC].

DISCOURSE UNIT: 2:3–11 [AB]. The topic is a tearful letter.

2:3 And I-wrote this very-thing/for this reason,[a] so-that having-come, I not have grief from those-of-whom it-should-(be)[b] for-me to-rejoice.[c]
LEXICON—a. αὐτος (LN 58.31) (BAGD 1.h. p. 123): '(this) very' [AB, BAGD ICC2, Lns, NTC], 'just (this)' [HNTC], '(this) same' [KJV]. The phrase 'I wrote this very thing' is translated 'I wrote as I did' [WBC; CEV, NAB, NIV, NJB, NLT, NRSV, TNT], 'this is precisely the point I made in my letter' [REB], 'that is why I wrote that letter to you' [TEV].
   b. imperf. act. indic. of δεῖ (LN 71.21) (BAGD 6.b. p. 172): 'should' [BAGD, LN, NTC; CEV, NAB, NJB, NRSV, TEV], 'ought' [AB, BAGD, HNTC, ICC2, LN, Lns, WBC; KJV, NIV, NLT, REB, TNT].
   c. pres. act. infin. of χαίρω (LN 25.125) (BAGD 1. p. 873): 'to rejoice' [BAGD, LN], 'to be glad' [BAGD, LN]. The phrase 'those of whom it should be for me to rejoice' is translated 'those who ought to make me rejoice' [AB, WBC; NIV], 'those who should have made me rejoice' [NRSV], 'from whom I ought to have joy' [HNTC], 'those over whom I ought to have rejoiced' [ICC2], 'them of whom I ought to rejoice' [KJV], 'them from whom I ought to be getting joy' [Lns], 'those who should have made me glad' [NTC], 'you should make me feel happy' [TEV], 'those who should rejoice my heart' [NAB], 'people who should have given me joy' [NJB], 'ones who ought to give me the greatest joy' [NLT], 'people who ought to have made me happy' [REB], 'people who should make me glad' [TEV], 'those who ought to make me happy' [TNT].
QUESTION—When Paul says 'I wrote' in this and the following verse, to what letter is he referring and how does it fit into the sequence of his visits and other correspondence?
   It refers to a letter previously written in anguish and tears [AB, Car, EBC, EGT, He, HNTC, Ho, ICC1, Lns, My, NIC1, NIC2, NTC, SP, TNTC, WBC; NLT, REB, TEV].
   1. After writing canonical 1 Corinthians, Paul paid a brief but 'sorrowful' visit to Corinth, after which he wrote the severe letter in anguish and tears that is described in this verse. This letter has not been preserved. Then he wrote canonical 2 Corinthians [Car, EBC, HNTC, NIC2, NTC, SP, TNTC, WBC], or a portion thereof consisting of chapters 1–8 [ICC2] or 1–9 [AB].

2. After writing canonical 1 Corinthians, Paul paid a brief but 'sorrowful' visit to Corinth, after which he wrote his severe letter which is preserved, in whole or in part, in chapters 10–13 of 2 Corinthians [He, ICC1]. He then wrote and sent another letter which is chapter 9, and then a final letter which consists of chapters 1–8 [He].
3. After founding the church in Corinth, Paul paid a second visit which was brief but 'sorrowful', after which he wrote a letter (now lost) which is referred to in 1 Corinthians 5:9. He then wrote 1 Corinthians, which is the severe letter, and then wrote 2 Corinthians [EGT, Ho, Lns, NIC1].

QUESTION—Is τοῦτο αὐτό used adverbially 'for this very reason' to express why he wrote, or objectively 'this very thing' to refer to what he wrote?
1. It is objective, stating what he wrote [AB, EGT, HNTC, Ho, ICC2, My, NIC2, NTC; KJV, REB]: I wrote this very thing. It refers to his previous letter [HNTC, ICC2]. It refers to his change of plan [EGT]. It refers to his statement that he did not come in order to spare them [ICC1]. It refers to his instructions about the incestuous man [Ho].
2. It is adverbial, stating why he wrote [He, Lns, TG; TEV]: I wrote for this reason.

QUESTION—What does he mean when he says 'I wrote…so that having come, I not have grief'?
1. He decided to write a letter instead running the risk of having a painful visit [AB, EGT, He, HNTC, ICC1, ICC2, NIC2, TNTC; CEV, REB, TEV].
2. He wrote as he did so that his next visit will not be painful [EBC, Ho, Lns, My, NIC1, NTC, TH, WBC; NAB, NIV, NLT, NRSV, TNT].

having-confidence[a] in you all that my joy[b] is (the joy) of-all of-you.
LEXICON—a. perf. act. participle of πείθω (LN 31.82) (BAGD 2.a. p. 639): 'to have confidence in' [ICC2, LN, Lns, NTC; KJV, NIV, REB], 'to put one's confidence in (someone)' [BAGD], 'to be confident' [HNTC, WBC; NRSV], 'to be convinced' [AB; NAB, TEV], not explicit [CEV, NLT]. This perfect participle is also translated as a prepositional phrase: 'in the conviction' [NJB]; as a verbal phrase 'I know you well enough to say that' [TNT], 'I know you well enough to be convinced' [NAB]. In the perfect tense πείθω has a present tense meaning [AB, BAGD, LN; NAB, NRSV, TEV, TNT].
b. χαρά (LN 25.123, 25.124) (BAGD 1. p. 875): 'joy' [AB, BAGD, HNTC, ICC2, LN (25. 123), Lns, NTC, WBC; KJV, NIV, NJB, NRSV], 'cause or reason for joy' [LN (25.124)], 'happiness' [NAB, NLT]. This noun is also translated as a verb: 'to be happy' [CEV, REB, TEV, TNT].

QUESTION—What does Paul mean by saying that his joy is the joy of them all?
1. Their joy is mutually dependent because of their close relationship [AB, EBC, EGT, He, HNTC, ICC1, ICC2, Lns, My, NIC1, NIC2, NTC, SP, TG, TH, WBC; CEV, NIV, NJB, NLT, REB, TEV, TNT].

1.1 Paul's joy is the cause of the Corinthians' joy; that is, they will be happy because Paul is happy [He, HNTC, ICC1, ICC2, NIC2, TH; CEV, NIV, NJB, REB, TEV, TNT]. Paul is confident that it will give them joy to please him [ICC1]. They will eventually share the joy he felt after hearing of their positive response to his severe letter [NIC2].

1.2 Paul's joy is based on the Corinthians' joy; that is, he is happy if they are happy [EGT, NTC, WBC; NLT].

2. Their mutual joy derives from the same common source. They would share his joy in that what causes him to rejoice will also cause them to rejoice [EBC, Ho]. What makes Paul happy is the obedience of the Corinthians which will bring purity and prosperity to the church, and happiness to them as a result [Ho].

2:4 For out-of much affliction^a and anguish^b of-heart, I-wrote to you through^c many tears,

LEXICON—a. θλῖψις (LN 22.2) (BAGD 2. p. 362): 'affliction' [BAGD, HNTC, Lns, NTC; KJV], 'trouble' [BAGD, LN], 'distress' [ICC2, WBC; NIV, NRSV, REB, TNT], 'sorrow' [NAB], 'trouble and suffering' [LN]. This noun is also translated as an adjective: 'troubled' [AB; TEV]. The phrase 'out of much affliction and distress of heart' is translated 'I was suffering terribly and my heart was broken' [CEV], 'in agony of mind' [NJB], 'how painful it was…(I was) heartbroken' [NLT]. See this word also at 1:4, 8.

b. συνοχή (LN **25.240**) (BAGD 2. p. 791): 'anguish' [BAGD, ICC2, WBC; KJV, NAB, NIV, NRSV, TNT], 'distress' [BAGD, HNTC, LN], 'dismay' [BAGD], 'anxiety' [Lns; REB], not explicit [CEV]. This noun is also translated as an adjective: 'anguished' [AB], 'distressed' [TEV]; and as a verbal phrase: 'my heart was broken' [CEV].

c. διά (BAGD A.III.1.c. p. 180): 'through' [AB, Lns, NTC, WBC], 'with' [BAGD, HNTC, ICC2; KJV, NAB, NIV, NRSV, TEV, TNT], not explicit [NJB]. The phrase 'through many tears' is translated 'my eyes were full of tears' [CEV], 'I cried over it' [NLT], 'how many tears I shed' [REB]. In this passage διά indicates attendant circumstance [BAGD].

QUESTION—What relationship is indicated by γάρ 'for'?

It refers to what he has said about his own grief and the motives for why he grieved the Corinthians [Ho, Lns]; since Paul sees himself as responsible for promoting the Corinthians' happiness his having grieved them gives him anguish of heart [Ho]. He is substantiating what he has just said about avoiding a visit [ICC2]. It refers to and explains his statement as to why he wrote as he did, which was to show his love, and the personal distress he felt when he did so [NIC2].

not in-order-that you-should-be-grieved^a but in-order-that you-may-know^b the love which I-have especially^c for you.

LEXICON—a. aorist pass. subj. of λυπέω (LN 25.275) (BAGD 2.a. p. 481): 'to be grieved' [AB, Lns; KJV], 'to grieve' [NIV, TNT], 'to be made sad'

[LN], 'to make sad' [NTC; NAB, TEV], 'to inflict sorrow upon' [HNTC], 'to be caused sorrow' [ICC2], 'to make sorrowful' [WBC], 'to make to feel bad' [CEV], 'to cause distress' [NJB], 'to hurt' [NLT], 'to cause pain' [NRSV, REB]. See this word also at 2:2.
  b. aorist act. subj. of γινώσκω (LN 28.1) (BAGD 1.a. p. 160): 'to know' [AB, BAGD, HNTC, ICC2, LN, NTC, WBC; CEV, KJV, NIV, NLT, NRSV, REB, TNT], 'to realize' [Lns; NAB, TEV], 'to come to know' [BAGD]. The subjunctive mood of this verb is also translated as an infinitive verb: 'to let you know' [CEV, NIV, NRSV, TNT], 'to show you' [NJB], 'to help you realize' [NAB], 'to make you realize' [TEV].
  c. περισσοτέρως (LN 78.31) (BAGD 2. p. 651): 'especially' [BAGD, Lns], 'most especially' [ICC2], 'specially' [HNTC], 'very great' [LN], 'great' [NAB], 'surpassing' [LN], 'the depth of' [NIV], 'more abundantly' [KJV], 'more abundant' [NTC], 'abundant' [NRSV], 'in great measure' [WBC], 'how much' [AB; CEV, TEV, TNT], 'how very much' [NJB, NLT], 'more than ordinary' [REB]. See this word also at 1:12.

QUESTION—What is communicated by the placing of τήν ἀγάπην 'the love' before the conjunction ἵνα 'in order that'?
  The unusual placement of 'love' before the conjunction gives it special emphasis [AB, EGT, HNTC, ICC1, ICC2, Lns, My, NIC1, NIC2, WBC]. The sense would be 'my love, that you may know it' [Lns].

QUESTION—How is the adverb περισσοτέρως used in this verse?
  1. This comparative form of the adverb is used not for comparison but to intensify the meaning [AB, EBC, EGT, HNTC, ICC1, NIC1, NIC2, TG, WBC; CEV, NAB, NIV, NJB, NLT, NRSV, REB, TEV, TNT].
  2. It is used comparatively [Ho, My, NTC]. Paul has more love for the Corinthians than for any other church [Ho]. Paul loves the Corinthians more now than when he was their pastor [NTC].

DISCOURSE UNIT: 2:5–17 [ICC1, TG, TH; CEV]. The topic is the treatment of the great offender and the result of the severe letter [ICC1], a plea for reconciliation [TG, TH], forgiveness [CEV].

DISCOURSE UNIT: 2:5–11 [EBC, TNTC; NAB, NIV, NLT, NRSV, TEV]. The topic is forgiveness for the offender [EBC, TNTC; NAB, NRSV, TEV], forgiveness for the sinner [NIV, NLT].

2:5 But[a] **if anyone has-caused-grief,[b] he-has-caused-grief not to-me, but in part,[c] lest I-exaggerate,[d] to you all.**
LEXICON—a. δέ (LN 89.124): 'but' [HNTC, ICC2, LN, Lns, NTC, WBC; CEV, KJV, NRSV], 'now' [AB; TEV], not explicit [NAB, NIV, NJB, NLT, TNT].
  b. perf. act. indic. of λυπέω: (LN **25.275**): 'to cause grief' [AB, NTC; KJV, NIV, TNT], 'to cause sorrow' [HNTC, ICC2, WBC], 'to grieve' [Lns], 'to make someone feel bad' [CEV], 'to make somebody sad' [LN; TEV], 'to give offense' [NAB], 'to cause distress' [NJB], 'to cause trouble' [NLT],

'to cause pain' [NRSV]. This verb is also translated 'any injury that has been done' [REB]. The perfect tense indicates action in past time with results that continue into the present [NTC]. See this word also at 2:2, 4.

c. μέρος (LN 63.15) (BAGD 1.c. p. 506): 'in part' [BAGD, LN; KJV, TEV], 'to some extent' [AB, HNTC, NTC; NIV, NRSV, REB], 'to some degree' [ICC2], 'in some degree' [NJB], 'more or less' [Lns], 'in some measure' [WBC; NAB], 'practically (all)' [TNT], not explicit [CEV]. The idiomatic construction ἀπὸ μέρους 'in part' is also found at 1:14.

d. pres. act. subj. of ἐπιβαρέω (LN 57.224) (BAGD p. 290): 'to exaggerate' [AB, BAGD, HNTC; NJB, NRSV, TNT], 'to overstate it' [NLT], 'to say (no) more' [NAB], 'to be too severe' [BAGD, NTC], 'to put it too severely' [NIV], 'to be too hard on' [CEV, TEV], 'to labor the point' [ICC2], 'to put it too strongly' [WBC], 'to make too much of it' [REB], 'to burden' [LN, Lns], 'to overcharge' [KJV]. This verb could be viewed either as transitive, to be too hard on someone [EGT, Ho, ICC1, Lns, NTC, TG; CEV, TEV], or as intransitive, to exaggerate [AB, EBC, ICC2, NIC1, WBC; NAB, NIV, NJB, NLT, NRSV, REB, TNT].

QUESTION—Why does Paul use the conditional 'if anyone has caused grief'?

The conditional form represents an actual case of offense that really happened [AB, EBC, Lns, NTC, TH]. Paul speaks in vague generalities out of tactful consideration for the offender [EGT, Ho, ICC1, ICC2, TG].

QUESTION—What was the offense and who was the offender that Paul is referring to?

1. Someone had openly insulted or opposed Paul [AB, EBC, He, HNTC, ICC1, NIC2, NTC, SP, TG, TH, WBC]. The offender who opposed Paul may have been someone who supported attendance at the pagan temple ceremonies in Corinth, where the practice of sexual license was common, and who resisted Paul's admonition about such [NIC2]. He may have been an outsider who had intruded into the Corinthian congregation [HNTC, WBC].
2. Paul is referring to the case of incest mentioned in 1 Corinthians 5 [EGT, Ho, My, NIC1, TNTC]. The incestuous man is the person who led opposition to Paul [TNTC].
3. Someone in Corinth had misappropriated funds from the collection and thereby threatened Paul's control over the congregation [ICC2].

QUESTION—What does ἀπὸ μέρους 'in part' qualify?

1. It qualifies the verb [EGT, He, HNTC, ICC2, Lns, WBC; NAB, NIV, NJB, NLT, NRSV, REB, TEV]; to some extent he has grieved all of you; or, Paul was grieved, but only in part [KJV].
2. It qualifies the object of the grieving, that is, part of the Corinthians were grieved, but some were not [Ho, ICC1, NTC; CEV, TNT].

QUESTION—How would the grief have affected them all?

It blunted the church's outreach to others in Corinth [NTC]. It created division [NIC2]. An attack on the apostle threatened the validity of the church he founded [AB, HNTC]. It was an insult to the community that Paul had founded [He]. It affected the unity of the church [WBC]. Sexual sin, as in the case of incest, would infect the whole congregation [TNTC]. A misappropriation of funds would not only deprive the church of its intended contribution to the collection but also would pain the church that one of their own would do such a thing [ICC2].

QUESTION—When Paul says that 'he has not caused grief to me' does he mean that literally or is it used in a relative sense?

1. It is used relatively [EBC, ICC1, ICC2, Lns, NIC2, NTC, TG, TH, TNTC, WBC; NAB, NLT]: 'he has caused trouble not as much to me as to all of you'.
2. It is used literally and refers to the case of incest [EGT, Ho, My]: 'the offense was not to me at all, it was to you'.

2:6 The punishment/reproof[a] to such-a-one[b] by the majority[c] (is) sufficient,[d]

LEXICON—a. ἐπιτιμία (LN 38.6) (BAGD p. 303): 'punishment' [AB, BAGD, LN, NTC; CEV, KJV, NAB, NIV, NJB, NRSV], 'penalty' [ICC2, Lns; REB], 'reproof' [HNTC], 'censure' [WBC]. This noun is also translated as a verb: 'to be punished' [NLT, TEV], 'to condemn' [TNT].

b. τοιοῦτος (LN 92.31) (BAGD 3.a.α. p. 821): 'such a one' [Lns; NAB], 'such a person' [AB, BAGD; NJB, NRSV], 'of such a kind' [LN], 'the person in question' [HNTC], 'this sort of person' [ICC2], 'this particular person' [NTC], 'this person' [TEV], 'that person' [WBC; CEV], 'to such a man' [KJV], 'him' [NIV, TNT], not explicit [NLT, REB].

c. πολύς (BAGD II.2.a.α., III..2.aγ. p. 689): 'the majority' [AB, BAGD ICC2, Lns, WBC; NAB, NIV, NJB, NRSV, TNT], 'most of you' [NTC; CEV, NLT, TEV], 'many' [KJV], 'the main body' [HNTC], 'the general meeting' [REB], 'the others, the rest' [BAGD].

d. ἱκανός (LN 78.14, **78.50**) (BAGD 1.a. p. 374): 'sufficient' [BAGD, HNTC, ICC2, **LN** (78.50), Lns; KJV, NIV], 'enough' [AB, LN (78.50), NTC, WBC; CEV, NAB, NLT, NRSV, TEV, TNT], 'quite enough' [NJB], 'well enough' [REB], 'adequate' [BAGD], 'great, extensive' [LN (78.14)].

QUESTION—What is implied by the term 'majority'?

1. It refers to a majority that made a decision regarding the offender's guilt [AB, ICC2, My, NIC1, TH]. It implies a deliberative session that voted on the action taken [AB, NIC1]. It implies that the vote was not unanimous, that a minority was in disagreement [Lns].
1.1 There was a minority who sided with the man, in opposition to Paul [EGT, NIC2, NTC, WBC].
1.2 There was a group of people supportive of Paul who felt that the penalty should be more severe [EBC, ICC1].
2. It simply means 'the many', that is, the whole church acting as a body and does not imply anything about a minority [He, HNTC, Ho].

2 CORINTHIANS 2:6

QUESTION—What is the ἐπιτιμία 'punishment/reproof'?
This appears to have been a legal or forensic term [ICC1, Lns, NTC, TNTC].
1. The guilty person was punished. The action taken would have been excommunication [Ho, Lns, My, TNTC] or form of exclusion [AB, EGT, NIC2], such as exclusion from the fellowship [He, NIC1, NTC, TG, WBC], from church activities and the eucharist [ICC2], or from the agape meal [WBC].
2. The guilty person was given a reproof or censure [HNTC, ICC1].

QUESTION—In what way was the punishment sufficient?
It was sufficient in terms of duration [AB, Ho, ICC2, NIC2, TH]. Paul was saying that it was sufficient to bring about repentance from the offender, and for the church, for it to be able to forgive [ICC2]. It was sufficient in that it was fair, just, deserved, and not inordinate [TG]. It was sufficient in that it had the desired effect [TNTC]. It satisfied the requirements of the case [ICC1]. It was sufficient in terms of severity as well as duration [EGT]. Paul was saying that in fact it had been prolonged beyond a reasonable point [NIC2]. Paul was more lenient than the church was [Ho]. The majority had sufficiently complied with Paul's instructions about the offense [My].

2:7 so-that on-the-contrary^a rather^b you (ought) to-forgive^c and encourage^d (him),

LEXICON—a. τοὐναντίον (LN 89.134): 'on the contrary' [LN], 'instead' [ICC2, LN], 'rather' [LN], 'on the other hand' [HNTC, WBC], 'contrariwise' [Lns; KJV], 'by contrast' [NTC], not explicit [CEV, NAB, TNT]. This word is also conflated with the following word μᾶλλον and translated 'now instead' [AB; NIV, NRSV], 'now however' [TEV], 'now by contrast' [NJB], 'now' [NAB, NLT, REB].
b. μᾶλλον (LN 89.126) (BAGD 3.a.β. p. 489): 'rather' [HNTC, ICC2, Lns, NTC, WBC; KJV], 'but rather' [LN], 'on the contrary' [LN; TNT], 'instead' [LN], not explicit [CEV].
c. aorist mid. (deponent = act.) infin. of χαρίζομαι (LN 40.10) (BAGD 2. p. 877): 'to forgive' [AB, BAGD, HNTC, ICC2, LN, Lns, NTC, WBC; all versions except NAB], 'to pardon' [BAGD], 'to relent' [NAB]. This verb and the following one may represent a single act of the congregation in that forgiving will bring comfort to the one restored [Lns].
d. aorist act. infin. of παρακαλέω (LN 25.150) (BAGD 4. p. 617): 'to encourage' [BAGD, LN; NJB, TEV, TNT], 'to comfort' [BAGD, HNTC, ICC2, Lns, NTC; KJV, NIV, NLT], 'to console' [LN, WBC; CEV, NRSV], 'to deal kindly' [AB], 'to support' [NAB], 'to put heart into' [REB]. See this word also at 1:4 and 1:6.

QUESTION—What is implied by τοὐναντίον μᾶλλον 'on the contrary rather'?
It calls for an action opposite to what has been going on [NIC1, NIC2], a reversal of the disciplinary process [AB]. It calls for a clear change of

attitude [ICC1, ICC2]. Some people, possibly the minority, may have refused to forgive the rebel [ICC1].

lest such-a-one be-swallowed-up[a] by excessive[b] sorrow.[c]
LEXICON—a. aorist pass. subj. of καταπίνω (LN **25.285**) (BAGD 1.c. p. 416): 'to be swallowed up' [BAGD, HNTC, Lns, WBC; KJV], 'to be overwhelmed' [AB, BAGD; NIV, NJB, NRSV, TNT], 'to be engulfed' [ICC2], 'to be overcome' [NTC], 'to be crushed' [NAB]. The phrase 'to be swallowed up by excessive sorrow' is translated 'to become so discouraged he won't be able to recover' [NLT], 'so sad as to give up completely' [TEV], 'give up in despair' [CEV], 'so severe as to overwhelm him' [REB], 'to grieve to the point of giving up, to despair so as to give up completely' [LN]. This compound form with the κατα- prefix has intensive force, 'to be swallowed up' [NIC2], or possibly being drowned by one's own tearful grieving [AB].

b. περισσότερος (LN 78.31) (BAGD 1. p. 651): 'excessive' [BAGD, HNTC, ICC2, LN, Lns, NTC, WBC; NIV, NRSV, TNT], 'immoderate' [AB], 'overmuch' [KJV], 'too great a weight' [NAB], 'the extent of' [NJB], 'severe' [REB]. See the adverbial form of this word at 1:12 and 2:4.

c. λύπη: (LN 25.273) (BAGD p. 482): 'sorrow' [HNTC, ICC2, NTC, WBC; KJV, NAB, NIV, NRSV], 'grief' [AB, Lns], 'despair' [CEV], 'distress' [NJB, REB], 'grief' [TNT]. See this word also at 2:1.

2:8 Therefore,[a] I-urge[b] you to-affirm[c] (your)[d] love[e] to/for him;
LEXICON—a. διό (LN 89.47): 'therefore' [ICC2, LN, NTC; NAB, NIV, REB], 'wherefore' [Lns; KJV], 'so' [HNTC, WBC; NRSV, TNT], 'and so' [TEV], 'thus' [AB], 'that is why' [NJB], 'for this reason' [LN], not explicit [CEV, NLT]. Διό reinforces the statement of the previous verse that they should restore and forgive the man [Ho, Lns, NIC2].

b. pres. act. indic. of παρακαλέω (LN 33.168) (BAGD 2. p. 617): 'to urge' [AB, BAGD, ICC2, Lns, WBC; NIV, NJB, NRSV, REB], 'to exhort' [BAGD, NTC], 'to appeal' [BAGD, LN], 'to ask' [HNTC], 'to beseech' [KJV], 'to beg' [NAB, TEV, TNT], not explicit [CEV, NLT]. See this word also at 1:4, 6; 2:7.

c. aorist act. infin. of κυρόω (LN **70.6**) (BAGD 2. p. 461): 'to affirm' [NTC, WBC], 'to reaffirm' [NAB, NIV, NRSV], 'to confirm' [BAGD, HNTC; KJV], 'to ratify' [AB, BAGD ICC2, Lns], 'to show something to be real' [LN]. The phrase 'to affirm love to him' is translated 'to reassure him of your love' [REB, TNT], 'show him you still love him' [NLT], 'to give your love definite expression' [NJB], 'let him know you really do love him' [TEV], 'make them sure of your love' [CEV].

d. There is no lexical entry for 'your', it is implied [AB, EGT, HNTC, ICC2, NTC, WBC; CEV, KJV, NAB, NIV, NJB, NRSV, REB, TNT].

e. ἀγάπη (LN 25.43) (BAGD I.1.b.β. p. 5): 'love' [AB, BAGD, HNTC, ICC2, LN, Lns, NTC, WBC; all versions].

QUESTION—Does the verb κυρόω indicate that the forgiveness was to be formal or that it required an official resolution by the church?

The verb κυρόω is a legal term [AB, EBC, HNTC, ICC2, Lns, NIC2, NTC, TH, TNTC, WBC]. Its juxtaposition with ἀγάπη 'love' is striking because of the difference [AB, EBC, HNTC, ICC2, WBC], involving a seeming paradox [ICC2] or oxymoron [AB], with one being a legal term and the other an ethical principle [NTC]. The use of this term indicates that some sort of a formal resolution was needed [AB, EBC, Ho, ICC2, Lns, NIC1, NIC2, TH, TNTC], or, if not a formal action, at least a change in attitude from censure to affection [ICC1].

QUESTION—Is εἰς αὐτόν 'to/for him' connected with the verb κυρόω 'affirm (to him)' or the noun ἀγάπην 'love (for him)'?

1. It is associated with the noun [AB, EGT, He, HNTC, ICC1, ICC2, NTC, WBC; KJV, NAB, NIV, NJB, NRSV]: 'love for him.'
2. It is the object of the verb [Lns, My; TNT]: 'ratify to him' [Lns], 'reassure him' [TNT].
3. It is used with both [CEV, NLT, REB, TEV]: 'show him you still love him' [NLT], 'reassure him of your love for him' [REB], 'let him know of your love for him' [TEV], 'make them sure of your love for them' [CEV].

2:9 **For to this (purpose)[a] also I-wrote, that I-may-know[b] the proof[c] of-you, whether you-are obedient[d] in everything.**

LEXICON—a. There is no lexical entry for 'purpose', the meaning being implied in the phrase εἰς τοῦτο γάρ 'for to this'. This phrase is translated 'for this purpose' [AB, Lns, NTC], 'for this reason' [ICC2; NRSV], 'the reason (I wrote)' [WBC; NAB, NIV], 'this was my reason' [NJB], '(I wrote) because' [CEV, TEV], 'to this end' [KJV], 'this is why (I wrote)' [TNT]. Purpose is also expressed by the use of the infinitive 'to (find out/see)' [HNTC; NLT, REB].

b. aorist act. subj. of γινώσκω (LN 28.1): 'to know' [AB, LN (28.1); KJV], 'to learn' [LN (27.2)], 'to test' [NTC; NJB], 'to test you and see' [TNT], 'to test you to see' [NTC], 'to test and learn' [NAB], 'to test and know' [NRSV], 'to test and find out' [CEV], 'to find out' [HNTC, LN (27.2)], 'to ascertain' [ICC2]. This word is translated in conjunction with the next word δοκιμή 'proof': 'to find out how you would stand the test' [HNTC], 'to find out how far you would go' [NLT], 'to see if you would stand the test' [NIV], 'to see if you would pass the test' [WBC], 'to see how you stand the test' [REB], 'to find out how well you had stood the test' [TEV], 'to get to know the (real) genuineness of you' [Lns].

c. δοκιμή (LN 72.7) (BAGD 1. p. 202): 'proof' [KJV], 'proof of genuineness' [LN], 'genuineness' [Lns], 'character' [BAGD], 'quality of character' [ICC2], 'quality' [NJB], not explicit [AB, HNTC, NTC, WBC; CEV, NAB, NIV, NLT, NRSV, REB, TEV, TNT]. As a noun δοκιμή is used in the NT only by Paul, and is rarely found outside of the NT; it represents evident character that is known or 'proved' by testing [ICC2, NIC1].

d. ὑπήκοος (LN 36.16) (BAGD p. 842): 'obedient' [AB, BAGD, HNTC, ICC2, LN, Lns, NTC, WBC; KJV, NAB, NIV, NJB, NRSV], 'wholly obedient' [TNT]. This adjective is also translated as a verbal phrase: 'to follow my instructions' [CEV], 'in obeying me' [NLT], 'to fully accept my authority' [REB], 'to obey my instructions' [TEV].

QUESTION—What is the purpose for which Paul wrote?

He wanted to test their obedience, since their failure to deal with the problem before threatened their very existence as a church by threatening Paul as their founder [AB]. Paul wanted to see if they regarded him as their apostle and would demonstrate their obedience in the case of church discipline as well as by forgiveness of the offender now [NIC2]. Paul wanted to prove their willingness to acknowledge the authority God had given him [EBC]. Paul wanted to see if they would be obedient to Christ in all things in which they needed to be obedient as a congregation [Lns]. Paul wanted to see if they were really genuine in spiritual matters [NTC].

QUESTION—What is the function of the word καί 'also'?

It indicates the agreement of this letter with the previous one [ICC1]. It connects the previous letter to this one, meaning that then as now he is writing about the same case [Lns]. He is adding a second purpose to the first purpose, which was that he not have sorrow from them [NIC1]. It intensifies εἰς τοῦτο γάρ 'for to this (purpose)', giving the sense of 'indeed' [NIC1]. It gives prominence to 'I wrote', meaning, I also wrote for this purpose, in addition to doing other things toward that end [Ho]. It means that Paul gave verbal instructions and also written ones [My].

QUESTION—What is the 'obedience' for which Paul was looking for proof?

He was testing their acceptance of and obedience to his apostolic authority [EGT, NIC1, TG; CEV, NLT, REB]. Paul wanted to see how they had stood the test of their difficult experience as well as to know how ready they were to obey his instructions [TEV]. Paul sees their obedience to himself as obedience to Christ [ICC2]. Paul was looking for their compliance in discipline as well as in restoration of the sinner [NTC]. This was a test of whether or not their was any future in Paul's relationship with the Corinthians [NIC2]. Paul was looking for their obedience to the gospel and its implications [TNTC]. Paul wanted to see whether they would be obedient to do their duty in the matter with regard to the principles of the gospel [ICC1]. The obedience Paul was looking for was their Christian character as well as their obedience to the his own legitimate authority [Ho]. Paul was looking for the evidence of their piety and wisdom via their obedience to Christ [He]. Paul wanted to test whether they were really committed to him and his teachings, in contrast to others who opposed him [TH]. It included his instructions concerning punishment of the incestuous man [My].

2:10 And,[a] to-whom you-forgive[b] anything, I also (forgive);
LEXICON—a. δέ (LN 89.94, 89.124): 'and' [ICC2, LN (89.94)], 'but' [HNTC, LN (89.124); NJB, REB], 'moreover' [Lns], not explicit [AB, NTC, WBC; CEV, KJV, NAB, NIV, NLT, NRSV, TEV, TNT].
   b. perf. indic. mid. (deponent = act.) of χαρίζομαι (LN 40.10) (BAGD 2. p. 876): 'to forgive' [AB, BAGD, HNTC, ICC2, LN, Lns, NTC, WBC; all versions].
QUESTION—Is Paul expressing a general standing principle in his relationship with them by this statement or is he referring to the particular circumstance at hand?
   Though stated in general terms, he is referring to the specific situation of church discipline [EGT, Ho, ICC1, ICC2, TH; NLT]. It is a general principle to which the present case applies [My].
QUESTION—Who is taking initiative in forgiving, Paul or the Corinthians?
   1. Paul lets them take the lead in this matter; that is, he is willing to forgive if they are [EGT, He, HNTC, Ho, ICC1, Lns, NTC, TG, WBC].
   2. Paul expects them to follow his lead in this matter; that is, they ought to forgive because he already has done so [EBC, NIC1, NIC2, TNTC].

for indeed what I-myself have-forgiven, if I-have-forgiven anything, (it is) for-the-sake-of[a] you in the-presence[b] of Christ,
LEXICON—a. διά with accusative object (LN 90.38, 90.44): 'for the sake of' [AB, LN (90.38); CEV, KJV, NAB, NIV, NJB, NRSV, REB, TNT], 'for the benefit of' [LN (90.38); NLT], 'because of' [LN (90.44); TEV], 'on account of' [HNTC, ICC2, LN (90.44), Lns, NTC, WBC].
   b. πρόσωπον (LN 85.26) (BAGD 1.c.γ. p. 721): '(in the) presence of' [AB, HNTC, ICC2, LN, Lns, NTC, WBC; NJB, NRSV, TEV, TNT], '(in the) sight of' [NIV], '(before) the face of' [BAGD], '(in the) person of' [KJV]. The phrase 'in the presence of Christ' is translated 'with Christ as my witness' [CEV], 'before Christ' [NAB], 'with Christ's authority' [NLT], 'as a representative of Christ' [REB]. See this word also at 1:11.
QUESTION—What is meant by εἴ τι κεχάρισμαι 'if I have forgiven anything'?
   'If I have forgiven anything' [AB, HNTC, ICC2; KJV, NJB, NRSV, TNT], can mean 'if there was anything to forgive' [Lns, NTC, WBC; NIV, TEV], or may simply be a way to state the idea in general terms: 'whatever needed to be forgiven' [CEV], 'any forgiving I have done' [NAB], 'for whatever is to be forgiven' [NLT], 'so far as there is anything to forgive' [REB]. Paul is either saying that the man's sin was not against Paul, it was against the church [AB, HNTC, Lns, NIC1], and that the responsibility to forgive was primarily theirs, not his [NIC1]; or he is graciously minimizing the offense [EBC, ICC1, NTC, TG, TH], downplaying his own hurt [TNTC]. Paul does not want to overstate the case, but has in fact forgiven the offense [NIC2].

QUESTION—What relationship is indicated by διά 'for the sake of'?
Paul means that it is for their benefit [HNTC, ICC1, ICC2, Lns, NTC, TG, TH, TNTC]: either to build up the church [HNTC], or so they won't be taken advantage of by Satan [Lns, NIC2]. It was for their benefit in that it freed the Corinthians to forgive and restore a sense of well-being [TNTC]. It is to their benefit in that it encourages and facilitates their forgiveness and restoration of the offender [ICC1, ICC2]. Paul's statement 'for your sake' means 'for your benefit, because I care for you' [TG]. It is to their benefit in that Paul exonerates them in the presence of Christ in case they have any ill-will toward him [NTC]. Paul was concerned entirely for their best interests since the offense was not an affront to himself personally [Ho]. It was for their benefit in that his forgiveness would prompt them to forgive also [My].

QUESTION—What is meant by 'in the presence of'?
Paul summons Christ as witness and guarantor of his actions [WBC]. Paul's forgiveness is not irresponsible, but is done in Christ's presence and under his judgment [HNTC]. Christ looks on as a witness [BAGD, EBC, ICC2, My, TG], and approves the forgiveness [BAGD, EBC, ICC2]. It means that Paul has placed the matter before Christ [NTC]. Paul is not thoughtless as he takes this action before Christ, who will approve or condemn his action [ICC1]. Paul, in the presence of Christ but absent from the Corinthians, participates in the formalities of judging and forgiving [NIC2]. It means that Paul's relationship with the Corinthians was through Christ [Lns]. It reflects the Hebrew expression *liphne* 'in the presence of' [AB, NIC1]. This demonstrates the sincerity and humility of Paul who sees all of life as lived before God as the ultimate judge [NIC1]. It is a kind of solemn oath with the final judgment in view, that whatever he forgave was for their sakes [AB]. Paul does what he does as a representative of Christ [REB] or with Christ's authority [NLT]. Paul did what he was aware that Christ wanted him to do [TH]. It refers to Paul's union with Christ [SP].

2:11 in-order-that[a] we- not -be-taken-advantage-of[b] by Satan; for we-are-not -ignorant-of[c] his designs.[d]

LEXICON—a. ἵνα (LN 89.59): 'in order that' [LN]. The phrase ἵνα μή 'in order that...not' is translated 'lest' [KJV], 'in order that...might not' [NIV, TEV] 'so that...will not' [NLT], 'so that...may not' [NRSV], 'to prevent' [NAB], 'to avoid' [NJB], The phrase 'lest we be taken advantage of by Satan' is translated 'I have done this to keep Satan from getting the better of us' [CEV], 'in order to keep Satan from getting the upper hand over us' [TEV], 'for Satan must not be allowed to get the better of us' [REB], 'we must not let him get the better of us' [TNT].

b. aorist pass. subj. of πλεονεκτέω (LN 88.144) (BAGD 1.b. p. 667): 'to be taken advantage of' [LN, Lns], 'to be exploited' [ICC2, LN], 'to be outwitted' [BAGD, NTC; NJB, NRSV], 'to be cheated' [AB, BAGD]. This passive verb is also translated actively with Satan as the agent; 'to take advantage of' [HNTC, WBC], 'to get an advantage of' [KJV], 'to get

the better of' [CEV, REB, TNT], 'to get the upper hand' [TEV], 'to outwit' [NAB, NIV], 'to outsmart' [NLT]. This verb implies treachery and cunning [TH].
c. pres. act. indic. of ἀγνοέω (LN **28.13**) (BAGD 1. p. 11): 'to be ignorant of' [BAGD, HNTC, ICC2, **LN**, Lns; KJV, NRSV], 'to be unaware of' [LN, NTC; NIV], 'to be oblivious to' [AB]. This verb is also stated positively without the οὐ 'not': 'to know' [WBC; CEV, NAB, NJB, REB, TEV, TNT], 'to be familiar with' [NLT]. The double negative consisting of the particle οὐ with the alpha-privative of the verb gives emphasis [NTC, WBC; NAB, NJB, NLT, REB]: 'we know well.' See this word also at 1:8.
d. νοήμα (LN 30.15) (BAGD 2. p. 540): 'designs' [AB, BAGD, HNTC, ICC2, NTC, WBC; NRSV], 'thought' [LN], 'purpose' [BAGD], 'devices' [Lns; KJV], 'plot' [BAGD], 'guile' [NAB], 'scheming' [NJB], 'evil schemes' [NLT], 'wiles' [REB], 'plans' [TEV], 'tricks' [TNT]. This noun is also translated by a phrase 'what goes on in his mind' [CEV]. The noun νοήμα 'designs' may be a play on words with ἀγνοοῦμεν 'we are (not) ignorant' having the sense of 'we are not unmindful of what's on his mind' [AB, ICC1].

QUESTION—What designs of Satan for taking advantage of believers is Paul talking about?

Paul was concerned that Satan might gain the victory if the offender would be 'swallowed up' by despair through not being forgiven [HNTC, Ho, My, NIC1], or by disruption of the fellowship of love in the church by undue harshness and excessive discipline [Ho, NIC1]. Satan would try to cheat the church of one of its members [ICC1, ICC2, TNTC, WBC], if not by the sin, then by unforgiveness of the sin [ICC1, WBC]. Satan's design is to alienate the Corinthians from Paul [Lns]. Satan would try to turn the man's repentance into downfall through excessive grief and to create division and discord in the church, either between the congregation and the offender, or between the church and the dissident minority who support the offender [EBC]. Satan would try to divide the church by the exclusion of the offender [He]. His design is to create discord and division that would jeopardize the gospel witness [AB]. Satan wants to sift them like wheat, causing spiritual ruin and use despondency and despair to recapture a pardoned sinner [NTC]. Satan's design is to draw them back into the darkness of unforgiveness and to create a rift between Paul and the church over this [NIC2]. Satan attempts to seduce those who desire to follow God's will [TH].

DISCOURSE UNIT: 2:12–4:6 [NTC; NJB]. The topic is the new covenant [NTC], the move from Troas to Macedonia and the importance of the apostolate [NJB].

DISCOURSE UNIT: 2:12–3:6 [NIV, NLT]. The topic is ministers of the new covenant.

DISCOURSE UNIT: 2:12–24 [NAB]. The topic is Paul's anxiety and relief.

DISCOURSE UNIT: 2:12–17 [NRSV]. The topic is Paul's anxiety in Troas.

DISCOURSE UNIT: 2:12–13 [AB, EBC, NIC2, TNTC, WBC]. The topic is a trip to Macedonia [AB], restlessness at Troas [EBC], Paul in Troas: turmoil in ministry [NIC2], waiting for Titus [TNTC], Paul's concern for Corinth [WBC], Paul's anxiety in Troas [TEV].

2:12 But (after) having-come to Troas for[a] the gospel of-Christ and a door[b] having-been-opened to-me by/in[c] the Lord,

LEXICON—a. εἰς (LN 89.57): 'for' [Lns, NTC], 'for the purpose of' [ICC2, LN], 'on behalf of' [AB], 'for the sake of' [NJB], 'to proclaim' [HNTC, WBC; NRSV, TNT], 'to preach' [CEV, KJV, NAB, NIV, NLT, REB, TEV].

b. θύρα (LN 7.49, 71.9) (BAGD 2.c. p. 366): 'door' [AB, HNTC, ICC2, LN (7.49), Lns, NTC; KJV, NIV, NJB, NRSV, TNT], 'door of opportunity' [NAB], 'opportunity' [WBC], 'way' [TEV]. The phrase 'a door having been opened' is also translated 'the door was wide open' [TNT], 'a door stood open' [HNTC], 'there being an opportunity opened' [WBC], '(God) gave me tremendous opportunities' [NLT], '(the Lord) had prepared the way' [CEV], '(the Lord) had opened the way' [TEV], 'an opening awaited me' [REB], 'to have been made possible' [LN (71.9)].

c. ἐν (LN 90.6): 'in' [AB, HNTC, Lns, NTC; NJB, NRSV], 'by' [ICC2, LN, WBC; NAB], 'of' [KJV], 'to serve' [TNT], 'for serving' [REB], not explicit [CEV, NIV, NLT, TEV].

QUESTION—What is the function of δέ 'but'?

It marks the transition to a new section [Lns, NIC2]. It resumes a topic [EGT, Ho, ICC2, My], probably from 2:4 [Ho, ICC2, My].

QUESTION—What relationship is indicated by εἰς 'for'?

It indicates purpose, which is to proclaim the gospel [HNTC, ICC1, ICC2, Lns, NIC1, NTC, TG, TH, TNTC, WBC; CEV, KJV, NAB, NIV, NLT, NRSV, REB, TEV, TNT], or to establish churches through preaching the gospel [NIC2].

QUESTION—How are the nouns related in the genitive phrase the 'gospel of Christ'?

Christ is the content of the gospel [NIC1]. It is the gospel that is about Christ [ICC2, NIC2, NTC, TH], and that belongs to Christ [NTC]. It is the gospel of which Christ is the author [Ho].

QUESTION—What is the significance of the tense and voice of the perfect passive participle ἀνεῳγμένης 'having been opened'?

The perfect tense indicates a lasting or enduring effect, that it stayed open [AB, HNTC, Lns, NIC1, NIC2, NTC, WBC], and the passive voice indicates that God was the agent of the action [AB, NIC1, NTC, WBC]. This clause is concessive 'despite the fact that a door had been opened, I left' [AB, HNTC, NTC, SP, WBC].

QUESTION—What is meant by ἐν κυρίῳ 'by/in the Lord'.
1. It indicates agency, that the door was opened 'by the Lord' [AB, He, ICC2, TH, WBC; CEV, KJV, NAB, NIV, NLT, TEV].
2. It indicates the sphere within which the opportunity for service lay [AB, EGT, Ho, ICC1, My, NIC1, NIC2; REB, TNT]. It indicates that it is connected with the Lord [Lns].

QUESTION—Who is 'the Lord'?
1. He is referring to Christ [NIC1, TG, TH, WBC].
2. He is referring to God [NIC2, NTC].

2:13 not finding Titus my brother[a] I-did- not -have rest[b] in my spirit, but (after) having-said-farewell[c] to-them I-departed into Macedonia.

LEXICON—a. ἀδελφός (LN 11.23): 'brother' [AB, HNTC, ICC2, Lns, NTC, WBC; KJV, NAB, NIV, NJB, NRSV, TEV, TNT], 'dear brother' [NLT], '(Christian) brother' [LN], 'fellow believer' [LN], 'friend' [CEV], 'colleague' [REB]. This term emphasizes the importance of Titus to Paul, as well as the equality of status of Jew and Gentile in the church [AB]. See this word also at 1:1, 8.

b. ἄνεσις (LN 22.36) (BAGD 2. p. 65): 'rest' [BAGD; KJV], 'relief' [BAGD, HNTC, LN, Lns, WBC; NJB, REB, TNT], 'ease' [ICC2]. The phrase 'I did not have rest in my spirit' is translated 'my anxiety was unrelieved' [AB], 'I was worried' [CEV], 'I was deeply worried' [TEV], 'I was inwardly troubled' [NAB], 'I had no peace of mind' [NIV], 'I had no relief from anxiety' [NJB], 'I couldn't rest' [NLT], 'my mind could not rest' [NRSV], 'I found/had no relief of mind' [REB, TNT]. The term πνεῦμα 'spirit' here is used interchangeably with σάρξ 'flesh' in a similarly worded phrase in 7:5, both of which are used in place of the personal pronoun and refer to Paul himself [HNTC, ICC2, NIC2, WBC].

c. aorist mid. participle ἀποτάσσω (LN 15.55) (BAGD 1. p. 100): 'to say farewell to' [BAGD; NRSV], 'to bid farewell to' [WBC; TNT], 'to make farewells to' [ICC2], 'to take leave of' [AB, BAGD, LN, Lns; KJV, REB], 'to say good-bye' [HNTC, LN; NAB, NIV, NJB, NLT, TEV], 'to leave' [CEV].

QUESTION—What is the function of the negated aorist infinitive with the dative article τῷ μὴ εὑρεῖν 'not finding' ?

It expresses cause [AB, He, HNTC, ICC2, Lns, My, NTC, WBC; KJV, NAB, NIV, NLT, NRSV, REB, TEV, TNT]: 'because I did not find Titus'.

DISCOURSE UNIT: 2:14–7:16 [WBC]. The topic is the main theme: Paul's apostolic ministry.

DISCOURSE UNIT: 2:14–7:4 [EBC, HNTC, ICC2, NIC2]. The topic is the apostolic ministry described [EBC], the purpose expressed in mission and ministry [HNTC], defense of the apostolic ministry [ICC2], defense of the ministry of the new covenant [NIC2].

DISCOURSE UNIT: 2:14–5:19 [AB]. The topic is comments on apostolic service.

DISCOURSE UNIT: 2:14–4:6 [EBC, ICC2, NIC2, NTC]. The topic is the grandeur and superiority of the apostolic ministry [EBC], the ministry of the new covenant and its glory [ICC2], Paul defends his ministry [NIC2], the new covenant [NTC].

DISCOURSE UNIT: 2:14–3:6 [AB, ICC2, WBC]. The topic is an introduction to comments on apostolic service [AB], introduction to Paul's ministry to the Corinthians [ICC2], the apostle's adequacy for ministry [WBC].

DISCOURSE UNIT: 2:14–3:3 [HNTC]. The topic is the Christian mission and its divine support.

DISCOURSE UNIT: 2:14–17 [EBC, NIC2, TNTC]. The topic is the privilege of apostolic service [EBC], God's victory procession [NIC2], being led in triumph [TNTC].

2:14 **But to-God (be) thanks, to-the-one always leading-us-in-triumph/ causing-us-to triumph^a in Christ**

LEXICON—a. pres. act. participle of θριαμβεύω (LN 39.59, **39.60**) (BAGD 1. p. 363): 'to lead in triumph' [BAGD, WBC; TNT], 'to triumph over, to be completely victorious over' [LN (39.59)], 'to lead in triumphal procession' [BAGD, ICC2, NTC; NIV, NRSV], 'to lead in triumphal train' [NAB], 'to put on display' [AB], 'to lead to victory' [CEV], 'to cause to triumph' [**LN**, Lns; KJV]. The participial phrase πάντοτε θριαμβεύοντι ἡμᾶς 'always leading us in triumph/causing us to triumph' is translated 'always puts us on display (as if we were prisoners in a triumphal procession)' [AB], 'who goes always at our head in a triumphal progress' [HNTC], 'who unfailingly leads us on in Christ's triumphal train' [NAB], 'who always gives us a part in Christ's triumphal procession' [NJB], 'who always makes us his captives and leads us along in Christ's triumphal procession' [NLT], 'who continually leads us as captives in Christ's triumphal procession' [REB], 'we are always led by God as prisoners in Christ's victory procession' [TEV], 'who continually leads us in triumph as Christians' [TNT].

QUESTION—What relationship is indicated by δέ 'but'?

It is used in an adversative sense; that is, notwithstanding all these problems, thanks be to God [HNTC]. It introduces a digression wherein Paul offers thanks to God despite all the problems of the human condition [NIC1]. It introduces a long digression that continues to 7:11 [EGT]. It changes the tone of the text from a depressing narrative to a hymn of praise [NTC]. It functions to introduce a second beginning to the letter, parallel to the initial benediction. It also contrasts the greatness of God to the human predicament [NIC2]. It marks the beginning of a new section [TH].

2 CORINTHIANS 2:14

QUESTION—What is meant by θριαμβεύοντι ἡμᾶς 'always leading us in triumph/causing us to triumph'?

The imagery here is that of a Roman victory parade in which the conquering general would lead prisoners into the capital of the empire, accompanied by the fragrance of incense being burned as a thank offering to the gods [EGT, HNTC, Lns, NIC1, NIC2, NTC, TG, TH, TNTC]. After the parade was finished, the captives would normally be executed; hence, the fragrance would signify victory for the conquerors, but impending death for the conquered [Lns, NTC].

1. God leads them in triumph as conquered captives or prisoners [AB, ICC1, ICC2, Kim, My, NIC1, NIC2, NTC, SP, WBC; NLT, REB, TEV].
1.1 This expression is in harmony with Paul's strength-in-weakness theme [NAC, NIC2, WBC]. God is the victorious general, Paul is the conquered prisoner who is being led to his death as a suffering slave or servant because of his preaching of the word of God, and whose work is also on display [NTC]. They are on exhibit to the world as subdued by the power of mercy and grace [NIC1]. This verb means to display someone as humbled, but not necessarily as being conquered [AB]. Paul is asserting the theme of power and weakness in this world; he has been captured by love, and his 'defeat' results in his salvation [NAC].
1.2 The focal point is not the humiliation or death of Paul or others, but the glory of God's victory, and the demonstration of God's power through Paul's apostolic activity [ICC2]. God, who leads them as captives, uses them as instruments of his glory [EGT, ICC1]. They are conquered by their conversion [My]. Paul does not present himself as a conquered prisoner but as a conquered missionary who is driven by the God who sends him out [SP]. Paul is conscious of the fact that though he was God's conquered enemy, God did not lead him to his execution but has reconciled Paul to himself and made him his own ambassador (cf.5:19–20) [Kim].
2. God leads them in triumph as participants in his victory [He, HNTC, Ho, Lns, TG, TNTC], or causes them to have victory [He, Ho; CEV, KJV]. The triumphal procession metaphor is used to celebrate the victory Paul has just experienced through Titus' positive report about the outcome of his ministry in Corinth [Lns]. This verb, like some other Greek verbs ending in -εύω has a causative sense like the Hebrew hifil stem [He, Ho]: 'he causes us to triumph'.

QUESTION—What is meant by ἐν Χριστῷ 'in Christ'?

It refers to living in union with Christ [Ho, Lns, TG], or being a member of the body of Christ [EGT]. It means that they are united with Christ, ever conscious of him and working in his service [ICC1]. It means to be in the sphere and influence of Christ, but also to be mystically and really in him [NIC1]. It reflects agency as well as instrumentality, since it is through the death and resurrection of Christ that God displays his power in the apostle's ministry [ICC2]. The words ἐν Χριστῷ mean in the cause of Christ [WBC].

It is in Christ that the knowledge of God is manifested [HNTC]. It is in Christ that Paul is a captive [NTC]. It is in Christ that God leads him [NIC2]. God's constant triumph is in the sphere of Christ, having a specifically Christian quality [My].

and manifesting[a] through[b] us the fragrance[c] of-the knowledge of-him in every place;

LEXICON—a. pres. act. participle of φανερόω (LN **28.36**) (BAGD 1.a. p. 852): 'to manifest' [AB, HNTC], 'to make manifest' [Lns; KJV], 'to make known' [BAGD, **LN**, NTC, WBC], 'to disclose' [LN], 'reveal' [BAGD, ICC2, LN], 'to spread' [NIV, NJB, NLT, NRSV, REB, TNT], 'to make to spread' [TEV], 'to help us spread (the knowledge)' [CEV], 'to employ (us) to diffuse (the fragrance of the knowledge)' [NAB]. The phrase 'manifesting through us the fragrance of the knowledge of him' is translated 'uses us to tell others about the Lord and to spread the Good News like a sweet perfume' [NLT], 'God helps us spread the knowledge about Christ everywhere, and this knowledge is like the smell of perfume' [CEV].

b. διά with genitive object (LN 90.4): 'through' [AB, HNTC, ICC2, LN, NTC, WBC; NIV, NJB, NRSV], 'by means of' [Lns], 'by' [KJV]. The phrase 'through us' is translated 'God helps us' [CEV], 'God employs us' [NAB], '(God) uses us' [NLT, REB, TEV, TNT].

c. ὀσμή (LN 79.45) (BAGD 2. p. 586): 'fragrance' [AB, NTC, WBC; NAB, NIV, NJB, NRSV, REB], 'sweet fragrance' [TEV], 'scent' [ICC2, LN], 'smell' [LN; CEV], 'odor' [HNTC, LN, Lns], 'savor' [KJV], 'like sweet perfume' [NLT, TNT]. This word may be used of pleasant or unpleasant odors [AB, ICC2, LN]. The translation of this word in a positive or pleasant sense is derived from the use of εὐωδία, which has a positive connotation, in the following verse.

QUESTION—What is meant by δι' ἡμῶν 'through us'?

'Through us' means through the gospel ministry they are carrying out [NIC2]. The apostles are a medium through which the knowledge spreads [Lns]. God uses them [NIC1, NTC, TG]. They are instruments [NIC1, NTC] or vessels for God's use [NIC1]. 'Through us' also forms the logical basis for the statement in the next verse 'for we are the aroma of Christ to God' [HNTC, NIC2].

QUESTION—How are the nouns related in the genitive construction γνῶσις αὐτοῦ 'knowledge of him'?

'Him' is objective, referring to knowing him or knowing about him [AB, EGT, He, HNTC, ICC1, ICC2, Lns, NIC1, NIC2, NTC, TG, TNTC; CEV, NJB, NLT, NRSV, REB, TEV].

QUESTION—To whom does 'of him' refer?

1. It refers to God [AB, He, HNTC, ICC2, NTC, TNTC, WBC; NJB, REB].
2. It refers to Christ [EGT, Ho, ICC1, Lns, My, NIC1, NIC2, TG, TH; CEV, TEV, TNT].

QUESTION—What is meant by 'every place'?
    God is at always at work in the apostles wherever they go [HNTC, Ho, Lns, NIC2]. God's objective is that his servants manifest him in all the world [ICC2, NIC1]. It is a complement to the word 'always' [ICC1, WBC], and refers to the universal scope and character of Paul's mission [AB, WBC]. God's triumph does not cease either in time or in space [ICC1].
QUESTION—Who is the 'us' he is speaking about?
    It refers to Paul himself [NIC2, NTC, WBC]. It refers primarily to Paul himself, although he is also speaking for all the apostles [ICC2]. It refers to Paul and his associates [HNTC, Lns, TH], to Paul and the apostolic ministry [NIC1]. It is the apostles, not just Paul [ICC1]. It is all who proclaim the gospel [TG].
QUESTION—What is the background for the metaphor of fragrance?
    1. It is taken from Jewish religious tradition [AB, He, ICC2, WBC]. It comes from the temple sacrifices made by the Jewish priests; Paul sees his ministry as a priestly service where sacrifices are burned at the altar [ICC2]. In rabbinic literature the torah was described as a medicine that brought either life or death, and Paul is saying that the fragrance is the knowledge of God which is like such a medicine [WBC]. The fragrance represents the presence of God, and therefore the knowledge of God, as in some texts from Hebrew wisdom literature [AB, He].
    2. It comes from the imagery of the Roman victory procession, and refers to the incense during the procession [EBC, HNTC, ICC1, Lns, My, NIC1, NIC2, TG, TNTC]. It describes the odor of the sacrifices to the gods during the victory procession [NTC].

2:15 **for we-are an aroma^a of-Christ to-God among those being-saved^b and among those perishing,^c**

LEXICON—a. εὐωδία (LN 79.46) (BAGD p. 329): 'aroma' [AB, BAGD, LN, NTC, WBC; NAB, NIV, NRSV], 'fragrance' [BAGD, LN; NJB, NLT, TNT], 'sweet scent' [ICC2], 'sweet odor' [Lns], 'sweet savor' [KJV], 'sweet savor of sacrifice' [HNTC], 'as perfume' [CEV], 'sweet smelling incense' [TEV], 'incense' [REB]. This word indicates a pleasant or sweet-smelling odor [AB, LN, WBC].
    b. pres. pass. participle of σῴζω (LN 21.27) (BAGD 2.b. p. 798): 'to be saved' [AB, BAGD, LN, Lns, NTC; all versions except REB], 'to be on the way/road to salvation' [HNTC, ICC2, WBC; REB]. The use of the present participles σῳζομένοις 'those being saved' and ἀπολλυμένοις 'those perishing' indicates that neither this condition of being saved nor of that of perishing are completed facts, but are conditions in progress [EGT, He].
    c. pres. pass. participle of ἀπόλλυμι (LN 20.31) (BAGD 2.a.α. p. 95): 'to perish' [AB, BAGD Lns, NTC; KJV, NLT, NRSV], 'to be destroyed' [BAGD, LN], 'to die' [BAGD], 'to be on the way to destruction' [HNTC;

92   2 CORINTHIANS 2:15

NAB, NIV, NJB, REB, TNT], 'to be on the road to perdition' [ICC2], 'to be on the road to ruin' [WBC], 'to be lost' [CEV, TEV].

QUESTION—What relationship is indicated by ὅτι 'for'?

It introduces the reason that God diffuses the knowledge of Christ, which is that it is a pleasing aroma to him [Ho]. It introduces an explanation for the statement just made that the manifestation of the knowledge of God is διά ἡμῶν 'through us', because they themselves are the fragrance [HNTC, ICC2, NIC2, NTC]. Not only is the fragrance of the knowledge of God made known through them, they are that fragrance to the extent that they realize and manifest their membership of Christ [EGT].

QUESTION—What is the imagery of aroma and fragrance here?

1. It is a continuation of the metaphor of the incense of the triumphal procession [EGT, Ho, My, TG, TNTC]. The lives of the saints are sweet and penetrative [EGT].
2. It is a metaphor drawn from the OT sacrificial offerings [HNTC, Lns, NIC2, NTC]. Paul and his associates are the fragrance of Christ's sacrifice that ascends to honor God [NTC]. It is drawn both from the metaphor of sacrifice as well as the tradition in Hebrew wisdom literature that divine wisdom is like a fragrant smell [ICC2].
3. It is drawn from the rabbinic concept of the law as being a medicine beneficial to the obedient but lethal to those rejecting it [EBC, TNTC]. It is related to the verb χρίεν 'to anoint', which is related to Χριστός 'Christ', which relates this to the medicine imagery of the previous verse [WBC].
4. It is not sacrificial imagery, but simply indicates that the gospel is dispersed abroad as a fragrance would be, and Christ is communicated [AB]. His thought is not primarily of sacrifice, but of the effect produced through the gospel [ICC1, NIC1].

QUESTION—What does 'an aroma of Christ' mean?

The word Χριστοῦ 'of Christ' comes first for emphasis [AB, ICC1, NIC1, NIC2], just as with τῷ θεῷ 'to God' in 2:14 [ICC1].

1. It is a fragrance of Christ, emanating from him [EBC, HNTC, Ho, ICC1, ICC2, My, NIC1, NIC2, NTC, TNTC; KJV, NAB, NIV, NJB, NRSV, TNT]. It is a fragrance of Christ, that is, the gospel about him which is proclaimed among men [EBC, Ho, TNTC]. Paul is the scent of which Christ is the content [ICC2, NIC1].
2. It refers to something offered or presented by Christ as a pleasing sacrifice [Lns, TG, TH; REB, TEV].

QUESTION—What does 'an aroma of Christ to God' mean?

As Paul carries out his ministry the smoke of Christ's sacrifice goes up, pleasing God and dispersing the truth to men [HNTC, ICC2]. God is pleased with that particular grace of which he himself is the author, and it is also communicated to other people [NIC1]. In spreading the fragrance of the knowledge of God they are themselves a fragrance to God [ICC1]. The gospel that Christ's preachers proclaim among men is offered to God by

Christ [Lns]. The proclamation of Christ's gospel is pleasing to God, because it concerns his beloved son [EBC]. It refers to the fact that Christ's sacrifice was pleasing to God [NTC]. Paul's sacrifice of himself in ministry is pleasing to God just as Christ's sacrifice of himself was [NIC2]. 'To God' means to the glory of God [He], or to the honor of God and for the benefit of God's people all over the world [AB].

2:16 **to-these (we are) an odor^a from^b death unto^c death, to-those a fragrance^d from life unto life.**
LEXICON—a. ὀσμή: 'odor' [HNTC, Lns; NAB], 'fragrance' [NRSV], 'stench' [AB], 'deadly stench' [TEV], 'scent' [ICC2], 'deadly fume' [WBC; REB], 'smell' [NIV, NJB], 'bad smell' [CEV], 'fearful smell' [NLT], 'savor' [KJV], 'perfume' [TNT].
  b. ἐκ (LN 89.3): 'from' [AB, LN, Lns; NRSV], 'issuing from' [HNTC], 'arising from' [ICC2], 'of' [NTC; KJV, NIV, NJB], 'that means' [TNT], 'has (a smell)' [CEV]. The phrase 'from death unto death...from life unto life' is translated 'dealing death...bringing life' [NAB], 'of death...of life' [NIV], 'of death and doom...life-giving perfume' [NLT], 'deadly fume/stench that kills...fragrance that brings life' [REB, TEV].
  c. εἰς (LN 89.48): 'unto' [KJV], 'for' [AB, Lns], 'leading to' [HNTC; NJB], 'resulting in' [ICC2], 'to' [NTC; NRSV], 'of' [NIV], 'leads them to' [CEV], 'that brings' [REB, TEV], 'that means' [TNT].
  d. ὀσμή: 'fragrance' [AB, WBC; NIV, NRSV, REB, TEV], 'odor' [HNTC, Lns], 'scent' [ICC2], 'aroma' [NTC], 'smell' [NJB], 'sweet smell' [CEV], 'savor' [KJV], 'breath' [NAB], 'perfume' [NLT, TNT].
QUESTION—What categories of people are signified by οἷς μέν...οἷς δέ, 'to these...to those'?
  The order of presentation represents an inversion or chiasmus, in which the first group οἷς μέν 'to these' represents the last ones mentioned in 2:15, 'those perishing', and the second group οἷς δέ 'to those' represents the first ones mentioned in 2:15, 'those being saved' [AB, ICC1, ICC2, Lns, NIC2, NTC, TH, WBC; CEV, NAB, NJB, NLT, REB, TEV, TNT].
QUESTION—What is meant by ἐκ...εἰς 'from...unto' as it is used with 'death' and 'life'?
  In Hebrew literature the word *sam* is used both of a lethal drug and of a sweet-smelling perfume or spice [EBC, HNTC]. The rabbis taught that the Torah was like such a medicine, able to bring either life or death to people [EGT, HNTC, Ho, ICC1, ICC2, NIC2, NTC, WBC].
  1. The formula ἐκ...εἰς 'from...unto' is a semitic idiom expressing emphasis [AB, EGT, NIC1, NIC2, NTC, TG, TH]. It is used emphatically to describe a result [TG; CEV, TEV]. It expresses a superlative 'ultimate death/life' [AB], or comprehensiveness, 'death/life from beginning to end' [NTC].
  2. It represents a progression from one stage to another, at least for those perishing, a movement from a bad condition to a worse one [ICC1].

94   2 CORINTHIANS 2:16

3. Ἐκ defines the source, and εἰς the result or destination [HNTC, Ho, ICC2, Lns, My, WBC]. Christ is the life and the source of life, but those who refuse his life draw death from him [Lns]. To some he is dead, and yields only a savor of death and is the source of death; but to believers he is alive and he and his gospel are the source of life [Ho]. The gospel issues from a scene of death, and for those who regard Jesus as no more than a dead Jew, they will become as dead as they imagine he is. If he is recognized as alive, he becomes the source of life [HNTC]. The fragrance of the gospel issuing from Jesus' risen life leads a person to eternal life [WBC]. To those who refuse the gospel the gospel is a smell of death that leads to their death, but for those who believe it is an aroma emerging from life and producing life [NTC]. For the perishing who reject Christ, the fragrance of the death of Christ which they encounter in Paul's ministry is a sign of their own eternal death. The fragrance of the risen Christ smelled in Paul by those who turn to Christ is a sign of their own eternal life [NIC2].

And for these-things[a] who (is) sufficient[b]?

LEXICON—a. ταῦτα (neuter plural form of demonstrative adj. οὗτος) (LN 92.29): 'these things' [KJV, NRSV], 'all this' [TNT], 'such a mission' [NAB], 'such a task' [NIV, NJB, NLT, TEV], 'such a calling' [REB], 'to do this work' [CEV].

b. ἱκανός (LN **75.2**) (BAGD 2. p. 374): 'sufficient' [HNTC, Lns; KJV, NRSV], 'adequate' [AB, ICC2, **LN**, WBC; NLT, TNT], 'qualified' [LN; NAB], 'competent' [BAGD, NTC], 'qualified, worthy' [BAGD], 'equal to the task/calling' [NIV, NJB, REB], 'capable' [TEV]. The question 'who is sufficient for these things?' is translated 'no one really has what it takes to do this work' [CEV]. See this word also at 2:6.

QUESTION—What are 'these things'?

It is the work of the ministry [NTC, WBC; CEV, NAB], the heavy responsibilities of such a ministry [AB, TH, TNTC], the effects of the ministry of the gospel [NIC1]. It is the task of proclaiming the good news which causes a division among people, bringing life to those who believe, but death to those who don't [EGT, Lns, My, NIC2, TG]. 'These things' comes first in the sentence for emphasis [AB, Lns, NTC].

QUESTION—What is the implied answer to this question?

1. The implied answer is that no one is sufficient [HNTC, SP, TH]. The question is posed to show the futility of claiming adequacy in oneself for such an awesome responsibility, not to claim adequacy for Paul [AB].
2. The implied answer is 'we are' [EGT, He, Ho, Lns, My]. Paul is implying that he is sufficient because his ministry has its source in God, but his opponents are not sufficient [ICC1, ICC2, Lns, NIC2]. No one is sufficient in himself for such a ministry, but God enables Paul for it [Ho, NIC1, NTC, TG, TNTC].

2:17 For we are not as many,[a] peddling-for-profit[b] the word[c] of God,

LEXICON—a. πολύς (LN 59.1): 'many' [LN; KJV, NLT], 'our many opponents' [WBC], 'the many' [Lns], 'so many' [AB; NAB, NIV, NJB, NRSV, REB], 'so many others' [TEV], 'so many people' [TNT], 'the majority' [HNTC], 'most people' [ICC2], 'a lot of people' [CEV].
   b. pres. act. participle of καπηλεύω (LN **57.202**) (BAGD p. 403): 'to peddle for profit' [**LN**; NIV], 'to peddle' [NTC], 'to huckster' [AB, LN], 'to engage in petty trading' [ICC2], 'to trade on' [NAB], 'to get rich from' [CEV], 'to haggle' [Lns], 'to handle as cheap merchandise' [TEV], 'to traffic in trivial things' [TNT], 'to adulterate' [WBC; NJB], 'to adulterate for profit' [REB], 'to corrupt' [KJV]. This participle is also translated as a noun: 'peddlers' [NRSV], or a noun clause: 'hucksters who preach just to make money' [NLT]. This word had a generally negative connotation [HNTC, ICC1, ICC2, NIC1, NIC2, NTC, TNTC, WBC].
   c. λόγος (LN 33.260) (BAGD 1.b.β. p. 478): 'the word (of God)' [AB, HNTC, ICC2, Lns, NTC; KJV, NAB, NIV, NJB, REB], '(God's) word' [NRSV], 'gospel' [BAGD, LN], 'what is preached' [LN], 'the Christian message' [BAGD], 'God's message' [WBC; CEV, NLT, TEV, TNT]. See this word also at 1:18.

QUESTION—What relationship is indicated by γάρ 'for'?
1. It introduces the answer to the question just raised; that is, we are sufficient because we are not like those others [Ho, ICC1, NIC2, WBC].
2. It introduces a reason for having raised the rhetorical question 'who is sufficient for these things?'; that is, Paul feels the heavy burden of responsibility of responsibility because he does not tamper with the message or remove its offence, or peddle it as others do [Lns, TH, TNTC].

QUESTION—What is implied by the use of the term οἱ πολλοί 'the many'?
It means that there were many of them [EBC]. It refers to the fact that there were many of them in many places [Lns, NTC]. It compares the many, in various places with the few true apostles [NIC1]. It refers to the practice of most people who had preached in Corinth [HNTC]. It refers to the many false teachers, but not the majority of teachers [Ho]. It refers to those ordinary teachers in Corinth who were not worthy to fill a such high office [EGT]. It is pejorative, referring to the 'mob' of false apostles [He, ICC1]. It is rhetorical and pejorative, but not necessarily numerical [AB, NIC2]. It refers not to their number but their influence [WBC]. It is a disparaging way to refer to some [ICC2].

QUESTION—What is implied by the word καπηλεύοντες 'peddling-for-profit'?
Merchants were often viewed as cheats who would adulterate their wares for dishonest gain [AB, NIC2]. This word implies both deceptiveness as well as greedy motives [LN], adulterating something for the purpose of improper gain [AB, EBC, EGT, HNTC, Ho, ICC2, NIC1, NIC2, WBC]. It implies that the false teachers were like merchants who would peddle inferior goods for the sake of gain and then leave [Lns]. They were defrauding the Corinthians

by selling them a watered-down message [NTC], motivated by personal gain [TG], garbling it for profit [ICC1]. The diluted gospel others preached was not potent enough either to save or to lead to destruction [Provence].

QUESTION—What is 'the word of God' of which he speaks?

It is God's message [CEV, NLT, TEV, TNT], that is, the gospel message [AB, EGT, ICC1, NIC2, NTC, TG, TH, WBC].

but as from[a] sincerity,[b] but as from[c] God we-speak in-the-presence[d] of-God in[e] Christ.

LEXICON—a. ἐκ (LN 89.85): 'from' [AB, LN, Lns], 'comes from' [ICC2], 'out of' [HNTC], 'of' [KJV], 'with' [LN; NIV, NLT, TEV, TNT], 'in' [REB]. The phrase 'as from sincerity' is translated 'as men of sincerity' [NTC], 'as persons of sincerity' [NRSV], 'as those who do so with sincerity' [WBC], 'we are sincere' [CEV], 'pure in motivation' [NAB], 'it is in all purity' [NJB].

b. εἰλικρίνεια (LN **88.42**) (BAGD p. 222): 'sincerity' [BAGD, HNTC, LN, Lns, NTC, WBC; KJV, NIV, NLT, NRSV, REB, TEV, TNT], 'sincere motives' [ICC2], 'sincere' [CEV], 'purity' [NJB], 'purity of motives' [BAGD, LN], 'pure motives' [AB], 'pure in motivation' [NAB]. This word refers to examining something in the light of the sun [NTC]. See this word also at 1:12.

c. ἐκ (LN 90.16): 'from' [AB, HNTC, ICC2, LN, Lns; REB, TNT], 'of' [KJV]. The phrase 'as from God' is translated as having an implied verb 'sent': 'sent from' [NTC; NIV, TEV], 'sent by' [NAB], 'we are God's messengers' [CEV], 'as envoys of God' [NJB]; or as implying the source of their message: '(whose word is) from (God)' [WBC].

d. κατέναντι (LN **83.42**) (BAGD 2.b. p. 421): 'in the presence of' [LN, Lns; NJB, TNT], 'standing in his presence' [NRSV], 'in his presence' [TEV], 'in the sight of' [AB, ICC2], 'in (God's) sight' [REB], 'before' [HNTC, LN]. The phrase 'in the presence of God' is translated 'with God as our witness' [CEV], 'God is watching us' [NLT].

e. ἐν: 'in' [AB, HNTC, Lns, NTC; KJV, NIV, NJB, NRSV, TNT], 'under the direction of' [ICC2], 'as servants of' [WBC; TEV], 'by the power of' [CEV], 'in (Christ's) name' [NAB], 'with Christ's authority' [NLT], 'as members of (Christ)' [REB].

QUESTION—Why does the repetition of ἀλλ' ὡς 'but as' signify?

It gives emphasis in ascending order [ICC1, NIC1, SP]. Paul emphatically distinguishes himself from those who peddle the word of God [Lns, NTC, WBC].

QUESTION—What is meant by ὡς ἐξ εἰλικρινείας 'as from sincerity'?

It refers to the subjective and human side of the genuineness of Paul's ministry which complemented the objective and external side, which was the authority which came 'as from God', that is, from God's call and commission [EGT, ICC1, NTC].

QUESTION—What is meant by ὡς ἐχ θεοῦ 'as from God'?
They were messengers sent by God [Lns, TG; CEV, NAB, NIV, NJB, NLT, NRSV, TEV], and under his direction [TG]. Not only were they sent from God, they were also like God, godly [Ho]. They were conscious that God was the source of their commission as messengers [EBC, EGT, NTC], but also of the message itself [EGT, He, ICC1, ICC2, NIC1, NIC2, NTC]. It means that their adequacy was from God [AB].

QUESTION—What is the speaking that he is referring to?
It is the preaching of the gospel message [ICC1, NIC2, NTC]. It is the entire apostolic witness to Christ, not only the preaching [AB]. It is speech inspired by the Holy Spirit [SP].

QUESTION—What is meant by ἐν Χριστῷ 'in Christ'?
It means in communion with Christ, as a member of his body [EGT, Ho], moved by his spirit [Ho]. It means that he does what he does as a Christian, as one whose act is determined by Christ and not by himself, with Christian insight and motivation [HNTC]. It means under the direction of Christ [ICC2]. His standing in God's presence is in connection with Christ [Lns]. It refers to the divine authority and power of his message [EBC]. It means incorporation into Christ [NIC1, NIC2]. Paul was incorporated into Christ at his conversion and his message flows from that [NIC2]. In refers to the manner in which Christ's servant ought to operate [WBC].

QUESTION—What is meant by the phrase κατέναντι θεοῦ 'in the presence of God'?
Paul is aware that he is seen by God and will be judged by him [HNTC, Lns]. Paul is aware that he must answer to God [AB, ICC2]. It means to be conscious of being in God's presence [EGT, Ho] and of his inspection [Ho]. It means that he does what he does with humility and fear [NIC1]. Since Paul stands in God's presence he represents God and can only speak what God has given him to speak [NTC]. Paul recognizes his accountability to an omniscient God for what he speaks in his name [NIC2]. Paul recognizes his responsibility and his dependence on God [EBC]. He knows that God judges wrongdoing so he speaks openly and truthfully [TH]. It means that God is our witness [CEV]. Paul is conscious of God's presence as his witness [My].

DISCOURSE UNIT: 3:1–6:13 [TG, TH]. The topic is Paul's apostolic commission and ministry.

DISCOURSE UNIT: 3:1–5:10 [REB]. The topic is Paul's commission as an apostle.

DISCOURSE UNIT: 3:1–4:10 [ICC1]. The topic is the glory of the apostolic office.

DISCOURSE UNIT: 3:1–18 [CEV, NAB, NRSV, TEV]. The topic is God's new agreement [CEV], ministers of the new covenant [NAB, NRSV], servants of the new covenant [TEV].

DISCOURSE UNIT: 3:1–11 [ICC1]. The topic is the superiority of the new ministration to the old.

DISCOURSE UNIT: 3:1–3 [TNTC]. The topic is letters of recommendation.

3:1 **Are-we-beginning to-commend[a] ourselves again?[b]**

LEXICON—a. pres. act. infin. of συνίστημι (LN **33.344**) (BAGD I.1.b. p. 790): 'to commend' [BAGD, HNTC, ICC2, NTC; KJV, NIV, NJB, NRSV, TNT], 'to recommend' [AB, BAGD, LN, Lns, WBC], 'to brag about' [CEV], 'to boast about' [TEV], 'to speak well of' [NAB], 'to tell how good we are' [NLT], 'to produce credentials' [REB]. Of the 16 occurrences of this word in the NT, half are in this epistle [WBC].

b. πάλιν (LN 67.55): 'again' [HNTC, ICC2, LN, Lns, NTC, WBC; KJV, NAB, NIV, NLT, NRSV, TEV, TNT], 'once again' [CEV], 'once more' [AB], 'afresh' [NJB], 'all over again' [REB].

QUESTION—What is meant by 'again'?

Paul has been charged with self-commendation before [EBC, Ho, ICC1, NIC1, TG]. His first self-commendation would have been his becoming their spiritual father at the time of the founding of the church in Corinth [NTC]. It refers to what he has said about himself in 1 Corinthians [EGT, Lns]. His defense of himself in chapter 1 might be seen as self-commendation [Ho, TNTC].

Or do-we-need[a] (surely not[b]) as some (do), letters-of-recommendation[c] to you or from you?

LEXICON—a. pres. act. indic. of χρῄζω (LN 57.39) (BAGD p. 885): 'to need' [AB, BAGD, HNTC, ICC2, LN, Lns, NTC; all versions], 'to have need of' [BAGD], 'to require' [WBC].

b. μή (LN 69.15): 'surely not' [AB, ICC2; NRSV]. This word indicates an expected negative response to a question [AB, He, ICC1, LN, Lns, NTC, TG, TNTC]. The linking of these two rhetorical questions with the conjunction ἤ 'or' means that a negative answer is expected for both [EBC, ICC2, NIC2]. The rhetorical question is presented as grounds for the conclusion reached in the previous verse that his ministry is valid [Moore, NOT 97, 10–83, p.9].

c. συστατικός (LN **33.345**) (BAGD 795): 'of recommendation' [AB, BAGD, ICC2, LN, NTC, WBC; NAB, NIV, NLT, NRSV, TEV, TNT], 'commendatory' [BAGD, HNTC, LN], 'recommendatory' [Lns], 'of commendation' [KJV, NJB], 'of introduction' [REB], 'introducing' [BAGD], '(letters) to tell about us' [CEV].

QUESTION—Is Paul condemning the use of commendatory letters?

He is not condemning the use of commendatory letters [AB, EBC, HNTC, ICC1, ICC2, Lns, NIC1, NTC, TNTC]. Since the Corinthian believers did not exist as a congregation when he first came, there would have been no one to present such a letter to, and now their existence as a congregation is the attestation of his apostleship [AB].

3:2 You-yourselves[a] are our letter, written[b] on[c] our hearts,[d] known[e] and read[f] by all men,[g]

TEXT—Instead of καρδίαις ἡμῶν 'our hearts', some manuscripts have καρδίαις ὑμῶν 'your hearts'. GNT selects the reading 'our hearts' with an A rating, indicating that the text is certain. The reading 'your' is taken by HNTC, ICC2, WBC; NAB.

LEXICON—a. ὑμεῖς (LN 92.7): 'you yourselves' [AB, NTC, WBC; NIV, NJB, NLT, NRSV, TEV, TNT], 'you' [HNTC, ICC2; CEV, KJV, NAB]. This word and its order in the sentence give added emphasis [AB, He, LN, Lns, NIC2, NTC, WBC].

b. perf. pass. participle of ἐγγράφω (LN 33.62) (BAGD 2. p. 214): 'to write in' [BAGD, LN]. This participle is translated as a participle: 'written' [HNTC, ICC2, Lns, NTC, WBC; all versions except CEV], 'inscribed' [AB]; as a verbal phrase: 'you are in (our hearts)' [CEV]. This verb is to be distinguished from the more generic γράφω (LN 33.61) 'to write' by the fact that ἐγγράφω is more specific and refers to engraving [NTC] or to the act of recording or writing in or upon something [LN]. It emphasizes the element of documentation, as in an official list or credential [AB]. The perfect tense indicates a permanent result [ICC1, NIC1, NIC2, NTC].

c. ἐν (LN 83.47): 'on' [AB, LN, NTC; NAB, NIV, NRSV, REB, TEV, TNT], 'in' [HNTC, Lns, WBC; CEV, KJV, NJB, NLT], 'within' [ICC2].

d. καρδία (LN 26.3) (BAGD 1.b.γ. p. 404): 'heart' [AB, BAGD, HNTC, ICC2, LN, Lns, NTC, WBC; all versions]. The heart is to be understood as the center of personhood and focal point of the activity of the Holy Spirit [WBC], the inmost self and most authentic being [AB].

e. pres. pass. participle of γινώσκω (LN 28.1): 'to know' [LN]. This participle is translated as a participle: 'known' [AB, HNTC, ICC2, Lns, NTC; KJV, NAB, NIV, TNT], 'recognized' [WBC]. It is also translated as an infinitive: 'to be known' [NRSV]; as a verbal phrase 'for (everyone) to understand' [CEV], 'that (everyone) can understand' [NJB], 'that (everyone) can recognize' [NLT], '(anyone) can see it for what it is' [REB], 'for (everyone) to know' [TEV].

f. pres. pass. participle of ἀναγινώσκω (LN 33.68) (BAGD 1. p. 51): 'to read' [BAGD, LN]. This participle is translated as a participle: 'read' [AB, HNTC, ICC2, Lns, NTC, WBC; KJV, NAB, NIV, TNT]; as an infinitive: 'to be read' [NRSV]; as a verbal phrase: 'for (everyone) to read' [CEV, TEV], 'everyone can read' [NJB, NLT], 'anyone can read it' [REB]. The present tense of both these verbs indicates that the Corinthians are continually known and read [NIC2].

g. ἄνθροπος (LN 9.1): This noun in the plural form is translated 'men' [HNTC, ICC2, Lns, NTC; KJV, NAB, TNT], 'people' [LN, WBC]. This noun is translated with πάντων 'all' as 'everyone' [AB; CEV, NJB, NLT, TEV], 'everybody' [NIV], 'anyone' [REB], 'all' [NRSV].

QUESTION—Does 'our letter' mean our letter of recommendation or our letter that we wrote?

The Corinthians are a letter of recommendation [AB, EBC, EGT, He, HNTC, My, NIC1, NIC2, TG, TNTC, WBC]. They are a letter he wrote, but also a testimony of his ministry [NTC].

QUESTION—What is the effect of the two participles γινωσκομένη καὶ ἀναγινωσκομένη 'known and read' being used together as they are in this context?

This is a play on words because of their similar sound [He, ICC1, NIC2, NTC]. The second word intensifies the first [AB, NIC2]. Everyone who knows Paul will be talking about the Corinthian church [NTC]. This is similar to his word-play in 1:13 with very similar verbs [ICC1, NIC1]. It means to be known and to be known well (as by reading) [AB, NTC].

QUESTION—In what way were they a letter written on the apostles' hearts, known and read by all men? (Note: He, HNTC, ICC2, WBC, TNTC take the reading 'your' following the textual variant, whereby the Corinthians would be a letter written on their own hearts.)

They are in his heart as dearly loved [NTC]. Paul took them into his heart by loving them [NIC2], and they were secure in his affections [NIC1]. The deep affection they felt and their thankfulness for the Corinthians' conversion, whose changed lives became an object lesson for everyone, tell Paul and his associates that the Corinthians are their validation in ministry [ICC1]. Paul's own heart testifies that the Corinthians are his credentials, and people hear about them from Paul wherever he goes as he speaks about their faith [EBC]. The deep love for them in his heart is apparent to everyone [TG]. The Corinthians, who were indelibly impressed on Paul's heart by his ministry there, are a 'letter' which is not evident for the world to see, but the one written by Christ on their hearts is open for the world to see [EGT]. The function of a letter of recommendation is to unite the hearts of those who receive it to those who are recommended; this letter from Christ is written on both sets of hearts, and the public nature of the letter comes from the idea that it is like a large stone monument, greater than a letter of paper and ink [Lns]. Something written on the heart is subjective knowledge of which the certainty is based on inward experience; Paul knew in his heart that the certainty of the Corinthians' conversion was his recommendation for ministry [Ho]. The Corinthians themselves are a letter the apostles carry in their hearts, but Paul also broadens his metaphor and says that the Corinthians are also Christ's letter written in their own hearts, the evidence of the work of the Spirit of God [AB].

3:3 being-manifested[a] **that you are a letter of-Christ**[b] **administered**[c] **by us,**

LEXICON—a. aorist pass. participle of φανερόω (LN 28.36) (BAGD 2.b.α. p. 853): 'to be made known' [BAGD, LN], 'to be revealed' [LN], 'to clearly show (yourselves to be)' [WBC], 'to clearly be' [NAB, NLT, TNT], 'to show (that)' [AB; NIV, NRSV], 'to be clear (that)' [TEV], 'to

be plain (that)' [NJB, REB], 'to be evident (that)' [NTC], 'to be manifest (that)' [HNTC], 'to be manifestly declared' [KJV], 'to be revealed' [ICC2], 'on public display' [Lns], not explicit [CEV]. This verb means to cause an invisible reality to become visible [NIC2]. The present tense indicates ongoing action [NTC]. See this word also at 2:14.
   b. Χριστοῦ: There is no lexical entry for the preposition 'of', the genitive case being used to express the relation between 'letter' and 'Christ'. It is translated 'of Christ' [HNTC, Lns, WBC; KJV, NAB, NRSV], 'from Christ' [NTC; NIV, NJB, NLT, TNT], 'that has come from Christ' [REB], 'written by Christ' [CEV], 'Christ's' [AB, ICC2], 'Christ himself wrote this letter' [TEV].
   c. perf. pass. participle of διακονέω (LN 35.37) (BAGD 3. p. 184): 'to be cared for' [AB, BAGD], 'to be taken care of' [BAGD, LN]. The participial phrase διακονηθεῖσα ὑφ' ἡμῶν is translated 'cared for by us' [AB], 'supplied by us' [HNTC], 'serviced by us' [ICC2], 'ministered by us' [KJV], 'ministerially by us' [Lns], 'delivered by us' [NTC; CEV, TNT], 'which I have delivered' [NAB], 'composed by our ministry' [WBC], 'the result of our ministry' [NIV], 'entrusted to our care' [NJB], 'prepared by us' [NLT, NRSV], 'sent by us' [TEV], 'given to us to deliver' [REB].

QUESTION—Is φανερούμενοι 'being manifested' a middle or passive participle, and how does that affect the meaning?
   1. It is passive: it is made evident that you are a letter of Christ [HNTC, ICC2, My, NTC, TG; KJV, NAB, NJB, NLT, REB, TEV, TNT]. God is the implied agent of the passive [NTC].
   2. It is middle: you show yourselves to be a letter of Christ [AB, He, NIC2, SP, WBC; NIV, NRSV].

QUESTION—How are the nouns related in the genitive phrase ἐπιστολή Χριστοῦ 'letter of Christ'?
   The letter is a letter from Christ [AB, EBC, He, ICC1, My, NTC, TG, WBC; NIV, NJB, NLT, REB, TNT], a letter of which Christ is the author [EBC, NIC2, NTC; CEV, TEV].

QUESTION—What does διακονέω 'administered' signify with regard to a letter in this context?
   Paul is the amanuensis or scribe that wrote Christ's letter which the Corinthians are [AB, EBC, EGT, Ho, My, TNTC], or the carrier that delivered it [AB, NTC, TG], by virtue of his ministry in Corinth when the church was founded [AB]. Paul served (διακονέω) the believers by administering or delivering the letter [NTC]. Paul was instrumental in the letter being written [He, ICC2], being used by Christ to bring the letter, that is the church, into existence [HNTC, ICC1]. The letter is caused by Paul's ministry [WBC]. The metaphor of a letter is limited [ICC1, NIC2]. Paul discontinues the metaphor at this point and is simply referring to his ministry at the founding of the church [NIC2]. It means 'ministerially by us' referring to their ministry to the Corinthians [Lns].

having-been-written not with-ink[a] **but with-(the)-Spirit**[b] **of the living God, not on stone tablets but on tablets which are hearts of-flesh.**[c]

LEXICON—a. μέλαν (LN **6.57**): 'ink' [AB, HNTC, ICC2, LN, Lns, NTC, WBC; all versions]. There is no lexical entry for the preposition 'with', the dative case being used to express the fact that ink is used as a medium of writing. The dative μέλανι is translated 'with ink' [AB, HNTC, ICC2, Lns, NTC; KJV, NAB, NIV, NJB, NRSV, REB, TEV, TNT], 'with pen and ink' [CEV, NLT], 'in ink' [WBC].

b. πνεῦμα (LN 12.18): 'Spirit' [AB, HNTC, ICC2, LN, Lns, NTC, WBC; all versions]. There is no lexical entry for the preposition 'with', the dative case being used to express the fact that the Spirit is the medium or means of the writing: 'with the Spirit' [AB, HNTC, ICC2, Lns, NTC; KJV, NIV, NJB, NLT, NRSV, REB, TEV, TNT]; or that the Spirit is the agent of the writing: 'by the Spirit' [WBC; CEV, NAB].

c. σάρκινος (LN 79.4) (BAGD 1. p. 743): 'of flesh' [BAGD, HNTC, ICC2; NAB], 'fleshly' [KJV], 'fleshen' [Lns], 'human' [AB, LN, NTC, WBC; NIV, NJB, NLT, NRSV, REB, TEV, TNT], not explicit [CEV].

QUESTION—How is the term σάρκινος 'of flesh' used in this context?

This refers to living substance as opposed to non-living material [AB, ICC2, NIC1, NIC2, TNTC]. It speaks of living receptivity [My], of that which is sensitive and feeling as opposed to lacking feeling [ICC1, ICC2].

QUESTION—What is the line of reasoning in Paul's extended metaphor of 'writing'?

The metaphor is not hard and fixed, but fluid [NIC2, NTC], with several streams of thought [WBC]. The two ideas conveyed here are that the letter that Christ wrote on the hearts of the Corinthians is spiritual in nature, not material or physical, and is internal, not external [Ho, NTC]. The two streams of thought of letters and covenant are linked by the Spirit who writes Christ's message on the heart, marking the coming of the new covenant age [WBC]. Paul shifts his metaphor from letter writing, where pen and ink contrast with the ministry of the Spirit, to the contrast of stone vs. human hearts [TNTC]. Paul shifts from a message written physically on paper or on the slabs of a public stone monument to the idea of a message written on a large public monument of fleshen hearts which is visible for all to see [Lns]. The contrast is between people who have ink-written letters they can carry with them and who promote a covenant written on stone, with Paul and his associates who have spirit-written letters written on people's hearts in a new covenant [NIC2]. Paul shifts his metaphor from a commendatory letter to the gospel, written on men's hearts and as opposed to the law [HNTC]. Paul's letter of recommendation is the new covenant written on fleshly, human hearts instead of stone hearts [Provence].

DISCOURSE UNIT: 3:4–18 [HNTC]. The topic is the old covenant and the new, the old ministry and the new.

DISCOURSE UNIT: 3:4–6 [TNTC]. The topic is ministers of the new covenant.

3:4 And[a] such confidence[b] we-have through[c] Christ before/toward[d] God.

LEXICON—a. δέ (LN 89.94): 'and' [ICC2, Lns, NTC; KJV], 'moreover' [Lns], not explicit [AB, HNTC, WBC; CEV, NAB, NIV, NJB, NLT, NRSV, REB, TEV, TNT].

b. πεποίθησις (LN **31.82**) (BAGD 2. p. 643): 'confidence' [AB, BAGD, HNTC, ICC2, LN, Lns, NTC, WBC; NAB, NIV, NJB, NRSV, TEV, TNT], 'trust' [KJV]. The phrase 'we have such confidence' is translated 'we are sure about all this' [CEV], 'it is in full reliance (upon God) that we make such claims' [REB], 'we are confident of all this because of our great trust (in God)' [NLT], 'we say this because we have confidence (in God)' [TEV], 'we say this because of the confidence we have' [TNT]. The phrase 'such confidence' receives emphasis by its initial position in the sentence [AB]. See this word also at 1:15.

c. διά with genitive object (LN 90.44): 'through' [AB, HNTC, ICC2, Lns, NTC, WBC; all versions except CEV]. The statement 'we have such confidence through Christ' is translated 'Christ makes us sure' [CEV].

d. πρός with accusative object (LN 89.112): 'before' [AB, HNTC, ICC2, LN; NIV], 'in the presence of' [WBC; CEV], 'in facing' [NJB], 'in regard to' [Lns], 'with' [LN], 'toward' [NTC; KJV, NRSV], 'in' [NAB, NLT, TEV, TNT], 'upon' [REB].

QUESTION—What relationship does this sentence have with the overall context?

1. It refers to 2:16–17 [EGT]. It refers to what immediately precedes it, and answers the question in 2:16 'who is sufficient for these things' [AB, NIC2, TNTC]. It connects the word 'confidence' with 2:17 where Paul discusses speaking with sincerity in Christ before God [NTC]. It also refers back to the use of the perfect tense of πείθω 'to be confident' in 1:9; Paul is expressing his confidence in God's power to save and vindicate [AB]. It connects the passage to 2:16–3:3 [HNTC, Ho, Lns, NIC2, Provence, WBC]. It is referring to 3:1–3 [EBC, ICC1, ICC2, NIC1], to 3:2–3 [TH], to 3:3 [TG].
2. It refers to what follows in 3:5–6 regarding the competence that God gives [TNTC].

QUESTION—What is Paul's confidence?

He is confident that the existence of the Corinthian church is his credential validating his ministry [EBC, ICC1, ICC2, NIC2, TG, TH]. He is confident that their faith validates his apostleship and that they are the evidence that the tablets of the law are superseded by the new covenant [HNTC]. The Corinthians are an epistle of Christ written by the Spirit, which gives him confidence in his ministry [NIC1]. He is sure of his apostleship and the fruit of its ministry [Lns]. He is confident in the sufficiency of his apostleship [EGT, Ho]. He is confident that he is acting as a true minister of the new covenant [WBC]. His confidence is the competence that God gives to be servants of the new covenant of the Spirit [TNTC]. It is the courage to approach God and be in his presence [AB]. It is the same confidence in Jesus that he spoke of in 1:14–15, which is linked to God's revelatory work in Jesus Christ and is connected to the day of the Lord Jesus [NTC]. It is that the Corinthians are a letter ministered by Paul and written by the Holy Spirit [SP].

QUESTION—What relationship is indicated by διά 'through'?

Christ is the basis or sphere of his confidence [AB]. It is through Paul's relationship with Christ and the work Christ does through him that he has such boldness [HNTC]. It expresses the fact that it was from Christ that Paul received the calling to be an apostle [Ho]. It refers to the fact that Christ has worked through Paul [WBC]. Paul's confidence is through Christ as opposed to self-confidence such as he would have had prior to his pre-conversion [NIC2]. It is Christ who gives them confidence in God [TG]. Christ is the channel through which confidence flows to them [Lns]. Paul's confidence comes from Christ, who is the author of the letter of recommendation which the Corinthian church is for Paul [ICC2]. Christ is the source of Paul's confidence because he brought Paul to conversion, called him to ministry, encouraged him in his ministry and fulfilled his promises to him [NTC]. Christ makes him sure of what he has asserted [CEV].

QUESTION—What is meant by confidence that is πρὸς τὸν θεόν 'before/toward God'?

1. It is confidence before God or in the presence of God [EBC, HNTC, Ho, ICC2, Lns, NTC, WBC; CEV, NIV, NJB]. Paul has a proper sense of limitation in the presence of an almighty God [ICC2]. God's presence is the sphere in which he exercises his ministry [WBC].
2. It is confidence in God himself [AB, EGT, HNTC, NIC1, NIC2, TG; NAB, NLT, REB, TEV, TNT]. It is confidence in God's power to save or vindicate [AB].
3. It is confidence that looks to God as its source [ICC1].

3:5 Not that we-are competent[a] of[b] ourselves to-think[c] anything as from[d] ourselves,

LEXICON—a. ἱκανός (LN 75.2) (BAGD 2. p. 374): 'competent' [BAGD, NTC; NIV, NJB, NRSV], 'adequate' [AB, ICC2, LN, WBC], 'qualified' [BAGD, LN], 'sufficient' [HNTC, Lns; KJV], 'having sufficient power' [REB], 'entitled to take credit' [NAB], 'able to do anything of lasting value' [NLT]. This clause is also translated 'we don't have the right to claim that we have done anything on our own' [CEV], 'there is nothing in us that allows us to claim that we are capable of doing this work' [TEV]. See this word also at 2:6, 16.

b. ἀπό (LN 90.15) (BAGD V.5. p. 88): 'of' [AB, BAGD, HNTC, ICC2, Lns, NTC; KJV, NAB, NRSV], 'from' [LN], 'in' [WBC; NIV, REB, TEV, TNT], 'by' [NLT], not explicit [CEV, NJB].

c. aorist mid. (deponent = act.) infin. of λογίζομαι (LN 31.1) (BAGD 2. p. 476): 'to think' [BAGD; KJV, NLT], 'to consider' [BAGD, HNTC, ICC2, LN, NTC], 'to claim' [Lns; NIV, NRSV, REB, TEV, TNT], 'to claim credit' [NJB], 'to regard' [LN], 'to evaluate' [AB], 'to reckon' [WBC], not explicit [CEV]. The phrase 'to think anything as from ourselves' is translated 'to take credit for anything' [NAB].

d. ἐκ (LN 90.16): 'from' [LN; TNT], 'coming from' [NRSV], 'proceeding from' [HNTC], 'deriving from' [ICC2], 'emanating from' [Lns], 'originating with' [AB], 'of' [KJV], not explicit [NLT, TEV]. The phrase 'anything as from ourselves' is translated 'anything to our credit' [WBC], '(to take) credit for anything' [NAB], '(to claim) anything/any credit for ourselves' [NIV, NJB], '(to claim) anything as our own' [REB].

QUESTION—What relationship is there between the infinitive λογίσασθαι 'to think' with the adjective ἱκανός 'competent'?

1. They would not consider or reckon themselves sufficient such that anything could come from themselves [AB, EGT, HNTC, ICC2, Lns, NIC1, TG, WBC; CEV, NIV, NJB, NLT, NRSV, REB, TEV, TNT]. He is not sufficient in himself even to the most basic of processes, which is thinking adequately concerning effective ministry, much less the doing of it [Ho]. He cannot rightly judge the methods that should be used in ministry [EGT].
2. They are not sufficient to judge, assess, or form an estimate of the results of ministry [EBC, ICC1] or of the means and ways of discharging his ministry [My].

QUESTION—What is implied by the use of the word ἱκανός 'competent'?

In the Septuagint (LXX) this word is used twice in Ruth and three times in Job for the divine name *El Shaddai*, mistakenly translated 'the sufficient One' (HNTC, ICC1, NIC1); Paul is saying that God is the sufficient one from whom comes the sufficiency of his ministers [ICC1, NIC1, NIC2]. Whereas Moses in Ex 4:10 (LXX) insists οὐκ ἱκανός εἰμι 'I am not sufficient' (as does Paul in 1 Cor. 15:9), here Paul is claiming that by the grace of God he is ἱκανός 'sufficient' (as in 1 Cor 15:10) [AB, NIC2].

but[a] our competence[b] (is) from[c] God

LEXICON—a. ἀλλά (LN 89.125): 'but' [LN, NTC, WBC; KJV, NIV], 'rather' [AB, HNTC], 'on the contrary' [ICC2, Lns], not explicit [CEV, NAB, NJB, NLT, NRSV, REB, TEV, TNT].

b. ἱκανότης (LN **75.1**) (BAGD p. 374): 'competence' [NTC; NIV, NJB, NRSV], 'adequacy' [AB, ICC2, **LN**, WBC], 'sufficiency' [HNTC, Lns; KJV], 'power' [REB], 'power and success' [NLT], 'capacity' [TEV], 'resources' [TNT], 'what it takes' [CEV], 'sole credit' [NAB].

c. ἐκ (LN 90.16): '(is) from' [LN, NTC; NAB, NRSV], '(comes) from' [HNTC, WBC; NIV, NJB, NLT, REB, TEV, TNT], '(derives) from' [ICC2], '(is emanating) from' [Lns], '(is) of' [KJV]. This clause is translated 'God gives us what it takes to do all that we do' [CEV].

3:6 who also made- us -competent^a (to be) ministers^b of a new covenant,^c

LEXICON—a. aorist act. indic. of ἱκανόω (LN **75.3**) (BAGD p. 374): 'to make competent' [NIV, NRSV], 'to give the competence (to be)' [NJB], 'to give adequacy' [WBC], 'to make adequate' [ICC2, **LN**], 'to enable to be adequate' [AB], 'to enable (to represent)' [NLT], 'to enable (to be)' [NTC], 'to make able (to be)' [KJV], 'to make capable (of)' [TEV], 'to give sufficiency' [HNTC], 'to make sufficient' [BAGD, LN, Lns], 'to empower as' [REB], 'to qualify' [LN], 'to make qualified (ministers)' [NAB], 'to make worthy to be' [CEV], 'to give all we need' [TNT]. The aorist form of this verb is a constative aorist (in which an action is viewed in its entirety), and refers to the whole of Paul's ministry [NTC].

b. διάκονος (LN 35.20) (BAGD 1.a. p. 184): 'minister' [AB, HNTC, Lns; KJV, NAB, NIV, NJB, NRSV, REB, TNT], 'servant' [BAGD, LN, NTC, WBC; CEV], 'agent' [ICC2]. This noun is also translated as a verb: 'to represent' [NLT]; as a gerund 'serving' [TEV].

c. διαθήκη (LN 34.44) (BAGD 2. p. 183): 'covenant' [AB, BAGD, HNTC, ICC2, LN, NTC, WBC; all versions except CEV, KJV], 'testament' [Lns; KJV], 'agreement' [CEV]. The διαθήκη 'covenant' is a one-sided or unilateral agreement, as opposed to a mutual agreement between two more or less equal parties [HNTC, ICC1, Lns, NIC1, NIC2, TG, TH].

QUESTION—What relationship is indicated by καί 'also'?

It is a simple conjunctive 'and' [NTC], 'also' [EGT, Lns; KJV], 'indeed' [WBC]. 'And who' is equivalent to 'for he' as in Luke 8:13 and elsewhere, indicating cause or reason [Ho]. It is not translated by AB, HNTC, ICC2; all versions except KJV.

QUESTION—To what event does ἱκάνωσεν ἡμᾶς 'he made us competent' refer?

He is referring to the Damascus road experience [AB, EBC, ICC1, NIC1, NIC2, TH]. (If one takes the view that the enabling was the call and conversion on the Damascus road, then Paul's use of the first person plural would be viewed as primarily referring to himself, but also to his associates by extension, as in other places.)

QUESTION—How are the nouns related in the genitive construction 'ministers of a new covenant'?

They serve the new covenant [My; TEV], represent the new covenant [REB], or serve in the way provided for by the new covenant [TG]. The words 'new' and 'covenant' are fused into one descriptive phrase which modifies 'ministers'; they are new testament ministers as opposed to ministers of another sort [Lns].

QUESTION—What is implied by the use of the adjective καινή 'new' as opposed to νέος 'new'?

The term καινή 'new' indicates a superior quality [AB, EBC, HNTC, ICC1, NIC1, NIC2, NTC]. It speaks of a new chapter in God's dealings with the human race and not just a renovated Judaism [WBC]. It contrasts with the old covenant of the Judaizers [NIC1]. It indicates that which is fresh and effective as opposed to the old and obsolete [ICC1, NIC2]. It reflects the wording of the LXX in Jer. 31 and the tradition of the last supper [ICC2, NTC], and may not represent any conscious choice on Paul's part [ICC2].

not of-letter/of-(the)-letter[a] but of-spirit/of-(the)-Spirit;[b] for the letter kills,[c] but the Spirit gives-life.[d]

LEXICON—a. γράμμα (LN 33.50) (BAGD 2.c. p. 165): 'writing' [LN]. This word has no definite article, and is in the genitive case, which expresses its grammatical function. It is translated 'of letter' [Lns; NRSV], 'of the letter' [NTC; KJV, NIV], 'based on letter' [HNTC], 'based on the letter' [WBC], 'characterized by letter' [ICC2], 'of written letters' [NJB], 'just a written code' [TNT], 'the written law' [REB], 'from a written law' [CEV], 'of a written law' [NAB, TEV], 'of written laws' [NLT], 'written' [AB]. It is translated without the definite article by AB, HNTC, ICC2, Lns; CEV, NAB, NJB, NLT, NRSV, TEV, TNT; with the definite article by NTC, WBC; KJV, NIV, REB. This word is distinguished from ἐπιστολή 'letter, epistle' which appears in 3:1–3.

b. πνεῦμα (BAGD 5.g.γ. p. 677): 'spirit' [BAGD]. This word has no definite article, and is in the genitive case, which expresses its grammatical function. It is translated 'of spirit' [Lns; NAB, NRSV], 'of the spirit' [KJV], 'of the Spirit' [NTC; NIV, NJB, NLT, TEV], 'from the Holy Spirit' [CEV], 'based on Spirit' [HNTC], 'based on the Spirit' [WBC], 'characterized by Spirit' [ICC2], 'spiritual' [AB; REB, TNT]. It is translated without the definite article by AB, HNTC, ICC2, Lns; NAB, NRSV, REB, TNT; with the definite article by NTC, WBC; CEV, KJV, NIV, NJB, NLT, TEV. It is capitalized by HNTC, ICC2, NTC, WBC; CEV, NIV, NJB, NLT, TEV.

c. pres. act. indic. of ἀποκτείνω (LN 20.61) (BAGD 1.b. p. 94): 'to kill' [AB, BAGD, HNTC, ICC2, LN, Lns, NTC, WBC; KJV, NAB, NIV, NJB, NRSV], 'to bring death' [CEV, TEV, TNT], 'to condemn to death' [REB]. The phrase 'the letter kills' is translated 'the old way ends in death' [NLT].

d. pres. act. indic. of ζῳοποιέω (LN 23.92) (BAGD 1. p. 341): 'to give life' [AB, BAGD, HNTC, LN, NTC; all versions except CEV], 'to make alive' [BAGD, Lns], 'to make live' [LN], 'to produce life' [ICC2], 'to impart life' [WBC], 'to bring life' [CEV].

QUESTION—What is the antecedent of the genitive phrases 'of letter/of (the) letter' and 'of spirit/of (the) spirit'?

1. The antecedent is διαθήκη 'covenant'; the new covenant is a covenant not of the letter but of the Spirit [AB, EBC, He, HNTC, ICC2, Lns, NIC1, NIC2, NTC, SP, TG, TH; CEV, NAB, NJB, NLT, REB, TEV, TNT].
2. The antecedent is διάκονοι 'ministers'; they are ministers, not of the letter but of the Spirit [EGT, Ho, ICC1, My, TNTC].

QUESTION—Is the word 'spirit' used in the same sense in both places in this sentence?
1. It refers to the Spirit of God in both places [EBC, EGT, He, HNTC, ICC1, ICC2, NIC2, NTC, TG, TH, TNTC; CEV, NIV, NJB, NLT, TEV].
2. The first occurrence (without the definite article) refers to the inner or spiritual dimension [AB, Ho, NIC1; NAB, NRSV, REB, TNT], an inward living force that is in contrast to the letter of the law [Lns]. The first occurrence means that which is of the heart, and the second occurrence is parallel to it and refers to the gospel [Ho].

QUESTION—What is the distinction being made between 'letter' and 'spirit'?
Letter and spirit refer to the external and internal dimension [NIC1]. It refers to the written code as opposed to the operation of the Spirit in the gospel [ICC1]. It is a contrast between the law and the gospel [Ho]. Only the Spirit changes a person's heart, bringing an internal obedience to the law as opposed to an external conformity [NTC, Provence]. It refers to dependence on the Mosaic law to establish one's own righteousness instead of the Holy Spirit to mediate life by the gospel [TNTC]. It is the difference between the freeing and enlivening power of the Spirit, which is based on promise, and performance of what is written, which is destructive and kills because it estranges a person from the grace he needs [AB]. It is a distinction between the literal meaning of the law versus the true spiritual meaning which only the Spirit can give; the law does not give the Spirit [He]. It refers to the opposition of the written regulations of the outward law which is imposed on rebellious hearts, versus the law of God being written inwardly on the minds and hearts of forgiven people [NIC2]. The law presents condemnation to the sinner and kills those who try to gain life by it instead of by promise, whereas the Spirit quickens and gives life [Lns]. It contrasts the written code which pronounces a sentence of death because it is powerless to transform versus the indwelling Spirit that brings transformation [EBC]. It refers to human and divine action respectively. The letter is based on external human performance and does not reach the heart [HNTC]. It refers to the fact that we obey the Spirit of God and not a written law [TG]. The law, which is external and written on stone, evokes fear and a sense of slavery, but is powerless to evoke the behavior it demands; the new order operates in the heart by the power of the Spirit [ICC2]. These are two different ways of service, one of which is obligation to the laws of Torah under the old covenant, and the other which is service that is guided and strengthened by the indwelling Spirit of God under the new covenant [Westerholm]. Letter and spirit characterize the manner in which the respective covenants occur and subsist [My]. The law and the Holy Spirit are the regulating principles and the motivating powers of the two respective covenants [Dunn]. It is a salvation-historical contrast between the written law, which is powerless, and God's new covenant wherein the spirit is active [SP].

QUESTION—What does he mean that 'the letter kills'?
The written law cannot transform life, it can only give a sentence of death [EBC]. Facing the letter of the law without the Spirit brings death [NTC]. A person who believes he is obeying the law but has only conformed outwardly, having missed its true intent, remains in rebellion and is condemned for not really keeping the law [Provence]. The letter kills because it is man-centered, enslaving a person to the idea that righteousness comes from one's doing of the law instead of as a gift from God, and estranging the person from the grace he really needs [AB, HNTC]. The letter kills because it leads to the false expectation of saving oneself by works, but does not conquer the sin which brings death [He]. The law condemns dead hearts [NIC2] and the sins of the transgressor [NIC1]. The law cannot help sinners or make them alive, it can only present them their death warrants [Lns]. The duty required by the written code kills hope and love because it sets up high standards that it cannot meet and then it condemns, imposing a death sentence [ICC1]. The law produces a sense of guilt through the knowledge of sin, and then exasperates the soul which is unable to obey, thus bringing condemnation for disobedience [Ho]. It brings eternal death in that it awakens evil desires which lead to sin and to the consequent condemnation and divine anger that result from breaking the law [My].

DISCOURSE UNIT: 3:7–4:6 [AB, EGT]. The topic is the ministry of the new covenant [AB], digression on the ministry of the new covenant [EGT].

DISCOURSE UNIT: 3:7–18 [ICC2, TNTC, WBC; NIV, NLT]. The topic is the glory of the new covenant [NIV, NLT], Paul's ministry and the ministry of Moses [ICC2], two ministries compared and contrasted [TNTC], life under the two covenants [WBC].

3:7 Now/but[a] if the ministry[b] of-death[c]
LEXICON—a. δέ (LN 89.124): 'now' [AB, ICC2, Lns, NTC, WBC; NIV, NJB, NRSV], 'but' [HNTC, LN; KJV], not explicit [CEV, NAB, NLT, REB, TEV, TNT].
  b. διακονία (LN 35.21) (BAGD 3. p. 184): 'ministry' [AB, BAGD, HNTC, LN, Lns, NTC, WBC; NAB, NIV, NRSV, REB], 'ministration' [KJV], 'administering' [NJB], 'agency' [ICC2], 'the law' [TEV], 'the Law of Moses' [CEV], 'the old system of law' [NLT], 'the giving of the law' [TNT].
  c. θάνατος (LN 23.99): 'death' [AB, HNTC, ICC2, LN, Lns, NTC, WBC; all versions except TEV], not explicit [TEV]. 'Of death' is translated 'of the death' [Lns], 'that resulted in death' [NTC], 'that leads to death' [WBC], 'that brought death' [NIV, REB], 'the promise of death' [CEV]. The phrase 'the ministry of death' is translated 'the Law of Moses brought only the promise of death' [CEV], 'the old system of law led to death' [NLT], 'the giving of the law has ended in death' [TNT].

2 CORINTHIANS 3:7

QUESTION—What relationship is indicated by δέ 'now/but'?
1. It is continuative [AB, ICC2, Lns, My, NTC, WBC; NIV, NJB, NRSV]: 'now'.
2. It is adversative [EGT, HNTC; KJV]: 'but'.

QUESTION—How is εἰ 'if' used in this sentence?
It introduces the first of three 'if...then' statements that constitute an argument from lesser to greater concerning the comparative glory of the new and old covenants [AB, ICC2, NIC2, TH, WBC]. It is a condition of reality [Lns, TH], and acknowledges the fact to set up the argument [TNTC].

QUESTION—How are the nouns related in the genitive construction 'ministry of death'?
The ministry is named for its effect [Lns]. It condemns to death [TG], it deals in death [AB], it brings death [Ho, NIC1, NIC2, TH; NIV, REB], it leads to death [WBC; NLT], it results in death [NTC]. It is the instrument of death in that it condemns [EGT], it leads to condemnation [He], it dispenses death to those who can't keep its requirements [TNTC], it is the ministry leading to the rule of death [My].

QUESTION—How is the term διακονία 'ministry' used in this context?
1. It is impersonal and refers to the dispensation or administration of the old covenant [ICC1, TH, WBC; CEV, NLT, TEV, TNT]. It refers to the effect of the old covenant and its effect on disobedient people [NTC]. It refers to the Law of Moses that was engraved on the tablets of stone [CEV].
2. It is personal and refers to the ministry or service of Moses [HNTC, My]. It refers to the circumstances surrounding the ministry of Moses in its effects on Israel [Dumbrell].
3. It is both personal and impersonal, referring to both the system of law as well as Moses the law-giver [AB, ICC2]. Moses serves as a go-between and his service consists in mediation or acting as an agent of God's law [ICC2].

having-been-engraved[a] in letters[b] on-stones[c] came[d] in/with[e] glory[f]
LEXICON—a. perf. pass. participle of ἐντυπόω (LN **33.67**) (BAGD p. 270): 'to engrave' [HNTC, ICC2, LN, Lns, WBC; KJV, NIV, NJB, REB], 'to carve' [BAGD, **LN**; CEV, NAB, TEV, TNT], 'to chisel' [AB, NTC; NRSV], 'to etch' [NLT]. Grammatically the subject of the participle ἐντετυπωμένη 'having been engraved' is διακονία 'ministry'; it is the ministry that is engraved on stone, not the letters [AB, EGT, HNTC, ICC1, ICC2, Lns, NTC, WBC].
b. γράμμα: 'letters' [AB, HNTC, ICC2, Lns, NTC, WBC; NIV, NJB, NRSV, TEV, TNT], not explicit [CEV, NLT]. The phrase 'in letters' is translated 'written' [KJV], 'in written form' [REB], 'in writing' [NAB].
c. λίθος (LN 2.23, 2.24) (BAGD 1.e. p. 474): 'stone' [AB, BAGD, HNTC, ICC2, LN (2.23, 2.24), Lns, NTC, WBC; all versions except NRSV, TEV], 'stone tablets' [NRSV, TNT]. This plural noun is translated in the singular 'in stone' or 'of stone' as indicating the material or medium [LN

(2.23)] upon which the law was written [AB, NTC, WBC; NAB, NIV, NJB, NLT, REB, TNT].
- d. aorist pass. (deponent = active) indic. of γίνομαι (LN 13.80, 13.3) (BAGD II.4.a. p. 160): 'to come' [NIV, NRSV, TNT], 'to come to exist' [LN (13.80)], 'to be' [BAGD, LN (13.3), Lns; KJV], 'to come into being' [HNTC, ICC2], 'to take place' [AB], 'to occur' [NJB], 'to appear' [NTC, WBC], 'to be inaugurated' [NAB, REB], 'to begin' [NLT]. The phrase 'came in glory' is translated 'to be given in a wonderful way' [CEV], 'God's glory appeared when it was given' [TEV].
- e. ἐν (LN 13.8): 'in' [HNTC, LN, NTC; NJB, NRSV], 'with' [AB, ICC2, LN, WBC; NAB, NIV, NLT, REB, TNT], 'in connection with' [Lns], not explicit [CEV, KJV, TEV].
- f. δόξα (LN 79.18) (BAGD 1.a. p. 203): 'glory' [HNTC, ICC2, LN, Lns, NTC, WBC; NAB, NIV, NJB, NLT, NRSV, REB], 'God's glory' [TEV], 'splendor' [AB, BAGD, LN; TNT], 'brightness, radiance' [BAGD]. The phrase 'in glory' is translated 'glorious' [KJV], 'in a wonderful way' [CEV], 'with attendant glory' [ICC2], 'in connection with glory' [Lns]. The phrase 'came in glory' is translated 'God's glory appeared' [TEV].

QUESTION—What is implied by the phrase 'in letters engraved on stone'?
1. It is two separate things: it was in letters, and it was engraved on stone; that is, 'written (but possibly never read) but also on heavy and dead material' [ICC1]. The perfect tense indicates the enduring nature of the effect, that it stands engraved forever [Lns]. Being written and in stone, the covenant was an external economy and not a spiritual one [Ho].
2. It refers to one thing: it was written by engraving on stone [CEV, NAB, NLT]

QUESTION—How is the verb γίνομαι 'came' used in this sentence?
Here in the protasis of this conditional clause this verb is used in its aorist form in place of εἶναι 'to be', which lacks an aorist form, and is parallel to the use of εἶναι in its future tense in the apodosis of the sentence, and is used as the implied verb in verses 9 and 11 [AB, Lns; KJV]. It means 'to come' in the sense of coming into existence [AB, EGT, HNTC, ICC2, NIC1; NIV, NJB, NLT, NRSV, TNT], or being inaugurated [ICC1].

such-that[a] the sons[b] of Israel were- not -able to-gaze[c] on the face of Moses because-of[d] the glory[e] of his face, the fading/being-set-aside [f] (glory),

LEXICON—a. ὥστε (LN 89.52) (BAGD 2.a.β. p. 900): 'such that' [AB, WBC; NAB, NJB, NLT, REB, TNT], 'so that' [BAGD, HNTC, ICC2, LN, Lns, NTC; CEV, KJV, NIV, NRSV, TEV], 'as a result' [LN]. This word indicates result as opposed to expressing purpose [AB, BAGD].
- b. υἱός (LN 11.58) (BAGD 1.b.α. p. 833): This plural noun is translated 'sons' [ICC2, Lns], 'children' [HNTC; KJV], 'descendants' [BAGD], 'people (of Israel)' [LN; CEV, NLT, NRSV, TEV]. 'The sons of Israel' is translated 'the Israelites' [AB, NTC, WBC; NAB, NIV, NJB, REB, TNT].

c. aorist act. infin. of ἀτενίζω (LN **24.49**) (BAGD p. 119): 'to gaze' [AB, HNTC, ICC2, Lns; NRSV], 'to look at/on' [NTC; CEV, NAB, NLT, TNT], 'to look steadily at/in' [NIV, NJB], 'to fix the eyes upon' [WBC], 'to keep the eyes on' [REB], 'to keep the eyes fixed on' [TEV], 'to stare at, to keep one's eyes fixed on' [LN], 'to look intently at' [BAGD], 'to behold steadfastly' [KJV].

d. διά (LN 90.44): 'because of' [BAGD, HNTC, ICC2, Lns, NTC, WBC; NAB, NIV, NJB, NRSV, TNT], 'because' [AB], 'on account of' [BAGD], 'for' [KJV, NLT], not explicit [CEV, REB, TEV].

e. δόξα (LN 14.49, 79.18) (BAGD 1.a. p. 203): 'glory' [HNTC, Lns, NTC, WBC; KJV, NAB, NIV, NJB, NRSV, REB], 'the glory of God' [NLT], 'radiance' [ICC2, LN (14.49); TNT], 'brightness' [LN (14.49); TEV], 'shining' [LN (14.49)], 'splendor' [AB]. The phrase 'the glory of his face' is translated '(the Law made) Moses' face shine brightly' [CEV].

f. pres. pass. participle of καταργέω (LN 13.163) (BAGD 2. p. 417): 'to fade' [REB, TEV], 'to fade away' [NLT], 'to be set aside' [BAGD, NTC; NRSV], 'to be put to a stop' [LN (13.163)], 'to be put to an end' [LN (13.100)], 'to be done away with' [Lns; KJV], 'to be abolished' [BAGD], 'to be annulled' [AB], 'to be in the process of abolition' [HNTC], 'to be in the process of effacement' [ICC2], 'to be transient' [WBC]. This passive participle is also translated as an adjective: 'fading' [CEV, NAB, NIV, TNT], 'transitory' [BAGD; NJB]. The position of this word in the sentence shows emphasis [EGT]. It is used here in a concessive sense, 'although' [EGT, He, Lns, NTC, TG, TH, WBC; CEV, NAB, NIV, NJB, NLT, REB, TEV, TNT]. The present participle has an imperfect sense because the action was contemporary with the action of the aorist main verb ἐγενήθη 'came' [AB, HNTC, Ho, ICC1, ICC2]. This participle is used again in 3:11, where it refers to the ministry of the old covenant.

QUESTION—Is the participle καταργουμένην middle 'fading', or passive 'being set aside'?

1. It is passive [AB, BAGD, Dumbrell, Hafemann, Hanson, ICC1, Lns, NIC1, NIC2, NTC; KJV, NRSV]; it is being abolished or set aside. God is the agent of the passive [Lns, NIC2]. The abolition began at the time of inauguration [AB, NIC2].

2. It is middle in force [EGT, He, Ho, ICC2, My, SP, TG, TH, WBC; CEV, NAB, NIV, NJB, NLT, REB, TEV, TNT]; it is transient or fading away. It is a passive or deponent passive with a middle meaning [EGT, ICC2].

QUESTION—Was the glory that was fading the glory of Moses' face or of the law?

1. It is the glory of Moses' face that was fading or being abolished [AB, EGT, He, HNTC, Ho, ICC1, ICC2, Lns, My, NIC2, SP, TG, TH, WBC].

2. It is the glory of the old covenant that was set aside [NTC]. Paul uses this word because the law and the old covenant were being abolished [HNTC]. When Paul uses this word with reference to the glory of Moses' face he is referring to the passing away of the old covenant [Hanson].

3. The glory of Moses' face was transient, but it was symbolic of the whole ministry of the law [Ho]. The fading of the glory of his face was a type of the ceasing of his ministry [My].

QUESTION—What made Moses' face shine?

The presence and glory of God had made Moses' face shine [Lns, My, NTC, Provence, TG]. It was the glory of the ministration of the law that made his face shine [Ho], or the law itself that made his face shine [CEV].

QUESTION—Why were they not able to look at Moses' face?
1. The people were not able to keep looking at Moses because of the brightness of the glory that shone from his face [EGT, He, HNTC, Ho, ICC1, ICC2, Lns, My, NTC, SP, TG, TNTC, WBC; CEV, KJV, NAB, NIV, NJB, NLT, NRSV, REB, TEV, TNT], and because of the contrast with their own idolatry [NTC, Provence]. The glory of God reflected in the face of Moses produced fear and turning away in hearts hardened by rebellion [Provence].
2. They could not look because the glory was being annulled or abolished [AB, NIC2].

3:8 how^a will the ministry^b of-the Spirit not be^c even-more^d in glory?

LEXICON—a. πῶς (LN 92.16) (BAGD 1.d. p. 732): 'how' [BAGD, ICC2, LN, Lns, NTC, WBC; KJV, NAB, NJB, NRSV, REB, TEV, TNT]. The rhetorical question introduced by πῶς οὐχί 'how will not' is translated as 'will not' [AB], 'does not this mean' [HNTC], 'how shall not' [ICC2, Lns; KJV], 'how much (more)' [NTC, WBC; NJB, NRSV], 'how much (greater)' [NAB, REB, TEV, TNT], 'won't' [CEV], 'will not' [NIV], 'shouldn't we expect' [NLT]. The phrase πῶς οὐχὶ μᾶλλον'how... not...more' introduces a rhetorical question typical of the rabbinic style in which the argument proceeds from lesser to greater [AB, HNTC, NIC2, NTC, WBC]: if this is true, that is much more. The rhetorical question demands an affirmative answer [ICC2, Lns, NTC, TG, TH, WBC].

b. διακονία: 'ministry' [AB, HNTC, Lns, NTC, WBC; NAB, NIV, NJB, NRSV, REB], 'ministration' [KJV], 'agency' [ICC2]. The phrase 'the ministry of the Spirit' is translated 'the agreement that the Spirit brings' [CEV], 'when the Holy Spirit is giving life' [NLT], 'the activity of the Spirit' [TEV], 'the giving of the Spirit' [TNT]. See this word also at 3:7.

c. fut. indic. act. of εἰμί (BAGD III. 4. p. 225): 'to be' [AB, BAGD, HNTC, ICC2, Lns, NTC, WBC; CEV, KJV, NAB, NIV, REB, TEV, TNT], 'to occur' [NJB], 'to come' [NRSV], not explicit [NLT].

d. μᾶλλον (LN 78.28) (BAGD 2.b. p. 489): 'even more' [HNTC, LN; CEV, NIV], 'more' [LN], 'much more' [NTC, WBC; NJB, NRSV], 'yet more certainly' [ICC2], 'more than, to a greater degree' [LN], 'greater' [AB], 'much greater' [NAB, REB, TEV, TNT], 'far greater' [NLT], 'rather' [Lns; KJV].

QUESTION—How are the nouns related in the genitive construction 'ministry of the Spirit'?
1. It is the ministry that gives the Spirit [AB, HNTC, ICC1, Lns, NIC2, NTC, SP, TNTC, WBC; TNT].
2. It is the ministry that the Spirit performs [My, TG, TH; TEV].
3. It is the ministry that the Spirit brings [CEV].
4. It is a spiritual ministry [Ho].

QUESTION—What is meant by the future tense in the verb phrase ἔσται ἐν δόξῃ 'will be in glory'?

The use of the present tense verb περισσεύει 'abounds' in the following verse indicates that ἔσται 'will be' refers to the condition present at the time of Paul's writing [Ho, ICC1].
1. It is a real future tense from the standpoint of the time of the giving of the old covenant, but which is contemporary for Paul as he writes [NIC2, TG, TH; TEV].
2. It is a logical future which expresses the certainty of the conclusion he is drawing from the rhetorical question, and which is contemporary for Paul as he writes [HNTC, Ho, ICC2]. He speaks of the glory that belongs to the ministry of the gospel in which he is now engaged [Ho].
3. It is both a logical future as well as a real future from the standpoint of the time of Paul's writing. That is, the ministry of the Spirit, in which Paul is now engaged, is more glorious and will continue to be so [AB, ICC1, NTC].
4. It is a logical future but primarily expresses the eschatological future which has not yet fully occurred [My, WBC].

QUESTION—How is μᾶλλον 'much more' used here?
1. It means that the ministry of the Spirit will be characterized by greater glory, or will be more glorious [AB, EBC, HNTC, ICC1, Lns, NIC2, NTC, TG, TH, WBC; CEV, NAB, NIV, NLT, REB, TEV, TNT].
2. It refers to the force of the argument, that it is much more certain or sure that the ministry of the Spirit will have glory [ICC2, SP].

QUESTION—What is the glory to which he refers?

It is the light of God's presence within the soul [Ho, NIC1]. It is God's power which expresses his nature, and which the ministers of the new covenant receive [ICC2]. It is transformation into Christ's likeness [NTC]. It is the life changing experience of those who know God through the preaching of the gospel [NIC2]. It is the glory of the coming age [My].

3:9 For[a] if in-the-ministry of condemnation[b] (there is)[c] glory,

TEXT—Instead of τῇ διακονίᾳ 'in the ministry' (in the dative case) some manuscripts have ἡ δακονία 'the ministry' (in the nominative case), making it the subject and not the object of the implied verb. The sense is the same however and variations in English versions would be due to stylistic considerations and not to the textual variant.

LEXICON—a. γάρ (LN 89.23): 'for' [AB, HNTC, ICC2, LN, Lns, WBC; KJV, NJB, NRSV], 'then' [NTC], 'and' [TNT], not explicit [CEV, NAB, NIV, NLT, REB, TEV]. This introduces the second point of comparison which is explanatory of the first [ICC1, Lns], continuing the argument begun in 3:7 [TH].
- b. κατάκρισις (LN **56.31**) (BAGD p. 412): 'condemnation' [AB, BAGD, HNTC, ICC2, LN, Lns, NTC, WBC; all versions except CEV]. The genitive phrase 'the ministry of condemnation' is translated 'the ministry of the condemnation' [Lns], 'the ministry that leads to condemnation' [WBC], 'something that brings the death sentence' [CEV], 'the ministry of the covenant that condemned' [NAB], 'to administer condemnation' [NJB], 'the old covenant, which brings condemnation' [NLT], 'the ministry that brought condemnation' [REB], 'the system which brings condemnation' [TEV], 'the giving of the Law which brings condemnation' [TNT].
- c. There is no lexical entry for this implied verb. The implied verb is translated 'there is (glory)' [AB], 'there was (glory)' [NRSV], 'was a matter of (glory)' [HNTC], '(glory) belongs to' [ICC2], 'is (glory)' [Lns], 'be (glory)' [KJV], 'is (glorious)' [CEV, NIV, NJB], 'was (glorious)' [WBC; NLT, TEV], 'had (glory)' [NAB], '(glory) was conferred' [NTC], '(glory) accompanied' [REB], 'was accompanied by (such splendor)' [TNT].

QUESTION—How are the nouns related in the genitive construction 'ministry of condemnation'?

It is the old ministry that brings condemnation [AB, EBC, HNTC, ICC1, ICC2, Lns, NAC, NIC2, NTC, TG, TH, WBC; CEV, NAB, NJB, REB, TEV, TNT].

how-much more^a the ministry of righteousness^b abounds^c in glory.

LEXICON—a. μᾶλλον: The phrase πολλῷ μᾶλλον 'how much more' is translated 'how much more' [AB, NTC, WBC; NIV, NLT, TEV, TNT], 'much more' [HNTC; KJV, NRSV], 'much more certainly' [ICC2], 'by how much more' [Lns], 'even more' [CEV], 'greater by far' [NAB]. This phrase is translated in conjunction with the following verb περισσεύω 'abounds' as 'to be far richer in' [NJB], 'to be much richer in' [REB]. This is a continuation of the lesser-to-greater argument begun in the previous verse [AB, ICC1, ICC2, NIC2, NTC, TH, TNTC].
- b. δικαιοσύνη (LN 34.46) (BAGD 3. p. 197): 'righteousness' [AB, HNTC, ICC2, Lns, NTC, WBC; KJV, NIV], 'the righteousness bestowed by God' [BAGD], 'a right relationship' [LN], 'saving justice' [NJB], 'justification' [NRSV], 'acquittal' [REB]. The phrase 'the ministry of righteousness' is translated 'the ministry that leads to righteousness' [WBC], 'the ministry that brings righteousness' [NIV], 'something that makes us acceptable to God' [CEV], 'the ministry that justifies' [NAB], 'the new covenant, which makes us right with God' [NLT], 'the ministry that brings

acquittal' [REB], 'the activity which brings salvation' [TEV], 'the giving of the Spirit which makes us right with God' [TNT].
   c. pres. act. indic. of περισσεύω (LN 59.52) (BAGD 1.a.γ. p. 651): 'to abound' [AB, HNTC, ICC2, LN, Lns, WBC; NRSV], 'to be abundant' [BAGD, NTC], 'to overflow' [BAGD], 'to be extremely rich' [BAGD], 'to be far richer (in glory)' [NJB], 'to be much richer (in glory)' [REB], 'to exceed' [KJV], 'to be greater by far' [NAB], 'to be much more (glorious)' [NIV, NLT, TEV], 'to be much more (splendid)' [TNT], 'to be even more (glorious)' [CEV]. See this word also at 1:5.
QUESTION—How are the nouns related in the genitive construction 'ministry of righteousness'?
   It is the new ministry that leads to, brings, or confers righteousness [EBC, He, HNTC, ICC1, Lns, My, NIC2, NTC, TG, TH, WBC; NIV, REB, TEV]. It is the ministry under which men are counted as righteous [TNTC]. It deals in righteousness [AB]. It preaches the gospel which is the means of justification that leads to righteousness [ICC2]. It reveals the righteousness by which men are justified [Ho].
QUESTION—Does δικαιοσύνη 'righteousness' refer to an ethical or forensic righteousness?
   It is a forensic righteousness conferred by God [BAGD, He, Ho, ICC1, ICC2, Lns, NIC1, NIC2, NTC, TNTC, WBC]. It is an acquittal by God that puts people into right relationship [TG, TH]. It is the ground of justification [Ho]. It is a relational righteousness but also represents the abiding and indwelling power of God [HNTC]. It is forensic and relational in that God declares righteous those whom he reconciles [NTC].

3:10 For[a] indeed[b] that-which has-been-glorified has not been-glorified[c] in this respect[d] on-account-of[e] the surpassing[f] glory.
LEXICON—a. γάρ (BAGD 2. p. 152): 'for' [BAGD, HNTC, ICC2, Lns, NTC; KJV, NIV], not explicit [AB, WBC; CEV, NAB, NJB, NLT, NRSV, REB, TEV, TNT].
   b. καί (LN 91.12): 'indeed' [AB, ICC2, LN, NTC, WBC; NAB, NJB, NRSV, REB, TNT], 'even' [Lns; KJV], not explicit [HNTC; CEV, NIV, NLT]. The phrase καὶ γάρ 'for indeed' is translated 'in fact' [CEV, NLT], 'we may say' [TEV].
   c. perf. pass. indic. of δοξάζω (LN 87.24) (BAGD 2. p. 204): 'to be glorified' [BAGD, LN], 'to be glorious' [CEV, NLT], 'to have glory' [KJV, NIV], 'to have splendor' [AB]. This verb is translated in conjunction with the negative particle οὐ as 'to lose splendor' [TNT], 'to lose glory' [WBC; NRSV], 'to be glorious no longer' [CEV], 'to be declared no glory' [NAB], 'to lose all claims to glory' [NJB], 'to be no glory' [REB], 'the glory that was is gone' [TEV]. The extent of the comparison expressed by οὐ δεδόξασται τὸ δεδοξασμένον 'that which has been glorified has not been glorified' is intensified by the addition of

'at all' to this perfect passive verb [HNTC, ICC2; CEV, NAB, NLT, REB].
d. μέρος (LN 89.5) (BAGD 1.b.θ. p. 506): 'about, in the case of, with regard to' [LN]. The phrase ἐν τούτῳ τῷ μέρει is translated 'in this case' [AB, BAGD], 'in this respect' [ICC2, NTC; KJV], 'in this point' [Lns], 'partial' [WBC], 'limited' [NAB], not explicit [HNTC; all versions except KJV, NAB].
e. εἵνεκεν (LN 89.31) (BAGD p. 226): 'on account of' [BAGD, ICC2, LN, Lns], 'because of' [AB, LN, NTC; NRSV, TEV], 'by reason of' [KJV]. Εἵνεκεν 'on account of' functions semantically to indicate the reason for the diminished glory of the old covenant, which is the comparison with the surpassing glory of the new covenant. This implied comparison is made explicitly by the following versions: 'in comparison with' [HNTC; NIV], 'compared with' [WBC; NLT], 'when you compare' [NAB], 'by contrast with' [NJB], not explicit [CEV]. The comparative relation of the lesser to the greater is translated 'it is outshone by' [REB], 'it has given place to' [TNT].
f. pres. act. participle of ὑπερβάλλω (LN 78.33) (BAGD p. 840): 'to surpass' [AB, BAGD, HNTC, ICC2, NTC, WBC; NAB, NIV], 'to excel' [KJV], 'to transcend' [NJB], 'far more, much greater, to a far greater degree' [LN], not explicit [CEV, TEV]. This participle is translated as an adjective: 'transcendent' [Lns], 'overwhelming' [NLT], 'greater' [NRSV], 'still greater' [REB], 'even greater' [TNT].

QUESTION—What relationship is indicated by γάρ?
It clarifies and further supports the forgoing argument [AB, TH]. It introduces the grounds for the previous statements [My, WBC]. It introduces a further explanation of the reference in 3:9 to abundant glory [ICC2]. Καί γάρ 'for indeed' intensifies Paul's arguments [NIC2].

QUESTION—To what does τό δεδοξασμένον 'that which has been glorified' refer?
It refers to the old covenant [NIC2; CEV]. It refers to the ministry of Moses [ICC1]. It refers to the ministry of Moses, and by extension, to the old covenant, of which he was the mediator [Ho, ICC2].

QUESTION—What does ἐν τούτῳ τῷ μέρει 'in this respect' mean here?
1. It means 'in this respect' as in 9:3, and qualifies οὐ δεδόξασται 'has not been glorified' with reference to the surpassing glory of the gospel [AB, BAGD, EGT, HNTC, Ho, ICC1, ICC2, My, NIC1, NTC, SP, TH; KJV]. That is, with respect to the greater glory of the gospel the old covenant has not been glorified [AB, ICC1, ICC2, NTC]. It means 'in this case', that is, in comparison with the splendor of the ministry of righteousness [SP]. Paul is clarifying his use of a metaphor and setting limits on how he is using it; 'in one sense, at least' the fading of visual glory was comparable to the temporal nature of the Mosaic economy [Aber NOT1].
2. It means 'in this respect' and refers to the power to confer righteousness and life described in the clause immediately preceding it ἡ διακονία τῆς

δικαιοσύνης δόξῃ 'the ministry of righteousness abounds in glory' [Dumbrell]. That is, with respect to conferring these things, the full potential of the old covenant was never realized, even though it was glorious.

3. It means 'in this point', a specific part of the larger matter [Lns]. That is, Moses' ministry was glorious, but in one respect God has not glorified Moses ministry in that he has not made it as glorious as the ministry of the gospel.
4. It means 'partial' or 'partially' in the same manner as ἀπο μέρους 'in part' does in 1:14 and 2:5. It qualifies τό δεδοξασμένον 'that which has been glorified', and sets limits on the glory of the first covenant [He, WBC; NAB].

QUESTION—What is meant by the paradoxical statement 'that which has been glorified has not been glorified'?

The idea is similar to comparing the light of the sun to any lesser light which would pale in the sun's brightness [EBC, Ho, ICC1, NIC1, TG].
1. Paul's absolute statement is a rhetorical device for emphasis; the oxymoron is true by way of comparison [EGT, He, Ho, ICC2, NTC, SP, TH, TNTC]. That is, the glory of the old covenant is nothing compared to the greater glory of the gospel. The old covenant has not been glorified to the fullest because of the new [NTC]. The oxymoron and paradox are made more pointed by the use of the perfect tense [AB].
2. It means that what was once glorified has been made not-glorious [NIC1, NIC2, WBC]. It has been de-glorified by being out-glorified [NIC2]. It has lost whatever glory it had [WBC].
3. It means that the old covenant was glorified in all but one respect, which is that it is not as glorious as the ministry of the gospel [Lns].

3:11 For if that-which is-being-set-aside/is-fading-away[a] (came) with[b] glory, much more[c] that-which is-remaining[d] (is) in[e] glory

LEXICON—a. pres. pass. participle of καταργέω (LN 13.163, 76.26) (BAGD 2. p. 417): 'to be set aside' [NTC; NLT, NRSV], 'to fade away' [CEV, NIV, REB, TNT], 'to be abolished' [ICC2, LN (76.26)], 'to be put to a stop' [LN (13.163)], 'to be annulled' [AB], 'to be in process of abolition' [HNTC], 'to be done away' [Lns; KJV], 'to be destined to pass away' [NAB], 'to last for a while' [TEV]. This participle is also translated as an adjective: 'transient' [WBC], 'transitory' [NJB].
b. διά with genitive object: This preposition, in conjunction with the implied verb, which must be supplied for English style, is translated 'was with' [AB], 'was accompanied by' [HNTC], 'was attended by' [ICC2], 'appeared with' [NTC], 'had its moments of' [WBC], 'was given with' [CEV], 'was given in' [NAB], 'came with' [NIV], 'had' [NJB], 'was full of' [NLT], 'came through' [NRSV], 'had its (glory/splendor)' [REB, TNT], 'there was (glory) in' [TEV], 'was (glorious)' [KJV], '(is being

done away with) despite (glory)' [Lns]. This preposition indicates attendant circumstances [BAGD, ICC2].
- c. μᾶλλον: The phrase πολλῷ μᾶλλον is translated 'much more' [HNTC, Lns; KJV, NRSV], 'how much more' [AB, NTC; TEV], 'much more certainly' [ICC2], 'how much' [WBC], 'still greater' [REB], 'much greater' [CEV], 'how much greater' [NIV, NJB, TNT], 'greater by far' [NAB], 'far greater' [NLT].
- d. pres. act. participle of μένω (LN 13.89) (BAGD 1.c.β. p. 504): 'to remain' [BAGD, LN, Lns, NTC; KJV, NLT], 'to endure' [AB, ICC2, WBC; NAB, REB], 'to abide' [HNTC], 'to last' [NIV, NJB, TEV, TNT]. This participle is also translated as a verbal phrase: 'it will never fade away' [CEV]; and as an adjective: 'permanent' [NRSV].
- e. ἐν (LN 13.8): 'in' [HNTC, LN, NTC; NRSV], 'with' [LN, Lns], not explicit [AB; CEV, NAB, NIV, NJB, NLT, REB, TEV, TNT]. This preposition is translated in conjunction with an implied verb: 'shall continue in' [HNTC], 'is characterized by' [ICC2], 'appears in' [NTC], 'is filled with' [WBC], 'has come in' [NRSV], 'is (glorious)' [KJV], 'is (the glory)' [NAB, NIV, NJB, REB], 'is (the splendor)' [TNT], 'has (glory)' [NLT], 'there is (glory)' [TEV].

QUESTION—What is the nature of the contrast between the glory of the two covenants that is set forth in these two verses?

In 3:9 there is a contrast of degree, and in 3:10 one of duration [NIC2, TG].

QUESTION—What relationship is indicated by γάρ 'for'?

It introduces the next lesser-to-greater argument as in 3:9 [AB]. It introduces additional grounds for the assertions of superiority [Ho]. It explains and supports the contrast that precedes [ICC1]. It explains 3:7 and 10 [NIC2]. It introduces an explanation for the one point that is still not yet resolved, which is why Moses' ministry is not equal to the apostles' ministry [Lns].

QUESTION—Is the participle τὸ καταργούμενον middle in meaning, 'that which is fading away', or passive in meaning, 'that which is being set aside'?

1. It is passive [AB, Dumbrell, Hafemann, Ho, ICC2, Lns, NIC2, NTC]. In Paul's typical use of this word the act of nullification also involves the abolishing of the effects of the thing nullified [Hafemann].
   1.1 God, who is setting aside the old covenant, is the agent of the passive [Lns, NIC2].
   1.2 The gospel, which is doing away with the law, is the agent of the passive [Ho]. The new covenant is doing away with the old [AB]. The death of Christ and the preaching of the gospel are doing away with the old covenant [ICC2].
   1.3 Disobedient people, who are setting aside the law by breaking it, are the agents of the passive [NTC].
2. It is middle in meaning: it is passing or fading away [EBC, EGT, ICC1, My, SP, TNTC]. It is temporary or transient in nature [He, TG, WBC].

QUESTION—What is the relationship between the present participle τὸ καταργούμενον 'that which is being set aside/that which is fading away' and the tense of the implied verb?
1. The implied verb is past tense and the present participle takes on an imperfect tense when used with a past tense verb [AB, NIC2; NIV, TNT]: what was being annulled or fading away came with glory.
2. The implied verb is in the past tense and the participle is used in the past tense also [CEV, NLT, NRSV, TEV]: what was set aside came with glory.
3. The implied verb is in the past tense and the participle is a future tense [NAB, REB]: what was going to pass away came in glory.
4. The implied verb is in the past tense but the participle is present in meaning [EGT, HNTC, ICC2, NTC; KJV], or is adjectival and without temporal reference [He, WBC; NAB]: what is fading away came with glory.
5. The present participle is a substantivized present and functions as the implied verb [Lns]: 'what is being done away with (is being done away with) despite glory'.
6. Both the participle and the implied verb are present tense [My]: that which ceases is glorious.

QUESTION—To what does the participle τὸ καταργούμενον 'that which is being set aside/that which is fading away' refer?

It refers the ministry of the old covenant [AB, EGT, ICC2, NIC2, NTC], the ministry of condemnation [Lns, SP], the old dispensation and its ministry [Ho], the ministry of the law [TNTC]. In 3:7 the verb refers to the glory of Moses' face, whereas here it refers to that glory as well as the administration that Moses represents [ICC2]. It refers to the function and ministry of Moses [My].

QUESTION—Is there a difference in meaning between the prepositions διά 'with' and ἐν 'in' in this sentence?
1. They are used here with essentially the same sense [AB, HNTC, Ho, ICC2, My, WBC].
2. Διά 'with' implies transience, while ἐν 'in' implies permanence [EGT, ICC1, NIC1, NIC2]. Διὰ δόξης is adjectival and means 'glorious', and ἐν δόξῃ describes the abiding element, that which is established in the sphere of glory [NIC1].
3. Διά has the meaning 'despite' as it does in Romans 2:27 and 4:11 [Lns].

DISCOURSE UNIT: 3:12–4:6 [ICC1]. The topic is the great boldness of the new ministers.

3:12 Therefore[a] having such[b] hope[c] we act[d] with much boldness[e]
LEXICON—a. οὖν (LN 89.50) (BAGD 1. p. 593): 'therefore' [BAGD, ICC2, LN, Lns, NTC; NIV, NJB], 'then' [BAGD, HNTC, LN, WBC; KJV, NRSV], not explicit [CEV, NAB, NLT, REB, TEV, TNT].

b. τοιοῦτος (LN 92.31, 64.2) (BAGD 2.a.β. p. 821): 'such' [AB, BAGD, HNTC, ICC2, LN (64.2), Lns, NTC, WBC; all versions except CEV, NJB], 'this wonderful' [CEV], 'like this' [LN (64.2); NJB].
c. ἐλπίς (LN 25.59) (BAGD 2.b. p. 253): 'hope' [AB, BAGD, HNTC, ICC2, LN, Lns, NTC, WBC; all versions except NLT], 'confidence' [NLT].
d. pres. mid. or pass. (deponent = act.) indic. of χράομαι (LN 41.4) (BAGD 2. p. 884): 'to act' [AB, BAGD; NRSV], 'to behave toward' [LN], 'to behave' [ICC2], 'to proceed' [BAGD], 'to exercise (freedom)' [HNTC], 'to continue using' [Lns]. The phrase πολλῇ παρρησίᾳ χρώμεθα 'we act with much boldness' is translated 'we are very bold' [NTC; NIV, TEV], 'we can be very bold' [NLT], 'we speak with great freedom' [WBC], 'we feel like speaking freely' [CEV], 'we use great plainness of speech' [KJV], 'we speak with full confidence' [NAB], 'we speak with great confidence' [TNT], 'we can speak with complete fearlessness' [NJB], 'we speak out boldly' [REB]. See this word also at 1:17.
e. παρρησία (LN 25.158) (BAGD 1. p. 630): 'boldness' [AB, LN; NRSV], 'courage' [LN], 'freedom' [HNTC], 'great freedom' [WBC], 'outspokenness' [BAGD], 'frankness' [BAGD], 'confident frankness' [ICC2], 'full openness of speech' [Lns], 'plainness of speech' [BAGD], 'great plainness of speech' [KJV], 'full confidence' [NAB], 'great confidence' [TNT], 'complete fearlessness' [NJB]. This noun is also translated as an adverb describing the manner of speaking: 'boldly' [REB], 'freely' [CEV]; or as a predicate adjective describing Paul and his co-workers: 'bold' [NTC; NIV, NLT, TEV].

QUESTION—What relationship is indicated by ἔχοντες 'having'?
It is causal [AB, HNTC, Ho, Lns, My, NIC2, NTC, Van Unnik, WBC; NIV, NLT, NRSV, TEV, TNT]: because we have such hope, therefore we act with boldness.

QUESTION—What is the hope to which he refers?
It is that the glory of the gospel is permanent [AB, HNTC, ICC1], or that the new covenant is a permanent one [TNTC, Van Unnik]. It is that they have a ministry with transcendent glory [Lns]. It is that they have an enduring covenant, the Holy Spirit, and a ministry of righteousness [NTC]. It is that at the coming of Christ the ministry of the gospel will have a glory far greater than that of Moses' ministry [My]. It is that the gospel and its ministry are superior to the law and Moses' ministry [Ho]. It is the glorious ministry of the Spirit referred to in 3:8 [EGT]. It is the eschatological reality (already present) depicted in 3:7–11, especially that which endures [SP].

QUESTION—Who is included in the "we"?
It refers to Paul and his co-workers [AB, Lns, NTC]. It refers to the servants of the gospel [ICC1]. It refers to Paul himself [ICC2, TH]. Paul refers to himself and his co-workers as representative of all believers [NIC2].

QUESTION—How is the term παρρησία 'boldness' used?
Paul is probably referring to having one's head or face uncovered and thus appearing openly or boldly [NTC, Van Unnik]. There is confidence and freedom, especially in relationship with other men [Van Unnik]. It is a frankness and unreservedness with people [My]. It is outspokenness and frankness as opposed to concealment [Ho], complete openness as opposed to secrecy [NIC1]. It is speaking openly without withholding, with no reservation [Lns]. It is openness [EBC, ICC2], frankness [HNTC, ICC1, ICC2], confidence [AB, EBC, ICC1], and courage [ICC1]. It means that Paul is bold in evangelizing [TH]. It is not being ashamed in his relationship with others [AB]. It is openness as opposed to having a veil or barrier, and being sighted as opposed to being blind [NIC2]. It is bold, fearless candor [EBC].

3:13 and not as[a] Moses who would-put[b] a veil[c] over his face
LEXICON—a. καθάπερ (LN 64.15) (BAGD p. 387): 'as' [HNTC, Lns; KJV, REB], 'just as' [BAGD, LN], 'like' [AB, NTC, WBC; CEV, NAB, NIV, NJB, NLT, NRSV, TEV, TNT], 'in the same way' [ICC2].
b. imperf. act. indic. of τίθημι (LN 85.32) (BAGD I.1.a.β. p. 816): 'to put' [AB, BAGD, HNTC, ICC2, LN, Lns, NTC, WBC; all versions except CEV, NAB]. The phrase 'to put a veil over' is translated 'to cover' [CEV], 'to hide with a veil' [NAB]. This imperfect verb is translated as a simple past tense: 'put' [HNTC; KJV, NJB, NLT, NRSV, REB, TEV], 'covered' [CEV]; as an ongoing or habitual action in time past: 'used to put' [AB, ICC2, NTC; TNT], 'kept putting' [Lns], 'was in the habit of putting' [WBC], 'would put' [NIV], 'used to hide' [NAB].
c. κάλυμμα (LN **6.177**) (BAGD 1. p. 400): 'veil' [AB, BAGD, HNTC, ICC2, LN, Lns, NTC, WBC; all versions except CEV], not explicit [CEV].
QUESTION—What relationship is indicated by οὐ καθάπερ 'and not as'?
It contrasts Paul's openness and boldness with Moses' covering of his face [HNTC, ICC1, SP, TH, Van Unnik]. It contrasts plainness of speech with concealment, as Moses had to speak in parables and types [Ho]. It contrasts Paul's ministry with that of Moses [Lns].

in order[a] that the sons of Israel would not stare[b] at the end[c] of what was fading away/being nullified.[d]
LEXICON—a. πρός (LN 89.60) (BAGD III.3.a. p. 710): 'for the purpose of, in order to' [LN]. The phrase πρὸς τό 'in order that' is translated 'so that' [ICC2, Lns, NTC; NAB, NJB, TEV], 'so' [AB; NLT], 'that' [HNTC; KJV, TNT]. The phrase πρὸς τὸ μή 'in order that...not' is translated 'to prevent' [WBC], 'to keep...from' [CEV, NIV, NRSV, REB].
b. aorist act. infin. of ἀτενίζω (LN 24.49) (BAGD P. 119): 'to stare' [LN, NTC], 'to look intently' [BAGD], 'to gaze' [AB, ICC2, Lns; NIV, NRSV, REB], 'to fix the eyes' [LN, WBC], 'to look steadfastly' [KJV], 'to watch' [NJB, TNT], 'to see' [CEV, NAB, NLT, TEV].

c. τέλος (LN 67.66; 89.55) (BAGD 1.a. p. 811): 'end' [AB, BAGD, HNTC, ICC2, LN (67.66), Lns, NTC; KJV, NJB, NRSV, REB], 'termination, cessation' [BAGD], 'purpose, intent, goal' [LN (89.55)], 'significance' [WBC], not explicit [CEV, NLT]. The phrase τὸ τέλος οὗ ταργουμένου 'the end/outcome of what was being nullified/fading away' is translated 'the final fading' [NAB], 'while it was fading away' [NIV], 'fade and disappear' [TEV, TNT].

d. pres. pass. participle of καταργέω (LN 13.100) (BAGD 2. p. 417): 'to fade' [NAB, TEV, TNT], 'fade away' [CEV, NIV, NLT, REB], 'to be caused to end' [LN], 'to be transitory' [BAGD; NJB], 'to be annulled' [AB], 'to be abolished' [HNTC; KJV], 'to be in process of effacement' [ICC2], 'to be done away with' [Lns, WBC], 'to be set aside' [NTC; NRSV].

QUESTION—What relationship is indicated by πρὸς τό 'so that'?
1. It indicates purpose [AB, EGT, He, HNTC, Ho, ICC1, ICC2, My, NIC1, NIC2, NTC, TG, WBC; all versions].
2. It indicates result [Lns].

QUESTION—What is meant by τέλος 'end'?
1. It refers to the end or fading of the glory of Moses' face [AB, Aber NOT1, BAGD, EGT, HNTC, Ho, ICC1, My, NIC1, NTC, TG; all versions].
   1.1 Combined with εἰς τό 'at/until' it refers to the duration [NIC1]; that is, so that they would not stare without interruption right on to the end of it.
   1.2 It is a pleonasm or redundancy with τοῦ καταργουμένου 'what was being nullified/rendered inoperative', both referring to the same thing [NTC]. Moses was preventing them from staring at the radiance which happened to be passing away and which signified something that was passing away.
2. It refers to purpose, goal, or outcome [Dumbrell, Hafemann, ICC2, Lns, NIC2, Provence].
   2.1 The end or goal is faith in Christ [Provence]. It refers to the goal of the splendor of the old revelation, which looked beyond itself to a higher fulfillment [Dumbrell]. The goal in view or fulfillment is the glory of the pre-existent Christ which Moses saw in the tabernacle [Hanson]. The goal or end would be the eschatological fulfillment by the new era which is of greater glory [NIC2]. The law ends in the righteousness of being justified by faith in Christ, both as its goal as well as its termination point [Lns]. Moses concealed the ultimate purpose of his own ministry under the old covenant [ICC2].
   2.2 The outcome would be judgment that would occur if sinful people were to gaze continually on the glory of God [Hafemann, NAC].
3. It refers to significance or meaning [He, WBC]. That is, they were not to see the significance of the veil or of the Mosaic administration [WBC].

QUESTION—To what does the neuter participle τοῦ καταργουμένου 'what was fading away/being nullified' refer?

This participle is neuter (or possibly masculine), whereas the same participle in 3:7 which refers to the glory of Moses' face is feminine in form, in agreement with and modifying the feminine noun δόξα 'glory'.

1. It refers to the glory of Moses' face [Aber NOT1, EGT, Ho, ICC1, NIC1, TH; CEV, NAB, NIV, NLT, TEV, TNT].
2. It refers to the covenant of which Moses was a minister [Dumbrell, EBC, Hanson, My, NIC2, SP]. The fading of the glory of his face represents the cessation of his ministry [My]. It refers either to the administration of law or to the veil itself [WBC]. This participle is neuter because it refers to the neuter participles of 3:10 and 11 which refer to the entire framework of the old covenant [HNTC]. It speaks of the end of Moses' ministry and its covenant [NTC].
3. It refers to the radiance of Moses' face, but also to the law and the old covenant ministry [AB, ICC2, TNTC].
4. It refers to the effect that would result from seeing the glory of God; in mercy toward the people, Moses veiled his face so that seeing the glory of God would not bring judgment for their sin and hard-heartedness [Hafemann].

QUESTION—What was Moses' motive for covering his face?

1. Moses covered his face to hide the glory from the Israelites [Hafemann, Hanson, My, NAC, NIC1, NIC2, NTC, Provence].
   1.1 Moses covered his face because of the Israelites' sinfulness and hardness of heart. Moses covered his face because the people were unworthy to behold the divine glory [NIC1]. Moses veiled himself to nullify the effect that the glory of God would produce, which would be judgment because of their hardness of heart [Hafemann]. Moses veiled himself so that God's glory would not have its natural effect of bringing judgment on sinful people [NAC]. Moses veiled his face so that they would not see the goal of the law as well as the glory of God revealed on his face, which goal would be to lead them to faith in Christ for salvation. The reason for his veiling was that their hearts were hard [Provence]. Moses hid his face because the Israelites were afraid to approach him due to the fact that their hearts were hard and they did not want to see the glory of God that came with the giving of his law [NTC].
   1.2 Moses covering of his face was educational and preparatory in that he did not want to diminish the Israelites' perception of the value of the law. He therefore covered his face to prevent the Israelites from contemplating the passing away of his covenant or ministry as they saw the fading of the glory of his face [My].
   1.3 Moses covered his face so the people would not see the ultimate significance of what was being abolished because they failed to

comprehend what the radiance was all about and what it pointed forward to [He, WBC]. The veiling was also for reverential reasons [WBC].

1.4 Moses' intent was to hide the glory of the pre-existent Christ whom he had seen in the tabernacle. This was because in the divine economy the blindness of Israel would result in the evangelization of the Gentiles [Hanson].

2. Moses covered his face to hide the fact that the glory was fading from his face of the glory from the Israelites [AB, Dunn, HNTC, Ho, ICC1, ICC2, TG, TNTC; CEV, NAB, NLT, TEV, TNT].

2.1 Moses did this to prevent them from seeing the temporary nature of the law and the old covenant [Dunn, ICC2], or seeing how soon the brightness ended [Ho]. This is a figurative way of saying that Moses taught obscurely because God's plan was to reveal the plan of redemption gradually [Ho].

2.2 Moses did this to prevent them from thinking less of him as someone of only temporary significance [HNTC], or that he was a minister of a fading covenant [TNTC].

3. Moses covered his face to keep the Israelites from gazing while it was fading [NIV], or from gazing in amazement until it went away [EBC], and also to teach them that the newly given order of the law would eventually pass away and be eclipsed [EBC]. Moses did not want the people to stare at him while his face was radiant [Aber NOT1].

4. Moses covered his face in order to suggest to Israel that there was a dimension of the covenant in which they were not sharing, though this was not understood because their minds were hardened [Dumbrell].

3:14 But[a] their minds[b] were-hardened.[c] For[d] until this-very day the same[e] veil remains[f] at the reading of the old covenant,[g]

LEXICON—a. ἀλλά (LN 89.125): 'but' [AB, HNTC, LN, Lns, NTC, WBC; NIV, NJB, NLT, NRSV], 'instead' [LN], 'on the contrary' [LN], 'to the contrary' [ICC2], 'of course' [NAB], 'indeed' [TEV], 'in any case' [REB], not explicit [CEV, TNT].

b. νοήμα (LN 26.14) (BAGD 1. p. 540): 'mind' [AB, BAGD, HNTC, ICC2, LN, NTC, WBC; all versions except CEV], 'thoughts' [BAGD], 'considerations' [Lns], not explicit [CEV].

c. aorist pass. indic. of πωρόω (LN **27.51**) (BAGD p. 732): 'to be hardened' [AB, BAGD, HNTC, ICC2, NTC; NLT, NRSV], 'to be made dull' [BAGD; NAB, NIV, TNT], 'to be made like stone' [Lns], 'to be blinded' [BAGD; KJV], 'to be obtuse' [WBC], 'to be caused to be completely unwilling to learn' [LN], 'to be closed' [**LN**], 'to cause the mind to be closed' [LN; NJB, REB, TEV]. The phrase 'their minds were hardened' is translated 'the people were stubborn' [CEV]. The aorist is ingressive, expressing action begun with ongoing results: their minds became dull [ICC1, NIC2].

d. γάρ (LN 89.23): 'for' [HNTC, ICC2, LN, Lns, NTC, WBC; KJV, REB, TNT], 'indeed' [NJB, NRSV], 'and' [CEV, TEV], 'and even' [NLT], 'because' [LN], not explicit [AB; NAB].
e. αὐτός (LN 58.31): 'same' [AB, HNTC, ICC2, LN, Lns, NTC, WBC; KJV, NIV, NJB, NRSV, REB, TEV, TNT]. The phrase 'the same veil' is translated 'the veil' [NAB], 'a veil' [NLT], 'something' [CEV].
f. pres. act. indic. of μένω (LN 13.89, 68.11) (BAGD 1.a.α. p. 503): 'to remain' [AB, BAGD, HNTC, ICC2, LN (13.89, 68.11), Lns, NTC, WBC; KJV, NAB, NIV, NJB, TNT], 'to continue' [LN (13.89, 68.11)], 'to be still there' [NRSV], 'to be there' [REB], not explicit [CEV, NLT, TEV]. The clause 'the same veil remains, unlifted' is translated 'something still keeps them from seeing the truth' [CEV], 'a veil covers their minds' [NLT], 'their minds are covered with the same veil' [TEV]. See this word also at 3:11.
g. διαθήκη (LN 34.44) (BAGD 2. p. 183): 'covenant' [AB, BAGD, HNTC, ICC2, LN, Lns, NTC, WBC; NAB, NIV, NLT, NRSV, REB, TEV, TNT], 'law' [CEV], 'testament' [KJV, NJB]. See this word also at 3:6.

QUESTION—What relationship is indicated by ἀλλά 'but'?

1. It contrasts the bold or open speech of the apostles in 3:2 with the hardness of the people of Israel [My]. Paul speaks freely, but his Jewish contemporaries don't understand either Paul's plain speech or the significance of the fading glory [ICC1]. It emphasizes that they are blind to the glory of their covenant and have no hope; in contrast to Paul who has hope and speaks freely [NIC2].
2. It contrasts Moses, who is not to be blamed, with the people, whose minds were hardened [SP, TH, TNTC]. It clarifies Moses' action; it was not that he sought to deceive, but rather that their hearts were hard [AB]. It contrasts Moses and his ministry with the people who did not understand or respond properly to Moses; on the contrary, they grew obstinate [Ho, Lns]. It points to the reason that Moses covered his face, which is that the people were afraid due to the fact that their hearts were hardened [NTC].
3. It contrasts the hardening of their minds with seeing the end of what was fading away and understanding its significance. They did not see that the covenant was eventually to pass away [EBC]; on the contrary, their minds were blinded into thinking that its glory remained [EGT].
4. It contrasts the hardening of their minds with the idea of seeing the τέλος, the purpose or significance in 3:13 [Dumbrell, ICC2, WBC]. They did not see the goal of the fading old covenant because their hearts were too hard [Provence]. They did not see the purpose of the glory on Moses' face, which was to communicate the potential of a covenant relationship with God. Moses gave the commandments in the same way he received them, with an unveiled face, and the consequent glory of his face was clearly meant to be seen by Israel as an authentication of the commandments [Dumbrell].

5. It contrasts the hardening of their minds with Moses' motive for hiding the fading of the glory. Moses hoped that by hiding the fading of the glory he and the covenant he mediated would not lose prestige, and the people would be more likely to accept the truth he had revealed; but instead, their minds were hardened [HNTC].
6. It gives an additional point in an emphatic way [Van Unnik; NAB]. Not only did Moses veil his face, but the hearts of the people were veiled as well [Van Unnik]. It emphasizes that their minds were closed [NAB, REB, TEV]; 'of course' their minds were dulled [NAB]; 'in any case' their minds were closed [REB]; 'indeed' their minds were closed [TEV].

QUESTION—What is meant by νοήμα 'mind'?

It means thoughts, the exercise of reason [My], thinking process, thought patterns [NTC], thinking faculty [ICC1], perception and reasoning of the mind [AB], the thoughts and affections of the inner man [Ho].

QUESTION—Who is the agent of the hardening?

God is the agent of the hardening [ICC2, TH]. God and the people themselves are the agent of the hardening [NIC2]. The self-hardening of the people was followed by God's judicial hardening as a punishment [Lns]. The hardening comes as a consequence of refusing and suppressing divine truth [NIC1]. God, Satan, and the people themselves are all involved in the hardening [ICC1]. This represents a hardening of the will as opposed to an obscuring of the powers of perception; the reason for their not seeing the goal of the fading old covenant was their spiritual condition of a hardened mind, which Paul symbolizes as a veil on their heart [Provence].

QUESTION—What relationship is indicated by γάρ 'for'?

It explains how and why their minds were hardened [HNTC]. It explains why the veil remains and they don't understand the law; it is because their minds were hardened [He, Ho, Lns, NIC2]. The reason Paul can say that their minds were hardened is that the same veil remains today [ICC2].

QUESTION—What does Paul mean by 'the same veil remains'?

He means a veil of the same nature [Dumbrell, EBC], or with the same effect [ICC1, WBC]. He is saying that neither the people of Moses' day nor the Jews of Paul's day recognized the transitory nature of the law [ICC1]. He means that the same hardness of mind that characterized the Israelites also characterizes the Paul's Jewish contemporaries [TNTC]. The veil is a metonymy for the hardness of heart under the old covenant [Hafemann, NTC]. It means that they have the same condition of being unable or unwilling to understand [TG], the same barrier to the understanding of the Mosaic covenant [ICC2], the same obscurity with regard to understanding the truth in that they don't perceive what the rituals of the law signify [Ho]. Paul's use of the idea of the veil means that they don't realize that Moses' glory is gone; it is as though the veil that covered the ending of that glory of the law still hides the fact that the glory has faded [Lns]. It represents the inability to recognize the end of Moses' ministry [My]. Moses' veil was an outward indicator of Israel's inward rebellion and unbelief which kept them from seeing and understanding the glory of God, and which now prevents them from seeing the glory of Christ and the gospel [NIC1]. He is referring to the same chronic hardening of the mind from the time of Moses until now [NIC2].

QUESTION—What is meant by ἐπὶ τῇ ἀναγνώσει 'at the reading'?

It refers to the public reading in the synagogue [AB, EGT, ICC2, My, TG, TH, WBC; REB].

QUESTION—What is meant by τῆς παλαιᾶς διαθήκης 'the old covenant'?

It refers to 'the covenant of long ago', to distinguish it from something which lasts a long time [LN (67.24)]. It is old in the same sense as worn out or obsolete [ICC1].

1. It refers in general terms to the old covenant [AB, NIC2, NTC], and not to its writings.
2. It refers to the Hebrew scriptures [EBC, He, HNTC, TH], to the Old Testament [NJB]. It refers to the law of Moses [CEV], to the Torah or Pentateuch [EGT, Lns, My, WBC], and to the unfulfilled promise of what is to come that fills the Pentateuch [Lns]. The phrase 'old covenant' is a metonymy for the books of the old covenant [Ho; TEV, TNT], which contain the covenant [Ho].

not being-unveiled,[a] because[b] in[c] Christ it is removed/abolished.[d]

LEXICON—a. pres. pass. participle of ἀνακαλύπτω (LN **79.117**) (BAGD p. 55): 'to be unveiled' [BAGD, LN], 'to be lifted' [AB, ICC2, Lns, WBC; NAB, NJB, REB, TEV, TNT], 'to be uncovered' [BAGD, LN, NTC; NLT], 'to be removed' [HNTC; NIV], 'to be taken away' [KJV], not explicit [CEV, NRSV].

b. ὅτι (LN 89.33, 90.21): 'because' [AB, ICC2, LN (89.33), Lns, NTC; NIV, REB], 'for' [HNTC; NJB], 'since' [NRSV], 'that' [LN (90.21), WBC], not explicit [CEV, KJV, NAB, NLT, TEV, TNT].

c. ἐν (LN 90.6): 'in' [AB, HNTC, ICC2, Lns, NTC, WBC; KJV, NAB, NIV, NJB, NRSV, REB, TNT], 'by' [LN], not explicit [CEV]. The phrase 'in Christ' is translated 'by believing in Christ' [NLT], 'when a person is joined to Christ' [TEV].

d. pres. pass. indic. of καταργέω (LN 13.100, 76.26) (BAGD 2. p. 417): 'to be removed' [BAGD, NTC; NLT, TEV], 'to be taken away' [NAB, NIV, REB], 'to be caused to come to an end' [LN (13.100)], 'to disappear' [TNT], 'to be caused not to function' [LN (76.26)], 'to be abolished' [HNTC, ICC2, LN (76.26)], 'to be annulled' [AB], 'to be set aside' [NRSV], 'to be done away with' [Lns; NJB], 'to be done away' [WBC; KJV]. The phrase 'in Christ it is set aside' is translated 'only Christ can take (it) away' [CEV]. See this word also at 3:7, 11, 13.

QUESTION—What is the relationship between the verb μένει, 'remains' and the participle μὴ ἀνακαλυπτόμενον 'not being unveiled'?
1. The verb and the participle are in apposition as they both describe the veil and should be separated by a comma [AB, GNT, He, HNTC, ICC2, NIC2, WBC; NIV, NJB, REB]; it remains, it is not lifted.
2. The verb is a copula or linking verb, and a comma should not be used [EGT, Ho, ICC1, Lns, NIC1, NTC, SP, TG; KJV, NAB, TNT]; it remains unlifted.

QUESTION—What is meant by 'in Christ'?
It means being joined to Christ [TEV], being in union with and in connection with Christ by faith [Lns], being in living relationship with Christ [AB, NTC]. It refers to believing in Christ [NLT]. It means being in the Christian community as opposed to the synagogue where the old covenant is read [ICC2]. It refers to people becoming believers in Christ [TNTC], when they turn to the Lord as in 3:16 [NIC2]. This phrase is placed in an emphatic position in the clause; that is, in Christ and only in Christ [ICC1]. It refers to becoming members of Christ [ICC1]. It means only Christ himself can remove the veil [CEV].

QUESTION—What relationship is indicated by ὅτι 'because'?
1. It indicates reason [AB, He, HNTC, Ho, ICC1, ICC2, Lns, NIC2, NTC, SP, TNTC; NIV, NJB, NRSV, REB]: the veil remains because only in Christ is it removed (and they are not in Christ).
2. It is demonstrative 'that' [Dumbrell, My, WBC]: it is evident that it is done away with in Christ. This requires treating the negated participle μὴ ἀνακαλυπτόμενον '(it is) not unveiled (because)' as a nominative or accusative absolute 'it is not evident (that)'.
3. It is a relative pronoun ὅ τι '(the) which' [KJV]: which veil is done away in Christ.

QUESTION—What is the subject of καταργεῖται 'removed/abolished'?
1. The subject is the veil, which is removed [BAGD, HNTC, Ho, ICC1, ICC2, NIC1, NIC2, NTC, SP, TG, TH, TNTC; all versions]. It is the veil as well as the unbelief that it represents [NIC1]. There is a play on words here in that the veil which covered the glory of a covenant that was being abolished is itself abolished in Christ who reveals God's glory [NIC2].
2. The subject is the ministry of the old covenant and its glory, which is being abolished or annulled, just as in 3:7, 11, and 13 [AB, Dunn, Hanson, WBC].

3:15 But[a] until today whenever Moses is-read, a veil lies[b] on the heart[c] of-them.
LEXICON—a. ἀλλά (LN 89.125, 89.96, 91.2): 'but' [HNTC, LN (89.125), WBC; KJV], 'instead, on the contrary' [LN (89.125)], 'and' [LN (89.96)], 'what is more' [ICC2], 'and, yet' [LN (91.2)], 'even (now)' [NAB, TEV], 'even (to this day)' [NIV], 'even (today)' [TEV], 'yes, even (today)'

[NLT], 'yes' [NTC; TNT], 'indeed' [AB; NRSV, REB], 'as it is' [NJB], 'yea' [Lns], not explicit [CEV].
- b. pres. mid. or pass. (deponent = act.) indic. of κεῖμαι (LN 13.73) (BAGD 1.b. p. 426): 'to lie' [AB, BAGD, HNTC, ICC2, Lns, WBC; NRSV, REB], 'to cover' [NTC; NAB, NIV, NJB, NLT, TEV, TNT], 'to exist' [LN], 'to be upon' [KJV]. The phrase 'a veil lies on the heart of them' is translated 'they have their minds covered over with a covering' [CEV].
- c. καρδία (LN 26.3) (BAGD 1.b.β. p. 403): 'heart' [AB, HNTC, ICC2, LN, Lns, NTC; KJV, NIV, NJB, NLT], 'mind' [BAGD, LN, WBC; CEV, NRSV, REB, TEV, TNT], 'understanding' [NAB].

QUESTION—What relationship is indicated by ἀλλά 'but'?
1. It is continues and carries forward the thought of the previous verse [AB, Dumbrell, ICC2, Lns, NTC, TH; NAB, NIV, NJB, NLT, NRSV, REB, TEV, TNT]. It restates more intensely what was just said [ICC2, TH]. It continues the thought of a barrier that exists between Judaism and Christ [Dumbrell].
2. It is adversative or contrastive with reference to the clause immediately preceding [HNTC, Ho, My, Van Unnik]. It contrasts Moses and the people of Israel [Van Unnik]. It contrasts with the veil not being taken away; on the contrary, it is still there [Ho]. It contrasts with it not being disclosed that in Christ the old covenant is done away with; on the contrary, there is still a hindrance to their insight [My].
3. The contrast begun in 3:13 by οὐ καθάπερ Μωϋσῆς is really a series of three statements, the second and third of which are found in vv.14 and 15 and begin with ἀλλά. These statements are both contrastive and continuative in that they further the ongoing contrast of the covenants, their ministers, and the effects upon the people who receive the covenants [Aber NOT1].

QUESTION—What is meant by 'Moses'?
It refers to the law of Moses [EGT, TG, TH; CEV, REB, TEV], the Torah [HNTC, NCBC, WBC], the Pentateuch [AB, ICC2, Lns], the old covenant [NIC2], the writings of Moses [NLT], the books of Moses [TNT]. Paul is speaking of the portion of the law contained in Exodus 19–34 [Dumbrell].

QUESTION—What is meant by καρδία 'heart'?
It is the center of practical intelligence [ICC1, My] and the seat of affections [ICC1]. It corresponds to, and is parallel with, νοήματα 'minds' in 3:14 [AB, TH, WBC; CEV].

QUESTION—Upon whose heart does the veil lie?
The veil is upon the hearts of the Jews [AB, HNTC, My, NTC]. The lack of the definite article here indicates that the veil that lies on the heart represents a slight shift in the metaphor, just as he shifted the metaphor about the letter previously [Dumbrell, EGT, ICC1]. The first veil was external, hiding the fading of the glory of the law, but the veil in this verse is internal, obscuring the coming of the glory of the gospel, and is the veil referred to in 3:16 [ICC1].

2 CORINTHIANS 3:16

3:16 But[a] whenever someone/he[b] turns[c] to the Lord, the veil is removed.[d]

LEXICON—a. δέ (LN 89.124): 'but' [HNTC, ICC2, LN, NTC; NAB, NIV, NLT, NRSV, REB, TEV], 'on the other hand' [LN], 'nevertheless' [KJV], 'yet' [Lns, WBC; TNT], 'and' [NJB], not explicit [AB; CEV].

b. There is no lexical entry for this word, as the third person singular verb ἐπιστρέψῃ 'turns' does not require an explicit subject to be stated. The implied subject is translated 'anyone' [AB, NTC; NIV, NLT], 'one' [NRSV], 'it' [HNTC, Lns; KJV], 'he' [ICC2; NAB, REB, TEV, TNT], 'those who (turn)' [CEV]. This phrase 'whenever someone/he turns' is translated 'whenever there is a turning' [WBC], 'not until they turn' [NJB].

c. aorist act. subj. of ἐπιστρέφω (LN 31.60) (BAGD 1.b.β. p. 301): 'to turn to' [AB, BAGD, HNTC, ICC2, LN, Lns, NTC, WBC; all versions], 'to come to believe, to come to accept' [LN].

d. pres. pass. indic. of περιαιρέω (LN **15.204**) (BAGD 1. p. 645): 'to be removed' [AB, BAGD, ICC2, **LN**, Lns, NTC, WBC; CEV, NAB, NRSV, REB, TEV, TNT], 'to be taken away' [KJV, NIV, NJB, NLT], 'to take away' [HNTC], 'to take from around' [BAGD, LN]. The compound form of this verb implies a sudden or complete removal [AB, He, ICC1, Lns].

QUESTION—What relationship is indicated by δέ 'but'?

It contrasts being unveiled, which is the mark of the new covenant, with being veiled, the mark of the old covenant, and also begins a new section [NIC2]. Paul used ἀλλά twice in 3:14-15 to describe the failure of the old covenant, but he now switches to δέ to signal that he is shifting from the negative side of his comparison to the positive side. Now in vv. 16–18 he furthers his contrast of the two covenants with several statements concatenated with a string of four occurrences of δέ [Aber NOT1].

QUESTION—Is this intended to be seen as a quote from Scripture?

1. It is a quote [Dunn, ICC2, NTC, WBC; NAB, REB, TEV, TNT]. It is an adaptation of the Exodus text [TNTC]. The wording is adapted and modified to suit Paul's argument [NTC].
2. It is not intended as a quotation [NIC2]. The wording has been modified so extensively that it is not a citation [AB, Wong]. It is an allusion, not a quote [EBC].

QUESTION— What is the implied subject of ἐπιστρέψῃ 'he/someone turns'?

1. The indefinite pronoun τις 'someone, anyone' is the implied subject [AB, NIC2, NTC, Wong; NIV, NLT]. Paul uses the text about Moses to fit a more general context, but he is also referring to his own experience on the Damascus road [NIC2]. The verb is singular to show that conversion occurs on an individual basis [NTC].
2. The subject is Moses, who turned to God in the tent of meeting [Dunn, ICC2, Van Unnik; NAB, REB, TEV, TNT]. Moses is the subject (taken from the OT allusion), but Paul intends the application to apply for anyone, Moses being the example [Van Unnik]. Moses is the example of

anyone who turns to Christ [ICC2]. Paul deliberately leaves the subject ambiguous so that it might apply to Moses as well as the Jews [Dunn].
3. The subject is 'the heart' from 3:15 [HNTC, My; KJV]: whenever it shall turn to the Lord. Paul is referring to the conversion of Israel [My].
4. The subject is Paul's Jewish contemporaries [EBC, SP, TNTC; NJB], or the Jew who hears the Torah read [ICC1]. It is Israel itself [He].
5. The subject is general; whenever there is a turning to the Lord [Lns, WBC].

QUESTION—What does ἐπιστρέψῃ πρὸς κύριον 'turns to the Lord' mean here?

It refers to conversion [AB, Dumbrell, He, HNTC, Ho, Lns, NIC1, NIC2, NTC, SP, WBC]. It means to believe in Christ [My]. It means to recognize Christ as Yahweh [Ho]. Paul is recalling his own conversion [NIC1, NIC2].

QUESTION—Who is 'the Lord'?
1. It is Yahweh [AB, Dunn, EBC, EGT, ICC2, TH, TNTC]. While he is primarily referring to Yahweh, the Lord as Christ is not far from Paul's mind [Dumbrell].
2. It is Christ [Hanson, He, HNTC, Ho, ICC1, Lns, My, NIC1, NIC2, NTC, TG].
3. It is the Holy Spirit [Van Unnik, Wong].

3:17 Now[a] **the Lord is the Spirit; and where the Spirit of the Lord (is), (there is) freedom.**[b]

LEXICON—a. δέ: 'now' [AB, HNTC, ICC2, Lns, NTC; KJV, NIV, NJB, NLT, NRSV, REB, TEV], not explicit [WBC; CEV, NAB, TNT].
b. ἐλευθερία (LN **37.133**) (BAGD p. 250): 'freedom' [AB, BAGD, HNTC, ICC2, LN, NTC, WBC; KJV, NAB, NIV, NJB, NLT, NRSV, TEV, TNT], 'liberty' [BAGD, Lns; REB]. The phrase 'where the Spirit of the Lord is, there is freedom' is translated 'the Lord's Spirit sets us free' [CEV].

QUESTION—What relationship is indicated by δέ 'but'?

It is an unemphatic connective [AB]. It introduces an exegetical explanation of the previous verse [Ho, ICC2, My, SP]. It introduces the reason that turning to the Lord removes the veil, which is that the Lord is the Spirit [Ho].

QUESTION—What does ὁ δὲ κύριος τὸ πνεῦμά ἐστιν 'but the Lord is the Spirit' mean?

Paul is indicating dynamic function, work, or action, not an identity of person [AB, EBC, Hanson, He, HNTC, Ho, Lns, My, NCBC, NIC2, TNTC, WBC]. The Lord (Christ) communicates himself in the Holy Spirit, who is the living principle of the influence and indwelling of Christ [My]. The Lord is the Spirit in our experience; just as Moses turned to Yahweh, so the Jew should turn to the Spirit [Dunn, Hanson]. The Yahweh of the OT signifies the Spirit of the NT in terms of the new relationship through Christ; that is, the immediacy of God's presence such as Moses experienced happens to the believer by means of the Spirit [Dumbrell]. The Holy Spirit is the one to whom one turns at conversion, and who removes the veil of hardheartedness [Wong]. Paul experienced God and Christ as well as the freedom of the new covenant through the Spirit [Dunn]. Christ and the Spirit work in the same way and produce the same effect [ICC1]. Paul is contrasting the administration of Moses and the law with that of Christ and the spirit; Moses is (by metonymy) 'the law', and the Lord is the Spirit in that those who rely on Moses get only the law, and those who turn to the Lord (Christ) receive the Spirit [Aber NOT1].

QUESTION—In what sense does he use the word ἐστιν 'is'?

1. It is epexegetical, further explaining what 'the Lord' of the previous verse means [AB, Dumbrell, Dunn, EBC, EGT, HNTC, ICC2, NAC, NCBC, WBC, Wong; NJB, REB, TEV, TNT]. The Lord of the previous verse means for us the Spirit [WBC]. The lord of the previous verse is the Holy Spirit, who is the one to whom a believer turns and by whom the veil is removed and freedom given [Van Unnik, Wong]. The identity of Christ and the Holy Spirit is one of our experience and not of their own essence; that is, Christ is known to us as spirit [Hanson]. The Lord is to us the Spirit under the new covenant [TNTC]. The Lord to whom they turned at conversion is the God of the new covenant which is of the Spirit, not of the letter [AB]. The Lord to whom the Jew must turn is the life-giving spirit of the living God [EBC]. It identifies to whom the Jew must turn, which is the Spirit [Dunn, EBC, ICC2], who is the transforming power and essential characteristic of the new covenant [ICC2]. The Spirit is the agent by which the veil of hardheartedness is removed when one turns to God [Provence].

2. It is associational and refers to the entire economy of the Spirit, to that which spiritual in nature as opposed to the law, and which includes also the personal ministry of the Holy Spirit [NIC1, NIC2]. He is referring to the contrast between the letter and the Spirit in 3:6; Christ is the way into that spiritual freedom that brings life [NIC1]. Turning to the Lord means turning to the lord of the new covenant of the Spirit, and who is himself a 'life giving spirit' (from 1 Cor. 15:45) [NIC2].

3. Paul is commenting on the relationship between Christ and the Spirit [Lns, NTC]. He emphasizes that in Christ it is the Spirit who takes away the veil from the reading of the old covenant [NTC]. He is saying that they are of one essence but are two persons and do the same work; the Spirit is where the Lord is, and where the Lord is the Spirit is [Lns].

4. Paul is saying that Christ and the Spirit are one and the same [CEV].

5. It is used in a comparative sense, comparing and contrasting Moses and Christ; Christ 'is' the Spirit in the same sense that Moses 'is' the law, each representing a separate covenant and its means of implementation [Aber NOT1].

QUESTION—Who is 'the Lord'?
   Paul is clarifying a statement he has just made. This is indicated by the addition of a demonstrative pronoun: 'this Lord' [NJB], 'the Lord is that spirit' [KJV]; by the addition of an explanatory phrase: 'the Lord of whom this passage speaks' [REB]; or by the fact that the words 'the Lord' are shown in quotes [AB, HNTC, ICC2, WBC; TEV, TNT].
   1. It is Yahweh, referring to the Exodus 34 passage that Paul has been commenting on [AB, Dumbrell, Dunn, EBC, EGT, ICC2, NAC, Provence, TG, TNTC].
   2. It is Christ [Aber NOT1, Hanson, He, HNTC, Ho, ICC1, Lns, My, NIC1, NIC2, NTC, SP, TG].
   3. It is the Holy Spirit [Van Unnik, Wong].
QUESTION—What is the freedom that he is referring to?
   It is a freedom from sin, death, and the law [Ho, ICC2, NTC, TG, Van Unnik]. It is a freedom from bondage to sin and the law [ICC1], or to sin, death, and the law as a means to righteousness [WBC]. It is freedom from the sinful nature, to live a new life [NTC]. It is freedom from the letter of the law, which is the antithesis of the Spirit, and from the veil of blindness which kept them bound to it [NIC2]. It is freedom from the letter of the law that brings condemnation and death [Lns]. It is freedom from the veil [Hafemann, My, NAC, NIC2, Wong]. It is freedom from the condemnation and bondage of the old covenant and freedom to be children of God, to walk by the Spirit and to be bold, as Paul was [TNTC]. It is freedom from Satan, from corruption and decay, from ignorance and error, and freedom to be the sons of God [Ho]. It is freedom from bondage to the law and from the kind of servile fear shown by the people of Israel in the Exodus passage [EGT]. It is freedom of access to God [EGT], a freedom from the veil [Wong]. It is the freedom to speak and act without fear [AB]. It is knowing and proclaiming Christ openly and freely [Hanson]. It is a freedom from the judgment of other men, and freedom to an open relationship with God [Van Unnik]. It is a freedom to be a son of God and call him father [ICC2]. It is the dynamic liberty of the Spirit as opposed to the bondage of the letter [NIC1]. It is a freedom from the negative aspects of the old covenant and freedom to justification, life, boldness and transformation [SP].
QUESTION—What is Paul intending to communicate in this verse?
   He is concerned with the contrast between two covenants, not with trinitarian ontology [Aber NOT1, NIC1]. When people turn to God under the new covenant they see that the new covenant of the Spirit has begun and they experience the Lord as spirit [TNTC]. By turning to Christ we partake of the Holy Spirit because Christ and the Spirit are one [Ho]. As Moses turned to Yahweh, so under the new covenant people turn to the Spirit [EGT, ICC2]. It is the Spirit of the Lord that grants us access to God [WBC]. Just as Moses saw Christ openly in the tabernacle, so also today we know Christ as spirit and experience transformation and freedom [Hanson]. Whereas the letter of the law binds and condemns, we may turn to Christ and be freed through the

Spirit [Lns]. The work of the Spirit is to replace the authority (as κύριος 'lord') of the letter of the law [HNTC]. The Spirit enables believers to understand God's revelation, and through that word changes them and leads them to freedom in Christ [NTC]. 3:17 constitutes a syllogism that explains 3:16–18 [ICC1, My]. The points of the syllogism are: Where the Spirit of the Lord is, there is liberty; the person converted to the Lord has this Spirit because the Lord is the Spirit; therefore, those who are converted have no veil, only freedom [My]. Or: Where the Spirit of the Lord is there is freedom; the Lord is the Spirit; therefore where the Lord is, the bondage of the letter has been removed [ICC1]. Paul's statement is a comparison, referring in summary form to the whole economy of the Spirit, describing that which is spiritual in nature as opposed to the law, as well as the personal ministration of the Holy Spirit. In this comparison Moses, whose name is used as a metonymy in v. 15 (and elsewhere) to signify the law, and who represents the covenant of law, corresponds to 'the Lord', who not only represents the covenant of spirit but is also the giver of the Spirit. Said more concisely, Moses is the law and the Lord is the Spirit; those who stubbornly stick with Moses get only the law, but those who turn to the Lord get the Spirit [Aber NOT1].

3:18 And[a] we all with face having-been-unveiled[b] reflecting/beholding-as-in-a-mirror[c] the glory of the Lord

LEXICON—a. δέ (LN 89.94): 'but' [HNTC, ICC2, Lns; KJV], 'and' [AB, LN, NTC, WBC; NIV, NJB, NLT, NRSV, REB, TNT], 'so' [CEV], 'then' [TEV], not explicit [NAB].
- b. perf. pass. participle of ἀνακαλύπτω (LN **79.117**) (BAGD p. 55): 'to be unveiled' [AB, BAGD, HNTC, ICC2, LN, Lns; NAB, NIV, NJB, NRSV, TNT], 'to have the veil removed' [NLT], 'to be uncovered' [BAGD, LN, NTC, WBC; TEV], 'to be not covered' [CEV]. The phrase 'with face having been unveiled' is translated 'open face' [KJV], 'there is no veil over the face' [REB].
- c. pres. mid. participle of κατοπτρίζω (LN **14.52, 24.44**) (BAGD p. 424): 'to reflect' [BAGD, LN (14.52); NIV, NJB, TEV], 'to show the bright glory' [CEV], 'to reflect as in a mirror' [Lns], 'to reflect as mirrors' [TNT], 'to behold and reflect' [NTC], 'to behold as in a mirror' [AB, WBC], 'to behold as in a glass' [HNTC, ICC2; KJV], 'to see as in a mirror' [LN (24.44); REB], 'to view as in a mirror' [BAGD], 'to gaze on (the glory)' [NAB], 'to contemplate' [BAGD]. The entire phrase 'reflecting/beholding as in a mirror the glory of the Lord' is translated 'and all of us have had that veil removed so that we can be mirrors that brightly reflect the glory of the Lord' [NLT] 'all of us, then, reflect the glory of the Lord with uncovered faces' [LN (14.52)], 'and all of us, with unveiled faces, seeing the glory of the Lord as though reflected in a mirror' [NRSV], 'and we all with uncovered faces behold the glory of the Lord as in a mirror' or '…by reflection' [LN (24.44)].

2 CORINTHIANS 3:18

QUESTION—What relationship is indicated by δέ 'and'?

It is continuative [AB, Ho, NTC]. It carries forward the idea of freedom in 3:17 to describe its meaning [AB] or to express its natural consequence [Ho]. It is transitional [ICC1, My, TH]. It moves from the concept of freedom in 3:17 to the people who are free [ICC1, My].

QUESTION—Who is the 'we' in this verse?

It refers to all Christians [AB, Dumbrell, EBC, EGT, HNTC, Ho, ICC1, ICC2, Lambrecht, My, NCBC, NIC1, NIC2, NTC, TG, TH, TNTC]. It is inclusive, referring to Paul and the Corinthians [Lns].

QUESTION—What does he mean by 'unveiled face'?

Paul is drawing upon his Semitic background in which the concept of unveiling the face represents freedom, boldness, and confidence, as opposed to veiling the face to express mourning or shame [NCBC, NTC, Van Unnik]. It refers to unrestricted access to God in Christ [Dumbrell]. The face represents spiritual intuition and knowledge, which is now free and unconfined [My]. It means that God has given sight to believers, having removed their blindness [NIC1, NIC2]. It refers to openness of fellowship with the Lord, in whose presence believers live [NTC].

1. It is an implied contrast.

    1.1 It is a contrast with Moses [Dunn, EGT, ICC1, ICC2, Lambrecht, Lns]. It contrasts believers with Moses, who veiled his face [EGT, ICC1, Lambrecht, Lns]. Believers have nothing to fear or conceal [ICC1], they are without veil or disguise and are confident [EGT], they don't hide the glory of God that they reflect [Lns]. It contrasts believers, whose perception of Christ is continuous, with Moses, who veiled and unveiled his face [ICC2]. It contrasts believers, whose glory increases, with Moses, whose glory faded [Dunn].

    1.2 It is a contrast with the people of Israel [AB, EBC, Ho, Lambrecht, Provence, TH, Wong]. It contrasts believers with the people of Israel, who lack sight [Ho, Lambrecht], who are veiled [Wong], and who could not gaze on the glory of God [TH, Wong]. It contrasts the hearts of believers with the veiled hearts of the Jews [EBC]. It contrasts the believer's transformation by the Spirit with the hard-hardness of the Jewish people which is symbolized by the veil [Provence]. It contrasts with the veiling of the understanding of the Jewish people that attends the reading of the old covenant as well as with the fact that they would not look at the glory [AB].

2. It is an implied comparison of believers with Moses who related to God openly, with face unveiled [He, NTC]. It compares Moses, who reflected glory, with believers, who reflect even more glory [He]. It compares Moses, who saw the pre-incarnate Christ in the tabernacle, with Christians who are able to see Christ [Hanson].

QUESTION—What does the participle κατοπτριζόμενοι 'reflecting/beholding' mean in this context?
1. It means to reflect as in a mirror [Aber NOT1, EGT, He, ICC1, Lns, NAC, Van Unnik; CEV, NIV, NJB, NLT, TEV, TNT]. Because the passage is portraying a relationship with God that is face to face and open, and goes on in 4:6 to describe the spiritual radiance shining out of a believer's life, we may judge that Paul uses the metaphor of reflecting to say that the believer is like Moses, who reflected the glory that he saw [Aber NOT1].
2. It means to behold as in a mirror [AB, HNTC, Ho, ICC2, Lambrecht, My, NIC1, NIC2, TH, TNTC, Wong; KJV, NRSV, REB]. The gospel is the mirror in which we behold Christ [Lambrecht, My, NIC1], who is also himself a mirror as well as the reflected image of God [Lambrecht, NIC2]. It means to observe, even if indirectly or in a reflection [Provence]. It also implies transformation through vision [Ho, ICC2, NIC2].
3. It means to behold and to reflect what is beheld [Dunn, EBC, NCBC, NTC]. Like Moses, they reflect what they have beheld [NTC].
4. It means to behold [Dumbrell, Hanson; NAB].
5. It is contemplating what one beholds; as they see, they contemplate and are transformed [Hanson].

QUESTION—What does he mean by 'the glory of the Lord'?
1. The glory of the Lord is the glory of the exalted Christ [ICC1, Lns, My], or the divine excellence of Christ [Ho]. Jesus Christ is the glory of God [EBC, EGT, ICC2], the glory and image of God [Wong], the glorified image of God [NIC2].
2. The glory of the Lord refers to the glory of Yahweh, and is found in the gospel [Dumbrell].

are-being-transformed[a] to the same[b] image[c] from[d] glory to glory just-as[e] from[f] the Lord, the Spirit.

LEXICON—a. pres. pass. indic. of μεταμορφόω (LN 13.53) (BAGD 2. p. 511): 'to be transformed' [AB, HNTC, ICC2, LN, Lns, NTC, WBC; NAB, NIV, NJB, NRSV, REB, TEV, TNT], 'to be changed' [BAGD, LN; KJV], 'to be made like' [CEV], 'to become like' [NLT].
b. αὐτός (LN 58.31): 'same' [AB, HNTC, ICC2, LN, Lns, NTC, WBC; KJV, NRSV, TNT], not explicit [CEV]. The phrase 'the same image' is translated 'his very image' [NAB], 'his likeness' [NIV, REB, TEV], 'the image that we reflect' [NJB], 'like him' [NLT], 'like our Lord' [CEV].
c. εἰκών (LN 58.35) (BAGD 2. p. 222): 'image' [AB, HNTC, ICC2, Lns, WBC; KJV, NAB, NJB], 'likeness' [LN, NTC; NIV, REB, TEV, TNT], 'same form' [LN], 'form' [BAGD], not explicit [CEV, NLT, NRSV].
d. ἀπό (LN 13.62) (BAGD II.3.b. p. 87): 'from' [AB, BAGD, HNTC, ICC2, LN, Lns, NTC, WBC; KJV, NAB, NRSV]. The expression 'from glory to glory' is translated 'with ever increasing glory' [NIV, REB], 'in an ever greater degree of glory' [TEV], 'more and more like our glorious Lord'

[CEV], 'in brighter and brighter glory' [NJB], 'more and more like him' [NLT].
  e. καθάπερ (LN 64.15) (BAGD p. 387): 'just as' [BAGD, LN, NTC], 'as' [AB, HNTC, Lns; CEV, NLT], 'even as' [KJV], 'as happens in' [ICC2], not explicit [WBC; NAB, NIV, NJB, NRSV, REB, TEV, TNT].
  f. ἀπό (LN 90.7, 90.15) (BAGD V.4. p. 88): 'from' [BAGD, LN (90.7, 90.15)], 'by' [LN (90.7, 90.15)]. The phrase 'just as from (the Lord)' is translated 'this is the work of (the Lord)' [WBC], 'by (the Lord)' [NAB], 'which comes from (the Lord)' [NIV], 'this is the working/work of (the Lord)' [NJB, TNT], 'as (the Spirit of the Lord) works within us' [NLT], 'for this comes from (the Lord)' [NRSV], 'through the power of (the Lord)' [REB]. This word indicates source, cause or agency [AB, BAGD, EBC, HNTC, Ho, ICC2, NIC1, NIC2, NTC, TG, TH, TNTC, Van Unnik, Wong].

QUESTION—What is meant by τὴν αὐτὴν εἰκόνα 'the same image'?
  1. It is the image of the Lord [NAB, NIV, NLT, REB, TEV], the image of Christ [AB, EGT, He, Ho, Lambrecht, Lns, My, NIC2, NTC, Wong; CEV]. It is the likeness of God expressed in Christ [TNTC]. They are being transformed to the same image they behold in the mirror [Lambrecht, Wong], the same image of God which is Christ's [Lambrecht]. The image is Christ's, and believers become like him as that image presents itself on them [My]. Believers are transformed through Christ who is the image of God [Dumbrell]. It refers to an exact image of an original, and not just similarity of one thing to another [Lns]. He is thinking of the image of both Christ and God at the same time, because Christ is the image of God [AB]. He is speaking of the likeness of the glorified Christ in a moral and spiritual sense [NIC2]. The image is the same one that we reflect [NJB].
  2. It means that the goal of transformation is the same for all believers [Dumbrell, Van Unnik]. They are being transformed into one and the same image through Christ as the image into which they grow [Dumbrell]. The same image is the image or likeness which all believers have in common [Van Unnik].

QUESTION—What is meant by the phrase ἀπὸ δόξης εἰς δόξαν 'from glory to glory'?
  1. It refers to transformation progressing in degrees from one stage of glory to another [AB, Dunn, EBC, EGT, HNTC, Ho, ICC1, ICC2, Lambrecht, Lns, NIC1, NTC, TG, TH, TNTC, Wong; CEV, NIV, NJB, NLT, NRSV, REB, TEV, TNT]. The first glory is the glory seen in the heart through the gospel when a person turns to the Lord, and the ultimate glory is the glory of the Lord that will be revealed at the last day [NIC2].
  2. It means that the source or cause of transformation is glory and the destination is glory [He, My]. The glory of our transformation occurs as a result of beholding the glory of Christ [My]. The glory of the Lord is what

causes the progressive transformation from one degree of glory to another [TEV].

QUESTION—What relationship is indicated by καθάπερ 'just as'?

1. It is comparative and indicates that which is in accord with, appropriate to, or what one would normally expect in a given situation or condition [AB, EGT, Ho, ICC1, ICC2, Lns, NIC2].
2. It is causative and indicates that the Spirit is the agent that produces the change [He, SP, Wong].
3. It introduces a 'just as…so also' comparison. Just as Moses reflected God's glory and was transfigured, so also we are transformed progressively into his image [NTC].

QUESTION—What is meant by the double genitive κυρίου πνεύματος 'the Lord, the Spirit'?

1. The two words are in apposition [AB, Dunn, EBC, EGT, Hanson, HNTC, Ho, Lns, NCBC, Van Unnik, WBC, Wong; NAB, NIV, NJB, NRSV, REB, TEV, TNT]; that is, from the Lord, who is the Spirit.
    1.1 It associates the Lord and the Spirit in terms of work or function, but not in exact identity [AB, EBC, Ho, Lns, NCBC]. It is a reference to 3:17 in which he expresses the dynamic oneness between the risen Lord and the Spirit by whom the life of the Lord is imparted and maintained [NCBC]. He is saying that Christ and the Spirit are so united in power and work, as well as in the divine essence in the trinity, that one is in the other [Lns]. It refers to 3:17 which explicates 3:16, which describes the Lord that Moses saw in the tabernacle as spirit, not in identity but in function [EBC]. It means that the Lord (Christ) and the Spirit are one in power and glory and the same in substance, and that Christ is where the Spirit is and does what the Spirit does [Ho]. There is an association of 'Lord' and 'spirit' but not an absolute identification of the two [AB].
    1.2 It is a clarification that by 'the Lord' he means the Holy Spirit [Van Unnik, Wong].
2. It is a reference to the believer's experience of the Lord [Dunn, Hanson, TNTC, WBC]. The Lord is present by the Spirit and experienced as the Spirit [TNTC]. We know Christ as spirit [Hanson]. In our experience, the Lord (Yahweh), who is referred to earlier in 3:16 from the Exodus 34 passage, is spirit [Dunn], or is experienced by us as the Holy Spirit [WBC].
3. It is an ellipsis [NIC2, NTC]. It means 'the Lord who gives the Spirit and whose covenant is characterized by spirit' [NIC2]. It is from 'the Lord, by and through the Spirit' that our transformation is effected [NTC]. The word 'spirit' receives emphasis from its position at the end of the verse and summarizes all the references to the Spirit in the chapter [NTC].
4. It means the Spirit of the Lord [ICC2, SP, TH; CEV, KJV, NLT].
5. It means the Lord who is spirit [ICC1, NIC1], where 'spirit' means spiritual agency as transforming power [NIC1].

6. It means the Lord of the Spirit [My]; that is, Christ sends the Spirit and is revealed by him.

DISCOURSE UNIT: 4:1–18 [NIV, NLT]. The topic is treasures in jars of clay [NIV], treasure in perishable containers [NLT].

DISCOURSE UNIT: 4:1–15 [CEV, NAB, TEV]. The topic is treasure in clay jars [CEV], treasure in earthen vessels [NAB], spiritual treasure in clay pots [TEV].

DISCOURSE UNIT: 4:1–6 [HNTC, ICC2, TNTC, WBC]. The topic is the treasure that the ministry dispenses [HNTC], the conduct of Paul's ministry [TNTC], a further defense of personal ministry; the content of the gospel [WBC], apostolate, kerygma, ministry [WBC].

4:1 **Because-of**[a] **this, having**[b] **this ministry just-as**[c] **we-received-mercy,**[d] **we-do- not -lose-heart**[e]

LEXICON—a. διά with acc. (LN 89.26): 'because of, on account of, by reason of' [LN]. The phrase διὰ τοῦτο 'because of this' is translated 'on account of this' [NTC], 'therefore' [AB, WBC; KJV, NIV, NJB, NRSV], 'for this reason' [HNTC, Lns], 'on this account' [ICC2], 'since' [REB], 'and so' [NLT, TEV], 'so' [TNT], 'that's why' [CEV], not explicit [NAB].

b. pres. act. participle of ἔχω (LN 90.65): 'to have' [AB, HNTC, ICC2, LN, Lns, NTC, WBC; KJV, NIV], 'to possess' [NAB], not explicit [CEV, NJB]. The phrase 'having this ministry' is translated 'God has given us this ministry' [NLT, REB, TEV], 'God has given us this commission' [TNT], 'we are engaged in this ministry' [NRSV], 'God has been kind enough to trust us with this work' [CEV]. This participle is translated as having causal force: 'since' [HNTC, ICC2, WBC; NIV, NLT, NRSV, REB], 'as' [TNT], 'seeing' [KJV], 'because' [NAB].

c. καθώς (LN 64.14): 'just as' [LN, NTC], 'as' [AB, ICC2, WBC; KJV], 'even as' [Lns], not explicit [CEV, NAB, NIV, NJB, NLT, NRSV, REB, TEV, TNT].

d. aorist pass. indic. of ἐλεέω (LN 88.76) (BAGD p. 249): 'to receive mercy' [ICC2, Lns, NTC; KJV], 'to be shown mercy' [BAGD, LN, WBC]. The phrase 'just as we received mercy' is translated 'as recipients of mercy' [AB], 'in the mercy of God' [HNTC], 'God in his mercy' [NLT, REB, TEV, TNT], 'through God's mercy' [NAB, NIV], 'by God's mercy' [NJB, NRSV], 'God has been kind' [CEV].

e. pres. act. indic. ἐγκακέω (LN 25.288) (BAGD 2. p. 215): 'to lose heart' [BAGD, LN; NIV, NRSV, REB], 'to become discouraged' [LN, WBC; TEV, TNT], 'to give in to discouragement' [NAB], 'to give up' [LN; CEV, NLT], 'to despair' [BAGD, NTC], 'to faint' [Lns; KJV], 'to waver' [NJB], 'to shrink back' [AB], 'to neglect one's duty' [HNTC], 'to grow lax' [ICC2]. This word stands in contrast to the boldness and confidence discussed in the previous chapter and initiates a series of four negations begun in the next verse [NIC2].

2 CORINTHIANS 4:1

QUESTION—What relationship is indicated by διὰ τοῦτο 'because of this'?
1. It refers to the great privilege of the ministry described in chapter 3 as the reason for not losing heart [AB, HNTC, Ho, ICC1, ICC2, Lns, My, NCBC, NIC2, TH, TNTC; CEV, KJV, NAB, NIV, NLT, NRSV, REB, TEV, TNT].
2. It refers to the next clause concerning divine mercy as the reason for not losing heart [WBC], or as the basis for Paul's ministry [TG].
3. It refers to his discussion of the ministry as well as to his having received mercy as the bases for his encouragement [Lns, NTC].

QUESTION—What relationship is indicated by the present participle ἔχοντες 'having'?

It indicates the reason for not losing heart [AB, EBC, HNTC, Ho, ICC1, ICC2, Lns, My, NCBC, NIC1, NIC2, NTC, TH, WBC; CEV, KJV, NAB, NIV, NJB, NLT, NRSV, REB, TEV, TNT]: because we have received this ministry through God's mercy, we therefore do not lose heart.

QUESTION—What does Paul refer to when he says 'just as we received mercy'?

It refers to the mercy God showed to Paul in granting him his ministry [AB, EBC, He, HNTC, Ho, ICC1, ICC2, My, NIC1, TG, TH, TNTC, WBC]. It refers to Paul's conversion as well as to the ministry that he has [Lns, NIC2]. It refers to God's merciful sustaining of Paul in his ministry [NTC].

QUESTION—Of whom does Paul speak when he says 'we'?

He is referring primarily to himself [EBC, HNTC, Ho, ICC1, ICC2, NIC1, NIC2, TNTC, WBC]. He is referring primarily to himself but also to his co-workers [AB, Lns, NCBC, NTC, TG].

4:2 but^a we-have-renounced^b the hidden-things of-shame^c

LEXICON—a. ἀλλά (LN 89.125): 'but' [HNTC, LN, Lns; KJV], 'instead' [LN], 'on the contrary' [ICC2, LN], 'rather' [AB; NAB, NIV], 'however' [NTC], not explicit [WBC; CEV, NJB, NLT, NRSV, REB, TEV, TNT].
  b. aorist indic. mid. of ἀπεῖπον (ἀπολέγομαι) (LN **13.156, 33.220**) (BAGD p. 83): 'to renounce' [AB, BAGD, HNTC, ICC2, **LN** (13.156), Lns, NTC; KJV, NIV, NJB, NRSV, REB, TNT], 'to repudiate' [WBC; NAB], 'to denounce' [LN (33.220)], 'to put aside' [LN (13.156); TEV], 'to reject' [**LN** (13.156); NLT], 'to refuse to become involved in' [LN (13.156)], 'to not do' [CEV]. The middle voice construction means 'for our part' [AB], 'for ourselves' [HNTC], 'as far as we are concerned' [HNTC].
  c. αἰσχύνη (LN 25.189, 25.191) (BAGD 1. p. 25): 'shame' [BAGD, HNTC, LN (25.189), Lns, NTC; REB, TNT], 'disgrace' [LN (25.189)], 'disgraceful conduct' [ICC2], 'that which causes shame' [LN (25.191)], 'dishonesty' [KJV]. (The KJV rendering of 'dishonesty' reflects a sense that is no longer associated with this word, in which 'honesty' could mean that which is 'honorable' and 'dishonesty' could mean 'disgrace' [ICC1].) This noun in the genitive is also translated as an adjective: 'shameful' [AB, WBC; CEV, NAB, NIV, NJB, NLT, NRSV, TEV]. The phrase

τὰ κρύπτα τῆς αἰσχύνης 'the hidden things of shame' is translated 'the shameful things one hides' [AB; NRSV], 'the behavior that shame hides' [HNTC], 'the secretive practices of disgraceful conduct' [ICC2], 'the secret things of shame' [NTC], 'shameful practices devised in secret' [WBC], 'what one conceals from a feeling of shame' [BAGD], 'the deeds that people hide for very shame' [REB], 'shameful things that must be kept secret' [CEV], 'shameful, underhanded practices' [NAB], 'shameful and underhanded methods' [NLT], 'secret and shameful ways' [NIV], 'secret and shameful deeds' [TEV], 'shameful secrecy' [NJB], 'deeds of darkness and of shame' [TNT].

QUESTION—What relationship is indicated by ἀλλά 'but'?
 1. It is contrastive with what he has just said about losing heart [NIC2, TH], about shrinking back [AB], or about being remiss in ministry [Ho]. (This ἀλλά 'but' is followed by μή 'not', μηδέ 'nor', and ἀλλά 'but' which further the contrast with the previous verse [NIC2].)
 2. It is not contrastive, but introduces an explanation of his ministry [NTC].

QUESTION—How are the nouns related in the genitive construction 'the hidden things of shame'?
 1. It refers to things that are considered shameful or disgraceful in an objective sense [AB, ICC2, Lns, NIC2, TG; CEV, NAB, NIV, NJB, NLT, NRSV, TEV]. The genitive phrase is descriptively stronger than the adjective [Lns].
 2. It refers to things that are hidden in order to avoid a subjective feeling of shame [HNTC, My; REB]. What follows this phrase are the specifics which a sense of shame would hide, namely trickery and adulterating the message of God [My].

QUESTION—Does the fact that he renounced shameful ways mean that he was once guilty of such ways?
 Paul is not indicating a fault which he practiced but has since turned from [AB, EGT, HNTC, ICC1, ICC2, NIC1, NTC, TG, TH]. He simply states what they do not do [NTC], that they decided never to have anything to do with such ways [TG, TH].

QUESTION—Is the aorist ἀπειπάμεθα 'we have renounced' a timeless/ingressive aorist or a true aorist representing a single action occurring at a specific point in time?
 1. It is a true aorist representing an action occurring at a definite point in time, probably at his conversion [ICC2, NIC1, NIC2].
 2 It is an ingressive or timeless aorist, indicating the inception of an action or state that continues to the present [AB, ICC1, SP].

not going-about[a] in trickery[b] nor falsifying[c] the word of God
LEXICON—a. pres. act. participle of περιπατέω (LN 41.11) (BAGD 2.a.δ. p. 649): 'to go about' [BAGD], 'to go about doing' [LN], 'to walk' [Lns; KJV], 'to live' [LN; TNT], 'to behave' [ICC2, LN], 'to conduct oneself' [AB], 'to act' [TEV]. The phrase 'going about in' is translated 'to

practice' [HNTC; NRSV, REB], 'to resort to' [NTC; NAB], 'to employ' [WBC], 'to try to' [CEV, NLT], 'to use' [NIV].
- b. πανουργία (LN 88.270) (BAGD p. 608): 'trickery' [BAGD, NTC; NAB], 'craftiness' [BAGD, LN, Lns; KJV], 'deception' [NIV], 'deceit' [TEV], 'guile' [TNT], 'treachery' [LN], 'cunning' [BAGD; NRSV, REB], 'cunning methods' [WBC], 'underhanded methods' [NLT], 'knavery' [HNTC], 'disgraceful conduct' [ICC2]. The phrase ἐν πανουργίᾳ 'in trickery' is translated as an adverb: 'craftily' [AB]. The phrase μὴ περιπατοῦντες ἐν πανουιργίᾳ 'not going about in trickery' is translated 'we don't try to fool anyone' [CEV], 'we do not try to trick anyone' [NLT], 'it is not our way to be devious' [NJB]. This word connotes the willingness to do anything to achieve one's ends [He, Ho, ICC1, ICC2, Lns, NIC2, WBC].
- c. pres. act. participle of δολόω (LN **72.9**) (BAGD p. 203): 'to falsify' [BAGD, ICC2, NTC; NAB, NJB, NRSV, TEV], 'to distort' [LN; NIV, NLT, REB, TNT], 'to adulterate' [AB, BAGD, HNTC, Lns], 'to tamper with' [WBC], 'to twist' [CEV], 'to handle deceitfully' [KJV].

QUESTION—What is meant by 'the word of God'?

It refers to the message of the gospel [AB, EGT, He, HNTC, Ho, ICC1, ICC2, My, NCBC, NIC1, NIC2, NTC, TG, TH, WBC]. It is the OT scriptures as well as the gospel, as the OT scriptures are fulfilled in Christ [NTC]. It may also refer to how Paul handled the OT scriptures [WBC]. The phrase 'the word of God' is parallel with 'our gospel' in the next verse and the proclamation of Jesus Christ as Lord in 4:5 [NIC2].

QUESTION—What does he mean by μηδὲ δολοῦντες 'nor falsifying'?

He does not falsify or water down the message [NCBC]. He does not alter it or mix in foreign elements [My, TNTC]. He does not mix in untrue elements to make it more pleasing and acceptable to men [ICC2, Lns]. The fact that he does not require observance of the Mosaic law is not a watering down of the gospel [HNTC, NIC2] or of the scriptural revelation [NTC]. He does not rob the gospel of its content and glory by implying that the old covenant is still in force [NIC1]. He does not misrepresent the relation of the old covenant to the new through false arguments [ICC1]. He does not falsify or adulterate the truth for personal gain [AB]. He does not adulterate it with the traditions of men [Ho].

but^a by^b the manifestation^c of the truth commending^d ourselves to every conscience^e of-men before^f God.

LEXICON—a. ἀλλά (LN 89.125): 'but' [HNTC, ICC2, LN, Lns, NTC, WBC; KJV, NRSV, TNT], 'instead' [AB, LN; NJB], 'on the contrary' [LN; NIV], not explicit [CEV, NAB, NLT, REB, TEV].
- b. There is no lexical entry for this word, the grammatical relation being indicated in the Greek by the dative case of the noun φανέρωσις 'manifestation'. This relation is translated 'by' [AB, HNTC, ICC2, Lns,

WBC; KJV, NIV, NJB, NRSV, REB], 'with' [NTC], not explicit [CEV, NAB, NLT, TEV, TNT].

c. φανέρωσις (LN 28.36) (BAGD P. 853): 'manifestation' [ICC2; KJV], 'disclosure' [BAGD, NTC], 'full disclosure' [AB], 'announcement' [BAGD], 'open proclamation' [BAGD], 'open declaration' [WBC], 'open statement' [NRSV], 'revelation' [LN], 'publishing' [Lns], 'showing' [NJB], 'showing forth' [HNTC], 'setting forth' [NIV], 'declaring' [REB]. The phrase 'the manifestation of the truth' is translated 'we speak only the truth' [CEV], 'we proclaim the truth openly' [NAB], 'we tell the truth' [NLT], 'in the full light of truth' [TEV]. See the verb form of this word at 2:14 and 3:3.

d. pres. act. participle of συνίστημι (LN 33.344) (BAGD I.1.b. p. 790): 'to commend' [BAGD, HNTC, ICC2, Lns, NTC; KJV, NAB, NIV, NJB, NRSV, TEV, TNT], 'to recommend' [AB, BAGD, LN, WBC; REB]. The phrase 'commending ourselves to every conscience of men' is translated 'so others will be sure that we can be trusted' [CEV], 'and all who are honest know that' [NLT]. See this word also at 3:1.

e. συνείδησις (LN 26.13) (BAGD 2. p. 786): 'conscience' [AB, BAGD, HNTC, ICC2, LN, Lns, NTC, WBC; KJV, NAB, NIV, NJB, NRSV, REB, TNT], 'good conscience' [TEV], not explicit [CEV, NLT]. The phrase 'every conscience of men' is translated 'every human conscience' [AB, ICC2, NTC], 'the conscience of all men' [HNTC], 'every man's conscience' [Lns; KJV, NAB, NIV, TNT], 'everyone's conscience' [WBC; NRSV], 'everyone's good conscience' [TEV], 'every human being with a conscience' [NJB], 'conscience of our fellow-men' [REB]. See this word also at 1:12.

f. ἐνώπιον (LN 90.20) (BAGD 2.b. p. 270): 'before' [NTC; NAB, NLT], 'in the sight of' [AB, BAGD, HNTC, ICC2, LN, Lns, WBC; KJV, NIV, NJB, NRSV, REB, TEV, TNT]. The phrase 'before God' is translated 'God is our witness' [CEV].

QUESTION—What is meant by 'the manifestation of the truth'?

He is referring to the truth of the gospel message [AB, EBC, EGT, HNTC, Ho, ICC1, ICC2, Lns, My, NCBC, TG, WBC], or of the truth he teaches [He]. The gospel is proclaimed openly in the full light of truth, in contrast with shameful practices that must be hid [TH]. He is referring to the open display of the genuineness of his own conscience and motives [NIC1]. He is referring to the open preaching of the word of God [SP].

QUESTION—What is meant by 'every conscience of men'?

It is every possible variety of the human conscience [EGT]. It is the total moral and intellectual understanding of others [NIC2]. It is the ability to decide on the rightness or wrongness of someone else's behavior [AB, TH]. Paul's integrity should be recognized by anyone who has the capacity for moral judgment [HNTC], or who is true to his conscience [TNTC]. It means that everyone becomes answerable for not heeding the truth [Lns]. It means that no type or variety of the human conscience could in good conscience give a bad report about Paul's ministry [NIC1]. He appeals to every kind of conscience of men in a wider range than the individual or a particular class [ICC1]. There is a general human ability to recognize the gospel as true [ICC2]. All men who have a moral and religious capacity can recognize the validity of his message [He]. People employ the conscience to judge the content of Paul's preaching [SP].

QUESTION—To what does 'before God' refer to?
1. It refers to the verb phrase 'we commend ourselves'; it is with God as his witness and for his ultimate approval that Paul ministers [AB, HNTC, Ho, ICC1, My, NCBC, NIC1, NIC2, TG, TH, TNTC; CEV, NJB, NLT, TEV, TNT, and probably all other versions]. What Paul commends about himself to everyone's conscience is that he lives in God's sight [WBC].
2. It refers to 'every conscience of men' [Lns, NTC], that is, men's consciences before God. Valid scrutiny of Paul and his ministry may come from those whose consciences are attuned to God's presence [NTC].

4:3 And^a even if our gospel is veiled,^b it is veiled to^c those-who-are-perishing^d

LEXICON—a. δέ (LN 89.94): 'and' [AB, LN, NTC; NIV, NRSV], 'moreover' [HNTC], 'for' [TEV, TNT], 'but' [ICC2, Lns; KJV], 'yet' [WBC], not explicit [CEV, NAB, NJB, NLT, REB].
  b. perf. pass. participle καλύπτω (LN 28.79) (BAGD 2.b. p. 401): 'to be veiled' [AB, HNTC, ICC2, Lns, NTC, WBC; NAB, NIV, NJB, NLT, NRSV, REB, TNT], 'to be hidden' [BAGD, LN; CEV, KJV, TEV].
  c. ἐν (LN 90.56): 'to' [AB, LN, NTC, WBC; CEV, KJV, NIV, NJB, NRSV], 'with respect to' [LN], 'for' [HNTC; NAB, REB], 'in' [Lns], 'amongst' [ICC2], 'from' [NLT, TEV, TNT].
  d. pres. pass. participle ἀπόλλυμι (LN 20.31) (BAGD 2.a.α. p. 95): 'to be perishing' [AB, BAGD, Lns, NTC; NIV, NLT, NRSV], 'to be being destroyed' [BAGD, LN], 'to be on the way to destruction' [HNTC; NJB, REB], 'to be on the road/way to perdition' [ICC2, WBC], 'to be headed toward destruction' [NAB], 'to be lost' [CEV, KJV], 'to be being lost' [TEV], 'to be on the way to being lost' [TNT].

QUESTION—What relationship is indicated by εἰ δὲ καί 'and even if'?
1. It is concessive, indicating a condition that actually exists: the gospel is veiled to some [AB, EBC, Ho, ICC1, Lns, NCBC, NIC1, NIC2, NTC, TG, TH, WBC].
2. It is not concessive, but admits only of the possibility: even if the gospel were veiled [ICC2].

QUESTION—What is meant by 'our' gospel?
It is the gospel of which he and his associates are ministers [Lns], the gospel which they preach [ICC1, My, NTC, TG]. It refers to their act of preaching the gospel [WBC]. It implies no distinction between what Paul preaches and what anyone else preaches [ICC2, Lns, NIC1, TH], nor does it imply that he

shapes the content of it [AB]. The possessive pronoun 'our' shows personal involvement and commitment to the gospel [TH].

4:4 in^a whom the god of this age^b has-blinded^c the minds^d of unbelievers^e

LEXICON—a. ἐν (LN 90.56): 'in' [HNTC, ICC2, Lns; KJV], 'to' [LN, NTC, WBC]. The phrase ἐν οἷς 'in whom' is translated 'in their case' [NRSV], not explicit [CEV, NAB, NIV, NJB, NLT, REB, TEV, TNT].

b. αἰών (LN 67.143, 41.38) (BAGD 2.a. p. 27): 'age' [AB, BAGD, HNTC, ICC2, LN (67.143), NTC, WBC; NIV], 'present age' [NAB], 'passing age' [REB], 'eon' [Lns], 'world' [LN (41.38); CEV, KJV, NJB, NRSV, TEV], 'evil world' [NLT]. The phrase 'the god of this age' is translated 'the god who rules this world' [CEV], 'the evil god of this world' [TEV].

c. aorist act. indic. τυφλόω (LN 32.43) (BAGD p. 831): 'to blind' [AB, BAGD, HNTC, Lns, NTC, WBC; all versions except TEV], 'to make someone not understand' [LN], 'to induce blindness' [ICC2], 'to keep in the dark' [TEV]. This aorist verb is represented as a perfect tense for the sake of English style [AB, HNTC, ICC2, NTC, WBC; all versions except REB].

d. νόημα (LN 26.14) (BAGD 1. p. 540): 'mind' [AB, BAGD, HNTC, ICC2, LN, NTC, WBC; all versions], 'thought' [BAGD, Lns]. See this word also at 3:14.

e. ἄπιστος (LN 31.98) (BAGD 2. p. 85): 'unbeliever' [AB, ICC2, LN (31.106), Lns, NTC; CEV, NIV, NJB, NRSV, TNT], 'those who do not believe' [HNTC; NLT], 'them which believe not' [KJV], 'nonbelievers' [WBC], 'unbelieving' [BAGD, LN (31.98); NAB, REB]. This noun is also translated as a verbal phrase: 'they do not believe' [TEV]. The phrase τὰ νοήματα τῶν ἀπίστων 'the minds of unbelievers' is translated 'their unbelieving minds' [NAB, REB].

QUESTION—What is meant by ὁ θεός τοῦ αἰῶνος 'the god of this age'?

It refers to Satan [AB, EBC, EGT, HNTC, Ho, ICC1, ICC2, Lns, My, NCBC, NIC1, NIC2, NTC, TG, TH, TNTC, WBC]. He is called 'god' of the present age because he has usurped the authority of God and is followed as a god by his fellow rebels [HNTC]. He holds sway over the world during this present age and the unregenerate serve him as though he were God [ICC1, NIC1, NIC2]. The title 'god' may refer to Psalm 8:5 where the Hebrew *elohim* is rendered 'angels' in the LXX [NTC].

QUESTION—What is the relationship between those who are perishing, those who are being blinded, and those who don't believe?

1. The three groups are co-extensive; they are the same people and the descriptive phrases are appositional [AB, EBC, He, HNTC, Ho, ICC1, ICC2, Lns, NCBC, NIC1, NIC2, NTC, TG, WBC]. The phrase 'among whom/in whom' might seem to be specifying a subgroup to 'those who are perishing', but the fact that Paul dictated this letter explains the awkward syntax in this sentence [NIC2]. Though the blindness is caused

by Satan, his use of the term 'unbeliever' adds a note of human culpability as well [SP].
2. The group of unbelievers is a larger group than those who are perishing, because some who don't believe become believers and are saved [My].

so-as-to not see/shine-forth[a] the illumination[b] of the gospel of the glory of Christ,
LEXICON—a. aorist act. infin. αὐγάζω (LN **28.37**) (BAGD 1., 2. p. 120): 'to see' [AB, BAGD (1), HNTC, WBC; CEV, NAB, NIV, NJB, NLT, NRSV, TEV, TNT], 'to behold' [ICC2], 'to shine forth' [BAGD (2)], 'to shine unto' [KJV], 'to get to dawn' [Lns], 'to dawn and bring light' [REB]. The whole clause is translated 'so that the light of the gospel of the glory of Christ would not be evident (to them)' or 'so that they would not see the light of the good news about the glory of Christ' [LN]. This word does not occur elsewhere in the NT.
b. φωτισμός (LN **72.3**) (BAGD 1. p. 873): 'illumination' [BAGD, HNTC, Lns, NTC], 'enlightenment' [AB, BAGD], 'light' [ICC2; CEV, KJV, NRSV, TNT], 'the light shining' [NJB, NLT, TNT], 'revealed splendor' [WBC], 'splendor' [NIV], 'truth' [**LN**]. The phrase αὐγάσαι τὸν φωτισμὸν 'see/shine forth the illumination' is translated as two verbs: 'dawn upon them and bring them light' [REB]. 'Truth' is a figurative extension of the meaning of 'light' [LN]. The noun φωτισμός is an action word indicating the act of illumination [NTC].
QUESTION—Does εἰς τό μή 'so as to not' indicate purpose or result?
1. It indicates the purpose of Satan, which is to blind the unbelievers [EBC, He, HNTC, My, NIC2, NTC, TH, WBC; KJV, NRSV, TNT].
2. It indicates the result of Satan's work, which is being unable to see the light [ICC1, ICC2, Lns, NIC1; CEV, NAB, NIV, NJB, NLT, REB, TEV].
QUESTION—Is φωτισμός 'illumination' the subject or the object of the verb αὐγάζειν 'to see/shine forth'?
In this clause the verb could be transitive 'to see' or 'to illumine', or it could be intransitive 'to shine forth'. Because the verb is an articular infinitive following a preposition of purpose, the accusative noun φωτισμόν could be the subject 'the light shines', or the object 'see the light' or 'shine the light'.
1. The verb is used transitively and φωτισμός 'illumination' is its object [AB, EBC, He, HNTC, ICC2, NIC1, NIC2, NTC, SP, TG, WBC; CEV, NAB, NIV, NJB, NLT, NRSV, TEV, TNT]: they do not see the illumination.
2. The verb is used intransitively and φωτισμός 'illumination' is its subject [EGT, Ho, Lns, My; KJV, REB]: the illumination does not shine.
QUESTION—How are the nouns related in the genitive construction τὸν φωτισμὸν τοῦ εὐαγγελίου 'the illumination of the gospel'?
The gospel is the source or origin of the illumination [AB, HNTC, ICC1, ICC2, Lns, NTC, SP, TG, TH]. The light or illumination is described in detail as 'the gospel of the glory of Christ' [TH].

QUESTION—How are the nouns related in the genitive construction τοῦ εὐαγγελίου τῆς δόξης 'the gospel of the glory'?
The gospel is about or concerning the glory of Christ [SP, TG, TH, TNTC; TEV]. The glory of Christ is the content of the gospel [EGT, Lns, My]. The gospel is derived from the glory that belongs to Christ [NTC]. The gospel contains and proclaims the glory of Christ [ICC1], and unfolds the glory of Christ [NCBC]. The illumination or revealed splendor of the gospel is the glory of Christ [WBC]. The phrase τῆς δόξης 'of the glory' is used adjectivally [CEV, KJV]: 'our glorious Christ' [CEV], 'the glorious gospel' [KJV].

who is the image[a] of God.
LEXICON—a. εἰκών (LN 6.96) (BAGD 1.b. p. 222): 'image' [AB, BAGD, HNTC, ICC2, LN, Lns, NTC, WBC; KJV, NAB, NIV, NJB, NRSV, REB], 'likeness' [BAGD, LN; TNT], 'exact likeness' [NLT, TEV], not explicit [CEV]. The phrase 'the image of God' is translated 'who shows what God is like' [CEV].
QUESTION—What is meant by 'the image of God'?
This phrase implies both personality and distinctiveness when describing the relation of Christ to God [EBC]. Here it signifies that Christ is a perfect manifestation of God, whose being he shares [NIC1], and is the full representation of God and the expression of his nature [WBC].

4:5 For[a] we-do- not -preach[b] ourselves, but Jesus Christ (as) Lord, and ourselves (as) your servants[c] for-the-sake-of[d] Jesus.
TEXT—Instead of Ἰησοῦν Χριστὸν 'Jesus Christ', some manuscripts read 'Christ Jesus'. GNT selects the reading 'Jesus Christ' with a B rating, indicating that the text is almost certain. The reading 'Christ Jesus' is taken by HNTC, Lns, KJV, NAB, NJB, NLT, REB, TNT.
LEXICON—a. γάρ (LN 89.23): 'for' [AB, HNTC, ICC2, LN, Lns, NTC, WBC; KJV, NIV, NRSV, TEV], 'because' [LN], not explicit [CEV, NAB, NJB, NLT, REB, TNT].
   b. pres. act. indic. κηρύσσω (LN 33.256) (BAGD 2.b.β. p. 431): 'to preach' [AB, BAGD, ICC2, LN, Lns, NTC; CEV, KJV, NAB, NIV, NLT, TEV], 'to proclaim' [BAGD, HNTC, WBC; NJB, NRSV, REB, TNT].
   c. δοῦλος (LN 87.76) (BAGD 1.e.α. p. 205): 'servant' [ICC2, NTC, WBC; all versions except NRSV], 'slave' [AB, BAGD, LN, Lns; NRSV].
   d. διά with accusative object (LN 90.44): 'for the sake of' [AB, HNTC, NTC, WBC; KJV, NAB, NIV, NJB, NRSV, REB, TEV, TNT], 'because of' [ICC2, LN, Lns], 'on account of' [LN]. The phrase 'servants for the sake of Jesus' is translated 'Jesus sent us to be your servants' [CEV], 'we are your servants because of what Jesus has done for us' [NLT].
QUESTION—What relationship is indicated by γάρ 'for'?
It ties this sentence to what has been said previously, especially in 4:4 [AB, TG]. It introduces Paul's role in the gospel he has been discussing in the last

part of 4:4 [NIC2]. It introduces Paul's explanation of the content of his preaching referred to in 4:4 [NTC]. It explains what is meant by the statement in 4:4 about 'the gospel of the glory of Christ', which is that he is proclaimed as Lord [NCBC]. It ties 4:4 to 4:5 and explains Paul's statement about 'our gospel', that it is really the gospel about Christ's glory and not about themselves [Ho, ICC1, My, TH]. It introduces an explanatory note; in the whole matter of the gospel light in 4:3–4, to which so many were being blinded by Satan, to explain that Paul plays only a minor part as a servant and is not the object of the preaching [Lns].

QUESTION—What does it mean to preach oneself?

It means to commend oneself [WBC], to craft one's own message or draw attention to oneself [NCBC], to promote one's own authority or importance [TNTC], to promote oneself and one's own interests [AB], to proclaim one's own merits [ICC1]. It is to attract admiration and homage of others to oneself [Ho], to offer one's own insight, importance, or interest as the content and aim of preaching [My], or to seek worldly advantage for oneself by preaching one's own thoughts and doctrines [Lns]. It is to lord it over someone else's faith [HNTC]. It is self-aggrandizement instead of glorifying Christ [NIC1]. In making this statement Paul is countering the charge that he exaggerated and overemphasized his own conversion experience because of self-interest and the desire to be in a position of control over others [ICC2].

QUESTION—In what sense is Paul the servant of the Corinthians?

He serves them by doing the will and work of the Lord [My], just as Christ himself was a servant [ICC1]. In Jewish religious tradition being a servant meant being chosen by God [WBC]. Paul served them by preaching to them and evangelizing them [Lns, NIC2, TG, TH], and by encouraging new converts in the faith [TG]. The term δοῦλος 'servant' is contrasted to the term κύριος 'Lord' [AB, Lns, NIC1, NTC, WBC]. Paul was not their overlord, but served them as a concerned father [EBC]. Instead of lording over them, Paul is willing to spend and be spent for them as in 12:15 [AB]. Paul assumes a very humble status so that all glory will go to God [NIC1].

QUESTION—Why does Paul use the name 'Jesus' without or apart from the title 'Christ'?

1. The name 'Jesus' is associated with his state of humiliation when he emptied himself and took the form of a bondservant [ICC1, NIC1]. It calls attention to the historical Jesus and the example he set in serving others [Lns, NTC]. Like 4:10–12 in this chapter it focuses on the human name of Jesus and the suffering he went through on earth [WBC]. Paul is thinking of Jesus in his suffering and as an example for himself. His use of the name 'Christ' refers to Jesus who died and rose, and 'Lord' to Jesus as alive, exalted and reigning [SP].

2. There is no particular significance to his using the name 'Jesus' without the title 'Christ' because the context is still the confession that Jesus Christ is Lord [AB].

QUESTION—What relationship is indicated by διὰ Ἰησοῦν 'for the sake of Jesus'?

They serve on account of Jesus [My, NIC2], and for Jesus' sake [HNTC, ICC2, SP]. Paul serves because Jesus himself did so [HNTC, ICC2, NIC1]. He serves on account of his loyalty to the gospel [WBC], and because of Jesus' interest in the Corinthians [Lns]. He serves in obedience to Jesus' command [Lns, TNTC], doing his will [My]. Paul serves out of love for Jesus [Ho, NTC], out of dedication to him [TG], and because he is his bond-slave [AB].

4:6 For[a] God, the one-having-said 'light shall-shine[b] out of darkness' (is he) who shone[c] in our hearts

LEXICON—a. ὅτι (LN 89.33) (BAGD 3.b. p. 589): 'for' [BAGD, HNTC, LN, NTC, WBC; KJV, NAB, NIV, NLT, NRSV, REB, TNT], 'because' [AB, ICC2, LN, Lns], not explicit [CEV, NJB, TEV].
  b. fut. act. indic. of λάμπω (LN 14.37) (BAGD 1.b. p. 466): 'to shine' [AB, HNTC, ICC2, LN, Lns, NTC, WBC; all versions except NLT], 'to shine out, to shine forth' [BAGD], 'to give light' [LN]. The future tense λάμψει is translated as a command: 'light shall shine!' [AB, HNTC, ICC2, Lns, WBC; REB, TEV, TNT], 'let light shine' [NTC; NAB, NIV, NJB, NRSV], 'let there be light' [NLT], 'God commanded light to shine' [CEV, KJV].
  c. aorist act. indic. of λάμπω (LN 14.37) (BAGD 2. p. 466): 'to shine' [BAGD, HNTC, ICC2, LN, Lns, WBC; CEV, KJV, NAB, NJB, NRSV, TNT], 'to shine forth' [NTC], 'to cause light to shine' [AB; REB], 'to make light to shine' [NIV, TEV], 'to make us understand' [NLT]. This aorist verb is translated in the perfect tense [AB, NTC, WBC; KJV, NAB, NIV, NJB, NLT, NRSV, REB], and in the present tense [CEV].

QUESTION—What relationship is indicated by ὅτι 'for'?

It refers back to 4:4 and furthers the contrast between light and dark [WBC]. It is a link to 4:5 [NTC]. It introduces grounds for 4:5 [AB]. It introduces a confirmation of the entire content of 4:5 [My]. It introduces an explanation for 4:5, which is that Paul preaches Jesus as Lord because the glory of God is revealed in him [Ho, ICC2, TNTC]. It explains why Paul and the apostles preach Christ and not self, which is that God has illumined them [ICC1, Lns, TH]. It introduces his reason for being a slave, which is that God illuminated him so he would evangelize others [NIC2].

QUESTION—What is the relationship of the two clauses in this sentence?

1. The subject of the sentence is God, the clause introduced by ὁ εἰπών 'the one having said' is an explanatory clause, the implied principle verb is ἐστίν 'is', and the clause introduced by ὅς ἔλαμψεν 'who shone' is the complement of the subject [HNTC, ICC1, ICC2, Lns, My, NIC2, WBC; NJB, NRSV, TEV]: the God who said 'Let light shine out of darkness' is the one who has shone in our hearts.

2 CORINTHIANS 4:6   151

2. The subject of the sentence is God, the clause introduced by ὁ εἰπών 'the one having said' is an explanatory clause, the main verb is ἔλαμψεν [AB; KJV, NAB, NIV, NLT, REB, TNT]: God, who said 'Let light shine out of darkness', has caused a light to shine in our hearts. This construction is parallel to that of 4:4 [AB].
3. The two clauses are balanced and can be separate sentences [NTC; CEV]: God is the one who said 'Let light shine out of darkness'. God has shone forth in our hearts.

QUESTION—Is the verb ἔλαμψεν 'shone' used transitively or intransitively?
1. It is used intransitively [EGT, HNTC, ICC1, ICC2, Lns, NCBC, NIC1, NIC2, NTC, WBC; CEV, KJV, NAB, NJB, NRSV, TNT]: God, who is light, 'shone'.
2. It is used factitively in the sense that God caused the light to shine in us [AB, My, SP; NIV, REB, TEV].
3. It is used transitively [Ho]; God, the subject, illuminated us, the object.
4. It is used metaphorically for giving understanding [NLT]: God has caused us to understand.

QUESTION—Is the statement 'light shall-shine out of darkness' a quotation from the OT?

It is a loosely worded reference to Genesis 1:3 [AB, EBC, HNTC, ICC1, ICC2, Lns, My, NCBC, NIC1, NIC2, NTC, TG, TH, TNTC], possibly influenced by the wording of Isaiah 9:2 [ICC2, NIC1, TNTC]. There may also be allusion to the servant of Yahweh passages in Isaiah such as 42:6 or 49:6 where the servant is called to be a light to the nations [NIC2, WBC].

for[a] illumination[b] of the knowledge[c] of the glory of God in the face[d] of Jesus Christ.

TEXT—Instead of Ἰησοῦ Χριστοῦ 'of Jesus Christ', some manuscripts read Χριστοῦ 'Christ'. GNT shows Ἰησοῦ 'Jesus' in brackets but does not rate the variant. The reading 'Christ' is taken by HNTC, WBC; NAB, NIV, NJB, TEV, TNT.

LEXICON—a. πρός with accusative object (LN 89.60) (BAGD 3.a. p. 710): 'for' [BAGD], 'for the purpose of' [BAGD, LN, Lns], 'with a view to' [HNTC], 'in order to' [LN], 'to (with infinitive)' [WBC; NJB], 'to give' [KJV, NIV, NRSV], 'to provide' [AB, NTC], 'to bring' [TEV], 'to effect' [ICC2], not explicit [CEV]. The phrase 'for illumination of the knowledge' is translated 'that we in turn might make known' [NAB], 'that we might understand' [NLT], 'which is knowledge' [REB], 'to bring to light the knowledge' [TNT]. This word is used to indicate purpose [AB, EGT, He, HNTC, Ho, ICC2, Lns, My, WBC].
  b. φωτισμός (LN **28.36**) (BAGD 2. p. 873): 'illumination' [HNTC, Lns, NTC], 'light' [NRSV, REB], 'enlightenment' [AB, ICC2], 'revelation' [LN], 'revealing' [BAGD], not explicit [WBC; CEV, NAB, TEV]. The phrase πρὸς φωτισμόν 'for illumination' is translated as an infinitive verb: 'to illumine' [WBC], 'to enlighten' [NJB], 'to bring to light'

[BAGD; TNT], 'to give the light' [KJV, NIV], 'to let you know' [CEV]. The phrase 'who shone in our hearts for illumination of the knowledge of the glory of God' is translated 'has made us understand that this light is the brightness of the glory of God' [NLT].

c. γνῶσις (LN 28.17) (BAGD 2. p. 163): 'knowledge' [AB, BAGD, HNTC, ICC2, LN, Lns, NTC, WBC; KJV, NIV, NJB, NRSV, REB, TEV, TNT], not explicit [CEV, NAB, NLT]. The phrase 'for illumination of the knowledge' is translated 'to let you know that' [CEV], 'that we in turn might make known' [NAB].

d. πρόσωπον (LN 8.18) (BAGD 1.a. p. 720): 'face' [AB, BAGD, ICC2, LN, Lns, NTC; KJV, NAB, NIV, NJB, NRSV, REB, TEV, TNT]. The phrase 'in the face of' is translated 'seen in the face of' [HNTC, WBC; NLT], 'shining on/in the face of' [NAB, TEV], and 'seen in' [CEV]. See this word also at 1:11; 2:10.

QUESTION—Of whom is Paul speaking when he says 'our hearts'?
1. He is speaking of the illumination of his own heart at his conversion on the road to Damascus [EBC, HNTC, ICC1, NCBC, NIC1, NIC2, WBC].
2. He is referring both to himself and to his associates [AB, Lns, My; CEV].
3. He is referring to all believers [He, Ho, NTC].

QUESTION—Does πρὸς φωτισμὸν 'for illumination' refer to receiving an inward illumination concerning Christ or giving a public proclamation of Christ?
1. Πρὸς φωτισμὸν 'for illumination' refers to the receiving of inward, subjective illumination concerning Christ [AB, He, Ho, ICC2, Lns, NCBC, NIC1, NTC, TNTC, WBC; KJV, NIV, NJB, NLT, NRSV, REB, TEV, TNT].
2. Πρὸς φωτισμὸν 'for illumination' refers to the giving of a public proclamation of Christ [EGT, HNTC, ICC1, My, NIC2, SP; CEV, NAB]. God shone in Paul's heart for the sake of using him to bring the illumination of the knowledge of the glory of God to others.

QUESTION—How are the nouns related in the genitive construction φωτισμὸν τῆς γνώσεως 'illumination of the knowledge'?
1. The illumination is or consists of the knowledge of God's glory [He, HNTC, NIC1; CEV, REB, TEV].
2. The illumination comes from the knowledge of God's glory [AB, EBC, ICC1], or by means of the knowledge [Lns, NTC, TG].
3. The illumination is God's action of bringing us the knowledge of God's glory [NLT, TNT].
4. In the phrase πρὸς φωτισμὸν τῆς γνώσεως, the first two words πρὸς φωτισμὸν indicate the action of making something known and the last two words τῆς γνώσεως represent the knowledge that is made known. That is, God shines in our hearts that we might illuminate others with the knowledge [EGT; NAB]. God's glory became visible in Jesus Christ [SP]

QUESTION—What does Paul mean when he says 'in the face of Jesus Christ'?
It is in the person of Christ himself that God's glory is embodied and revealed [EBC, EGT, HNTC, Ho, Lns, NIC1, TG, TNTC]. This is contrasted with 3:7 where Moses' face showed a temporary and fading reflection of God's glory [AB, HNTC, ICC1, NCBC, NIC1, NTC, TH, WBC]. Paul is remembering his experience on the road to Damascus where he saw the glory of God in the face of Christ [ICC1, NIC2].

DISCOURSE UNIT: 4:7–5:10 [AB, EBC, ICC1, ICC2, NTC; NJB]. The topic is earthly and heavenly dwellings [NTC], the hardships and hopes of the apostolate [NJB], the suffering and glory of the apostolic ministry [EBC], the sufferings and supports of an apostle [ICC1], Paul's distress and future glory [ICC2], the ministry and mortality [AB].

DISCOURSE UNIT: 4:7–18 [HNTC, WBC]. The topic is Paul's ministry: its glory and frailty [WBC], the ministry—the earthenware vessel in which the treasure is contained [HNTC].

DISCOURSE UNIT: 4:7–15 [ICC2, NIC2]. The topic is the ministry: life and death [NIC2], Paul's inglorious lifestyle [ICC2].

DISCOURSE UNIT: 4:7–12 [TNTC]. The topic is treasure in earthen vessels.

4:7 But/and[a] we-have[b] this treasure[c] in vessels[d] of-clay,[e]

LEXICON—a. δέ (LN 89.94, 89.124): 'but' [HNTC, ICC2, LN (89.124), Lns, WBC; KJV, NIV, NJB, NLT, NRSV, REB; 'yet' [TEV, TNT], 'now' [AB], 'and' [LN (89.94), NTC], not explicit [CEV, NAB].

b. pres. act. indic. of ἔχω (LN 57.1): 'to have' [AB, HNTC, ICC2, LN, Lns, NTC, WBC; KJV, NIV, NRSV, REB, TEV], 'to hold' [NJB], 'to possess' [NAB]. This is also expressed in the passive: 'to be stored in' [CEV, TNT], 'to be held' [NLT].

c. θησαυρός (LN 65.10) (BAGD 2.b.γ. p. 361): 'treasure' [AB, BAGD, HNTC, ICC2, LN, Lns, NTC, WBC; all versions except NLT, TEV], 'precious treasure' [NLT], 'spiritual treasure' [TEV].

d. σκεῦος (LN 6.118) (BAGD 2. p. 754): 'vessel' [BAGD, HNTC, LN, Lns; KJV, NAB], 'jar' [BAGD; CEV, NIV, NRSV, REB], 'container' [ICC2, LN; NLT], 'pot' [AB, NTC, WBC; NJB, TEV, TNT].

e. ὀστράκινος (LN **2.20**) (BAGD P. 587): 'clay' [BAGD, **LN**, WBC; CEV, NIV, NRSV, TEV, TNT], 'earthen' [AB, Lns; KJV, NAB], 'made of earth' [BAGD], 'earthenware' [HNTC, ICC2, LN, NTC; NJB, REB]. This word is also translated as indicating perishability: 'perishable containers, that is, in our weak bodies' [NLT]; or as indicating commonness: 'common clay pots' [TEV].

QUESTION—What relationship is indicated by δέ 'but/and'?
1. It is contrastive [EGT, ICC1, ICC2, Lns, NIC1, TH, WBC; KJV, NIV, NJB, NLT, NRSV, REB, TEV, TNT]: but. It contrasts the glory of God with the Christian messengers [TH]. It contrasts with the glory spoken of

in 4:6 [EGT, ICC1, ICC2, WBC]. It introduces the contrast between the splendor he has been discussing and the humble containers of it [NIC1].
2. It is continuative [AB, My, NIC2, NTC]: and. It continues his train of thought regarding his high vocation and compares it with his outward condition [My]. He is explaining the paradox introduced in 2:14–16 regarding God's victory in his humiliation [NIC2].

QUESTION—Who is included in the 'we'?
1. Paul is primarily talking about himself, or about himself and his associates in ministry [AB, EBC, HNTC, ICC2, Lns, NCBC, NIC1, NIC2, TH, TNTC, WBC]. He is primarily talking about himself, but applies it more generally to all believers [NIC2] or to any servant of Christ [NIC1]. He is primarily describing his own condition [EBC, ICC2].
2. The 'we' is inclusive, and refers to all believers [NTC].

QUESTION—What is the treasure?
It is the gospel [HNTC, NTC], the glory of the gospel [WBC], the light of the gospel [TNTC], the inward enlightenment from God [My]. It is the gospel of God's glory revealed in Christ [ICC2]. It is the light of the knowledge of the glory of God [EBC, EGT, ICC1, NCBC, NIC1, NIC2]. It is God's shining in our heart to fill us with his grace [Lns]. It is the task of preaching the gospel [Ho, TG]. It is the light of the gospel as well as the ministry of spreading it [AB, TH]. It is Paul's ministry [SP].

QUESTION—What is the point of his comparison regarding the clay vessels?
It compares the low value of the vessel with the treasure it contains [AB, HNTC, Lns, My, NCBC, NIC2, NTC, TG, TH, TNTC]. It compares the weakness and fragility of the vessel with the treasure it contains [AB, EBC, EGT, He, Lns, My, NCBC, NIC2, NTC, SP, TG, TH, TNTC, WBC]. It compares the imperfection and weakness of the ministers with the glorious effect of the ministry [Ho]. It highlights the unworthiness of the containers [NIC1], their insignificance [EBC], and their unimpressiveness [ICC2]. It also refers to the fact of Paul's being God's chosen vessel (cf. Acts 9:15) and an instrument in the potter's hand (cf. Jer. 18:1–11) [NTC, WBC].

QUESTION—Are the 'vessels of clay' their bodies or themselves as persons?
Paul does not see the relationship of body and soul in dualistic terms as the Greeks did, with the body being only a 'vessel' or container for the soul [AB, EBC, HNTC, Lns, NIC2]. Rather, both body and soul are aspects of a unified being [AB, EBC, Lns, NIC2].
1. Paul is referring to the body and its condition [EGT, He, My, TH]. Paul is referring to the visible outer person, but the whole person, both inner and outer experiences the tribulations of apostolic ministry [SP].
2. Paul is talking about the whole person, not just the body [EBC, Ho, ICC1, NTC, TG].

in-order-that the exceeding-greatness[a] **of the power**[b] **might-be**[c] **(seen to-be) from**[d] **God and not from**[e] **us.**

LEXICON—a. ὑπερβολή (LN **78.33**) (BAGD p. 840): 'exceeding greatness' [Lns], 'extraordinary quality' [BAGD], 'far greater degree' [LN], 'immensity' [NJB], 'excellency' [KJV], 'preeminence' [HNTC]. This noun is also translated adjectively: 'beyond any comparison' [AB], 'surpassing' [NAB], 'all-surpassing' [NIV], 'transcendent' [REB], 'overwhelming' [ICC2], 'supreme' [LN; TEV, TNT], 'preeminent' [WBC], 'glorious' [NLT], 'extraordinary' [**LN**, NTC; NRSV], 'real' [CEV]. This word describes a transcending of normal limits [NIC1]. See 1:8 for an adverbial expression containing this word.

b. δύναμις (LN 76.1): 'power' [AB, HNTC, ICC2, Lns, NTC, WBC; all versions]. See this word also at 1:8.

c. pres. act. subj. of εἰμί (BAGD IV.5. p. 225): 'to be' [HNTC, Lns, NTC; KJV, NJB]. The phrase 'that the exceeding greatness of the power might be from God' is translated 'the real power comes from God' [CEV]. The subordinating conjunction ἵνα with the subjunctive of the verb 'to be' indicates purpose, that the power 'might be from God', but with the implied meaning that the power be seen or recognized as being from God. It is translated as 'that it might be seen' [AB], 'that it may prove to be' [ICC2], 'this proves' [REB], 'to show' [WBC; NIV, TEV], 'showing' [TNT], 'to make it clear' [NAB], 'so everyone can see' [NLT], 'that it may be made clear' [NRSV].

d. There is no lexical entry for this word, the relationship being indicated by the genitive case of the word θεός 'God'. This relationship is translated 'from God' [CEV, NAB, NIV, NLT, TNT], 'of God' [Lns, NTC; KJV], 'belongs to God' [AB; NRSV, TEV], 'God's' [HNTC, ICC2, WBC; NJB], 'God's alone' [REB].

e. ἐκ (LN 90.16): 'from' [ICC2, LN, Lns; CEV, NAB, NIV, NRSV, REB, TNT], 'derived from' [HNTC], 'of' [KJV], 'out of' [NTC], 'belongs to (us)' [AB; TEV], 'our own' [WBC; NJB, NLT].

QUESTION—What is the power that is from God?

It is the message of the gospel [AB, EBC, HNTC, Ho, Lns, TG], which brings enlightenment [My, NIC2] and salvation [AB, NIC2]. It is the power to endure great hardships [ICC2]. It is the power of Paul's preaching, plus the miracles he did and his endurance, all of which produced conversion in people [ICC1]. It is the power of God's word [NTC]. It is the very great power contained in Paul's preaching and which also is operative in the difficult circumstances within which his ministry is carried out [SP].

4:8 **In every**[a] **(way) (we are) being-pressed**[b] **but not being-crushed;**[c]

LEXICON—a. πᾶς (LN 59.23): 'every, all' [LN]. The phrase ἐν παντί 'in every (way)' is translated 'in every way' [AB, ICC2, NTC, WBC; NRSV, TNT], 'in every way possible' [NAB], 'at all times and in every way' [HNTC], 'on every side' [Lns; KJV, NIV, NLT], 'every kind of

(hardship)' [NJB], 'often' [CEV, TEV], not explicit [REB]. The initial position of ἐν παντί in the sentence gives it emphasis [TH].
   b. pres. pass. participle of θλίβω (LN 22.15) (BAGD 3. p. 362): 'to be pressed' [Lns; TNT], 'to be hard pressed' [ICC2, WBC; NIV, REB], 'to be pressed by trouble' [NLT], 'to be oppressed' [BAGD], 'to be afflicted' [AB, BAGD, HNTC, NTC; NAB, NRSV], 'to be troubled' [LN; KJV, TEV], 'to suffer hardship' [LN], 'to be subjected to hardship' [NJB], 'to suffer' [CEV]. See this word also at 1:6.
   c. pres. pass. participle of στενοχωρέω (LN **22.19**) (BAGD p. 766): 'to be crushed' [AB, HNTC, WBC; CEV, NAB, NIV, NRSV, TEV], 'to be crushed and broken' [NLT], 'to be caused to be in great trouble' [LN], 'to be hard pressed' [NTC], 'to be cornered' [REB, TNT], 'to be hemmed in with difficulty' [LN], 'to be hemmed in' [Lns], 'to be trapped' [ICC2], 'to be distressed' [KJV, NJB].
QUESTION—With what is ἐν παντὶ 'in every way' to be taken?
   1. It is used with reference to all four antithetical pairs of participles that follow [AB, HNTC, Ho, ICC1, ICC2, My, SP]. It refers to all kinds of hardships, and taken with πάντοτε 'always' in 4:10 and ἀεί 'always' in 4:11 emphasizes their intensity and scope [AB].
   2. It is used with reference to only the first participle that follows, and means to be subjected to every kind of hardship [NJB], to be hard pressed or afflicted in every direction [EGT, Lns; NIV], on every side [KJV, NLT], often [CEV, TEV], or in every way [NTC, WBC; NAB, NRSV, TNT], that is, physically, mentally, socially, and spiritually [NTC].
QUESTION—How is this series of participles used?
   They are used absolutely, that is, as verbs [ICC2, NIC2, NTC]. They carry the imagery of combat [EBC, EGT, Ho, ICC1, NTC, TH]. It is the imagery of a chase and a fight [Lns]. Paul is like a soldier who is pressed hard in battle, surrounded, pursued, and then thrown down [EGT, Ho], though never finally killed [Ho]. The first half of each contrast corresponds with Jesus' death, the second to his life, and describe a real change in Paul's actual situation [ICC2]. Paul is describing four cases where their weaknesses could have been fatal but were not [ICC1]. The four pairs are in steps, increasing to the most extreme [NIC2]. The present tense is the iterative present, indicating an ongoing experience [Ho, Lns, NIC1, TG].

being-perplexed[a] but not despairing,[b]
LEXICON—a. pres. mid. participle of ἀπορέω (LN 32.9) (BAGD p. 97): 'to be perplexed' [NTC; KJV, NIV, NLT, NRSV, TNT], 'to be thrown into perplexity' [WBC], 'to be bewildered' [REB], 'to be at a loss' [BAGD, HNTC, LN, Lns], 'to be full of doubts' [NAB], 'to be in doubt' [BAGD, LN; TEV], 'to not know what to do' [CEV], 'to be despairing' [AB], 'to be near-desperate' [ICC2], 'to see no way out' [NJB].
   b. pres. mid. or pass. (deponent = act.) participle of ἐξαπορέω (LN 25.237) (BAGD p. 273): 'to despair' [BAGD; NAB, NJB, TNT], 'to be in despair'

[KJV, NIV, TEV], 'to be left to despair' [WBC], 'to be driven to despair' [NRSV], 'to despair completely, to be in utter despair' [LN], 'to be wholly desperate' [ICC2], 'to be utterly desperate' [AB], 'to give up' [CEV], 'to give up and quit' [NLT], 'to be thoroughly perplexed' [NTC], 'to be at wit's end' [REB], 'to be completely baffled' [HNTC], 'to have lost out' [Lns]. The form of this word ἐξαπορούμενοι, is identical to the verb preceding it ἀπορούμενοι, except for the addition of the intensifying prefix ἐξ. With the similarity of the two words Paul is making a play on words or paronomasia with the second being stronger than the first [AB, NTC]. This is shown in translation as 'despairing but not utterly desperate' [AB], 'near-desperate but not wholly desperate' [HNTC], 'at a loss but not having lost out' [Lns], 'perplexed but not thoroughly perplexed' [NTC]. See this word also at 1:8.

QUESTION—In what way can this statement be reconciled with 1:8 where he says that they despaired of life?

Ἐξαπορέομαι can signify being trapped, with no outlet of way of escape [He, Ho]. He is saying that even when it sometimes appears as though there is no way of escaping with their life (as in 1:8), they do escape somehow [Ho, Lns]. The verb ἐξαπορέομαι in 1:8 is used in the same way that ἀπορέω is used in this verse, in that while perplexed with a seemingly hopeless situation, they still don't despair completely or lose faith in God altogether [AB]. In 1:8 he describes what seemed to be the inevitability of death, but here he is saying that he is not confounded to a hopeless degree [NIC1]. The expectation of death is still compatible with the confidence that all will end well [ICC1]. Even when Paul had earlier concluded that he would not escape death, he did not feel abandoned by God [WBC]. It is the difference between a single instance and a more general mental attitude [My]. They are not contradictory since in this verse he is speaking of the ultimate effect or outcome of God's power [SP].

4:9 being-persecuted^a but not being-abandoned^b

LEXICON—a. pres. pass. participle of διώκω (LN 39.45) (BAGD 2. p. 201): 'to be persecuted' [AB, BAGD, HNTC, ICC2, LN, Lns, NTC; KJV, NAB, NIV, NRSV], 'to be harassed' [LN, WBC], 'to be pursued' [NJB, TNT], 'to be hunted' [REB], 'to be hunted down' [NLT]. This passive participle is also translated 'there are many enemies' [TEV], 'in times of trouble' [CEV].

b. pres. pass. participle of ἐγκαταλείπω (LN 35.54) (BAGD 2. p. 215): 'to be abandoned' [BAGD, Lns, NTC, WBC; NAB, NIV, NLT], 'to be abandoned to one's fate' [REB], 'to be forsaken' [AB, BAGD, ICC2, LN; KJV, NRSV, TNT], 'to be deserted' [BAGD, HNTC, LN], 'to be cut off' [NJB]. The idea of not being abandoned is expressed 'God is with us' [CEV], 'God never abandons us' [NLT], 'we are never without a friend' [TEV].

QUESTION—By whom is Paul not abandoned?
He is not abandoned by God [ICC1, Lns; CEV, NLT].

being-knocked-down[a] but not being-destroyed,[b]

LEXICON—a. pres. pass. participle of καταβάλλω (LN **19.10, 20.21**) (BAGD 1. p. 408): 'to be knocked down' [LN (19.10), WBC; CEV, NJB, NLT, TNT], 'to be struck down' [AB, BAGD, HNTC, ICC2, NTC; NAB, NIV, NRSV, REB], 'to be thrown down' [BAGD, Lns], 'to be cast down' [KJV], 'to be badly hurt' [LN (20.21); TEV].

b. pres. mid. or pass. participle of ἀπόλλυμι (LN 20.31): 'to be destroyed' [AB, HNTC, ICC2, LN, Lns, NTC; KJV, NAB, NIV, NRSV, TEV, TNT], 'to be killed' [REB], 'to be ruined' [LN], 'to be knocked out' [WBC]. The phrase 'being knocked down but not being destroyed' is translated 'when we are knocked down we get up again' [CEV], 'knocked down, but still have some life left in us' [NJB], 'we get knocked down, but we get up again and keep going' [NLT].

4:10 always[a] carrying-about[b] in the[c] body[d] the death[e] of Jesus,

LEXICON—a. πάντοτε (LN 67.88): 'always' [AB, HNTC, ICC2, LN, Lns, NTC, WBC; KJV, NIV, NJB, NRSV, TNT], 'continually' [NAB], 'constantly' [NLT], 'at all times' [LN; TEV], 'every day' [CEV], 'wherever we go' [REB].

b. pres. act. participle of περιφέρω (LN **15.190**) (BAGD 1. p. 653): 'to carry about' [AB, BAGD, HNTC; NAB, TNT], 'to carry around' [LN, NTC; NIV], 'to carry with (us)' [NJB, REB], 'to carry' [NRSV, TEV], 'to bear about' [ICC2; KJV], 'to bear around' [Lns], 'to bear' [WBC]. The phrase 'always carrying about in the body the dying of Jesus' is translated 'our bodies show what his death was like' [CEV], 'these bodies of ours always share in the death of Jesus' [NLT].

c. Although there is no possessive pronoun 'our' in this clause, it is present in the following clause, and is therefore translated as implied here: 'our (body/bodies)' [ICC2, NTC; CEV, NAB, NIV, NJB, NLT, REB, TEV, TNT].

d. σῶμα (LN 8.1) (BAGD 1.b. p. 799): 'body' [AB, BAGD, HNTC, ICC2, LN, Lns, NTC; all versions except TEV], 'mortal bodies' [TEV], 'bodily existence' [WBC]. This singular noun is also translated as plural: 'bodies' [CEV, NAB, NLT, TEV].

e. νέκρωσις (LN **23.99**) (BAGD 1. p. 535): 'death' [AB, BAGD, ICC2, LN, NTC; CEV, NIV, NJB, NLT, NRSV, REB, TEV], 'putting to death' [BAGD, Lns], 'killing' [HNTC], 'dying' [WBC; KJV, NAB, TNT]. The phrase 'the death of Jesus' is translated 'the death that Jesus died' [REB]. The phrase 'always carrying about in the body the dying of Jesus' is translated 'we face death every day because of Jesus' [CEV], 'through suffering, these bodies of ours constantly share in the death of Jesus' [NLT].

QUESTION—Does νέκρωσις 'death' represent death itself or the process of dying?
1. It represents a putting to death or killing [AB, EGT, HNTC, Lns, My, NCBC, TG] or the process of dying [ICC1, NIC1, NIC2, WBC]. It is the whole course of Paul's life being given up to death [AB]. It is the continuing process of people attacking Paul physically [Lns]. Here Paul sums up the four antitheses in 4:8–9 in the word νέκρωσις [ICC1, NCBC, NIC2, SP]. It is like a continual ascent to the cross [NIC1]. It is a process of mortification [EGT, HNTC]. This word describes the entire process of weakening, dying, and decay. Here it represents both his suffering and his death [NTC]. It is that which causes death during Paul's entire life [SP].
2. Νέκρωσις means 'death' as a state, not a process [ICC2]. It is parallel to θάνατος 'death' in the next verse (just as 'body' and 'flesh' are parallel) and is used for stylistic reasons only [TNTC].

QUESTION—What does it mean to carry around Jesus' death?
It speaks of the physical aspect of suffering in Paul's apostolic career [AB, WBC]. Paul is subject to treatment that would lead to death [TNTC]. The 'death of Jesus' is a reference to his own physical sufferings and the participle 'carrying about' refers to his missionary journeys [He]. He faces the risk of death wherever he goes [ICC1, TG, TH]. He is constantly exposed to the danger of being killed for the gospel's sake [My]. He carries around Jesus' death by being persecuted just as Jesus was [Lns]. This statement is a summary of all the affliction of 4:8–9 [EBC, NIC2]. He shares in the sufferings of Christ through daily exposure to danger and death for Jesus' sake [NCBC]. It is as though a process of death is clinging to them and will one day claim them [My]. Paul's intimate union with Christ and his sufferings is manifested in his own bodily experience of suffering [EGT]. Paul is speaking of the process of daily mortification, but also of the fact that his ministry was killing him [HNTC]. Paul is conscious of a union with Christ that brings him a unity of experience with his life and his death, both in terms of his being in constant jeopardy as well as in terms of self-denial [NIC1]. Because of his union with Christ, Christ's death is being manifested in Paul as he demonstrates the nature of the crucified Christ through his own physical existence; he is a picture of Christ's death [ICC2]. Paul carries about the dying of Jesus as he always proclaims Jesus' death and also as he demonstrates his willingness to suffer for him [NTC].

QUESTION—What does he mean by the use of the word 'always' in 4:10?
It means that he always proclaims Christ, in season and out of season [NTC]. Hardship is the normal and essential characteristic of his ministry, not the exception [AB]. He is describing a normal pattern [HNTC], one that is daily, constant and perpetual [NIC1], unrelieved [NIC2], always and everywhere [He]. It means there are constant occasions of peril and deliverance [ICC2]. It repeats the emphatic ἐν παντί 'in every way' and signifies that he is perpetually in peril [ICC1]. It corresponds to ἐν παντί in 4:8 [My, NIC2]

and ἀεί in 4:11 [My]. The danger of death is a constantly present experience [NCBC].

in-order-that the life[a] of Jesus also might-be-manifested[b] in our body.
LEXICON—a. ζωή (LN 23.88) (BAGD 1.a. p. 340): 'life' [AB, BAGD, HNTC, ICC2, LN, Lns, NTC, WBC; all versions].

  b. aorist pass. subj. of φανερόω (LN 28.36) (BAGD 1.b. p. 852): 'to be manifested' [AB, HNTC], 'to be made manifest' [KJV], 'to be made publicly manifest' [Lns], 'to be revealed' [BAGD, ICC2, LN, NTC; NAB, NIV, REB], 'to be made known' [LN], 'to be displayed' [WBC], 'to be seen' [CEV, NLT, TEV], 'to be shown' [TNT], 'to be made visible' [NJB, NRSV]. The placement of this verb at the end of the sentence gives it emphasis [WBC]. The subjunctive mood of the verb indicates that ἵνα introduces a purpose clause, as it also does in the next verse. See this word also at 2:14; 3:3.

QUESTION—In what way would the life of Jesus be manifested?
  Whenever Paul would face imminent death, Christ constantly renewed his life in that he was repeatedly spared and strengthened [NTC]. God used Paul to disclose the power of his resurrection life in terms of being renewed and transformed by the Holy Spirit [AB]. The life of Jesus was manifested through being saved from the four states described in 4:8–9 and through repeated deliverances from death [EBC]. The life of Jesus was manifested by Paul's ministry of life to others as well as by his physical survival [He]. The life is Jesus is manifested through constant occasions of being delivered from mortal peril [ICC1, ICC2], but also through the power to endure suffering without being defeated by it [ICC2]. He is primarily referring to his future bodily resurrection, but also to his present inward renewal and physical deliverance from death [HNTC]. He is describing spiritual power for living now, but ultimately also the glorification of the resurrected body [NIC1]. Being rescued from the danger of death is like the resurrection of Jesus [My]. The deliverances represented by the four participles introduced by 'but not' in 4:8–9 illustrate the death and resurrection of Jesus [NIC2]. It is that the Holy Spirit gives assurance of experiencing Jesus' resurrection life and gives the power of Jesus' risen life here and now [NCBC]. It is the spiritual life which they minister through preaching [Lns]. It is the display of divine power in a weak man [WBC]. Jesus' life is manifested as Paul is continually upheld, preserved, and caused to triumph [TNTC]. Survival of persecution is evidence that Jesus is alive [TG]. The purpose clauses in 4:7b and 10b frame 4:7–10, and 'the power of God' in 7b corresponds to 'the life of Jesus' in 10b; Paul's dying allows a visible, bodily demonstration of Jesus' life, that is, of God's power [SP].

2 CORINTHIANS 4:11

4:11 For[a] we the-ones-living[b] always[c] are-being-handed-over[d] to death for-the-sake-of/because-of[e] Jesus,

LEXICON—a. γάρ (LN 89.23): 'for' [AB, HNTC, ICC2, LN, Lns, NTC, WBC; KJV, NIV, NRSV, TNT], 'indeed' [NJB], 'yes' [NLT], not explicit [CEV, NAB, REB, TEV].
  b. pres. act. participle of ζάω (LN 23.88) (BAGD 1.a.α. p. 336): 'to live' [BAGD, LN]. The phrase 'we the ones living' is translated 'we who are alive' [AB, ICC2; NIV], 'we which live' [KJV], 'we living men' [HNTC], 'we, the ones living' [Lns], 'we as living persons' [WBC], 'we, though living' [TNT], 'while we live' [NAB, NRSV], 'while we are still alive' [NJB], 'all our life, we' [REB], 'throughout our lives we (are always in danger)' [TEV], 'we live (under constant danger)' [NLT], not explicit [CEV].
  c. ἀεί (LN 67.86) (BAGD 3. p. 19): 'always' [LN, NTC, WBC; KJV, NIV, NRSV, TEV], 'always in process' [ICC2], 'continually' [BAGD, HNTC, LN; NJB], 'constantly' [AB, BAGD, LN; NAB], 'forever' [Lns], 'every day' [CEV], 'all the time' [TNT], 'constant' [NLT]. The phrase 'we the living ones always' is translated 'we are all our life' [REB]. This word occurs first in the Greek sentence, giving it emphasis [AB, TH].
  d. pres. pass. indic. of παραδίδωμι (LN 57.77) (BAGD 1.b. p. 615): 'to be handed over' [BAGD, HNTC, LN, WBC; NJB, REB], 'to be given over' [LN; NIV], 'to be given up' [AB; NRSV], 'to be delivered' [Lns, NTC; KJV, NAB], 'to be delivered up' [TNT], 'to be in process of deliverance' [ICC2]. The phrase 'to be handed over to death' is translated 'we face death' [CEV], 'to live under danger of death' [NLT], 'to be in danger of death' [TEV].
  e. διά with accusative object (LN 90.44, 90.38): 'for the sake of' [HNTC, LN (90.38), WBC; KJV, NAB, NIV, NJB, NRSV, REB, TEV, TNT], 'because of' [LN (90.44), Lns, NTC; CEV], 'on account of' [AB, ICC2, LN (90.44)]. The phrase 'for the sake of/because of Jesus' is translated 'because we serve Jesus' [NLT].

QUESTION—What relationship is indicated by γάρ 'for'?
  It shows that the structure and content of 4:10 and 11 are parallel [AB, NTC, TNTC], with 4:11 amplifying [EBC], repeating [HNTC, ICC2], explaining [EGT, Ho, ICC2], elucidating [ICC1, My], confirming [Ho], supporting [AB, TH], or intensifying [ICC1] 4:10. It introduces a clarification of his statements about death in the previous verse [SP]. It introduces an explanation of how the effect of 4:10 is brought about [Lns].

QUESTION—What does he mean by 'being handed over to death'?
  They always run the risk of death or are exposed to death because of the ministry [HNTC, TG, TH]. Suffering is required as a part of apostolic life [WBC]. They are subject to the same fate as Jesus because of the gospel [TNTC]. The same hate that followed Jesus follows them because they preach Jesus and his life [Lns]. Paul lives expecting death, as a condemned man would [Ho]. The apostles are like living prey being fed to a monster

[ICC1]. He not only tells of Jesus' passion, he experiences it in his sufferings as a missionary [NIC2]. Paul voluntarily gives himself to deadly peril for Jesus' sake [NTC]. He is subject to mortal danger but also wastes away outwardly [AB].

QUESTION—What relationship is indicated by διὰ Ἰησοῦν 'because of/for the sake of Jesus'?

1. It means because of or on account of Jesus [AB, ICC2, NIC2; CEV], on account of loyalty to the gospel [WBC]. It means because of Paul's connection with Jesus, that is, because of faith in him and because of the ministry [Lns].
2. It means for Jesus' sake or benefit [HNTC, ICC1, NIC1, NTC; all versions except CEV, NLT]. It means for Jesus' sake in the performance of apostolic ministry; Paul is describing the fact that he has a union with Christ and what Christ experienced that conforms itself to how Christ lived [HNTC]. It indicates Paul's motive for ministry [NIC1].

QUESTION—Is the 'we' inclusive or exclusive?

It is exclusive; Paul is talking about the difficulties of the apostolic ministry [AB, EBC, He, HNTC, ICC2, Lns, NIC2, NTC, TG, WBC].

QUESTION—What is the function of the participial phrase οἱ ζῶντες 'we the ones living'?

It accents the contrast between life and death, living and mortal [ICC2, My, NIC1, NIC2], or the idea of constant dying [AB]. It accents the new life that they have [He]. It is a picture of being delivered alive to wild beasts [NIC1]. Paul is saying that he is a living prey every day that he lives [ICC1]. It is set in apposition to 'the life of Jesus' and refers to the spiritual life they have [Lns]. It focuses on the peculiar condition of living as though always being delivered to death [Ho]. It refers to those who have not died before the parousia, which Paul hoped to live to see [HNTC].

QUESTION—Is there any difference between πάντοτε 'always' in 4:10 and ἀεί 'always' in 4:11?

They are used synonymously in parallel construction [AB, NIC2, NTC, TNTC].

in-order-that the life of Jesus also might-be-manifested in our mortal[a] flesh.[b]

LEXICON—a. θνητός (LN 23.124) (BAGD p. 362): 'mortal' [AB, BAGD, HNTC, ICC2, LN, Lns, NTC, WBC; all versions except CEV, NLT], 'dying' [NLT]. The phrase 'that the life of Jesus might be manifested in our mortal flesh' is translated 'our bodies show what his death was like, so that his life can also be seen in us' [CEV].

b. σάρξ (LN 8.4) (BAGD 5. p. 744): 'flesh' [AB, HNTC, ICC2, Lns, NTC; KJV, NAB, NJB, NRSV], 'body' [LN; NIV, NLT, REB, TEV], 'physical body' [LN], 'life here on earth' [BAGD], 'nature' [WBC; TNT], not explicit [CEV]. See this word also at 1:17.

QUESTION—What is the relation of σῶμα 'body' in 4:10 and σάρξ 'flesh' in 4:11?

They are used synonymously [He, Lns, NTC, TG, TNTC, WBC]. They are used in parallel, but the shift to σάρξ 'flesh' emphasizes the vulnerability of the body [AB]. It is a stylistic variation with the same basic meaning, but with the added nuance that even our self-serving nature (σάρξ) is transformed by the Holy Spirit [HNTC]. They are used synonymously, but σάρξ emphasizes the weakness and mortality of this life [Ho, ICC2]. Σάρξ 'flesh' intensifies the meaning of σῶμα 'body' as being that part of us that is subject to death [ICC1]. He uses σάρξ to emphasize the weakness and transitoriness of the body [My]. They are used interchangeably, but the modifier 'mortal' heightens the idea of vulnerability [NIC2], or of temporality [TH]. The words 'mortal flesh' describe the body more emphatically and literally [EGT].

QUESTION—What does he mean by 'the life of Jesus' being manifested?

It refers to the living presence of Jesus within by virtue of union with Christ [NTC]. Paul is referring to how the resurrection life of Jesus shows the incomparable power of God in his weakness [AB]. It is the transforming power of the spirit [HNTC]. He is referring to how his repeated escapes and restored courage manifest Jesus' life [EBC, NIC1]. The pattern of continual peril and rescue are images of Christ's death and resurrection [ICC2]. The life and power of the risen Christ are shown in Paul's being kept alive and by his successful ministry [ICC1]. He is referring to daily deliverance as well as ultimate eschatological deliverance [NIC2]. The life of Jesus in that which continually upholds Paul and enables him to triumph even in his mortal body, despite being subject to forces that would lead to death [TNTC]. The life of Jesus is shown by Paul's physical survival and by his bringing the life of Jesus to others [He]. The life of Jesus is the fountain of eternal life that Jesus himself is and which flows from Jesus [Lns]. It is the power of Jesus' risen life and the enabling of his life-giving spirit which also guarantees Paul's sharing the resurrection life [NCBC]. He is referring to the power of the life of Christ, which enables Paul to do and suffer all that he did, despite his weakness [Ho].

4:12 So-then,[a] death is-at-work[b] in[c] us, but life in[d] you.

LEXICON—a. ὥστε (LN 89.52) (BAGD 1.a. p. 899): 'so then' [LN, Lns; KJV, NIV], 'and so' [HNTC, LN; TNT], 'so' [BAGD, NTC; NLT, NRSV], 'then' [NJB], 'therefore' [BAGD, LN], 'for this reason' [BAGD], 'as a result' [LN], 'accordingly' [AB], 'consequently' [ICC2], 'thus' [WBC; REB], 'this means' [CEV, TEV], not explicit [NAB].

b. pres. mid. indic. of ἐνεργέω (LN 42.3) (BAGD 1.b. p. 265): 'to be at work' [BAGD, HNTC, LN, WBC; NAB, NIV, NJB, NRSV, REB, TEV, TNT], 'to work' [BAGD, LN; KJV], 'to be working' [CEV], 'to keep working' [Lns], 'to be effective' [BAGD], 'to operate' [BAGD], 'to be operative' [ICC2], 'to be active' [NTC], 'to be made active' [AB]. The

phrase 'death is at work' is translated 'we live in the face of death' [NLT]. This verb is not repeated in the second clause, but is repeated in translation by NTC; CEV, NIV, TEV. This verse is translated 'so we live in the face of death, but it has resulted in eternal life for you' [NLT].
- c. ἐν (LN 83.13): 'in' [AB, HNTC, ICC2, LN, Lns, NTC, WBC; all versions except NLT], 'for' [NLT].
- d. ἐν (LN 83.13): 'in' [AB, HNTC, ICC2, Lns, NTC; all versions except NLT], 'for' [NLT].

QUESTION—What relationship is indicated by ὥστε 'so then'?

It is inferential, introducing the logical consequence of what has just been said [AB, HNTC, Ho, Lns, My, NIC2, NTC, SP, TG; CEV, TEV].

QUESTION—In what sense is death at work in Paul?

The death of which he speaks is the persecution he suffers because of his ministry [Lns, NCBC, NIC1, NTC], or the danger and risk of death he faces because of the ministry [EBC, TG, TH, TNTC]. It is suffering which is leading to death [Ho]. It is the suffering related to his ministry which is metaphorically represented as death [NIC2].

QUESTION—In what way is 'life' at work in the Corinthians because of Paul's sufferings?

1. The suffering is an attendant circumstance of the ministry which brings life; the life the Corinthians experience is the result of the ministry for which he is persecuted [ICC1, ICC2, Lns, NIC1, NTC, WBC].
2. The suffering is part of what makes the ministry effective [AB, EBC, HNTC, Ho, My, NIC2, SP, TNTC]. There is a cause and effect relation between his suffering and the life the Corinthians receive [EBC, He, TG, TH].
   2.1 Both 'the death' and 'the life' are manifested in Paul [Ho, My, TNTC]. The death is his own suffering and dying and the life is the divine life of Jesus manifested in him, supporting him and making his ministry effect for benefit to the Corinthians [Ho, TNTC]. By continual exposure to death in their work, and by the fact that they still live, the are able to minister to the Corinthians [My].
   2.2 Through his union with Christ Paul sees himself as suffering vicariously for them in some way [AB, SP]. The disclosure of the saving death of Christ through the apostles' experience produces life for those who come to faith [AB]. Paul's sufferings are an extension of Christ's vicarious sufferings, though of a different order in that Paul suffers as a messenger in imitation of Christ's sufferings [NIC2]. His sufferings have a vicarious quality in that as the leader of the Christian movement he draws upon himself the brunt of the suffering and others are spared it, but the consequence is that spiritual benefit comes to others because of his ministry [HNTC]. Death is imposed from the outside through persecution but also works itself out from within because of his union with the crucified Christ [HNTC].

2.3 The life that he ministers is mediated to them through the comfort he receives from God in his sufferings and which he then passes on [EBC].

QUESTION—What is the relation of the first clause ὁ θάνατος ἐν ἡμῖν ἐνεργεῖται 'death is at work in us' to the second clause ἡ δὲ ζωὴ ἐν ὑμῖν 'but life in you'?

The normal construction for two contrasting clauses like this would be μέν...δέ, the μέν being untranslatable in English but which sets up the expected contrast made explicit by δέ 'but'. The lack of μέν here adds impact to the contrast expressed by the second clause because its conclusion is unexpected [AB, ICC1, My, NIC2].

1. The thought is parallel; the verb in the first clause is implied in the second clause and the preposition ἐν 'in' indicates the sphere wherein death is at work [AB, HNTC, ICC2, Lns, NTC; CEV, KJV, NAB, NIV, NJB, NRSV, REB, TEV, TNT]: death is at work in us, but life is at work in you.
2. The ἐν ἡμῖν 'in us' of the first clause is the sphere wherein death is at work, but the ἐν ὑμῖν of the second clause is a dative of advantage 'for you' [WBC; NLT]: 'it is life for you' [WBC], 'it has resulted in eternal life for you' [NLT].

DISCOURSE UNIT: 4:13–15 [TNTC] The topic is the spirit of faith.

4:13 But[a] having[b] the same spirit of-faith according-to[c] the (thing) having-been-written,[d]

LEXICON—a. δέ (LN 89.124): 'but' [HNTC, ICC2, LN, Lns, WBC; NJB, NLT, NRSV, REB, TNT], not explicit [AB, NTC; CEV, KJV, NAB, NIV, TEV].

b. pres. act. participle of ἔχω (LN 57.1): 'to have' [AB, HNTC, ICC2, Lns, NTC; all versions except NIV, REB, TEV], 'to possess' [LN, WBC]. The phrase 'having the same spirit' is translated 'with the same spirit' [NIV], 'in the same spirit' [REB, TEV].

c. κατά (LN 89.8): 'according to' [Lns], 'in accordance with' [ICC2, LN; NRSV], 'according as' [KJV], 'as' [AB], 'as that referred to' [HNTC], 'as that shown by' [WBC], 'that corresponds to' [NTC], 'as is described in' [NJB], not explicit [CEV, NAB, NIV, NLT, REB, TEV, TNT].

d. perf. pass. participle of γράφω (LN 33.61) (BAGD 2.c. p. 166): 'to be written' [BAGD, LN, Lns, NTC; KJV, NIV]. The phrase 'the same spirit of faith according to the thing having been written' is translated 'the same spirit of faith as the one who wrote' [AB], 'the same spirit of faith as that referred to in the Scripture passage' [HNTC], 'the same spirit of faith as is described in Scripture' [NJB], 'the same spirit of faith, in accordance with the written text' [ICC2], 'the same spirit of faith that corresponds to the one of who it is written' [NTC], 'the same spirit of faith as that shown by the Scripture writer' [WBC], 'that spirit of faith of which the Scripture says' [NAB], 'the same kind of faith the psalmist had when he said' [NLT], 'the Scripture says...(we have) that same kind of faith' [CEV], 'it is written...with that same spirit of faith (we also)' [NIV], 'the Scripture says...in the same spirit of faith (we also)' [TEV], 'the Scripture says...(and we too,) in the same spirit of faith' [REB], 'the Scripture says...(we too have) the same spirit of faith' [TNT].

QUESTION—What relationship is indicated by δὲ 'but'?
1. It contrasts with what was just said in 4:12 [EGT, HNTC, Ho, ICC1, ICC2, Lns]: despite these sufferings and perils this is why we minister.
2. It elucidates what was just said in 4:12, namely that the reason life is at work in the Corinthians is that Paul believes and speaks the gospel [My].
3. It begins a new thought [AB, NIC2, SP].

QUESTION—What is the function of the participle?
It is causal [AB, HNTC, Ho, ICC1, ICC2, My, NIC2, NTC, SP, TNTC, WBC]; because we have the same spirit of faith, we believe and speak. It picks up on the theme of the revelatory nature of the apostolic office, as in 4:1 where the same participle appears [NIC2]. It comes first in the sentence for emphasis [NTC].

QUESTION—How does he use the word 'spirit' here?
1. It means the same disposition or attitude of faith [EGT, ICC1, ICC2, Lns, NIC1, NTC, TNTC], the same kind of faith [TG; CEV, NLT], a shared conviction [EBC].
2. It refers to the Holy Spirit [AB, He, HNTC, Ho, My, NIC2]. The Holy Spirit is designated by the effect produced [Ho].

'I-believed,[a] therefore[b] I-spoke',[c] we also believe, therefore we also speak,

LEXICON—a. aorist act. indic. of πιστεύω (LN 31.35) (BAGD 2 p. 662): 'to believe' [AB, HNTC, ICC2, Lns, NTC, WBC; all versions except CEV, NLT, TNT], 'to believe in God' [NLT], 'to have faith' [CEV, TNT].
b. διό (LN 89.47): 'therefore' [HNTC, ICC2, LN, Lns, NTC; KJV, NIV, NJB, REB, TNT], 'so then' [LN], 'and so' [AB, WBC; NLT, NRSV]. The phrase 'I believed, therefore I spoke' is translated 'I spoke because I had faith' [CEV], 'I spoke because I believed' [NAB, TEV].
c. aorist act. indic. of λαλέω (LN 33.70): 'to speak' [AB, HNTC, ICC2, LN, Lns, NTC, WBC; all versions except NAB, REB], 'to speak out' [NAB, REB]. This aorist verb is translated as a perfect tense: 'I have spoken' [NTC; KJV, NIV]; as present tense 'I speak' [NLT].

QUESTION—What is the speaking he is talking about?
It is the preaching of the gospel message [AB, EBC, He, HNTC, Ho, ICC2, Lns, My, NIC2, NTC, SP, TG, TNTC, WBC].

QUESTION—What is the relation between Psalm 116:10 and Paul's use of it here?
Paul is quoting verbatim from the LXX, in which this psalm is divided into two psalms (114 and 115) and in which this verse appears as the first verse of the second psalm. The Hebrew text of this verse is unclear, but may mean 'I believed when I spoke' or 'I believed for I spoke'.
1. Paul is referring to the context of the entire psalm in Hebrew in which the psalmist speaks of deliverance from death [EBC, Ho, ICC2, Lns, NIC1,

NIC2, NTC, TH, WBC], or faith that persists despite suffering [TNTC]. Speaking proceeds from faith [He, My], or is the effect and proof of faith [Ho]. The psalmist talks about life and death and as Paul meditates on that he shares the same spirit of faith in God as the psalmist [NTC].
  2. Paul has made use only of the wording of the psalm, but without reference to its context [AB, HNTC, SP].

4:14 knowing[a] that the one-having-raised[b] the Lord Jesus also will-raise[c] us with Jesus and will-present[d] us with you.
TEXT—Instead of τὸν κύριον Ἰησοῦν 'the Lord Jesus', some manuscripts have τὸν Ἰησοῦν 'Jesus'. GNT selects the reading 'the Lord Jesus' with a B rating, indicating that the text is almost certain. The reading 'Jesus' is taken by HNTC and WBC.
LEXICON—a. perf. act. participle οἶδα (LN 28.1): 'to know' [AB, HNTC, ICC2, Lns, NTC; all versions except NJB], 'to realize' [NJB]. The participle 'knowing that' is translated 'in the knowledge that' [WBC].
  b. aorist act. participle of ἐγείρω (LN 23.94) (BAGD 1.a.β. p. 214): 'to raise' [AB, BAGD, ICC2, NTC; NIV, NLT, NRSV, REB, TEV, TNT], 'to raise up' [BAGD, HNTC, Lns, WBC; KJV, NAB, NJB], 'to raise to life' [LN; CEV].
  c. fut. act. indic. of ἐγείρω (LN 23.94) (BAGD 1.a.β. p. 214): 'to raise' [AB, BAGD, ICC2, Lns, NTC; NIV, NLT, NRSV, REB, TNT], 'to raise up' [BAGD, HNTC, WBC; KJV, NAB, NJB, TEV], 'to raise to life' [LN; CEV].
  d. fut. act. indic. of παρίστημι (LN 85.14) (BAGD 1.e. p. 628): 'to present' [AB, LN, Lns; KJV, NIV, NLT], 'to bring before' [BAGD], 'to bring us to (himself)' [NJB], 'to bring into (his presence)' [ICC2; CEV, NRSV, REB, TNT], 'to place in (his presence)' [NTC; NAB], 'to lead into (his presence)' [WBC], 'to take us into (his presence)' [TEV], 'to make stand' [HNTC].
QUESTION—What is the function of εἰδότες ὅτι 'knowing that'?
  It shows a reason for speaking [AB, EBC, HNTC, Ho, ICC1, My, NIC2, NTC, SP, TH, TNTC, WBC; CEV, NIV, NRSV]. It states the knowledge which is the basis for his belief and speech [HNTC, Ho, NIC2, TH]. Paul believes and speaks because he knows of Jesus' resurrection and our future resurrection [My, NTC, SP]. The conviction that Christ's resurrection guarantees his own enables him to preach [EBC, TNTC]. It identifies God as the object of faith and therefore the source of the boldness in speech [AB]. Paul preaches based on his firsthand experience of conversion on the Damascus Road [NIC2]. Knowledge is the ground of faith [ICC1, WBC], or strengthens faith which then prompts preaching [TNTC].
QUESTION—What does he mean by 'raise us with Jesus'?
  It denotes union with Christ [Ho, Lns, My, NIC1, NIC2, SP, TH]. It indicates an association in principle with the resurrection of Christ as one event, a harvest of which Christ is the first fruits of all the rest [EBC, Lns,

My, NIC1, NIC2, NTC, TNTC]. Jesus' resurrection is the prototype and ground of the resurrection of all believers [EBC]. It means in the company of Jesus [AB] or in fellowship with him [Ho, WBC]. Jesus will be with them in God's presence [NTC], they will share his destiny [NIC1]. They will share his company, be in communion with him and be in his retinue [He]. It means they will be raised as he was [HNTC, TG], and they will be with him forever [HNTC]. It means to be with him in his resurrection existence [ICC2]. Their resurrection is dependent on his and they will share his glory [ICC1].

QUESTION—In what way would God 'present' Paul with them?

1. It is a reference to eternal reward [AB, He, HNTC, Ho, ICC1, ICC2, Lns, NTC, SP, TNTC]. It means that God will bring them into his glorious presence [Ho]. It is to be presented in honor as opposed to banishment [Lns]. It is living eternally in God's presence [AB, ICC2, SP, TNTC]. He will present them as a bride is presented to her husband [ICC1]. It means to stand blameless in his presence [HNTC]. They will be present before God in communion with Christ [He]. It is appearing before God with all the multitude of the redeemed [NTC].

2. It is a reference to being brought before the seat of judgment [My, NIC2]. They are led into God's presence at the final consummation, but there is also a note of judgment [WBC].

4:15 For^a all-things^b (are) for-the-sake-of^c you,

LEXICON—a. γάρ (BAGD 2. p. 152): 'for' [BAGD, HNTC, ICC2, Lns, NTC, WBC; KJV], 'so' [AB], 'indeed' [NAB, REB], 'you see' [NJB], 'yes' [NRSV], not explicit [CEV, NIV, NLT, TEV, TNT].

b. πᾶν (LN 59.23) (BAGD 2.b.β. p. 633): 'all things' [BAGD; KJV], 'all these things' [HNTC, Lns, NTC; NLT], 'all this' [WBC; CEV, NIV, REB, TEV, TNT], 'all' [LN], 'everything' [AB, ICC2; NAB, NJB, NRSV].

c. διά with accusative object (LN 90.38): 'for the sake of' [AB, ICC2, LN; KJV, NRSV, REB, TEV, TNT], 'on account of' [HNTC, NTC, WBC], 'because of' [Lns], 'for' [CEV], 'for your benefit' [NIV, NJB, NLT], '(ordered) to your benefit' [NAB].

QUESTION—What relationship is indicated by γάρ 'for'?

It introduces an explanation of 4:7–14, especially 4:13–14 [NIC2]. It explains the words 'with you' in 4:14 and expresses the reason for Paul's confidence of being raised and presented in glory with the Corinthians, which is that they were to be partakers of the benefit from all his work and suffering [Ho, ICC2, Lns]. All these things are for sake of the Corinthian believers because God wants all of them present and giving thanks at the resurrection [Lns].

QUESTION—What is meant by πάντα δι' ὑμᾶς, 'all things (are) for the sake of you'?

It refers to his sufferings and hard work in the ministry which were endured for their benefit [AB, EBC, Ho, ICC1, ICC2, Lns, My, NIC1, NIC2, NTC,

SP, TG, TH, TNTC]. It refers to all his experiences of affliction or comfort [HNTC]. It refers to his sufferings as well as their future resurrection [WBC]. It repeats what he has said in 4:12, that death works us and life works in you [NCBC].

so-that[a] **the grace having-extended**[b] **through**[c] **the many,**[d] **the thanksgiving**[e] **may-increase**[f] **to the glory of-God.**

LEXICON—a. ἵνα (LN 89.59): 'so that' [ICC2, LN, NTC, WBC; CEV, NAB, NIV, NJB, NRSV, REB], 'that' [HNTC; KJV], 'in order to' [LN], 'in order that' [HNTC, Lns], not explicit [NLT, TEV, TNT].

b. aorist act. participle of πλεονάζω (LN **59.67**) (BAGD 1.a. p. 667): 'to extend, to be extended' [AB, WBC; NRSV], 'to grow' [BAGD], 'to increase' [BAGD; TNT], 'to become more and more' [LN], 'to multiply' [LN], 'to be expanded' [HNTC], 'to enlarge scope' [ICC2], 'to multiply, to be multiplied' [LN, Lns, NTC], 'to be bestowed in abundance' [NAB], 'to reach (more and more people)' [NIV, TEV], 'to spread' [NJB], not explicit [CEV, NLT, REB]. This verb is also translated as a noun: 'abundant' [KJV]. The phrase 'so that the grace having extended through the many' is translated 'so that more and more people will know how kind God is' [CEV], 'as God's grace brings more and more people to Christ' [NLT], 'as the abounding grace of God is shared by more and more' [REB].

c. διά with genitive object (LN 84.29, 89.76, 90.4): 'through' [AB, HNTC, ICC2, LN (84.29, 90.4), NTC; KJV], 'by means of' [LN (89.76), Lns], 'to' [WBC; NRSV], 'among' [NJB], not explicit [CEV, NAB, NIV, NLT, REB, TEV, TNT]. The phrase 'grace having increased through the many' is translated 'the abounding grace of God is shared by more and more' [REB], 'God's grace reaches more and more' [TEV], 'the grace bestowed in abundance' [NAB], 'the grace that is reaching more and more people' [NIV], 'God's grace brings more and more people to Christ' [NLT].

d. πολύς (LN 59.1) (BAGD II.2.a.β. p. 689): 'many' [BAGD, LN; KJV, NAB], 'a great number of' [LN], 'more and more' [BAGD; REB], 'more and more people' [NTC; CEV, NIV, NJB, NLT, NRSV, TEV], 'ever more' [AB], 'yet more' [NTC], 'the growing numbers' [ICC2], 'the multiplied number' [Lns], 'the majority' [HNTC], not explicit [TNT].

e. εὐχαριστία (LN 33.349) (BAGD 2. p. 328): 'thanksgiving' [BAGD, ICC2, LN, Lns, NTC; KJV, NIV, NJB, NLT, NRSV, TNT], 'the chorus of thanksgiving' [REB], 'prayers of thanksgiving' [TEV], 'gratitude' [HNTC, WBC], not explicit [CEV]. The phrase 'that the thanksgiving may increase to the glory of God' is translated 'people will praise and honor him' [CEV]. This word is also translated as a verb: 'to give thanks' [NAB]. There is a play on words between ἡ χάρις 'grace' and τὴν εὐχαριστίαν 'thanksgiving' [AB, HNTC, ICC1, NTC, SP].

f. aorist act. subj. περισσεύω (LN 59.52) (BAGD 2.a. p. 651): 'to increase' [NTC; TNT], 'to cause to increase' [ICC2], 'to abound' [LN], 'to cause to abound' [BAGD, HNTC, Lns, WBC], 'to be in abundance' [LN], 'to overflow' [NJB], 'to cause to overflow' [AB; NIV], 'to redound' [KJV], 'to be many' [NAB], 'to be great' [NLT], 'to be greater' [REB], not explicit [CEV, NAB]. The verb is used transitively: 'that grace may increase thanksgiving' [NTC]; and intransitively 'that thanksgiving may overflow' [NJB], 'that grace might redound to the glory of God' [KJV], 'God's grace will increase' [TNT]. The phrase 'that thanksgiving may increase to the glory of God' is translated 'there will be great thanksgiving, and God will receive more and more glory' [NLT], 'they will offer to the glory of God more prayers of thanksgiving' [TEV]. See this word also at 1:5 and 3:9.

QUESTION—What is meant by ἡ χάρις πλεονάσασα 'grace having extended'?

1. The verb is intransitive and refers to grace extending to more people [AB, Lns, NIC1, NIC2, NTC, TG, TH, TNTC, WBC], or growing in influence among the Corinthians [EBC, HNTC, ICC2].

    1.1 It refers to the spread of the good news; the gospel is spread geographically [TH], or through more and more people being converted [AB, Lns, NIC1, NIC2, NTC, TG, TNTC, WBC]. The result is that thanks is given to God.

    1.2 It refers to God's power as an influence at work in the lives of the Corinthian believers [EBC, He, HNTC, ICC2]. Grace increases among them through the growing numbers within whom it is operative [ICC2], or through the majority of the church recognizing their dependence on God's grace [HNTC]. God's grace expands in their hearts so that they reach more people for Christ who in turn give thanks [EBC]. God's grace spreads among the multitude of believers causes thanksgiving to abound to God's glory [He].

2. The verb is intransitive and refers to God's grace for Paul [EGT, ICC1, NCBC]. God's grace is multiplied toward Paul for his ministry [EGT]. God's grace is granted to Paul in his afflictions [NCBC]. The grace for Paul's ministry is augmented by the fact of the growing numbers of believers, which is an encouragement for Paul, and by the fact that more people pray for his ministry [ICC1].

3. The verb is transitive and the object is τὴν εὐχαριστίαν 'thanksgiving' [SP]; grace, that is, the gift of the ministry, increases thanksgiving among the people.

DISCOURSE UNIT: 4:16–5:10 [NIC2, TNTC; CEV, NAB, NRSV, TEV]. The topic is living by faith [NAB, NRSV, TEV], hope in the face of dying and death [NIC2], faith in the Lord [CEV], the object of faith [TNTC].

DISCOURSE UNIT: 4:16–18 [ICC2]. The topic is the link between present and future.

2 CORINTHIANS 4:16

4:16 Therefore[a] we do not lose-heart,[b] even though[c] our outer[d] self[e] is-being-decayed,[f]

LEXICON—a. διό (LN 89.47): 'therefore' [HNTC, ICC2, LN, Lns, NTC; NIV], 'so then' [LN], 'so' [WBC; NRSV], 'thus' [AB], 'for this reason' [LN; TEV, TNT], 'for which cause' [KJV], 'that is why' [NJB, NLT], 'no wonder' [REB], not explicit [CEV, NAB].

b. pres. act. indic. of ἐγκακέω (LN 25.288) (BAGD 2. p. 215): 'to lose heart' [BAGD, LN, NTC; NAB, NIV, NRSV, REB], 'to faint' [Lns; KJV], 'to become discouraged' [LN, WBC; TEV, TNT], 'to give up' [LN; CEV, NLT], 'to shrink back' [AB], 'to waver' [NJB], 'to neglect one's duty' [HNTC], 'to grow lax' [ICC2], 'to despair' [BAGD]. See this word also at 4:1.

c. ἀλλ' εἰ καί 'even though' [AB; NAB, NRSV, TEV], 'but though' [HNTC, NTC; KJV], 'though' [NIV, NLT, REB], 'instead, although' [ICC2], 'indeed, though' [NJB], 'even if' [TNT], 'but even if' [WBC], 'on the contrary, even if' [Lns], not explicit [CEV]. The phrase ἀλλ' εἰ καί introduces a concessive clause which states a matter of fact [AB, EGT, HNTC, ICC1, ICC2, NTC, SP, TG; NAB, NIV, NLT, NRSV, REB, TEV].

d. ἔξω (LN 83.20) (BAGD 1.a.γ. p. 279): 'outer' [AB, BAGD, Lns, NTC; NJB, NRSV], 'outward' [HNTC, ICC2, WBC; KJV, REB], 'outside' [LN], not explicit [CEV, NAB, NLT]. The phrase 'outer self' is translated 'body' [CEV, NAB, NLT], 'physical being' [TEV, TNT], 'outwardly' [NIV]. The phrase 'our outer self is being decayed' is translated 'outwardly we are wasting away' [NIV].

e. ἄνθρωπος (LN **8.3**) (BAGD 2.c.α. p. 68): 'self' [ICC2, NTC], 'man' [BAGD, HNTC, Lns; KJV], 'person' [AB, WBC], 'being' [NAB, TEV, TNT], 'body' [LN; CEV, NLT], 'human nature' [NJB], 'nature' [NRSV], 'humanity' [REB]. The phrase 'outer self' is translated 'outwardly' [NIV]. This designation is used here to represent the two sides of human nature, the inner man being the spiritual and immortal aspects of a person and the outer man being the material, transitory or sinful aspects of a person [BAGD].

f. pres. pass. indic. of διαφθείρω (LN 23.146) (BAGD 1. p. 190): 'to decay' [HNTC], 'to fall into decay' [NJB], 'to decay gradually' [TEV], 'to be in decay' [REB], 'to be in process of decay' [TNT], 'to waste away' [LN, WBC; NIV, NRSV], 'to be wasted away' [AB], 'to be destroyed' [BAGD, **LN**, Lns, NTC; NAB], 'to be in process of destruction' [ICC2], 'to die' [NLT], 'to gradually die' [CEV], 'to perish' [KJV]. The present tense indicates an ongoing process [AB].

QUESTION—What relationship is indicated by διό 'therefore'?

It indicates the conclusion of his discourse on the resurrection and it also links that discussion with what follows in 5:1–10 about our living either in our earthly body or with the Lord [NTC]. It resumes the sentiment of 4:1 and extends the argument 4:1–15 to what follows [NIC1, NIC2]. It sums up everything he has said in 4:7–15 and returns to the idea of 4:1 [AB]. It looks back to the faith that Paul expresses in 4:13–14 [ICC2]. It looks back to 4:1 and to 4:14–15 and gives Paul's reasons for not giving up, which are his commission to be a minister of a superior covenant, the hope of the resurrection, and his concern for the welfare of the Corinthians [EBC]. Paul is saying that he is not discouraged because of the hope of the resurrection mentioned in 4:14 [EGT, HNTC, ICC1, Lns, My, WBC]. Paul is confident because he knows that God raised Jesus and will raise him, and because of the renewal that happens day by day [SP]. Paul is confident because of the hope of the resurrection and because he knows that his suffering and labor will advance God's glory [Ho]. It links 4:16 with what was just said in 4:15, which is that they don't lose heart because God's grace is spread to more people [TH]. Paul is saying that he does not lose heart because of the renewal of the inner man [TNTC; NAB].

QUESTION—Who is the 'we'?

It refers to Paul, or to Paul and his associates in ministry [Lns, My, NIC2, NTC, SP]. However, it may be applied to all believers, particularly what follows about the inner self and outer self [Lns, NIC2, NTC, TG].

QUESTION—What does he mean by 'outer self'?

It is the outwardly visible, mortal frame [SP], the physical part of human existence [Ho, TG, TH], the visible bodily nature with its phenomenal existence [My], the physical aspect as opposed to the higher, spiritual life [ICC2]. It is the body and the physical powers with the emotions and appetites [ICC1]. It is that aspect of man's mortal physical nature which experiences hardships [AB], it is the outward, physical self of this age which is subject to decay and death [HNTC]. It is his life as a mere man, that which is mortal [WBC]. It is the self in its mortal creatureliness, and which is of this age [EBC], that 'clay jar' which experiences the 'dying of Jesus' and which belongs to this physical world that is passing away [NIC2]. It is the natural life as it exists in the outer world [Lns]. It refers to the body as an entity and is that which is exposed to temptation, danger and decay [NTC].

QUESTION—What is the relation between the 'outer self' and the 'old self' of which Paul speaks in Romans 6 and 7?

1. The outer self is man seen in its perishable physical aspect and is not the same as the old self [AB, EGT, ICC1, ICC2, Lns, NIC1, NIC2, SP].
2. The outer self corresponds to the old self [HNTC, NTC].

QUESTION—Is Paul expressing an anthropological dualism?

Although Paul uses terminology here that was also used in Hellenistic spirit/matter dualism [AB, SP], he does not hold such dualistic ideas, but sees the human being as a unified person which may be seen from two aspects [AB, EBC, HNTC, ICC1, Lns, NIC1, NIC2, NTC, SP, TNTC, WBC]. That Paul sees man as a whole entity is evidenced by his belief in the resurrection of the outer self [NTC, WBC]. If there is any dualism to Paul's thought it is not anthropological but eschatological, a dualism which sees the

Christian as simultaneously living in the present age as well as the age to come [He, HNTC, NIC2].

yet^a our inner^b (self) is-being-renewed^c day by day.^d

LEXICON—a. ἀλλά (LN 91.2) (BAGD 4. p. 38): 'yet' [BAGD, HNTC, ICC2, LN; KJV, NIV, REB, TEV, TNT], 'nevertheless' [Lns], 'at the same time' [NJB], 'but' [CEV], not explicit [AB, NTC, WBC; NAB, NLT, NRSV].

b. ἔσω (LN **26.1**) (BAGD 2. p. 314): 'inner' [AB, BAGD, LN, Lns, NTC; NAB, NJB, NRSV], 'inward' [WBC; KJV]. The phrase 'our inner (self)' is translated 'we ourselves' [CEV], 'inwardly' [NIV, REB, TNT], 'our spirits' [NLT], 'our spiritual being' [TEV].

c. pres. pass. indic. of ἀνακαινόω (LN 58.72) (BAGD p. 55): 'to be renewed' [AB, BAGD, HNTC, Lns, NTC, WBC; all versions except CEV], 'to be in process of renewal' [ICC2], 'to be made stronger' [CEV].

d. ἡμέρα (ἡμέρᾳ καὶ ἡμέρᾳ (BAGD 2. p. 347): 'day by day' [ICC2, Lns, NTC, WBC; KJV, NIV, NJB, NRSV, REB, TNT], 'day after day' [BAGD; TEV], 'daily' [HNTC], 'each day' [CEV, NAB], 'every day' [NLT].

QUESTION—What does he mean by 'inner self'?

It is the heart, the new person [WBC]. It is the new person of the age to come [EBC, HNTC]. It is the higher spiritual life [ICC2]. It is the believer's regenerate spiritual existence [Lns], the spiritual part of his being [TG]. It is the heart, the source of will, emotion, thought and affection [TNTC]. It is the moral personality which is self-aware, thinking, and willing and the life-principle of spirit [My]. It is the spiritual nature, the higher nature, the soul as the subject of the divine life [Ho]. It is the new creation spoken of in 5:17 [AB, NCBC, TH]. It is that part of us that communes with God and is strengthened by the Holy Spirit [NTC]. It is the part of our immaterial being that is opposed to worldliness and is rooted in God, and which can be the home of the Holy Spirit and ruled by him [ICC1].

QUESTION—What is the renewal?

It is growth in knowledge, righteousness, and holiness [NTC]. It is gaining new strength [Ho, My, TG, TH]. It is a daily act of faith that receives and appropriates the life of Jesus [AB]. It is the renewal of Christian existence which requires continual contact with Christ [HNTC]. It is a continual and ever-increasing re-creation in prospect of the coming age of glory [NIC2]. It is the increase in strength by divine grace that continues until death [ICC1, Lns]. It is the gradual transformation in Christian character into the divine likeness, of which he spoke in 3:18 [ICC2]. The renewal occurs because of the hope of the resurrection [WBC].

4:17 For^a the momentary^b light^c (weight) of-our affliction^d

LEXICON—a. γάρ (LN 89.23): 'for' [AB, HNTC, ICC2, Lns, NTC, WBC; NIV, NLT, NRSV], not explicit [CEV, NAB, NJB, REB, TEV, TNT].

b. παραυτίκα (LN **67.109**) (BAGD p. 623): 'momentary' [AB, BAGD, HNTC, Lns, WBC; NIV, NRSV, TNT], 'for a moment' [KJV], 'temporary' [LN, NTC; NJB, TEV], 'transient' [ICC2], 'for the present' [BAGD; NAB, NLT], 'short lived' [REB], not explicit [CEV].

c. ἐλαφρός (LN 86.2) (BAGD 1. p. 248): 'light' [BAGD, HNTC, ICC2, LN, WBC; KJV, NAB, NIV, NJB, TNT], 'trifling' [AB, NTC], 'little' [CEV], 'small' [TEV], 'quite small' [NLT], 'slight' [NRSV, REB]. This adjective is translated as modifying 'affliction' [AB, ICC2, Lns, NTC, WBC; all versions except NAB, NJB]; as modifying the implied noun 'burden' which would correspond with βάρος 'weight' in the second clause of this verse [HNTC; NAB, NJB]. It is also translated as a noun: 'lightness' [Lns].

d. θλῖψις (LN 22.2) (BAGD 1. p. 362): 'affliction' [AB, BAGD, HNTC, ICC2, Lns, NTC, WBC; NRSV, TNT], 'trial' [NAB], 'hardship' [NJB], 'trouble' [LN; CEV, NIV, NLT, REB, TEV]. See this word also at 1:4, 8; 2:4.

produces[a] for-us a greatly-exceeding[b] eternal weight[c] of glory,[d]

LEXICON—a. pres. mid. or pass. (deponent = act.) indic. of κατεργάζομαι (LN 13.9) (BAGD 2. p. 421): 'to produce' [BAGD, HNTC, WBC; NLT, TNT], 'to result in' [LN], 'to bring about' [AB, BAGD, LN], 'to bring' [TEV], 'to work' [NTC; KJV], 'to work out' [Lns], 'to achieve' [NIV], 'to earn for us' [NAB, NJB], 'to get us ready for' [CEV], 'to prepare us for' [NRSV]. This verb is also translated as a noun: 'the outcome' [REB].

b. ὑπερβολή (LN 78.33) (BAGD p. 840): 'far more exceeding' [KJV], 'to a far greater degree, far more' [LN], 'far beyond all measure' [TNT], 'beyond all measure and proportion' [BAGD], 'beyond all comparison' [NAB], 'utterly incomparable' [NJB], 'absolutely incomparable' [AB], 'out of all proportion' [HNTC, WBC], 'immeasurably' [NLT], 'to an utterly extraordinary degree' [ICC2], 'beyond all measure' [Lns; NRSV], 'that exceeds all limits' [NTC]. The expression καθ' ὑπερβολὴν εἰς ὑπερβολὴν is translated 'that will make all our troubles seem like nothing' [CEV]. In conjunction with βάρος 'weight' it is translated 'much greater than' [TEV], 'that far outweighs them' [NIV, REB]. See this construction at 1:8 and 4:7.

c. βάρος (LN **78.23**) (BAGD 3. p. 134): 'weight' [ICC2, Lns, WBC; KJV, NAB, NJB, NRSV, TNT], 'fullness' [BAGD, NTC], 'great' [NLT], 'tremendous, very great' [LN], 'greater (than)' [TEV], 'abundance' [AB], 'load' [HNTC], not explicit [CEV, NIV, REB].

d. δόξα (LN 79.18) (BAGD 1.b.β. p. 203): 'glory' [AB, BAGD, HNTC, ICC2, LN, Lns, NTC, WBC; all versions].

QUESTION—What is the relation of afflictions to glory?

1. Afflictions do not earn or merit glory [AB, Ho, ICC1, Lns, NIC1, NIC2, NTC, SP]. Afflictions produce glory [Ho]. The verb κατεργάζεται 'produces' does not refer to merit since the point of his statement is that there is no correspondence between the suffering and the glory, but rather a great contrast between them [AB, NIC1]. It is God who produces or

brings about glory through affliction [AB, NTC, SP]. Suffering does not cause or merit glory, but is the medium through which God accomplishes his purposes in us [Lns]. The verb means 'working out' as opposed to 'working for' glory [NIC2]. The glory is bestowed by the mercy and grace of God [NIC1].
   2. Trials and affliction earn for us a weight of glory [NAB, NJB].

4:18 we (are) not looking-at[a] the things-which-are-seen[b] but the things-which-are- not -seen; for the things-which-are-seen (are) temporary,[c] but the things-which-are- not -seen are eternal.[d]

LEXICON—a. pres. act. participle of σκοπέω (LN **30.20**) (BAGD p. 756): 'to look at' [NTC; NLT, NRSV, TNT], 'to keep one's eyes on' [BAGD, ICC2, Lns], 'to keep one's eyes fixed on' [HNTC], 'to fix one's eyes on' [NIV, REB], 'to fix one's attention on' [LN; TEV], 'to fix one's gaze on' [NAB], 'to set one's gaze on' [WBC], 'to let one's mind dwell on' [**LN**], 'to keep one's mind on' [CEV], 'to keep thinking about' [LN], 'to focus one's attention on' [AB], 'to look at' [KJV], 'to aim for' [NJB].
   b. pres. pass. participle of βλέπω (LN 24.7) (BAGD 1.b. p. 143): 'to be seen' [AB, BAGD, HNTC, ICC2, LN, Lns, NTC, WBC; all versions except NJB], 'to be visible' [NJB]. The contrast between what is seen and what is unseen is an eschatological contrast between the current temporal reality and the eternal reality to come, not a metaphysical dualism between the real and the ideal or a philosophical dualism between a visible and an invisible world [EBC, HNTC].
   c. πρόσκαιρος (LN 67.109) (BAGD p. 715): 'temporary' [AB, BAGD, HNTC, LN; NIV, NRSV, TNT], 'temporal' [KJV], 'transitory' [BAGD, ICC2; NAB, NJB], 'transient' [Lns, WBC; REB], 'for the moment' [NTC], 'for a while' [LN], 'for a little while' [LN], 'lasts only for a time' [TEV], 'don't last forever' [CEV], 'will soon be over' [NLT].
   d. αἰώνιος (LN 67.96) (BAGD 3. p. 28): 'eternal' [AB, BAGD, HNTC, ICC2, LN, Lns, NTC, WBC; KJV, NIV, NJB, NRSV, REB, TNT], 'lasts forever' [CEV, NAB, NLT, TEV].

QUESTION—What is the function of the genitive absolute μὴ σκοπούντων ἡμῶν τὰ βλεπόμενα 'not looking at the things which are seen'?
   1. It states the grounds for making the preceding claim [ICC1, NTC; NJB, NRSV, TEV, TNT]. Momentary affliction prepares us for an eternal weight of glory because we don't look at what can be seen but what cannot be seen [NRSV]. When we focus attention on the eternal things we minimize hardships [NTC]. We are sure that hardships are light and momentary compared to the glory which they work out for us because we direct our attention to the lasting realities we don't see yet [ICC1].
   2. It states one of the reasons that Paul does not loose heart, which is that he does not focus on what is seen [TNTC].

3. It states the subject about whom what is said in 4:17 is true [Lns, SP]: those for whom affliction produces a weight of glory are those who are not looking at the things which are seen.
4. It states the attendant circumstance of what is said in 4:17 [HNTC, ICC2, WBC; KJV]: affliction produces a weight of glory while we keep our eyes on unseen and eternal things.
5. It is conditional [EBC, He, Ho, WBC; REB]: affliction produces a weight of glory provided that they don't look at the things which are seen.
6. It states the conclusion drawn from believing what is said in 4:17 [NIV, NLT]: light troubles achieve a weight of glory that far outweigh them, so we don't fix our eyes on what is unseen.
7. It states the conclusion to be drawn from the following statement [CEV].
8. There is no causal relation to what was said previously [AB, TG, TH; NAB].

QUESTION—What is the meaning of the paradox 'not looking at the things which are seen'?

It means that they don't focus attention on sufferings and afflictions [NIC1, NIC2, TH]. They don't strive for the goods and enjoyments of the present time [My]. They don't fix attention upon ordinary earthly things, including the things of the outer man [Lns], or on things that are not of ultimate significance [AB]. They don't fix attention on life's conditions and trials but on God's rule over all [WBC]. They don't keep thinking about the things of this life but of the one to come [TG]. Visible troubles will end soon, but future joys are eternal [NLT].

DISCOURSE UNIT: 5:1–10 [HNTC, ICC2, WBC; NIV, NLT]. The topic is a digression illustrating further the relative unimportance of the earthenware container [HNTC], our heavenly dwelling [WBC; NIV], new bodies [NLT], the future beyond death [ICC2].

5:1 For^a we-know that if our earthly^b house^c of-the tent^d be-destroyed^e

LEXICON—a. γάρ (LN 89.23): 'for' [AB, HNTC, ICC2, LN, Lns, NTC, WBC; KJV, NJB, NLT, NRSV, TEV, TNT], 'indeed' [NAB], 'now' [NIV], not explicit [CEV, REB].
   b. ἐπίγειος (LN 1.41) (BAGD 1. p. 290): 'earthly' [AB, BAGD, HNTC, ICC2, NTC, WBC; KJV, NAB, NIV, NLT, NRSV, REB], 'here on earth' [Lns; CEV, TEV], 'on earth' [LN; NJB, TNT].
   c. οἰκία (LN 7.3) (BAGD 1.b. p. 557): 'house' [AB, BAGD, HNTC, LN, Lns; KJV], 'dwelling' [BAGD, ICC2, LN]. The phrase 'our earthly house of the tent' is translated 'the tent that houses us on earth' [NJB], 'the earthly tent in which we dwell' [NAB], 'the earthly tent we live in' [NTC, WBC; NIV, NLT, NRSV], 'the earthly frame that houses us today' [REB], 'this tent we live in—our body here on earth' [TEV], 'our bodies are like tents that we live in here on earth' [CEV], 'our bodily home on earth' [TNT], 'our earthly bodily dwelling' [ICC2].

2 CORINTHIANS 5:1

d. σκῆνος (LN **8.5**): 'tent' [HNTC, Lns, NTC, WBC; NAB, NIV, NJB, NLT, NRSV, TEV], 'tent-like' [AB], 'tabernacle' [KJV], 'body' [LN], 'bodily' [ICC2; TNT], 'frame' [REB]. The metaphor of the tent is also applied to the manner of the destruction of the body: 'if our bodily home on earth should be pulled down like a tent' [TNT].

e. aorist pass. subj. of καταλύω (LN 20.54, 20.55) (BAGD 1.b.β. p. 414): 'to be destroyed' [AB, BAGD, ICC2, LN (20.55); CEV, NAB, NIV, NRSV], 'to be torn down' [BAGD, LN (20.54); TEV], 'to be taken down' [BAGD, HNTC, Lns, NTC], 'to be dismantled' [WBC], 'to be folded up' [NLT], 'to be dissolved' [KJV], 'to be demolished' [REB], 'to be pulled down like a tent' [TNT].

QUESTION—What relationship is indicated by γάρ 'for'?

1. It explains the previous context [EBC, EGT, ICC1, Lns, NIC2, TNTC]. It explains the previous verse, and how 'focusing on the things unseen' lifts us above all 'the things that are seen', which are persecution and death [Lns]. It shows that the preceding statement about momentary affliction that produces glory is related to what follows [TNTC]. It introduces an explanation for 4:17–18 [EGT, NIC2]. It introduces an explanation about what was said in 4:16 about not losing heart [ICC1]. Paul specifies how the believer who faces death receives divine comfort through knowledge of the future spiritual body and being with Christ after death [EBC].
2. It continues the theme of 4:16–18 [NTC, SP, WBC]. It ties 5:1–5 closely to 4:17–18 [AB, TH]. It indicates a continuation of the thought just stated [SP]. It links his statements in 4:16–18 about the inner and outer man and the temporal and eternal things with the discussion that follows in which he reminds them of his teaching on the resurrection [NTC].
3. It indicates the grounds for a preceding statement [AB, Ho, My, NIC2] It is the grounds for saying that tribulation produces eternal glory in 4:17, which is that we know that we have an eternal heavenly home [Ho, My]. It is a strong resumptive, echoing 'therefore we don't lose heart' in 4:16 and anticipating 'therefore we are always confident' in 5:6 [NIC2]. It introduces both the supporting statement for 'we do not lose heart' in 4:16, as well as the support for the argument that earthly tribulation is only temporary [AB]. It introduces a conclusion to what has been said about the visible and invisible, present and future, which is that we can focus on the eternal because we know this about a dwelling in heaven [HNTC].

QUESTION—Is the 'we' of οἴδαμεν 'we know' inclusive or exclusive?

1. It is inclusive of the readers [AB, EGT, HNTC, NIC1, NIC2, NTC, WBC].
2. It is exclusive of the readers [Ho, Lns, My, NCBC]. It refers to Paul and his associates [Lns, My]. It refers only to Paul, who is stating his own conviction: 'I know' [Ho]. It is Paul's own confidence, but one which all believers can share [NCBC].

QUESTION—What is the basis for this knowledge?

This is a reference to commonly held Christian teaching or tradition [He, HNTC, NIC2], or Paul's earlier teaching [NTC]. Paul uses this verb with reference to knowledge that is gained intuitively or by revelation as opposed to γινώσκω, which would be knowledge that is gained by human means such as teaching or investigation [ICC1, NIC1, WBC].

QUESTION—How is ἐάν 'if' used in this sentence?

1. It is used in a conditional statement which states the relation 'if this, then that' [AB, HNTC, ICC2, Lns, NIC2, NTC, WBC; KJV, NIV, NRSV, REB, TNT]. When ἐάν occurs with the aorist subjunctive followed by a present indicative it indicates an axiomatic formula and states that when one condition prevails, then so will the other [AB, NIC2]. It is used in its normal sense of 'if', positing an uncertain possibility of whether or not they would die prior to the parousia [ICC1, Lns, My, NIC1, TG, WBC]. Paul expects them to live to see the parousia but this states the exception for those who don't [ICC1]. He is saying that even if, as it may turn out, his sufferings prove fatal, he has another home in heaven [Ho].
2. It is used in the sense of 'when' [He, TH; CEV, NAB, NJB, NLT, TEV]. It expresses uncertainty only of when it will happen, not that it will happen [TH].

QUESTION—What does he mean by his analogy of the tent which is dismantled?

He is referring to the impermanence and vulnerability of mortal earthly existence [AB, Lns, TH]. He is referring to the body [He, Ho, TG, WBC], which is like a tent in that it is transient [EBC, My, TH], fragile, and impermanent [NIC1, NIC2]. He is referring to the body's vulnerability [EBC, NIC2], its susceptibility to death through persecution [TNTC], its impermanence and insecurity [HNTC]. It is reminiscent of the tabernacle in the wilderness [NIC1, NTC]. It emphasizes the temporary character of the body [NCBC]. Paul is saying that life here is a pilgrimage [ICC1]. The tent represents transitoriness, and the dismantling of the tent represents the end of earthly existence [NTC]. He is using the analogy of the body as a dwelling place for the soul, somewhat in the fashion of Hellenistic philosophy [EGT, ICC2].

we-have[a] a building[b] from[c] God, a house not-made-by-hands[d] eternal in the heavens.

LEXICON—a. pres. act. indic. of ἔχω (LN 57.1): 'to have' [AB, HNTC, ICC2, LN, Lns, NTC, WBC; KJV, NAB, NIV, NLT, NRSV], 'to possess' [REB]. The phrase 'we have' is translated 'there is' [NJB]. The phrase 'we have...from God' is translated 'God will give each of us' [CEV], 'God will have for us' [TEV], 'God has for us' [TNT]. This verb is translated in the present tense by AB, HNTC, ICC2, Lns, NTC, WBC; KJV, NAB, NIV, NJB, NRSV, REB, TNT; in the future tense by NLT, CEV, TEV.

2 CORINTHIANS 5:1

b. οἰκοδομή (LN **42.34**) (BAGD 2.b. p. 559): 'building' [AB, BAGD, HNTC, ICC2, Lns; CEV, KJV, NIV, NRSV, REB], 'a solid building, a house' [TNT], 'house' [NTC; NJB] 'a house to live in' [TEV], 'home' [NLT], 'construction' [LN], 'dwelling' [NAB], 'a place to live' [CEV], not explicit [WBC; NJB].

c. ἐκ (LN 90.16) (BAGD 3.c. p. 235): 'from' [AB, BAGD, ICC2, LN, Lns, NTC, WBC; NIV, NJB, NRSV], 'that comes from' [HNTC], 'of' [KJV], 'provided by' [NAB], 'made by' [NLT], 'which God has provided' [REB], 'God will give' [CEV], 'God will have' [TEV], 'God has' [TNT].

d. ἀχειροποίητος (LN **42.33**) (BAGD p. 128): 'not made by hands' [NAB], 'not made with hands' [AB, HNTC, Lns, NTC; KJV, NRSV, TNT], 'not made by human hands' [BAGD, ICC2, **LN**; NJB, NLT, REB], 'not built by human hands' [WBC; NIV], 'not man-made' [LN], 'not buildings someone has made' [CEV], not explicit [TEV].

QUESTION—What is the 'building'?
1. It is the spiritual or resurrection body [EBC, EGT, He, HNTC, ICC1, ICC2, My, NAC, NCBC, NIC1, NIC2, SP, TG, TNTC, WBC; NLT].
1.1 It is the new body which is received at the parousia [EBC, EGT, He, HNTC, ICC1, My, NCBC, NIC1, NIC2, SP, TG, TNTC, WBC].
1.2 It is a new body received immediately upon death [ICC2, NAC].
2. It is a mansion in heaven which is the believer's dwelling [Ho].
3. It is God's presence which covers the believer with eternal glory immediately upon death [NTC].
4. It is an image for the new age to which believers belong, the new eschatological Jerusalem [AB].
5. It is our heavenly existence, and which corresponds to what he has already referred to as an eternal weight of glory [Lns].

QUESTION—What contrast is implied by the adjective ἀχειροποίητος 'not made by hands'?

It contrasts earthly bodies, which are brought to birth through human effort, with the resurrection body [He, NTC]. It contrasts bodies that are from the earth with something that comes wholly from God and is permanent [WBC]. It contrasts that which is natural with what is supernatural or spiritual [AB, ICC1, ICC2, TH]. It emphasizes the supernatural character and origin of the heavenly body [EGT, My]. It contrasts with 'the things which are seen' in 4:18 and is parallel with the 'things which are not seen' which are from God [HNTC]. The contrast applies to the figure of the heavenly building, which is not made with hands, and not to the natural body; that is, we have a house but it is a supernatural one and not a natural or man-made one [Ho, My]. Ἀχειροποίητος means that it is entirely of divine origin [NCBC, NIC2, TH]. The tent represents our earthly existence, which is based on what our hands make and do for us, and contrasts with the heavenly existence which is based on what God does [Lns].

5:2 For[a] indeed[b] in this[c] we-groan[d] longing[e] to-be-clothed-with[f] our dwelling[g] from heaven,

LEXICON—a. γάρ (LN 89.23) (BAGD 1.e. p. 152): 'for' [BAGD, HNTC, ICC2, LN, Lns, NTC], 'also' [AB], 'and' [WBC], not explicit [CEV, NAB, NIV, NLT, REB, TNT].

    b. καί (LN 91.12): 'indeed' [AB, ICC2, LN, NTC, WBC], 'in addition' [Lns], 'and' [NJB, TEV], not explicit [KJV, NAB, NIV, NLT, NRSV, REB, TNT]. The phrase καὶ γὰρ 'for indeed' is translated 'also, indeed' [AB], 'indeed' [TNT], 'and indeed' [WBC], 'and' [NJB, TEV], 'for' [HNTC; KJV, NRSV, TNT], not explicit [NAB, NIV, NLT, REB].

    c. οὗτος (LN 92.29) (BAGD 1.b.α. p. 597): 'this' [LN]. The phrase ἐν τούτῳ 'in this' is translated 'in this' [Lns; KJV], 'in this dwelling' [ICC2], 'in this earthly state' [NJB], 'in this present body' [REB], 'in our present bodies' [NLT], 'in this tent' [NTC, WBC; NRSV], 'while we are in this tent' [TNT], 'while we are here' [NAB], 'while we are here on earth' [CEV], 'meanwhile' [NIV], 'now' [TEV], 'in view of this' [AB], 'for this reason' [BAGD].

    d. pres. act. indic. of στενάζω (LN 25.143) (BAGD p. 766): 'to groan' [BAGD, HNTC, ICC2, LN, Lns, NTC, WBC; KJV, NAB, NIV, NJB, NRSV, REB], 'to sigh' [AB, BAGD, LN; CEV, TEV], 'to cry out for' [TNT], 'to grow weary' [NLT].

    e. pres. act. participle of ἐπιποθέω (LN 25.18) (BAGD p. 297): 'to long' [AB, BAGD, HNTC, ICC2, LN, Lns, NTC, WBC; NIV, NJB, NLT, NRSV], 'to want' [CEV], 'to earnestly desire' [KJV], 'to yearn' [NAB, REB, TNT]. The participle ἐπιποθοῦντες 'longing' is translated 'so great is our desire' [TEV].

    f. aorist mid. infin. of ἐπενδύομαι (LN **49.2**) (BAGD p. 285): 'to be clothed with' [NIV, NRSV], 'to be clothed over with' [NTC], 'to be clothed upon with' [KJV], 'to clothe ourselves' [AB], 'to be covered by' [REB], 'to put on' [BAGD, Lns, WBC], 'to put on over' [HNTC, LN; NJB], 'to be put on over us' [TEV], 'to put on like new clothing' [NLT], 'to put on as an overgarment' [ICC2], 'to have (our heavenly habitation) envelope us' [NAB], not explicit [CEV]. The phrase τὸ οἰκητήριον ἡμῶν τὸ ἐξ οὐρανοῦ ἐπενδύσασθαι ἐπιποθοῦντες 'longing to be clothed with our dwelling from heaven' is translated 'we yearn for the protection of our heavenly dwelling' [TNT].

    g. οἰκητήριον (LN **85.68**) (BAGD 2. p. 557): 'dwelling' [AB, BAGD, NTC; NIV, NRSV, TNT], 'dwelling place' [**LN**], 'home' [LN; CEV, NJB, TEV], 'habitation' [BAGD, HNTC, ICC2, Lns; NAB, REB], 'house' [WBC; KJV]. The phrase 'to be clothed with our dwelling from heaven' is translated 'to put on our heavenly bodies like new clothing' [NLT].

QUESTION—To what does ἐν τούτῳ 'in this' refer?

    1. It means 'in this body or tent' [EGT, He, HNTC, Ho, ICC1, ICC2, Lns, My, NIC2, NTC, SP, WBC; NLT, NRSV, REB, TNT].

2. It means 'meanwhile, in this time' [NIC1; NIV, TEV], 'in this situation' [TNTC], 'in this earthly existence or state' [TH; CEV, NAB, NJB].
3. It is causal, meaning 'in view of this' [AB]. That is, in view of the fact that we know that we have a building from God, we sigh.

QUESTION—What is the nature of the groaning?

It is a hopeful longing, not of fear [NIC2]. It expresses the desire for something that a believer expects to receive [WBC]. It is a yearning for the full experience of salvation [NIC1]. The groaning is a reflection of the believer's painful suffering and his desire for the new body, as well as the proof of his knowledge of what the future holds for him [SP]. The groaning is because of the present hardships [NCBC]. It is the groaning of frustration, sadness, and unfulfilled desire [TG]. It is a longing based on the inward assurance of the fact of being clothed with the new dwelling [My]. It is a sigh of desire for something good and not a groaning of pain [TH]. It is a longing for the heavenly home, not of sorrow over afflictions [Ho]. The groaning arises out of intense, eager longing [NTC]. The groaning arises out of frustration with mortal existence with all its limitations and decay [EBC]. It arises primarily out of a longing for fulfillment, but partly out of affliction as well [HNTC]. It expresses the tension between suffering and hope [ICC2]. The yearning is the evidence of the reality that he hopes for [ICC1]. It is the sighing of hope and not of despair, indicating the presence of the Holy Spirit within them and confirming that they already belong to the coming age [AB].

QUESTION—What is meant by being clothed with a heavenly dwelling?

1. It is having a new body put over the existing body, which would happen to a person who is still alive at the parousia [EGT, He, HNTC, ICC1, ICC2, My, NIC1, NIC2, NTC, SP, TG, WBC].
2. It is having a new body at the time of death [NAC, NCBC]. The new body is received immediately at the death of a believer [NAC]. Paul does not clearly say when it is received, but implies that it is given as soon as the believer dies [NCBC]. Although the believer receives a new body immediately upon death, here Paul is talking about the preference to receive the new body at the parousia and not to have to go through death [ICC2].
3. It is a polemic against a proto-Gnosticism that denied any eternal bodily existence; Paul is saying that we don't want to be without a body in heaven, but to have a body in heaven [EBC].
4. It means that all who go to heaven receive a heavenly mansion as a dwelling [Ho].
5. It is entering into our heavenly existence at the time of death [Lns]. It is eschatological fulfillment, when mortality is dissolved by immortality and salvation is complete [AB].

5:3 **if indeed^a having-been-clothed^b we-will-be-found^c not naked.^d**

TEXT—Instead of ἐνδυσάμενοι 'having-been-clothed', some manuscripts have ἐκδυσάμενοι 'having-been-unclothed'. GNT selects the reading 'having-been-unclothed' with a C rating, indicating difficulty in deciding which variant to place in the text. The reading 'having-been-unclothed' is taken only by GNT and NRSV ('if indeed, when we have taken it off we will not be found naked').

LEXICON—a. γε καί (LN 91.6, 91.12) (BAGD 3.a. p. 152): 'then, indeed' [LN (91.6) (γέ), 91.12 (καί)]. The phrase εἴ γέ καί is translated 'if so be' [KJV], 'if indeed' [BAGD, NTC; NJB, NRSV], 'presupposing, of course' [AB], 'provided' [NAB], 'since indeed' [WBC], 'because' [NIV], 'inasmuch as' [BAGD], 'on the certain condition that' [ICC2], 'since also' [Lns], 'for' [NLT], 'so that' [TNT], 'in the hope that' [HNTC; REB], not explicit [CEV, TEV].
  b. aorist mid. participle of ἐνδύω (LN 49.1) (BAGD 2.a. p. 264): 'to clothe' [LN], 'to clothe over' [NTC], 'to clothe oneself' [AB, BAGD], 'to be clothed' [KJV, NAB, NIV, NJB, REB, TEV], 'to dress' [LN], 'to put on' [BAGD, HNTC, ICC2, LN, Lns, WBC], 'to put on like clothes' [CEV], 'to put on new heavenly bodies' [NLT], 'to be under (its) covering' [TNT]. NRSV translates the variant ἐκδυσάμενοι 'to take off' [NRSV].
  c. fut. pass. indic. of εὑρίσκω (LN 90.70) (BAGD 2. p. 325): 'to be found' [AB, BAGD, Lns, NTC, WBC; KJV, NAB, NIV, NJB, NRSV, TNT], 'to find oneself' [REB], 'to come into an experience' [LN], 'to be discovered to be' [HNTC], 'to prove to be' [ICC2], 'to be' [CEV, TEV], not explicit [NLT].
  d. γυμνός (LN 49.22) (BAGD 4. p. 168): 'naked' [AB, HNTC, ICC2, LN, Lns, NTC, WBC; CEV, KJV, NAB, NIV, NRSV, REB], 'uncovered' [BAGD], 'stripped bare' [NJB], '(to be) spirits without bodies' [NLT], '(to be) without a body' [TEV], 'unprotected' [TNT].

QUESTION—What is the function of εἴ γε καί 'if indeed'?
  1. It assumes the validity of what was supposed, expressing certainty and not doubt [AB, EGT, HNTC, Ho, ICC1, Lns, NCBC, NIC2, NTC, SP, WBC; NIV, NLT].
  2. It indicates the purpose of the protection of the heavenly dwelling, which is not being found naked [TH; CEV, REB, TEV, TNT].

QUESTION—What is the state of nakedness to which he is referring?
  1. Nakedness would be the soul's existence in a bodiless state [EGT, He, HNTC, ICC1, ICC2, My, NAC, NCBC, NIC1, NIC2, NTC, SP, TH, TNTC, WBC; NLT, TEV].
  2. Nakedness is being homeless, that is, without the heavenly home [Ho, Lns], as are those who are cast out into outer darkness [Lns].
  3. Nakedness is alienation from Christ as opposed to being clothed with Christ, because of having denied one's baptism in some way [AB].

5:4 For[a] indeed, we the-ones being in the tent[b] groan being-burdened,[c]

LEXICON—a. γάρ (LN 89.23) (BAGD 3. p. 152): 'for, because' [BAGD, LN]. The phrase καὶ γάρ 'for indeed' is translated 'for indeed' [ICC2, NTC], 'indeed' [AB; REB], 'for' [HNTC, WBC; KJV, NIV, NRSV, TNT], 'for also' [Lns], 'yes, indeed' [NJB], not explicit [CEV, NAB, NLT, TEV].

b. σκῆνος (LN 8.5) (BAGD p. 755): 'tent' [AB, BAGD, HNTC, Lns, NTC, WBC; CEV, NAB, NIV, NJB, NRSV], 'tabernacle' [KJV], 'earthly frame' [REB], 'earthly tent' [TEV], 'bodily tent' [TNT], 'bodily dwelling' [ICC2], 'body' [LN], 'dying body' [NLT]. The participial phrase οἱ ὄντες ἐν τῷ σκήνει 'the ones being in the tent' is translated as a temporal adverbial phrase: 'while (we are in this tent)' [AB, NTC, WBC; NAB, NIV, NJB, NRSV, TEV, TNT]. See this word also at 5:1.

c. pres. pass. participle of βαρέω (LN 22.18) (BAGD p. 133): 'to be burdened' [BAGD, HNTC, LN, NTC, WBC; KJV, NIV], 'to be weighted down' [ICC2, Lns; NAB], 'to be weighed down' [BAGD], 'to be oppressed' [REB], 'to be troubled' [LN]. The participle βαρούμενοι 'being burdened' is translated 'under a burden' [AB; NJB, NRSV, TNT], 'like a heavy burden' [CEV], 'with a feeling of oppression' [TEV], not explicit [NLT]. See this word also at 1:8.

QUESTION—What is the nature of the groaning?

The groaning is from suffering [Ho, Lns, SP, TH, TNTC], or from a feeling of oppression [TG]. It expresses aversion to the thought of being bodiless [HNTC, ICC1, My, NTC, SP]. It expresses Paul's aversion to the process of dying [ICC2]. It is a groaning from the burden that bodily existence entails [He]. It is a sigh of longing for better things [NCBC, NIC2], a yearning for the new spiritual body [WBC].

QUESTION—What is the burden of which he speaks?

It is the apprehension concerning the bodiless state [HNTC, ICC1, My, NTC]. It is the burden of frailties and limitations [NIC1], or the mortal bodily existence [He]. It is the burden of his sufferings [Ho, ICC2, Lns, NCBC, NIC2, SP, TNTC, WBC].

because[a] not do-we-want to-be-unclothed[b] but to-be-clothed,[c]

LEXICON—a. ἐφ ᾧ(ἐπὶ τούτῳ ὅτι) (BAGD II.1.b.γ. p. 287; also I.11.d. p. 585): 'because' [AB, BAGD, HNTC, ICC2, NTC, WBC; CEV, NAB, NIV, NJB, NRSV, REB], 'for this reason that' [BAGD, Lns], 'for that' [KJV], 'it is (not) that' [NLT, TEV], not explicit [TNT].

b. aorist mid. infin. of ἐκδύω (LN 49.18) (BAGD 2. p. 239): 'to be unclothed' [NTC, WBC; KJV, NIV, NRSV], 'to put off clothing' [ICC2], 'to put off' [Lns], 'to unclothe oneself' [AB], 'to undress' [BAGD], 'to take off clothes, to strip off' [LN], 'to strip' [BAGD, HNTC], 'to be stripped naked' [NAB], 'to be stripped of covering' [NJB], 'to have the old body stripped off' [REB], 'to get rid of our earthly body' [TEV], 'to lose the old body' [TNT], 'to leave these bodies that will die' [CEV], 'to die and have no body' [NLT].

c. aorist mid. infin. of ἐπενδύομαι (LN 49.2) (BAGD p. 285): 'to be clothed' [WBC], 'to be clothed with our heavenly dwelling' [NIV], 'to be clothed upon' [KJV], 'to be clothed over' [NTC], 'to clothe oneself over' [AB], 'to be covered with a second garment on top' [NJB], 'to be further clothed' [NRSV], 'to put on' [BAGD, Lns], 'to put on over' [LN], 'to put on over our body the habitation that comes from heaven' [HNTC], 'to put on an overgarment' [ICC2], 'to have the heavenly dwelling envelop us' [NAB], 'to be covered by the new body put on over it' [REB], 'to have the heavenly body put on over us' [TEV], 'to slip into our new bodies' [NLT], 'to gain the protection of our new body' [TNT], not explicit [CEV].

QUESTION—What is the logical relation indicated by ἐφ ᾧ 'because'?
  1. It indicates the reason for what has just been said about groaning [ICC1, My, NIC2, SP; CEV, NAB, NIV, NJB, NRSV, REB]: we groan and are burdened, because we don't want to be unclothed, but clothed.
  2. It introduces an explanatory comment 'not that', indicating that the second half of the clause that follows is the reason for the groaning [NLT, TEV]: it's not that we want to die, but rather to have new bodies.
  3. It indicates the logical conclusion of what has preceded [Ho]: because we are burdened, we therefore do not wish to die, but to be clothed.

QUESTION—What is meant by being unclothed and clothed?
  1. It refers to being in a bodiless state after death as opposed to having the new spiritual body at the parousia [EBC, EGT, He, HNTC, ICC1, ICC2, My, NIC1, NIC2, SP, TG, TH, TNTC, WBC].
  2. It refers to being in a bodiless state after death as opposed to having the new spiritual body immediately upon death [NAC, NCBC].
  3. It means to lay aside the earthly tent of this existence and enter into one's heavenly home or mansion [Ho].
  4. It means to be clothed with the new life after having received the Holy Spirit by faith [AB].

so-that^a the mortal^b may-be-swallowed-up^c by life.^d

LEXICON—a. ἵνα (LN 89.59): 'so that' [ICC2, LN, NTC; NAB, NIV, NJB, NLT, NRSV, REB, TEV], 'that' [AB, HNTC; KJV], 'in order that' [Lns, WBC; TNT], 'it is because we want' [CEV].
  b. θνητός (LN 23.124) (BAGD p. 362): 'mortal' [BAGD, HNTC, LN, Lns, NTC, WBC; NAB, NIV, NJB, NRSV, TEV, TNT], 'these dying bodies' [NLT], 'mortality' [AB, ICC2; KJV, REB]. See this word also at 4:11.
  c. aorist pass. subj. of καταπίνω (LN 13.43) (BAGD 2. p. 416): 'to be swallowed up' [BAGD, HNTC, LN, Lns, NTC, WBC; KJV, NIV, NJB, NLT, NRSV, TNT], 'to be engulfed' [AB, ICC2], 'to be absorbed' [NAB, REB], 'to be transformed' [TEV], 'to be caused to end' [LN]. The clause καταποθῇ τὸ θνητὸν ὑπὸ τῆς ζωῆς 'the mortal may be swallowed up by life' is translated 'to change them for bodies that will never die' [CEV].

d. ζωή (LN 23.88) (BAGD 1.a. p. 340): 'life' [AB, BAGD, HNTC, ICC2, LN, Lns, NTC, WBC; KJV, NAB, NIV, NJB, NRSV, TEV, TNT], 'everlasting life' [NLT], 'life immortal' [REB], 'bodies that will never die' [CEV]. In the phrase τὸ θνητὸν ὑπὸ τῆς ζωῆς 'the mortal...by life' both nouns have the definite article, thus creating a grammatical or structural balance between 'mortal' and 'life'. The correspondence between the two nouns is represented in translation as 'the mortal...by the life' [Lns], 'mortality...by life' [AB, HNTC, ICC2; KJV], 'what is mortal...by life' [NTC, WBC; NAB, NIV, NJB, NRSV, TEV, TNT], 'these dying bodies...by everlasting life' [NLT], 'mortality...life immortal' [REB].

QUESTION—How would the mortal be swallowed up by life?
1. The immortal heavenly body replaces the mortal earthly body [EBC, EGT, He, HNTC, NCBC, NIC1, TG, TH, TNTC, WBC; CEV, TNT].
2. Death and mortality in this age will be replaced by the immortal life of the coming age [Ho, ICC1, ICC2, Lns, My, NIC2, NTC, SP]. When salvation is complete everything that pertains to mortal existence is overcome [AB].

5:5 Now^a the one-having-prepared^b us for this very^c (thing) (is) God,

LEXICON—a. δέ (LN 89.94): 'now' [Lns; KJV, NIV], 'and' [ICC2], not explicit [AB, HNTC, NTC, WBC; CEV, NAB, NJB, NLT, NRSV, REB, TEV, TNT].
b. aorist mid. participle (act. = deponent) of κατεργάζομαι (LN **77.6**) (BAGD 3. p. 421): 'to prepare someone for something' [BAGD, HNTC, LN, NTC, WBC; NLT, NRSV, TEV, TNT], 'to make ready' [LN], 'to equip' [AB], 'to begin production' [ICC2], 'to work something' (transitive) [Lns; KJV], 'to fashion' [NAB], 'to make' [NIV], 'to design' [NJB]. The participial phrase ὁ δὲ κατεργασάμενος ἡμᾶς εἰς αὐτὸ τοῦτο θεός 'now the one having prepared us for this very thing is God' is translated 'God is the one who has made all this possible' [CEV], 'it is for this destiny that God himself has been shaping us' [REB]. The past tense of this participle is translated as 'he who wrought us' [Lns; KJV]. See this word also at 4:17.
c. αὐτὸ τοῦτο 'this very thing' [AB, Lns; NAB, NRSV], 'the selfsame thing' [KJV], 'this very purpose' [HNTC, NTC, WBC; NIV, NJB, TNT], 'this very end' [ICC2], 'this destiny' [REB], 'this change' [TEV], 'all of this' [CEV], 'this' [NLT]. The Greek construction indicates specificity: 'just this thing (and not something else)' [TH].

QUESTION—Is κατεργασάμενος 'having prepared' a reference to God's creation of the believer or to a 'preparation' at some point in the believer's life?
1. It refers to God's creating work and design [NIC1, WBC; NAB, NIV, NJB].
2. It refers to a preparatory work he does in a believer's life [AB, EBC, He, HNTC, Ho, ICC1, ICC2, My, NTC, SP, TG, TH, TNTC; REB, TEV]. The

two actions represented by aorist participles, preparing and giving the Spirit, occur at the same point in time [ICC2, NIC2]. It refers to the act of regeneration [ICC1], or to the giving of the Spirit [NIC2]. The preparation is a producing or shaping of the person toward a certain goal [ICC2, SP; REB].

QUESTION—What is it that God has prepared them for?

The preparation is for the mortal being swallowed up by life [AB, EGT, ICC2, Lns, My, NIC2, SP]. It is the change from a mortal body to an immortal body [EBC, ICC1, NCBC, NTC, TG, TH]. It is for the new life and its restoration of perfect fellowship [WBC]. God has prepared them for a glorious future [TNTC], for the glorious state after the resurrection [He], for the glory of being clothed upon with immortality [Ho, NIC1].

the-one having-given to-us the pledge^a of the spirit.

LEXICON—a. ἀρραβών (LN 57.170) (BAGD p. 109): 'pledge' [BAGD, LN, Lns, WBC; NAB, NJB, REB], 'installment and pledge of what is to come' [TNT], 'first installment' [BAGD, LN], 'first installment of his whole gift' [HNTC], 'guarantee' [LN; NLT, NRSV], 'guarantee of all that he has in store for us' [TEV], 'down payment' [AB, BAGD, LN], 'deposit' [BAGD, ICC2], 'deposit guaranteeing what is to come' [NIV], 'earnest' [KJV]. This noun is also translated as a purpose clause: 'to make us certain that he will do it' [CEV]. See this word also at 1:22.

QUESTION—How are the nouns related in the genitive phrase τὸν ἀρραβῶνα τοῦ πνεύματος 'the pledge of the spirit'?

The words 'pledge' and 'Spirit' are in apposition, that is, the Holy Spirit is the pledge [AB, EBC, EGT, He, HNTC, Ho, ICC1, ICC2, My, NCBC, NIC1, NIC2, NTC, SP, TG, TNTC, WBC; CEV, NAB, NIV, NJB, NLT, NRSV, REB, TEV, TNT].

5:6 Therefore,^a always^b being-confident^c and knowing^d

LEXICON—a. οὖν (LN 89.50): 'therefore' [AB, HNTC, ICC2, LN, NTC; KJV, NAB, NIV, REB, TNT], 'so' [LN; CEV, NLT, NRSV, TEV], 'accordingly' [LN, Lns, WBC], 'then' [LN; NJB].

b. πάντοτε (LN 67.88): 'always' [AB, HNTC, ICC2, LN, Lns, NTC, WBC; all versions except NAB, REB]. This adverb is translated in conjunction with the present participle it modifies as 'we continue (to be confident)' [NAB], 'we never cease (to be confident)' [REB].

c. pres. act. participle of θαρρέω (LN **25.156**) (BAGD p. 352): 'to be confident' [AB, BAGD, HNTC, ICC2, NTC, WBC; KJV, NAB, NIV, NLT, NRSV, REB], 'to be full of confidence' [NJB], 'to be cheerful' [CEV], 'to have courage' [LN; TNT], 'to be full of courage' [**LN**; TEV]. This participle is translated as a participle [AB, ICC2, Lns]; as a present tense indicative verb [HNTC, NTC, WBC; KJV, NAB, NIV, NJB, NLT, NRSV, REB, TEV, TNT]; as an imperative [CEV].

d. pres. act. participle of οἶδα (LN 28.1): 'to know' [AB, HNTC, ICC2, LN, Lns, NTC, WBC; all versions except CEV, NJB], 'to realize' [NJB], not explicit [CEV].

QUESTION—What relationship is indicated by οὖν 'therefore'?

It cites the assurance given by the Spirit in 5:5 as the basis for the confidence expressed in 5:6 [EGT, Ho, ICC1, ICC2, NIC1, NIC2, NTC, TG, WBC]. It draws a conclusion from 4:18 about fixing our eyes on the unseen things and from 5:5 about the assurance given by the Spirit [NCBC]. It cites the hope of eventually receiving the glorified body discussed in 5:1 and the assurance given by the Spirit in 5:5 as the basis for confidence [EBC]. It introduces a conclusion drawn from all that is said in 4:6 through 5:5; because all that is true, we are both confident and certain [Lns]. It refers back to 5:1–5 [HNTC]. It resumes the thought of 4:1 and 4:16, and introduces what follows on the basis of what has been asserted in 4:16 through 5:5 [AB, TH]: that is, because the inner man is being renewed, we look at the unseen things, and we have a dwelling in heaven and the earnest of the Spirit, and therefore we are confident [AB].

QUESTION—What is the relationship of the second participle εἰδότες 'knowing' to the first participle θαρροῦντες 'being confident'?

1. The participles are coordinate [AB, Ho, ICC1, Lns, My, NIC2, NTC, SP, WBC; NAB, NIV, REB, TEV]: they are confident and they know.
2. Εἰδότες 'knowing' is causal [HNTC, NIC1; TNT]: they are confident because they know.
3. Εἰδότες is concessive [He; NLT, NRSV]: they are confident, even though they know.
4. Εἰδότες is the basis for what follows in 5:8 [EBC]: because we know, we prefer.

that (while)[a] being-at-home[b] in the body we-are-away-from-home[c] from the Lord,

LEXICON—a. There is no lexical entry for this word, the grammatical function being expressed by the present tense participle. It is represented in translation as a temporal adverb: 'while' [AB, HNTC, ICC2, Lns, NTC, WBC; KJV, NAB, TNT]; as an adverbial phrase: 'as long as' [CEV, NIV, NJB, NLT, NRSV, TEV], 'so long as' [REB].

b. pres. act. participle of ἐνδημέω (LN **23.91**) (BAGD p. 263): 'to be at home' [AB, BAGD, HNTC, ICC2, Lns, NTC, WBC; KJV, NIV, NJB, NRSV, REB, TEV, TNT], 'to dwell' [NAB], 'to live' [NLT], 'to be alive (here on earth)' [LN], 'to be (in these bodies)' [CEV]. This verb does not occur elsewhere in Scripture.

c. pres. act. indic. of ἐκδημέω (LN **85.21**) (BAGD p. 238): 'to be away from home' [AB, ICC2, Lns], 'to be not at home' [NLT], 'to be away' [BAGD, LN, NTC, WBC; CEV, NAB, NIV, NRSV, TNT], 'to be absent' [HNTC, **LN**; KJV], 'to be exiled' [NJB], 'to be an exile' [REB]. The phrase 'to be away from home from the Lord' is translated 'to be away from the Lord's home' [TEV]. This verb does not occur elsewhere in Scripture.

QUESTION—Does 'body' refer to the human body or the church as the body of Christ?

It is the physical human body [AB, EBC, EGT, HNTC, ICC2, Lns, My, NCBC, NIC1, NTC, TG, TH, WBC; CEV, NAB, NLT].

5:7 for[a] we-live[b] by[c] faith,[d] not by[e] sight,[f]

LEXICON—a. γάρ (LN 89.23): 'for' [AB, HNTC, ICC2, LN, Lns, NTC, WBC; KJV, NRSV, TEV], 'because' [LN], 'this is why' [NLT], 'but' [CEV], not explicit [NAB, NIV, NJB, REB, TNT].

b. pres. act. indic. of περιπατέω (LN 41.11): 'to live' [LN, WBC; CEV, NIV, NLT, TNT], 'to live one's life' [ICC2], 'to conduct one's life' [HNTC], 'to conduct oneself' [AB], 'to behave' [LN], 'to go about doing' [LN], 'to walk' [Lns, NTC; KJV, NAB, NRSV], 'to be guided' [NJB]. The phrase 'we live by faith' is translated 'faith is our guide' [REB], 'life is a matter of faith' [TEV].

c. διά with genitive object (LN 90.8): 'by' [NTC, WBC; CEV, KJV, NAB, NIV, NJB, NLT, NRSV, TNT], 'by means of' [LN], 'by way of' [Lns], 'through' [LN], 'according to' [AB], 'on the basis of' [HNTC], 'in the sphere of' [ICC2], not explicit [REB, TEV].

d. πίστις (LN 31.85) (BAGD 2.d.β. p. 663): 'faith' [AB, BAGD, HNTC, ICC2, LN, Lns, NTC, WBC; all versions except NLT], 'believing' [NLT].

e. διά with genitive object (LN 90.8): All versions and commentaries translate this second use of διά exactly like the first one except ICC2 which renders the second one 'in the presence of (his visible form)' [ICC2].

f. εἶδος (LN **24.1**) (BAGD 1.a. p. 220): 'sight' [LN, Lns, NTC, WBC; KJV, NAB, NIV, NJB, NRSV, REB, TEV, TNT], 'seeing' [**LN**; NLT], 'what is seen' [LN; CEV], 'appearance' [AB], 'the appearance of things' [HNTC], '(in the presence of) his visible form' [ICC2].

QUESTION—What relationship is indicated by γάρ 'for'?

It introduces an explanatory comment about the clause immediately preceding it in 5:6 about being absent from the Lord when at home in the body [AB, EBC, EGT, HNTC, Ho, ICC1, ICC2, Lns, My, NIC1, NIC2, TG, TNTC, WBC]. That is, faith is only possible when Christ is not visible [HNTC].

QUESTION—Is 'faith' objective or subjective?

1. It is the subjective quality of trusting [EBC, HNTC, ICC1, ICC2, Lns, NIC1, NTC, SP, TG, TNTC, WBC; NLT].

2. It is the objective faith concerning what is believed [AB, NIC2, TH].

QUESTION—What relationship is indicated by διά 'by'?

It means 'through the sphere of' [My], or 'in the realm of' [EBC]. It indicates manner [AB, NIC2, NTC], or 'on the basis of' [AB, HNTC]. It is 'by means of' faith and 'with' or 'in the presence of' what is seen, that is, the object of our faith [Ho].

QUESTION—Does 'sight' refer to the faculty of seeing or to what is seen?
1. It refers to what is seen, to appearances; that is, we go by what we believe, not by what we see at the moment [AB, HNTC, Ho, ICC2, My, NIC1, NTC, TH]. We do not see the visible form of Christ [HNTC, ICC2, My]. We do not go by the appearance of things but by faith in God [NTC].
2. It refers to the faculty of sight; that is, we go by believing, not by seeing [EBC, EGT, He, Lns, NIC2, SP, TG, TNTC, WBC; NLT]. Believing is present, seeing is future [SP].

5:8 **we-are-confident, then**[a] **and we-are-pleased**[b] **rather to be-away-from-home**[c] **from the body and to-be-at-home**[d] **with the Lord.**

LEXICON—a. δέ (BAGD 3. p. 171): 'then' [ICC2, Lns; NJB], 'indeed' [NTC], 'yes' [NLT, NRSV], 'I say' [HNTC; KJV, NIV, REB, TNT], 'I repeat' [WBC; NAB], not explicit [AB; CEV, TEV]. This particle is treated as resuming the thought introduced at the beginning of 5:6 [HNTC, ICC2, Lns, NTC, WBC; KJV, NAB, NIV, NJB, NLT, NRSV, REB, TNT].

b. pres. act. indic. of εὐδοκέω (LN 30.97) (BAGD 1. p. 319): 'to be well-pleased' [Lns], 'to prefer' [LN, NTC; NIV, TNT], 'to resolve' [BAGD], 'to be resolved' [AB], 'to be content' [HNTC], 'to be ready' [ICC2], 'to long' [NJB]. The phrase εὐδοκοῦμεν μᾶλλον 'we are pleased rather' is translated 'we would rather' [WBC; CEV, NLT, NRSV, REB], 'we would much rather' [NAB], 'we are willing rather' [KJV], 'we would prefer' [NIV, TNT], 'we would much prefer' [TEV], 'we long instead' [NJB].

c. aorist act. infin. of ἐκδημέω (LN **23.111**) (BAGD p. 238): 'to be away from home (out of the body)' [Lns], 'to be away (from the body)' [NTC, WBC; NAB, NIV, NLT, NRSV], 'to leave (the body)' [BAGD, ICC2; CEV], 'to leave our home (in the body)' [TEV], 'to be absent (from the body)' [HNTC; KJV], 'to go away (from the body)' [TNT], 'to get away from being at home (in the body)' [AB], 'to be exiled (from the body)' [NJB, REB], 'to die' [LN]. This word does not occur in any other passage of Scripture.

d. aorist act. infin. of ἐνδημέω (LN **85.20**) (BAGD p. 263): 'to be at home (with)' [BAGD, ICC2, LN, Lns, NTC, WBC; CEV, NAB, NIV, NJB, NLT, NRSV, TEV, TNT], 'to begin to be at home (with)' [ICC2], 'to make our home (with)' [REB], 'to be present (with)' [HNTC; KJV]. This verb is translated in conjunction with the following pronoun πρός as 'get on home to (the Lord)' [AB]. This word does not occur in any other passage of Scripture.

5:9 **Therefore**[a] **also we-aspire,**[b] **whether being-at-home or being-away-from-home, to-be well-pleasing**[c] **to him.**

LEXICON—a. διό (LN 89.47): 'therefore' [ICC2, LN, Lns, NTC], 'wherefore' [KJV], 'for this reason' [HNTC, LN], 'and so' [WBC; NJB], 'so then'

[LN], 'this being so' [NAB], 'so' [NIV, NLT, NRSV, TNT], 'accordingly' [AB], 'that is why' [REB], not explicit [CEV, TEV].

b. pres. mid. or pass. (deponent = act.) indic. of φιλοτιμέομαι (LN 25.78) (BAGD p. 861): 'to aspire' [BAGD, LN], 'to have as one's ambition' [BAGD, LN], 'to make it one's ambition' [AB, HNTC; NJB], 'to make it one's goal' [NIV], 'to make it one's aim' [ICC2; NAB, NRSV], 'to make it one's honor aim' [Lns], 'to consider it one's aim' [NTC], 'to try' [CEV], 'to be eager' [TNT], 'to labor' [KJV]. The verb phrase 'we aspire' is translated 'our ambition is' [WBC; REB], 'our aim is' [NLT], 'more than anything else, we want' [TEV].

c. εὐάρεστος (LN 25.94) (BAGD 1. p. 318): 'pleasing' [BAGD, HNTC, ICC2, LN], 'well-pleasing' [Lns], 'acceptable' [AB, BAGD; REB], 'accepted' [KJV]. The phrase εὐάρεστοι αὐτῷ εἶναι 'to be well-pleasing to him' is translated 'to please him' [NTC, WBC; CEV, NAB, NIV, NJB, NLT, NRSV, TEV, TNT].

QUESTION—What relationship is indicated by διό 'therefore'?

It introduces the climax or conclusion of the discussion in the preceding verses [AB, NTC]. It introduces the conclusion to be drawn from his statement in 5:8 where he says that he would rather be with the Lord; that is, because we want to be with the Lord, we want to please him [Ho, ICC1, ICC2, My, NIC1]. It introduces the implications for behavior from 5:1–8; that is, because death will bring us into the presence of Christ, we try to please him [EBC]. It introduces a conclusion based on the idea that Christ's coming will bring final meaning to their existence [HNTC]. It introduces a conclusion about the kind of conduct that should flow from the sentiments expressed in 5:6–8 [Lns].

QUESTION—How does εἴτε ἐνδημοῦντες εἴτε ἐκδημοῦντες 'whether being at home or being away from home' fit into the logic of this sentence?

1. It means that the important thing is that they want to be pleasing to Christ regardless of whether or not they are going to continue to live on this earth [AB, EGT, HNTC, ICC1, Lns, My, NIC1, TNTC, WBC]. That is, their aim is to please the Lord in this life, not later [EBC, ICC2].
2. It means that they want to be pleasing to Christ whether in this life or the next [Ho, TG, TH]. It means they want to be pleasing to him now in this life as they no doubt will when they are with him in the next [NCBC].

5:10 For[a] it-is-necessary-that we all[b] be-revealed/appear[c] before the judgment-seat[d] of Christ,

LEXICON—a. γάρ (LN 89.23): 'for' [AB, HNTC, ICC2, LN, Lns, NTC, WBC; all versions except CEV, NAB], 'because' [LN], 'after all' [CEV], not explicit [NAB].

b. πάντος ἡμᾶς 'we all' [AB, BAGD, HNTC, ICC2, Lns, WBC; KJV, NIV, NJB, NLT, REB, TNT], 'all of us' [NTC; NRSV, TEV], 'the lives of all of us' [NAB], 'each of us' [CEV].

c. aorist mid. or pass. infin. of φανερόω (LN 28.36) (BAGD 2.b.β. p. 853): 'to be revealed' [BAGD, LN], 'to have one's life revealed' [NAB], 'to be made known' [LN], 'to be made manifest publicly' [Lns], 'to be seen for what one is' [NJB], 'to have one's life laid open' [REB], 'to appear' [AB, HNTC, ICC2, NTC, WBC; KJV, NIV, NRSV, TEV], 'to stand before' [NLT, TNT], not explicit [CEV]. See this word also at 2:14; 4:10.

d. βῆμα (LN **7.63**) (BAGD 2. p. 140): 'judgment seat' [HNTC, LN, Lns, NTC, WBC; KJV, NIV, NJB, NRSV, TNT], 'tribunal' [BAGD, ICC2; NAB, REB], 'judicial bench' [AB]. The phrase 'appear before the judgment seat of Christ' is translated 'stand before Christ to be judged' [NLT], 'appear before Christ to be judged by him' [TEV], 'Christ will judge us' [CEV].

QUESTION—Does πάντος ἡμᾶς 'all of us' refer to all people or only to believers?

    1. It refers to all believers [AB, EBC, He, ICC1, ICC2, My, NIC1, SP, TG, TNTC, WBC].

    2. It refers to Paul and all the Corinthians [NTC], or to Paul and his helpers and the Corinthians [Lns]. It refers to Paul and the Corinthians, but applies to all believers [NCBC].

    3. It refers to all men [HNTC, Ho].

QUESTION—Is φανερωθῆναι a passive or middle verb form?

    1. It is middle [AB, HNTC, ICC2, NTC, TG, WBC; KJV, NIV, NLT, NRSV, TEV]: we must appear before the judgment seat.

    2. It is passive [EBC, EGT, He, ICC1, Lns, NIC1, SP; NAB, NJB, REB]: we must be made manifest or exposed before the judgment seat.

a) so-that each may-receive-back[a] the-things according-to[b] what he-did[c]
b) so that each may-receive-back[a] according-to[b] the-things which he-did[c]

LEXICON—a. aorist mid. subj. of κομίζω (LN **90.92**) (BAGD 2.a. p. 443): 'to receive back' [AB], 'to receive' [KJV], 'to receive recompense' [BAGD, HNTC, ICC2, NTC, WBC; NAB, NRSV], 'to receive what is due' [NIV, REB], 'to receive one's due' [TNT], 'to receive what one deserves' [NJB, NLT, TEV], 'to be repaid' [LN], 'to carry away' [Lns]. The aorist subjunctive middle verb phrase ἵνα κομίσηται ἕκαστος 'that each may receive' is also translated as a future indicative active: 'Christ will judge us' [CEV].

    b. πρός (LN **89.9**) (BAGD III.5.d. p. 710): 'according to' [AB, LN, Lns; KJV, NAB, TEV], 'in accordance with' [BAGD, LN], 'in relation to' [HNTC, ICC2], 'matched to' [NJB], 'for' [NTC, WBC; CEV, NIV, NLT, NRSV, REB, TNT].

    c. aorist act. indic. of πράσσω (LN **42.8**) (BAGD 1.a. p. 698): 'to do' [AB, BAGD, HNTC, ICC2, LN, Lns, NTC, WBC]. The verb phrase τὰ διὰ τοῦ σώματος πρὸς ἃ ἔπραξεν 'the things which he did in the body' is translated 'his life in the body' [NAB], 'his conduct in the body' [REB].

QUESTION—What is the nature of the judgment and reward that he describes here?

It is not a question of salvation but rather of particular reward for those who are saved [AB, EBC, HNTC, Ho, ICC1, ICC2, NIC1, NTC, TNTC, WBC]. The judgment will be based on the sum of each person's life—the habitual practice and not the individual acts [ICC1, Lns, NIC1, WBC]. The judgment is in terms of reward or loss of reward [TNTC], or praise and blame [NCBC]. Judgment is based on life and actions [ICC2], on faithfulness [TNTC], on the presence or absence of faith as evidenced by actions [Lns], on obedience [WBC], on commitment to the Lord [AB], on actions and character that stem from faith [EBC], on the life that is built upon justification [HNTC], on how believers glorify God in their living [NIC1].

in-the-body, whether good[a] or bad.[b]
LEXICON—a. ἀγαθός (LN 88.1): 'good' [AB, HNTC, ICC2, Lns, NTC, WBC; all versions], 'something good' [Lns].
  b. φαῦλος (LN 88.116) (BAGD 2. p. 854): 'bad' [ICC2, LN, NTC, WBC; CEV, KJV, NAB, NIV, NJB, REB, TEV, TNT], 'something bad' [Lns], 'evil' [AB, BAGD, ICC2, LN; NLT, NRSV].
QUESTION—Does the phrase εἴτε ἀγαθὸν εἴτε φαῦλο 'whether good or bad' refer to what a person has done or the nature of the recompense?
  1. It refers to the conduct that is judged to be either good or bad [He, Ho, ICC1, ICC2, Lns, My, NIC1, NTC, SP, TG, WBC; CEV, NLT, TEV, TNT].
  2. It refers to the nature of the recompense, which is either good or bad [BAGD, NCBC, TNTC; NAB].
  3. It describes both the works and the recompense [AB, HNTC].

DISCOURSE UNIT: 5:11–7:4 [ICC2, TNTC]. The topic is further considerations of Paul's ministry [ICC2], the ministry of reconciliation [TNTC].

DISCOURSE UNIT: 5:11–7:1 [NIC2]. The topic is ministers of God.

DISCOURSE UNIT: 5:11–6:13 [CEV, NAB, NRSV, REB, TEV]. The topic is bringing people to God [CEV], the message of reconciliation [NAB, NRSV, REB], friendship with God through Christ [TEV].

DISCOURSE UNIT: 5:11–6:10 [EBC, ICC1; NJB]. The topic is the function and exercise of the apostolic ministry [EBC], the life of an apostle [ICC1], the apostolate in action [NJB].

DISCOURSE UNIT: 5:11–6:2 [NIV, NLT]. The topic is the ministry of reconciliation [NIV], being God's ambassadors [NLT].

DISCOURSE UNIT: 5:11–21 [HNTC, ICC2, NTC]. The topic is the treasure: the ambassador's message of reconciliation and new creation arising out of the death of Christ [HNTC], the ministry of reconciliation [NTC], motivation and character; basis in the Christ-event [ICC2].

2 CORINTHIANS 5:11   193

DISCOURSE UNIT: 5:11–19 [AB]. The topic is the ministry of reconciliation.

DISCOURSE UNIT: 5:11–15 [WBC]. The topic is the motives for Paul's preaching and living.

5:11 Therefore[a] knowing[b] the fear[c] of the Lord we-persuade[d] people,

LEXICON—a. οὖν (LN 89.50): 'therefore' [AB, LN, NTC, WBC; KJV, NRSV], 'so' [LN; TNT], 'and so' [NJB], 'accordingly' [LN, Lns], 'since then' [HNTC; NIV], 'then' [ICC2], not explicit [CEV, NAB, REB, TEV]. The causal relation implied by this particle used with the participle is also expressed by the phrase 'it is because (we know)' [NLT].

b. perf. act. participle of οἶδα (LN 28.1) (BAGD 2. p. 556): 'to know' [AB, HNTC, ICC2, LN, Lns, NTC, WBC; CEV, KJV, NIV, NLT, NRSV, TEV, TNT]. The phrase 'knowing the fear of the Lord' is translated 'standing in awe of the Lord' [NAB], 'with the fear of the Lord always in mind' [NJB], 'with this fear of the Lord before our eyes' [REB], 'we know what it is/means to fear the Lord' [NIV, TEV]. This present participle is also translated as a past participle: 'having come to know' [Lns]; as a finite verb: 'we know' [HNTC, NTC, WBC; CEV, NIV, NLT, TNT]. This Greek verb does not have a present tense form, so where a present tense meaning is intended, the form of the perfect tense is used.

c. φόβος (LN 53.59) (BAGD 2.b.α. p. 864): 'fear' [AB, HNTC, ICC2, Lns, NTC, WBC; NJB, NRSV, REB], 'solemn fear' [NLT], 'reverence' [BAGD, LN], 'awe' [LN; NAB], 'respect' [BAGD], 'terror' [KJV]. This noun in also translated as a verb: 'to fear' [CEV, NIV, TEV, TNT], 'to respect' [CEV].

d. pres. act. indic. of πείθω (LN 33.301) (BAGD 1.b. p. 639): 'to persuade' [AB, BAGD, HNTC, ICC2, LN; KJV, NRSV], 'to convince' [LN], 'to appeal to' [BAGD], 'to address an appeal to' [REB], 'to be busy persuading' [Lns], 'to attempt to persuade' [NTC, WBC], 'to work hard to persuade' [NLT], 'to try to persuade' [NAB, NIV, TEV, TNT], 'to try to win people over' [NJB]. The phrase ἀνθρώπους πείθομεν 'we persuade people' is translated 'we encourage everyone to turn to him' [CEV]. See this word also at 1:9; 2:3.

QUESTION—What relationship is indicated by οὖν 'therefore'?

It links what he says in this verse about knowing the fear of the Lord back to his reference to the judgment seat of Christ in 5:10 [AB, EGT, Ho, ICC1, ICC2, My, NIC1, NTC, SP, TG, TH, TNTC, WBC]. They try to persuade people to respond to the gospel because they know that everyone must appear before the judgment seat [Aber NOT2]. It draws a conclusion based on what he has said in 5:10 about judgment [SP]. It links 5:11 with what he says in 5:9 about pleasing the Lord and in 5:10 about the judgment seat of Christ [Lns]. It connects what follows with 5:10 and opens a new phase of the discussion [AB]. It marks the conclusion of his digression on ministry and opens a new discussion on reconciliation [WBC]. It resumes his excursus on his ministry in 2:14–4:16 [NIC2]. It links what he has said about

Christ's judgment seat with his fear of the Lord, showing that his whole life and ministry is under God's scrutiny [TNTC].

QUESTION—Who is 'the Lord' that Paul fears?
1. It is Christ [EBC, Ho, ICC1, ICC2, My, NIC2, SP, TG].
2. It is God the Father [AB, He].

QUESTION—What is the nature of that fear?
It is a reverential fear [EBC], a pious reverence [Ho]. It is the fear, though not the dread, of divine judgment [NTC]. It relates not to condemnation but to commendation or the lack of it [NIC2]. This fear is a holy fear that is combined with trust and love, which only believers experience, in contrast with the dread which the ungodly have [Lns]. This fear is inseparable from the hope of 3:12 which makes him bold [NCBC]. It is reverence and awe toward the master he serves in love, and who will also be his judge [NIC1, WBC].

QUESTION—What is meant by 'persuade'?
The present tense is used in a conative sense to indicate what Paul is attempting to do [AB, HNTC, NCBC, NIC2, SP, TG, TH]: 'we try to persuade'. It is used in a durative sense to indicate an ongoing action [Lns, NIC2, WBC]: 'we are busy persuading'. Paul may be quoting his opponents' pejorative use of this word in their criticism of him [ICC1, ICC2].
1. Paul wants to persuade people about his sincerity and integrity, and about the validity of his ministry [EBC, EGT, Ho, ICC1, NIC1, NTC, TG]. Paul is saying that although he is manifest before God, who knows his integrity, he must persuade people to recognize it [ICC1].
2. Paul wants to persuade people to accept the gospel message [AB, EBC, HNTC, ICC2, Lns, NCBC, NIC2, SP, TH, TNTC]. Paul is saying that his preaching is done in integrity and without deception [AB, ICC2, TNTC], that is, with the gospel and not with human argumentation [Lns]. Paul wants to convince people of the truth of the gospel, but also about the purity and sincerity of his motives and the validity of his ministry [EBC, WBC]. This statement is comparable to 4:2 and anticipatory of 5:20 [NIC2].
3. Paul tries to persuade people to make it their goal to be pleasing to the Lord, as he says of himself in 5:9 [My].

and have-been-made-manifest[a] to-God; and I-hope we-have-been-manifest in your consciences[b] as well.

LEXICON—a. perf. pass. indic. of φανερόω (LN **28.36**) (BAGD 2.b.α. p. 853): 'to be made manifest' [Lns; KJV], 'to be made known' [AB, BAGD, LN], 'to be revealed' [LN, NTC], 'to be well known' [NRSV], 'to be fully known' [**LN**], 'to stand open to' [HNTC, WBC], 'to be open to scrutiny' [ICC2]. The phrase θεῷ δὲ πεφανερώμεθα 'to be made manifest to God' is translated 'God himself knows what we are like' [CEV], 'what we are is known to God' [NAB], 'what we are is plain to God' [NIV], 'God sees us for what we are' [NJB], 'God knows we are

sincere' [NLT], 'to God our lives are open' [REB], 'God knows us completely' [TEV], 'God knows us as we really are' [TNT]. The perfect tense refers to something that has effect in the present [AB, HNTC, ICC2, Lns, NTC, WBC]. This word is used in 5:10 of being revealed (or appearing) before the judgment seat; Paul is as transparently open before the Lord now as he will have to be at the judgment [ICC1, NCBC]. See this word also at 2:14; 3:3; 4:10.
- b. συνείδησις (LN 26.13) (BAGD 2. p. 786): 'conscience' [AB, BAGD, HNTC, ICC2, LN, Lns, NTC, WBC; KJV, NAB, NIV, NJB, NRSV], 'moral consciousness' [BAGD], 'heart' [TEV], 'heart of hearts' [REB]. The phrase ἐλπίζω δὲ καὶ ἐν ταῖς συνειδήσεσιν ὑμῶν πεφανερῶσθαι 'and I hope we have been manifest in your consciences as well' is translated 'I hope you also know what kind of people we are' [CEV], 'I hope you know this too' [NLT], 'I hope that you too understand us as we are' [TNT]. See this word also at 1:12; 4:2.

QUESTION—How would they be 'manifest' in the consciences of the Corinthians?

Paul appeals to their consciences, to what they really know in their hearts to be true about him [ICC1, NIC1, TNTC, WBC]. Paul hopes that in the judgment of their consciences his integrity will be obvious to them [ICC2]. He expected that the church as a whole had an inward conviction of his integrity based on their knowledge of his life and character when he was among them [Ho, TG]. He appeals to their unbiased judgment when he says 'your consciences', which is said more searchingly than if he had said 'to you' [Lns]. He hopes that they will recognize his pure motives if they will only be objective about it [HNTC]. His words and actions in ministry are known openly to them and he asks them to attest to his truthfulness and sincerity [NIC2, NTC]. Paul expects that this letter will show his sincerity and honesty [SP].

5:12 We-are- not -commending^a ourselves to-you again but (are) giving to-you an opportunity^b of-boasting^c on-behalf-of us,

LEXICON—a. pres. act. indic. of συνίστημι (LN 33.344) (BAGD I.1.b. p. 790): 'to commend' [HNTC, ICC2, NTC, WBC; KJV, NIV, NJB, NRSV, TNT], 'to recommend' [AB, BAGD, LN, Lns; NAB, REB, TEV], 'to brag' [CEV], 'to pat (ourselves) on the back' [NLT]. See this word also at 3:1; 4:2.
- b. ἀφορμή (LN 22.46) (BAGD p. 127): 'opportunity' [BAGD, ICC2, LN; NAB, NIV, NJB, NRSV, TNT], 'chance' [REB], 'occasion' [BAGD, HNTC, LN, NTC, WBC; KJV], 'a suitable basis' [AB], 'starting point' [Lns], 'favorable circumstances' [LN], 'a good reason' [TEV], 'reason' [NLT], not explicit [CEV].
- c. καύχημα (LN 33.371, 33.372) (BAGD 2. p. 426): 'boast' [BAGD], 'what one boasts about' [BAGD, LN (33.371)], 'the right to boast' [LN (33.372)]. This noun is translated as an infinitive verb: 'to boast' [NTC,

WBC; NAB, NRSV], 'to be proud' [AB, BAGD; NLT, TEV], 'to take pride in' [NIV, NJB], 'to show yourselves proud' [REB], 'to brag' [CEV], 'to glory' [KJV]; as a participle: 'boasting' [HNTC, ICC2], 'glorying' [Lns], 'showing pride' [TNT]. See this word also at 1:14.

that you-may-have (such) toward those boasting in appearance[a] and not in heart.[b]

LEXICON—a. πρόσωπον (LN 24.24) (BAGD 1.d. p. 721): 'appearance' [BAGD, HNTC, LN; KJV, NJB], 'outward appearance' [ICC2; NRSV], 'external appearances' [NAB], 'people's appearance' [TEV], 'what is outward' [AB], 'outward show' [REB], 'what is observable' [NTC], 'what is seen' [WBC; NIV], 'external things' [BAGD], 'what is on their faces' [Lns], 'a spectacular ministry' [NLT], 'the superficial' [TNT]. The phrase 'those boasting in appearance and not in heart' is translated 'those who are not sincere and brag about what others think of them' [CEV]. See this word also at 1:11; 2:10; 4:6.

b. καρδία (LN 26.3) (BAGD 1.b.α. p. 403): 'heart' [BAGD, HNTC, LN, Lns, NTC, WBC; KJV, NAB, NIV, NRSV], 'a sincere heart before God' [NLT], 'inner self' [LN], 'what is within' [AB], 'character' [TEV], 'inner reality' [NJB], 'inward worth' [REB], 'the deeper things' [TNT]. The phrase 'not in heart' is translated 'not sincere' [CEV].

QUESTION—What does he mean by the contrast of boasting 'in appearance and not in heart'?

The message of Paul's opponents has to do with externals and not about the heart being right with God [NTC], or about the inward motive of the message [EGT]. It is a focus on externals as opposed to the inner attitudes [BAGD], on the superficial as opposed to what is genuine [NIC1]. It is a focus on appearance versus reality or real intentions [AB, He], on what is showy as opposed to what is sincere and truthful [HNTC]. He is talking about those who boast in such credentials as Jewish orthodoxy or descent [AB, EBC, EGT, Ho, ICC1, NTC, TNTC], acquaintance with Jesus during his earthly ministry [EBC, EGT, HNTC], letters of recommendation [EGT, HNTC, NTC, SP, TNTC], visions or revelations [AB, EBC, EGT, HNTC, NTC, TNTC], signs or miracles [NTC, TNTC], eloquence [EGT, NTC, SP], forcefulness of character [HNTC], or their experiences and success [SP, TNTC]. He is speaking of the attempt to validate ministry based on the measure of ecstatic speech [NIC2]. Such people appear to be confident in what they teach, but it is a pretense because they care little about spiritual issues [NIC1]. They are deficient in honesty and sincerity [SP]. They appear to be righteous but in their hearts they are wicked because they tear down Paul's work [Lns]. They have the appearance of holiness, zeal and love on their face (πρόσωπον) but lack the reality in their heart [My]. These are non-Christian Jews who boast of the glorified face of Moses and refuse to see the realization of the new covenant in people whose hearts are changed

[ICC2]. They focus on external characteristics and the superficial advantages and privileges of being Jewish, but not on character [ICC1].

5:13 For if we-are-out-of-our-minds,[a] (it is) for[b]-God; if we-are-in-our-right-mind[c] (it is) for[d]-you.

LEXICON—a. aorist act. indic. of ἐξίστημι (LN 30.24) (BAGD 2.a. p. 276): 'to be out of one's mind' [LN, NTC, WBC; CEV, NIV], 'to not be in one's right mind' [LN], 'to lose one's mind' [BAGD], 'to lose one's wits' [Lns] 'to be insane' [LN; TEV], 'to be crazy' [NLT], 'to be out of one's senses' [BAGD], 'to be beside oneself' [AB, HNTC; KJV, NRSV], 'to be mad' [TNT], 'to be in ecstasy' [ICC2], 'to be caught up out of oneself' [NAB], 'to be unreasonable' [NJB]. The phrase 'for if we are out of our minds, it is for God' is translated 'if these are mad words, take them as addressed to God' [REB]. The aorist tense may refer to a specific event or to habitual or occasional conduct referred to as one event [EBC, HNTC]. It is translated as a present tense: '(if) we are' [HNTC, WBC; NIV, NRSV, TNT], '(if) we are ever' [NAB], '(whether) we be' [KJV], '(if) we seem' [CEV, NLT], '(if these) are (mad words)' [REB]; as a perfect tense: '(if) we have been' [NJB], '(if) we have ever been' [AB], '(if) we have' [Lns, NTC]; as a past tense: '(if) we were' [ICC2]. The phrase εἴτε γὰρ ἐξέστημεν 'for if we are out of our minds' is translated as a rhetorical question: 'are we really insane?' [TEV].
  b. There is no lexical entry corresponding to the word 'for', the dative case of θεῷ 'God' being used to indicate that it is the indirect object of the implied verb 'to be'. This relation is translated 'for God' [AB, HNTC, Lns, NTC, WBC; NJB, NRSV], 'for God's sake' [TEV, TNT], 'for the sake of God' [NIV], 'to God' [KJV], 'it was God's concern' [ICC2], 'it is between God and us' [CEV], 'God is the reason' [NAB], 'it is to bring glory to God' [NLT], 'take them as (words) addressed to God' [REB].
  c. pres. act. indic. of σωφρονέω (LN **30.22**) (BAGD 1. p. 802): 'to be in one's right mind' [AB, ICC2, LN, NTC; CEV, NIV, NLT, NRSV], 'to be of sound mind' [BAGD, HNTC, WBC], 'to be sane' [TEV, TNT], 'to keep one's wits' [Lns], 'to be sober' [KJV], 'to be brought back to one's senses' [NAB], 'to be reasonable' [NJB], '(if these words are) sound sense' [REB].
  d. There is no lexical entry corresponding to the word 'for', the dative case of ὑμῖν 'you' being used to indicate that it is the indirect object of the implied verb 'to be'. This relation is translated 'for you' [AB, HNTC, Lns, NTC, WBC; NIV, NJB, NRSV], 'for your sake' [NAB, TEV, TNT], 'for your good' [CEV], 'for your cause' [KJV], 'for your benefit' [NLT], '(it is) your concern' [ICC2], '(take them) as addressed to you' [REB].

QUESTION—In what way would Paul and his co-workers be beside themselves for God or in their right minds for the Corinthians?
  Paul is repeating and responding to a criticism of him current among some of the Corinthians [Ho, Lns, My, SP, TG, TH], and is probably using irony

[BAGD]. Paul has been accused of losing his equilibrium and being carried away [Lns], of being extravagant and exceeding the bounds of discretion in his self-commendation [Ho]. He is accused of being fanatical [NIC1], or of being mad because of his zeal [EGT, Lns, My]. He is criticized for being out of his mind because of his willingness to go to extremes and engage in unreasonable hardship and danger [My, NIC1], or because of his visions and ecstatic experiences [EGT, ICC1, ICC2, My, NIC2, SP, WBC], his worship of God [EGT], or his sudden conversion [ICC1, My]. Paul's opponents disputed his claim to apostleship on the basis of the Damascus road vision, which they ridiculed as madness [Kim]. In contrasting ἐξίστημι 'to be out of one's mind' with σωφρονέω 'to be in one's right mind' Paul is contrasting exceptional conditions of life and ordinary conditions [ICC1, NIC1]. In neither case does Paul serve himself [HNTC, ICC1]. Paul is responding to the Corinthians' perception that he was deficient in his experience of religious ecstasy, which in the Greek world was seen in a very favorable light and as a validator of religious superiority and knowledge [AB, ICC2]. Paul is saying that an ecstatic experience would be between himself and God and would not validate his ministry [AB, ICC2, NIC2, SP]. Paul is saying that if he speaks in tongues it is for God, and not a part of his public ministry, in which he is sensible and in control of himself, using plain reason in order to benefit them [HNTC, NTC, TNTC]. He is saying that if he seems out of his mind, that is God's concern [NCBC; CEV]. Paul divides his behavior into two categories: the ecstatic, which is toward God, and the rational and controlled, which is toward the Corinthians; but whichever is the case, all of his actions are directed toward someone else [WBC]. Because of the persecution and difficulties he endures, very little about his life seems either normal or enviable. And if social respectability and prestige are the marks of a successful minister of the gospel, Paul and his coworkers are so far beyond the pale that they have to be out of their minds [Aber NOT2].

5:14 **For the love of-Christ controls[a] us,**
LEXICON—a. pres. act. indic. of συνέχω (LN **37.17**) (BAGD 7. p. 789): 'to control' [ICC2, **LN**, NTC; NLT, REB, TNT], 'to control our actions' [HNTC], 'to cause to act (in a certain way)' [LN], 'to compel' [WBC; NIV], 'to constrain' [Lns; KJV], 'to urge' [BAGD], 'to urge on' [NRSV], 'to impel' [BAGD; NAB], 'to lay claim to' [AB], 'to rule' [CEV, TEV], 'to overwhelm' [NJB].
QUESTION—Does ἡ ἀγάπη τοῦ Χριστοῦ 'the love of Christ' mean Christ's love for Paul or Paul's love for Christ?
   1. Christ is the subject of the love; that is, he is the one who loves Paul and his co-workers, and his love controls them [AB, EBC, EGT, HNTC, Ho, ICC1, ICC2, LN, Lns, NCBC, NIC1, NIC2, NTC, SP, TG, TNTC, WBC; CEV, NIV, NLT, TNT]: we are controlled by Christ's love for us.

2. Christ is the object of the love; that is, he is the one whom Paul and his co-workers love, and their love for him controls them [He]: we are controlled by our love for Christ.

QUESTION—What does it mean that Christ's love συνέχει ἡμᾶς 'controls us'?

Christ's love controls and governs Paul [Ho] and the direction of Paul's ministry [NIC2]. It restrains him from self-seeking and self-serving [Ho, ICC1, ICC2, My, NIC2, TG], such that he serves God and other people instead [Ho, ICC1, My]. Christ's love holds Paul in its grip as the all-determining factor in his life [SP]. It is the compelling power in his life and ministry [WBC]. Paul is both compelled and limited, having no other option than to love and serve Christ [EBC]. Christ's love confines him to one supreme allegiance [NIC1], and to the task of ministry [EGT, ICC1, Lns]. It controls and motivates him [AB, HNTC, TNTC], and impels him to live for Christ [AB, ICC2]. Christ's love confines him to the conclusion that he draws about the meaning of the death of Christ stated in 5:14 [NCBC]. Paul's opponents are governed by their selfish ambition, but Paul, and all believers, are governed by the love of Christ such that they live for him [NTC]. They are possessed by a love for Christ which is not coerced but which is based on the fact that he died for them [He]. Christ's love, is their all governing motivation for ministry, urging them on in what they do and limiting or constraining them in what they don't do [Aber NOT2].

QUESTION—Who is the 'us' who are controlled by the love of Christ?

The 'us' is Paul himself [ICC2, WBC], or Paul and his co-workers [EGT, HNTC, Lns, My, TG, TH]. It refers to Paul but also to all believers [AB, Ho, NIC2, NTC]. It is autobiographical, referring to his conversion experience, but also represents all believers [NIC2].

having-concluded[a] this, that one died for[b] all,[c] therefore all[d] died;

LEXICON—a. aorist act. participle of κρίνω (LN 30.75) (BAGD 2. p. 451): 'to conclude' [WBC], 'to reach a conclusion' [REB], 'to come to a conclusion' [LN; TNT], 'to be convinced' [NTC; NIV, NRSV], 'to reach a conviction' [NAB], 'to make up one's mind' [HNTC, LN], 'to consider' [BAGD; NJB], 'to judge' [Lns; KJV], 'to make a judgment' [ICC2], 'to be certain' [CEV], 'to believe' [NLT], 'to recognize' [TEV]. This participle is also translated as a phrase: 'our decision having been this' [AB].

b. ὑπέρ (LN 90.36) (BAGD 1.c. 839): 'for' [AB, ICC2, LN, Lns, NTC, WBC; all versions], 'on behalf of' [BAGD, HNTC, LN], 'for the sake of' [LN], 'in place of, instead of' [BAGD].

c. πᾶς (LN 59.23) (BAGD 2.b.α. p. 633): 'all' [AB, BAGD, HNTC, ICC2, LN, Lns, NTC, WBC; KJV, NAB, NIV, NJB, NRSV, REB, TNT], 'everyone' [NLT, TEV], 'everyone else' [CEV].

d. πᾶς: 'all' [AB, HNTC, ICC2, NTC, WBC; KJV, NAB, NIV, NJB, NRSV, TEV, TNT], 'they all' [Lns], 'all of us' [CEV], 'we all' [NLT], 'all mankind' [REB].

QUESTION—What relationship is indicated by the participial phrase κρίναντας τοῦτο 'having judged this'?
1. It indicates the reason the love of Christ controls them [He, HNTC, Ho, ICC2, My, NTC, SP, TNTC, WBC; KJV, NAB, NIV, NJB, NRSV, REB, TEV]: the love of Christ controls us because we are convinced that Christ died for all. This conclusion was reached at the time of Paul's conversion or shortly thereafter [Ho, ICC1, NIC1, NIC2, WBC]. Here Paul states the rational ground of his security in Christ [NIC1, WBC]. Paul's judgment about Christ was changed at his conversion such that he came to understand the significance of Christ's vicarious death, and no longer understood it in a fleshly way as a sign of his having been cursed [Kim]. This verb is used in the sense of judging or evaluating the subject under discussion [Danker].
2. The participle is modal, and expresses a decision or conclusion that accompanies the experience of the love of Christ but is not the basis for it [AB, TH; REB].
3. It indicates the grounds for believing that all have died [NLT]: since he died for all, therefore all have died.

QUESTION—What relationship is indicated by ὑπέρ 'for'?
1. It means that Christ died in behalf of or for the benefit of people [EGT, HNTC, ICC1, ICC2, My].
2. It indicates substitution; Christ died instead of or in the place of people [Lns, NCBC, NIC1, NIC2, NTC, SP, TNTC]. He is their representative [NCBC, NTC, SP], their proxy [WBC]. Christ died as a substitute for people, but that means he also died in their behalf [EBC, WBC]. Christ's representation is inclusive substitution [SP].

QUESTION—Who is the 'all' for whom Christ died and who is the 'all' that died?
When he says 'one died for all' he may be quoting from an early creedal statement [AB, HNTC, ICC2, NTC, SP], a baptismal formula [WBC], or a hymn [NIC2].
1. Christ died for all people [AB, Aber NOT2, EBC, EGT, HNTC, ICC1, Lns, NAC, SP, Stagg].
1.1 All people died [AB, EGT, ICC1, Lns, NAC, SP]. All people are drawn into God's saving purpose and power [AB]. Paul is using a theological shorthand to say that Christ died the death that all should have died, and bore the penalty of their sins. He states the conclusion of a syllogism of which the first two premises are not stated because the Corinthians already know them, which is that all people were subject to the penalty of death for their sins, Christ identified with all sinful people and died, and therefore all died. [NAC].
1.2 All people have potentially died, but only believers have actually died [Aber NOT2, EBC, HNTC, Stagg]. The effect of Christ's death included all people such that all people are redeemed and ransomed and their guilt expiated, but this must be appropriated through faith [Lns]. Just as

Paul can assert in Eph 2:14-18 that Christ's death reconciled Jews and Christians to each other and both groups to God, even though in actual fact there was still deep enmity and much unbelief, so also he can assert that Christ's death was the death of all, even though many people remain in their sin and unbelief. That is, in their place Christ died the death they all deserved because of their sin. In v.14 the 'all' for whom Christ died corresponds in v.19 to 'the world' which God was reconciling to himself through Christ [Aber NOT2].
2. Christ died for all believers, and all believers died [Danker, Ho, Lewis, Mead, NCBC, NIC2, NTC, TH, TNTC, WBC]. The word 'all' is inclusive of Paul's readers, that is, 'all of us' [TH]. The word 'all' is modified and limited by the governing love of Christ and the pronoun 'us' in 5:14 [NTC], and is used in harmony with similar passages in Rom 5:18 and 1 Co. 15:22 [Ho, NTC]. 'All' is used in the same sense as 'world' in 5:19, and both are used in the same sense as in Rom 4:9–12 where God's blessing to Abraham is extended both to circumcised and to uncircumcised, though not to every human being [TNTC]. The second 'all' has the definite article, indicating that it refers to the first 'all', and both are synonymous with the second use of 'many' in Rom 5:15, 19 [NCBC]. Christ died for the all who died when he did; just as Adam's sin became the sin of all united to him, so the work of Christ was the work of all united to him [Ho]. The 'all' is potentially inclusive of all who die in Adam, but in actuality is limited to those who are 'in Christ' through a faith commitment [NIC2]. When Paul uses πάντες ἀνθρόποι 'all men' he refers to all humanity, but when he uses πάντες 'all' he is focusing on allness as opposed to separateness and saying that there are no exceptions or separate ways for Jews or Gentiles. Here πάντες is parallel to and elaborated by τις ἐν Χριστῷ of 5:17, and refers to believers [Danker]. The 'all' for whom he died is 'all of us' who are believers and the 'all' who died are those who have joined Christ in death [Lewis]. Although Paul states elsewhere that Christ died for every person, the purpose clause of 5:15 shows what Paul was intending to stress in this passage, which is that Christ died for believers, especially those in Corinth [Mead].

QUESTION—What relationship is indicated by ἄρα 'therefore'?
1. It draws a conclusion from the statement 'one died for all', which is that all died with him [AB, My, NIC1, NIC2, NTC, SP, TG, TNTC]. It introduces the point that Paul is trying to make [My], which is that because Christ died in their place, then logically all died [TNTC]. It expands the statement that 'one died for all' [HNTC].
2. It draws a conclusion from the statement 'one died for all', which is that all must have been dead [Murphy-O'Connor; KJV]; that is, 'if one died for all, then all were dead' [KJV].
3. It introduces an objection being raised to the statement he just made, and which will be refuted in the next verse; 'Yet, someone will say, all died. True, but . . .' [He].

QUESTION—What was the nature of the death they died?
1. In Christ they died a spiritual death to the old life of sin and self [Ho, My, NIC1, NIC2, NTC, SP, TG, WBC]. Christ's death was a death to sin and self for his people who are united to him in his death [Ho, NIC1, NTC], and who are then able to live for him because they are united with his life [Ho, NTC]. Those who died with Christ have risen with him to be able to live in newness of life [NCBC]. The literal death of Christ brings them a metaphorical death [SP], an ethical death [My], a figurative death, which is the removal of the curse of death [NTC].
2. Because of Christ's death they have potentially died to sin and self, a death which becomes actual through repentance and faith [Aber NOT2, EBC, HNTC, Lns]. To die means they are free to live a life with different goals and purposes [HNTC].
3. They died in the sense that God caused everything old to come to an end when he established a new creation and drew everyone and everything into his saving purpose [AB]. Sinful mankind's pursuit of self-interest was extinguished by Christ's act of love, and his life of love was kindled in them [ICC1].
4. They were already dead, and the death of Christ only proves or demonstrates that state of spiritual death that already existed [Murphy-O'Connor; KJV]. Christ's death shatters the illusion that self-centered living is normal or right and reveals that those who are only alive physically must become alive spiritually through dedication to Christ. [Murphy-O'Connor].

5:15 and he-died for all so-that the-living-ones[a] may-live[b] for-themselves no-longer[c] but (may-live) for-the-one (who) for-them having-died and having-been-raised.

LEXICON—a. pres. act. participle of ζάω (LN 23.88): 'to live' [LN]. This participle is translated 'those who live' [AB, ICC2, NTC; KJV, NAB, NIV, NJB, NRSV, REB, TEV, TNT], 'the living' [HNTC], 'those living' [Lns], 'those who receive his new life' [NLT], 'we' [CEV].
b. pres. act. subj. of ζάω (BAGD 3.b. p. 337): 'to live for (someone or something)' [BAGD]. This verb with the dative plural reflexive pronoun ἑαυτοῖς is translated 'to live for themselves' [HNTC, ICC2, NTC, WBC; NAB, NIV, NJB, NRSV, REB, TEV, TNT], 'to live to themselves' [AB], 'live to please themselves' [NLT], 'to live unto themselves' [Lns; KJV], 'to live for ourselves' [CEV].
c. μηκέτι (LN 67.130) (BAGD 1. p. 518): 'no longer' [AB, BAGD, HNTC, ICC2, LN, Lns, NTC, WBC; CEV, NAB, NIV, NLT, NRSV, TEV, TNT], 'not from now on' [BAGD], 'not henceforth' [KJV], 'not any more' [NJB], 'cease' [REB].

QUESTION—Who are 'the living ones' and in what way do they 'live'?
1. They are those who believe and are spiritually alive in Christ by having died to the old life and the sinful self [AB, EBC, Ho, Lns, My, NAC,

NCBC, NIC1, NIC2, NTC, SP, TG, WBC; NLT]. They are those who view themselves as dead but alive for God and his purposes [Danker].
2. They are all people who are physically alive [Aber NOT2, HNTC, ICC1, ICC2]. Because the participle 'living ones' stands in complementary contrast to 'he died' it would seem more likely for the participle to carry the non-metaphorical sense of 'people who are alive'. By contrast, the mood of the verb 'would live' is subjunctive, indicating a desired effect but not a certain outcome. It is the desired effect that living people would who should have died would chose to die to self and live for him who died for them [Aber NOT2].

QUESTION—Does ὑπὲρ αὐτῶν 'for them' refer to both participles ἀπο θανόντι 'having died' and ἐγερθέντι 'having been raised' or only to ἀποθανόντι 'having died'?
  1. It refers to both participles [EGT, He, ICC1, My, NIC1, NIC2, NTC, SP, WBC]. Although it refers to both participles, with ἐγερθέντι 'having been raised', ὑπὲρ αὐτῶν 'for them' does not mean substitution as it does with ἀποθανόντι 'having died' [NTC].
  2. It refers only to ἀποθανόντι 'having died' [Lns].

DISCOURSE UNIT: 5:16–21 [WBC]. The topic is living in the new age.

5:16 Therefore[a] from now (on)[b] we-know[c] no-one according-to[d] (the) flesh;[e]

LEXICON—a. ὥστε (LN 89.52): 'therefore' [LN, WBC; NRSV, REB], 'wherefore' [Lns; KJV], 'so' [AB, LN; NIV, NLT, TNT], 'then' [NJB, TEV], 'consequently' [ICC2], 'because of this' [NAB], 'hence' [NTC], 'the consequence of this' [HNTC], not explicit [CEV].
  b. ἀπὸ τοῦ νῦν: 'from now on' [AB, ICC2, Lns, NTC, WBC; NIV, NRSV], 'from now onwards' [NJB, TNT], 'henceforth' [HNTC; KJV], not explicit [CEV]. This phrase is expressed in combination with the negation contained in οὐδένα 'no-one' as 'no longer' [NAB, TEV], '(we) have stopped' [NLT], '(worldly standards) have ceased' [REB].
  c. perf. act. indic. of οἶδα (BAGD 2. p. 556): 'to know' [BAGD, HNTC, ICC2, Lns, NTC; KJV], 'to regard' [AB; NIV, NRSV], 'to look on' [NAB], 'to consider' [NJB], 'to judge' [WBC; CEV, TEV], 'to assess' [TNT], 'to evaluate' [NLT]. The phrase 'we know no one according to the flesh' is translated 'worldly standards have ceased to count in our estimate of anyone' [REB]. This Greek verb does not have a present tense form, so where a present tense meaning is intended, the form of the perfect tense is used.
  d. κατά (LN 89.4) (BAGD II.5.b.β. p. 407; II.7.a. p. 408): 'according to' [AB, BAGD, HNTC, LN; NJB], 'after' [KJV], 'in terms of' [NAB], not explicit [CEV, NIV, NLT, NRSV, REB, TEV, TNT].
  e. σάρξ (LN 26.7) (BAGD 6. p. 744): 'human nature' [LN], 'the external side of life' [BAGD]. The phrase 'according to the flesh' is translated 'from a human point of view' [BAGD; NRSV], 'from an outward point of

view' [WBC], 'from a worldly point of view' [NIV], 'from a worldly perspective' [NTC], 'as far as externals are concerned' [BAGD], 'by what they seem to be' [CEV], 'by what the world thinks of them' [NLT], 'in a merely human fashion' [ICC2], 'in a fleshly way' [Lns], 'in terms of mere human judgment' [NAB], 'by human standards' [NJB, TEV], 'by worldly standards' [TNT], 'worldly standards (have ceased to count)' [REB]. See this word also at 1:17; 4:11.

QUESTION—What relationship is indicated by ὥστε 'therefore'?

It indicates a conclusion drawn from what was said in 5:14–15 [AB, EBC, EGT, HNTC, Ho, ICC2, Lns, My, NIC1, NTC, SP, TNTC, WBC]. It connects the discussion of Christ's death in 5:14–15 to the change of thinking that results from it, and which he now describes [NTC]. It connects the idea of being dead to self and alive for Christ in 5:14–15 to the new perspective he now describes [WBC]. Since Paul recognized that Christ died for all, the love of Christ has changed his whole outlook [TNTC]. Paul now draws a conclusion based on the conviction that believers should no longer live for themselves [EGT, NIC1]. It introduces the effect of the Christ event described in 5:14–15 on the way one evaluates other people [ICC2]. He draws the inference from 5:14–15 that they don't judge according to the flesh as their opponents do [My]. Paul is saying that since he has been changed by knowing the love of Christ he does not judge according to the flesh [Ho]. Because of Christ's love he has a new kind of knowledge [SP]. It introduces a parenthetical remark based on what has just been stated [ICC1]. It introduces an exposition of 5:14–15 about how the love of Christ governs them in their relating to others [Lns].

QUESTION—What is the reference point in time for ἀπὸ τοῦ νῦν 'from now (on)'?

It means from the time of Paul's conversion on [EBC, Ho, ICC2, NCBC, NIC1, SP, TG, TH]. It refers to the time that he came to the conclusion described in 5:14 [HNTC, ICC1, My, TNTC], and that conviction mastered him [EGT]. It refers to Christ's death and resurrection but also to the time of conversion, Paul's as well as that of any believer [NIC2]. It refers to the transformation that occurred when Christ died on the cross, because from that point on they could not see the world in the same way [NTC]. It refers to the death of Christ in which God acted decisively [WBC]. It refers to the eschatological 'now' of God's saving love as expressed through Christ's death [AB]. The phrase ἀπὸ τοῦ νῦν focuses more on the resultant idea or consequence than on temporality [Lns].

QUESTION—Who is the 'we'?

1. It is Paul [EBC, Ho, ICC2, SP], or Paul and his associates in ministry [ICC1, Lns]. It is Paul's autobiographical experience, but is expressed in a way that is true of all believers [NIC2]. The ἡμεῖς is emphatic [EGT, Lns, My]: it emphasizes a contrast between Paul and his opponents [EGT, My, NIC2], or between Paul and the Corinthians themselves [Lns, NIC2].

2. It is all Christians [AB].

QUESTION—What does Paul mean by the verb οἶδα 'know'?
It means to evaluate or form an estimation of someone [AB, HNTC, Ho, ICC1, Lns, NCBC, SP, TG, TH, WBC; CEV, NAB, NIV, NJB, NLT, NRSV, REB, TEV, TNT]. It is an appraisal and acknowledgement of others [NIC1]. It refers to how they interact with people as followers of Christ [NTC].

QUESTION—What does κατὰ σάρκα 'according to the flesh' modify?
1. It modifies the verb οἴδαμεν 'we know' [AB, Danker, EBC, EGT, HNTC, ICC1, ICC2, My, NCBC, NIC2, NTC, SP, TG, TH, WBC; CEV, NAB, NIV, NJB, NLT, NRSV, REB, TEV, TNT].
2. It modifies οὐδένα 'no one'. Paul no longer takes account of people on the basis of who they used to be in their old sinful way of living prior to conversion instead of according to their new life as renewed people [He].

QUESTION—What is meant by knowing κατὰ σάρκα 'according to the flesh'?
1. It is objective, referring to the standards by which a person is evaluated; Paul no longer evaluates people from a worldly perspective, in merely human terms or by external standards [AB, Danker, EBC, HNTC, Ho, ICC1, ICC2, My, NCBC, NIC1, NTC, TG, TH, TNTC, WBC; CEV, NAB, NIV, NJB, NLT, REB, TEV, TNT]. It is evaluating a person by appearance instead of by who he or she is as a new creation [EBC, My]. It is judging by the world's standards of outward appearance, social status, race or wealth [NIC1]. It is evaluating by external qualifications for ministry such as eloquence or Jewish ethnicity [EGT]. Paul is addressing the perspective of his opponents whose Jewish nationalism or charismatic manifestations overly valued an impressive outward appearance [Kim].
2. It is subjective, referring to the motives and attitudes of the person who evaluates others; Paul no longer evaluates people according to a fleshly, self-centered, wrong, or sinful approach [HNTC, ICC2, Lns, SP]. He is no longer controlled by natural or carnal ideas and unregenerate motives [Lns].

Even if[a] we-have-known[b] Christ according-to (the) flesh, yet[c] now no-longer we-know (him this way).

LEXICON—a. εἰ καί: 'even if' [NJB, REB, TEV], 'if' [NAB, TNT], 'if indeed' [AB], 'if also' [Lns], 'though' [HNTC, NTC, WBC; CEV, NIV], 'even though' [NRSV], 'although' [ICC2], 'yea though' [KJV]. The phrase εἰ καὶ ἐγνώκαμεν 'even if we have known' is translated 'once I (mistakenly) thought' [NLT].

b. perf. act. indic. γινώσκω (BAGD 1.b. p. 161): 'to know' [BAGD, HNTC, ICC2, Lns, NTC; KJV, NRSV], 'to regard' [AB; NAB, NIV], 'to think of' [NLT], 'to judge' [WBC; CEV, TEV], 'to assess' [TNT], 'to be familiar with' [NJB], not explicit [REB]. This verb is in the perfect tense. It may be that Paul shifts to this verb to show a perfect tense meaning, 'we have known' since οἶδα (used in the previous sentence) conveys a present tense meaning in its perfect tense form [AB, HNTC, NIC1].

c. ἀλλά (LN 89.125) (BAGD 4. p. 38): 'yet' [BAGD, HNTC, ICC2, Lns; KJV], 'but, instead, on the contrary' [LN]. This word is not translated by AB, NTC, WBC; all versions except KJV.

QUESTION—Does the εἰ καί 'even if' refer to a real condition or a hypothetical one?

    1. Εἰ καί introduces a concessive statement about what actually occurred. [EGT, HNTC, ICC1, ICC2, Lns, My, NIC1, NIC2, NTC, SP, TG, WBC].

       1.1 Paul acknowledges that he did once know Christ according to the flesh, but now does so no longer [EGT, HNTC, ICC1, ICC2, Lns, My, NIC1, NIC2, NTC, SP, TG; CEV, KJV, NIV, NLT, NRSV]. The statement is concessive, but also indicates indifference, as though he were saying that it is unimportant what they once did because they don't do so now [Lns].

       1.2 Paul concedes that there may be people who acknowledge Jesus as an earthly messiah, a merely human achievement (κατὰ σάρκα), but who are unable to see past that to acknowledge him as Lord of creation [WBC].

    2. Paul is speaking hypothetically, not about something that actually happened [AB].

QUESTION—Who is the 'we' of this verse?

    1. It is Paul [EBC, ICC2, TG], or Paul and his associates in ministry [ICC1]. The first 'we' is Paul and anyone else, such as his opponents, who may have known Jesus personally during his earthly life, but with the second 'we' he speaks for all believers in terms of his own conversion experience [NIC2].

    2. It is all Christians [AB].

QUESTION—What does knowing Christ 'according to the flesh' refer to?

    1. Paul is referring to a viewpoint that is based only on external, worldly standards [AB, TG, TH; NIV, TEV, TNT]. Paul judged Jesus from superficial human standards of what the Christ should be [EBC, EGT, Ho, ICC1, ICC2, Kim, My, TNTC]. Paul judged Jesus according to what the world thought of him and as though he were only a human being [NLT]. Even though Paul would probably have had some acquaintance with Christ during his earthly life, he is referring to a superficial, worldly or misguided perspective of him [NIC1, NIC2, NTC], a perspective which refused to honor him as God's Son and as the Christ [NTC]. It is an approach to Christ that is fleshly, wrong and sinful [SP]. It is a false estimate of Jesus which does not lead to being controlled by Christ [HNTC]. Paul is referring to how some people, such as his opponents, would view Jesus only in terms of human achievement, as an earthly messiah [WBC]. His opponents focused only on the historical Jesus as a miracle worker or eschatological prophet like Moses, but this would have been looking at him from a purely earthly perspective as Paul did when he judged that Christ could not possibly be the messiah [Kim].

2. Paul is referring to a knowledge of Jesus during his earthly life. He is defending himself from those who will only accept as apostles those disciples who were Jesus' contemporaries [He].

QUESTION—How do they know Christ now?

They know him according to his true, higher spiritual nature [My]. They know him as he really is [NIC1, NIC2], according to the Spirit [NIC2]. Paul knows him as messiah and Lord [EBC]. He knows him by the Spirit and faith [HNTC], and according to his new standing with Christ in the new creation [HNTC]. By faith and the Spirit they must know him for who he fully is, as Christ [WBC]. Now with spiritual vision he sees the meaning and value of Christ's death which he did not see before [NTC]. Paul knows him according to a whole new set of spiritual values [ICC2]. Instead of knowing him according to the flesh they know him in terms of the cross, just as Paul first preached him to the Corinthians [AB].

QUESTION—Does κατὰ σάρκα 'according to the flesh' refer to the verb 'know' or to the persons 'Christ' and 'no one'?

1. It is adverbial and refers to the verb 'know' [AB, EGT, HNTC, Ho, ICC1, ICC2, Lns, My, NTC, SP, TH, TNTC, WBC].
2. It refers to the persons 'Christ' and 'no one' [He].
3. It refers both to the verb 'know' and to the persons [NIC2]. Paul is saying that he knew the historical Jesus, the Jesus 'according to the flesh', and that he knew him in a way that was superficial and misguided, in a fleshly manner [NIC2].

QUESTION—What point of time do the temporal adverbs 'now' and 'from now on' refer to?

The phrase ἀλλὰ νῦν 'but now' means that Paul discarded his old view of things at his conversion [Danker, EGT, HNTC, ICC1, ICC2, My, NIC1, NIC2, NTC, SP, TG, TNTC]. It refers to the time they came to be governed by Christ's love [Lns]. It refers to the eschatological 'now' of God's saving love through Christ's death [AB]. It refers to the new eschatological situation, the new creation in which believers now live [WBC].

5:17 Therefore[a] if anyone (is) in[b] Christ, (he is/there is)[c] a new creation.[d]

LEXICON—a. ὥστε (LN 89.52): 'therefore' [LN; KJV, NIV], 'wherefore' [Lns], 'so' [AB, LN, NTC, WBC; NJB, NRSV], 'consequently' [ICC2], 'a further consequence is' [HNTC], 'this means that' [NAB], 'what this means is that' [NLT], not explicit [CEV, REB, TEV, TNT].

b. ἐν (LN 89.119): 'in' [AB, HNTC, ICC2, LN, Lns, NTC, WBC; KJV, NAB, NIV, NJB, NRSV, TNT], 'in union with' [LN], 'united to' [REB], 'joined to' [TEV]. The phrase εἴ τις ἐν χριστῷ 'if anyone is in Christ' is translated 'anyone who belongs to Christ' [CEV], 'those who become Christians' [NLT].

c. There is no lexical entry for 'he is/there is'. The verb ἐστί 'he is' or ἔστι 'there is' is implied. The implied verb is translated 'he is' [Lns; CEV,

KJV, NAB, NIV, TEV]; 'there is' [AB, HNTC, NTC, WBC; NJB, NRSV, REB, TNT].

d. κτίσις (LN 42.38) (BAGD 1.b.α. p. 455): 'creation' [AB, LN, Lns, NTC, WBC; NAB, NIV, NJB, NRSV, REB], 'act of creation' [HNTC; TNT], 'creature' [BAGD, LN; KJV], '(new) being' [TEV], '(newly created) being' [ICC2], '(new) person' [CEV, NLT]. Some commentaries and versions see this word as representing God's new act of creation [EBC, HNTC, Lns; TNT]. This would correspond with LN 42.35 'creation' which refers to God's activity in creation, as opposed to LN 42.38 'creation, creature' which refers to what results from that activity.

QUESTION—What relationship is indicated by ὥστε 'therefore'?

1. It introduces a second conclusion to be drawn from 5:14–15 [EBC, HNTC, Ho, ICC2, Lns, NIC1, NIC2, NTC, SP, TH], 5:16–17 being parallel and analogous [HNTC, ICC2, NTC, TH]. The conclusion being drawn is that in Christ's death the old way of life ended so that a newly created person could come into being [ICC2, NIC1]. It introduces a summary of what he said earlier about the unity a believer has with Christ [NTC]. It introduces a second parenthetical remark based on what was just said in 5:15 [ICC1]. It also introduces a reason for no longer judging according to the flesh (5:16), which is that they are new people in Christ [Lns].
2. It broadens the point made in 5:16; not only have they abandoned worldly standards, they are part of a new creation [AB].
3. It makes an inference from 5:16: if believers no longer judge by human standards they are different than they were before [My].
4. It states the consequence of taking a higher view of Christ (5:16), which is that those who come to know Christ for who he really is become a new creation [EGT].

QUESTION—What is meant by ἐν Χριστῷ 'in Christ'?

It means to be in union with Christ [Ho, TG, TH; REB, TEV]. It speaks of the personal unity of the believer with Christ [ICC2], or of participation in Christ [SP]. It is to be a member of Christ or of his body [EBC, Ho, ICC1, NTC], existing in intimate fellowship with him [NTC]. It means to be in union and communion with Christ in a living spiritual connection with him [Lns]. It is a union between Christ and a believer in which both remain distinguishable persons but bound inseparably in dying and living together, as well as a union with the body of Christ the church [Stagg]. It means someone who has become a Christian [NLT], who belongs to Christ [CEV], or who has experienced the spiritual death and resurrection described in 5:14–15 [NIC2]. It is an eschatological reality which objectively means being drawn under the rule of his love, and subjectively means a total reorientation of values and principles [AB]. It is someone who has experienced conversion and experienced the eschatological reality of being transferred from the present age to the age to come [HNTC]. 'In Christ' is a summation of the meaning of redemption [NIC1].

QUESTION—Is the καινὴ κτίσις 'new creation' subjective or objective?
1. It is subjective: the person in Christ is a new creation [Aber NOT2, He, Ho, ICC1, ICC2, Lns, My, NCBC, NIC1, SP, TG; CEV, KJV, NAB, NIV, NLT, TEV]. Because redemption fulfils God's original purpose in creation the believer is called a new creation, and as a new person is a microcosm of the eschatological new heavens and earth [NIC1]. While both are true, the focus in this passage is on the individual. Paul is stating the basis for not judging people according to human standards, which is that they are totally different now, they are new creations [Aber NOT2].
2. It is objective: for the person in Christ there exists a new creation [AB, EBC, EGT, HNTC, NAC, NIC2, NTC, TNTC; REB]. It is objective, because God's plan of salvation affects the whole created order, but the primary focus here is on the believer as a part of that order [TNTC]. It is primarily objective, but also subjective; there is a objective new creation out of which the personal and subjective new creation flows [NIC2]. The total environment of those in Christ is new and their previous lifestyles and associations are gone [NTC]. The believer is part of a whole new creation and a whole new age [AB]. In the death and resurrection of Christ there is a whole new act of creation which takes effect subjectively in a believer at conversion [HNTC]. Christ's death and resurrection signal a radical eschatological transition from the old age to the new [NAC].

the old[a] passed-away,[b] look[c] new-(things)[d] have-come.[e]
TEXT—Many manuscripts include τὰ πάντα 'all things' either before or after καινά 'new'. It is omitted by GNT with an A rating, indicating that the text is certain. 'Things' is included either because of the textual variant or by implication by HNTC, Lns, NTC; CEV, KJV, NAB, NRSV.
LEXICON—a. ἀρχαῖος (LN 67.98) (BAGD 2. p. 111): This neuter plural adjective and implied noun which it modifies is translated 'the old' [ICC2; NIV, TEV, TNT], 'what is old' [BAGD], 'everything old' [AB; NRSV], 'all old things' [HNTC], 'old things' [KJV], 'the old things' [Lns, NTC], 'the old order' [WBC; NAB, NJB, REB], 'the past' [CEV], 'the old life' [NLT].
b. aorist act. indic. of παρέρχομαι (LN 13.93) (BAGD 1.b.α. p. 626): 'to pass away' [BAGD, ICC2, LN, Lns, NTC; KJV, NAB, NRSV], 'to cease to exist' [LN], 'to come to an end' [AB, BAGD], 'to go' [HNTC, WBC; NIV, NJB, REB, TEV, TNT]. The phrase τὰ ἀρχαῖα παρῆλθεν 'the old passed away' is translated 'the past is forgotten' [CEV], 'they are not the same anymore, for the old life is gone' [NLT]. The aorist form παρῆλθεν is translated as a having a perfect tense meaning by AB, HNTC, ICC2, Lns, NTC, WBC; NAB, NIV, NRSV, REB, TNT; as a present with a perfect tense meaning 'is gone' [CEV, NJB, NLT, TNT], 'are passed away' [KJV].
c. ἰδού (LN 91.13) (BAGD 1.a. p. 371): 'look' [BAGD, LN, NTC], 'behold' [AB, BAGD, HNTC, ICC2; KJV], 'listen' [LN], 'lo' [Lns], 'see' [BAGD;

NRSV], not explicit [WBC; CEV, NAB, NIV, NJB, NLT, REB, TEV, TNT]. This interjection sounds a note of triumph or jubilation [ICC1, My, NIC1, NIC2, Stagg], and expresses that something of great importance has suddenly happened [Stagg].
- d. καινός (LN 58.71) (BAGD 3.b. p. 394): 'new' [BAGD, LN, Lns; CEV, KJV, NAB, NRSV], 'the new' [ICC2, WBC; NIV, TEV, TNT], 'new things' [AB, HNTC], 'the new things' [NTC], 'things...new' [Lns; KJV], 'a new being' [NJB], 'a new life' [NLT].
- e. perf. act. indic. of γίνομαι (LN 13.80, 13.48): 'to come to exist' [LN (13.80)], 'to become' [LN (13.48)]. The phrase γέγονεν καινά 'new things have come' is translated 'things have become new' [Lns], 'the new has come' [NIV], 'the new things have come' [NTC], 'a new life has begun' [NLT], 'the new has come' [TEV, TNT], 'new things have come to be' [AB], 'new things have come into being' [HNTC], 'the new has come into existence' [ICC2], 'to be replaced by the new' [WBC]. Those versions which reject the textual variant τὰ πάντα 'all things' see 'new (things)' as the subject and γίνομαι takes the meaning 'to come to exist': new things have come. Those which include the textual variant τὰ πάντα see 'new' as a predicate adjective and γίνομαι takes the meaning 'become': all things have become new. (A neuter plural subject such as τὰ καινά or τὰ ἀρχαῖα takes a singular verb.)

QUESTION—What are the old things that have come to an end?
1. The old things are all previous conditions and relationships [EBC], the old form of human life [ICC2], the former sinful condition [ICC1, Lns], the pre-conversion life and lifestyle [My, NTC, TG, TH, TNTC; CEV, NLT]. It is all old allegiances, desires, affections, and viewpoints [Ho]. It is all old things and relationships that were characterized by κατὰ σάρκα 'according to the flesh' [HNTC, SP]. It is all the distinctions, prejudices, enslavements and misunderstandings of the pre-conversion life [NIC1]. Paul is saying that if anyone is in Christ he is no longer judged by the old, fleshly criteria such as the distinctions between Jew and Gentile [Danker, Stagg]. Paul is saying that the sinful past of the believer is forgotten [CEV] or gone [NLT]. It is the former dispensation [ICC1, NIC2], as well as the former self-centered fleshly life of the believer [NIC2]. It is the Jewish ritual observance, old understandings of what the messiah should be and do, and old understandings of God, sin, and salvation [EGT].
2. The old things would be the totality of creation [AB, He, NCBC], the old order [REB]. It is the first or original order as opposed to the new order [AB, He], the present transient age, which is replaced by the coming new age [NCBC].

QUESTION—What is the relationship between καίνα 'new' and the verb γέγονεν 'has become'?
1. Καίνα is a predicate adjective; something old is now new or has become (γέγονεν) new [EGT, Ho, My, NIC1, NIC2; CEV, KJV, NAB, NRSV]. The old things have become new, having received a fresh coloring [EGT].

There is a continuity with the old, not only for the believer, but for the cosmos as well [NIC1]. The cosmos is renewed and transformed but not replaced [NIC2]. The person has become new [Ho, My].
2. Καίνα is the subject; new things have come (γέγονεν) [AB, Aber NOT2, Danker, EBC, He, HNTC, ICC1, ICC2, Lewis, Lns, NCBC, NTC, SP, Stagg, TH, TNTC; NIV, NJB, NLT, REB]; a new order has come [REB], a new age has come [NCBC], a new condition has come [ICC1], new things have come into being [AB], a new being has come [NJB, TEV], a new creation has come [NIV], a new act of creation has come [TNT], a new life has come [NLT]. New relationships [EBC, HNTC] and new conditions have come [EBC], and especially a new attitude toward Christ and other people [EBC]. A whole new way of interacting with one's environment has come [HNTC]. The new order has come or become reality as opposed to the old order of things [Danker]. New outlooks, motives, relationships and actions have come to replace the unconverted existence [Lewis]. He speaks of new things that replace the old, not a renewal of old things [AB, Stagg]. There is a discontinuity with the old, which has passed away [Lns].

5:18 Now[a] all-(things/these-things)[b] (are) from[c] God the-one-having-reconciled[d] us to-himself through Christ

LEXICON—a. δέ (LN 89.94): 'now' [Lns], 'and' [ICC2, LN, NTC, WBC; KJV], not explicit [AB, HNTC; all versions except KJV].
  b. πᾶς (LN 59.23): 'all things' [AB, NTC; KJV], 'all these things' [Lns], 'all' [LN; NJB], 'it all' [CEV, TNT], 'all these consequences' [HNTC], 'all this' [ICC2; NAB, NIV, NRSV, REB, TEV], 'this new order' [WBC], 'all this newness of life' [NLT].
  c. ἐκ (LN 90.16): 'from' [AB, HNTC, ICC2, LN, Lns, NTC; NIV, NLT, NRSV, TNT], 'of' [KJV]. The phrase τὰ πάντα ἐκ τοῦ θεοῦ 'all things are from God' is translated 'God has done it all' [CEV], 'all this has been done by God' [NAB], 'all this is done by God' [TEV], 'it is all God's work' [NJB], 'all this has been the work of God' [REB], 'all this newness of life is from God' [NLT], 'it all comes from God' [TNT], 'all these consequences come from God' [HNTC], 'and this new order in all respects is God's doing' [WBC].
  d. aorist act. participle of καταλλάσσω (LN **40.1**) (BAGD 1. p. 414): 'to reconcile' [AB, BAGD, HNTC, ICC2, LN, Lns, NTC, WBC; all versions except CEV, NLT, TEV]. The phrase τοῦ καταλλάξαντος ἡμᾶς ἑαυτῷ διὰ Χριστοῦ 'the one having reconciled us to himself through Christ' is translated 'he sent Christ to make peace between himself and us' [CEV], 'who brought us back to himself through what Christ did' [NLT], 'who through Christ changed us from enemies into his friends' [TEV].
QUESTION—What is the function of δέ 'now'?
  (Most English versions leave δέ untranslated).

1. It continues the thought expressed in the previous few verses [AB, ICC2, LN, Lns, NTC, WBC; KJV].
2. It indicates contrast [EGT, He, ICC1, NIC2, SP]. It signals a change from a Christocentric view to a theocentric view; Christ is the agent of reconciliation, but it was God is its source and who took the initiative to accomplish it [NIC2, SP]. Paul is pointing out that God is the ultimate source of creation [He], or of these blessings [EGT], or that the new life doesn't just happen spontaneously or come from man, it is from God [ICC1].

QUESTION—To what does τὰ πάντα 'all things' refer?
1. It refers to all the new things, not all things [Lns]. It refers to the new attitudes and new creation of 5:16–17 [EBC, HNTC]. It is all that God renews and recreates for his children [NTC]. It refers to all Paul's mission and ministry activity [Danker]. It refers to the new conditions or new creation which have their source in God [ICC1]. It is all the personal life that has become new [My]. It refers to the content of 5:14–17 [ICC2, NIC2, SP]. It refers to the personal change he has been speaking of [Ho], the change to being a new creature and the removal of the old way of life [TG]. It is God's work in new creation in 5:17 [TH]. It is all the things he has spoken of, the new era, philosophy, moral code, society [EGT]. It refers to God's plan of salvation [TNTC].
2. It is the new order which is God's creation [AB, NCBC]. It refers to everything created, the universe [He]. It refers to the new age, the new creation and the new ground for reconciliation [Stagg].

QUESTION—What is the nature of the reconciliation of which Paul speaks?
By God's act through the death of Christ, God's displeasure against sinful humanity was appeased and enmity between God and humanity was totally and objectively removed [EBC]. From his side God removed the objective obstacle to peace with himself, which is human sin [NIC2]. What Christ did effected an objective reconciliation, but it is incomplete without the human response [ICC2]. God himself removed the barrier caused by sin and thereby removed the curse and wrath resulting from sin [Ho]. The reconciliation occurs not within God but within man since the estrangement is in man [ICC1]. In the act of reconciliation God is the subject and people are the object [NTC].

QUESTION—What is meant by διὰ Χριστοῦ 'through Christ'?
It means through the death of Christ [AB, HNTC, Ho, NIC2, SP, TH], or through his death and resurrection [NTC]. It means through what Christ did [TG], or that Christ was God's agent [EBC]. What this means is explained in 5:21 [NCBC].

QUESTION—Who is the 'us'?
1. It is Paul [Danker], or Paul and his associates [ICC1, Lns]. It is Paul and his associates, but could include all believers [SP]. It refers primarily to Paul, but also includes all believers [NCBC, NIC2].

2. It is all believers [AB, Ho, ICC2, My, NTC, TH]. It is all believers, and potentially all people [TG].
3. It is all mankind [EGT], or all men potentially [HNTC].

and having-given[a] to-us the ministry[b] of-reconciliation,[c]
LEXICON—a. aorist act. participle of δίδωμι (LN 57.71): 'to give' [AB, HNTC, ICC2, LN, Lns, NTC, WBC; all versions except REB]. The phrase θέμενος ἐν ἡμῖν 'and having given to us (the ministry)' is translated 'and has enlisted us (in this ministry)' [REB].
  b. διακονία (LN 35.21) (BAGD 3. p. 184): 'ministry' [AB, BAGD, HNTC, ICC2, LN, Lns, NTC, WBC; KJV, NAB, NIV, NJB, NLT, NRSV], 'work' [CEV], 'task' [LN; REB, TEV, TNT]. See this word also at 3:7, 8.
  c. καταλλαγή (LN 40.1) (BAGD p. 414): 'reconciliation' [AB, BAGD, HNTC, ICC2, LN, Lns, NTC, WBC]. The phrase τὴν διακονίαν τῆς καταλλαγῆς 'the ministry of reconciliation' is translated 'the work of making peace between himself and others' [CEV], 'the task of reconciling people to him' [NLT], 'the task of making others his friends also' [TEV], 'the task of reconciling others' [TNT].
QUESTION—Who is the 'us'?
1. It is a literary plural, and refers to Paul himself [EGT, ICC2, Stagg]. It refers to Paul and his associates [HNTC, Ho, ICC1, Lns, My, NTC, SP, TG, TH]. It refers primarily to Paul, but includes all believers [NCBC].
2. It refers to all believers [AB].

5:19 that[a] God was in[b] Christ reconciling[c] (the) world[d] to-himself
LEXICON—a. ὡς ὅτι (LN 90.21): 'that' [LN; NIV], 'how' [Lns], 'that is' [NTC; NRSV], 'as it is said' [AB], 'which bears the message that' [HNTC], 'our message is that' [TEV], 'likewise' [ICC2], 'its terms are that' [WBC], 'what we mean is' [CEV], 'I mean' [NJB], 'I mean that' [NAB], 'to wit' [KJV], 'for' [NLT], 'to show how' [TNT], not explicit [REB].
  b. ἐν (LN 90.6, 83.13): 'in' [AB, HNTC, ICC2, LN (89.119), Lns, NTC, WBC; all versions except TEV], 'through' [TEV].
  c. pres. act. participle of καταλλάσσω (LN **40.1**) (BAGD 1. p. 414): 'to reconcile' [AB, HNTC, ICC2, Lns, NTC, WBC; all versions except CEV, TEV]. The phrase 'God was reconciling the world to himself' is translated 'God was making all human beings his friends' [TEV]. The phrase 'God was reconciling the world to himself, not counting against them their trespasses' is translated 'God was offering peace and forgiveness to the people of this world' [CEV].
  d. κόσμος (LN 9.23) (BAGD 5.a., 7. p. 446): 'world' [AB, BAGD, HNTC, ICC2, Lns, NTC, WBC; all versions except CEV, TEV], 'people of the world' [LN], 'the people of this world' [CEV], 'all human beings' [TEV]. Κόσμος could be a reference to all people [BAGD (5.a)] or to the world as that which is in hostility to God [BAGD (7)].

QUESTION—What relationship is indicated by ὡς ὅτι 'that'?
1. It restates and further explains the meaning of what was just said [AB, EGT, ICC1, ICC2, Kim, Lns, NCBC, NIC1, NIC2, NTC, SP, TG, TH, TNTC, WBC; KJV, NAB, NIV, NJB, NRSV, REB]. It introduces a more precise statement of 5:18 [TG]. It further explains the ministry of reconciliation by reiterating what God has done [TNTC]. It introduces the content of the ministry of reconciliation [ICC1; TEV]. It repeats 5:18 [ICC2]. It continues the sentence of 5:18 [SP].
    1.1 It introduces all of 5:19 as an explanatory note about the ministry of reconciliation described in 5:18 [NTC].
    1.2 It introduces 5:19ab as an explanatory note about the ministry of reconciliation described in 5:18 and 19c [AB, Kim, SP, WBC]. The ὡς ὅτι introduces 5:19ab as a traditional doctrinal formula or a quotation [AB, WBC]. The ὡς ὅτι is a combination of the comparative function of ὡς and the causal function of ὅτι and introduces a parenthetical statement that serves as the grounds for what Paul has said in 5:18: 'as was the case, because...' [Kim, SP].
2. It introduces an explanation and confirmation of 5:18 [HNTC, Ho, My]. All of 5:19 comments on the first clause of 5:18 [Ho]: all this new creation is from God, because he was reconciling. 5:19 is the grounds for 5:18 and 5:20 is a consequence of 5:19 [HNTC]: since, according to the message, it was God who was reconciling.

QUESTION—What is meant by ἐν Χριστῷ 'in Christ'?
1. It refers to agency: God was reconciling through Christ [AB, EGT, He, HNTC, Ho, ICC1, NCBC, NIC2, NTC, SP, TG, WBC]. 'Through Christ' means through his death [Ho, NIC2, NTC]. God was at work in the person and work of Christ [My, TG]. God was reconciling through Christ, but God was also present in Christ [SP]. God was working in the personal destiny of Christ as representative man [ICC2]. It is parallel to the διὰ Χριστοῦ 'through Christ' of 5:18 except that here it emphasizes that God and Christ are one in this work [NCBC].
2. It refers to God being present in Christ: God was in Christ in order to reconcile the world, especially when Christ died [Lns].

QUESTION—Does the imperfect verb ἦν 'was' go with ἐν Χριστῷ 'in Christ' or with καταλλάσσων 'reconciling'
1. It goes with the participle καταλλάσσων as a periphrastic imperfect: θεός ἦν καταλλάσσων 'God was reconciling the world (in Christ)' [AB, He, HNTC, Ho, ICC1, ICC2, My, NCBC, NIC2, NTC, SP, TG, TH, WBC; NAB, NIV, NRSV, TEV, TNT]. It goes with καταλλάσσων 'reconciling' and with θέμενος 'having entrusted'; in Christ God was reconciling the world and in Christ God was entrusting the ministry to us [EGT].
2. It goes with 'Christ': θεός ἦν ἐν Χριστῷ 'God was in Christ (reconciling the world)' [Lns; CEV, KJV, NJB, NLT, REB].

2 CORINTHIANS 5:19

QUESTION—In what way is 'the world' reconciled to God?

This is reconciliation in the objective sense, in which God reconciled the world to himself by removing sin as the barrier to fellowship with himself through the death of Christ. There is also the subjective aspect of reconciliation in which that atoning work must be announced and appropriated for any person to be reconciled to God [Aber NOT2, ICC1, Kim, Lns, Marshall, WBC].

QUESTION—What is the meaning of κόσμος 'world' in this verse?

1. It is mankind [EBC, EGT, ICC1, ICC2, Lns, My, TG, TH; CEV, TEV]. It is sinful or rebellious humanity [Lewis, SP]. 'World' refers to the comprehensive scope with which reconciliation spans the entire world [ICC2, NIC2, NTC], encompassing Jew and Gentile alike [NIC2, NTC, TNTC]. 'World' expresses comprehensiveness, but 'to them' refers to those who benefit or will benefit from Christ's atonement [NTC]. It is parallel with and corresponds to 'us' 5:18 [AB, NTC]. It indicates the class of beings toward whom God is favorably disposed, though not meaning all people without regard to faith or unbelief, penitence or impenitence [Ho].
2. It is cosmic in scope, representing both man and the created order [NIC1].

not counting-against[a] them their trespasses[b] and having-entrusted[c] to us the message[d] of reconciliation.

LEXICON—a. pres. mid. or pass. (deponent = act.) participle of λογίζομαι (LN **29.4**) (BAGD 1.a. p. 476): 'to count against' [HNTC, ICC2, NTC; NAB, NIV, NLT, NRSV], 'to count' [BAGD], 'to keep an account of' [TEV, TNT], 'to take into account' [BAGD], 'to reckon to' [Lns], 'to keep a record' [LN], 'to charge to' [AB], 'to charge against' [WBC], 'to hold against' [NJB, REB], 'to impute' [KJV], 'to keep in mind' [**LN**], not explicit [CEV]. See this word also at 3:5.

b. παράπτωμα (LN 88.297) (BAGD 2.b. p. 621): 'trespass' [AB; KJV, NRSV], 'transgression' [BAGD, HNTC, ICC2, LN, Lns; NAB], 'sin' [BAGD, LN, NTC; NIV, NLT, TEV], 'offenses' [WBC; TNT], 'faults' [NJB], 'misdeeds' [REB], not explicit [CEV]. The phrase 'not counting against them their trespasses' is translated 'offering forgiveness' [CEV].

c. aorist mid. participle of τίθημι (LN 37.96) (BAGD II.1.a. p. 816): 'to entrust' [BAGD, ICC2, NTC, WBC; NAB, NJB, NRSV, REB, TNT], 'to appoint, designate, assign, give a task to' [LN], 'to establish' [AB, BAGD], 'to put in' [HNTC], 'to deposit to (our charge)' [Lns], 'to give' [CEV, NLT, TEV], 'to commit' [KJV, NIV].

d. λόγος (LN 33.98) (BAGD 1.b.β. p. 478): 'message' [HNTC, ICC2, LN, NTC, WBC; all versions except KJV], 'word' [AB, BAGD, LN; KJV], 'statement' [Lns]. See this word also at 1:18; 2:17.

QUESTION—Who is the 'us' in 5:18 and 19 to whom the ministry and message of reconciliation is entrusted?
1. It is Paul [HNTC, NIC2, SP, WBC], or Paul and his associates [Ho, Lns, My, NCBC, TG, TNTC], or ministers of the gospel [NIC1].
2. It is all believers [AB, NTC]. It is Paul and his associates, as well as all other believers [NTC].

QUESTION—What is the mutual relationship of the participial phrases in 5:18 and 19?

The following schema is used in the answers represented below:
18a = 'All these-things are from God, the one having-reconciled us to himself through Christ'
18b = 'and having given to us the ministry of reconciliation'
19a = 'that God was in Christ reconciling the world to himself'
19b = 'not counting against them their trespasses'
19c = 'and having entrusted to us the message of reconciliation'

1. 18a, 18b, and 19c together make a logically coherent statement, and 19a and b are a parenthetical comment on 'the ministry of reconciliation' in 5:18b [AB, Kim, Lns]. 18a, 18b, and 19c are bound together logically by past participles representing actions of God in which he accomplished reconciliation objectively for the world, and also accomplished it subjectively in Paul, entrusting the ministry to him; 19a and b use present participles which represent actions in progress whereby God is still at work to accomplish reconciliation subjectively in those who are not yet believers [Lns].
2. 5:19 elucidates and explains 5:18 [Danker, EGT, He, Ho, ICC2, NIC2, NTC, SP, TG].
2.1 The two participial phrases in 5:18 are coordinate, and the three in 5:19 form an explanatory statement about τὴν διακονίαν τῆς καταλλαγῆς 'the ministry of reconciliation' in 5:18 [NTC].
2.2 19b explains 19a [Danker, EGT, He, Ho, ICC2, NIC2, SP, TG].
2.2.1 18a is paralleled by 19a, 18b is paralleled by 19c, and 19b explains 19a [Danker, Ho, ICC2, SP, TG].
2.2.2 19a and c are co-ordinate and 19b explains 19a [EGT, NIC2]. That is, the ministry of reconciliation consists of God's reconciling the world to himself (by not counting their sins against them), and his entrusting the message to his messengers.
2.2.3 19a expresses a causal relation with 19c, 19b explains 19a, and 19c is the result of 19a. Because God has reconciled the world, which means not counting against them their transgressions, he has committed the proclamation of it to his ministers [He].
2.3 19b and c are co-ordinate and explain 19a [WBC]. That is, the ministry of reconciliation, which is God's reconciling the world to himself, consists of not counting their sins against them and of entrusting the message to his messengers.

- 2.4 18a is paralleled by 19a and b, and 18b is paralleled by 19c, which is then expanded upon in 5:20 [HNTC].
- 2.5 18a explains the new conditions of 5:17, and 19b and c explain how God brings the reconciliation about [ICC1].
- 2.6 19b and c are subordinate to 19a, explaining the mode of reconciliation, and 19c also elucidates 18b about the giving of the ministry of reconciliation [My].
- 3. Paul advances his exposition in progressive repetitions; the two phrases in 5:18 and the first two phrases in 5:19 describe reconciliation to God, and the third phrase in 5:19 is paired with 5:20, which describes the apostles as ambassadors of reconciliation [Lewis].

QUESTION—What is the significance of the tense of the present participles καταλλάσσων 'reconciling' and λογιζόμενος 'counting'?
- 1. They are used with ἦν, the past tense of the verb 'to be', as a periphrastic imperfect; 'God was reconciling and God was not counting' [EGT, ICC1, ICC2, My, NCBC, NIC1, NIC2, NTC, SP, WBC]. This adds an element of contingency and emphasizes the continuous aspect of the verb [WBC]. Although the reconciliation is completed from God's side, people may or may not accept it [ICC1, NCBC, WBC]. The periphrastic imperfect is more emphatic than the simple imperfect [EGT].
- 1.1 The sense of the periphrastic imperfect is present; God's reconciling activity is an ongoing one [My, NTC].
- 1.2 The tense of the participles is used with reference to an activity in the past [ICC2, NIC1, NIC2, SP]. The imperfect form is used for reasons of style and rhythm, but with an aorist sense [ICC2]. When seen with the aorist tense of the same verb in 5:18 it emphasizes that God's work is finished and complete [NIC2]. It refers to the activity which God was engaged in at the time of the crucifixion of Christ [NIC1, SP].
- 2. The past tense verb ἦν goes with 'in Christ' (God was in Christ), and the participles are used in the present durative sense of action that continues to go on; God reconciled the world to himself objectively in the cross, but is still working to reconcile men to himself subjectively by their own acceptance of the reconciliation [Lns].

DISCOURSE UNIT: 5:20–9:15 [AB]. The topic is appeals.

DISCOURSE UNIT: 5:20–6:10 [AB]. The topic is an appeal for reconciliation with God [AB].

5:20 Therefore[a] we-are-ambassadors[b] for Christ as-(if)[c] God (were)-entreating[d] through us;

LEXICON—a. οὖν (LN 89.50): 'therefore' [AB, HNTC, ICC2, LN, NTC; NIV, REB], 'then' [LN, WBC; TEV], 'so' [LN; NJB, NRSV, TNT], 'so then' [LN], 'now then' [KJV], 'accordingly' [LN, Lns], not explicit [CEV, NAB, NLT].

b. pres. act. indic. of πρεσβεύω (LN **37.88**) (BAGD p. 699): 'to be an ambassador' [BAGD, ICC2, LN, Lns, NTC, WBC; KJV, NAB, NIV, NJB, NLT, NRSV, REB, TNT], 'to serve as ambassadors for' [AB], 'to act as ambassador' [HNTC], 'to be a representative of' [**LN**], 'to speak for someone' [CEV, TEV].

c. ὡς (LN 64.12): 'as if' [HNTC; REB], 'as though' [KJV, NIV, NJB, TEV], 'as' [LN, NTC], 'as it were' [Lns; NAB], 'since' [NRSV], 'certain that' [ICC2], not explicit [AB, WBC; CEV, NLT, TNT].

d. pres. act. participle of παρακαλέω (LN 33.168) (BAGD 2. p. 617): 'to ask for earnestly' [LN], 'to exhort' [BAGD, HNTC], 'to plead' [LN], 'to urge' [BAGD], 'to beg (you) to listen' [CEV], 'to appeal' [AB, BAGD, LN; NJB, REB, TEV, TNT], 'to make an appeal' [ICC2, NTC; NIV, NRSV], 'to make a plea' [WBC], 'to plead' [LN; NLT], 'to admonish' [Lns], 'to beseech' [KJV], 'to implore' [NAB]. See this verb at 1:4, 6, and 2:7, 8.

QUESTION—What relationship is indicated by οὖν 'therefore'?

It draws a conclusion from 5:18–19 [EBC, EGT, Ho, ICC2, Lns, My, NTC, SP, TNTC]: since God has entrusted them with the message of reconciliation they therefore act as ambassadors. Because of all God has done for sinners Paul takes his commission to preach seriously, as representing God himself [NTC]. It connects what has just been said in 5:18–19 with the entreaty to be reconciled [AB, TH], but also connects the whole discussion of his apostolic ministry that began in 2:14 with the appeals in 5:20–9:15 [AB]. It introduces a statement based on the whole passage from 2:14 about the apostolic office [NIC2].

QUESTION—What relationship is indicated by ὡς 'as-(if)'?

The particle ὡς followed by the genitive absolute indicates that the supposition of the genitive absolute is an actual fact [AB, ICC1, ICC2, NIC1, NIC2, NTC, SP, Stagg]: we are ambassadors, seeing that God entreats through us.

we-urge[a] (you/people)[b] on-behalf-of[c] Christ, be-reconciled[d] to God.

LEXICON—a. pres. mid. or pass. (deponent = act.) indic. of δέομαι (LN 33.170) (BAGD 3. p. 175): 'to urge' [NLT], 'to entreat' [AB; NRSV], 'to implore' [ICC2; NAB, NIV, REB], 'to plead' [LN, NTC; TEV], 'to beg' [BAGD, HNTC, LN, Lns, WBC; TNT], 'to appeal' [NJB], 'to sincerely ask' [CEV], 'to pray (you)' [KJV].

b. The word 'you' is not in the Greek text, but is supplied based on the assumption that the second person plural imperative καταλλάγητε 'be reconciled' refers to the Corinthians. 'You' is expressed explicitly as the implied object of one or more of the verbs by HNTC, ICC2, Lns, NTC, WBC, and all versions. It is also possible that the implied object of the verbs is 'people' and that the imperative 'be reconciled to God' is the discourse content, introduced by δεόμεθα, of Paul's message when he preaches.

c. ὑπέρ (LN 90.36): 'on behalf of' [HNTC, ICC2, LN, NTC; NIV, NRSV, TEV, TNT], 'in behalf of' [WBC], 'in the stead of' [KJV], 'in the name of' [NAB, NJB, REB], 'for' [AB, LN, Lns; CEV]. The phrase 'on behalf of Christ' is translated 'as though Christ himself were here pleading with you' [NLT].

d. aorist pass. impera. of καταλλάσσω (LN **40.1**) (BAGD 2.a. p. 414): 'to be reconciled' [AB, BAGD, HNTC, ICC2, LN, Lns, NTC, WBC; all versions except CEV], 'to make peace with' [CEV]. The phrase 'be reconciled to God' is translated 'let God change you from enemies into his friends' [TEV].

QUESTION—How is the preposition ὑπέρ 'on behalf of' used?

Paul represents Christ [AB, EGT, He, HNTC, Ho], acting in his stead [HNTC, Ho, ICC2, Lns, NIC1, SP], in his interest [Danker, HNTC, ICC1], on his behalf [ICC1, Lns, NIC1, SP], in his service [ICC2]. Paul speaks with the authority of Christ as his representative [AB, NIC2].

QUESTION—To whom is the appeal addressed?

1. It is an appeal to the Corinthians themselves to be reconciled to God [AB, EGT, HNTC, NIC2, NTC, SP, TNTC, WBC; CEV, KJV, NAB, NIV, NJB, NLT, NRSV, REB, TEV, TNT]. Paul views doubts and questions about God's appointed ambassadors to mean that the gospel message itself was being called into question [Mead]. Because of the influence of Paul's opponents in Corinth there was a lack of trust in Paul and his authority [SP, TNTC]. It is an appeal to the Corinthians and to all people [NTC]. It is the content of his normal preaching, but applied specifically to the Corinthians, who have moved away from the gospel [WBC]. Paul is using the terminology of evangelism to appeal to them to accept him as their spiritual father, since accepting the gospel of reconciliation also means accepting the designated servant of reconciliation [Marshall]. They have drifted away from Paul, and away from the gospel and from God as a result, because their relationship with God and his salvation cannot be separated from their relationship with Paul; he appeals to them to be restored in their relationship with God and to confirm that they accept God's forgiveness [NIC2]. Though the Corinthians had intellectually received Christ, their lack of conformity to his character showed that there was the danger that his grace would be without meaningful effect, so Paul must appeal for their re-conversion [Murphy-O'Connor].

2. 'Be reconciled to God' is the content of what Paul's normal message that he preaches to all people as Christ's ambassador [Aber NOT2, EBC, ICC1, ICC2, Lns, My, NCBC, NIC1]. In chapter 7 he praises their spiritual health and loyalty to him and says how proud and encouraged he is about them, so an appeal for them to be reconciled to God seems out of place. But because this occurs in a context of an apologetic for his ministry it seems more likely that he is simply stating what his apostolic ministry is – it is a ministry that urges people to be reconciled to God [Aber NOT2].

5:21 The-one- not -knowing[a] sin he-caused (to be) sin[b] on-behalf-of[c] us,

LEXICON—a. aorist act. participle of γινώσκω (BAGD 6.a.α. p. 161): 'to know' [AB, BAGD, HNTC, Lns, NTC; KJV, NAB, NRSV]. The phrase τὸν μὴ γνόντα ἁμαρτίαν 'the one not knowing sin' is translated 'him who had no sin' [NIV], 'him who was without any acquaintance with sin' [WBC], 'the sinless one' [NJB], 'Christ never sinned' [CEV], 'who never sinned' [NLT], 'Christ was innocent of sin' [REB, TNT], 'Christ was without sin' [TEV]. In this context this verb means to know something by experience [AB, He, HNTC, ICC2, My, TH].

b. ἁμαρτία (BAGD 3. p. 43): 'sin' [AB, BAGD, HNTC, ICC2, Lns, NTC; KJV, NAB, NIV, NRSV], 'sin itself' [TNT], 'a sin-offering' [WBC], 'the offering for our sin' [NLT], 'a victim for sin' [NJB]. The phrase ἁμαρτίαν ἐποίησεν 'he caused (to be) sin' is translated 'God treated him as a sinner' [CEV], 'God made him one with human sinfulness' [REB], 'God made him share our sin' [TEV].

c. ὑπέρ (LN 90.36): 'on (our) behalf' [HNTC, ICC2, LN, NTC, WBC; TNT], 'on (our) part' [Lns], 'for' [KJV, NIV], 'for our sake' [NAB, NJB, NRSV, REB, TEV], 'for our sin' [NLT], not explicit [CEV].

QUESTION—What does it mean that Christ, who knew no sin, was made sin?

This statement is expressed as a paradox [Danker, He, Mead, SP]. Paul is using the abstract to refer to the concrete [My, NIC2, SP].

1. It conveys the idea of substitution. God made the one who was innocent to be the guilty one [Danker]. It means that God laid all sin on Christ [AB, Lns, NIC1, TG]. It means that God treated Christ as though he were a sinner [NAC, TG; CEV], placing on him the burden of human sin [TG]. It means that he was made to bear human sin [NTC], and the consequence of sin [TNTC]. He was made a victim for sin [NJB]. All sin was placed upon him as upon the scapegoat on the day of atonement [EGT]. God made him the object of his judgment and wrath against sin [HNTC, ICC2, My, NIC1]. It means that God treated him as he would treat sin [Mead]. Jesus stood in for sinful humanity and God dealt with him as he would have dealt with sinners [NAC].

2. It conveys the idea of identification. Christ was identified with sin [He, ICC1], and shared human sin [TEV], so that man could share God's own righteousness through union with Christ [ICC1; TEV]. Christ identified with human sinfulness [REB] and with sinful humanity [AB, TH], taking the place of sinners and representing them [SP]. Christ identified with the sin, guilt, and consequences of human separation from God [EBC]. It is metaphorical, and means that Christ's love for sinners is so great that, though he is not responsible for sin, he identifies with mankind and takes responsibility for sinners such that human sin becomes his own [Stagg]. It is a metonymy in which the abstraction 'to be made sin' is given for the concrete, which is the crucifixion, in which Christ's death was sin-laden [NIC2].

3. It conveys the idea of sacrifice in that God made Christ a sin-offering [Lewis, NCBC, WBC; NLT]. This follows the wording of Leviticus 5:12 and 6:5 [Lewis] or Is 53:10 [NCBC, WBC] where the sin offering is simply called 'sin'. Christ became a sin-offering, taking their sin and its judgment to himself [NCBC].

so-that we might-become (the) righteousness[a] of-God in[b] him.
LEXICON—a. δικαιοσύνη (LN 88.13) (BAGD 3. p. 197): 'righteousness' [AB, BAGD, HNTC, ICC2, LN, Lns, NTC, WBC; KJV, NIV, NRSV, REB, TEV], 'uprightness' [NJB], 'goodness' [TNT], 'the very holiness' [NAB]. The phrase ἵνα ἡμεῖς γενώμεθα δικαιοσύνη θεοῦ ἐν αὐτῷ 'so that we might become the righteousness of God in him' is translated 'so that Christ could make us acceptable to God' [CEV], 'so that we could be made right with God through Christ' [NLT], 'so that in him we might be made one with the righteousness of God' [REB], 'in order that in union with him we might share the righteousness of God' [TEV], 'that through him we might share the goodness of God' [TNT].
  b. ἐν (LN 89.119, 90.6): 'in' [AB, HNTC, ICC2, LN (89.119), NTC, WBC; KJV, NAB, NIV, NJB, NRSV, REB], 'in union with' [LN (89.119); TEV], 'in connection with' [Lns], 'through' [NLT, TNT], not explicit [CEV].
QUESTION—Who is the 'we'?
  1. It refers to believers [EBC, ICC2, NIC1, NIC2, NTC, TG, WBC]. Paul is speaking inclusively of himself as well as the readers [SP, TH].
  2. It refers to Paul and his associates in ministry [Lns].
QUESTION—What does it mean that believers are made 'the righteousness of God'?
  It means they are justified [HNTC, ICC2, My, NCBC], they are made right before God [NLT], they have a right standing before God [HNTC, ICC2, TG, TNTC], they are acceptable to God [CEV]. They are made one with the righteousness of God [REB], they share his righteousness [TEV] or his goodness [TNT]. It is not just a theoretical righteousness that is credited to those in Christ but a real righteousness which God brings about in them [Stagg]. Through identification with Christ believers are made righteous with a righteousness that is God's own [WBC]. The righteousness of God is the quality of God's own righteousness that is stamped upon believers when he acquits them of sin [Lns]. It means that in God's sight they are as righteous as the son of God [EGT]. Because of substitution and imputation they are treated as righteous in a forensic sense [Ho]. They have a forensic righteousness, but the term also possesses a moral sense because there is an implied imperative 'be righteous' [SP]. It refers to a sinner's justification in which Christ's righteousness is reckoned to him [NIC1]. Through Christ God places believers in the context of his own righteousness [NTC].

QUESTION—How are the nouns related in the genitive construction δικαιοσύνη θεοῦ 'righteousness of God'?
1. It is God's own righteousness [Lns, NTC], the righteousness that characterizes him [EBC, ICC1].
2. It is the righteousness that comes from God [Lns], which is bestowed by him [BAGD]. It means to be righteous in God's sight [Ho]. It is a technical term for God's powerful eschatological act in which he makes the world right with his own purpose through Christ [WBC].

DISCOURSE UNIT: 6:1–7:16 [NTC]. The topic is Paul's ministry.

DISCOURSE UNIT: 6:1–7:4 [ICC2]. The topic is Paul's ministry to the readers.

DISCOURSE UNIT: 6:1–13 [HNTC, ICC2, WBC]. The topic is an appeal for a response to God and his ambassador [HNTC], the beginning of direct appeal and further defense of apostolic conduct [ICC2], Paul's appeal for an open heart [WBC].

6:1 Working-together-with[a] (God/you) then[b] we-exhort[c] you also[d] not to-receive[e] the grace of God in vain.[f]

LEXICON—a. pres. act. participle of συνεργέω (LN 42.15) (BAGD p. 787): 'to work together with' [AB, BAGD, LN, NTC; CEV, NRSV], 'to work with' [HNTC]. This participle is translated 'in cooperation with' [ICC2], 'as co-workers' [WBC], 'as workers together' [KJV, TNT], 'as fellow workers' [NAB, NIV, NJB], 'as partners' [NLT], 'sharing in (God's) work' [REB], 'in our work together' [TEV].
b. δέ: 'then' [NTC; KJV, TEV], 'so' [AB], 'thus' [HNTC, WBC], 'and' [ICC2; CEV], not explicit [NAB, NIV, NJB, NLT, NRSV, REB].
c. pres. act. indic. of παρακαλέω (LN 33.168) (BAGD 2. p. 617): 'to exhort' [BAGD, HNTC, NTC, WBC], 'to urge' [BAGD, ICC2; NIV, NJB, NRSV], 'to beg' [CEV, NAB, NLT, TEV], 'to appeal' [AB, BAGD, LN], 'to make an appeal' [REB, TNT], 'to beseech' [KJV]. The direct object of this verb, ὑμᾶς 'you', comes last in the sentence for emphasis [AB, ICC2, Lns, NIC2]. See this word also at 1:4, 6; 2:7, 8, and 5:20.
d. καί (LN 89.93): 'also' [AB, HNTC, ICC2, LN, Lns; KJV, NRSV], 'and' [CEV], not explicit [NAB, NIV, NJB, NLT, REB, TEV]. The phrase καὶ παρακαλοῦμεν 'we exhort (you) also' is translated 'we make a further appeal' [TNT].
e. aorist mid. (deponent = act.) infin. of δέχομαι (LN 57.125) (BAGD 3.b. p. 177): 'to receive' [AB, HNTC, ICC2, LN, NTC, WBC; KJV, NAB, NIV, REB, TEV, TNT], 'to accept' [BAGD, LN, Lns; NRSV]. The phrase μὴ εἰς κενὸν τὴν χάριν τοῦ θεοῦ δέξασθαι 'not to receive the grace of God in vain' is translated 'make good use of God's kindness to you' [CEV], 'not to let your acceptance of his grace come to nothing' [NJB], 'not to reject this marvelous message of God's great kindness' [NLT].

f. κενός (εἰς κενόν) (LN 89.64) (BAGD 2.a.β. p. 428): 'in vain' [AB, BAGD, HNTC, LN, Lns, NTC, WBC; KJV, NAB, NIV, NRSV], 'to no effect' [ICC2], '(come) to nothing' [NJB, REB], not explicit [CEV, NLT]. The phrase 'to receive in vain' is translated 'to reject' [NLT], 'to let it be wasted' [TEV], 'to let it fail' [TNT].

QUESTION—With whom are they working together?
  1. They are working together with God [AB, EBC, EGT, He, HNTC, Ho, ICC1, ICC2, Lns, My, NAC, NCBC, NIC1, NIC2, NTC, SP, TH, TNTC, WBC; all versions except NAB].
  2. They are working together with the Corinthians [NAB].

QUESTION—What relationship is indicated by καί 'also'?
  It posits another exhortation in addition to the appeal to be reconciled in 5:20 [ICC1, ICC2, Lns, My, NIC2]. The appeal not to receive the grace of God in vain specifies more exactly what he means by the appeal to be reconciled [SP]. In addition to announcing that God made Christ an offering for sin, he also urges them not to receive God's grace in vain [Ho]. In 5:20 God entreated through them, and now Paul also entreats [NIC1].

QUESTION—Does the aorist tense of the infinitive δέξασθαι 'to receive' indicate a past tense meaning for the action of the verb?
  1. It is a timeless aorist referring to the act itself without reference to any point in time [AB, ICC2].
  2. Paul is urging a response in the present [EGT, He, Ho, ICC1, My, NTC, SP, TH]. Paul is urging a response in the present to what God did in the past [TH].
  2.1 Paul is urging an ongoing action or state [He, NTC].
  2.2 Paul is urging a response at a single moment in the present [SP].
  3. The aorist denotes the act in time past of having accepted God's grace in faith [Aber NOT2, Lns, NIC2]. He is telling them not to let all the good things God has done for them through the gospel and the grace that he has extended to them be wasted because of how they live and because they neglect the present opportunity [Aber NOT2].

QUESTION—To what does the phrase τὴν χάριν τοῦ θεοῦ 'the grace of God' refer?
  It refers to the kindness of God [TH; CEV, NLT]. It is all the favors and privileges continually offered to Christ's church [EGT]. It is what they experienced at conversion [TG]. It is the gospel of God's grace [AB, Aber NOT2, NCBC], and all it signifies [Aber NOT2]. It is God's reconciling work in Christ [NAC]. It is God's favor expressed in redemption of which he spoke in chapter 5 [Ho]. It is a reference to the reconciliation discussed in 5:18–21 [AB, Lns]. It is a reference to all that was proclaimed in the message of reconciliation that God accomplished through Christ and is offered in the ministry of the gospel [NIC2, TNTC]. It is a comprehensive term that includes all the various aspects of the grace of salvation [ICC2, SP], which would include reconciliation and justification [SP].

QUESTION—How might the Corinthians receive the grace of God in vain?

It would be the failure to understand and practice the moral requirements of their faith by living a life that contradicts and rejects divine grace [ICC2]. To receive the grace of God in vain would be to reject salvation [Ho], to fail to profit by it [ICC1], to let it go to waste by not making full use of it in their lives [TG], or to fail to live as reconciled people should [SP]. It would be to fail to express God's grace through good works and by abstaining from idol worship [NAC]. It would be to receive it without meaningful effect [AB], by an inactive response to God's word [NTC], or if it produced no fruit in their lives [He]. It would be to frustrate God's grace by not living as Christians should [TH], by not showing the moral results that would correspond to Christian faith [My]. To receive the grace of God in vain would be to allow the reconciliation which Paul brought to them to be threatened by those who challenge his apostolic authority, and by associating with idol worship [NIC2]. It would be to live in a manner inconsistent with Christian faith or by embracing a different gospel based on law-keeping as the basis for acceptance with God [EBC]. To receive the grace of God in vain would be to adhere to a different gospel [HNTC], or to fail to cease living for self and begin living instead for Christ [HNTC, NIC1, WBC]. It would be to receive the gospel in a superficial and empty way as hearers and not as doers of the message [Lns]. Paul feared that if the Corinthians were not grateful for God's grace they might frustrate grace by abandoning the message they had once accepted. They might also fail to respond to Paul's appeals and thereby oppose his ministry, or fail to mature in living under Christ's control [WBC]. Paul did not want their Christian experience to be adversely affected by criticism of the gospel or of himself as its messenger [TNTC]. To receive the grace of God in vain would be to resist Paul's appeals to be reconciled, to abandon the faith, or to revert to pagan ways [NCBC]. The grace of God is in vain or unprofitable apart from faith and obedience [EGT].

6:2 For he-says (at-a) favorable[a] time I-heard[b] you, and in a day of-salvation[c] I-helped[d] you.

LEXICON—a. δεκτός (LN **66.9**) (BAGD p. 174): 'favorable' [BAGD, NTC], 'acceptable' [HNTC, ICC2, Lns, WBC; NAB, NRSV], 'accepted' [KJV]. The phrase καιρῷ δεκτῷ 'at a favorable time' is translated 'when the time came' [CEV], 'at just the right time' [NLT], 'when the time came to show you favor' [TEV, TNT], 'at the time of my favor' [AB; NIV, NJB], 'in the hour of my favor' [REB].

b. aorist act. indic. of ἐπακούω (LN **24.60**) (BAGD 1. p. 282): 'to hear' [AB, BAGD, ICC2, NTC, WBC; KJV, NAB, NIV, NLT, TEV, TNT], 'to give favorable hearing' [Lns], 'to listen to' [BAGD, HNTC, LN; CEV, NRSV], 'to answer' [NJB, REB].

c. σωτηρία (LN 21.26) (BAGD 2. p. 801): 'salvation' [AB, BAGD, HNTC, ICC2, LN, Lns, NTC, WBC; KJV, NAB, NIV, NJB, NLT, NRSV, TNT], 'deliverance' [REB]. The phrase ἐν ἡμέρᾳ σωτηρίας 'in a day of

salvation' is translated 'when you needed help' [CEV], 'the day for me to save you' [TEV].
  d. aorist act. indic. of βοηθέω (LN 35.1): 'to help' [AB, LN, NTC, WBC; NAB, NIV, NJB, NLT, NRSV, TEV, TNT], 'to bring help' [HNTC], 'to come to (your) aid' [ICC2, Lns; REB], 'to come to save' [CEV], 'to succor' [KJV].

QUESTION—Who or what is the subject of λέγει 'he says'?
(What follows is a verbatim quotation of the LXX Is 49:18, in which God is the speaker.)
1. God is the subject [AB, EGT, HNTC, ICC1, ICC2, NIC1, NTC, SP, TG, TH, WBC; all versions].
2. The subject is impersonal 'the word is' [Lns].

Look,[a] now (is the) favorable[b] time, look, now (is the) day of salvation;
LEXICON—a. ἰδού (LN 91.13) (BAGD 2. p. 371): 'look' [NTC, WBC], 'lo' [Lns], 'behold' [AB, HNTC; KJV], 'see' [ICC2; NRSV], 'listen' [TEV], 'I tell you' [NIV], 'well' [NJB], 'indeed' [NLT], not explicit [CEV, NAB, REB, TNT]. When used with a noun and without a finite verb this particle may take the meaning 'here is, there is' [BAGD].
  b. εὐπρόσδεκτος (LN **22.44**) (BAGD p. 324): 'favorable' [ICC2], 'acceptable' [BAGD; NAB, NRSV], 'accepted' [KJV], 'highly acceptable' [Lns, NTC, WBC], 'truly favorable' [LN], 'welcome' [HNTC]. The phrase νῦν καιρὸς εὐπρόσδεκτος 'now is the favorable time' is translated 'God is ready to help you right now' [NLT], 'the time has come' [CEV], 'now is the time of God's favor' [NIV], 'now is the real time of favor' [NJB], 'this is the hour of favor' [REB], 'the special time of favor is now' [TNT], 'of favor' [AB], 'this is the hour to receive God's favor' [TEV], 'God is ready to help you right now' [NLT].

QUESTION—What period of time is represented by 'now'?
It is the time since the coming of Christ [HNTC], the gospel era [EBC]. It is the interval until the parousia [ICC1, My]. It is the time from Christ's coming until his return or our own death, which is a time of opportunity as well as of responsibility [WBC]. It is the eschatological now of life in Christ and in the new creation [AB], the current age of grace in which people may become new in Christ by rebirth [NIC1]. It is the era of God's good pleasure that will last until the consummation [NTC]. It is the current, final phase of salvation history [NIC2], the eschatological change of ages that was begun by Christ's death [NAC]. It is the critical present moment in which God's help is still available [ICC2]. It is the present moment as the apex of salvation history, in which God has worked reconciliation for the world through Christ's death and resurrection [SP].

QUESTION—In what way is the time 'favorable'?
1. It is a time acceptable to God [ICC2, Lns, NAC]. The time is chosen and appointed by God, not by man [NAC]. It is a time when people are acceptable to God [He, NIC2], the time of eschatological opportunity

[NIC2]. It is a time accepted by God as the right time for bringing grace to men [Lns, NIC1, TH, WBC]. It is a time acceptable to God because he appointed it, but it is appointed as a time of grace to man, an opportunity for which they must answer [NIC1].
2. It is a time favorable to man [ICC1, My], a time of God's favor to man [AB], a time when God mercifully accepts man [HNTC]. It is a welcome time [NTC], a time of God's good pleasure [NTC]. In the first clause the time was δεκτός 'acceptable' to God, a time in which he mercifully heeded them, but in the second clause the present time is a time which is εὐπρόσδεκτος 'acceptable' or welcome to the Corinthians [SP].
3. The point is not about to whom the time is acceptable or favorable, but that that time is now; the day of salvation is the day when someone who needs help gets it. God has chosen the time and man is benefited by it, so it is acceptable to God and favorable to man [Aber NOT2].

DISCOURSE UNIT: 6:3–13 [NIV]. The topic is Paul's hardships.

6:3 **giving nothing (as) cause-for-stumbling[a] in-anything/to-anyone,[b] so-that the ministry not be-discredited,[c]**

LEXICON—a. προσκοπή (LN **22.14, 25.183, 88.307**) (BAGD p. 716): 'reason for stumbling' [Lns], 'offense' [HNTC; KJV, NAB, REB], 'an occasion for taking offense' [BAGD], 'cause for offense' [ICC2], 'cause to take offense' [AB], 'opportunity to take offense' [NTC], 'something to cause offense' [LN (25.183)], 'that which causes someone to sin' [LN (88.307)], 'a stumbling block' [WBC; NIV], 'obstacle' [LN (22.14)], 'obstacle in anyone's way' [NJB, NRSV]. The phrase διδόντες προσκοπήν 'giving cause for stumbling' is translated 'to cause problems' [CEV], 'to be hindered' [NLT].

b. μηδέν (LN 92.23) (BAGD 1., 2.b.δ. p. 518): 'nothing' [LN]. The phrase μηδεμίαν ἐν μηδενί 'nothing…in anything' is translated 'no (offense) in anything' [KJV], 'not at all in any respect' [BAGD], 'no (offense) of any kind' [HNTC], '(avoid giving) any offense in anything' [REB], 'no one at anything' [AB], 'no (obstacle) in anyone's way' [NRSV], 'in no respect any (cause for offense) whatsoever' [ICC2], 'no reason in anything' [Lns], 'not (give) anyone (an opportunity)' [NTC]. The phrase μηδεμίαν ἐν μηδενὶ διδόντες προσκοπήν 'giving nothing as cause for stumbling in anything' is translated 'we try hard not to cause problems' [CEV], 'we avoid giving anyone offense' [NAB], 'we do not put a stumbling block in anyone's path/way' [NJB, TNT], 'we put no stumbling block in anyone's path' [NLT], 'we try not to put obstacles in anyone's way' [TEV], 'we try to live in such a way that no one will be hindered from finding the Lord by the way we act' [NLT].

c. aorist pass. subj. of μωμάομαι (LN **33.414**) (BAGD p. 531): 'to be discredited' [NIV], 'to be brought into discredit' [REB], 'to be faulted' [NTC, WBC], 'to be found fault with' [BAGD, **LN**; NRSV], 'to find fault with' [CEV, NLT, TEV, TNT], 'to be censured' [BAGD, HNTC, LN], 'to be subject to censure' [ICC2], 'to be blamed' [AB, BAGD, Lns; KJV, NAB]. The phrase ἵνα μὴ μωμηθῇ ἡ διακονία 'so that the ministry not be discredited' is translated 'so that no blame may attach to our work of service' [NJB].

QUESTION—Is ἐν μηδενί to be understood as a neuter pronoun '(in) nothing' or as masculine pronoun '(to) no one'?
1. It is neuter [EGT, He, HNTC, ICC1, ICC2, Lns, My, NIC2, SP, TH, WBC; KJV, REB]: giving nothing as cause for offense in anything. Ἐν μηδενί in 6:3 corresponds with the neuter expression ἐν παντί 'in everything' in 6:4, indicating that both are neuter [He, ICC2, My, SP, TH, WBC].
2. It is masculine [AB, NTC; NAB, NIV, NJB, NRSV, TEV, TNT]: giving no one a cause for offense in anything.

6:4 rather[a] as servants[b] of-God commending[c] ourselves in everything,

LEXICON—a. ἀλλά (LN 89.125): 'rather' [AB, WBC; NIV], 'but' [LN; CEV, KJV, NJB, NRSV], 'instead' [LN; TEV], 'on the contrary' [HNTC, ICC2, LN, Lns; NAB], 'however' [NTC], not explicit [NLT, REB, TNT].
b. διάκονος (LN 35.20) (BAGD 1.a. p. 184): 'servant' [BAGD, HNTC, ICC2, LN, NTC, WBC; CEV, NIV, NJB, NRSV, TEV, TNT], 'minister' [AB, Lns; KJV, NAB, NLT, REB]. See this word also at 3:6.
c. pres. act. participle of συνίστημι (LN **28.49**) (BAGD I.1.b. p. 790): 'to commend' [HNTC, ICC2, Lns, NTC, WBC; NIV, NRSV, TNT], 'to recommend' [AB; REB], 'to present' [BAGD; NAB], 'to show' [LN], 'to show to be' [CEV, TEV], 'to try to show to be true' [NLT], 'to approve' [KJV], 'to prove authentic' [NJB]. See this word also at 4:2 and 5:12.

QUESTION—What is the relationship of 'as servants of God' to this clause?
1. In everything they commend themselves as God's servants; that is, they present themselves as God's servants or demonstrate that they are God's servants [EBC; CEV, NIV, NJB, NLT, TEV].
2. As God's servants, they commend themselves in everything; that is, they are God's servants, and they commend themselves in the way God's servants should [AB, EGT, HNTC, Ho, ICC1, ICC2, Lns, My, NAC, NIC1, NIC2, NTC, SP, TH, WBC; NIV, NRSV, REB, TNT].

QUESTION—How is this statement to be understood with regard to what he says in 3:1 and 5:12 about not commending himself?
They have rejected the pretense and boasting in external things that their rivals have engaged in, but they do offer the kind of real credentials that ministers of God should demonstrate [AB]. Paul is not primarily promoting himself; his self-commendation is self-deprecating [WBC]. Paul recommends himself with regard to his God-given ministry, not in regard to himself personally [NTC, TNTC]. Paul did not have to commend himself in the way his opponents did [NIC1]. Paul is not being inconsistent with what he said in other passages because his method of commending is by his purity of motive and what he suffers to enrich others [HNTC]. Paul commends

himself by his actions and not by self-praise [Ho]. Paul rejects self-commendation based on self-praise for reasons of selfish ambition, but allows the better type that is exhibited through purity and suffering [ICC2]. Paul does not actively commend himself as his opponents do, but he expects that the quality of his service and ministry will commend him to them [NIC2]. Paul is not commending himself to the Corinthians; rather, this is how he commends himself to the world, and which is also how the Corinthians should commend him to others [NAC].

in[a] much endurance,[b] in afflictions,[c] in hardship,[d] in distresses,[e]

LEXICON—a. ἐν (LN 89.80): 'in' [HNTC, Lns, NTC, WBC; KJV, NIV], 'with' [AB, LN; NAB], 'by' [ICC2; CEV], not explicit [CEV, NLT]. In 6:4–5 this preposition is used primarily to indicate attendant circumstance (LN 89.80), as opposed to 6:6–7 where it is used to indicate the manner in which an event occurs (LN 89.84). In the string of prepositional phrases ἐν ὑπομονῇ πολλῇ, ἐν θλίψεσιν…ἐν πληγαῖς, 'in much endurance, in afflictions…in beatings' the ἐν…ἐν…ἐν 'in…in…in' is translated: 'by…in…in' [TNT], 'by…in situations of…on occasions of' [ICC2], 'by…in times of…when' [NAB], 'by…in…when' [REB], 'through…in…in' [NRSV], 'with…amid…amid' [NAB], 'with… in the course of…in the course of' [AB].

b. ὑπομονή (LN 25.174) (BAGD 1. p. 846): 'endurance' [AB, BAGD, HNTC, ICC2, LN, NTC, WBC; NAB, NIV, NRSV, REB], 'patience' [BAGD; KJV], 'perseverance' [BAGD, Lns; NJB], 'steadfastness' [TNT]. The phrase 'in much endurance' is translated 'we have always been patient' [CEV], 'we patiently endure' [NLT], 'patiently enduring' [TEV]. The plural used for this noun and the two following indicate a series of such situations [ICC2]. See this word also at 1:6.

c. θλῖψις (LN 22.2) (BAGD 1. p. 362): 'affliction' [AB, BAGD, HNTC, ICC2, NTC, WBC; KJV, NRSV, REB, TNT], 'tribulation' [BAGD, Lns], 'trial' [NAB], 'trouble' [CEV, NIV, NLT, TEV], 'hardship' [NJB], 'trouble and suffering' [LN]. See this word also at 1:4, 8; 2:4; 4:17.

d. ἀνάγκη (LN 22.1) (BAGD 2. p. 52): 'hardship' [NIV, NLT, NRSV, REB, TEV, TNT], 'anguish' [HNTC, NTC, WBC], 'distress' [BAGD, LN], 'calamity' [BAGD, ICC2], 'necessity' [Lns; KJV], 'trouble' [LN], 'catastrophe' [AB], 'suffering' [CEV], 'difficulty' [NAB, NJB].

e. στενοχωρία (LN 22.10) (BAGD p. 766): 'distress' [BAGD, HNTC, LN, NTC, WBC; KJV, NAB, NIV, NJB, REB], 'difficulty' [BAGD, LN; TEV], 'anguish' [BAGD], 'trouble' [BAGD, ICC2], 'pressure' [AB], 'anxiety' [Lns], 'hard times' [CEV], 'calamity' [NLT, NRSV], 'frustration' [TNT].

QUESTION—Is ἐν ὑπομονῇ πολλῇ 'in much endurance' logically connected to the participle 'commending ourselves' that precedes it or to the list of difficulties that follows it?
1. It goes with the list that follows; they commend themselves in these ways, the first of which is endurance [AB, HNTC, NTC, WBC; KJV, NIV, NJB, NLT, NRSV, TEV, TNT]. Endurance, which is one of the ways they commend themselves, relates to the three terms that follow; they endure in times of hardship, difficulties and distress [NJB, NLT, TEV, TNT].
2. It goes with what precedes; in much endurance, they commend themselves in the nine things that follow [EBC, EGT, He, Ho, ICC2, Lns, My, NAC, NCBC, NIC1, NIC2, SP, TG, TNTC; NAB, REB]. Affliction itself does not commend anyone, but endurance in affliction does [NAC]. 'In endurance' is amplified and explained by the nine words that follow [EGT], and serves as a title for that list of hardships [ICC2, NIC2, SP]. Endurance is his attitude throughout the nine misfortunes that follow [He].

6:5 in beatings,a in prisons,b in riots,c in labors,d in sleeplessness,e in fastings,f

LEXICON—a. πληγή (LN 19.1) (BAGD 1. p. 668): 'beating' [AB, ICC2, NTC, WBC; NAB, NIV, NRSV], 'flogging' [TNT], 'blow' [BAGD, LN], 'stripe' [Lns; KJV]. The phrase ἐν πληγαῖς 'in beatings' is translated 'beaten' [HNTC], 'we have been beaten' [CEV, NLT, TEV], 'when we are flogged' [NJB], 'when flogged' [REB].
b. φυλακή (LN 7.24) (BAGD 3. p. 867): 'prison' [BAGD, LN, Lns], 'imprisonment' [AB, ICC2, NTC, WBC; KJV, NAB, NIV, NRSV, TNT]. The phrase ἐν φυλακαῖς 'in prisons' is translated 'imprisoned' [HNTC; REB], 'sent to prison' [NJB], 'put in jail' [CEV, NLT], 'jailed' [TEV].
c. ἀκαταστασία (LN **39.36**) (BAGD 1. p. 30): 'riot' [AB, LN; NAB, NIV, NRSV], 'disturbance' [BAGD, ICC2], 'tumult' [Lns; KJV], 'civil disorder' [NTC; TNT], 'social disorder' [WBC]. The phrase ἐν ἀκαταστασίαις 'in riots' is translated 'mobbed' [HNTC; NJB, REB, TEV], 'being mobbed' [**LN**], 'hurt in riots' [CEV], 'faced angry mobs' [NLT].
d. κόπος (LN 42.47) (BAGD 2. p. 443): 'labor' [AB, BAGD, ICC2, Lns, WBC; KJV, NRSV], 'hard work' [LN], 'hard work' [NTC; NAB, NIV], 'toil' [BAGD, LN]. The phrase ἐν κόποις 'in labors' is translated 'laboring' [HNTC; NJB], 'overworked' [REB], 'worked to exhaustion' [NLT], 'we have been overworked' [TEV], 'we have worked hard' [CEV], 'without rest' [TNT].
e. ἀγρυπνία (LN **23.73**) (BAGD 1. p. 14): 'sleeplessness' [LN], 'watching' [KJV]. This plural noun is translated 'times of sleeplessness' [NTC, WBC], 'sleeplessnesses' [Lns], 'sleepless nights' [AB, BAGD, ICC2; NAB, NIV, NLT, NRSV]. The phrase ἐν ἀγρυπνίαις 'in sleeplessness' is translated 'sleepless' [HNTC; NJB, REB], 'we have gone without sleep' [CEV, TEV], 'without rest' [TNT].

f. νηστεία (LN **23.31**) (BAGD 1. p. 538): 'fasting' [BAGD, ICC2, Lns; KJV, NAB], 'times without food' [AB], 'without food' [TEV, TNT], 'times of hunger' [WBC], 'hunger' [NTC; NIV, NRSV], 'hungry' [HNTC], 'to be quite hungry' [LN], 'starving' [NJB, REB]. The phrase ἐν νηστείαις 'in fastings' is translated 'we have gone without food' [CEV, NLT].

QUESTION—What is the κόπος 'labor' of which he speaks?

Paul engaged in manual labor in his craft to support himself [AB, EBC, HNTC, Ho, NAC, NIC2]. It refers to the work of ministry [EBC, EGT, Ho, My, NAC, NIC1, NTC, WBC]. It also includes the rigors of travel [Ho]. It refers to labor in general, which may include his craft [ICC2]. This word emphasizes fatigue, showing they are truly overworked [TH].

QUESTION—What was the nature and cause of the sleeplessness?

1. Lack of sleep was due to physical necessity and not voluntary spiritual discipline [He, HNTC, ICC1, TG]. The rigors of travel made sleeping difficult [Ho, Lns, TNTC]. Paul missed sleep in order to gain time for ministry [ICC1, ICC2, NIC1, WBC] and for manual labor [AB, ICC1, ICC2]. Paul experienced sleeplessness due to the pressures of ministry [TNTC] and concern for churches [Ho, TNTC].
2. Paul missed sleep in order to pray [EBC, NTC].

QUESTION—What was the nature and cause of the fastings?

1. Paul experienced hunger through physical necessity because of financial lack or shortage of food [AB, He, HNTC, NTC, TH]. Paul lacked food because of the rigors of travel [Lns, NIC2] and the wish not to be a burden on anyone [NAC, NIC2]. Paul neglected eating to give time to preaching [Ho, ICC2, NAC, NIC1].
2. The hunger was from fasting as a voluntary spiritual discipline [EBC, My, NCBC, NTC].

6:6 in[a] purity,[b] in knowledge,[c] in patience,[d] in kindness,[e] in (the) Holy Spirit,[f] in genuine[g] love,

LEXICON—a. ἐν (LN **89.84**): 'in' [HNTC, Lns, NTC, WBC; NIV, NJB], 'with' [AB, LN], 'conducting ourselves with' [NAB], 'by' [ICC2; KJV, NRSV, TEV, TNT], 'we have proved ourselves by' [NLT], 'we recommend ourselves by' [REB], not explicit [CEV].

b. ἁγνότης (LN **88.29**) (BAGD p. 12): 'purity' [BAGD, ICC2, LN, Lns, NTC, WBC; NIV, NJB, NLT, NRSV, TEV, TNT], 'pureness' [KJV], 'sincerity' [BAGD], 'probity' [HNTC], 'innocence' [NAB], 'innocent behavior' [REB]. The phrase ἐν ἁγνότητι is translated 'we have kept ourselves pure' [CEV].

c. γνῶσις (LN 28.17, 32.16) (BAGD 2. p. 163): 'knowledge' [AB, BAGD, HNTC, ICC2, LN (28.17), Lns, NTC, WBC; KJV, NAB, NJB, NRSV, TEV, TNT], 'understanding' [LN (32.16); NIV, NLT], 'grasp of truth' [REB]. The phrase ἐν γνώσει is translated 'we have been understanding' [CEV].

d. μακροθυμία (LN 25.167) (BAGD 2.a. p. 488): 'patience' [BAGD, HNTC, LN, NTC, WBC; NIV, NJB, NLT, NRSV, REB, TEV, TNT], 'longsuffering' [Lns; KJV, NAB], 'forbearance' [AB, BAGD, ICC2]. The phrase ἐν μακροθυμίᾳ is translated 'we have been patient' [CEV]. This patience is a patience toward others [BAGD].
e. χρηστότης (LN 88.67) (BAGD 2.a. p. 886): 'kindness' [AB, BAGD, HNTC, ICC2, LN, Lns, NTC, WBC; KJV, NIV, NJB, NLT, NRSV, TEV, TNT], 'kindliness' [REB], 'sincere love' [NAB]. The phrase ἐν χρηστότητι is translated 'we have been kind' [CEV].
f. πνεῦμα ἅγιος (LN 12.18) (BAGD 5.c.β. p. 676): 'the Holy Spirit' [AB, BAGD, ICC2, LN, Lns, WBC; CEV, NAB, NIV, NJB, TEV, TNT], 'the Holy Ghost' [KJV], 'the power of the Holy Spirit' [NLT], 'gifts of the Holy Spirit' [REB], 'a holy spirit' [HNTC], 'holiness of spirit' [NRSV]. The phrase ἐν πνεύματι ἁγίῳ is translated 'the Holy Spirit has been with us' [CEV].
g. ἀνυπόκριτος (LN 73.8) (BAGD p. 76): 'genuine' [BAGD, ICC2, LN, NTC, WBC; NRSV], 'sincere' [BAGD, LN; NAB, NIV, NLT, TNT], 'without hypocrisy' [BAGD], 'unhypocritical' [Lns], 'authentic' [AB], 'undissembled' [HNTC], 'real' [CEV], 'true' [TEV], 'unfeigned' [KJV], 'free of affectation' [NJB], 'unaffected' [REB].

QUESTION—What is meant by ἐν πνεύματι ἁγίῳ 'in Holy Spirit' (without the definite article)?
1. It refers to the Holy Spirit [AB, EGT, He, Ho, ICC2, Lns, My, NAC, NIC2, NTC, SP, TH, TNTC, WBC; CEV, KJV, NAB, NIV, NJB, TEV, TNT].
2. It is a metonymy referring to the power of the Holy Spirit [NLT] or to the gifts and graces of the Holy Spirit [EBC, NIC1; REB], which would include personal holiness [NIC1].
3. It refers to a holy spirit or attitude [HNTC, ICC1; NRSV].

6:7 in (the) message[a] of-truth, in (the) power of God; through[b] the weapons[c] of righteousness of-(the)-right-hand and of-(the)-left-hand,

LEXICON—a. λόγος (LN 33.98) (BAGD 1.a.β. p. 477): 'message' [BAGD, LN, WBC; NAB, TEV], 'word' [AB, HNTC, LN, Lns, NTC; KJV, NJB], 'declaration' [ICC2], '(truthful) speech' [NIV, NRSV]. The phrase ἐν λόγῳ ἀληθείας 'in the message of truth' is translated 'we have spoken the truth' [CEV], 'we have faithfully preached the truth' [NLT], 'declaring the truth' [REB], 'preaching of the truth' [TNT]. See this word also at 1:18; 2:17; 5:19.
b. διά with genitive object (LN 89.76): 'through' [LN, WBC], 'by' [LN; KJV], 'with' [HNTC, NTC; NIV, NRSV, TNT], 'by means of' [ICC2, LN], 'between the aids of' [Lns], 'we wield' [REB], 'wielding' [NAB], 'we have' [NLT, TEV], 'having' [AB], 'by using' [NJB], not explicit [CEV].

c. ὅπλον (LN **6.29, 82.7**) (BAGD 2.b. p. 575): 'weapon' [AB, BAGD, ICC2, LN, NTC, WBC; all versions except CEV, KJV], 'armor' [HNTC; KJV], 'aid' [Lns], not explicit [CEV].

QUESTION—To what does ἐν λόγῳ ἀληθείας 'in the message of truth' refer?
1. It refers to the gospel message [AB, EBC, EGT, HNTC, ICC1, ICC2, Lns, NIC1, NTC, TG, TH, WBC; NAB], the true message which Paul preaches [Ho; NAB, NLT, TEV, TNT]. It is his proclamation of true doctrine [My].
2. It refers to truthful speech [NAC; NIV, NRSV]. Paul does not mince words [NAC].

QUESTION—What relationship is indicated by διά 'through'?
1. It is instrumental [EGT, ICC1, ICC2, My, NTC, SP].
2. It describes the manner or attendant circumstances of how they commend themselves [AB].

QUESTION—What is meant by ἐν δυνάμει θεοῦ 'in the power of God'?
It describes the manner in which Paul proclaims the truth [EBC]. It is the manifestation of God's power that attends Paul's preaching [HNTC, My, NIC1]. It means that Paul's speech is more than just human speech [WBC]. It is that which stands in contrast to human weakness [ICC2]. The effects of Paul's ministry stand in contrast to his weakness [ICC1]. It refers to God's power in a general sense that is always available to the apostles [TG]. It represents divine grace by which Paul carried out ministry [EGT, NIC2]. It complements 'in the Holy Spirit' since the power of the Holy Spirit is evident in his preaching of the gospel [NTC]. The gospel is the power of God [AB].

QUESTION—What is meant by the genitive construction τῶν ὅπλων τῆς δικαιοσύνης 'the weapons of righteousness?'
1. It refers to all the equipping that comes from righteousness, or which righteousness affords [AB, HNTC, Ho, ICC1, Lns, My, NTC]. The righteousness is the righteousness that is by faith [Ho, My]. Paul is strong because of his integrity [HNTC]. These are weapons that God's righteousness has provided [AB]. The aids that belong to this righteousness are stated in what follows: acknowledgment and despising, bad report and good report [Lns].
2. It refers to all the weapons that fit one for righteousness [SP], that promote righteousness [NTC], or that support the cause of righteousness [ICC1].
3. It refers to weapons that consist of righteousness; that is, righteous conduct is a weapon [ICC2, TG, TH].

QUESTION—What is meant by 'weapons…of the right hand and of the left hand'?
It refers to weapons for attack was well as for defense [BAGD, EGT, He, HNTC, Ho, LN, NIC2, NTC, SP, TG, TNTC]. It refers to being equipped to commend as well as to defend the faith [TH]. The presentation of the gospel is an offensive weapon [TNTC]. Having weapons for the right and left means that they are thoroughly equipped for their ministry task [HNTC,

ICC2, Lns, NIC2, WBC]. It means they are prepared to meet attack from any direction [NIC1]. Right and left refer to the positive and negative conditions that are stated in the following verses [Lns, NAC]. Neither adversity nor prosperity overcame Paul, who was indifferent to fame as well as to abuse [NAC].

6:8 through[a] glory[b] and dishonor,[c] through ill-repute[d] and good-repute;[e] as[f] deceivers[g] and (yet) true[h]

LEXICON—a. διά with genitive object (LN 67.136): 'through' [HNTC, NTC, WBC; NIV], 'by' [KJV], 'in' [NRSV, TNT], 'in circumstances of' [ICC2], 'in time of' [NJB]. The phrase διὰ δόξης καὶ ἀτιμίας 'through glory and dishonor' is translated 'being renowned and dishonored' [AB], 'we are honored and disgraced' [TEV], 'between acknowledgement and despising' [Lns], 'whether we were honored or dishonored' [CEV, NAB], 'whether people honor us or despise us' [NLT], 'honor and dishonor are alike our lot' [REB].

b. δόξα (LN 87.4): 'glory' [HNTC, NTC, WBC; NIV], 'honor' [ICC2, LN; KJV, NJB, NRSV, REB, TNT], 'honored' [CEV, NAB, NLT, TEV], 'respect' [LN], 'being renowned' [AB], 'acknowledgment' [Lns].

c. ἀτιμία (LN 87.71) (BAGD p. 120): 'dishonor' [BAGD, ICC2, LN, NTC, WBC; KJV, NIV, NRSV, REB, TNT], 'dishonored' [AB; CEV, NAB], 'disgrace' [BAGD, HNTC; NJB], 'disgraced' [TEV], 'shame' [BAGD], 'disrespect' [LN], 'despising' [Lns]. The phrase 'through dishonor' is translated 'people despise us' [NLT].

d. δυσφημία (LN **33.398**) (BAGD p. 210): 'ill repute' [BAGD; NRSV], 'ill report' [HNTC, ICC2], 'evil report' [KJV], 'bad report' [Lns, NTC, WBC; NIV], 'bad reputation' [TNT], 'slander' [BAGD, LN], 'blame' [NJB, REB], '(being) defamed' [AB], 'cursed' [CEV], 'spoken ill of' [NAB], 'insulted' [TEV]. The phrase 'through ill-repute' is translated 'they slander us' [NLT].

e. εὐφημία (LN **33.356**) (BAGD p. 327): 'good repute' [BAGD; NRSV], 'good report' [BAGD, HNTC, ICC2, Lns, NTC; KJV, NIV], 'good reputation' [WBC; TNT], 'praise' [LN; NJB, REB], 'praised' [AB; CEV, TEV], 'spoken of well' [NAB]. The phrase 'through good repute' is translated 'they praise us' [NLT].

f. ὡς (LN 64.12): 'as' [AB, HNTC, LN, Lns, NTC, WBC; KJV, NIV, NRSV], 'as though' [ICC2], 'taken for' [NJB], 'we are treated as' [TEV], 'we are regarded as' [TNT], 'we are called' [NAB], 'they call us' [NLT], not explicit [CEV, REB]. (Note: ὡς 'as' is also used in 6:9–10.)

g. πλάνος (LN 31.9) (BAGD 2. p. 666): 'deceiver' [AB, BAGD, HNTC, Lns, WBC; KJV, TNT], 'imposter' [BAGD, NTC; NAB, NIV, NJB, NLT, NRSV, REB], 'deceitful' [ICC2, LN], 'liar' [TEV], not explicit [CEV]. The phrase 'as deceivers and yet true' is translated 'we always told the truth about ourselves. But some people said we did not' [CEV].

h. ἀληθής (LN 88.39) (BAGD 1. p. 36): 'true' [AB, ICC2, Lns; KJV, NRSV, TNT], 'true men' [HNTC, NTC, WBC], 'truthful' [BAGD, LN; NAB], 'genuine' [NIV, NJB], 'honest' [BAGD, LN; NLT], 'who speak the truth' [REB], 'we speak the truth' [TEV], 'we always told the truth about ourselves' [CEV].

QUESTION—What relationship is indicated by διά 'through'?
1. It indicates attendant circumstances [AB, Ho, ICC1, ICC2, NTC, SP], or state or condition [EGT]. It indicates experiences through which Paul passes [HNTC].
2. It is instrumental [My]; both honor and shame contribute to his commendation.

QUESTION—What is implied in this series of contrasts?
These are complementary yet paradoxical truths about Paul's life and ministry [EBC, HNTC, NAC]. These reflect the varying opinions and reactions people have regarding Paul and his ministry [HNTC, ICC2, NIC1, NIC2, WBC]. These represent how Paul is judged by worldly standards as opposed to the standards of the eternal order [NCBC]. These are the false estimates of those who judge according to worldly standards as opposed to the true judgment of those who are in Christ [AB]. These circumstances in which Paul is both honored and slandered are the spiritual battles he fights with the weapons of righteousness [NTC]. These represent the contrast between the visible appearance and the essential reality of Paul's life [He]. The combination of all these contradictions in a single person demonstrates that he stands in a special relation to God [ICC1].

6:9 as unknown[a] and (yet) well-known,[b] as dying[c] and (yet) look, we live,[d] as punished[e] and (yet) not being-put-to-death,[f]

LEXICON—a. pres. pass. participle of ἀγνοέω (LN 28.13): 'unknown' [AB, ICC2, Lns, NTC, WBC; KJV, NIV, NJB, NRSV, TEV], 'unknown men' [REB], 'treated as unknown' [NLT], 'unknown to others' [CEV], 'ignored' [TNT], 'unrecognized' [HNTC], 'nobodies' [NAB]. See this word also at 1:8; 2:11.

b. pres. pass. participle of ἐπιγινώσκω (LN 31.27) (BAGD 1.a. p. 291): 'to be well-known' [ICC2, Lns, NTC, WBC; KJV, NAB, NLT, NRSV], 'to be well known to you' [CEV], 'to be known fully' [AB], 'to be known completely' [BAGD], 'to be known by all' [TEV], 'to be known' [NIV], 'to be recognized' [HNTC], 'to be acknowledged' [LN; NJB, TNT]. The phrase 'as unknown and yet well known' is translated 'the unknown men whom all men know' [REB].

c. pres. act. participle of ἀποθνῄσκω (LN 23.117) (BAGD 2. p. 91): 'to be dying' [AB, HNTC, ICC2, Lns, NTC, WBC; KJV, NIV, NJB, NRSV, REB], 'to seem to be dying' [CEV], 'to be as though dead' [TEV], 'to be about to die' [BAGD], 'to face death' [BAGD, LN], 'to be dead' [NAB], 'to live close to death' [NLT], 'to die' [TNT].

d. ζάω (LN 23.88): 'to live' [AB, ICC2, LN, NTC, WBC; KJV], 'to be alive' [HNTC, LN; NAB, NJB, NRSV], 'to be still alive' [CEV, NLT], 'to go on living' [Lns], 'to still live on' [REB], 'to live on' [NIV, TEV], 'to live' [LN; TNT]. The particle ἰδοὺ 'behold' heightens the contrast between 'we live' and the phrase before it 'as dying' [NIC2].

e. pres. pass. participle of παιδεύω (LN 38.4) (BAGD 2.b.α. p. 604): 'to be punished' [LN; CEV, NAB, NRSV, TEV], 'to receive punishment' [AB], 'to undergo punishment' [HNTC], 'to be disciplined' [BAGD, ICC2; TNT], 'to be disciplined by suffering' [REB], 'to be chastised' [Lns], 'to be chastened' [NTC, WBC; KJV], 'to be beaten' [NIV], 'to be scourged' [NJB]. The phrase 'as punished and yet not being put to death' is translated 'we have been beaten within an inch of our lives' [NLT].

f. pres. pass. participle of θανατόω (LN **20.65**) (BAGD 1. p. 351): 'to be put to death' [AB, HNTC, ICC2; NAB, TNT], 'to be killed' [BAGD, **LN**, NTC, WBC; CEV, KJV, NIV, NRSV, TEV], 'to be executed' [LN; NJB], 'to be made to die' [Lns], 'to be done to death' [REB], not explicit [NLT].

6:10 **as sorrowing[a] yet[b] always rejoicing, as poor[c] yet enriching[d] many,**

LEXICON—a. pres. pass. participle of λυπέω (LN 25.274) (BAGD 2.b. p. 481): 'to be sorrowing' [AB, HNTC, WBC], 'to be sorrowful' [BAGD, ICC2, NTC; KJV, NAB, NIV, NRSV], 'to be distressed' [BAGD, LN], 'to be sad' [LN], 'to be saddened' [TEV], 'to be grieved' [Lns], 'to be in pain' [NJB], 'to be afflicted' [TNT]. The participle λυπούμενοι 'as sorrowing' is translated 'our hearts ache' [NLT], 'in our sorrows' [REB], 'in times of suffering' [CEV]. See this word also at 2:2, 4, 5.

b. δέ (LN 89.124): 'yet' [NTC, WBC; KJV, NIV, NJB, NRSV, TNT], 'and yet' [ICC2], 'but' [AB, HNTC, LN, Lns; NLT], 'though' [NAB], not explicit [CEV, REB]. The phrase 'as sorrowing yet always rejoicing' is translated concessively: 'although saddened, we are always glad' [TEV].

c. πτωχός (LN 57.53) (BAGD 1.a. p. 728): 'poor' [BAGD, HNTC, LN, Lns, NTC, WBC; CEV, KJV, NAB, NIV, NJB, NLT, NRSV, REB], 'having nothing' [AB, ICC2], 'we have nothing' [TNT], 'we seem to have nothing' [TEV].

d. pres. act. participle of πλουτίζω (LN 57.29) (BAGD 2. p. 674): 'to make rich' [BAGD, HNTC, ICC2, LN, Lns, NTC, WBC; CEV, KJV, NIV, NJB, NRSV, TEV, TNT], 'to enrich' [AB, LN; NAB], 'to give spiritual riches to others' [NLT], 'to bring wealth to' [REB].

as having[a] nothing and-yet[b] possessing[c] everything.[d]

LEXICON—a. pres. act. participle of ἔχω (LN **57.1**) (BAGD I.2.a. p. 332): 'to have' [AB, BAGD, HNTC, ICC2, **LN**, Lns, NTC, WBC; KJV, NAB, NIV, NJB, NRSV, TNT], 'to seem to have' [TEV], 'to possess' [BAGD, LN], 'to own' [CEV, NLT]. The phrase 'having nothing' is translated 'penniless' [REB].

b. καί (LN 91.12): 'yet' [AB, HNTC, LN, WBC; NAB, TEV, TNT], 'and yet' [ICC2, Lns, NTC; KJV, NIV, NJB, NLT, NRSV], not explicit [REB].

The phrase 'as having nothing and yet possessing everything' is translated concessively: 'though we own nothing, everything is ours' [CEV].
  c. pres. act. participle of κατέχω (LN 57.1) (BAGD 1.b.γ. p. 423): 'to possess' [AB, BAGD, HNTC, ICC2, LN, NTC, WBC; KJV, NIV, NRSV, TEV, TNT], 'to have' [LN; NLT], 'to thoroughly have' [Lns], 'to own' [LN; NJB, REB]. The phrase 'possessing everything' is translated 'everything is ours' [CEV, NAB]. This participle is a compounded version of ἔχοντες 'having' and indicates a more intense ownership [ICC1, NIC1, NIC2, WBC].
  d. πᾶς (πάντα) (LN 59.23) (BAGD 2.a.δ. p. 633): 'everything' [AB, BAGD, Lns, NTC, WBC; CEV, NAB, NIV, NJB, NLT, NRSV, TEV, TNT], 'all things' [BAGD, HNTC, ICC2; KJV], 'all' [LN], 'the world' [REB].

QUESTION—In what sense do they possess all things?

They own all things in a metaphorical and spiritual sense [SP]. Though they are poor materially, they are rich spiritually [TG]. Paul is contrasting having temporal earthly riches with having eternal heavenly riches such as eternal security [WBC]. They possess a store of divine blessings that they impart to other people [My]. They have Christ, which is all that matters [TH]. By 'all things' he means the sum total of all eschatological and soteriological blessings [NIC2]. Earthly poverty is being contrasted with heavenly riches, because in Christ believers own everything [NTC]. All things belong to people who belong to Christ in the sense that they are no longer bound by the standards and claims of this present age [AB]. By faith they possess an inheritance in the age to come [HNTC]. Those who have Christ have everything [NIC1]. To have what Christians have is to have everything because God has appointed everything to work together for their good [Lns]. They possess all things in the sense that God holds and disposes all things for the benefit of his people for their present good and future glory, and they are joint heirs with Christ [Ho]. They possess all things in the sense that they already experience spiritual blessings as the first fruits of the age to come [TNTC].

DISCOURSE UNIT: 6:11–7:4 [EBC; NJB]. The topic is the openness and joy of the apostolic ministry [EBC], a warning [NJB].

DISCOURSE UNIT: 6:11–7:3 [AB]. The topic is an appeal for reconciliation with the Pauline apostolate.

6:11 Our mouth has-opened^a to you, Corinthians, our heart has-been-opened-wide.^b

LEXICON—a. perf. act. indic. of ἀνοίγω (LN **33.252**) (BAGD 2. p. 71): 'to open' [BAGD, Lns; KJV], 'to be open' [AB, ICC2], 'to speak freely' [NTC, WBC; NIV, TNT], 'to speak frankly' [NAB, NJB, NRSV, REB, TEV], 'to speak honestly' [NLT]. The phrase 'our mouth has opened to

you' is translated 'I have let my tongue run away with me' [HNTC], 'we are telling the truth' [CEV], 'we spoke the complete truth to you' [**LN**].
  b. perf. pass. indic. of πλατύνω (LN **25.53**) (BAGD 2. p. 667): 'to open (the heart) wide' [BAGD, NTC, WBC; NAB, NIV, TEV], 'to open (the heart)' [NJB, NLT, REB], 'to be wide' [AB], 'to be wide open' [HNTC; NRSV, TNT], 'to be enlarged' [BAGD, ICC2; KJV], 'to be expanded' [Lns], 'to make broad' [BAGD]. The phrase 'our heart has opened wide' is translated 'there is room in our hearts for you' [CEV], 'our heart is open' [LN]. 'To broaden the heart' is an idiom for making evident that one has affection for someone [LN].
QUESTION—What is meant by the metaphor of opening the heart?
It is an expression of love and affection [AB, HNTC, ICC2, Lns, My, NAC, NIC1, NIC2, NTC, TG, TH, TNTC], of warmth and acceptance [EBC], of expanding sympathy [EGT]. It means that he has revealed his own thoughts and feelings freely, holding nothing back [Ho, ICC1, Lns, TG].
QUESTION—What is the significance of the perfect tense with the two verbs?
  1. It is used in the durative sense of a past action with effect that continues into the present [HNTC, Lns, NIC2, NTC, SP, WBC; NAB, NIV, NJB, NLT, NRSV, REB, TEV].
  2. It is used with a present tense meaning [AB, He, Ho; CEV, KJV, TNT].

6:12 **You-are-constrained**[a] **not in/by**[b] **us, rather**[c] **you-are-constrained in your-own affections.**[d]
LEXICON—a. pres. pass. indic. of στεναχορέω (LN 37.18, **25.54**) (BAGD 766): 'to be restricted' [BAGD, LN (37.18)], 'to be cramped' [AB, BAGD], 'to lack space' [HNTC, ICC2], 'to suffer restraint' [Lns], 'to be straightened' [KJV]. The phrase 'you are constrained not in/by us' is translated 'we are not restricting our love to you' [NTC], 'we are not holding back on our love for you' [CEV], 'we have not closed our hearts to you' [LN (25.54)], 'we do not withhold our affection from you' [WBC; NIV], 'there is no lack of room in us' [NAB], 'any distress you feel is on your own side' [NJB], 'if there is a problem between us, it is not from lack of love on our part' [NLT], 'there is no restriction in our affections' [NRSV], 'there is no constraint on our part' [REB], 'it is not we who have closed our hearts to you' [TEV], 'we are not restraining you' [TNT].
  b. ἐν: 'in' [Lns; KJV, NAB, NRSV], 'within' [ICC2], 'by' [HNTC], 'on (my side)' [HNTC], 'on (our side)' [NJB], 'on (our part)' [NLT, REB], not explicit [NTC, WBC; CEV, NIV, TEV, TNT].
  c. δέ (LN 89.124): 'rather' [AB], 'but' [HNTC, ICC2, NTC, WBC; CEV, KJV, NIV, NLT, NRSV], 'only' [Lns], not explicit [NAB, NJB, REB, TEV, TNT].
  d. σπλάγχνον (LN **25.54**) (BAGD 1.b. p. 763): The plural form is translated 'affections' [ICC2, LN, Lns; NRSV], 'affection' [WBC; NIV], 'feelings' [AB, HNTC; TNT], 'love' [NTC; CEV, NLT], 'heart' [BAGD; TEV], 'bowels' [KJV], not explicit [NAB, NJB, REB].

QUESTION—How is the metaphor σπλάγχνον 'affections' used here by Paul?
It refers to the affections, and is synonymous with καρδία 'heart' [AB, EGT, He, HNTC, Ho, ICC1, ICC2, Lns, My, NIC1, NIC2, NTC, SP, TH].

6:13 **As a response[a] of-like-kind,[b] I-speak as to-(my)-children,[c] open-wide[d] yourselves as well.**

LEXICON—a. ἀντιμισθία (LN **38.15**) (BAGD p. 75): 'response' [AB], 'recompense' [HNTC, ICC2; KJV], 'exchange' [BAGD; NAB, NIV, NJB, REB], 'reciprocal exchange' [LN], 'reciprocation' [Lns], 'in return' [NTC, WBC; NRSV, TNT], not explicit [CEV, NLT]. The phrase τὴν δὲ αὐτὴν ἀντιμισθίαν 'response of like kind' is translated 'show us the same feelings we have for you' [TEV].

b. αὐτός (LN 58.31): 'of like kind' [HNTC], 'in kind' [AB], 'same' [LN, Lns; KJV, TEV], 'in the same way' [NTC], 'equivalent' [ICC2], 'fair' [NAB, NIV, NJB, REB], not explicit [WBC; CEV, NLT, NRSV, TNT].

c. τέκνον (LN 9.46) (BAGD 2.b. p. 808): 'child' [BAGD, LN]. This noun in the plural is translated 'children' [AB, Lns; NRSV], 'my children' [HNTC, ICC2, NTC, WBC; KJV, NIV], 'my own children' [CEV, NLT], 'to children of mine' [NJB], '(as) a father to his children' [NAB, TNT], 'if I may speak to you like a father' [REB], '(as though) you were my children' [TEV].

d. aorist passive imperative of πλατύνω (LN **25.53**) (BAGD 2. p. 667): 'to open wide (your hearts)' [BAGD; NAB, NIV, NRSV, TEV, TNT], 'to open (your hearts)' [NJB, NLT, REB], 'to be wide open' [HNTC], 'to widen' [AB], 'to enlarge' [ICC2], 'to be enlarged' [KJV], 'to be expanded wide' [Lns], 'to widen (your hearts)' [NTC], 'to make room (in your hearts)' [CEV], not explicit [WBC].

QUESTION—What does Paul mean by saying that he speaks to them ὡς τέκνοις 'as children'?
Paul's relationship with them is that of a father with his own children [EBC, EGT, He, HNTC, Ho, ICC1, ICC2, Lns, My, NIC1, NIC2, NTC, TG, TH, TNTC; CEV, KJV, NAB, NIV, NJB, NLT, REB, TEV, TNT]. It speaks of endearment, not of immaturity [AB].

DISCOURSE UNIT: 6:14–7:16 [REB]. The topic is church life and discipline.

DISCOURSE UNIT: 6:14–7:4 [HNTC, ICC2]. The topic is response to God is exclusive [HNTC], ethical exhortation and conclusion of direct appeal [ICC2].

DISCOURSE UNIT: 6:14–7:1 [TG, WBC; CEV, NAB, NIV, NLT, NRSV, TEV]. The topic is not being yoked with unbelievers [NIV], the temple of the living God [WBC; CEV, NAB, NLT, NRSV], warning against pagan influences [TG, TH; TEV].

2 CORINTHIANS 6:14

6:14 Don't be misyoking[a] with-unbelievers, for what partnership[b] (have) righteousness and lawlessness[c] or what fellowship[d] has light with darkness?

LEXICON—a. pres. act. participle of ἑτεροζυγέω (preceded by and used in conjunction with γίνομαι 'to be or become') (LN **34.9**) (BAGD p. 314): '(to be) misyoked' [AB], '(to be) unevenly yoked' [BAGD, NTC], '(to be) unequally yoked' [KJV], '(to be) incongruously yoked' [ICC2], '(to try to be) heterogeneously yoked up' [Lns], '(to be) yoked together' [NIV], '(to be) mismated' [BAGD, WBC], '(to be) wrongly matched' [**LN**], '(to be) mismatched' [LN; NRSV], 'to yoke oneself in a mismatch' [NAB], 'to get into double harness' [HNTC], 'to harness oneself in an uneven team' [NJB], 'to team up with' [NLT, REB, TNT], 'to work together as equals with' [TEV], not explicit [CEV]. The phrase 'do not be misyoking with unbelievers' is translated 'stay away from people who are not followers of the Lord' [CEV].

b. μετοχή (LN **34.7**) (BAGD p. 514): 'partnership' [HNTC, **LN**, Lns, WBC; NRSV, REB], 'sharing' [BAGD, LN], 'fellowship' [KJV], 'participation' [BAGD], '(to have) in common' [AB, BAGD, ICC2, NTC; NAB, NIV, TNT], 'to be partners' [NJB, NLT, TEV], not explicit [CEV]. The phrase 'what partnership have righteousness and lawlessness' is translated 'can someone who is good get along with someone who is evil' [CEV].

c. ἀνομία (LN **88.139**) (BAGD 1. p. 71): 'lawlessness' [AB, BAGD, ICC2, LN, Lns, NTC, WBC; NAB, NRSV], 'law-breaking' [NJB], 'iniquity' [HNTC], 'unrighteousness' [KJV], 'wickedness' [NIV, NLT, REB], 'wrong' [TEV, TNT], 'someone who is evil' [CEV].

d. κοινωνία (LN 34.5) (BAGD 1. p. 439): 'fellowship' [BAGD, ICC2, LN, NTC, WBC; NAB, NIV, NRSV], 'association' [BAGD], 'partnership' [AB, HNTC; TNT], 'communion' [BAGD, Lns; KJV], '(to have) in common' [NJB], not explicit [CEV, NLT, REB, TEV]. The phrase 'what fellowship has light with darkness' is translated 'are light and darkness the same' [CEV], 'how can light live with darkness' [NLT], 'how can light and darkness live together' [TEV], 'can light associate with darkness' [REB].

QUESTION—What is the force of the present active participle used in the prohibition μὴ γίνεσθε ἑτεροζυγοῦντες 'don't be misyoking'?
  1. He is telling them not to become yoked with unbelievers [AB, EGT, He, ICC1, ICC2, Lns, NAC, NIC2, TNTC]. Some were on the verge of doing what he is forbidding [NIC2].
  2. He is telling them to stop being yoked with unbelievers [NIC1, NTC, WBC].

QUESTION—What is the 'yoking' with unbelievers that Paul is referring to?
  This included engaging in pagan ceremonies or idolatrous worship [HNTC, Ho, NAC, NCBC, NIC2, NTC, SP, TNTC], eating meat offered to idols [ICC2, NAC, WBC], moral defilement [HNTC], mixed marriage [EBC, EGT, He, Ho, ICC2, SP, WBC], engaging in business partnerships [ICC2, SP], condoning the practices of unbelievers [ICC1], collaborating with them

[He, TG], or bringing lawsuits before unbelievers [EBC]. It was a prohibition against forming very close relationships with unbelievers [EBC, EGT, Ho, ICC1, NIC1, SP], of taking common cause with their efforts and aims wherein the unbeliever forms the standard for thinking and action [My]. It is close relationships with unbelievers that result in linking up with the world [WBC]. It is a very general appeal [AB].

QUESTION—What relationship is indicated by γάρ 'for'?

It introduces the logical conclusion to the preceding clause, which demands a distinction between believers and unbelievers [WBC]. It substantiates or explains the command with the rhetorical questions that follow [Lns, NIC2, SP].

6:15 And what agreement[a] (is there) of-Christ with Beliar,[b] or what share[c] (has) a-believer with an-unbeliever?

LEXICON—a. συμφώνησις (LN **31.15**) (BAGD p. 781): 'agreement' [BAGD, LN; NRSV], 'agreeing' [Lns], 'concord' [AB; KJV], 'accord' [NAB], 'harmony' [HNTC, NTC, WBC; NIV, NLT]. This noun is also translated as a verb: 'to agree' [REB, TEV, TNT]; a verb phrase: 'to be a friend of' [CEV], 'to come to an agreement with' [NJB].

b. Βελιάρ (LN **93.69**) (BAGD p. 139): 'Beliar' [AB, HNTC, ICC2, Lns; NJB, NRSV, TNT], 'Belial' [BAGD, LN, NTC, WBC; KJV, NAB, NIV, REB], 'Satan' [CEV], 'the Devil' [NLT, TEV]. ('Belial' is the form that occurs in the OT, but both forms occur in inter-testamental literature.)

c. μερίς (LN **63.13**) (BAGD 2. p. 505): 'share' [AB, BAGD, **LN**], 'sharing' [NJB], 'portion' [BAGD, LN, Lns, WBC], 'part' [KJV], 'common lot' [HNTC; NAB]. This noun is also translated as a verb: 'to share' [NRSV, TNT]; as a verb phrase: 'to possess in common' [ICC2], 'to have in common' [NTC; CEV, NIV, TEV], 'to be a partner with' [NLT], 'to join with' [REB].

QUESTION—What is the meaning of the question 'what share has a believer with an unbeliever'?

Paul is saying that believers and unbelievers have nothing in common [ICC2]. He is referring to the particular things about unbelievers the Lord has changed in believers, not to those things that all people share [NIC1]. Paul is saying that one cannot be a believer and an unbeliever at the same time [NIC2]. An unbeliever has no share in the community and promises of believers [NAC]. A believer is joined to Christ and the church, but an unbeliever has no such connection [NIC2]. Believers must fully disassociate with pagan idolatry and dedicate themselves to Christ [NTC]. Believers and unbelievers are subject to different lords [Lns, My]; only believers have righteousness, pardon and hope of eternal life, in which unbelievers have no part [Lns]. Believers and unbelievers do not share the same objectives and principles; their interior lives are different and they move in entirely different spheres [Ho]. There is a difference in matters of faith and morality

[TG]. He is saying that a believer should not take part in pagan worship [TNTC].

QUESTION—Who is 'Beliar'?

It is Satan [AB, EGT, He, HNTC, Ho, ICC1, ICC2, Lns, NAC, NIC1, NTC, SP, TG, TH, WBC]. It is the personification of evil, equivalent here to Antichrist [NCBC].

6:16 And what agreement[a] (has) (the) temple[b] of-God with idols? For we are (the) temple of (the) living God, just-as[c] God has said:

TEXT—Instead of ἡμεῖς 'we are', some manuscripts have ὑμεῖς 'you are'. GNT selects the reading 'we are' with a B rating, indicating that the text is almost certain. The reading 'you are' is taken by KJV and NAB.

LEXICON—a. συγκατάθεσις (LN **31.18**) (BAGD p. 773): 'agreement' [AB, BAGD, HNTC, NTC, WBC; KJV, NAB, NIV, NRSV], 'union' [BAGD; NLT], 'accord' [ICC2, Lns], 'common ground' [TNT]. This noun is also translated as a verb phrase: 'to compromise with' [NJB], 'to come to terms with' [TEV]. The phrase 'what agreement has the temple of God with idols' is translated 'do idols belong in the temple of God' [CEV], 'can there be a compact between the temple of God and idols' [REB].

b. ναός (LN 7.15) (BAGD 2. p. 533): 'temple' [AB, BAGD, HNTC, ICC2, LN, NTC, WBC; all versions], 'sanctuary' [LN, Lns]. The definite article, though lacking, is assumed and supplied by all commentaries and versions. This word indicated the shrine or sanctuary of a temple, as opposed to ἱερόν 'temple' which was the larger structure in which the shrine was located [ICC1, Lns, NIC1, NIC2, NTC, WBC].

c. καθώς (LN 64.14): 'just as' [LN, NTC; NAB], 'as' [AB, HNTC, ICC2, WBC; CEV, KJV, NIV, NLT, NRSV, TEV, TNT], 'even as' [Lns]. The phrase 'as God has said' is translated 'we have God's word for it' [NJB], 'God's own words are' [REB].

QUESTION—Is the metaphor of being the temple of God a reference to the individual or to the church?

It refers to the church [AB, EBC, EGT, Ho, ICC1, ICC2, NAC, SP, TG, TH, TNTC, WBC]. It is a corporate temple, though one made up of individual persons in whom he also dwells as a temple [HNTC, NIC2]. It is the church, but implies the necessity of purity for each individual [NIC1].

QUESTION—What relationship is indicated by γάρ 'for'?

It drives home the point about being misyoked by the use of OT quotes [HNTC]. It introduces the reason that the Christian has no room for idolatry [WBC]; because the temple of God is incompatible with idols, they should not participate in pagan worship [TNTC]. It draws a conclusion from the five rhetorical questions, especially the last one, stated in an assertion that is made emphatic by the use and placement of the pronoun ἡμεῖς 'we' [NIC2].

I-will-dwell^a **among**^b **them and I-will-walk-among**^c **(them) and I-will-be their God and they-will-be my people.**

LEXICON—a. indic. fut. act. of ἐνοικέω (LN 85.73) (BAGD p. 267): 'to dwell' [AB, BAGD, HNTC, ICC2, LN, Lns, NTC, WBC; KJV, NAB, TNT], 'to live' [BAGD, LN; CEV, NIV, NLT, NRSV, REB], 'to fix one's home' [NJB], 'to make one's home' [TEV].

b. ἐν (LN 83.9): 'among' [LN; NJB, REB], 'amongst' [ICC2], 'in' [AB; KJV, NLT, NRSV, TNT], 'in the midst of' [HNTC], 'with' [LN; CEV, NAB, NIV, TEV].

c. fut. act. indic. of ἐμπεριπατέω (LN **85.81**) (BAGD p. 256): 'to walk among' [HNTC, NTC; CEV, NAB, NIV, NLT, NRSV, TNT], 'to walk about among' [AB, BAGD], 'to walk about in' [Lns], 'to walk with' [WBC], 'to walk in' [KJV], 'to move among' [BAGD], 'to move amongst' [ICC2], 'to move about among' [REB], 'to live among' [LN; NJB, TEV].

6:17 Therefore^a **come-out**^b **from the midst**^c **of-them and be-separated**^d **says the Lord**

LEXICON—a. διό (LN 89.47): 'therefore' [AB, ICC2, LN, NTC, WBC; NAB, NIV, NLT, NRSV, TNT], 'and therefore' [REB], 'wherefore' [Lns; KJV], 'so then' [LN], 'so' [HNTC], 'and so' [TEV], not explicit [NJB]. This conjunction is translated as a verb phrase: 'The Lord also says' [CEV].

b. aorist act. impera. of ἐξέρχομαι (LN 15.40) (BAGD 1.b.β. p. 275): 'to come out' [AB, HNTC, ICC2, Lns, NTC, WBC; KJV, NAB, NIV, NLT, NRSV, TNT], 'to come away' [BAGD], 'to come away and leave' [REB], 'to leave' [CEV, TEV], 'to get away' [NJB].

c. μέσος (LN 83.9) (BAGD 2. p. 508): 'midst' [AB, HNTC, ICC2, Lns, NTC, WBC; TNT], not explicit [CEV, NIV, NJB, NLT, NRSV, REB, TEV]. The phrase 'from the midst of them' is translated 'from among them' [BAGD; KJV, NAB], 'from them' [CEV, NIV, NJB, NLT, NRSV].

d. aorist passive imperative of ἀφορίζω (LN 63.28) (BAGD 1. p. 127): 'to be separated' [BAGD, LN, Lns], 'to be separate' [AB, BAGD, HNTC, ICC2, NTC, WBC; KJV, NIV, NRSV], 'to separate oneself' [NAB, NLT, REB, TEV], 'to purify oneself' [NJB], 'to stay away' [CEV], 'to leave' [TNT].

QUESTION—What relationship is indicated by διό 'therefore'?

It presses home the meaning of the passage just quoted [NIC1]. It introduces practical conclusions to be drawn from 6:14–16 [ICC1]. It introduces the appeal in 6:17 on the basis of the citation in 6:16 [AB, Ho, TH]; because God dwells in them they must keep themselves from the pollutions of the world [HNTC, Ho, ICC2, NIC2]. Because Christians are God's people, therefore they must be pure [SP]. It is an inference from the larger passage; because believers and unbelievers have drastically different ways of life, and because the church is God's temple and he promises to dwell among them, they must separate themselves [WBC].

2 CORINTHIANS 6:17

And do- not -touch^a (any) unclean-thing;^{b} and I-will-welcome^c you

LEXICON—a. pres. mid. impera. of ἅπτω (LN 24.73) (BAGD 2.a. p. 102): 'to touch' [AB, BAGD, HNTC, ICC2, LN, NTC, WBC; all versions except TEV], 'to have nothing to do with' [TEV]. This present negative imperative is also translated in the sense of discontinuing an activity: 'stop touching' [Lns].
- b. ἀκάθαρτος (LN 53.39) (BAGD 1. p. 29): 'unclean' [AB, BAGD, HNTC, ICC2, Lns, NTC, WBC; all versions except CEV, NLT], 'that isn't clean' [CEV], 'filthy' [NLT], 'impure' [BAGD].
- c. fut. mid. (deponent = act.) indic. of εἰσδέχομαι (LN **34.53**) (BAGD p. 232): 'to welcome' [BAGD, ICC2, LN; CEV, NAB, NJB, NLT, NRSV, TNT], 'to receive' [AB, BAGD, HNTC, **LN**, Lns, NTC, WBC; KJV, NIV], 'to accept' [LN; REB, TEV].

QUESTION—In what way did Paul expect the Corinthians to 'come out', 'be separated' and 'not touch anything unclean'?

They were to separate from the pagan way of life [EBC, ICC2, TNTC]. They were to withdraw morally and spiritually from the pagan way of life [ICC1]. They were to keep away from moral impurity [HNTC, NIC1, SP, TH, WBC] and idolatry [HNTC, NAC, NIC1, NIC2, WBC]. They were to avoid all ethical impurity, anything incompatible with holiness [NCBC]. They were to avoid unbelievers [AB], or avoid their influence [TH], to abstain from all heathen habits [My].

6:18 and I-will-be a father to-you and you will-be sons and daughters to-me says the Lord almighty.^{a}

LEXICON—a. παντοκράτωρ (LN 12.7) (BAGD p. 609): 'the Almighty' [AB, BAGD, HNTC, ICC2, LN, Lns, NTC, WBC; all versions except CEV], 'all-powerful' [CEV], 'the one who has all power' [LN].

QUESTION—What is Paul saying about the basis of a believer's relationship with God?

God will accept them if they become separate from unbelievers [TH]. Separation from the world will lead to friendship with God [ICC1]. God welcomes those who turn from idols to him [TNTC]. It is a warning that if they want to be God's people they must separate from idol worship [NAC]. As a father with his children God will receive into his favor those who keep themselves aloof from contaminating influence [Ho]. Unless they leave idolatry and are received by their father, they are denying their relationship to him as father [NIC2]. It is not a call to earn holiness, but a call to live the holiness to which God has called them [WBC]. The adoption promise from 2 Sam. 7:14, applied now to Christians, will be kept if they do what is required in 6:17 [SP]. The future-tense verbs signify things that have already occurred and promises that are already fulfilled; believers must become what they already are in the Pauline tension of 'already' and 'not yet' [ICC2]. It is not about becoming his child, but about being acceptable to a holy father; God's children must be holy for him to approve of them and take them in

[NTC]. God's acceptance and approval of his people is contingent on their obedience to his commands [EBC].

7:1 Therefore^a having these promises, beloved,^b let-us-cleanse^c ourselves

LEXICON—a. οὖν (LN 89.50) (BAGD 1.b. p. 593): 'therefore' [AB, BAGD, LN, NTC; KJV, REB, TNT], 'so' [BAGD, LN; CEV], 'then' [BAGD, LN], 'so then' [ICC2; TEV], 'since then' [HNTC, WBC], 'since' [NAB, NIV, NJB, NRSV], 'consequently' [BAGD, LN], 'accordingly' [BAGD, LN, Lns], 'because' [NLT].

b. ἀγαπητός (LN 25.45) (BAGD 2 p. 6): 'beloved' [AB, BAGD, ICC2, LN, Lns, WBC; NAB, NRSV], 'dearly beloved' [KJV], 'dear friends' [NIV, NLT, REB, TNT], 'my dear friends' [HNTC, NTC; NJB, TEV], 'my friends' [CEV].

c. aorist act. subj. of καθαρίζω (LN 53.28) (BAGD 2.b.α. p. 387): 'to cleanse' [AB, HNTC, ICC2, LN, Lns, NTC, WBC; KJV, NLT, NRSV, REB, TNT], 'to purify' [LN; NAB, NIV, TEV], 'to wash clean' [NJB]. The phrase 'let us cleanse ourselves from every defilement of flesh and spirit' is translated 'we should stay away from everything that keeps our bodies and spirits from being clean' [CEV]. By using the first person plural (i.e., hortatory subjunctive) Paul identifies with the readers: 'let us...' [ICC1, ICC2, Lns, My, NTC, TNTC].

QUESTION—What relationship is indicated by οὖν 'therefore' with the present active participle ἔχοντες 'having'?

It indicates a consequence or conclusion drawn from the facts just stated [HNTC, ICC2, NIC1, NIC2, NTC, SP, TG, WBC]; that is, because we have these promises, let us cleanse ourselves.

QUESTION—Which promises is he referring to?

They are the promises of 7:16–18 concerning God's dwelling among them as in a temple [AB, HNTC, ICC2, My, NAC, NIC1, NIC2, NTC, SP, TH, TNTC, WBC]. They are the promises of being God's dwelling place and the benefits of obedience to God [EBC], of God's indwelling and his favor [Ho]. The word ταύτας 'these' occurs first in the sentence, indicating emphasis [EBC, EGT, HNTC, ICC1, NTC].

from every defilement^a of flesh^b and spirit,^c

LEXICON—a. μολυσμός (LN 53.35) (BAGD p. 527): 'defilement' [AB, BAGD, HNTC, ICC2, LN, NTC, WBC; NAB, NRSV, TNT], 'stain' [Lns], 'filthiness' [KJV]. The phrase 'every defilement' is translated 'all that can defile' [REB], 'everything that can defile' [NLT], 'everything that contaminates' [NIV], 'everything that pollutes' [NJB], 'everything that keeps (our bodies and spirits) from being clean' [CEV], 'everything that makes (body or soul) unclean' [TEV].

b. σάρξ (LN 8.4) (BAGD 2. p. 743): 'flesh' [AB, HNTC, ICC2, Lns, NTC, WBC; KJV, NAB, REB], 'body' [BAGD, LN; CEV, NIV, NJB, NLT, NRSV, TEV, TNT]. See this word also at 1:17; 4:11; 5:16.

c. πνεῦμα (LN 26.9) (BAGD 3.a. p. 675): 'spirit' [AB, BAGD, HNTC, ICC2, LN, Lns, WBC; all versions except TEV], 'soul' [TEV].

QUESTION—What are the defilements of flesh and spirit they are to avoid?

This word μολυσμός 'defilement' is used only here in the NT and in three places in the LXX, where it represents religious defilement [TNTC]. He is calling them to avoid any association with idolatry or pagan worship [EBC]. He is saying that the Corinthians must avoid the spiritual and physical contaminations of idolatrous worship and the cultic prostitution associated with it [NTC, TNTC]. The sins of the flesh are drunkenness and debauchery, which desecrate the body as the temple of the Holy Spirit, and the sins of the spirit are pride and malice [Ho]. Paul is making a connection between purity, which the people of that day considered necessary for entering any temple, and the idea of the people as a temple of God [NAC]. Paul's exhortation in 6:17 'do not touch any unclean thing' is applied now to separation from the temple cults [NIC2].

QUESTION—How does Paul use the terms 'flesh' and 'spirit'?

Σάρξ 'flesh' is used as the seat of the principle of sin, the physical-psychical part of our nature; the two terms include each other, and represent wrong actions as well as wrong thoughts, desires, or doctrines [Lns, My]. Sins of the flesh are physical in nature and sins of the spirit have to do with attitudes [Ho]. 'Flesh' and 'spirit' represent the whole of human nature [ICC1, WBC], the material and the immaterial [ICC1], the body and the soul [Lns], the biological and the intellectual [He], the physical and spiritual [NTC, TNTC]. It is the totality of one's physical and emotional being [NIC2], the total personality outwardly and inwardly in relation to God and to other people [EBC]. It is the entire person in its inward and outward aspects [AB, HNTC, NAC, TG]. Defilement of flesh and spirit refers to every possible kind of defilement [ICC2, NIC1], whether external or internal, seen or unseen, public or private [NIC1]. If one aspect of the person is defiled the other is defiled also [ICC1, WBC].

perfecting[a] holiness[b] in (the) fear[c] of-God.

LEXICON—a. pres. act. participle of ἐπιτελέω (LN 68.22) (BAGD 2. p. 302): 'to perfect' [HNTC, ICC2, NTC, WBC; KJV, NIV], 'to make perfect' [AB; NRSV], 'to complete' [BAGD, LN; REB], 'to bring to its goal' [Lns], 'to bring to completion' [NJB]. The phrase 'perfecting holiness' is translated 'we should try to be completely like him' [CEV], 'strive to fulfill our consecration perfectly' [NAB], 'to work toward complete purity' [NLT], 'be completely holy' [TEV], 'live a life of perfect holiness' [TNT]. The present participle indicates a continual advancing in holiness [AB, NIC1].

b. ἁγιωσύνη (LN 88.25) (BAGD p. 10): 'holiness' [AB, BAGD, HNTC, ICC2, LN, Lns, NTC, WBC; KJV, NIV, NRSV, TNT], 'consecration' [NAB, REB], 'sanctification' [NJB], 'purity' [NLT], '(being) holy' [TEV], not explicit [CEV].

246   2 CORINTHIANS 7:1

c. φόβος (LN 53.59) (BAGD 2.b.α. p. 864): 'fear' [AB, HNTC, ICC2, Lns, NTC, WBC; KJV, NAB, NJB, NLT, NRSV, REB], 'reverence' [BAGD, LN; NIV], 'respect' [BAGD], 'awe' [LN; TEV, TNT], '(to) honor (God)' [CEV].

QUESTION—In what way might holiness become 'perfect'?

Holiness is the positive aspect of that for which cleansing is the negative [Ho, SP]. The negative aspect is purity and the positive aspect is moral excellence [Ho].

1. It refers to a process of progressive sanctification. It is the repeated act of consecrating oneself [ICC1, WBC]. It is turning away from sin in every instance of temptation, and thus attaining holiness in that case [Lns]. It is to give oneself completely to consecration [ICC1], to living God's way [TG]. It is a continuing process in which believers apply themselves to fostering complete holiness [NTC]. The holiness is ethical in nature and progresses as Christians keep up sustained efforts and don't thwart the Holy Spirit [He]. To perfect holiness is to establish complete holiness in oneself [My]. To perfect holiness is the process of pressing on toward the goal of perfection in reverence and devotion as well as in awe of God and concern for ultimate judgment [NIC1]. It is a striving to purify the inward self and the outward behavior, to be completely holy as is fitting for those who are a temple in which God dwells [ICC2].
2. It refers to a covenant relation with God in which they fulfill their commitment to him by withdrawing from any unholy alliance or association with idolatry [NAC, NIC2, TNTC].

DISCOURSE UNIT: 7:2–16 [TG, TH, WBC; CEV, NAB, NIV, NLT, NRSV, TEV]. The topic is Paul's joy [TG, TH; NIV, TEV], joy over repentance [NAB], Paul's joy at the church's repentance [NLT, NRSV], the final appeal and Titus' good report [WBC], the church makes Paul happy [CEV].

DISCOURSE UNIT: 7:2–4 [NIC2]. The topic is epilogue: words of encouragement.

7:2 Make-room[a] for-us (in your hearts); we-wronged[b] no-one, we-corrupted[c] no-one, we-took-advantage-of[d] no-one.

LEXICON—a. aorist act. impera. of χωρέω (LN **34.13**) (BAGD 3.b.α. p. 890): 'to make room for' [BAGD, ICC2, Lns, NTC, WBC; NAB, NIV, NRSV, TEV, TNT], 'to provide room for' [AB], 'to make a place for' [CEV, REB], 'to keep a place for' [NJB], 'to take (us) into' [HNTC], 'to receive' [KJV], 'to open one's heart to' [**LN**; NLT], 'to be friendly to' [LN]. The implicit qualifier 'in your hearts' is made explicit by BAGD, HNTC, ICC2, LN, NTC, WBC; CEV, NAB, NIV, NJB, NLT, NRSV, REB, TEV, TNT.

b. aorist act. indic. of ἀδικέω (LN 88.22) (BAGD 2.a. p. 17): 'to wrong' [AB, BAGD, HNTC, ICC2, NTC, WBC; KJV, NIV, NRSV, REB, TEV],

'to do wrong to' [NLT], 'to do injustice to' [Lns], 'to treat unjustly' [BAGD; TNT], 'mistreat' [CEV], 'to injure' [NAB, NJB].
c. aorist act. indic. of φθείρω (LN **20.23**) (BAGD 2.a. p. 17): 'to corrupt' [AB, NTC; KJV, NAB, NIV, NRSV], 'to lead astray' [NLT], 'to ruin' [BAGD, HNTC, ICC2, **LN**, WBC; NJB, REB, TEV, TNT], 'to cause harm' [LN], 'to damage' [Lns], 'to hurt' [CEV]. The 'ruin' implied by this word may be financial ruin [BAGD (1.a. p. 17), LN].
d. aorist act. indic. of πλεονεκτέω (LN 88.144) (BAGD 1.a. p. 667): 'to take advantage of' [BAGD, LN, Lns, WBC; NJB, NLT, NRSV, TEV, TNT], 'to defraud' [AB, BAGD, HNTC, NTC; KJV], 'to exploit' [LN; NIV, REB], 'to cheat' [CEV, NAB]. See this word also at 2:11.

QUESTION—Why does he plead with them to make room in their hearts for him?

Paul wants to be accepted into their affections [TG, TH]. He wants them to reciprocate his own love for them [AB, HNTC, Lns, NIC1, TNTC, WBC]. He wants a greater inclusion of himself in their affections and a corresponding decrease in their tolerance of idolatry [NAC]. Paul wants them to understand his intentions [He]. Making room for Paul also means ousting Paul's opponents who proclaim a different gospel [NTC].

QUESTION—What is implied by Paul's three statements in this verse?

He is defending himself against accusations or insinuations of these same things [EBC, EGT, HNTC, ICC1, ICC2, My, NCBC, NIC1, NIC2, NTC, SP, TH, WBC]. Some people may be thinking that these things are true of Paul, though not openly accusing him [Lns]. The 'we' indicates a contrast; Paul did not do these things, although someone else had wronged him, and someone else was corrupting the minds of the Corinthians [NIC2]. The repetition and placement of οὐδένα 'no one' before each of the verbs makes it emphatic [AB, ICC1, ICC2, Lns, WBC].

QUESTION—What is the nature of the corruption that Paul claims not to have done?

It is financial ruin [EBC, HNTC, Ho] or bribery [TH]. It is a moral corruption [EBC, SP, TNTC]. It is corruption or damage to someone's faith [Lns, NIC2, SP, TG], which would be caused by diverting away from a focus on Christ [NIC2]. It is personal ruin brought by excessively severe judgment [NIC1].

7:3 I do- not -say (this) for (your) condemnation;[a] for I-have-said (already) that you-are in our hearts to-die-together[b] and to-live-together.[c]

LEXICON—a. κατάκρισις (LN 56.31) (BAGD p. 412): 'condemnation' [AB, BAGD, HNTC, ICC2, LN, Lns]. This noun is also translated as a verb: 'to condemn' [NTC, WBC; KJV, NAB, NIV, NJB, NLT, NRSV, TEV, TNT], 'to be hard on' [CEV]. The phrase 'for (your) condemnation' is translated 'my words are no reflection on you' [REB]. See this word also at 3:9.

b. aorist act. infin. of συναποθνῄσκω (LN 23.118) (BAGD p. 785): 'to die together' [AB, LN, Lns, NTC; NJB, NLT, NRSV], 'to die with' [BAGD, ICC2, WBC; KJV, NIV], 'to be bound up in death' [HNTC]. The phrase 'to die together and to live together' is translated 'whether we live or die' [CEV, TEV], 'even to the sharing of death and life together' [NAB], 'so that together we live and together we die' [NJB], 'come death, come life' [REB], 'come life or death' [TNT].
   c. pres. act. infin. of συζάω (LN **23.96**) (BAGD p. 775): 'to live together' [AB, BAGD, LN, Lns, NTC; NJB, NLT, NRSV], 'to live with' [ICC2, **LN**, WBC; KJV, NIV], 'to be bound up with in life' [HNTC], 'whether we live (or die)' [CEV, TEV], 'to the sharing of (death and) life together' [NAB], '(come death) come life' [REB], 'come life (or death)' [TNT].

QUESTION—What relationship is indicated by γάρ 'for'?

It indicates the grounds for his statement that he did not say this to condemn them [Ho, NIC2, TH].

QUESTION—To what earlier statement is he referring?

He is referring to his statement in 6:11 that he and his associates have opened wide their hearts [EBC, HNTC, ICC2, My, NAC, NIC1, NIC2, NTC, TG, TH, WBC]. He is referring to 6:12 where he says that they are not withholding affection from the Corinthians [Ho, ICC2]. He is referring to 3:2 where he says they are his letter written on his heart, as well as to 6:11 [EGT]. He is referring to 4:10–15 where he claims that death working in him brings life to them [Lns].

QUESTION—How does Paul die together or live together with the Corinthians?

The Corinthians have a permanent and secure place in his affections [EBC]; neither death nor circumstance will sever the friendship [Ho, TG]. It is a lasting friendship that will endure no matter what happens [TH]. Whether they live or die, the Corinthians are in their hearts [AB, EGT, ICC1]. Paul gives himself to them without reserve [HNTC], and his commitment to them includes risking his life to minister to them [NTC]. He will go to any length to preserve their relationship [WBC]. They have a sense of comradeship and unity, not an actual dwelling together in the same place [LN]. There is a deep bond of union [He, SP]. The normal order is reversed due to the Christian perspective [TNTC]; physical death precedes eternal life [SP]. The text order is reversed in translations to present the normal order: to live or die together [CEV, NIV, NJB, NLT, TEV, TNT]. Paul is speaking of their sharing together in the resurrection life [ICC2]. Paul is saying that it is the Corinthians who died and are living together with Paul, because they died to sin through faith and live a spiritual life along with Paul [Lns].

DISCOURSE UNIT: 7:4–9:15 [AB]. The topic is the collection for Jerusalem.

DISCOURSE UNIT: 7:4–16 [AB]. The topic is preliminary assurances of confidence.

7:4 **I-have much boldness/confidence[a] toward/in[b] you, I have much boasting[c] about you;**
LEXICON—a. παρρησία (LN 25.158) (BAGD 3.a. p. 630): 'boldness' [BAGD, LN], 'boldness of speech' [KJV], 'freedom of speech' [HNTC], 'outspokenness' [Lns], 'confidence' [BAGD, NTC, WBC; NIV, NLT, TNT]. The phrase 'I have boldness/confidence toward/in you' is translated 'I feel I can speak quite candidly to you' [AB], 'I am very candid with you' [ICC2], 'I speak to you with utter frankness' [NAB], 'I can speak with the greatest frankness to you' [NJB], 'I am speaking to you with great frankness' [REB], 'I trust you completely' [CEV], 'I boast about you' [NRSV], 'I am sure of you' [TEV]. See this word also at 3:12.
  b. πρός (LN 90.25, 90.58): 'to' [LN (90.58)], 'about' [LN (90.25)]. Those who translate παρρησία in terms of boldness, candidness, or freedom of speech translate this pronoun as 'to (you)' [AB; NAB, NJB, REB, TNT], 'toward (you)' [HNTC, Lns; KJV], 'with (you)' [ICC2]. Those who translate παρρησία in terms of confidence translate the pronoun as 'in (you)' [NTC, WBC; NIV, NLT], 'about (you)' [NRSV], 'of (you)' [TEV].
  c. καύχησις (LN **25.204**) (BAGD 1. p. 426): 'pride (in you)' [AB, BAGD, ICC2, LN, NTC, WBC; NIV, NJB, NLT, NRSV, REB, TEV, TNT], 'glory (about you)' [Lns], 'glorying (of you)' [KJV]. This noun is also translated as a verb phrase: 'I am proud (of you)' [**LN**; CEV], 'I boast (about you)' [HNTC; NAB]. See this word also at 1:12.
QUESTION—Does παρρησία πρὸς ὑμᾶς refer to Paul's openness of speech toward the Corinthians or his confidence in them?
  1. It is his frankness or boldness of speech [EGT, HNTC, ICC2, Lns, NAC, NCBC, NIC1, NIC2, SP, TH; KJV, NAB, NJB, REB]. Boldness of speech is based on confidence [NAC, NIC1, TH].
  2. It is his confidence in them [He, ICC1, My, NTC, TNTC, WBC; CEV, NIV, NLT, NRSV, TEV]. His great confidence prompted bold and open speech toward them [NTC].

I-have-been-filled[a] with-encouragement,[b] I-overflow[c] with-joy in all our affliction.[d]
LEXICON—a. perf. pass. indic. of πληρόω (LN 59.37) (BAGD 1.b. p. 671): 'to be filled with' [AB, BAGD, ICC2, LN, Lns, NTC; KJV, NAB, NJB, NRSV, TNT], 'to be full of' [HNTC; REB, TEV]. The phrase 'I have been filled with encouragement' is translated 'I am greatly encouraged' [CEV, NIV], 'my encouragement is complete' [WBC], 'you have greatly encouraged me' [NLT].
  b. παράκλησις (LN 25.150) (BAGD 3. p. 618): 'encouragement' [LN, WBC; NJB, TNT], 'courage' [TEV], 'comfort' [AB, BAGD, HNTC, ICC2, NTC; KJV], 'consolation' [BAGD, Lns; NAB, NRSV, REB]. This noun is also translated as a verb: 'you encouraged me' [NLT], or as a predicated adjective: 'I am encouraged' [CEV, NIV, NLT]. See this word also at 1:3–7.

250 2 CORINTHIANS 7:4

   c. pres. pass. indic. ὑπερπερισσεύω (LN 59.49) (BAGD 2. p. 841): 'to overflow' [BAGD, HNTC, ICC2, NTC, WBC; NJB, REB, TNT], 'to be overcome' [AB], 'to be more abundant' [LN], 'to be made to abound' [Lns], 'to run over' [TEV]. The phrase 'I overflow with joy' is translated 'I am very happy' [CEV], 'I am exceeding joyful' [KJV], 'my joy knows no bounds' [NAB, NIV], 'you have made me happy' [NLT], 'I am overjoyed' [NRSV].
   d. θλῖψις (LN 22.2) (BAGD 1. p. 362): 'affliction' [AB, BAGD, HNTC, ICC2, NTC; NAB, NRSV, TNT], 'tribulation' [BAGD, Lns; KJV], 'suffering' [LN], 'trouble and suffering' [LN], 'trouble' [CEV, NIV, NLT, REB, TEV], 'distress' [WBC], 'hardship' [NJB]. See this word also at 1:4, 8; 2:4; 4:17; 6:4. The phrase ἐπὶ πάσῃ τῇ θλίψει ἡμῶν 'in all our affliction' is also found in 1:4.

QUESTION—What relationship does 7:2–4 have to the rest of the epistle?

The verses immediately preceding conclude the long excursus on Paul's ministry begun in 2:14 and are a hinge connecting the two main parts of the epistle; Paul's repetition of words and ideas from earlier passages that he will carry forward in subsequent passages indicate that this is a transitional or bridge passage [NIC2]. Everything in between 2:13 and 7:4 has been a digression or interlude [EBC, My, NTC, TG, TNTC].

DISCOURSE UNIT: 7:5–9:15 [HNTC, NIC2]. The topic is Paul's plans for Corinth and their working out in the future [HNTC], Paul in Macedonia: Titus brings news from Corinth [NIC2].

DISCOURSE UNIT: 7:5–16 [EBC, HNTC, ICC1, ICC2, NIC2, TNTC; NJB]. The topic is Paul in Macedonia; he is joined by Titus [NJB], the effects of the severe letter [NIC2], Paul's reconciliation with the Corinthians [EBC], the reconciliation completed [ICC1], self-defense concluded [ICC2], narrative resumed, penitence opens the door to the future [HNTC], Paul's joy after a crisis resolved [TNTC].

7:5 For indeed,[a] (after) having-come into Macedonia our body[b] had no rest,[c]

LEXICON—a. καὶ γάρ 'for indeed' [ICC2, NTC], 'indeed' [AB], 'for even' [HNTC, Lns; NRSV], 'for' [WBC; KJV, NIV], 'even' [NJB, REB, TEV], 'it is true that' [TNT], not explicit [CEV, NAB, NLT].
   b. σάρξ (LN 8.4) (BAGD 2. p. 743): 'body' [BAGD, LN, NTC, WBC; NIV, NJB, NRSV], 'flesh' [HNTC, Lns; KJV], 'vulnerable human nature' [ICC2]. The phrase 'our body' is translated '(for) us' [AB; NLT], 'we' [CEV, REB, TEV, TNT], 'I' [NAB]. See this word also at 1:17; 4:11; 5:16; 7:1.
   c. ἄνεσις (LN 22.36) (BAGD 2. p. 65): 'rest' [BAGD, NTC, WBC; KJV, NIV, NJB, NLT, NRSV, TEV], 'chance to rest' [CEV], 'relief' [AB, BAGD, HNTC, LN, Lns; REB, TNT], 'ease' [ICC2]. The phrase 'our body had no rest' is translated 'I was restless and exhausted' [NAB]. The

negative used here οὐδεμίαν 'not even any' is intensive [NIC2]. See this word also at 2:13.
QUESTION—What relationship is indicated by καὶ γάρ 'for indeed'?
It introduces the particulars (in 7:4) of what Paul was talking about in 7:3 concerning his afflictions [AB, Ho, ICC2, SP, WBC]. It introduces an explanatory concessive clause which is followed by a contrastive 'not...but' clause [NIC2]; even when we came, we did not find rest but rather we were afflicted.
QUESTION—How does his statement 'our body (σάρξ) had no rest' compare with 'I did not have rest in my spirit (πνεῦμα)' in 2:13?
1. The two words σάρξ 'body' and πνεῦμα 'spirit' are used in essentially the same sense in these two passages [EBC, EGT, HNTC, Ho, NCBC, NIC1, SP, TG]. Both are used loosely in a non-theological sense [HNTC, NIC1]. They are used loosely to refer to the whole person [EBC, EGT, HNTC, ICC2, TG, TH]. One implies the other [NIC1]. Σάρξ 'flesh' implies weakness, vulnerability, and frailty [Ho, ICC2, NAC, NCBC, SP, TH]. Σάρξ here is the circumstances of daily life [He].
2. In Troas his mind was troubled but in Macedonia he was affected physically [Lns].
QUESTION—What connection is there between this verse and the very similar statement in 2:12–13?
After a long digression Paul now resumes what he was discussing in 2:13 [EBC, He, HNTC, ICC1, ICC2, Lns, NAC, NIC1, NIC2, NTC, SP, TH, TNTC, WBC].

but being-afflicted[a] in every way;[b] battles[c] outside,[d] fears[e] inside.[f]
LEXICON—a. pres. pass. participle of θλίβω (LN 22.15) (BAGD 3. p. 362): 'to be afflicted' [AB, BAGD, Lns; NRSV], 'to suffer affliction' [HNTC], 'to suffer hardship' [LN], 'to be troubled' [ICC2, LN; KJV], 'to be in trouble' [TNT], 'to be distressed' [BAGD, NTC, WBC], 'to be harassed' [NIV], 'to be beset by hardship' [NJB], not explicit [NLT]. The phrase 'being troubled in every way' is translated 'we were faced with all kinds of problems' [CEV], 'I was under all kinds of stress' [NAB], 'trouble met us at every turn' [REB], 'there were troubles everywhere' [TEV]. This present participle is translated in the past tense by AB, HNTC, ICC2, NTC, WBC, and all versions. See this word also at 1:6 and 4:8.
b. ἐν παντί (LN 59.23): 'in every way' [AB, ICC2, Lns; NRSV], 'in every respect' [NTC], 'on all sides' [WBC; NJB], 'on every side' [KJV, TNT], 'at every turn' [NIV, REB], 'from every direction' [NLT], 'everywhere' [TEV], 'all kinds of (problems/stress)' [CEV, NAB], 'every kind of (affliction)' [HNTC]. See the phrase ἐν παντὶ θλιβόμενοι at 4:8.
c. μάχη (LN **39.23**) (BAGD p. 496): 'battle' [BAGD], 'dispute' [AB, BAGD, ICC2; NRSV], 'struggle' [**LN**], 'fight' [HNTC, LN, NTC; REB], 'fighting' [BAGD, Lns; KJV], 'strife' [BAGD, WBC], 'quarrel' [BAGD; NJB, TEV, TNT], 'quarrel with others' [NAB], 'conflict' [NIV, NLT].

The phrase 'battles outside' is translated 'we were troubled by enemies' [CEV].

d. ἔξωθεν (LN 83.20) (BAGD 1.b.α. p. 279): 'outside' [BAGD, LN, Lns, NTC; NIV, NLT, TNT], 'without' [AB, HNTC, WBC; KJV, NRSV, REB], 'outwardly' [ICC2], 'all around us' [NJB], not explicit [CEV, NAB]. The phrase 'battles outside' is translated 'quarrels with others' [NAB, TEV].

e. φόβος (LN **25.251**) (BAGD 2.a.α. p. 863): 'fear' [AB, BAGD, HNTC, ICC2, LN, Lns, NTC, WBC; all versions except NJB], 'misgivings' [NJB].

f. ἔσωθεν (LN 83.16) (BAGD 2. p. 314): 'inside' [BAGD, Lns, NTC; NLT], 'on the inside' [LN], 'within' [AB, BAGD, HNTC, LN, WBC; KJV, NIV, NRSV, REB, TNT], 'within myself' [NAB], 'within us' [NJB], 'inwardly' [ICC2], 'in our hearts' [TEV]. The phrase 'fears within' is translated 'troubled by fears' [CEV].

QUESTION—What was the nature of the 'battles outside'?

Paul was faced with adversaries in Macedonia [NCBC]. There were quarrels within the Macedonian churches [NIC1, NTC]. There was opposition or persecution from the outside [NIC1, NTC, TH]. There were opponents in Philippi whom Paul referred to in Phil 3:2 as 'dogs' and 'workers of evil' [AB]. The 'battles' were conflicts with unbelievers [ICC2].

QUESTION—What was the nature of the 'fears inside'?

Paul was concerned about the welfare of the Corinthian church [EGT, ICC1, Lns, NTC, SP] and about why Titus is delayed [Lns, NTC]. He was concerned for Titus' safety in travel [AB, HNTC, ICC2, Lns] and the outcome of his mission in Corinth [AB, HNTC, ICC2, Lns, NCBC, NIC2]. He was worried about the Corinthians' response to his severe letter [NIC2]. Paul was worried that if the Corinthians did not respond positively to his letter, his work among them would prove to be in vain and the Gentile mission would be jeopardized because of it [EBC, NAC]. Paul was troubled by opposition in Macedonia [EBC]. Paul experienced depression caused by illness [He]. Paul was concerned for peace and purity in the churches and about the possibility of apostasy [Ho].

7:6 But the-one-encouraging[a] the downcast,[b] God, encouraged us by the arrival[c] of Titus,

LEXICON—a. pres. act. participle of παρακαλέω (LN 25.150) (BAGD 4. p. 617): 'to encourage' [BAGD, LN, WBC; NJB, NLT, TEV, TNT], 'to comfort' [AB, BAGD, HNTC, ICC2, Lns, NTC; KJV, NIV], 'to bring comfort to' [REB], 'to console' [LN; NRSV], 'to cheer up' [BAGD; CEV], 'to give heart to' [NAB]. All versions translate this word the same in both occurrences in this verse except NAB which translates 'to give strength' the second time. The word order of this clause ('but the one encouraging...God') gives emphasis to 'God' [HNTC, Lns, NIC2] and

reinforces its contrast with the previous verse [NIC2]. See this word also at 1:4, 6, 2:7, 8; 5:20, and 6:1.
b. ταπεινός (LN **25.295**) (BAGD 1. p. 804): 'downcast' [AB, HNTC, ICC2, **LN**, NTC, WBC; NIV, NRSV, REB], 'lowly' [BAGD, Lns], '(those that are) cast down' [KJV], 'dejected' [LN; TNT], 'downhearted' [BAGD, LN; TEV], '(people) in need' [CEV], '(those who are) low in spirit' [NAB], '(all those who are) distressed' [NJB], '(those who are) discouraged' [NLT].
c. παρουσία (LN **15.86**) (BAGD 2.a. p. 630): 'arrival' [HNTC, ICC2, Lns; NAB, NJB, NLT, NRSV, REB, TNT], 'coming' [AB, BAGD, LN, NTC, WBC; KJV, NIV, TEV]. The phrase 'the arrival of Titus' is translated 'when he sent Titus to us' [CEV].

7:7 **and not only by his arrival but also by the encouragement by which he-was-encouraged among/about^a you,**
LEXICON—a. ἐπί (LN 83.9, 89.27) (BAGD II.1.a.δ. p. 287): 'among' [BAGD, HNTC, LN (83.9)], 'because of' [LN (89.27)], 'about' [AB; NRSV, REB], 'in' [KJV], 'in regard to' [Lns], 'on (your) account' [ICC2], 'from' [NAB]. The phrase ἐφ᾽ ὑμῖν 'among/about you' is translated 'that you imparted to him' [NTC], 'that you gave to him' [WBC], 'that you had given him' [NIV, NJB], 'he received from you' [NLT], 'he received among you' [TNT], 'the way you (cheered him up)' [CEV], 'you encouraged him' [TEV].
QUESTION—What relationship is indicated by the preposition ἐπί in the phrase ἐφ᾽ ὑμῖν 'over you'?
 1. When Titus was 'among' them he was encouraged by them [He, HNTC, NTC, WBC; CEV, NAB, NIV, NJB, NLT, TEV, TNT].
 2. Titus was encouraged 'about' them [AB, Ho, ICC1, ICC2, Lns, SP; NRSV, REB].

reporting to-us your longing,^a your mourning,^b your zeal^c for me^d so-that I rejoiced^e more.
LEXICON—a. ἐπιπόθησις (LN **25.18**) (BAGD p. 298): 'longing' [AB, BAGD, HNTC, ICC2, Lns, NTC; NAB, NIV, NRSV], 'desire' [WBC], 'desire to see us' [NJB], 'earnest desire' [KJV]. This noun is also translated as a verb: 'to long' [LN; REB]; as a verb phrase: 'how much you were looking forward to my visit' [NLT], 'how much you want to see me' [TEV], 'how you longed to see me' [TNT]. The nouns 'longing' and 'zeal' are conflated and translated 'how concerned you were (about me)' [CEV].
b. ὀδυρμός (LN **52.3**) (BAGD p. 555): 'mourning' [BAGD, NTC, WBC; KJV, NRSV], 'grief' [NAB], 'lamenting' [LN], 'lamentation' [HNTC, ICC2, Lns], 'sorrowing' [AB], 'deep sorrow' [NIV], 'how sorry you are' [REB, TEV], 'how sorry you were' [CEV, NJB, TNT], 'how sorry you were about what happened' [NLT].
c. ζῆλος (LN **25.46**) (BAGD 1. p. 337): 'zeal' [AB, BAGD, HNTC, ICC2, Lns, NTC, WBC; NRSV], 'ardor' [BAGD], 'ardent concern' [NAB,

NIV], 'earnest concern' [LN], 'fervent mind' [KJV]. The phrase 'your zeal for me' is translated 'how concerned you were about me/for us' [CEV, NJB], 'how warmly you supported me' [TNT], 'how ready you are to defend me' [TEV], 'how loyal your love is for me' [NLT], 'how eager to take my side' [REB].

d. ὑπὲρ ἐμοῦ: 'for me' [AB, NTC, WBC; NAB, NIV, NLT, NRSV, REB], 'about me' [CEV], 'toward me' [KJV], 'on my behalf' [ICC2], 'on my own behalf' [Lns], 'on our behalf' [HNTC], 'for us' [NJB], not explicit [TEV]. This prepositional phrase is also translated as a direct object of implied verbs: 'you longed to see me...you supported me' [TNT]. The phrase 'for me' is explicitly paired with the first and last of the three nouns in this clause ('longing' and 'zeal') by NTC, WBC; NIV, NJB, NLT, REB, TEV, TNT.

e. aorist pass. (deponent = act.) infin. of χαίρω (LN 25.125) (BAGD 1. p. 874): 'to rejoice' [AB, BAGD, HNTC, ICC2, LN, Lns, NTC; KJV, NRSV], 'to be joyful' [NJB], 'to be filled with joy' [NLT], 'to be glad' [BAGD, LN], 'to be happier' [TEV], 'to make (me) happier' [CEV, REB, TNT]. This verb is also translated as a noun: 'joy' [WBC; NAB, NIV]. See this word also at 2:3.

QUESTION—For what were the Corinthians longing?
They longed to see Paul [AB, EBC, EGT, He, HNTC, Ho, Lns, NAC, NCBC, NIC1, NTC, TH, WBC], to restore good relations with him [EBC, Ho, ICC1, NIC1], to receive his approval of how they had responded to him and his assistants [Lns].

QUESTION—What was their mourning about?
They regretted having caused Paul trouble [ICC1, TG, WBC] or having offended him [Ho]. They were sorry for how they had treated Paul during his previous visit [NIC1, NIC2, NTC, SP], and for the wrong things they had done and tolerated [NIC1]. They regretted their disloyal behavior [EBC] and their strained relationship with Paul [NCBC, TH]. They regretted that Paul had not come and the problems that prompted him to stay away [HNTC]. They were mourning because of the rebuke he sent them [EGT].

QUESTION—With which of these nouns is 'for me' to be associated?
It is associated with 'mourning' and 'zeal' [AB, HNTC, ICC1, NIC2, NTC, SP, WBC; NIV, NJB, NLT, REB, TEV, TNT]. It is associated with all three nouns [TH].

7:8 For even if[a] I-grieved[b] you by the letter, I do- not -regret-it;[c]

LEXICON—a. εἰ καί: 'even if' [NTC, WBC; NIV, NRSV, REB, TEV, TNT], 'even though' [AB; CEV], 'though' [HNTC, Lns; KJV, NJB, NLT], 'although' [ICC2], 'if' [NAB].

b. aorist act. indic. of λυπέω (LN 25.275) (BAGD 1. p. 481): 'to grieve' [AB, BAGD, ICC2, Lns, NTC; TNT], 'to cause sorrow' [NIV], 'to make sad' [LN; TEV], 'to sadden' [LN; NAB], 'to hurt' [HNTC, WBC; REB], 'to hurt someone's feelings' [CEV], 'to make sorry' [KJV, NRSV], 'to

distress' [NJB]. The phrase 'I grieved you' is translated 'it was painful to you' [NLT]. See this word also at 2:2, 4, 5, and 6:10.
  c. pres. mid. or pass. (deponent = act.) indic. of μεταμέλομαι (LN **25.270**) (BAGD p. 511): 'to regret' [BAGD, HNTC, **LN**, Lns, NTC, WBC; NIV, NJB, NRSV, REB], 'to have regrets' [AB; NAB], 'to feel regret' [ICC2], 'to feel sad about' [LN], 'to feel bad' [CEV], 'to repent' [KJV], 'to be sorry' [NLT, TEV, TNT].

even if[a] I-did-regret-it—for I-see that that letter grieved you, even if[b] (only) for-a-moment—[c]
TEXT—The word γάρ 'for' (first occurrence, 'for I see') does not occur in some manuscripts. It is included by GNT in brackets, indicating doubt about its authenticity. It is taken by most versions and commentaries as being in the text or at least implied, since its absence leaves the sentence syntactically difficult and the logic of the sentence unclear. It is not included by HNTC and REB.
LEXICON—a. εἰ καί: 'even if' [NJB, TNT], 'even though' [AB], 'though' [HNTC, Lns, WBC; KJV, NIV, NLT, NRSV], 'although' [ICC2, NTC], 'or if' [NAB], not explicit [CEV, REB]. The phrase 'even if I did regret it' is translated 'I could have been sorry' [TEV].
  b. εἰ καί: 'even if' [AB], 'if (only)' [TNT], 'even though' [NJB], 'though' [Lns; NRSV, REB], 'though it were' [KJV], 'albeit' [ICC2], not explicit [HNTC; CEV, NAB, NLT, TEV]. The phrase 'even if only for a moment' is translated 'but for a little while' [NTC], 'but only for a little while' [NIV].
  c. πρὸς ὥραν (LN 67.109) (BAGD 2.a.β. p. 896): 'for a moment' [BAGD], 'for a while' [BAGD, ICC2, LN, WBC; CEV, TEV], 'for a little while' [NTC; NLT], 'only for a little while' [NIV], 'for a time' [Lns; NAB], 'only for a time' [REB, TNT], 'for a season' [KJV], 'temporarily' [AB], 'it was only temporary' [HNTC], 'not for long' [NJB], 'only briefly' [NRSV].
QUESTION—What relationship is indicated by εἰ καί 'even if' in the phrase εἰ καὶ μετεμελόμην 'even if I did regret it'?
  1. It is concessive [AB, EGT, He, HNTC, ICC1, ICC2, Lns, NCBC, NIC1, NIC2, NTC, SP, WBC; all versions except TEV, TNT]: although I did regret grieving you then, I don't now.
  2. It expresses a contrary to fact situation, that is, he could have regretted it, but did not do so. [TG; TEV, TNT]: even if I had been sorry, I wouldn't be now.
QUESTION—What is the logical relationship within its context of Paul's statement βλέπω [γὰρ] ὅτι ἡ ἐπιστολὴ ἐκείνη 'for I see that that letter…'?
(The word γάρ 'for' is not accepted as a part of the text by HNTC and REB, who take the phrase βλέπω ὅτι ἡ ἐπιστολὴ ἐκείνη as introducing a new and different thought. That is, though I did regret hurting you, I see that the hurt was only for a moment.)

1. It is parenthetic, explaining why he felt regret [AB, EBC, EGT, He, Ho, ICC1, Lns, My, NIC1, NTC, SP, WBC]. That is, I felt regret because I see that the letter grieved you.
2. It begins a new sentence, and is loosely connected with Paul's statement at the beginning of 7:8 that he grieved them [ICC2, TG]. That is, Although I grieved you…and I see that I did in fact grieve you….

7:9 **now I-rejoice, not that you-were-grieved but that you were grieved to**^{a} **(the point of) repentance;**^{b}

LEXICON—a. εἰς (LN 89.48) (BAGD 4.e. p. 229): 'to' [AB; KJV], 'unto' [Lns], not explicit [CEV]. This preposition is also translated as a verb phrase: 'led to' [HNTC, NTC, WBC; NAB, NIV, NJB, NRSV, REB], 'resulted in' [ICC2; TNT], 'caused you to have' [NLT], 'made you (change)' [TEV].

b. μετάνοια (LN 41.52) (BAGD p. 512): 'repentance' [AB, BAGD, ICC2, LN, Lns, NTC, WBC; KJV, NAB, NIV, NJB, NRSV, TNT], 'contrition' [AB], 'a change of heart' [REB]. This noun is also translated as a verb phrase: 'to change your ways' [TEV], 'to have remorse and change your ways' [NLT]. The phrase 'grieved to (the point of) repentance' is translated 'God used your hurt feelings to make you turn back to him' [CEV].

for you-were-grieved according-to^a **God, so-that**^{b} **in nothing did-you-suffer-loss/you-might-suffer-loss**^{c} **because-of**^{d} **us.**

LEXICON—a. κατά (LN 89.8): The phrase 'according to God' is translated 'as God willed' [AB], 'in the way of God's will' [HNTC], 'in accordance with the will of God' [ICC2], 'according to God's will' [NTC], 'according to God's way' [Lns], 'after a godly manner' [KJV], 'the kind that God approves' [NJB], 'the kind God wants his people to have' [NLT]. The phrase 'you were grieved according to God' is translated 'you experienced godly sorrow' [WBC], 'God used your hurt feelings' [CEV], 'you were filled with a sorrow that comes from God' [NAB], 'you felt a godly grief' [NRSV], 'you bore the pain as God would have you bear it' [REB], 'you became sorrowful as God intended' [NIV], 'you bore your grief as God intended' [TNT], 'that sadness was used by God' [TEV].

b. ἵνα (LN 89.59, 89.49): 'so that' (purpose) [LN (89.59)], 'that' [AB; KJV], 'in order that' [HNTC], 'in order to' [LN (89.59)], 'so as a result' [LN (89.49)], 'so that' (result) [ICC2, LN (89.49), Lns, NTC, WBC; NRSV, TNT]. The subjunctive clause 'so that in nothing you might suffer loss' is translated as an indicative result clause: 'and none of you were harmed' [CEV], 'thus you did not suffer' [NAB], 'so you were not harmed' [NIV, NLT], 'and so you have come to no harm' [NJB], 'and so you came to no harm' [REB], 'so we caused you no harm' [TEV].

c. aorist pass. subj. of ζημιόω (LN 57.69) (BAGD 1. p. 338): 'to suffer loss' [BAGD, LN, Lns, NTC, WBC; NAB, TNT], 'to sustain a loss' [AB], 'to suffer damage' [HNTC, ICC2], 'to receive damage' [KJV], 'to be

harmed' [CEV, NIV, NLT, NRSV], 'to come to harm' [NJB, REB]. This passive verb is also translated as active: 'we caused you no harm' [TEV].
   d. ἐκ (LN 89.25) (BAGD 3.e.α. p. 235): 'because of' [AB, BAGD, HNTC, LN, NTC], 'by' [BAGD; CEV, KJV, NIV, NLT, NRSV], 'through' [WBC; NJB, TNT], 'from' [Lns; NAB]. The phrase ἐξ ἡμῶν 'because of us' is translated 'at our hands' [ICC2], 'from what we did' [REB], 'we caused' [TEV].
QUESTION—Does the subjunctive verb clause ἵνα ἐν μηδενὶ ζημιωθῆτε ἐξ ἡμῶν 'so that in nothing did you suffer loss through us' indicate purpose or result?
   1. It indicates result [He, ICC2, Lns, NAC, NIC2, NTC, TG, TNTC]; so that you did not suffer loss.
   2. It indicates purpose [AB, EGT, HNTC, Ho, ICC1, My, NIC1, TH, WBC]; so you would not suffer loss.
QUESTION—What is the loss of which he is speaking?
   It is the loss of ultimate reward at the judgment [NAC, NIC1, TNTC, WBC], or a loss in some sense with respect to salvation [My, NAC]. The loss would be that Paul would not return to Corinth [He]. The loss would be having the resentment and sense of injury that characterizes worldly regret [EBC, HNTC, ICC2]. He is referring to spiritual harm [SP, TG]. Paul is saying that they were not spiritually hurt, they were helped by his letter [Ho, TG], or that God intended the rebuke to help, not hurt [EGT]. The loss would be the spiritual benefit they actually received from his letter [NCBC, NTC].

7:10 For[a] the sorrow[b] according-to[c] God

LEXICON—a. γάρ (LN 89.23): 'for' [HNTC, ICC2, LN, Lns, NTC, WBC; KJV, NJB, NLT, NRSV, TEV], 'because' [LN], 'indeed' [NAB], not explicit [AB; CEV, NIV, REB, TNT].
   b. λύπη (LN 25.272) (BAGD p. 482): 'sorrow' [BAGD, NTC, WBC; KJV, NAB, NIV, NLT], 'grief' [AB, ICC2, Lns; NRSV, TNT], 'hurt' [HNTC], 'pain' [REB], 'sadness' [LN; TEV]. This noun is also translated as a verb: 'to feel sorry' [CEV], 'to be distressed' [NJB]. See this word also at 2:1, 7.
   c. κατά (LN 89.8): 'in accordance with, in relation to' [LN]. The phrase κατὰ θεόν 'according to God' is translated 'according to God's way' [Lns], 'according to God's will' [NTC], 'that God wills' [AB], 'in the way of God's will' [HNTC], 'borne in God's way' [REB], 'borne as God intends' [TNT], 'in a way that God approves' [NJB], 'godly' [ICC2, WBC; KJV, NIV, NRSV], 'for God's sake' [NAB], 'that is used by God' [TEV]. The phrase 'sorrow according to God' is translated 'when God makes you feel sorry' [CEV], 'God can use sorrow' [NLT].

produces[a] repentance leading-to[b] salvation[c] without-regret;[d]

LEXICON—a. pres. mid. or pass. (deponent = act.) indic. of ἐργάζομαι (LN 13.9) (BAGD 2.c. p. 307): 'to produce' [NTC, WBC; NAB, NRSV, TNT], 'to result in' [LN], 'to bring about' [AB, BAGD, LN], 'to bring'

[NIV, REB, TEV], 'to effect' [HNTC, ICC2], 'to work' [Lns; KJV], 'to lead to' [NJB], not explicit [CEV, NLT].
- b. εἰς (LN 89.48): 'leading to' [ICC2; NAB, REB], 'leads to' [AB, HNTC, WBC; NIV, NJB, NRSV, TEV], 'to cause' [LN], 'to' [KJV], 'for' [Lns], 'that effects' [NTC], 'that results in' [TNT], not explicit [CEV, NLT].
- c. σωτηρία (LN **21.25**) (BAGD 2. p. 801): 'salvation' [AB, BAGD, HNTC, ICC2, LN, Lns, NTC, WBC; all versions except CEV], 'to be saved' [CEV].
- d. ἀμεταμέλητος (LN **25.271**) (BAGD 1. p. 45): 'without regret/s' [BAGD; NAB], 'unregrettable' [Lns], 'unregretted' [AB], 'not to be regretted' [BAGD, HNTC, ICC2], 'cannot be regretted' [NTC], '(that) leaves no regret' [WBC; NIV], 'leaves no regrets' [TNT], 'with no regrets' [NJB], 'brings no regret' [NRSV, REB], 'we will never regret' [NLT], 'there is no regret (in that)' [TEV], 'not regretful, not feeling sorry about' [LN], 'not to be repented of' [KJV]. This word is translated 'you don't have anything to feel bad about' [CEV].

QUESTION—With which noun is ἀμεταμέλητος 'without regret' associated?
1. It is associated with repentance [AB, EBC, EGT, He, HNTC, ICC1, ICC2, Lns, NAC, NCBC, NIC2, NTC; NAB, NIV, NLT, NRSV, REB, TNT]: repentance that leads to salvation is not to be regretted. This statement is almost an oxymoron, possibly made for rhetorical effect; that is, repentance is the kind of regret that you don't regret [AB, NCBC].
2. It is associated with salvation; salvation is not to be regretted [Ho, My, NIC2, TG; TEV].

But the sorrow of-the-world[a] produces[b] death.
LEXICON—a. κόσμος (LN 41.38) (BAGD 7. p. 446): 'world' [BAGD, LN, Lns; KJV]. The phrase τοῦ κόσμου 'of the world' is translated 'worldly' [HNTC, ICC2, NTC, WBC; NAB, NIV, NRSV, TNT], 'of a worldly kind' [AB], 'the world's kind' [NJB], 'borne in the world's way' [REB], 'that is merely human' [TEV]. The phrase 'sorrow of the world' is translated 'when this world makes you feel sorry' [CEV], 'sorrow without repentance' [NLT].
- b. pres. mid. or pass. (deponent = act.) indic. of κατεργάζομαι (LN 13.9) (BAGD 2. p. 421): 'to produce' [BAGD, ICC2, NTC; NRSV, TNT], 'to bring about' [AB, BAGD, LN], 'to result in' [LN; NLT], 'to end in' [NJB], 'to effect' [HNTC], 'to work' [KJV], 'to work out' [Lns], 'to lead to' [WBC], 'to cause' [CEV, TEV], 'to bring' [NAB, NIV, REB].

7:11 **For look,[a] this very-thing having-been-grieved[b] according-to God worked in-you such[c] earnestness,[d]**
LEXICON—a. ἰδού (LN 91.13) (BAGD 1.c. p. 371): 'look' [HNTC, LN, NTC; CEV, NAB, NJB, REB], 'lo' [Lns], 'see' [AB, ICC2, WBC; NIV, NLT, NRSV, TEV, TNT], 'behold' [KJV], 'consider' [BAGD]. See this word also at 5:17; 6:2.

b. aorist pass. infin. of λυπέω: 'to be grieved' [Lns, NTC], 'to grieve' [AB], 'to be caused grief' [ICC2], 'to bear grief' [TNT], 'to be hurt' [HNTC], 'to be made to feel distress' [NJB], 'to sorrow' [KJV]. This verb is also translated as a noun: 'sorrow' [WBC; NAB, NIV, NLT], 'grief' [NRSV], 'sadness' [TEV]. The phrase 'having been grieved according to God' is translated 'what God has done by making you sorry' [CEV], 'you bore your pain in God's way' [REB]. See this word also at 2:2, 4, 5; 6:10; 7:8.

c. πόσος (LN 78.13) (BAGD 1. p. 694): 'such' [NLT], 'what' [HNTC, ICC2, Lns, NTC, WBC; KJV, NAB, NIV, NJB, NRSV, TNT], 'how great' [BAGD, LN], 'how much' [AB, BAGD, LN], 'intense' [LN], not explicit [CEV, REB, TEV].

d. σπουδή (LN 25.74) (BAGD 2. p. 763): 'earnestness' [AB, BAGD, HNTC, Lns, NTC; NIV, NLT, NRSV], 'devotion' [LN], 'eagerness' [BAGD, ICC2, LN, WBC; TNT], 'carefulness' [KJV], 'a measure of holy zeal' [NAB], 'concern' [NJB]. The phrase 'such earnestness' is translated 'you sincerely wanted' [CEV], '(it made you) take the matter seriously' [REB], '(it has made you) earnest' [TEV].

such^a defense,^b such indignation,^c such fear,^d

LEXICON—a. ἀλλά (LN **89.96**) (BAGD 5. p. 38): 'and' [LN]. Its use six times in succession indicates a repetition of πόσος: 'such…such… such…such' [NLT], 'how much…such…such…such' [AB], 'how… how…such… such…such' [TEV], 'how much…more, what…more, what…more, what' [ICC2], 'what…yea…yea…yea' [Lns], 'what…and… and…and' [HNTC], 'what…yea, what…yea, what…yea, what' [KJV], 'what… what… what…what' [NIV, NJB, NRSV, TNT], 'what…also what…what…what' [NTC, WBC], 'you want…you are… you are…you are' [CEV], 'what…not to speak of…what…what' [NAB], not explicit [REB]. The repetition of this word before each adjective has an ascending, intensifying, and climactic effect [BAGD, ICC2, My, NIC2, WBC].

b. ἀπολογία (LN 33.436) (BAGD 2.b. p. 96): 'defense' [BAGD, HNTC, LN, Lns; NJB], 'self-defense' [ICC2], 'concern to defend yourselves' [AB], 'concern to clear yourselves' [NLT], 'eagerness to clear yourselves' [NTC; NIV, NRSV], 'clearing of yourselves' [KJV], '(it made you) vindicate yourselves' [REB], 'self-vindication' [TNT], 'eager to prove your innocence' [TEV], 'you want to prove that you are innocent' [CEV], 'readiness to defend yourselves' [NAB].

c. ἀγανάκτησις (LN **88.186**) (BAGD p. 4): 'indignation' [AB, BAGD, HNTC, ICC2, **LN**, Lns, NTC, WBC; KJV, NAB, NIV, NJB, NLT, NRSV, TNT], 'anger' [LN; TNT]. The phrase 'such indignation' is translated 'you are angry' [CEV], 'it made you indignant' [REB].

d. φόβος (LN 53.59) (BAGD 2.a.α. p. 863): 'fear' [BAGD, ICC2, Lns, NTC, WBC; KJV, NAB, TNT], 'fearful respect' [HNTC], 'reverence' [LN], 'alarm' [AB; NIV, NJB, NLT, NRSV, TEV]. The phrase 'such fear' is translated 'you are shocked' [CEV], 'it made you apprehensive' [REB].

QUESTION—What does Paul mean by ἀπολογία 'defense'?

They acted to clear themselves of complicity in the wrongdoing [EBC, HNTC, ICC2, My, NIC1]. They showed that they had not participated in the offense nor condoned it [ICC1]. They cleared themselves by apologizing for having allowed the sin to go unaddressed [Ho].

QUESTION—What was the cause of the ἀγανάκτησις 'indignation'?

They were angry at the offender for what he had done [AB, EBC, He, ICC2, Lns, My, NAC, TH]. They were angry at themselves [ICC2, NIC1, WBC]. They were indignant about the shame caused to the church [ICC1]. They were angry that they had troubles with Paul [TG].

QUESTION—What was the nature of their φόβος 'fear'?

It was a fear of God [He, ICC1]. It was a fear of punishment by God and Paul [Ho]. It was a reverence or fearful respect of Paul [HNTC, WBC], or a fear of being punished by Paul [ICC2]. They were alarmed at their own behavior and its effects [EBC]. They were fearful of the possible damage to their Christian fellowship [TG], or of the consequences of continued indifference to what had happened [AB]. They were fearful of not doing all that they should do [Lns].

such longing,[a] such zeal,[b] such rendering-of-justice.[c]

LEXICON—a. ἐπιπόθησις (LN 25.18) (BAGD p. 298): 'longing' [AB, BAGD, HNTC, ICC2, Lns, NTC, WBC; NAB, NIV, NRSV, TNT], 'longing (to see me)' [NLT], 'longing (for me)' [REB], 'deep desire' [LN], 'vehement desire' [KJV], 'yearning' [NJB], 'feelings' [TEV]. The phrase 'such longing, such zeal, such rendering of justice' is translated 'you are eager to see that justice is done' [CEV].

b. ζῆλος (LN 25.46) (BAGD 1. p. 337): 'zeal' [AB, BAGD, HNTC, ICC2, Lns, NTC, WBC; KJV, NLT, NRSV, TNT], 'ardent desire' [NAB], 'readiness' [NIV], 'enthusiasm' [NJB], 'eagerness' [REB], 'concern' [NIV], 'earnest concern' [LN], 'ardor' [BAGD], 'devotion' [REB, TEV], not explicit [CEV]. This word is associated with the following word, ἐκδίκησις by CEV, NAB, NLT; that is, their zeal was that justice be done.

c. ἐκδίκησις (LN 38.8, 39.33) (BAGD p. 238): 'punishment' [BAGD, LN (38.8), NTC, WBC; NRSV], 'infliction of punishment' [ICC2], 'retribution' [LN (39.33)], 'revenge' [KJV], 'vengeance' [BAGD], 'desire for vengeance' [HNTC], 'reprisal' [AB], 'action of justice' [Lns], 'justice done' [NJB], 'desire to see justice done' [TNT], 'desire to restore the balance of justice' [NAB], 'readiness to see justice done' [NIV], 'eagerness to see justice done' [REB], '(you are eager) to see that justice is done' [CEV], 'readiness to punish the wrongdoer' [NLT], 'readiness to punish wrongdoing' [TEV].

QUESTION—What is the focus of their ἐπιπόθησις 'longing'?

They longed to see Paul [AB, EBC, He, HNTC, Ho, My, TG], and restore their relationship with him [NAC, NIC1, TG, WBC]. They were longing for Paul's approval [Ho, ICC1], and for him to visit them again [ICC1].

QUESTION—What was the object of their ζῆλος 'zeal'?

It was a zeal for Paul [AB, HNTC, ICC2, WBC], a zeal for his message [WBC], a zeal to honor him and his ministry [NIC1]. It was a zeal for justice to be done [CEV, NAB, NLT], a zeal for the punishment of the offender [Ho, My] or for his reformation [Ho]. It was a zeal to do all that they should [Lns]. Their zeal is a reversal of the apathy that had previously characterized them [NAC]. Their ζῆλος was a concern that Paul might exercise discipline when he visited them again [EBC].

QUESTION—What does Paul mean by ἐκδίκησις 'rendering of justice'?

It was the punishing of the offender [EBC, He, HNTC, ICC1, ICC2, NCBC, NIC1, NTC, TG, WBC]. This is the punishment referred to in 2:6 [NCBC].

In everything you-showed[a] yourselves to-be innocent[b] in the matter.

LEXICON—a. aorist act. indic. of συνίστημι (LN 28.49) (BAGD I.1.c. p. 790): 'to show' [AB, BAGD, HNTC, ICC2, LN, NTC; NLT, TEV], 'to demonstrate' [BAGD, LN, WBC], 'to display' [NAB], 'to establish' [TNT], 'to prove' [CEV, NIV, NRSV], 'to approve' [KJV], 'to commend' [Lns], 'to clear (of blame)' [NJB, REB]. See this word also at 3:1, 4:2, 5:12, and 6:4.

b. ἁγνός (LN 88.28) (BAGD 1. p. 12): 'innocent' [AB, BAGD, HNTC, ICC2; NIV, TNT], 'pure' [LN, Lns], 'completely right' [CEV], 'clear' [KJV], 'guiltless' [NRSV], 'without fault' [TEV]. This adjective is also translated as a noun: 'innocence' [WBC; NAB]. The phrase συνεστήσατε ἑαυτοὺς ἁγνοὺς εἶναι 'you showed yourselves to be innocent' is translated 'you have cleared yourselves of blame' [NJB, REB], 'you showed that you have done everything you could to make things right' [NLT].

QUESTION—In what way were they innocent?

They were now innocent because they had repented [Lns, NAC]. They showed that they had not been involved in the offense [EGT, My, TG, TNTC], and they proved that by disciplining the offender [TNTC]. They were not guilty of approving or countenancing the offense and they cleared themselves by apologizing for letting it go unaddressed [Ho]. They were not guilty in what happened, and their repentance had to do with their neglect in dealing with it [AB, HNTC, ICC2]. They were innocent by virtue of having done what they should have to right the wrong [EBC, He, NIC1, NIC2]. They were innocent because they were no longer complacent, and they sided with Paul [WBC].

7:12 So[a] even though/when[b] I-wrote to you, (it was) not for[c] the wrongdoer nor for the one-wronged[d]

LEXICON—a. ἄρα (LN 89.46) (BAGD 4. p. 104): 'so' [BAGD, HNTC, LN, Lns, NTC; NAB, NJB, NRSV, TEV], 'and so' [REB], 'so then' [ICC2, WBC; TNT], 'then' [BAGD, LN], 'as a result, consequently' [BAGD, LN], 'thus' [AB], 'wherefore' [KJV], 'therefore' [NAB], not explicit [CEV, NLT].
- b. εἰ καί: 'even though' [AB; NIV, TEV, TNT], 'though' [HNTC, Lns; KJV], 'although' [ICC2, NTC; NJB, NRSV, REB], 'when' [WBC; CEV], not explicit [NAB, NLT].
- c. ἕνεκεν (LN 89.31) (BAGD p. 263): 'for' [NAB], 'for the sake of' [BAGD; NJB, TNT], 'for the cause of' [KJV], 'because of' [AB, BAGD, LN; TEV], 'on account of' [BAGD, HNTC, ICC2, LN, Lns, NTC, WBC; NIV, NRSV]. The phrase 'not for the wrongdoer' is translated 'it wasn't to accuse the one who was wrong' [CEV], 'my purpose was not to write about' [NLT], 'it was not the offender...that most concerned me' [REB].
- d. aorist pass. participle of ἀδικέω (LN 88.22) (BAGD 2.a. p. 17): 'to be wronged' [AB, BAGD, HNTC, LN; NLT, NRSV, TEV], 'to be treated unjustly' [BAGD, LN; TNT], 'to suffer injustice' [Lns], 'to suffer wrong' [KJV], 'to be offended' [NTC, WBC; NAB, NJB], 'to be hurt' [CEV], 'to be injured' [NIV]. The phrase 'the one wronged' is translated 'victim' [REB]. See this word also at 7:2.

QUESTION—What relationship is indicated by εἰ καί 'even though'?
1. It is concessive [AB, EGT, He, HNTC, Ho, ICC2, Lns, NIC2, NTC; KJV, NIV, NJB, NRSV, REB, TEV, TNT]; 'although I wrote to you'.
2. It is referential; 'when I wrote to you' [WBC; CEV, NAB].

QUESTION—What relationship is indicated by οὐχ...οὐδέ 'not...nor'?
1. It is a comparative relationship; I wrote not as much for reason A or reason B as for reason C [AB, EBC, EGT, HNTC, ICC1, ICC2, Lns, NAC, NCBC, NIC1, NIC2, NTC, WBC; REB]. This is a Semitic way of expressing a comparative relationship [NIC1].
2. It is an absolute relationship; I wrote not for reason A, nor reason B, but for C [My, TH; CEV, KJV, NAB, NIV, NJB, NLT, NRSV, TEV, TNT].
3. It is an absolute relationship; you were comforted not because of the wrongdoer or the one wronged, but because your solicitude for us was clearly shown [He].

QUESTION—What is the identity of the wrongdoer?
1. The wrongdoer was someone who insulted Paul or challenged his authority [AB, EBC, HNTC, ICC1, NAC, NCBC, NIC2, NTC, SP, TG, TH, WBC].
2. The wrongdoer was the incestuous man referred to in 1 Corinthians 5 [EGT, Ho, My, NIC1, TNTC]. The incestuous man had also insulted and challenged Paul [TNTC].
3. The wrongdoer was someone who had misappropriated funds from the collection [ICC2].

2 CORINTHIANS 7:12

QUESTION—What is the identity of the person who had been wronged?
1. Paul was the offended party [AB, HNTC, ICC1, NAC, NCBC, NIC2, NTC, SP, TG, TH, TNTC, WBC]. The whole community had also been wronged [NAC, NCBC, NTC].
2. The offended party was the father of the incestuous man [EGT, Ho, My, NIC1].

but for^a manifesting^b to you your earnestness^c for us before^d God.

TEXT—Instead of τὴν σπουδὴν ὑμῶν τὴν ὑπὲρ ἡμῶν 'your earnestness for us', some manuscripts have τὴν σπουδὴν ἡμῶν τὴν ὑπὲρ ὑμῶν 'our earnestness for you'. GNT does not mention this alternative. Only KJV accepts this reading, which it translates 'our care for you'.

LEXICON—a. ἕνεκεν (LN **89.58**) (BAGD p. 263): 'for' [LN], 'for the sake of' [BAGD, LN], 'in order that' [AB, BAGD, HNTC, **LN**; NRSV], 'so that' [ICC2, NTC; CEV, NJB, NLT], 'that' [KJV, NIV], 'on account of' [Lns], 'on (your) account, so that' [WBC], 'to (with infinitive)' [NAB, REB, TEV, TNT].

b. aorist pass. infin. of φανερόω: (LN 28.36) (BAGD 1.b. p. 852): 'to be manifested' [HNTC], 'to be publicly manifested' [Lns], 'to be made known' [LN; NRSV], 'to become known' [BAGD], 'to be revealed' [BAGD, LN, NTC], 'to be made plain' [ICC2, LN], 'to make plain' [NAB, REB, TEV], 'to be disclosed' [AB, LN], 'to appear' [KJV], 'to show' [NLT, TNT]. The phrase 'for manifesting to you...before God' is translated 'so that before God you could see' [WBC; NIV], 'so that God would show you' [CEV], 'that you yourselves should fully realize' [NJB]. See this word also at 2:14; 3:3; 4:10; 5:10, 11.

c. σπουδή (LN **25.74**) (BAGD 2. p. 763): 'earnestness' [AB, BAGD, HNTC, Lns, WBC], 'eagerness' [BAGD, LN], 'devotion' [BAGD, ICC2, **LN**; NAB, TEV], 'zeal' [NRSV], 'good will' [NTC], 'concern' [NJB], 'care' [KJV]. The phrase 'earnestness for us' is translated 'how much you do care for us' [CEV, NLT], 'how devoted to us you are' [NIV, REB], 'how eager you are on our behalf' [TNT]. See this word also at 7:11.

d. ἐνώπιον (LN 83.33) (BAGD 4. p. 270): 'before' [BAGD, HNTC, LN, NTC, WBC; NIV, NRSV, TNT], 'in the sight of' [AB, ICC2, Lns; KJV, NAB, NJB, NLT, REB, TEV], not explicit [CEV].

QUESTION—What are they earnest about?
It is their good will toward Paul [ICC2, NTC]. It is an earnestness to right the wrong committed against Paul [AB] or to be reconciled to him [WBC]. It is their sincerity of devotion to Paul [ICC1, My, NIC1, NIC2] or their zeal for him [TG]. It is their indebtedness and loyalty to Paul [HNTC].

7:13 Because-of^a this we-have-been-encouraged.

TEXT—KJV has 'therefore we were comforted in your comfort', linking this phrase with the phrase that follows in 7:13 and taking a textual variant ὑμῶν 'your' in place of ἡμῶν 'our'. GNT does not mention this variant.

LEXICON—a. διά with accusative object (LN 89.26): 'because of' [LN, WBC], 'by' [NIV, NLT], 'on account of, by reason of' [LN], 'through' [NTC], 'in' [NRSV], not explicit [CEV]. The phrase διὰ τοῦτο 'because of this' is translated 'this is why' [AB; TNT], 'that is why' [REB, TEV], 'for this reason' [HNTC, Lns], 'therefore' [ICC2; KJV], 'this done' [NAB], 'that is what (I have found encouraging)' [NJB]. See the phrase διὰ τοῦτο also at 4:1.

QUESTION—What is the reason for Paul's encouragement?

Paul is encouraged by Titus' report of their positive response to his letter in 7:6 [NIC1, NIC2]. He is encouraged because his purpose stated in 7:12 was attained [ICC1, Lns, My, NCBC, NTC, TNTC, WBC; NAB]. He is encouraged because his letter led to repentance [Ho].

But in-addition-to[a] our encouragement we rejoiced much[b] more at[c] the joy of Titus,

LEXICON—a. ἐπί (BAGD II.1.b.β. p. 287): 'in addition to' [AB, BAGD, ICC2, Lns, NTC, WBC; NIV, NJB, NLT, NRSV, TNT], 'in' [HNTC; KJV], 'beyond this' [NAB], 'besides (being encouraged)' [REB], 'not only' [TEV], not explicit [CEV]. The phrase ἐπὶ δέ is translated 'although' [CEV].

b. περισσοτέρως (LN **78.31**) (BAGD 1. p. 489): 'very great, extremely, all the more, much greater' [LN]. The phrase περισσοτέρως μᾶλλον 'much more' is translated 'very much more' [AB], 'far more' [TNT], 'still more' [BAGD; NRSV], 'even more' [NAB], 'even more greatly' [**LN**], 'all the more' [NJB], 'exceedingly' [NTC], 'exceedingly the more' [KJV], 'the more exceedingly' [Lns], 'the more especially' [HNTC], 'an especially greater degree' [ICC2], 'more than ever' [WBC]. The phrase 'we rejoiced much more' is translated 'we felt even better' [CEV], 'we were especially delighted' [NIV, NLT], 'we have also been delighted beyond everything' [REB], 'how happy (Titus) made us' [TEV]. See this word also at 1:12; 2:4.

c. ἐπί (LN 89.27): 'at' [AB, HNTC, Lns, NTC, WBC; NAB, NRSV, TNT], 'because of' [ICC2, LN], 'for' [KJV], 'by' [NJB], not explicit [TEV]. The phrase 'at the joy of Titus' is translated 'when we saw how happy Titus was' [CEV], 'to see how happy Titus was' [NIV, NLT], 'by seeing how happy Titus is' [REB].

because[a] his spirit[b] has-been-refreshed[c] by you all;

LEXICON—a. ὅτι (LN 89.33, 90.21): 'because' [AB, ICC2, LN (89.33), NTC, WBC; CEV, KJV, NAB, NIV, NRSV], 'for' [HNTC, LN (89.33)], 'now that' [NJB], 'at the way' [NLT], 'over the way' [TEV], 'that' [LN (90.21), Lns], not explicit [REB, TNT].

b. πνεῦμα (LN 26.9) (BAGD 3.b. p. 675): 'spirit' [BAGD, HNTC, ICC2, LN, Lns, NTC, WBC; KJV, NIV, NJB], 'mind' [AB; NAB, NLT, NRSV, REB]. The phrase 'his spirit' is translated 'he' [TNT]. The phrase 'his spirit has been refreshed by you' is translated 'you had shown that he had

nothing to worry about' [CEV], 'all of you helped to cheer him up' [TEV].
c. perf. pass. indic. of ἀναπαύω (LN 23.84) (BAGD 1. p. 59): 'to be refreshed' [BAGD, HNTC, ICC2, NTC, WBC; KJV, NIV, NJB, TNT], 'to be revived' [BAGD], 'to be given rest' [BAGD, LN], 'to receive rest from' [Lns], 'to be set at rest' [NAB, NRSV], 'to be set at ease' [AB], not explicit [CEV]. This passive verb is also translated as an active verb: 'you set his mind at ease' [NLT], 'you helped to set his mind completely at rest' [REB], 'you helped to cheer him up' [TEV].

QUESTION—What is the capacity referred to as 'spirit'?

It is a non-theological use of the term 'spirit' [HNTC, WBC], used more or less interchangeably with σπλάγχνα 'affections' [ICC1, WBC]. It is the mind [AB, TNTC], the soul [Lns], the inner life of feelings and will [TH], his human spirit [NIC2]. It is the self, the seat of the inward life [ICC2].

QUESTION—What is meant by Titus' spirit having been refreshed?

His mind was set at rest [TNTC; NAB, NLT, NRSV, REB], his worries were dispelled [TG; CEV]. Titus' visit was hopeful and encouraging [HNTC]. He was cheered up [TEV]. There was a temporary relief from conflict [ICC1, WBC]. There was a long-lasting sense of relief [NIC2].

QUESTION—How is the term 'all' to be understood here and in 7:15?

All the Corinthians responded positively to Titus [EBC, EGT, ICC2, NIC2]. There was a unity in their welcome of Titus [NIC1]. The entire community has restored relations with Paul [NTC]. They responded well with no significant exceptions [AB]. There was no minority still resisting [HNTC]. While a majority responded to Paul's severe letter, all responded positively to Titus [NIC2]. The majority, though not all, were in unity about supporting Paul [WBC].

7:14 because if[a] I-boasted[b] anything[c] to-him about you, I-was- not -put-to-shame,[d]

LEXICON—a. εἰ (LN 89.65): 'if' [AB, ICC2, LN, Lns; KJV, NJB, NRSV, TNT], 'if indeed' [NTC]. The phrase 'if I boasted' is translated 'in any boasts I had made' [HNTC], 'anything I may have said' [REB]. It is also translated as a statement of fact: 'I boasted' [WBC], 'I had boasted' [NIV], 'I did boast' [TEV], 'though I boasted' [NAB] 'we had told him' [CEV], 'I had told him' [NLT].
b. perf. (deponent = mid. or pass.) indic. of καυχάομαι (LN 33.368) (BAGD 2. p. 426): 'to boast' [BAGD, LN, NTC, WBC; KJV, NAB, NIV, NJB, TEV, TNT], 'to glory' [Lns], 'to tell how much we thought of you' [CEV], 'to tell (him) how proud I was' [NLT], 'to be boastful' [NRSV]. This verb is also translated as a noun: 'boast' [HNTC, ICC2]. The phrase 'if I boasted anything to him about you' is translated 'anything I said to show my pride' [REB].

c. τι (LN 92.12): 'anything' [LN; KJV, REB], 'any (boast)' [HNTC, ICC2], 'in any way' [NJB], 'at all' [TNT], 'some' [AB], 'somewhat' [Lns, NTC; NRSV], not explicit [WBC; CEV, NAB, NIV, NLT, TEV].

d. aorist pass. indic. of καταισχύνω (LN 25.194) (BAGD 2. p. 410): 'to be put to shame' [BAGD, Lns; NAB], 'to be ashamed' [ICC2; KJV], 'to be disgraced' [AB, HNTC, LN; NRSV], 'to be made to look foolish' [NJB]. This passive verb is translated as an active verb: 'you did not embarrass me' [NTC, WBC], 'you have not embarrassed me' [NIV], 'you did not disappoint us/me' [CEV, NLT], 'you have not disappointed me' [TEV], 'you have not let me down' [TNT]. The phrase 'if I boasted anything to him about you, I was not put to shame' is translated 'anything I may have said to him to show my pride in you has been justified' [REB].

but[a] **just-as we-spoke all-things**[b] **in truth**[c] **to you, so also our boasting to Titus proved**[d] **true.**

LEXICON—a. ἀλλά (LN 89.125): 'but' [HNTC, LN, Lns; KJV, NIV, NRSV], 'on the contrary' [AB, ICC2, LN], 'however' [NTC], 'rather' [NAB], 'and' [WBC], 'indeed' [NJB], not explicit [CEV, NLT, REB, TEV, TNT].

b. πᾶς (LN 59.23): 'all things' [Lns; KJV], 'all' [HNTC, LN], 'in all things' [NTC, WBC], 'everything' [AB; NAB, NIV, NRSV], 'in everything' [ICC2], 'every word' [REB], 'always' [CEV, NLT, TEV], 'anything' [NJB], 'nothing but (the truth)' [TNT].

c. ἀλήθεια (LN 72.2) (BAGD 1. p. 35): 'truth' [HNTC, LN, Lns, NTC, WBC; CEV, KJV, NLT, REB, TEV, TNT]. The noun phrase ἐν ἀληθείᾳ 'in truth' is also translated as an adverb: 'truthfully' [BAGD, ICC2]; as an adjective: 'true' [AB; NAB, NIV, NJB, NRSV].

d. aorist pass. indic. of γίνομαι (LN 13.48): 'to prove to be' [HNTC, WBC; CEV, NAB, NIV, NJB, NLT, NRSV, REB, TEV, TNT], 'to turn out to be' [AB, ICC2, Lns], 'to be found (a truth)' [KJV], 'to become' [LN], 'to come (true)' [NTC].

QUESTION—What are the things that Paul spoke in truth to the Corinthians?

Paul is claiming honesty in all his dealings with them [EBC, EGT, He, HNTC, Ho, ICC1, ICC2, Lns, NCBC, NTC, TG]. He is referring specifically to the question about his earlier travel plans [NIC2]. This is the same claim as he has made in 1:17–18 [EGT, HNTC, Ho, ICC2, My, NCBC, NIC2]. He is referring to his consistent character and reliability when he was with them in Corinth [NIC1]. He is speaking of his truthfulness in general and his gospel message in particular [WBC].

7:15 **And his affections**[a] **are more-abundantly**[b] **toward you, remembering**[c] **the obedience**[d] **of you all,**

LEXICON—a. σπλάγχνον (LN 26.11) (BAGD 1.b. 763): The plural form is translated 'affections' [HNTC], 'affection' [NTC, WBC; KJV, NIV], 'personal affection' [NJB], 'heart' [BAGD, ICC2, Lns; NAB, NRSV, REB, TNT], 'feelings' [AB, Lns], not explicit [CEV, NLT, TEV]. See this word also at 6:12.

b. περισσοτέρως (LN 78.31) (BAGD 2. p. 651): 'more abundant' [KJV], 'the more enlarged' [AB], 'more intensely' [Lns], 'more than ever' [NLT], 'all the more' [LN; NRSV, REB], 'all the more significant' [NTC], 'all the greater' [NIV], 'all the stronger' [NJB], 'much greater' [LN], 'especially' [BAGD, HNTC, ICC2]. The phrase 'his affections are more abundantly toward you' is translated 'his affection abounds toward you' [WBC], 'Titus loves all of you very much' [CEV], 'he cares for you more than ever' [NLT], 'his love for you grows stronger' [TEV], 'his heart embraces you with an expanding love' [NAB]. See this word also at 1:12; 2:4; 7:13.

c. pres. pass. participle of ἀναμιμνῄσκω (LN **29.9**) (BAGD p. 57): 'to remember' [AB, BAGD, HNTC, ICC2, **LN**, Lns, NTC; all versions except NAB, REB], 'to recall' [LN, WBC; NAB, REB]. This present participle is translated 'as he remembers/recalls' [AB, HNTC, ICC2; NAB, NRSV, REB, TEV, TNT], 'when he remembers' [Lns, NTC, WBC; CEV, NIV, NJB, NLT], 'whilst he remembers' [KJV].

d. ὑπακοή (LN 36.15) (BAGD 1.b. p. 837): 'obedience' [AB, BAGD, HNTC, ICC2, LN, Lns, NTC, WBC; KJV, NAB, NRSV]. The phrase 'the obedience of you all' is translated 'you obeyed' [CEV] 'you all obeyed' [TNT], 'you were all obedient' [NIV], 'how obedient you all have been' [NJB], 'you listened to him' [NLT], 'how ready you all were to do what he asked' [REB], 'all of you were ready to obey' [TEV].

QUESTION—What is the function of the comparative adverb περισσοτέρως 'the more abundantly'?

1. It functions as a comparative [He, Ho, ICC1, My, TG]. Titus loves them now even more than he did before [He, Ho, ICC1, My, TG]. Titus' love has grown stronger [TH]. His love is growing as he remembers their obedience [He].
2. It is used as a superlative and no comparison is intended [AB, ICC2, NIC1, NIC2, NTC]. Paul is expanding on his previous statement and is accustomed to using superlatives [NTC]. By the NT era the superlative form had been replaced by the comparative form [WBC].

as you-received[a] him with fear and trembling.[b]

LEXICON—a. aorist (deponent = mid.) indic. of δέχομαι (LN 34.53) (BAGD 1. p. 177): 'to receive' [AB, BAGD, HNTC, ICC2, LN, Lns, NTC, WBC; KJV, NAB, NIV, TNT], 'to welcome' [LN; CEV, NJB, NLT, NRSV, TEV], 'to meet' [REB].

b. τρόμος (LN 16.6) (BAGD p. 827): 'trembling' [AB, BAGD, HNTC, ICC2, LN, Lns, NTC, WBC; all versions except CEV, NLT]. The phrase 'you received him with fear and trembling' is translated 'you trembled with fear when you welcomed him' [CEV], 'you welcomed him with such respect and deep concern' [NLT].

QUESTION—What does 'fear and trembling' mean in this context?
It is anxiety over whether they might fail to do all that is required of them [AB, Ho, ICC1, My, WBC]. It is anxiety to do the will of God [NAC]. They were anxious lest they should fail to be in proper submission to Titus as Paul's emissary [AB, EBC, NIC1]. It is their positive response to Paul's assertion of his God-given authority [ICC2]. It is evidence of their respect for Paul and his associates [TNTC]. It was a readiness to obey the word of God that Titus brought from Paul [Lns]. It was evidence that they revered God and wanted to do his will as spoken through Titus, whom they considered to be God's ambassador [NTC]. It is an eschatological dread concerning the possibility of their being severed from Paul's apostolic ministry [NIC2]. They trembled because of the stern message regarding excommunication of the offender [EGT]. The fear and trembling is related to the alarm of 7:11 [NCBC].

7:16 I-rejoice that/because[a] I-have-confidence[b] in you in everything.

LEXICON—a. ὅτι (LN 89.33, 90.21): 'that' [HNTC, LN (90.21), Lns, NTC, WBC; CEV, KJV, NJB, TEV, TNT], 'because' [AB, LN (89.33); NAB, NLT, NRSV], not explicit [NIV, REB].

b. pres. act. indic. of θαρρέω (LN 25.156) (BAGD p. 352): 'to have confidence (in)' [AB, HNTC, ICC2, WBC; KJV, NJB, NLT, NRSV, REB], 'to be able to have confidence (in/about)' [NIV, TNT], 'to be confident' [BAGD], 'to be able to depend on someone' [BAGD, NTC; CEV, TEV], 'to be of good cheer in regard to' [Lns], 'to trust' [NAB]. The phrase ἐν παντὶ θαρρῶ ἐν ὑμῖν 'I have confidence in you in everything' is translated 'I have every confidence in you' [AB, HNTC; NJB], 'I have confidence in you in all things' [KJV], 'I have complete confidence in you' [WBC; NIV, NLT, NRSV, REB], 'in every respect I have confidence in you' [ICC2], 'I can be completely confident about you' [TNT], 'in everything I am of good cheer in regard to you' [Lns], 'I can depend completely on you' [NTC; TEV], 'I can depend on you' [CEV], 'I trust you utterly' [NAB]. See this word also at 5:6.

DISCOURSE UNIT: 8:1–24 [HNTC]. The topic is the collection.

DISCOURSE UNIT: 8:1–15 [AB, EBC, TH; CEV, NAB, NIV, NJB, NLT, NRSV, TEV]. The topic is the appeal proper [AB], the need for generosity [EBC], generous giving [CEV], liberal giving [NAB], generosity encouraged [NIV], why the Corinthians should be generous [NJB], a call to generous giving [NLT], encouragement to be generous [NRSV], Christian giving [TH; TEV].

DISCOURSE UNIT: 8:1–7 [ICC1]. The topic is the example of the Macedonian churches.

DISCOURSE UNIT: 8:1–6 [NTC, TNTC, WBC]. The topic is generosity shown [NTC], the commendation of the Macedonians [WBC], the example of the Macedonians [TNTC].

DISCOURSE UNIT: 8:1–5 [EBC]. The topic is the generosity of the Macedonians.

8:1 Now[a] we-make-known[b] to-you, brothers,[c] the grace[d] of God (which) has-been-given[e] to/among[f] the churches of Macedonia,

LEXICON—a. δέ: 'now' [Lns; NLT], 'and now' [ICC2; NIV], 'and' [NTC], 'next' [NJB], 'moreover' [KJV], not explicit [AB, HNTC, WBC; CEV, NAB, NRSV, REB, TEV, TNT]. This word marks transition to a new topic [EGT, Ho, ICC1, My, NIC2].
  b. pres. act. indic. of γνωρίζω (LN 28.26) (BAGD 1. p. 163): 'to make known' [BAGD, LN, NTC], 'to inform' [AB, Lns], 'to draw attention to' [HNTC], 'to draw notice to' [WBC], 'to tell' [NJB, NLT, REB]. The phrase 'we make known to you' is translated 'we want you to know' [CEV, NIV, NRSV, TEV, TNT], 'I should like you to know' [NAB], 'we have information for you' [ICC2], 'we do you to wit' [KJV].
  c. ἀδελφός (LN 11.23): 'brother' [HNTC, ICC2, Lns, NTC, WBC; KJV, NAB, NIV, NJB, TNT], 'fellow believer, Christian brother' [LN]. This plural noun is translated 'brothers and sisters' [AB; NRSV], 'friends' [REB], 'my friends' [CEV], 'our friends' [TEV], 'dear friends' [NLT]. The masculine plural form ἀδελφοί can refer to both males and females [LN, NTC]. See this word also at 1:1, 8; 2:13.
  d. χάρις (LN 88.66) (BAGD 4. p. 878): 'grace' [AB, BAGD, HNTC, ICC2, LN, NTC, WBC; all versions except CEV, NLT]. The phrase 'the grace of God' is translated 'how kind God is' [CEV], 'God in his kindness' [NLT]. See this word also at 1:2, 12.
  e. pres. pass. participle of δίδωμι (LN 57.71): 'to be given' [HNTC, LN, NTC, WBC], 'to be granted' [AB; NJB, NRSV], 'to be bestowed' [ICC2, Lns; KJV], 'to be conferred' [NAB]. This passive verb is also translated in the active voice 'to give' with God as the stated agent: 'the grace that God has given' [NIV, REB, TNT]. The phrase 'the grace of God which has been given to/among the churches of Macedonia' is translated 'the churches in Macedonia have shown others how kind God is' [CEV], 'what God in his kindness has done for the churches in Macedonia' [NLT], 'what God's grace has accomplished in the churches in Macedonia' [TEV].
  f. ἐν (LN 90.56, 83.9): 'to' [AB, HNTC, LN (90.56), NTC, WBC; NJB, NRSV, REB, TNT], 'among' [ICC2, LN (83.9)], 'in' [Lns; TEV], 'on' [KJV, NAB], 'for' [NLT], not explicit [CEV, NIV]. The phrase 'the grace of God which has been given to/among the Macedonian churches' is translated 'the grace that God has given the Macedonian churches' [NIV].

QUESTION—How is χάρις used here?
  It refers to God's grace, which causes the Macedonians to be generous [AB, HNTC, Ho, ICC1, ICC2, My, NAC, NCBC, NIC2, NTC, TG, TH, TNTC, WBC]. It refers to divine grace granted to and displayed by the Macedonians [HNTC]. It speaks of the effects produced by divine grace [BAGD]. It is the

grace of generous giving [EGT, NIC2]. Human generosity is given by God [NAC], and is a consequence of his saving grace [NTC].

QUESTION—Does ἐν mean 'to' or 'among'?
1. It means 'to': God's grace was given to the churches [AB, HNTC, NAC, NTC, WBC; NIV, NJB, NRSV, REB, TNT], or on the churches [NAB], or for the churches [NLT].
2. It means 'in' or 'among': God's grace was given in or among the churches [He, ICC1, ICC2, Lns, My, NIC2]. God's grace has accomplished something in the churches [TEV].
3. God's grace was given to as well as exhibited among the churches [EGT, NIC1].

8:2 that[a] in a great trial[b] of-affliction[c]

LEXICON—a. ὅτι (LN 90.21): 'that' [LN, NTC], 'that is' [LN], 'that is, that' [ICC2], 'how that' [WBC; KJV], 'and how' [NJB], 'namely' [LN, Lns], 'I mean' [HNTC], 'for' [AB; NRSV], not explicit [CEV, NAB, NIV, NLT, REB, TEV, TNT].
b. δοκιμή (LN **27.45**) (BAGD 2. p. 202): 'trial' [KJV, NAB, NIV], 'test' [BAGD, Lns], 'testing' [LN, NTC, WBC], 'severe testing' [AB], 'ordeal' [BAGD, ICC2; NRSV], 'ordeals' [NJB]. The phrase 'great trial of affliction' is translated 'severe trial' [NAB], 'most severe trial' [NIV], 'continual ordeals of hardship' [NJB], 'sorely tried by affliction' [HNTC], 'going through much trouble and hard times' [NLT], 'going through hard times' [CEV], 'the troubles they have been through have tried them hard' [REB], 'severely tested by the troubles' [**LN**; TEV], 'severely tested by tribulation' [TNT]. See this word also at 2:9.
c. θλῖψις (LN 22.2) (BAGD 1. p. 362): 'affliction' [AB, BAGD, HNTC, ICC2, Lns, NTC; KJV], 'trouble' [LN], 'adversity' [WBC], 'hardship' [NJB], not explicit [CEV]. This noun in the genitive case is also translated as an adjective modifying δοκιμή: 'severe (trial/ordeal)' [NAB, NIV, NRSV]; as an adverb 'severely (tested)' [TEV, TNT]. See this word also at 1:4, 8; 2:4; 4:17; 6:4; 7:4.

QUESTION—What relationship is indicated by ὅτι 'that'?
1. It is epexegetic, further explaining what the 'grace' in 8:1 was [EGT, HNTC, Ho, ICC1, ICC2, Lns, My, NIC1, NIC2, NTC, WBC; KJV, NJB]: 'that'.
2. It indicates a causal relation, giving the grounds for Paul's statement in 8:1 [AB, SP; NIV, NRSV]: 'for'.

QUESTION—What relationship is indicated by the genitive phrase 'great trial of affliction'?

They were tested by afflictions [AB, EGT, He, HNTC, ICC1, My, NIC2, NTC, SP, TG, WBC].

their abundance[a] of joy and their deep[b] poverty overflowed[c] into the wealth[d] of their generosity.[e]

- LEXICON—a. περισσεία (LN **78.31**) (BAGD p. 650): 'abundance' [AB, BAGD, ICC2; KJV], 'overflowing' [HNTC] 'excess' [Lns], The phrase 'abundance of joy' is translated 'overflowing joy' [NAB, NIV], 'unfailing joy' [NJB], 'wonderful joy' [NLT], 'abundant joy' [NRSV]; as a verb phrase: 'their joy was very great' [LN], 'their joy was so great' [TEV], 'they were glad' [CEV], 'they have been so exuberantly happy' [REB], 'their joy overflowed' [TNT].
- b. βάθος (LN **78.22**) (BAGD 2. p. 130): 'deep' [ICC2; KJV, NAB, NLT]. The phrase κατὰ βάθους is translated 'down to depth' [Lns], 'deep down' [WBC], 'the depths' [REB], 'profound' [AB], 'rock bottom' [HNTC], 'extreme' [BAGD, NTC; NIV, NRSV], 'intense' [NJB]. The phrase κατὰ βάθους πτωχεία 'deep poverty' is translated 'they were/are very poor' [CEV, TEV], 'they were extremely poor' [LN], 'they were desperately poor' [TNT].
- c. aorist act. indic. of περισσεύω (LN **59.52, 59.54**) (BAGD 1.a.γ. p. 651): 'to overflow' [AB, BAGD, HNTC, NTC; NJB, NLT, NRSV], 'to flow out in' [WBC], 'to abound' [LN (59.52); KJV], 'to abundantly result' [ICC2], 'to exceed' [Lns], 'to well up' [NIV], 'to cause to be abundant' [LN (59.54)]. The phrase 'overflowed into the wealth of their generosity' is translated 'produced an abundant generosity' [NAB], 'they have shown themselves lavishly open-handed' [REB], 'they were extremely generous in their giving' [TEV], 'they were glad to give generously' [CEV], 'they have been generous beyond measure in their giving' [TNT]. See this word also at 1:5, 3:9, 4:15.
- d. πλοῦτος (LN **78.15**) (BAGD 2 p. 674): 'wealth' [AB, BAGD, HNTC, ICC2, NTC, WBC; NJB, NRSV], 'abundance' [BAGD], 'riches' [Lns; KJV], not explicit [CEV]. The phrase 'the wealth of (their) generosity' is translated 'great generosity' [LN], 'abundant generosity' [NAB], 'rich generosity' [NIV, NLT], 'lavishly open-handed' [REB], 'extremely generous' [TEV], 'generous beyond measure' [TNT].
- e. ἁπλότης (LN 57.106) (BAGD 2. p. 86): 'generosity' [AB, BAGD, ICC2, LN, NTC, WBC; NAB, NIV, NJB, NLT, NRSV], 'liberality' [KJV], 'simple-hearted goodness' [HNTC], 'single-mindedness' [LN], not explicit [CEV]. This noun is also translated as an adjective: 'open-handed' [REB], 'generous' [TEV, TNT].

QUESTION—What is the logic of Paul's statement that abundant joy and deep poverty overflowed into a wealth of generosity?

Paul is using contrasts for emphasis [Lns, My]. The contrast here is between joy and poverty [NTC, TG]. Paul is stating a paradox [ICC2, WBC], which is that affliction can produce joy, and joy and poverty can produce generosity [NAC, NTC]. Paul's statement here concerning poverty overflowing into wealth is an oxymoron [AB, BAGD].

QUESTION—What relationship is indicated by the genitive phrase τὸ πλοῦτος τῆς ἁπλότητος 'the wealth of their generosity'
1. The noun πλοῦτος 'wealth' modifies ἁπλότης 'generosity'; that is, their generosity was very great [He, Ho, ICC2, My, NTC, TG; NAB, NIV, NJB, NLT, REB, TEV, TNT].
2. Their wealth consisted of their generosity [NAC, NIC2, WBC] or single-mindedness [Lns].

8:3 For[a] **according to (their) ability,**[b] **I-testify,**[c] **and beyond (their) ability, of-their-own-accord**[d]

LEXICON—a. ὅτι (LN 89.33, 90.21): 'for' [AB, HNTC, ICC2, LN (89.33), Lns, WBC; KJV, NIV, NLT, NRSV, TNT], 'because' [LN (89.33), NTC], 'that' [LN (90.21)], not explicit [CEV, NAB, NJB, REB, TEV].
b. δύναμις (LN 71.1): 'ability' [LN, Lns], 'means' [ICC2, Lns, NTC, WBC; NAB, NRSV], 'power' [KJV]. The phrase κατὰ δύναμιν 'according to their ability' is translated 'as they were able' [AB], 'up to their power' [HNTC], 'as much as they could afford' [CEV], 'as much as they could' [TEV], 'as much as they were able' [NIV], 'what they could afford' [NLT], 'as far as their resources would allow' [NJB], 'to the limit of their resources' [REB, TNT]. See this word also at 1:8; 4:7.
c. pres. act. indic. of μαρτυρῶ (LN 33.262) (BAGD 1.a. p. 492): 'to testify' [BAGD, ICC2, Lns, NTC, WBC; NAB, NIV, NJB, NLT, NRSV, REB], 'to witness' [LN], 'to bear witness' [HNTC], 'to bear record' [KJV], 'to swear' [AB], 'to assure' [TEV], 'to tell' [TNT], not explicit [CEV].
d. αὐθαίρετος (LN **25.66**) (BAGD p. 121): 'of their own accord' [AB, BAGD, HNTC, NTC; NJB], 'of their own free will' [LN; NLT, TEV, TNT], 'of their own volition' [ICC2], 'voluntarily' [Lns; NAB, NRSV], 'spontaneously' [WBC], 'entirely on their own' [NIV], 'on their own initiative' [REB], 'willing of themselves' [KJV]. This word is also translated 'simply because they wanted to' [CEV].

QUESTION—To what action of the Macedonians is Paul referring when he says 'according to their ability and beyond their ability'?
The sentence is long and elliptical, and the verb 'gave' in 8:5 is implied in this verse; that is, they gave according to their ability and beyond their ability [AB, He, HNTC, Ho, ICC1, ICC2, My, NIC1, NIC2, NTC, SP, WBC; NIV, NJB, NLT, NRSV, TEV, TNT].

QUESTION—What relationship is indicated by ὅτι 'that'?
1. It indicates the grounds for Paul's statements in 8:1–2 [AB, EGT, HNTC, Ho, ICC1, My, NTC, WBC; KJV, NIV, NLT, NRSV, TNT]: 'for'.
2. It is epexegetic, further explaining what Paul said in the previous verse [NIC1]: 'that'.

2 CORINTHIANS 8:3

QUESTION—With what action is αὐθαίρετος 'of their own accord' connected?

1. It is associated with the implied verb 'give' [AB, Ho, ICC1, ICC2, Lns, My, NCBC, NIC2, SP, WBC; CEV, KJV, NJB, NLT, NRSV]: of their own accord they gave.
2. It is associated with δέομαι 'to beg' (8:4) [EGT; NIV, REB, TEV, TNT]: of their own accord they begged to be included in the ministry.
3. It is associated with the desire to give as well as the plea to participate in the ministry [NTC].

8:4 with much entreaty^a begging^b us (for) the privilege^c and the sharing^d of the ministry^e to the saints,^f

TEXT—Some manuscripts include δέξασθαι ἡμᾶς 'that we would receive (the gift)' after εἰς τοὺς ἁγίους 'to the saints'. It only occurs in the margin of some manuscripts and is omitted by GNT. Only KJV accepts this variant.

LEXICON—a. παράκλησις (LN **33.168**) (BAGD 2. p. 618): 'entreaty' [KJV], 'pleas' [ICC2], 'appeal' [BAGD, LN]. The phrase 'with much entreaty' is translated as an adverb or adverbial phrase modifying the following verb: 'earnestly' [BAGD, NTC; NRSV], 'urgently' [NIV], 'most urgently' [AB], 'insistently' [NAB] 'most insistently' [NJB, REB], 'with great insistence' [WBC], 'with earnest request' [HNTC], 'with the utmost insistence' [TNT], 'with much urging' [Lns], 'again and again' [NLT], 'with earnest appeal' [LN]; as a verb: 'they begged' [TEV], 'they asked' [CEV].

b. pres. (deponent = mid. or pass.) participle of δέομαι (LN 33.170) (BAGD 2. p. 175): 'to beg' [BAGD, ICC2, LN, Lns, NTC, WBC; CEV, NAB, NLT, NRSV, REB, TNT], 'to implore' [AB; NJB], 'to plead' [LN; NIV, TEV], 'to ask' [HNTC], 'to pray' [KJV]. See this word also at 5:20.

c. χάρις (LN 57.103) (BAGD 3.a. p.878): 'privilege' [LN (**57.98**), NTC, WBC; NIV, NJB, NLT, NRSV, TEV], 'gracious privilege' [NLT], 'grace' [Lns], 'favor' [BAGD, ICC2; NAB, TNT], 'joy' [CEV], 'benefit' [AB], 'generosity' [HNTC], 'gift' [KJV]. This is also translated 'to be allowed' [REB]. See this word also at 1:15; 8:6, 19.

d. κοινωνία (LN **57.98**) (BAGD 4. p. 439): 'sharing' [BAGD, LN, NTC; NAB, NIV, NLT, NRSV, TNT], 'to share in' [REB], 'a share' [NJB], 'participation' [AB, BAGD], 'taking part' [BAGD], 'having a part' [TEV], 'partnership' [ICC2], 'joining in' [WBC], 'fellowship' [HNTC, Lns; KJV], not explicit [CEV]. See this word also at 6:14.

e. διακονία (LN 57.119) (BAGD 4. p. 184): 'ministry' [Lns; NRSV], 'ministering' [KJV], 'service' [HNTC; NAB, NIV, NJB, TNT], 'charitable service' [ICC2], 'act of service' [WBC], 'generous service' [REB], 'service of helping' [NTC], 'helping' [TEV], 'help' [LN], 'contribution' [BAGD, LN], 'giving their money' [CEV], 'gift' [NLT], 'support' [BAGD, LN], 'relief work' [AB]. See this word also at 3:7, 8; 5:18.

f. ἅγιος (LN 11.27): This plural form is translated 'saints' [AB, HNTC, ICC2, Lns, NTC, WBC; KJV, NIV, NRSV], 'God's people' [LN; CEV], 'God's holy people' [NJB], 'members of the church' [NAB], 'the Christians in Jerusalem' [NLT], 'fellow-Christians' [REB], 'God's people in Judea' [TEV]. See this word also at 1:1.

QUESTION—What is meant by χάρις 'privilege'?
1. It is receiving the favor or privilege of participating in the ministry [AB, EBC, EGT, Ho, ICC1, ICC2, My, NAC, NCBC, NIC1, NIC2, NTC, SP, TG, TH, TNTC, WBC; CEV, NAB, NIV, NJB, NLT, NRSV, TEV, TNT].
2. It is human generosity or love that they show [HNTC].

QUESTION—What is the sharing or fellowship expressed by κοινωνία?
It is having a share in the ministry [AB, EBC, Ho, ICC2, My, NAC, NIC2, NTC, SP, TH, TNTC, WBC]. It is being in communion with other churches who are sharing in the ministry [EBC, Lns, NCBC], as well as with those who receive benefit from it [EBC, NCBC].

QUESTION—What relationship is indicated by καί 'and' in the phrase 'the privilege and the sharing of the ministry to the saints'?
It is epexegetic, indicating what the privilege is [AB, EBC, Ho, ICC1, LN, Lns, My, NAC, NCBC, NIC1, NIC2, NTC, TH, WBC; KJV, NAB, NIV, NJB, NLT, NRSV, REB, TEV, TNT]: the privilege of sharing in the ministry to the saints.

QUESTION—Who are the 'saints'?
They are the believers in Jerusalem [AB, EBC, HNTC, ICC2, Lns, NAC, NCBC, NIC1, NIC2, NTC, TH] or in Judea [TEV].

8:5 and (this) not as we-expected[a] but they gave[b] themselves first[c] to the Lord and to us by[d] the will of God

LEXICON—a. aorist act. indic. of ἐλπίζω (LN 30.54) (BAGD 1. p. 252): 'to expect' [AB, ICC2, LN, NTC; NIV, NJB, NRSV], 'to hope' [BAGD, HNTC, LN, Lns, WBC; CEV, KJV, TEV]. This verb is also translated as a noun: 'expectations' [REB, TNT], 'hopes' [NAB, NLT]. The phrase οὐ καθὼς ἠλπίσαμεν 'not as we expected' is translated with the implied notion of the Corinthians having surpassed Paul's expectations: 'not merely as we had hoped/expected' [AB, Lns; NRSV], 'not just as we expected/hoped' [NTC, WBC], 'they did more than we had hoped' [CEV], 'their giving surpassed our expectations' [REB], 'this was beyond all our expectations' [TNT], 'beyond our hopes' [NAB], 'they went beyond our highest hopes' [NLT]. It is also translated as having taken Paul by surprise 'it was not something that we expected of them' [NJB].

b. aorist act. indic. of δίδωμι (LN **53.48**) (BAGD 6. p. 193): 'to give' [AB, HNTC, ICC2, LN, Lns, NTC, WBC; all versions except NJB, NLT], 'to give (oneself) up' [BAGD], 'to offer' [NJB], 'to dedicate' [NLT].

c. πρῶτος (LN 60.46, 65.52) (BAGD 2.c. p. 726): 'first' [AB, ICC2, LN, NTC; CEV, KJV, NAB, NIV, NRSV, TEV, TNT], 'first of all' [BAGD, HNTC; REB], 'in the first place' [Lns], 'their first action' [NLT], 'most

importantly' [LN (65.52), WBC]. This adverb is also translated by a verbal phrase: 'it began by' [NJB].
d. διά with genitive object (LN 89.26, 90.4) (BAGD A. III.1.d. p. 180): 'by' [AB, LN (90.4), WBC; KJV, NAB, NRSV, TEV, TNT], 'through' [BAGD, HNTC, ICC2, LN (90.4), Lns, NTC], 'because of' [LN (89.26)], 'at the prompting of' [NJB]. The phrase 'by the will of God' is translated 'just as God wanted them to do' [CEV], 'in keeping with God's will' [NIV], 'for whatever directions God might give them' [NLT], 'under God (to us)' [REB].

QUESTION—What does he mean by saying 'not as we expected'?
How the Macedonians responded exceeded all expectations [AB, EGT, He, HNTC, Ho, ICC1, Lns, My, NAC, NCBC, NIC2, NTC, SP, TG, TH, TNTC, WBC; CEV, NAB, NJB, NLT, NRSV, REB, TNT].

QUESTION—What was it that was unexpected?
The level of the Macedonians' generosity was unexpected [HNTC, My, NAC, NIC2, TH, WBC]. It was their unexpected dedication of themselves [NAB, NIC1]. It was their giving and their self-dedication [Ho, ICC1, Lns]. It was their eagerness to participate in the ministry to the saints [NCBC, NTC; NJB]. It was the level of commitment to personal service to Paul in the evangelistic ministry, in which a number of Macedonians were involved [EGT].

QUESTION—What does the adverb πρῶτον 'first' signify?
1. It indicates temporal sequence [HNTC, Lns, TG; CEV, NAB, NIV, NJB, NLT, TEV, TNT].
  1.1 First they gave themselves to the Lord, and then they gave themselves to us [CEV, NAB, NIV, TEV, TNT].
  1.2 First they gave themselves to the Lord and to us, and then they gave money [HNTC, Lns; NJB, NLT].
2. It indicates priority of importance; that is, most importantly they gave themselves [AB, EBC, Ho, ICC1, My, NAC, NIC2, WBC]. Most importantly, they gave themselves to the Lord, but also they gave themselves to us [AB, EBC, NIC2].
3. It indicates both priority of importance as well as temporal sequence [EGT, He, ICC2, NIC1, NTC].
  3.1 First, and most importantly, they gave themselves, then they gave their gifts [ICC2, NIC1].
  3.2 First, and most importantly, they gave themselves to the Lord, and then they gave themselves to us [He, NTC].

QUESTION—What does Paul mean by the phrase 'through the will of God'?
1. It was God's will for the Macedonians to give themselves to Paul and his associates [EBC, EGT, He, HNTC, ICC2, Lns, NCBC, NIC2, NTC, TG, TNTC]. They recognized Paul's God-given authority [NTC, TNTC]. Dedication to Christ means being dedicated to serving him by helping his servants [EBC]. They recognized Paul's apostleship as being through the will of God and responded to him accordingly [NIC2]. Acts and the

epistles of Paul reveal that a number of Macedonians assisted Paul at various points in his ministry [EGT].
2. It was God's will for the Macedonians to give themselves to God and to Paul and his associates [ICC1, My, SP, WBC]. God worked in their hearts to prompt them to devote themselves most importantly to God, but also to Paul [My]. The basis for the collection is that they recognize God's power at work in Paul's ministry and that that Paul was an apostle by the will of God [WBC].
3. It was God's will for the Macedonians to give themselves and their possessions [NIC1].
4. It was God's for the Macedonians to give of their possessions [Ho, NAC]. Their giving was God's will and their motive for generosity was his grace [NAC].

DISCOURSE UNIT: 8:6-12 [EBC]. The topic is a plea for liberal giving.

8:6 so-that[a] (we) urged[b] Titus, that just-as he-previously-began[c] thus also he-might-bring-to-completion[d] among[e] you this grace[f] as-well.

LEXICON—a. εἰς (LN 89.48): 'so that' [HNTC, Lns, WBC; NRSV], 'so that as a result' [LN], 'so' [CEV, NIV, NLT, TEV], 'with the consequence that' [ICC2], 'in consideration of this' [AB], 'that is why' [NAB, TNT], 'the upshot is' [REB], 'in the end' [NJB], 'insomuch that' [KJV].

b. aorist act. infin. of παρακαλέω (LN 33.168) (BAGD 2. p. 617): 'to urge' [AB, BAGD, ICC2, Lns, NTC; NIV], 'to encourage' [BAGD], 'to exhort' [NAB], 'to request' [LN, WBC], 'to appeal' [LN], 'to ask' [HNTC], 'to beg' [CEV], 'to desire' [KJV]. See this word also at 1:4, 6; 2:7, 8; 5:20; 6:1; 7:6.

c. aorist (deponent = mid.) indic. of προενάρχομαι (LN **68.4**) (BAGD p. 705). In the aorist tense this verb with its temporal prefix προ means 'to have begun previously' [LN], 'to have begun beforehand' [BAGD], 'to have launched previously' [ICC2]. It is translated 'he had begun' [KJV], 'who had already begun' [NAB], 'he had previously made a beginning' [AB], 'he had already previously made a beginning' [HNTC], 'he had earlier made a beginning' [NIV], 'he had already made a beginning' [NJB, NRSV, REB], 'he had already begun' [Lns], 'he had earlier begun' [NTC], 'he had previously begun' [WBC], 'who began (this work)' [TEV], '(Titus) was the one who got you started' [CEV], 'he was in charge of it at the beginning' [TNT], '(Titus) encouraged your giving in the first place' [NLT].

d. aorist act. subj. of ἐπιτελέω (LN 68.22) (BAGD 1. p. 302): 'to bring to completion' [NTC, WBC; NIV, NJB, REB], 'to bring to successful completion' [NAB], 'to complete' [AB, HNTC, LN, Lns; NRSV, TNT], 'to finish' [BAGD, LN; KJV], 'to finalize' [ICC2]. The phrase 'to bring to completion among you' is translated 'to have you finish' [CEV], 'to

encourage you to complete' [NLT], 'to continue it and help you complete' [TEV].
e. εἰς (LN 83.9, 90.41): 'among' [AB, LN (83.9); NAB, NJB, NRSV, TNT], 'in' [KJV], 'on (your part)' [NIV], 'for' [HNTC, ICC2, LN (90.41), Lns, NTC, WBC], not explicit [CEV, NLT, REB, TEV].
f. χάρις (LN 57.103) (BAGD 3.a. p. 878): 'grace' [HNTC, Lns; KJV], 'work of grace' [NTC], 'act of grace' [NIV], 'gracious gift' [LN], 'gracious deed' [BAGD], 'gracious service' [WBC], 'gracious enterprise' [ICC2], 'gift' [BAGD, LN; TNT], 'benefaction' [BAGD], 'benevolence' [AB], 'work of charity' [NAB], 'work of generosity' [NJB, REB], 'ministry of giving' [NLT], 'generous undertaking' [NRSV], 'good thing' [CEV], 'special service of love' [TEV]. See this word also at 1:15; 8:4, 19.

QUESTION—What does καί 'also' in the phrase καὶ ἐπιτελέσῃ '(thus) also he-might bring to completion' refer to?
1. It refers to the collection [He, ICC1, Lns, NIC1, NIC2, SP, TG, TNTC, WBC; CEV, NAB, NLT, TEV, TNT]: just as Titus began getting you interested in the collection, so also he will help you to complete it.
2. It refers to his ministry in Corinth of delivering the severe letter and restoring the relationship of Paul and the Corinthians [EBC, EGT, ICC2, NAC, NCBC]: just as Titus worked to bring reconciliation, so also he will help you to complete the collection. Titus' work of reconciliation was a manifestation of grace, and this will be another [NCBC].
3. It refers to Titus' ministry in general [AB, My, NTC]. In addition to what Titus has already done in Corinth, he will even complete this task of the collection as well [AB, NTC]. In addition to anything else Titus needs to complete among them, so also will he complete the work of the collection [My].

DISCOURSE UNIT: 8:7–15 [NTC, TNTC, WBC]. The topic is Paul's advice [NTC], exhortation to excel [TNTC], the appeal to the Corinthians [WBC].

8:7 Now[a] just-as you-abound[b] in everything, (in) faith and speech[c] and knowledge

LEXICON—a. ἀλλά (LN 91.2) (BAGD 6. p. 39): 'now' [AB, BAGD, NTC; NRSV], 'so now' [ICC2], 'and now' [WBC], 'and' [LN], 'yet' [LN], 'but' [NIV], 'only' [HNTC], 'more' [NJB], 'therefore' [KJV], not explicit [CEV, NAB, NLT, REB, TEV, TNT].
b. pres. act. indic. of περισσεύω (LN 59.52) (BAGD 1.b.β. p. 651): 'to abound' [HNTC, LN, Lns; KJV], 'to excel' [AB, BAGD, NTC; NIV, NLT, NRSV], 'to overflow' [WBC], 'to be rich' [NAB, NJB, REB, TEV, TNT], 'to be prolific' [ICC2], 'to do (everything) better' [CEV]. See this word also at 1:5; 3:9; 4:15; 8:2.
c. λόγος (LN 33.99) (BAGD 1.a.β. p. 477): 'speech' [AB, HNTC, ICC2, LN, NTC, WBC; NIV, NRSV, REB, TEV, TNT], 'speaking' [BAGD, LN], 'word' [BAGD], 'utterance' [KJV], 'discourse' [NAB], 'eloquence'

[NJB], 'doctrine' [Lns]. The phrase 'you abound in speech' is translated 'you speak better' [CEV], 'you have such gifted speakers' [NLT]. See this word also at 1:18; 2:17; 5:19; 6:7.

QUESTION—What relationship is indicated by ἀλλά?

1. It indicates a transition to another topic [Ho, ICC2, My, NIC1, NIC2]. It leads into the exhortation [ICC2, NIC1], and strengthens it [AB, ICC2, NIC2].
2. It indicates transition and contrast [ICC1, Lns, NTC]. He switches from discussing what the Macedonians did to what the Corinthians should do [NTC]. He contrasts what God has done for the Macedonians with what he has done for the Corinthians, who abound in everything [ICC1]. He shifts from what Titus was exhorted to do to what the Corinthians are exhorted to do [Lns].

and all[a] diligence[b] and the love from us in/for[c] you, (see) that[d] you-abound in this grace also.

TEXT—Instead of ἐξ ἡμῶν ἐν ὑμῖν ἀγάπῃ 'the love from us in you', some manuscripts have ἐξ ὑμῶν ἐν ἡμῖν ἀγάπῃ 'the love from you in us'. GNT selects the reading 'the love from us in you' with a C rating, indicating difficulty in deciding which variant to place in the text. The reading 'the love from you in us' is taken by Lns; CEV, KJV, NIV, NJB, NLT, REB, and TEV.

LEXICON—a. πᾶς (LN 78.44) (BAGD 1.a.β. p. 632): 'all' [ICC2, Lns, NTC, WBC; KJV, TNT], 'utmost' [AB; NRSV], 'every kind' [HNTC; REB], 'total' [NAB], 'complete' [LN; NIV], '(in) every respect' [BAGD], '(in) everything' [BAGD], '(for) everything' [NJB], 'such' [NLT], not explicit [CEV, TEV].

b. σπουδή (LN 25.74) (BAGD 2. p. 763): 'diligence' [BAGD; KJV], 'earnestness' [AB, BAGD, Lns; NIV], 'zeal' [BAGD, HNTC, ICC2], 'diligence' [NTC; REB], 'concern' [NAB, NJB], 'eagerness' [BAGD, LN, WBC; NRSV, TNT], 'eagerness to help' [TEV], 'enthusiasm' [NLT], 'devotion' [LN]. This word is translated by the phrase 'you are eager to give' [CEV]. See this word also at 7:11, 12.

c. ἐν (LN 90.56): 'in relation to' [LN], 'for' [AB, NTC; NIV, NJB, NLT, NRSV, REB, TEV], 'to' [LN, Lns; KJV], 'that reaches (you)' [HNTC], 'present in' [ICC2], not explicit [CEV]. The phrase τῇ ἐξ ἡμῶν ἐν ὑμῖν ἀγάπῃ 'the love from us in you' is translated 'the love we bear you' [NAB]. This preposition is also translated as indicating love that Paul and his associates had stimulated in the Corinthians: 'the love we have aroused in (you)' [WBC], 'the love we have awakened in you' [TNT].

d. ἵνα (LN 90.22): 'that' [LN]. In conjunction with the subjunctive verb περισσεύητε 'abound' this adverb is translated as introducing a wish: 'so may you' [NAB], 'I want you to' [NLT], 'we want you to' [NRSV, TEV]; as introducing an imperative: 'see that' [HNTC, NTC; KJV, NIV], 'make

sure' [WBC; NJB], 'you should surely' [REB], 'continue to' [Lns], 'you must' [CEV], 'do (become prolific)' [ICC2], not explicit [AB; TNT].
QUESTION—What does 'the love from us in/for you' mean?
(Note: In addition to the versions noted above, EGT, My, NAC, SP, TG, and TNTC take the variant reading 'your love in/for us'.)
1. It is the love that Paul has stimulated in them [ICC1, ICC2, NIC1, TH, WBC; TNT]. It is the love that Paul taught them to have [TH]. Love from Paul was in them, stimulating their actions [NIC1]. Paul's love wins love in return, uniting the Corinthians' hearts with the hearts of Paul and his associates [ICC1]. Paul has shown what real love is by the way he worked in Corinth, and thus is the originator of the Christian love they have [ICC2].
2. It is the love Paul has for them [NIC2; NAB, NRSV]: our love for you; or (following the variant reading) the love they have for Paul [CEV, KJV, NIV, NJB, NLT, REB, TEV]: your love for us.

DISCOURSE UNIT: 8:8–15 [ICC1]. The topic is the example of Christ.

8:8 **I-speak not by-way-of[a] command[b] but (as) testing[c] the genuineness[d] of your-own love also by-means-of[e] the diligence of others.**
LEXICON—a. κατά (LN 89.8) (BAGD II.5.b.β. p. 407): 'by way of' [HNTC, ICC2, Lns], 'by' [KJV], 'as' [AB, NTC, WBC; NJB, NRSV, REB]. The phrase 'I speak not by way of command' is translated 'I am not ordering you to do this' [CEV], 'I am not giving an order' [NAB], 'I am not commanding you' [NIV], 'I am not saying you must do it' [NLT], 'I am not laying down any rules' [TEV], 'this is not an order' [TNT].
b. ἐπιταγή (LN 33.326) (BAGD p. 302): 'command' [BAGD, HNTC, ICC2, LN, NTC; NRSV], 'commandment' [KJV], 'order' [AB, BAGD, LN, Lns, WBC; NAB, NJB, REB, TNT], 'decree' [LN], 'rule' [TEV], not explicit [CEV, NIV, NLT].
c. pres. act. participle of δοκιμάζω (LN 27.45): 'to test' [HNTC, LN, Lns, NTC; CEV, NAB, NIV, NJB, NRSV], 'to put to the test' [ICC2; REB], 'to verify' [AB], 'to try out' [WBC], 'to find out' [TNT], 'to try to find out' [TEV], 'to prove' [KJV, NLT]. This word implies a testing that results in or is intended to result in success, as opposed to a tempting intended to produce failure [ICC1, ICC2, NAC, NIC2].
d. γνήσιος (LN **73.1**) (BAGD 2. p. 163): 'genuineness' [BAGD, HNTC, Lns, NTC; NJB, NRSV], 'genuine quality' [ICC2], 'genuine' [LN; TNT], 'sincerity' [BAGD; KJV, NIV], 'reality' [AB, WBC], 'real' [CEV, NLT, TEV]. The phrase 'testing the genuineness of your own love' is translated 'testing your generous love' [NAB], 'I am putting your love to the test' [REB].
e. διά with genitive object (LN 90.8): 'by means of' [LN, Lns], 'by' [NTC], 'by occasion of' [KJV], 'by (mentioning)' [AB], 'by (using)' [WBC], 'by (comparing)' [CEV, NIV], 'by (telling)' [REB], 'by (showing)' [TEV],

'through' [ICC2, LN], 'against' [NAB, NJB, NRSV], not explicit [HNTC; NLT, TNT].

QUESTION—How does he test the genuineness of their love by the Macedonians' diligence?

The Macedonians' diligence is an example for the Corinthians to follow as well as an incentive to do so [ICC2, NAC, NCBC, NIC1]. Paul uses the diligence of the Macedonians as a standard by which the Corinthians may be evaluated [Lns, NIC1, NIC2, TH, WBC]. He is setting forth the behavior of the Macedonians as a standard by which the Corinthians may evaluate themselves [HNTC]. He uses the comparison to exhort the Corinthians to action which will prove their love [AB, NTC]. The way the Macedonians responded offers the Corinthians an opportunity to show or prove their love [He, TG]. Paul intends to prove that the Corinthians will indeed follow the good example of the Macedonians [ICC1]. The Corinthians' love will be proved and confirmed by their sharing in the collection [NIC2]. Paul is testing their love to see if it is real and not just professed [Ho].

QUESTION—What is the function of καί 'also'?

It correlates the diligence of the Macedonians with the genuineness of the Corinthians [AB, ICC1]. It correlates the two groups of people [ICC2, WBC]. It heightens the contrast between 'your' and 'of others' [NIC1].

8:9 For you-know the grace[a] of our Lord Jesus Christ, that being rich[b] he-become-poor[c] for-the-sake-of[d] you, so-that you by his poverty might-become-rich.[e]

LEXICON—a. χάρις (LN 88.66) (BAGD 2.a. p. 877): 'grace' [ICC2, LN; KJV, NIV, TEV, TNT], 'generosity' [WBC; NJB, REB], 'generous act' [NRSV], 'favor' [NAB], 'love and kindness' [NLT], 'kindness' [LN]. The phrase 'the grace of our Lord Jesus Christ' is translated 'our Lord Jesus Christ was kind' [CEV]. See this word also at 1:2, 12; 8:1, 4, 6.
- b. πλούσιος (LN 57.26) (BAGD 2. p. 673): 'rich' [AB, BAGD, HNTC, ICC2, LN, Lns, NTC; all versions except CEV, NLT], 'very rich' [NLT], 'riches' [CEV], 'wealthy' [BAGD, LN, WBC]. The participial phrase πλούσιος ὤν 'being rich' is translated concessively: 'though he was rich' [AB, HNTC, NTC, WBC; KJV, NAB, NIV, NJB, NLT, NRSV], 'he was rich, yet' [REB, TNT].
- c. aorist act. indic. of πτωχεύω (LN **57.4**) (BAGD p. 728): 'to become poor' [AB, BAGD, HNTC, LN, Lns, NTC, WBC; KJV, NIV, NJB, NLT, NRSV, REB, TNT], 'to become utterly poor' [ICC2], 'to give up one's riches' [CEV], 'to make oneself poor' [NAB, TEV]. This aorist is ingressive, indicating an action or event that begins an ongoing state or condition [AB, HNTC, ICC2, NTC, WBC]; that is, Christ entered into a condition of poverty.
- d. διά with accusative object (LN 90.38): 'for the sake of' [AB, HNTC, ICC2, LN, WBC; all versions except CEV], 'because of' [Lns], 'on account of' [NTC], 'on behalf of, for the benefit of' [LN], not explicit

[CEV]. The position of δι' ὑμᾶς at the beginning of the clause makes it emphatic [AB, ICC1, NIC1, WBC].
e. aorist act. subj. of πλουτέω (LN 57.25, 57.28) (BAGD 2. P. 674): 'to become rich' [AB, HNTC, ICC2, LN (57.28), Lns, NTC; CEV, NAB, NIV, NJB, NRSV, REB, TNT], 'to be rich' [BAGD, LN (57.25); KJV], 'to become wealthy' [LN (57.28), WBC]. The subjunctive verb phrase ἵνα ὑμεῖς πλουτήσητε 'that you might become rich' is also translated as indicative '(to) make you rich' [NLT, TEV].

QUESTION—What relationship is indicated by γάρ 'for'?

It introduces an argument for a self-sacrificial expression of love [Ho, NIC1]. It introduces a reason for participation in the collection [ICC2]. It introduces the motive for the Corinthians to show love to Paul, which is that he had told them of the love of Jesus [Lns]. It introduces an explanation for why he does not issue a command about the collection [AB, ICC1, NIC2], and why he wants to verify the reality of their love [AB].

QUESTION—Is 'grace' an attribute of Jesus or a specific act?
1. It is a gracious act [AB, EBC, EGT, ICC2, SP, TH]. It is the act of giving himself [EBC]. It is the incarnation [ICC2, SP, TH], or the incarnation and passion [AB]. It is the message of all that Christ has done to bring salvation and grant us his abiding presence [NTC].
2. It is his divine love expressed in action towards people [NAC, TNTC, WBC], his love manifested in the incarnation [Ho]. It is the great love or undeserved favor of Christ [Lns, TG], the life and character of Christ [NIC2]. It is his generosity [HNTC].

QUESTION—What were the riches and poverty of Christ?

Christ's poverty was the incarnation [EGT, ICC1, ICC2, Lns, NCBC, NIC1, NIC2, SP, TH, TNTC, WBC], becoming a mortal man [SP, TG], sharing the human condition [He] and the poverty of human existence [EBC, NTC, SP]. Christ's poverty was his earthly life, including his crucifixion [AB, HNTC, NAC, NTC]. The riches he forsook was the glory of his preexistence in heaven [AB, EBC, EGT, He, Ho, ICC1, ICC2, NAC, NCBC, NTC, TH, TNTC, WBC], the life of heaven [HNTC], his equality with God [NAC], the power and glory he shared with God [TG], the outward signs of deity [AB], or the use of his divine attributes during his earthly life [Lns]. Christ's poverty also included material poverty [NIC2, NTC] and the fact that he became a spiritual debtor by bearing our sin [NTC].

QUESTION—Does this passage have anything to say about Christ's preexistence?

Paul's statements in this passage assume the preexistence of Christ prior to the incarnation [AB, EBC, EGT, He, HNTC, Ho, ICC1, ICC2, NAC, NCBC, NIC1, NIC2, NTC, TH, TNTC, WBC].

QUESTION—What riches did Christ provide for the Corinthians by his poverty?

It is the riches of salvation [AB, ICC2, NAC, TNTC] and the blessings of the new age [ICC2, TNTC]. It is spiritual wealth and blessings [EBC, NAC,

TG], being rich as God sees it [TH]. It is the spiritual riches of being co-heirs with him now and in the world to come [NTC]. It is the righteousness of God which is given to believers [NAC]. It is the results of the atonement, righteousness, and grace gifts [NIC2], forgiveness of sins [NIC1], union with God in Christ [ICC1], and eternal life [ICC1, NIC1]. It is to be exalted by his grace out of the abasement of sin [Lns]. It is the graces of the incarnation [EGT], the riches of sharing in Christ's glory and in the divine nature [Ho]. It is the riches of the opportunity to act out their faith by giving [WBC].

QUESTION—What is conveyed by the use of the pronouns 'you' and 'his' in the phrase ὑμεῖς τῇ ἐκείνου πτωχείᾳ 'you by his poverty'?

Both the use of the pronouns as well as the word order show emphasis and contrast between 'his' and 'you' [AB, ICC1, ICC2, NIC1, NIC2, NTC].

8:10 And I-give (my) opinion[a] in this; for this benefits[b] you, who previously-began[c] last-year not only the doing but also the wanting;[d]

LEXICON—a. γνώμη (LN 31.3) (BAGD 2. p. 163): 'opinion' [BAGD, ICC2, LN, NTC, WBC; TEV, TNT], 'considered opinion' [NJB], 'advice' [HNTC; CEV, KJV, NAB, NIV, NRSV, REB], 'counsel' [AB], 'judgment' [Lns]. The phrase 'I give (my) opinion' is translated 'I suggest' [NLT].

b. pres. act. indic. of συμφέρω (LN 65.44) (BAGD 2. a. p. 780): 'to be advantageous' [BAGD, LN], 'to be of advantage' [Lns], 'to be beneficial for' [ICC2, NTC], 'to be in someone's interest' [AB], 'to be expedient' [HNTC; KJV], 'to be profitable, to be useful, to confer a benefit' [BAGD], 'to befit someone' [WBC], 'to help' [NAB], 'to be best for someone' [NIV], 'to be better for someone' [TEV], 'to be appropriate' [NRSV], not explicit [CEV, NLT, TNT]. The phrase τοῦτο γὰρ ὑμῖν συμφέρει 'for this benefits you' is translated 'this will be the right course for you' [NJB], 'I have your best interests at heart' [REB].

c. aorist (deponent = mid.) indic. of προενάρχομαι (LN 68.4) (BAGD p. 705). In the aorist tense this verb with its temporal prefix προ means 'to have begun previously' [LN], 'to have previously made a start' [ICC2], 'to have begun before' [KJV], 'to have begun beforehand' [BAGD], 'to be beforehand' [HNTC]. It is translated 'you already made a beginning' [AB], 'you made a good beginning' [REB], 'you…began' [Lns; NAB, NRSV, TEV], 'you were the first' [NTC, WBC; CEV, NIV, NJB, NLT, TNT]. See this word also at 8:6.

d. pres. active infin. of θέλω (LN 25.1, 30.58) (BAGD 2. p. 355): 'to want' [BAGD, LN (25.1)], 'to wish' [BAGD, LN (25.1)], 'to desire' [LN (25.1)], 'to purpose' [LN (30.58)], 'to prove willing' [ICC2]. This infinitive with the definite article is translated as a noun phrase: '(in) your determination' [HNTC], '(in) your willingness to do it' [REB]; as a participial phrase: '(in) wanting it' [AB], 'the willing' [Lns]; as an infinitive phrase: 'to decide on it' [WBC], 'to be forward' [KJV], 'to do so willingly' [NAB], 'to be willing to act' [TEV], 'to desire to do something' [NRSV], 'to have the desire to do so' [NIV], 'to conceive the project' [NJB], 'to propose' [NLT], 'to want to help' [TNT]; as a verb phrase: 'you wanted to' [CEV], 'you expressed the desire to do so' [NTC]. This verb is variously translated as expressing purpose [HNTC, WBC], desire [AB, NTC; CEV, NIV, NRSV, TNT], a plan or proposal of action [NJB, NLT, TEV], or willingness [REB].

QUESTION—What is he saying will benefit them?
1. His advice will benefit them [AB, He, ICC2, NIC2, SP, TH, WBC; NAB, REB].
2. Participation in the collection will benefit them [HNTC, Ho, Lns, NAC, NTC, TG, TNTC; NIV, NJB, NRSV, TEV].
3. His giving an opinion instead of a command is most appropriate for people like them [EGT, ICC1, WBC].

QUESTION—Does ἀπὸ πέρυσι mean 'last year' or 'a year ago'?
1. It means 'last year' [AB, EGT, He, HNTC, Ho, ICC1, NAC, NIC1, NIC2, NTC, TH, TNTC; NAB, NIV, NRSV, REB, TEV, TNT].
2. It means 'a year ago' [Lns; CEV, KJV, NJB, NLT].

QUESTION—To what does ἐν τούτῳ 'in this' refer?
1. Ἐν τούτῳ refers to the matter at hand about which he will give advice [AB, Ho, ICC2, NTC, TG, TH; NAB, NIV, NJB, NRSV, TNT].
  1.1 The matter under discussion is their participation in this collection [Ho, ICC2, NTC, TG, TH; NAB].
  1.2. The matter under discussion is the reality of their love [AB].
2. Ἐν τούτῳ refers to the content of the advice he gives; that is, 'In this that I am about to say I give my opinion' [NIC2; KJV, REB].

QUESTION—What does he mean by οἵτινες 'who'?
Οἵτινες is an emphatic pronoun meaning 'such as yourselves, who…'. That is, they are people who are characterized by a particular trait or action [He, HNTC, Ho, ICC1, Lns, TG, TH, WBC], which in this case is the fact that they are already motivated to give [He, ICC1, Lns, SP, TH, WBC]. The pronoun here implies a causal force; that is, because you are such people as who were already willing to give, contributing to the collection will benefit you [Lns].

8:11 but[a] now also complete[b] the doing, so-that just-as the eagerness[c] of-(the)-wanting (to), thus also the completing from what you-have.

LEXICON—a. δέ (LN 89.124): 'but' [AB, LN, NTC], 'however' [Lns], 'then' [NJB, TEV], 'now, then' [ICC2], not explicit [HNTC, WBC; CEV, NAB, NIV, NLT, NRSV, REB, TNT]. The phrase νυνὶ δέ 'but now' is translated 'now therefore' [KJV].
  b. aorist act. impera. of ἐπιτελέω (LN 68.22) (BAGD 1. p. 302): 'to complete' [AB, LN, NTC, WBC; NJB, TNT], 'to carry through to completion' [NLT], 'to carry through to a successful completion' [NAB], 'to bring to completion' [ICC2], 'to finish' [BAGD, LN, Lns; CEV, NIV,

NRSV], 'to go on and finish' [REB], 'to go on with it and finish' [TEV], 'to finish off' [HNTC], 'to perform' [KJV].
  c. προθυμία (LN 25.68) (BAGD p. 706): 'eagerness' [LN; NRSV], 'eager' [CEV, REB, TEV], 'eager willingness' [NIV], 'willingness' [BAGD], 'ready willingness' [ICC2], 'readiness' [BAGD, HNTC, Lns, NTC, WBC; KJV], 'ready resolve' [NAB], 'desire' [LN], 'goodwill' [AB, BAGD], 'enthusiasm' [NJB], 'enthusiastically' [NLT]. The phrase ἡ προθυμία τοῦ θέλειν 'the eagerness of the wanting to' is translated 'you were keen (to help)' [TNT].
QUESTION—What relationship is indicated by δέ in the phrase νυνὶ δὲ καί 'but now also'?
  It introduces a contrast between 'now' and 'a year ago' [ICC2, NIC2, SP]. It introduces a contrast between their initial willingness to participate in the collection and the actual completion of it [Ho].

8:12 **For if the eagerness exists,ᵃ (it is) acceptableᵇ according-toᶜ (what) he-may-have, not according-to (what) he-has not.**
LEXICON—a. pres. mid. or pass. (deponent = act.) indic. of πρόκειμαι (LN 13.75) (BAGD 2. p. 707): 'to exist openly or clearly' [LN], 'to be present' [AB, BAGD, HNTC, ICC2], 'to be there' [Lns, NTC, WBC; NIV, NJB, NRSV], 'to be' [KJV], not explicit [CEV, NAB, NLT, REB, TEV]. The phrase 'if the eagerness exists' is translated 'if a man is really keen to give' [TNT], 'how much you are willing (to give)' [CEV], 'if we give eagerly' [REB], 'if you are eager to give' [TEV].
  b. εὐπρόσδεκτος (LN 25.86) (BAGD 1. p. 324): 'acceptable' [AB, BAGD, ICC2, NTC, WBC; NIV, NJB, NRSV], 'acceptable to God' [REB], 'fully acceptable' [Lns], 'very acceptable' [LN], 'accepted' [KJV], 'acceptability' [HNTC], 'quite pleasing' [LN], not explicit [CEV, NAB, NLT]. The word εὐπρόσδεκτος '(it is) acceptable' is translated 'what matters is' [CEV], 'God wants (you to give)' [NLT], 'God will accept' [TEV], 'God...accepts' [TNT]. See this word also at 6:2.
  c. καθό (LN 78.53) (BAGD 2. p. 390): 'according to' [AB; KJV, NIV, NRSV, REB], 'in accordance with' [ICC2, WBC], '(should) accord with' [NAB], 'according as' [Lns], 'just as' [LN], 'to the degree that' [BAGD, LN], 'insofar as' [BAGD, NTC], 'on the basis of' [HNTC; TEV], 'the basis on which' [NJB], not explicit [CEV, NLT, TNT].
QUESTION—What is it that is acceptable?
  1. It is the gift [HNTC, NTC, SP, TG, TH; NIV, NRSV, TEV, TNT], or the fact of their giving [TNTC; REB], or the result of their giving [He] that is acceptable. It is the giver that is acceptable, but that really means that the gift is acceptable [ICC2].
  2. It is the intent or willingness that is acceptable [AB, Ho, NIC1, NIC2, WBC; NJB].

DISCOURSE UNIT: 8:13-15 [EBC]. The topic is the aim of equality.

8:13 For (it is) not that relief[a] (be) to-others, (and) affliction[b] to-you, but from[c] equality;[d]

LEXICON—a. ἄνεσις (LN **22.36**) (BAGD 2. p. 65): 'relief' [AB, BAGD, HNTC, ICC2, LN, Lns, NTC; NAB, NRSV], not explicit [NLT]. The phrase ἵνα ἄλλοις ἄνεσις 'that relief be to others' is translated 'relieving others' [WBC; REB], 'to relieve others' [TEV], 'to make life easier for others' [CEV], 'that other men be eased' [KJV], 'that others might be relieved' [NIV], 'to relieve other people's needs' [NJB], 'that the burden of others should be lightened' [TNT]. See this word also at 2:13 and 7:5.

b. θλίψις (LN 22.2) (BAGD 1. p. 362): 'affliction' [BAGD, HNTC, WBC], 'distress' [Lns], 'pressure' [NRSV], 'trouble and suffering' [LN], 'a hard time' [AB], 'hardship' [ICC2; NJB, REB], 'burden' [TEV, TNT]. The phrase ὑμῖν θλῖψις 'affliction to you' is translated 'and you be burdened' [NTC; KJV], 'making life harder for you' [CEV], 'to impoverish you' [NAB], 'you are hard-pressed' [NIV], 'that you suffer' [NLT]. See this word also at 1:4, 8; 2:4; 4:17; 6:4; 7:4; 8:2.

c. ἐκ (LN 89.85) (BAGD 3.i. p. 235): 'from' [LN], 'on the basis of' [BAGD, ICC2], 'based on' [TNT], 'in accordance with' [BAGD], 'with' [LN], 'a matter of' [AB, HNTC, WBC], 'due to' [Lns], 'by' [KJV]. In the phrase ἐξ ἰσότητος 'from equality' the preposition ἐκ/ἐξ is translated 'there should be' [NJB], 'that there should be' [NAB, NLT], 'that there be' [NTC], 'that there might be' [NIV], 'it is a question of' [NRSV, REB]. The entire phrase is translated 'it is only fair' [CEV, TEV]. This phrase is included in 8:14 by KJV, REB.

d. ἰσότης (LN **58.32**) (BAGD 1. p. 381): 'equality' [AB, BAGD, HNTC, ICC2, LN, NTC; KJV, NAB, NIV, NLT, REB], 'equalization' [Lns], 'fair' [CEV, TEV], 'fair shares' [WBC], 'fair balance' [NJB, NRSV], 'fairness' [TNT].

QUESTION—What relationship is indicated by οὐ γὰρ ἵνα 'for…not that'?
 1. It indicates purpose, stated negatively [AB, EGT, HNTC, ICC2, SP].
 2. It indicates result [NTC].
 3. It states the content of a proposition: not a question of this, but of that [WBC; REB].

QUESTION—What is meant by ἰσότης 'equality'?
Equality means that the needs of some are met from the surplus of others [AB, NCBC, NTC, TNTC], not a general equalizing of goods and property among believers [Ho, ICC2, NIC1, NTC, SP]. Equality is equal sharing of financial burdens resulting in an equal supply of the necessities of life [EBC]. It is giving proportionally in Christian partnership [AB]. Paul calls for giving based on equity, such that everyone should have enough, though not necessarily the same amount, and that no one gains a higher status over another through giving [NAC]. It is about spiritual fellowship and unity as well as material help [NIC2]. Equality means reciprocity [EGT]. He is calling for equilibrium, and a display of mutual affection and respect between fellow believers who are joint citizens of the kingdom [NIC1]. He is

calling for equal relief from the burden of being needy [Ho]. Paul appeals to a concept of communal equality as had been practiced in Greek law and politics [ICC2]. Equality is mutual giving and receiving in which believers render service to each other [ICC1]. Equality is equal opportunity to share in the blessing of God that comes through giving proportionally according to one's means, such that there is never a debit in Christian giving for giving too small a sum or a credit for giving a large sum; rather, we are always even [Lns]. Equality means that everyone should have a fair share [WBC].

QUESTION—What relationship is indicated by ἐκ 'from' in the phrase ἐξ ἰσότητος 'from equality'?

1. It indicates that basis of the desired action is the principle of equality [HNTC, ICC1, ICC2, Lns, NAC, NIC1, NIC2, SP; CEV, NRSV, REB, TEV, TNT]: according to equality.
2. It indicates that equality is the desired outcome of the action [AB, He, Ho, NTC, TG, TH, TNTC, WBC; NAB, NIV, NJB, NLT]: that there should be equality.

QUESTION—What relationship is there between the phrase ἀλλ' ἐξ ἰσότητος 'but from equality' and its context?

1. The contrastive conjunction ἀλλά 'but' introduces ἐξ ἰσότητος 'from equality' as the contrasting complement of the first half of 8:13 [AB, He, ICC2, Lns, NTC, SP, TG, WBC; NAB, NIV, NJB, NLT, REB, TNT]: not affliction for some and relief for others, but rather equality.
2. The contrastive conjunction ἀλλά 'but' conjoins the first half of 8:13 'not affliction for some and relief for others' with the contrasting complement beginning with ἐξ ἰσότητος and including all of 8:14 [EGT, HNTC, ICC2, NIC2; CEV, KJV, NRSV, TEV]: not affliction for some and relief for others, but by way of equality, your present abundance supplying their lack, etc.

8:14 In the present time your abundance[a] (might be) to their lack,[b] so-that also their abundance might-be to your lack, (and) thus equality might-be.

LEXICON—a. περίσσευμα (LN **59.53**) (BAGD 1. p. 650): 'abundance' [BAGD, HNTC, ICC2, LN, Lns; KJV, NRSV], 'surplus' [AB, NTC, WBC; NJB, REB, TNT], 'plenty' [NAB, NIV, NLT, TEV]. The phrase 'your abundance' is translated 'you have so much' [CEV].

b. ὑστέρημα (LN **57.38**) (BAGD 1. p. 849): 'need' [AB, BAGD; NAB, NRSV, REB, TEV], 'want' [BAGD, HNTC; KJV], 'insufficiency' [ICC2], 'deficiency' [BAGD, Lns, NTC, WBC], 'deficit' [NJB, TNT], 'what is lacking' [**LN**] 'what is needed' [LN], 'what they need' [NIV], not explicit [NLT]. The phrase 'their lack' is translated 'they have so little' [CEV].

QUESTION—What is the 'present time' that Paul refers to?

1. It is temporal, referring to the moment in time in which he was writing, and in which the Corinthians had material abundance [AB, EBC, EGT, HNTC, ICC1, ICC2, Lns, NIC1, NTC, SP, TG, TH, TNTC].

2. It is eschatological, referring to the era of salvation history in which they were living [NAC, NIC2, WBC]. It is the era of salvation and the spirit, of the new covenant of righteousness, and a worldwide covenant people within which there is to be equality until the parousia [NIC2]. It is the era of freedom-in-grace for the Gentiles [WBC].

QUESTION—What kind of possible reciprocation does Paul envision the Christians in Jerusalem being able to make to the Corinthians?
1. The reciprocation is material and Paul is saying that if circumstances somehow are reversed, the believers in Jerusalem will send money to Corinth [EGT, He, HNTC, ICC1, ICC2, NIC1, NTC, SP, TG, TH, TNTC]. He is talking about material reciprocation, though it is unlikely that it would ever actually happen [He].
2. The reciprocation is spiritual [EBC, Lns, NCBC, NIC2, WBC]. The Corinthians are giving a material reciprocation for spiritual benefits they have received from the believers in Jerusalem [EBC, NAC, NCBC]. The believers in Jerusalem can offer spiritual gifts such as their prayer and admonition [Lns]. Christians in Corinth have been enriched with grace gifts, and their sharing of material blessings demonstrates concern for ethnic Israel in its material poverty as well as its spiritual poverty of unbelief [WBC]. The reciprocation is primarily loving and prayerful spiritual fellowship, but could include material help if the circumstances were ever reversed [NIC2].
3. Neither material nor spiritual reciprocity is in view specifically, but more fundamentally the sharing of any kind of surplus one has with someone in need [AB].

8:15 **Just-as it-is-written,[a] The-one (gathering)[b] much[c] did- not -have-too-much,[d] and the one (gathering) little[e] did- not -have-too-little.[f]**

LEXICON—a. perf. pass. indic. of γράφω (LN 33.61): 'to be written' [LN]. This verb is translated 'it is written' [AB, HNTC, ICC2, NTC; KJV, NAB, NIV, NRSV], 'it has been written' [Lns], 'this is in line with scripture' [WBC], 'the scriptures say' [CEV], 'scripture says' [NJB, TNT], 'what the scriptures say' [NLT], 'scripture has it' [REB]. See this word also at 4:13.
  b. There is no lexical entry for this implied verb. It is represented as 'to gather' [AB, ICC2; CEV, KJV, NAB, NIV, NLT, REB, TEV, TNT], 'to have' [HNTC, Lns; NRSV], 'to increase' [NTC], 'to collect' [WBC; NJB].
  c. πολύς (LN 59.11) (BAGD I.2.c.α. p. 689): 'much' [AB, BAGD, HNTC, ICC2, LN, Lns, NTC, WBC; KJV, NAB, NIV, NRSV, TEV, TNT], 'too much' [CEV], 'a lot' [NLT], 'more' [NJB, REB].
  d. aorist act. indic. of πλεονάζω (LN **57.23**) (BAGD 1.b. p. 667): 'to have too much' [BAGD, LN, NTC, WBC; NIV, NJB, NRSV, REB, TEV, TNT], 'to have extra' [AB], 'to have surplus' [ICC2], 'to have (some) left' [CEV], 'to have (some) left over' [NLT], 'to have over' [KJV], 'to

have more' [HNTC, Lns], 'to have excess' [NAB]. See this word also at 4:15.
  e. ὀλίγος (LN 59.13) (BAGD 2.a. p. 563): 'little' [AB, BAGD, HNTC, LN, Lns, WBC; KJV, NAB, NIV, NRSV, TEV, TNT], 'only a little' [CEV, NLT], 'less' [NTC; NJB, REB], 'a small amount' [BAGD, ICC2, LN].
  f. aorist act. indic. of ἐλαττονέω (LN **57.41**) (BAGD P. 248): 'to have too little' [BAGD, ICC2, **LN**, NTC; NIV, NJB, NRSV, REB, TEV, TNT], 'to have less' [BAGD, HNTC, LN, Lns], 'to have shortage' [AB], 'to lack' [WBC], 'to have lack' [KJV, NAB]. This verb negated by οὐκ is translated '(they) had all they needed' [CEV], 'to have enough' [NLT].
QUESTION—What lesson is Paul drawing from the Exodus 16 quotation?
  1. In the Exodus passage Paul is focusing on the fact of equality and not how it came about [AB, HNTC, ICC1, ICC2, Lns, NAC, NIC2]. The equality achieved with regard to the manna in Exodus 16 was divinely imposed, but the equality to be achieved among the churches should be voluntary [EBC, HNTC, ICC1, NAC, NIC2]. There was neither excess nor deficiency, for everyone had what he needed [NCBC]. Paul is not exegeting the Exodus passage in detail [AB]. He is using the wording of Exodus 16, not in an exact sense but in a proverbial sense, to show that God provides for everyone [NTC]. Paul wants each church to have enough for necessities, not for luxuries [EGT]. Paul is saying that provision and need ought to be matched [WBC].
  2. The manna was redistributed after it was gathered so that the need of those who lacked was met out of the surplus of those who had more than enough [Ho, NIC1].

DISCOURSE UNIT: 8:16–9:5 [AB, EBC]. The topic is the mission of Titus and his companions [EBC], commendation of the representatives [AB].

DISCOURSE UNIT: 8:16–24 [EBC, ICC1, NTC, TH, TNTC, WBC; CEV, NAB, NLT, TEV]. The topic is Titus and his companions [TH; NAB, NLT, TEV], Titus and his friends [CEV], the visit of Titus [NTC], the new mission to be entrusted to Titus and two others [ICC1], the delegates and their credentials [EBC], commendation of those who will receive the collection [TNTC], the mission of Titus [WBC].

DISCOURSE UNIT: 8:16–9:5 [NIV, NJB]. The topic is Titus sent to Corinth [NIV], the delegates recommended to the Corinthians [NJB].

8:16 But[a] thanks[b] (be) to-God the-one-giving[c] the same[d] earnestness[e] for you into the heart of Titus,
LEXICON—a. δέ (LN 89.94, 89.124): 'but' [HNTC, LN (89.124), NTC; KJV, NRSV], 'and' [ICC2, LN (89.94)], 'now' [Lns, WBC], not explicit [AB; CEV, NAB, NIV, NJB, NLT, REB, TEV, TNT].
  b. χάρις (LN 33.350) (BAGD 5. p. 878): 'thanks' [AB, BAGD, HNTC, ICC2, LN, Lns, WBC; KJV, NAB, NRSV, TNT]. The phrase 'thanks be to God' is translated 'I thank God' [NTC; NIV, REB], 'we thank God'

[TEV], 'I am grateful' [CEV], 'I am thankful' [NLT], 'thank God' [NJB]. See this word also at 1:2, 12; 8:1, 4, 6, 9.
c. aorist act. participle of δίδωμι (LN 90.51) (BAGD 1.b.β. p. 193): 'to give' [ICC2, Lns; NLT], 'to place' [AB], 'to put' [NTC, WBC; KJV, NAB, NIV, NJB, NRSV], 'to kindle' [HNTC], 'to make (eager)' [TNT], 'to cause, to bring about, to produce' [LN]. The phrase 'God, the one giving earnestness for you into the heart of Titus' is translated 'God has made Titus care about you' [CEV], 'God has made Titus keen on your behalf' [REB], 'God has made Titus eager to help you' [TEV].
d. αὐτός (LN 58.31): 'the same' [AB, HNTC, ICC2, LN, Lns, NTC, WBC; NIV, NJB, NLT, NRSV], 'equal' [NAB], not explicit [CEV, REB, TEV, TNT].
e. σπουδή (LN 25.74) (BAGD 2. p. 763): 'earnestness' [AB, BAGD, Lns], 'earnest care' [KJV], 'eagerness' [BAGD, LN, NTC, WBC; NRSV], 'concern' [NIV], 'sincere concern' [NJB], 'zeal' [BAGD, HNTC, ICC2; NAB], 'enthusiasm' [NLT], not explicit [CEV, REB]. The phrase σπουδὴν ὑπὲρ ὑμῶν 'earnestness for you' is translated '(to) care about you' [CEV], 'keen about you' [REB], 'eager (to help you)' [TEV, TNT]. See this word also at 7:11, 12; 8:7.

QUESTION—To what does 'the same' refer?
Titus' earnestness or zeal is the same as that of Paul and his associates [AB, EBC, HNTC, Ho, ICC1, ICC2, Lns, NAC, NIC1, NIC2, NTC, TG, TH, TNTC, WBC; CEV, NIV, NLT, NRSV, REB, TEV, TNT].

8:17 for[a] not-only did-he-accept (our) appeal,[b] but being more-earnest[c] he-is going-out[d] to you of-his-own-accord.[e]
LEXICON—a. ὅτι (LN 89.33): 'for' [AB, HNTC, ICC2, LN, Lns, WBC; KJV, NIV, NRSV], 'because' [LN, NTC], not explicit [CEV, NAB, NJB, NLT, REB, TEV, TNT].
b. παράκλησις (LN 33.168) (BAGD 1., 2. p. 618): 'appeal' [BAGD (2), LN, NTC; NAB, NIV, NRSV], 'request' [BAGD (2), HNTC, ICC2, LN, WBC; NLT, REB, TEV], 'urging' [AB, Lns; NJB], 'exhortation' [KJV]. The noun παράκλησις '(our) appeal' is translated as a verb phrase 'we begged' [CEV], 'we asked' [TNT]. See this word also at 8:4.
c. σπουδαῖος (LN **25.75**) (BAGD p. 763). 'earnest' [BAGD, LN], 'eager' [BAGD, LN; NLT], 'ready' [TNT]. This adjective, occurring here in the comparative form σπουδαιότερος, is translated 'extremely earnest' [AB], 'the more earnest' [Lns], 'so eager' [**LN**; TEV], 'very eager' [NTC; NAB], 'more eager than ever' [NRSV], 'with all eagerness' [WBC], 'with much enthusiasm' [NIV], 'greater still (was his) enthusiasm' [NJB], 'more zealous' [BAGD, HNTC], 'yet more zealous' [ICC2], 'more forward' [KJV], 'so keen' [REB], 'he cared so much (for you)' [CEV].
d. aorist act. indic. of ἐξέρχομαι (LN 15.40) (BAGD 1.a.ε. p. 274): 'to go out' [AB, BAGD, LN, NTC], 'to go forth' [Lns], 'to go' [NAB, NRSV, TEV], 'to go off' [NJB], 'to go and see (you)' [NLT], 'to set off' [HNTC,

ICC2], 'to leave' [REB], 'to come' [NIV, TNT], 'to be on one's way' [WBC], not explicit [CEV]. The aorist verbs of going and sending in 8:17, 18, and 22 are considered epistolary aorists, meaning that, although the actions in view had not yet occurred at the time of the writing, they would already have occurred by the time the recipients received and read the letter [AB, EGT, HNTC, Ho, ICC1, ICC2, Lns, NIC1, NIC2, NTC, TH, WBC]. This verb is translated as present tense, i.e., 'he is leaving' [AB, NTC; NIV, NRSV, REB]; as aorist, i.e., 'he has left' [HNTC, ICC2, Lns, WBC; KJV, NAB, NJB].

e. αὐθαίρετος (LN 25.66) (BAGD p. 121): 'of one's own accord' [AB, BAGD, HNTC, ICC2, NTC; KJV, NJB, NRSV], 'of one's own free will' [LN; TEV, TNT], 'of one's own will' [Lns], 'of one's own initiative' [WBC; NIV], 'of one's own choice' [REB], 'freely' [NAB], not explicit [NLT]. This word is translated 'he wanted to' [CEV]. See this word also at 8:3.

QUESTION—What meaning is intended by the use of the comparative form σπουδαιότερος 'more earnest'?

1. It is an elative use of the comparative form, indicating emphasis and not comparison [AB, EGT, He, HNTC, ICC1, NAC, NIC2, NTC, WBC; CEV, NAB, NIV, REB, TEV]: that is, he is very earnest or eager.
2. It is comparative. Titus' earnestness was increasing [Lns], and he is more earnest than ever [SP; NRSV]. He is going of his own accord, and is therefore more enthusiastic than he would have been had he only been motivated by Paul's request [ICC2].

8:18 And we-are-sending with him the brother whose praise[a] in the gospel[b] (is) throughout[c] all the churches.

LEXICON—a. ἔπαινος (LN 33.354) (BAGD 1.a.α. p. 281): 'praise' [BAGD, HNTC, ICC2, LN, Lns; KJV], 'fame, recognition' [BAGD]. The phrase οὗ ὁ ἔπαινος 'whose praise (is)' is also translated 'who is renowned' [AB], 'who is famous' [NRSV], 'who is highly respected' [TEV], 'whose reputation is high' [REB], 'who is well known' [CEV], 'who is praised' [NTC, WBC; NIV, NJB, TNT], 'whom (the churches) praise' [NAB], 'he is highly praised' [NLT].

b. εὐαγγέλιον (LN 33.217) (BAGD 1.a. p. 318): 'gospel' [AB, BAGD, HNTC, LN, Lns, NTC, WBC; KJV, NAB, NIV], 'good news' [BAGD, LN; CEV, NLT, NRSV]. The phrase ἐν τῷ εὐαγγελίῳ 'in the gospel' is translated 'because of/for his work for the gospel' [AB, WBC], 'in the sphere of the gospel' [ICC2], 'in connection with the gospel' [Lns], 'in the service of the gospel' [NTC], 'for his work in spreading the good news' [TNT], 'for spreading the good news' [CEV] 'for proclaiming the good news' [NRSV], 'as a preacher of the good news' [NLT], 'for his preaching of the gospel' [NAB], 'for his work in preaching the gospel' [TEV], 'for his service to the gospel' [NIV, REB], 'as an evangelist' [NJB].

c. διά with genitive object (LN 84.29) (BAGD A.I.2. p. 179): 'throughout' [BAGD, Lns, WBC; KJV, TNT], 'through' [BAGD, LN], 'in' [AB, HNTC; CEV, NJB, NLT, TEV], 'among' [NRSV, REB], 'by' [NTC; NIV], not explicit [NAB]. This preposition is also translated as a verb 'pervades' [ICC2].

QUESTION—What is meant by the phrase ἐν τῷ εὐαγγελίῳ 'in the gospel'?
 1. He was distinguished for his service generally [AB, SP], for his labor in promoting the cause of the gospel [EGT, Ho], for general support of the gospel and those who preach it [TNTC]. He was faithful in Christian work [WBC].
 2. The service would be in the areas of preaching and evangelism [EBC, He, HNTC, ICC1, ICC2, Lns, NAC, NCBC, TNTC; CEV, NAB, NIV, NJB, NRSV, REB, TNT]. This service may also have included administration [EBC, HNTC].

QUESTION—What churches is Paul referring to?
He is referring to the Macedonian churches [He, HNTC, Ho, ICC1, Lns, NCBC, NIC2, SP, TG], or to the congregations in both Macedonia and Achaia [NAC]. He is referring to all the churches through which he had passed and which were interested in this ministry [EGT]. Paul is referring to the various churches he had founded [WBC]. The phrase is widely representative, including those in Macedonia [NTC].

8:19 And not only (this) but also^a having-been-appointed^b by the churches (as) our traveling-companion^c

LEXICON—a. The phrase οὐ μόνον ἀλλὰ καί 'not only but also' is translated 'not only this but also' [Lns, NTC; NRSV; similarly KJV, TNT], 'And not only this. On the contrary' [ICC2], 'in addition to this he has also' [WBC], 'in addition' [NIV], 'moreover' [AB, HNTC; REB], 'what is more' [NJB], 'in addition to this' [WBC], 'and besides that' [TEV], not explicit [CEV, NAB, NLT].
 b. aorist pass. participle of χειροτονέω (LN 30.101) (BAGD p. 881): 'to be appointed' [AB, HNTC, NTC, WBC; NAB, NLT, NRSV, TNT], 'to be chosen' [BAGD, **LN**; KJV, NIV, TEV], 'to be elected' [ICC2, LN; NJB], 'to be selected' [LN], 'to be voted (as)' [Lns]. This passive participle is also translated as an active finite verb: '(they) chose' [CEV], 'they appointed' [REB].
 c. συνέκδημος (LN 15.151) (BAGD p. 787): 'traveling companion' [BAGD, HNTC, LN, NTC, WBC; NAB, NJB, TNT], 'travel companion' [Lns]. This noun is also translated as a verb phrase 'to travel as our companion' [ICC2], 'to travel with us' [CEV, KJV, NRSV, REB, TEV], 'to accompany us' [AB; NIV, NLT].

with this gracious-gift^a being-administered^b by us for^c the glory of the Lord himself and (to-show)^d our readiness^e (to help),
TEXT—The word αὐτός 'himself' does not occur in some manuscripts. It is included in brackets by GNT with a C rating, indicating difficulty in

deciding whether or not to place it in the text. It is omitted or not translated by Lns; CEV, NAB, NJB, NLT, and TEV.

LEXICON—a. χάρις (LN 57.103) (BAGD 3.a. p. 878): 'gracious gift' [BAGD, LN], 'gift' [LN; CEV, TNT], 'gracious work' [NTC], 'grace' [HNTC, Lns; KJV], 'benevolence' [AB], 'benefaction' [BAGD, ICC2], 'beneficent work' [REB], 'offering' [NIV, NLT], 'work of charity' [NAB], 'work of generosity' [NJB], 'generous undertaking' [NRSV], 'service' [WBC], 'service of love' [TEV]. See this word also at 1:15, and 8:4, 6.

b. pres. pass. participle of διακονέω (LN 35.37) (BAGD 2. p. 184): 'to be administered' [AB; NJB], 'to be ministered' [Lns], 'to be carried on' [BAGD], 'to be taken care of' [LN]. This passive participle is also translated actively: 'to administer' [NTC; KJV, NIV, NRSV, TNT], 'to render' [WBC], 'to deal with' [HNTC], 'to take' [NLT], 'to carry' [CEV], 'to carry on' [NAB], 'to carry out' [TEV]. The phrase 'being administered by us' is translated 'which on our part is in process of organization' [ICC2]. The phrase 'our traveling companion with this gracious gift being administered by us' is translated 'to travel with us and help in this beneficent work' [REB]. See this word also at 3:3.

c. πρός (LN 89.60): 'for' [NTC; NAB, NJB, NRSV, TNT], 'for the sake of' [LN; TEV], 'in order to' [LN; NIV], 'to' [HNTC, NTC; KJV]. This preposition is used as a marker of purpose, pointing to the goal of an event or state [LN]. It is translated as an infinitive or verb phrase: 'to show' [AB, Lns], 'resulting in' [ICC2], '(that) will bring' [CEV]. The phrase πρὸς τὴν τοῦ κυρίου 'for the glory of the Lord' is translated 'that glorifies the Lord' [NLT], 'by which we do honor to the Lord' [REB], 'in order to honor the Lord' [NIV].

d. There is no lexical entry for the phrase 'to show', the relationship being understood as an implied repetition of the preposition πρός because of the presence of the conjunction καί 'and' after the phrase 'for the glory of the Lord'. The implied or stated relationship is translated 'to show' [AB, Lns, NTC; CEV, NIV, NLT, NRSV, REB, TEV], 'to prove' [WBC], 'for' [NJB], 'resulting in' [ICC2], 'as evidence of' [TNT], 'declaration of' [KJV], not explicit [NAB]. It is also translated in conjunction with προθυμία 'readiness' as 'at our suggestion' [HNTC].

e. προθυμία (LN **25.68**) (BAGD p. 706): 'readiness to help' [NTC, WBC], 'ready mind' [KJV], 'readiness' [BAGD, Lns], 'desire to help' [**LN**], 'how much we hope to help' [CEV], 'eagerness to help' [NIV, NLT], 'eagerness to serve' [REB], 'eagerness' [LN], 'goodwill' [AB, BAGD; NRSV], 'willingness' [BAGD], 'keenness' [TNT], 'complete satisfaction' [NJB]. This word is translated 'willingly' [NAB], '(at our) suggestion' [HNTC], 'to show that we want to help' [TEV].

QUESTION—What relationship is indicated by πρός 'for...to show'?

1. It indicates purpose [AB, EGT, He, Ho, ICC1, Lns, NAC, NIC1, NIC2, SP, TG, TNTC, WBC; NIV].

2. It indicates result [ICC2]. The result of the appointment was the glory of the Lord, etc.

QUESTION—What action was the antecedent to the phrase 'to the glory of the Lord' etc.?

1. The gift and its administration were to the glory of the Lord, etc. [EBC, EGT, He, Ho, ICC1, Lns, NAC, NIC2, NTC, SP, TG, TNTC, WBC; CEV, KJV, NAB, NIV, NJB, NLT, NRSV, REB, TEV, TNT].
2. The appointment of the brother was to the glory of the Lord, etc. [AB, HNTC, ICC2, NIC1].

8:20 **guarding-against**[a] **this, lest anyone blame**[b] **us concerning this generous-gift**[c] **being administered**[d] **by us;**

LEXICON—a. pres. mid. participle of στέλλω (LN **13.159**) (BAGD 2. p. 766): 'to avoid' [BAGD, LN; KJV, NAB, NIV], 'to try to avoid' [BAGD, NTC; TNT], 'to seek to avoid' [HNTC], 'to take precaution' [WBC], 'to guard against' [NLT, REB], 'to make preparation' [ICC2], 'to arrange...(so that)' [NJB], 'to be careful' [TEV], 'to take advance thought' [Lns], 'to intend (that)' [NRSV], 'to take action' [AB], not explicit [CEV].

b. aorist (deponent = mid.) subj. of μωμάομαι (LN 33.414) (BAGD p. 531): 'to blame' [AB, BAGD, HNTC, Lns, NTC, WBC; KJV, NRSV, TNT], 'to cast blame upon' [ICC2], 'to find fault with' [BAGD, LN; CEV], 'to criticize' [LN], 'to make accusation' [NJB]. This word is also translated as a noun: 'blame' [NAB], 'criticism' [NIV, REB], 'suspicion' [NLT], 'complaints' [TEV]. The phrase στελλόμενοι τοῦτο, μή τις ἡμᾶς μωμήσηται 'guarding against this, lest anyone blame us' is translated 'we don't want anyone to find fault' [CEV], 'we are being careful not to stir up any complaints' [TEV]. See this word also at 6:3.

c. ἁδρότης (LN **59.60**) (BAGD p. 19): 'generous gift' [LN, WBC; CEV, NLT, NRSV, TEV, TNT], 'lavish gift' [BAGD, ICC2, NTC], 'liberal gift' [NIV], 'generous collection' [NAB], 'large sum' [AB, HNTC; NJB, REB], 'bounty' [Lns], 'abundance' [BAGD; KJV]

d. pres. pass. participle of διακονέω (LN 35.37) (BAGD 2. p. 184): 'to be administered' [AB, HNTC; KJV], 'to be ministered' [Lns], 'to be organized' [ICC2]. This passive participle is also translated as an active finite verb: 'we administer' [NTC, WBC; NIV, NJB, NLT, NRSV], 'we handle' [CEV, TEV]; as a substantive: 'my/our handling' [NAB, REB], 'our administration' [TNT] See this word also at 3:3; 8:19.

8:21 **for we have-regard-for**[a] **(what is) right**[b] **not only before**[c] **the Lord but also before men.**

LEXICON—a. pres. act. indic. of προνοέω (LN 30.47) (BAGD 2. p. 708): 'to have regard for' [BAGD], 'to take thought for' [BAGD], 'to give attention to' [LN], 'to pay attention to' [AB], 'to be concerned' [HNTC; NAB], 'to take thought for' [ICC2], 'to take advance thought for' [Lns], 'to aim to do' [NTC], 'to take precaution' [WBC], 'to provide for' [KJV], 'to take pains (to do)' [NIV], 'to be careful (to do/be)' [NJB, NLT], 'to intend'

[NRSV]. The phrase 'we have regard for what is right' is translated 'our aims are entirely honorable' [REB], 'our purpose is to do what is right/good' [TEV, TNT].
  b. καλός (LN 88.4) (BAGD 2.b. p. 400): 'right' [NTC, WBC; NIV, NJB, NRSV, TEV], 'good' [BAGD, LN; TNT], 'morally good' [BAGD, ICC2], 'praiseworthy' [BAGD, LN], 'honorable' [AB, Lns; NLT, REB], 'a good reputation' [HNTC], 'honest' [KJV]. This entire clause is translated 'but we want to do what pleases the Lord and what people think is right' [CEV], 'we are concerned not only for God's approval but also for the good esteem of men' [NAB].
  c. ἐνώπιον (LN 90.20) (BAGD 3. p. 270): 'before' [NTC; NLT], 'in the opinion or judgment of' [BAGD, LN], 'in the sight of' [AB, ICC2, LN, Lns; KJV, NJB, NRSV, TEV, TNT], 'in the eyes of' [WBC; NIV, REB], 'with' [HNTC], not explicit [CEV, NAB].

8:22 **And[a] we-are-sending-with them our brother whom we-have-proved[b] in many-things[c] many-times[d] (as) being diligent,**
LEXICON—a. δέ (LN 89.94): 'and' [AB, ICC2, LN; KJV, NRSV], 'also' [NTC, WBC; CEV], 'and...also' [NLT], 'moreover' [Lns], not explicit [HNTC; NAB, NJB, TEV, TNT]. The phrase 'and we are sending' is translated 'we are sending another (of our company)' [REB], 'in addition we are sending' [NIV].
  b. aorist act. indic. of δοκιμάζω (LN 27.45) (BAGD 2.b. p. 202): 'to prove' [ICC2; KJV, NAB, NIV], 'to accept as proved, approve' [BAGD], 'to test and prove' [HNTC, WBC], 'to test' [BAGD, LN, Lns, NTC; NJB, NRSV, REB, TEV, TNT], 'to examine' [LN], 'to verify (the earnestness of)' [AB]. The phrase 'whom we have proved...as being' is also translated 'we approve (of this man)...he has already shown' [CEV], 'he has been tested and has shown' [NLT], 'tested and found' [NRSV, TEV]. See this word also at 8:8.
  c. πολύς (LN 59.1) (BAGD I.2.b.α. p. 688): 'many things' [BAGD, Lns; KJV], 'many ways' [AB, BAGD, NTC; NAB, NIV, NJB], 'many matters' [HNTC, WBC; NRSV], 'many respects' [ICC2], 'many circumstances' [TNT], 'thoroughly' [NLT], not explicit [CEV, REB, TEV].
  d. πολλάκις (LN 67.11) (BAGD p. 686): 'many times' [BAGD, LN; CEV, TEV], 'often' [AB, BAGD, LN, Lns, NTC, WBC; NIV, NRSV, TNT], 'oftentimes' [KJV], 'on many occasions' [HNTC; NLT], 'frequently' [BAGD, ICC2], 'over and over again' [NJB], 'repeated opportunities' [REB], not explicit [NAB].

and[a] now (he is) much more-diligent[b] because-of[c] (his) great confidence[d] in you.
LEXICON—a. δέ (LN 89.124): 'and' [HNTC, Lns, WBC; CEV, NIV, NJB, REB, TEV, TNT], 'but' [ICC2, LN; KJV, NRSV], not explicit [AB; NAB, NLT].

b. σπουδαῖος (LN 25.75) (BAGD p. 763): 'diligent' [KJV], 'earnest' [AB, BAGD, LN, Lns], 'eager' [LN, NTC, WBC; NAB, NJB, NRSV, TNT], 'eager to help' [TEV], 'zealous' [HNTC, ICC2; NIV], 'enthusiastic' [NLT], 'keen' [REB]. The phrase πολὺ σπουδαιότερον is translated 'much more diligent' [KJV], 'the more earnest' [AB], 'the more zealous' [HNTC], 'now even more zealous' [NIV], 'much more earnest' [Lns], 'much more zealous' [ICC2], 'much more eager' [NTC], 'now all the more eager' [WBC; NJB, TNT], 'now more eager than ever' [NAB, NRSV], 'all the more eager to help' [TEV], 'he wants to help more than ever' [CEV], 'now even more enthusiastic' [NLT], 'now all the more keen' [REB].
c. There is no lexical entry for the phrase 'because of', the grammatical relation being indicated in the Greek by the dative case of the noun πεποίθησις 'confidence'. It is translated 'because of' [NTC, WBC; NAB, NIV, NLT, NRSV, REB, TNT], 'because' [CEV, NJB], 'by reason of' [AB, ICC2], 'in view of' [HNTC], 'with' [Lns], 'upon' [KJV], not explicit [TEV].
d. πεποίθησις (LN 31.82) (BAGD 1. p. 643): 'confidence' [AB, BAGD, ICC2, LN, Lns, NTC, WBC; KJV, NIV, NLT, NRSV, REB, TEV, TNT], 'trust' [BAGD, LN; NAB]. The phrase πεποιθήσει πολλῇ τῇ εἰς ὑμᾶς 'because of his great confidence in you' is translated 'because he trusts you so much' [CEV], 'he has so much faith in you' [NJB]. See this word at 1:15, 3:4.

QUESTION—In what sense is the comparative form σπουδαιότερον 'more diligent' used in this clause?

His confidence in the Corinthians has caused his zeal or eagerness in this matter to increase [He, Ho, NIC1, NTC]. In this matter he is even more eager than usual [EBC, ICC1], more eager than ever [NAC]. He is more earnest than in other tasks Paul has given him [Lns].

8:23 If[a] (anyone asks) about Titus, (he is) my partner[b] and co-worker[c] with-respect-to[d] you;

LEXICON—a. εἴτε (LN 89.69): 'if' [HNTC, ICC2, LN, WBC; NJB, NLT, REB]. The construction εἴτε...εἴτε, used to introduce the two clauses of this verse, is translated 'if...if' [HNTC, ICC2, LN; NJB, NLT, REB], 'whether...or' [LN; KJV], 'whether...whether' [Lns], 'as for...as for' [AB, NTC; NAB, NRSV, TEV, TNT], not explicit [CEV, NIV]. The phrase εἴτε ὑπὲρ is translated 'if anyone asks about' [NLT], 'if there is any inquiry about' [HNTC; similarly ICC2; KJV], 'if there is any question about' [WBC; NJB, REB], 'whether anything comes up about' [Lns]. See this construction also at 1:6.

b. κοινωνός (LN 34.6) (BAGD 1.d. p. 440): 'partner' [AB, BAGD, HNTC, ICC2, LN, NTC, WBC; CEV, KJV, NIV, NJB, NLT, NRSV, REB, TEV, TNT], 'associate' [LN, Lns], 'companion' [NAB]. See this word also at 1:7.

c. συνεργός (LN 42.44) (BAGD p. 787): 'co-worker' [AB; NRSV], 'fellow-worker' [BAGD, HNTC, ICC2, LN, Lns, NTC, WBC; NAB, NIV, NJB, REB, TNT], 'fellow helper' [KJV]. This word is translated 'who works with me' [CEV, NLT], 'and works with me' [TEV]. See this word also at 1:24.

d. εἰς (LN 90.41): 'with respect to' [ICC2], 'in relation to' [HNTC], 'concerning' [KJV], 'for' [LN, Lns, NTC; TNT], 'in toiling for' [AB], 'on behalf of' [LN; NAB], 'in (your) interests' [NJB], 'in (your) service' [NRSV], 'to serve (you)' [CEV], 'to help (you)' [NLT, TEV], 'in dealings with (you)' [REB], 'among' [WBC; NIV].

if (anyone asks) about our brothers, (they are) representatives[a] of (the) churches, the glory[b] of-Christ.

LEXICON—a. ἀπόστολος (LN 33.194) (BAGD 1. p. 99): 'representative' [AB; NIV, NLT], 'messenger' [BAGD, LN; KJV, NRSV], 'delegate' [BAGD, ICC2, NTC, WBC; REB, TNT], 'envoy' [BAGD, HNTC], 'emissary' [NJB], 'apostle' [NAB], 'commissioner' [Lns]. The phrase 'representatives of the churches' is translated 'they are sent by the churches' [CEV], 'they represent the churches' [TEV].

b. δόξα (LN 25.205): 'glory' [AB, HNTC, ICC2, Lns, NTC; KJV, NAB, NJB, NRSV], 'honor' [WBC; NIV, TNT]. The phrase 'the glory of Christ' is translated 'they bring honor to Christ' [CEV, REB], 'they bring glory to Christ' [TEV], 'a splendid example of those who bring glory to Christ' [NLT].

QUESTION—Whom does the descriptive phrase 'the glory of Christ' describe?

1. It describes the men who represent the churches [AB, EBC, EGT, He, HNTC, Ho, ICC1, ICC2, Lns, NAC, NCBC, NIC1, NTC, SP, TG, TH, TNTC; CEV, KJV, NIV, NJB, NLT, REB, TEV, TNT].
2. It describes the churches [NIC2].

8:24 **Therefore[a] in (the) presence[b] of the churches (be)-proving[c] the proof of your love and our boasting[d] about you to them.**

LEXICON—a. οὖν (LN 89.52): 'therefore' [LN, NTC; NAB, NIV, NRSV], 'wherefore' [KJV], 'and so' [LN], 'so' [AB, HNTC; NLT, REB], 'so then' [LN; NJB], 'then' [ICC2; TNT], 'accordingly' [LN, Lns], 'for this reason' [WBC], not explicit [CEV, TEV].

b. πρόσωπον (LN 85.26) (BAGD 1.c.β. p. 721): 'in the presence of' [AB, NTC], 'in the sight of' [Lns], 'before' [BAGD, ICC2; KJV], 'openly before' [NRSV], 'in full view of' [NJB]. The phrase εἰς πρόσωπον 'in the presence of' (literally 'in/to the face of') is translated 'so that the churches/congregations can see' [HNTC, WBC; NIV], 'in such a way that the churches will see' [CEV], 'for all the churches to see' [NAB]. The phrase 'in the presence of the churches be proving the proof of your love' is translated 'show them your love, and prove' [NLT], 'show your love to them so that all the churches will be sure of it' [TEV], 'show them evidence of your love' [TNT], 'give them, and through them the churches, clear evidence of your love' [REB]. See this word also at 1:11; 2:10; 4:6; 5:12.

c. pres. mid. participle of ἐνδείκνυμι (LN 28.51) (BAGD 1. p. 262): 'to show' [BAGD, LN], 'to demonstrate' [AB, BAGD, LN]. The participial phrase ἔνδειξιν...ἐνδεικνύμενοι 'proving the proof' is translated as an imperative: 'clearly demonstrate' [AB], 'show them the proof' [HNTC, ICC2, WBC; KJV, NAB, NIV, NRSV], 'show them and prove' [NLT], 'show them the evidence' [TNT], 'give them clear evidence' [REB], 'give proof' [NJB], 'present proof' [NTC], 'display...the display' [Lns], 'show...so that they will be sure of it and know' [TEV].

d. καύχησις (LN 25.204) (BAGD 1. p. 426): 'boasting' [AB, BAGD; KJV, NLT, NRSV, TEV], 'boast' [HNTC, ICC2], 'glorying' [Lns], 'pride (in someone)' [BAGD, LN, NTC, WBC; NIV, REB, TNT]. The phrase 'our boasting about you' is translated 'why we bragged about you' [CEV], 'why we boast about you' [NAB], 'we were right to boast of you' [NJB]. See this word also at 1:12 and 7:4.

QUESTION—What was the nature of Paul's boast?

Paul's boast about the Corinthians is a general pride in them [EBC, HNTC, ICC1, NIC1, NTC, WBC; NIV, REB, TNT]. Paul has boasted about their readiness to give [EGT, TNTC]. He boasts about their loyalty to himself [NCBC].

DISCOURSE UNIT: 9:1–15 [HNTC; CEV, NAB, NLT, NRSV, TEV]. The topic is the collection [HNTC], the money for God's people [CEV], the offering for the saints [NAB], the collection for the Christians at Jerusalem [NLT, NRSV], help for needy believers [TEV], help for fellow Christians [TH].

DISCOURSE UNIT: 9:1–5 [EBC, ICC1, NTC, TNTC, WBC]. The topic is help for the saints [NTC], the need for readiness [EBC], exhortation to readiness [ICC1], commendation of the brothers to Achaia [WBC], be prepared to avoid humiliation [TNTC].

9:1 For[a] it-is superfluous[b] for-me to-write to-you concerning the ministry to the saints;

LEXICON—a. γάρ (BAGD 1.b. p. 151, 1.e. p. 152): 'for' [BAGD, HNTC, ICC2, Lns, NTC; KJV], 'so' [AB], 'now' [WBC; NRSV], not explicit [CEV, NAB, NIV, NJB, NLT, REB, TEV, TNT].

b. περισσός (LN **59.51, 71.40**) (BAGD 2.b. p. 651): 'superfluous' [AB, BAGD, HNTC, ICC2, LN (59.51), Lns; KJV, REB, TNT], 'unnecessary' [BAGD, LN (71.40)], 'not necessary' [NTC; NRSV], 'no necessity' [WBC], 'no need' [NAB, NIV, NJB, TEV], 'I don't need to' [CEV, NLT]. See the comparative form of this adjective at 2:7.

QUESTION—What relationship is indicated by γάρ 'for'?

It connects this verse with what was just said in 8:24 [EBC, HNTC, Ho, ICC1, NAC, NIC2, NTC, SP]. It resumes the preceding topic and explains his boasting in 8:24 [EBC;, NAB]. Paul urges them to receive the brothers hospitably, but because he is confident in their willingness to give he doesn't need to write about that [Ho, ICC1, NTC].

QUESTION—Why does Paul write if it is superfluous to do so?

Paul does not really need to write to motivate them to give, since they were already eager to do so [AB, EBC, EGT, NIC1, NIC2, NTC, TH, TNTC], though he also knows that they need help following through on it [AB, EGT, NIC1, NIC2, NTC]. He does not need to write because they already know about the collection, although they do need to be stimulated to complete it [Lns]. Paul knows that Titus will take care of details so he does not need to elaborate further, since he is confident in them again [NAC]. He means that it is not necessary to write what he has already written to them [WBC]. He means that it is not necessary to write more than what he has already written [NAC, SP]. It is Paul's polite way of affirming that they were already willing [Ho]. Paul is just being polite [TG], and is trying to soften what he really wants to say [ICC2].

9:2 For[a] I-know your willingness[b] which I-have-boasted about you to-the-Macedonians, that Achaia has-been-ready[c] since last-year,[d] and your eagerness[e] stirred-up[f] most-of-them.[g]

LEXICON—a. γάρ (LN 89.23): 'for' [HNTC, ICC2, LN, Lns, NTC, WBC; KJV, NIV, NJB, NLT, NRSV], 'because' [AB], not explicit [CEV, NAB, REB, TEV, TNT].

b. προθυμία (LN 25.68) (BAGD p. 706): 'willingness' [BAGD, ICC2; NAB], 'willing to help' [TEV], 'readiness' [BAGD, HNTC, Lns, WBC], 'eagerness' [LN, NTC; NRSV], 'eagerness to help' [NIV], 'how eager you are to help' [NLT, REB], 'how eager you are to give' [CEV], 'how keen you are to help' [TNT], 'enthusiasm' [NJB], 'forwardness' [KJV], 'goodwill' [AB]. See this word also at 8:11, 19.

c. perf. mid. indic. of παρασκευάζω (LN 77.8) (BAGD 2. p. 622): 'to be ready' [AB, BAGD, LN, NTC; CEV, KJV, NAB, NJB, NRSV], 'to be ready to help' [TEV], 'to be ready to give' [NIV], 'ready to send an offering' [NLT], 'to have everything ready' [REB], 'to be prepared' [HNTC, ICC2, LN, Lns, WBC], 'to prepare oneself' [BAGD],

d. πέρυσι (LN 67.204) (BAGD p. 633): 'last year' [AB, BAGD, HNTC, ICC2, LN, NTC, WBC; NAB, NIV, NRSV, REB, TEV, TNT], 'a year ago' [BAGD, Lns; KJV, NLT], 'for a year' [NJB], 'for a whole year' [CEV]. See the construction ἀπὸ πέρυσι at 8:10.

e. ζῆλος (LN 25.46) (BAGD 1. p. 337): 'zeal' [AB, BAGD, HNTC, ICC2, Lns, NTC, WBC; KJV, NAB, NRSV, REB, TNT], 'enthusiasm' [NIV, NJB, NLT], 'eagerness' [TEV], 'desire to give' [CEV]. See this word also at 7:7, 11.

f. aorist act. indic. of ἐρεθίζω (LN **90.55**) (BAGD p. 308): 'to stir up' [HNTC; NAB, NRSV, TEV], 'to stir up to begin helping' [NLT], 'to stir to action' [NIV], 'to spur' [WBC], 'to be a spur' [AB; NJB], 'to stimulate' [TNT], 'to give a stimulus' [ICC2], 'to incite' [Lns], 'to arouse'

[BAGD, NTC], 'to fire' [REB], 'to provoke' [KJV], 'to make them want to give' [CEV].

g. πολύς (BAGD II.2.a.α. p. 689): 'most of them' [AB, WBC; NAB, NIV, NRSV, REB, TEV], 'most' [BAGD], 'the majority' [BAGD, HNTC, ICC2, Lns], 'many of them' [NLT], 'many people' [NTC], 'many others' [NJB], 'very many' [KJV], not explicit [CEV]. See this word also at 2:6.

QUESTION—What relationship is indicated by γάρ 'for'?

It introduces the reason he does not need to write to them [AB, HNTC, NIC2].

QUESTION—When Paul uses the name Achaia is he referring to the entire province or only the city of Corinth?
1. He is referring to a broader area than just Corinth [EBC, Lns, NIC2, NTC, WBC]. Corinth is the principle church in Achaia [HNTC, NTC].
2. All the Christians in Achaia belonged to the church in Corinth, though they did not all live in Corinth [Ho]. Paul balances his reference to Macedonia, which is a province, with the name Achaia, which is also a province [NAC, SP].

QUESTION—In what way were they prepared last year?
1. They were prepared in the sense that they were willing to give to the collection [AB, EBC, HNTC, Ho, NAC, NIC1, NTC, WBC]. Paul had prepared them by informing them and by awakening readiness and zeal in them [Lns].
2. Paul thought that they were ready and willing to give, though now he sees that he was mistaken [ICC2]. Paul overstated their readiness to give; they are still not ready [SP].

9:3 But[a] I-sent[b] the brothers, lest our boast concerning you be-made-empty[c] in this matter,[d] that you-would-be-ready just-as I-have-been-saying.

LEXICON—a. δέ (LN 89.124): 'but' [AB, HNTC, ICC2, LN, NTC, WBC; NIV, NLT, NRSV], 'yet' [Lns; KJV], 'nonetheless' [NAB], 'all the same' [NJB], 'now' [TEV], not explicit [CEV, REB].

b. aorist act. indic. of πέμπω (LN 15.66) (BAGD 1. p. 641): 'to send' [AB, BAGD, HNTC, ICC2, LN, Lns, NTC, WBC; all versions]. This aorist verb is translated 'I have sent' [HNTC, WBC; KJV, NJB], 'I sent' [ICC2, Lns], 'I am sending' [AB, NTC; CEV, NIV, NLT, NRSV, TEV, TNT], 'I send' [NAB], 'my purpose in sending' [REB].

c. aorist pass. subj. of κενόω (LN 76.27) (BAGD 3. p. 428): 'to be made empty' [BAGD, Lns], 'to be proved (to be) empty' [HNTC; NRSV, REB], 'to be shown empty' [NAB], 'to turn out to be empty words' [TEV], 'to prove to be hollow' [NTC; NIV, NJB], 'to come to nothing' [ICC2], 'to lose its justification' [BAGD], 'to cause to lose power' [LN], 'to be in vain' [AB; KJV], 'to be proved to be in vain' [WBC]. The phrase 'lest our boast...be made empty' is translated 'to prove we were not wrong' [CEV], 'I don't want it to turn out that I was wrong' [NLT], 'to make sure that all we said...may be proved to be true' [TNT].

d. μέρος (LN 89.5) (BAGD 1.b.θ. p. 506): 'matter' [AB, BAGD, WBC; NIV, REB, TEV, TNT], 'affair' [BAGD], 'case' [BAGD, LN, NTC; NRSV], not explicit [CEV, NLT]. The phrase ἐν τῷ μέρει τούτῳ is translated 'in this respect' [HNTC, ICC2; NJB], 'in this part' [Lns], 'in this behalf' [KJV], 'in this regard' [NAB]. See this word also at 1:15; 2:5; 3:10.

QUESTION—What relationship is indicated by δέ 'but'?

This particle corresponds to the μέν (untranslated) in the phrase περί μέν γάρ 'for...concerning' in 9:1 [AB, EBC, EGT, HNTC, ICC1, ICC2, NIC2, SP, TH]. That is, on the one hand, he does not need to write, but on the other hand, he does send the brothers [ICC2]. The μέν...δέ construction suggests some limitation of the thought of 9:1; 'I know this, but nevertheless I am sending' [HNTC]. The μέν...δέ construction suggests some limitation of or contrast with the thought of 9:1; 'I know your eagerness, but nevertheless I am sending the brothers' [AB, EBC, HNTC, NIC2, SP, TH].

QUESTION—What does Paul intend to convey by the aorist form ἔπεμψα 'I sent'?

1. It is an epistolary aorist, which means that at the time of writing the sending is future, but when the letter is read it will have already happened [AB, EBC, EGT, He, HNTC, ICC1, NIC2, SP, TH].
2. Paul had already sent them when this part was written [WBC].

QUESTION—Does 'just as I have been saying' refer to something he had told someone earlier or to what he has just written?

1. It refers to his previous claims concerning the Corinthians' readiness [AB, EGT, He, ICC1, ICC2, NIC2, NTC, TNTC, WBC; CEV, NAB, NIV, NJB, NLT, NRSV, REB, TEV, TNT].
2. It refers to what he was saying in 9:2 [Lns].

QUESTION—What does Paul mean when he says ἐν τῷ μέρει τούτῳ 'in this matter'?

'In this matter' refers to the matter of the collection [AB, ICC1, ICC2, NIC2, TG, TH, TNTC, WBC], and to their readiness to participate [WBC]. It refers to 'the case' of his boasting about the Corinthians [NTC], or to the 'particular aspect' of his boast, which is their readiness or zeal [Lns]. It refers to the 'one respect' in which his boasting may be proved hollow, which is their completion of the collection [NIC1]. It refers to the particular aspect of actually gathering the money, as opposed to the willingness to do it [EGT].

9:4 lest if^a (any) Macedonians come with me and find you unprepared^b we, not to-mention you, be-ashamed^c in this undertaking.^d

TEXT—Some manuscripts include καύχεσις 'boasting' before or after τοῦτος 'this'. It is omitted by GNT with a B rating, indicating that the text is almost certain. It is included only by KJV.

LEXICON—a. ἐάν (LN 89.67): 'if' [AB, HNTC, ICC2, LN, Lns, NTC, WBC; NIV, NLT, NRSV, REB, TEV, TNT], 'if by chance' [NJB], not explicit

[NAB]. The phrase 'if any Macedonians come with me' is translated 'some followers from Macedonia may come with me' [CEV].
b. ἀπαρασκεύαστος (LN **77.9**) (BAGD p. 80): 'unprepared' [BAGD, HNTC, ICC2, LN, Lns, NTC, WBC; KJV, NIV, NJB], 'not prepared' [REB], 'not ready' [BAGD, LN; NLT, NRSV, TEV, TNT], 'unready' [AB; NAB], not explicit [CEV].
c. aorist pass. subj. of καταισχύνω (LN 25.194) (BAGD 2. p. 410): 'to be ashamed' [KJV, NIV, TEV], 'to be put to shame' [BAGD, HNTC, ICC2, LN, Lns, NTC, WBC; NAB, NJB, TNT], 'to be humiliated' [BAGD, LN; NLT, NRSV], 'to be disgraced' [AB, LN], 'to be embarrassed' [CEV]. The phrase 'lest...we be ashamed' is translated 'what a disgrace it will be to us' [REB]. See this word also at 7:14.
d. ὑπόστασις (LN **31.84**) (BAGD 2. p. 847): 'undertaking' [AB; NRSV], 'situation' [BAGD, NTC], 'condition' [BAGD], 'project' [ICC2], 'confidence' [HNTC, LN; NJB, REB], 'trust' [NAB], 'assurance' [Lns], not explicit [NLT]. The phrase ἐν τῇ ὑποστάσει ταύτῃ is translated 'to do this' [CEV], 'of having been so confident' [NIV], 'for feeling so sure of you' [TEV], 'for being over-confident' [TNT]. The variant ἐν τῇ ὑποστάσει ταύτῃ τῆς καυχήσεως is translated 'in this same confident boasting' [KJV].

QUESTION—What uncertainty is expressed by the conditional μή πως ἐάν 'lest if'?
1. Paul is not certain whether or not Macedonians will accompany him [AB, NTC, SP, TH; CEV].
2. Paul expects Macedonians to accompany him, so the only thing that is uncertain is whether or not the offering will be ready [EBC, ICC2, Lns, NIC1, NIC2, TG, TNTC, WBC].

QUESTION—What area of meaning is intended by ὑπόστασις 'undertaking'?
1. It indicates confidence or assurance [HNTC, ICC1, LN, Lns, NIC1, TG, TNTC; KJV, NAB, NIV, NJB, REB, TEV, TNT].
2. It refers to an undertaking or project [AB, ICC2, NAC, NTC, SP, TH; NRSV].
3. It refers to the eventuality or possibility of their not being ready [He, WBC].

QUESTION—What is Paul's real intent in this statement?
He trusts their willingness, but recognizes they need administrative help to carry it out lest they all be embarrassed [AB, EBC, EGT, HNTC, NIC1, NTC]. Paul wants to save face for himself and the Corinthians [ICC2, NAC, NTC, TNTC, WBC]. Paul wants to save face for the Corinthians [Ho, ICC1]. Paul wants to save face for the Corinthians, but mentions his own name first to avoid embarrassment to them [Ho]. Paul is seeking to keep the Corinthians from losing face, and to prevent damaged relations between the churches in the two provinces [NIC2]. Paul fears that the whole project may falter if the Corinthians default on their part of it [NAC]. Paul initially trusted their willingness, but now is unsure of it, and does not want them and

himself to lose face [ICC2]. Paul had awakened readiness and zeal in them, but if they do nothing the Macedonians could question whether Paul had really done what he claimed [Lns]. Paul is wanting to salvage his previously overstated claim that they were ready to give [SP]. Paul is concerned that if he and the Corinthians are embarrassed before the materially poorer Macedonians, there may be a lack of cohesion among the various churches involved in the ministry [AB].

9:5 So[a] I-thought (it) necessary[b] to-urge[c] the brothers, that they-go to you and prepare-in-advance[d] your promised[e] generous-gift,[f]

LEXICON—a. οὖν (LN 89.50): 'so' [HNTC, ICC2, LN, WBC; CEV, NIV, NJB, NLT, NRSV], 'therefore' [AB, LN; KJV], 'consequently' [LN], 'accordingly' [LN, Lns; REB, TEV], 'thus' [NTC], 'this is why' [TNT], not explicit [NAB].

b. ἀναγκαῖος (LN 71.39) (BAGD 1. p. 52): 'necessary' [AB, BAGD, HNTC, ICC2, LN, Lns, NTC; KJV, NAB, NIV, NJB, NRSV, REB, TEV, TNT], 'needful' [WBC], not explicit [CEV]. The phrase 'I thought it necessary to urge...that they go' is translated 'I thought I should send' [NLT].

c. aorist act. infin. of παρακαλέω (LN 33.168) (BAGD 3. p. 617): 'to urge' [AB, Lns, NTC; NIV, NRSV, TEV], 'to ask' [HNTC, WBC; CEV, REB, TNT], 'to request' [BAGD, ICC2, LN], 'to implore' [BAGD], 'to exhort' [KJV, NAB], 'to encourage' [NJB], 'to appeal to' [BAGD, LN], not explicit [NLT]. See this word also at 1:4, 6; 2:7, 8; 5:20; 6:1; 7:6; 8:6.

d. aorist act. subj. of προκαταρτίζω (LN **77.4**) (BAGD p. 707): 'to prepare in advance' [LN, NTC, WBC], 'to prepare' [HNTC], 'to make ready in advance' [**LN**], 'to make sure in advance' [NJB], 'to make up beforehand' [KJV], 'to get ready in advance' [BAGD; TEV], 'to arrange in advance' [BAGD; NAB, NRSV], 'to arrange beforehand' [TNT], 'to make arrangements in advance' [ICC2], 'to organize in advance' [AB], 'to fix up in advance' [Lns], 'visit you in advance and finish the arrangements' [NIV], 'ahead of me to make sure' [NLT], 'before I arrive...they can arrange' [CEV], 'to see that (it is) in order before I come' [REB].

e. perf. (deponent = mid. or pass.) participle of προεπαγγέλλομαι (LN 33.287) (BAGD p. 705): 'to have been promised beforehand' [BAGD, LN], 'to have been previously promised' [BAGD, ICC2], 'to have been promised in advance' [HNTC], 'to have been already provided' [WBC], 'to have had notice before' [KJV]. This participle is translated as an active verb: 'you promised' [NLT], 'you promised to make' [TEV], 'you have promised' [CEV, NIV, NRSV], 'you promised in advance' [Lns], 'you promised beforehand' [NTC], 'you have already promised' [NAB, NJB], 'you had already pledged' [AB]. It is also translated as an adjective: 'promised (bounty/gift)' [REB, TNT].

f. εὐλογία (LN **37.105**) (BAGD 3.b.β. p. 353, 5. p. 323): 'generous gift' [BAGD, ICC2, NTC; NIV], 'gift' [AB, BAGD, HNTC, **LN**, WBC; NJB,

NLT, TEV, TNT], 'bountiful gift' [NAB, NRSV], 'blessing' [BAGD, LN, Lns], 'bounty' [BAGD; KJV, REB], 'the money' [CEV], 'contribution' [LN].

this being ready thus[a] **as a-generous-gift**[b] **and not as something-grudgingly-given/a-compulsion.**[c]

LEXICON—a. οὕτως (LN 61.9): 'thus' [HNTC, LN, Lns], 'so' [NTC; NRSV], 'so that' [NJB], 'that' [AB; KJV], 'in this way' [LN], 'in such a way' [ICC2], 'then' [CEV, NIV, REB], not explicit [WBC; NAB, NLT, TEV, TNT].

b. εὐλογία. The contrast between this second occurrence of εὐλογία 'generous gift' and πλεονεξία 'something grudgingly given' which follows is accented in translation by modifiers added to εὐλογία: 'true blessing' [Lns], 'really a gift' [WBC], 'real gift' [NJB], 'willing gift' [NLT]; or by a change of modifier: 'gracious gift' [NAB], 'voluntary gift' [NRSV], 'genuine bounty' [REB]. Εὐλογία is also translated here as a verb phrase: 'give because you want to' [CEV, TEV], 'you give it freely' [TNT].

c. πλεονεξία (LN **88.144**) (BAGD p. 667): 'something grudgingly given' [NIV], 'in a grudging spirit' [TNT], 'grudgingly granted by avarice' [BAGD], 'something wrung from you' [HNTC, WBC], 'compulsion' [LN], 'covetousness' [ICC2, Lns; KJV], 'an exaction' [NAB], 'an imposition' [NJB], 'given under pressure' [NLT], 'torn away from greed' [NTC], 'because you feel forced to' [CEV], 'because you have to' [TEV], 'extortion' [AB; NRSV, REB], 'exploitation' [LN], 'being taken advantage of' [**LN**]. See the verb form of this word at 2:11; 7:2.

QUESTION—What questionable motives are implied in the use of the pejorative term πλεονεξία 'grudgingly given'?

1. The word refers to giving in a begrudging manner [EBC, He, HNTC, Ho, ICC1, ICC2, Lns, NAC, NIC1, NTC, SP, TG, TNTC, WBC; CEV, KJV, NIV, TEV, TNT].
2. The word refers to the use of extortionary tactics by Paul and his associates [AB, EGT, NIC2, TH; NRSV, REB]. Paul has previously been accused of having acted with fraudulent intent [AB].

DISCOURSE UNIT: 9:6–15 [AB, EBC, ICC1, TNTC, WBC; NIV, NJB]. The topic is closing remarks on generous giving [AB], an exhortation to be generous [TNTC], sowing generously [NIV], blessings to be expected from the collection [NJB], the results of generosity [EBC], exhortation to liberality [ICC1], the collection and the unity of the church [WBC].

DISCOURSE UNIT: 9:6–11 [EBC, NTC]. The topic is the enrichment of the giver [EBC], cheerful giving [NTC].

9:6 Now[a] (the point is)[b] this, the one-sowing[c] sparingly,[d] sparingly also will-reap,[e] and the one-sowing generously,[f] generously also will-reap.

LEXICON—a. δέ (LN 89.124): 'now' [Lns], 'but' [HNTC, LN; KJV, NJB], not explicit [AB, ICC2, NTC, WBC; CEV, NAB, NIV, NLT, NRSV, REB, TEV, TNT].

b. There is no lexical entry for the implied phrase 'the point is'. The phrase τοῦτο δέ 'now this' is translated 'now this' [Lns], 'the point is this' [ICC2, NTC; NRSV], 'I am saying this' [AB], 'let me say this much' [NAB], 'but this I say' [KJV], 'but, you know, this is true' [HNTC], 'to enforce the point' [WBC], 'remember' [REB], 'but remember' [NJB], 'remember this' [NIV, NLT, TNT], 'remember this saying' [CEV], 'remember that' [REB].

c. pres. act. participle of σπείρω (LN 43.6) (BAGD 1.b.α. p. 761): 'to sow' [AB, BAGD, HNTC, ICC2, LN, Lns, NTC, WBC; KJV, NAB, NIV, NJB, NRSV, REB, TNT], 'to plant' [NLT, TEV], not explicit [CEV].

d. φειδομένως (LN **59.61**) (BAGD p. 854): 'sparingly' [AB, BAGD, HNTC, ICC2, **LN**, Lns, NTC, WBC; KJV, NAB, NIV, NRSV, REB, TNT], 'sparsely' [NJB], 'in a limited manner' [LN]. The phrase 'the one sowing sparingly' is translated 'who plants few seeds' [NLT, TEV]. The clause 'the one sowing sparingly, sparingly also will reap' is translated 'a few seeds make a small harvest' [CEV].

e. fut. act. indic. of θερίζω (LN 43.14) (BAGD 2.a. p. 359): 'to reap' [AB, BAGD, HNTC, ICC2, LN, Lns, NTC, WBC; KJV, NAB, NIV, NJB, NRSV, REB, TNT], 'to harvest' [BAGD, LN]. The phrase 'reap sparingly' is translated 'make a small harvest' [CEV], 'get/have a small crop' [NLT, TEV].

f. εὐλογία (LN **59.56**) (BAGD 5. p. 323): 'an abundance' [LN]. The phrase ἐπ' εὐλογίαις is literally 'on (the basis) of blessings' [AB, LN, Lns]. It is translated 'generously' [NTC, WBC; NIV, NJB, NLT], 'bountifully' [BAGD, HNTC, ICC2; KJV, NAB, NRSV, REB], 'liberally' [AB], 'plentifully' [TNT]. The phrase 'generously also will reap' is translated 'will have a large crop' [TEV], 'make a big harvest' [CEV]. See this word also at 9:5.

9:7 Each (should give)[a] as he-has-previously-decided[b] in (his) heart,[c]

LEXICON—a. There is no lexical entry for the implied phrase 'should give'. This phrase is left as an ellipsis by Lns and KJV. It is translated 'let each person contribute' [AB], 'let each man/one give' [HNTC, NTC, WBC], 'each person/man/one should give' [NIV, NJB, REB], 'each should do' [ICC2], 'each of you must give' [NRSV], 'everyone must give' [NAB], 'you should each give' [TEV], 'each of you (must make up your own mind) about how much to give' [CEV, NLT, TNT].

b. perf. mid. indic. of προαιρέω (LN **30.84**) (BAGD 2. p. 702): 'to decide beforehand' [LN], 'to decide' [AB, BAGD, HNTC, NTC, WBC; NAB, NIV, NJB, REB, TEV], 'to determine' [BAGD], 'to make up one's mind'

[BAGD, ICC2; CEV, NLT, NRSV, TNT], 'to choose in advance' [Lns], 'to purpose' [KJV].
- c. καρδία (LN **26.3**) (BAGD 1.b.γ. p. 403): 'heart' [HNTC, LN, Lns; KJV, NIV], 'mind' [BAGD, ICC2, NTC, WBC; CEV, NLT, NRSV, TNT], not explicit [AB; TEV]. The phrase 'in his heart' is translated 'inwardly' [NAB], 'on his own initiative' [NJB], 'for himself' [REB].

not out-of grief[a] or out-of compulsion;[b] for God loves[c] a cheerful[d] giver.
- LEXICON—a. λύπη (LN **25.272**) (BAGD p. 482): 'grief' [BAGD, Lns], 'regret' [**LN**], 'unhappiness, sadness' [LN], 'sorrow' [BAGD]. The phrase ἐκ λύπης 'out of grief' is translated 'reluctantly' [BAGD, NTC; NIV, NJB, NLT, NRSV], 'grudgingly' [AB; KJV], 'regretfully' [ICC2, WBC], 'with regret' [TEV, TNT], 'sadly' [NAB], 'as if it hurt him' [HNTC], 'don't feel sorry (that you must give)' [CEV], 'there should be no reluctance' [REB]. See this word also at 2:1, 7; 7:10.
- b. ἀνάγκη (LN **71.30**) (BAGD 1. p. 52): 'compulsion' [AB, BAGD, ICC2, Lns; NIV, NJB, REB], 'necessity' [BAGD, HNTC, NTC; KJV], 'obligation' [LN], 'duty' [TEV], 'constraint' [WBC]. The phrase 'not out of compulsion' is translated 'freely' [TNT], 'not grudgingly' [NAB], 'not out of response to pressure' [NLT], 'don't feel that you are forced (to give)' [CEV]. See this word also at 6:4.
- c. pres. act. indic. of ἀγαπάω (LN **25.104**) (BAGD 1.b.α. p. 4): 'to love' [AB, BAGD, HNTC, ICC2, Lns, NTC, WBC; all versions], 'to take pleasure in' [LN].
- d. ἱλαρός (LN **25.117**) (BAGD p. 375): 'cheerful' [AB, BAGD, HNTC, ICC2, LN, Lns, NTC, WBC; KJV, NAB, NIV, NJB, NRSV, REB, TNT]. The phrase 'cheerful giver' is translated 'people who love to give' [CEV], 'person who gives cheerfully' [NLT], 'one who gives gladly' [TEV].

QUESTION—What does the verb ἀγαπάω 'love' mean in this context?
Here 'God loves' means 'God approves of' [AB, EBC, HNTC, NAC, NIC2, TH], 'God values' [AB, HNTC, TH], or 'God delights in' [Ho, TNTC]. God loves a cheerful giver because he is a cheerful giver himself [NAC, TNTC]. This is a reference to Prov. 22:8a LXX (not included in the Heb text) which says 'God blesses a cheerful and giving man' [AB, NIC1, NTC]. Paul may have been quoting a variant text and used 'loves' instead of 'blesses' [NIC1], or he may have used 'loves' as a more all-encompassing word than 'blesses', which refers only to an action [NTC].

9:8 **And[a] God is-able[b] (to-cause)-to-abound[c] to you all[d] grace[e]**
- LEXICON—a. δέ (LN **89.94**): 'and' [AB, ICC2, LN; KJV, NIV, NLT, NRSV, REB, TEV], 'moreover' [Lns], 'for' [NTC], not explicit [HNTC, WBC; CEV, NAB, NJB, TNT].
- b. pres. act. indic. of δυνατέω (LN **74.5**) (BAGD 2. p. 208): 'to be able to' [BAGD, HNTC, ICC2, LN, Lns, NTC, WBC; KJV, NIV, NRSV, TEV, TNT], 'to be perfectly able' [NJB], 'to have the power' [AB], 'can' [LN;

CEV, NAB]. The phrase δυνατεῖ δὲ ὁ θεός 'God is able' is translated 'it is in God's power' [REB], 'God will (generously provide)' [NLT].
  c. aorist act. infin. of περισσεύω (LN 59.54) (BAGD 1.b.α. p. 651): 'to abound' [BAGD], 'to make abound' [HNTC, Lns, NTC; KJV, NIV], 'to make to overflow' [WBC], 'to cause to be abundant' [LN]. The verb 'to abound' is translated 'abundantly' [ICC2]. The phrase 'to cause to abound to you all grace' is translated 'bless you with everything you need' [CEV], 'generously provide all you need' [NLT], 'to multiply his favors' [NAB], 'to enrich you with every grace' [NJB], 'to provide every benefit/blessing in abundance' [AB; NRSV], 'to provide all good gifts in abundance' [REB], 'to give you more than you need' [TEV; similarly TNT]. See this word also at 1:5; 3:9; 4:15; 8:2, 7.
  d. πᾶς (LN 59.23): 'all' [HNTC, ICC2, LN, NTC, WBC; KJV, NIV, NLT, REB, TNT], 'every' [AB, Lns; NJB, NRSV], not explicit [CEV, NAB, TEV]. The adjective πᾶς 'all' appears in the next verse in the phrases 'all things', 'all sufficiency', and 'every good work', and in 9:11 in the phrases 'in everything' and 'all generosity'.
  e. χάρις (LN 88.66) (BAGD 4.a. p. 878): 'grace' [BAGD, HNTC, ICC2, LN, Lns, NTC, WBC; KJV, NIV, NJB], 'benefit' [AB], 'favors' [NAB], 'blessing' [NRSV], 'good gifts' [REB]. The phrase 'all grace' is translated 'all/everything you need' [CEV, NLT], 'all you need and more' [TNT], 'more than you need' [TEV]. See this word also at 1:2, 12; 8:1, 4, 6, 9, 16, 19.
QUESTION—What area of meaning is intended by χάρις 'grace'?
  In this context it is material benefit or blessing [AB, Ho, NIC2, SP, TG, TH, TNTC]. It is God's generosity, presumably expressed in material blessings [HNTC]. It is all spiritual and material benefits and gifts [EBC, EGT, NTC]. It means that God gives material blessings and the spiritual motivation to share them [ICC1, ICC2, NAC]. It is God's gracious favor [WBC]. It is grace in the broadest sense of an active attribute of God, including the gifts of grace [Lns]. It is the enabling power that comes from God's love [NIC1].

so-that[a] always[b] having all sufficiency[c] in all-things[d] you-may-abound[e] in every[f] good work,[g]
LEXICON—a. ἵνα (LN 89.49): 'so that' [HNTC, ICC2, LN, NTC, WBC; NAB, NIV, NJB, NRSV, REB, TEV, TNT], 'in order that' [LN], 'that' [AB, LN; KJV]. The relation of result indicated by the phrase 'so that always having' is translated 'you will always have' [CEV, NLT].
  b. πάντοτε (LN 67.88): 'always' [ICC2, LN, NTC; CEV, KJV, NAB, NRSV, REB, TEV, TNT], 'at all times' [HNTC, LN, WBC; NIV, NJB, NLT], 'ever' [AB, Lns]. This word is a cognate of the adjective πᾶς (see comment above). There is a play on words in the phrase ἐν παντὶ πάντοτε πᾶσαν (literally 'in all always all') focusing on the superlative 'all'.

c. αὐτάρκεια (LN **75.6**) (BAGD 1. p. 122): 'sufficiency' [BAGD, HNTC, ICC2, **LN**, Lns; KJV], 'what is needed' [AB, LN, WBC; CEV, NIV, NLT, REB, TEV, TNT], 'enough' [BAGD, NTC; NAB, NJB, NRSV].
d. πάς: 'everything' [AB, Lns, NTC; CEV, NAB, NLT, NRSV], 'all things' [WBC; KJV, NIV], 'all ways' [HNTC], 'in every respect' [ICC2], 'every need' [REB], 'every conceivable need' [NJB], 'all (you need)' [TEV, TNT].
e. pres. act. subj. of περισσεύω: 'to abound' [AB, Lns, NTC; KJV, NIV], 'to overflow' [WBC; NJB], 'to be prolific' [ICC2], 'to share abundantly' [NRSV], 'do all kinds of (good things)' [CEV], 'to help (every good work)' [TNT], not explicit [HNTC; NAB, NLT, REB, TEV]. See this word also at 1:5; 3:9; 4:15; 8:2, 7.
f. πάς: 'every' [AB, ICC2, Lns, NTC; KJV, NIV, NRSV, REB, TEV, TNT], 'every kind of' [WBC], 'all kinds of' [HNTC; CEV, NJB], not explicit [NAB, NLT].
g. ἔργον (LN 42.42) (BAGD 1.c.β. p. 308): 'work' [AB, HNTC, ICC2, LN, Lns, NTC, WBC; KJV, NIV, NJB, NRSV, TNT], 'works' [NAB], 'deed' [BAGD], 'cause' [REB, TEV]. The phrase ἔργον ἀγαθόν 'good work' is translated 'good things for others' [CEV], 'to share with others' [NLT].

9:9 **as it-is-written, He-scattered-abroad,**[a] **he-gave**[b] **to the poor,**[c] **his righteousness**[d] **endures**[e] **forever.**
LEXICON—a. aorist act. indic. of σκορπίζω (LN **57.95**) (BAGD 2. p. 757): 'to scatter abroad' [AB, BAGD, HNTC, ICC2; NAB, NIV, NRSV], 'to scatter widely' [WBC], 'to scatter out' [Lns], 'to scatter' [NTC], 'to disperse abroad' [KJV], 'to distribute generously' [LN], 'to distribute' [BAGD], 'to distribute freely' [TNT]. The verb εσκόρπισεν 'he scattered abroad' is conflated with the phrase ἔδωκεν τοῖς πένησιν 'he gave to the poor' and translated 'he has scattered abroad his gifts to the poor' [NIV], 'God freely gives his gifts to the poor' [CEV], 'to the needy he gave without stint' [NJB], 'he lavishes his gifts on the needy' [REB], 'he gives generously to the needy' [TEV], 'godly people give generously to the poor' [NLT]. This verb is translated as past tense [AB, HNTC, ICC2, Lns, NTC, WBC; KJV, NAB, NIV, NJB, TNT]; as present tense [CEV, NLT, NRSV, REB, TEV]. The habitual actions represented in axioms and proverbs can be represented in Greek by past tense verbs [TH].
b. aorist act. indic. of δίδωμι (LN 57.71): 'to give' [AB, HNTC, ICC2, LN, Lns, NTC, WBC; KJV, NAB, NJB, NRSV, TNT]. This verb is also translated as a noun: 'gifts' [NIV, REB]. The aorist tense of this verb is translated as a perfect tense: 'he has given' [AB, NTC, WBC; KJV, TNT], 'he has scattered his gifts' [NIV]; as a present tense: 'he gives' [CEV, NRSV, TEV], '(they) give' [NLT], 'he lavishes gifts' [REB].
c. πένης (LN **57.50**) (BAGD p. 642): 'poor' [BAGD, HNTC, ICC2, **LN**, NTC, WBC; CEV, KJV, NAB, NIV, NLT, NRSV, TNT], 'poor laborers' [Lns], 'needy' [AB, BAGD, LN; NJB, REB, TEV].

d. δικαιοσύνη (LN 88.13, 34.46) (BAGD 2.a. p. 196): 'righteousness' [AB, BAGD, HNTC, ICC2, LN, Lns, NTC, WBC; KJV, NIV, NRSV], 'justice' [NAB], 'uprightness' [NJB], 'good deeds' [NLT], 'benevolence' [REB], 'kindness' [TEV], 'generosity' [TNT], 'charitableness' [BAGD]. The phrase 'his righteousness endures forever' is translated '(God) always does what is right' [CEV]. See this word also at 3:9; 5:21.

e. pres. act. indic. of μένω (LN 13.89) (BAGD 1.c.β. p. 504): 'to endure' [AB, NTC, WBC; NAB, NIV, NRSV], 'to remain' [BAGD, LN, Lns; KJV], 'to last' [BAGD; REB, TEV, TNT], 'to abide' [HNTC], 'to last' [ICC2], 'to continue' [BAGD, LN], 'to stand firm' [NJB], 'to continue to exist' [LN]. The phrase 'his righteousness endures forever' is translated 'their good deeds will never be forgotten' [NLT], '(God) always does right' [CEV].

QUESTION—Whom does Paul intend as the subject of this statement quoted from Ps 112:9?
1. The subject of the statement is the righteous person [AB, HNTC, Ho, ICC1, ICC2, NCBC, NIC1, NTC, SP, TG, TH, WBC; NLT].
2. The subject of the statement is God himself [NAC, NIC2; CEV].

QUESTION—What is the righteousness of which Paul speaks?
1. In this context the 'righteousness' is their charitable giving [AB, BAGD, EGT, Lns, NCBC, NTC, TH, TNTC, WBC]. It is a general virtue that is shown in charitable giving [Ho]. This righteousness is a token or expression of a right relation to God through forensic righteousness [WBC]. The man who obeys God's will in giving will maintain his justified relation with God [HNTC]. Paul is saying that the righteous acts of the righteous person continue throughout his life [ICC2].
2 The righteousness is God's covenant loyalty and faithfulness to his people [NIC2]. God is always gracious and merciful [NAC]. Although he is speaking of the pious man, God's righteousness, in which their charitable gifts are a participation, cannot be excluded [AB].
3. The 'righteousness' is the forensic justification imputed by God [Lns].

QUESTION—In what way does the righteousness endure forever?
His benevolent acts will never be forgotten [EBC, SP]. God remembers the generous man's righteous acts [TG]. His goodness will always be remembered and rewarded by God, both now and hereafter [ICC1]. God establishes the man's righteousness forever [TNTC]. The effect as well as the reward of righteous acts are lasting [NCBC]. The righteous person will always have the means to be benevolent [Ho]. Their charitable acts are a participation in God's righteousness, which endures forever [AB].

9:10 Now[a] the one-who-supplies[b] seed[c] to the-one-sowing[d] and bread[e] for food[f]

LEXICON—a. δέ: 'now' [NTC; KJV, NIV, NJB, REB], 'and' [AB, ICC2, Lns; TEV], 'for' [NLT], not explicit [HNTC, WBC; CEV, NAB, NRSV, TNT].

b. pres. act. participle of ἐπιχορηγέω (LN **35.31**) (BAGD p. 883): 'to supply' [BAGD, **LN**; NAB, NIV, NRSV, TEV], 'to provide' [BAGD, HNTC, ICC2, NTC, WBC; NJB, REB, TNT], 'to furnish' [Lns], 'to give' [CEV, NLT], 'to minister' [KJV].
c. σπόρος (LN 3.35) (BAGD p. 763): 'seed' [AB, BAGD, HNTC, ICC2, LN, Lns, NTC, WBC; all versions].
d. pres. act. participle of σπείρω (LN 43.6) (BAGD 1.a.α. p. 761): 'to sow' [BAGD, LN]. This participle is translated as a substantive: 'the sower' [AB, HNTC, ICC2, NTC, WBC; KJV, NAB, NIV, NJB, NRSV, TEV, TNT], 'farmer' [CEV, NLT], 'the one sowing' [Lns], 'sowing' [REB].
e. ἄρτος (LN 5.1) (BAGD 1.a. p. 110): 'bread' [AB, BAGD, HNTC, ICC2, Lns, NTC, WBC; all versions except CEV, NJB], not explicit [CEV, NJB].
f. βρῶσις (LN 5.1, 23.3) (BAGD 1. p. 148): 'food' [AB, ICC2, LN (5.1), WBC; CEV, KJV, NIV, NRSV, REB], 'food to eat' [NJB], '(for) eating' [BAGD, HNTC, LN (23.3), Lns; TNT], '(the) eater' [NTC; NAB], 'to eat' [NLT, TEV].

will-supply[a] and will-multiply[b] your seed and will-increase[c] the harvest[d] of your righteousness;[e]

TEXT—Instead of πληθυνεῖ καὶ αὐξήσει 'will multiply...and will increase' in the future indicative, many manuscripts have πληθύναι καὶ αὐξήσαι 'may he multiply and increase' in the optative, which indicates a hope or wish. GNT does not mention this alternative. Only KJV adopts the optative reading.

LEXICON—a. fut. act. indic. of χορηγέω: 'supply' [AB, HNTC, ICC2; NIV, NRSV, TEV], 'furnish' [Lns], 'provide' [NTC, WBC; NAB, NJB, REB, TNT], 'give' [NLT], not explicit [CEV, KJV].
b. fut. act. indic. of πληθύνω (LN 59.69) (BAGD 1.a. p. 669): 'to multiply' [AB, BAGD, HNTC, ICC2, LN, Lns, NTC; KJV, NAB, NRSV, REB], 'to increase' [BAGD, LN, WBC; CEV, NIV], 'to make it grow' [TEV, TNT]. The two verbs 'supply' and 'multiply' are conflated and translated as one action: 'increase' [CEV]. The phrase χορηγήσει καὶ πληθυνεῖ τὸν σπόρον ὑμῶν 'will supply and will multiply your seed' is translated 'will provide you with ample store of seed for sowing' [NJB], 'he will give you many opportunities to do good' [NLT].
c. fut. act. indic. of αὐξάνω (LN **59.63**) (BAGD 1. p. 121): 'to increase' [AB, BAGD, ICC2, **LN**, Lns, NTC; KJV, NAB, NRSV, TNT], 'to cause to increase' [LN], 'to make or cause to grow' [BAGD, HNTC], 'to augment' [WBC], 'to enlarge' [NIV], 'to make bigger' [NJB], 'to swell' [REB]. The phrase 'increase the harvest of your righteousness' is translated 'so that you can give even more to those in need' [CEV], 'produce a great harvest of generosity in you' [NLT], 'produce a rich harvest from your generosity' [TEV].

d. γένημα (LN 13.49) (BAGD p. 155): 'harvest' [BAGD, NTC, WBC; NIV, NJB, NLT, NRSV, REB, TEV, TNT], 'product' [BAGD, LN], 'yield' [AB, BAGD, LN; NAB], 'fruits' [BAGD, HNTC, Lns; KJV], 'products' [ICC2], not explicit [CEV].

e. δικαιοσύνη: 'righteousness' [AB HNTC, ICC2, Lns, NTC, WBC; KJV, NIV, NRSV], 'uprightness' [NJB], 'generosity' [NLT, TEV, TNT], 'benevolence' [REB], not explicit [CEV]. The genitive phrase τὰ γενήματα τῆς δικαιοσύνης ὑμῶν 'the harvest of your righteousness' is translated 'your generous yield' [NAB].

QUESTION—What is meant by the genitive phrase τὰ γενήματα τῆς δικαιοσύνης ὑμῶν 'the harvest of your righteousness'?

1. Paul is speaking of the 'harvest' or result that comes as a consequence of righteousness [AB, EBC, HNTC, Ho, ICC1, ICC2, NAC, NCBC, NIC1, NIC2, NTC, TG, TH, TNTC; CEV, TEV].
    1.1 The righteousness is the Corinthians' giving, and the harvest that results from it is greater blessing for themselves [ICC2, NCBC, NIC1, NTC].
    1.2 The righteousness is the Corinthians' giving, and the harvest that results from it is greater bounty provided by God so that they can give more to others [AB, EBC, Ho, NAC; CEV]. The result of their giving is a large harvest of good things for others [TG].
    1.3 The righteousness is the Corinthians' giving, and the harvest that results from it is greater unity, love, and thanksgiving [TNTC].
    1.4 The righteousness is God's justifying action, and the harvest or fruit it produces is the liberality of the Corinthians [NIC2].
2. It is epexegetical: the harvest is their righteousness [Lns; NLT, REB]. Paul is saying that the spiritual fruit of the godly life is righteousness [Lns]. He is saying that the harvest is the generosity of the Corinthians [NLT, REB].

9:11 in everything[a] being-enriched[b] for all generosity,[c] which produces[d] thanksgiving[e] to God through[f] us;

LEXICON—a. πᾶς: 'everything' [Lns; KJV], 'every way' [AB, HNTC, ICC2, NTC, WBC; CEV, NAB, NIV, NJB, NRSV, TNT], not explicit [NLT]. The phrase ἐν παντί is translated 'abundantly' [TNT]. The phrase ἐν παντὶ πλουτιζόμενοι εἰς πᾶσαν ἁπλότητα 'in everything enriched for all generosity' is translated 'always rich enough to be generous' [REB], 'always rich enough to be generous at all times' [TEV].

b. pres. pass. participle of πλουτίζω (LN **57.29**) (BAGD 2. p. 674): 'to be enriched' [AB, HNTC, LN, Lns; KJV, NAB, NLT, NRSV], 'to be made rich' [BAGD, **LN**, NTC, WBC; NIV, TEV], 'to be made abundantly rich' [TNT], 'to be rich enough' [NJB, REB], 'to be in process of enrichment' [ICC2], 'to be blessed' [CEV]. See this word also at 6:10.

c. ἁπλότης (LN 57.106) (BAGD 2. p. 86): 'generosity' [AB, BAGD, ICC2, LN, NTC; NJB, NRSV], 'liberality' [BAGD, LN; NAB], 'bountifulness' [KJV], 'integrity' [HNTC], 'single-mindedness' [Lns]. The phrase εἰς

πᾶσαν ἁπλότητα 'for all generosity' is translated 'so that you can be always generous' [WBC], 'so that you can be generous on every occasion' [NIV], 'be able to keep on being generous' [CEV], 'so that you can give even more generously' [NLT], 'always be rich enough to generous' [REB], 'rich enough to be generous at all times' [TEV], 'so that you may be generous in every way' [TNT]. See this word also at 1:12; 8:2.
   d. pres. mid. or pass. (deponent = act.) indic. of κατεργάζομαι (LN 13.7) (BAGD 2. p. 421): 'to produce' [BAGD, HNTC, NTC; NRSV], 'to bring about' [AB, BAGD, ICC2, LN], 'to work out' [Lns], 'to yield' [WBC], 'to result in' [LN; NAB, NIV], 'to issue in' [REB], 'to cause' [KJV], 'to make' [NJB, TNT], not explicit [CEV, NLT, TEV]. See this word also at 4:17; 5:5; 7:10.
   e. εὐχαριστία (LN 33.349) (BAGD 2. p. 328): 'thanksgiving' [AB, BAGD, HNTC, ICC2, LN, Lns, NTC, WBC; KJV, NIV, NLT, NRSV, REB], 'thanks' [NAB]. This noun is also translated as a verb: 'to thank' [CEV, NJB, TEV]; as an adjective: 'thankful' [TNT]. See this word also at 4:15.
   f. διά with genitive object (LN 90.4): 'through' [AB, HNTC, ICC2, LN, Lns, NTC, WBC; KJV, NAB, NIV, NRSV, REB], 'by' [LN]. The phrase δι' ἡμῶν 'through us' is translated 'working through us' [HNTC], 'through our agency' [ICC2], 'through our action' [REB], 'for what we have done' [NJB, TNT], 'when we deliver your gift' [CEV], 'when we take your gifts to those who need them' [NLT], 'your gifts which they receive from us' [TEV].
QUESTION—Does the use of the present passive participle πλουτιζόμενοι indicate that the enriching is a present condition or a future result?
   1. It indicates a future result [Ho, ICC1, Lns, NAC, NIC2, SP, TG, TH, TNTC, WBC; CEV, NIV, NJB, NLT, NRSV, REB, TEV, TNT]: you will be enriched. It is something that is being fulfilled and will be fulfilled [ICC2]. Paul uses a present tense as if it were already so because he is so confident that it will be so [AB, ICC2].
   2. It is a true present tense and indicates something that is already happening [HNTC, NTC; NAB]: you are being enriched.

DISCOURSE UNIT: 9:12-15 [EBC, NTC]. The topic is the offering of thanks to God [EBC], surpassing grace [NTC].

9:12 for[a] the administration[b] of this service[c] not only is providing-for[d] the needs[e] of the saints,
LEXICON—a. ὅτι (LN 89.33): 'for' [AB, HNTC, LN, NTC; KJV, NJB, NRSV, REB, TEV, TNT], 'because' [ICC2, LN, Lns], not explicit [WBC; CEV, NAB, NIV, NLT].
   b. διακονία (LN 35.19, 57.119) (BAGD 4. p. 184): 'administration' [ICC2; KJV], 'ministration' [AB], 'administering' [NAB], 'ministry' [NTC], 'rendering' [NRSV], 'service' [LN; TEV], 'execution' [HNTC], 'support' [BAGD, LN], not explicit [NLT]. This noun is also translated as a verb phrase: 'which you render' [WBC], 'which we are rendering' [TNT], 'that

312   2 CORINTHIANS 9:12

you perform' [NIV, TEV, TNT], 'what you are doing' [CEV], 'the help provided by (this contribution)' [NJB]. The phrase ἡ διακονία τῆς λειτουργίας ταύτης 'the administration of this service' is translated 'a piece of willing service' [REB]. See this word also at 3:7, 8; 5:18; 8:4.
- c. λειτουργία (LN 35.22) (BAGD 2. p. 471): 'service' [AB, BAGD, ICC2, LN, NTC, WBC; KJV, NIV, TEV, TNT], 'public service' [Lns], 'act of public service' [HNTC], 'public benefit' [NAB], 'contribution' [NJB], 'ministry' [NRSV], not explicit [CEV, NLT, REB].
- d. pres. act. participle of προσαναπληρόω (LN **35.34**) (BAGD p. 711): 'to supply' [AB, BAGD, HNTC, ICC2, **LN**, NTC; CEV, KJV, NAB, NIV, NRSV, TNT], 'to provide for' [WBC], 'to provide fully' [LN], 'to satisfy' [NJB], 'to meet' [NLT, TEV], 'to add (something) to fill up' [Lns], not explicit [REB].
- e. ὑστέρημα (LN 57.38) (BAGD 1. p. 849): 'need' [AB, BAGD, NTC, WBC; NAB, NIV, NJB, NLT, NRSV, REB, TEV, TNT], 'want' [BAGD, HNTC, ICC2; KJV], 'deficiency' [BAGD, Lns], 'what is lacking' [LN], 'what is needed' [LN], 'what they need' [CEV]. See this word also at 8:14.

but also overflows^a through^b many thanksgivings to God;
LEXICON—a. περισσεύω (LN 59.52) (BAGD 1.a.γ. p. 650): 'to overflow' [AB, BAGD, HNTC, Lns, NTC, WBC; NAB, NIV, NJB, NRSV, REB, TNT], 'to be abundant' [BAGD, LN; KJV], 'to be abundantly productive' [ICC2], 'to produce an outpouring of (gratitude)' [TEV], not explicit [CEV, NLT]. See this word also at 1:5; 3:9; 4:15; 8:2, 7; 9:8.
- b. διά with genitive object (LN 89.76): 'through' [ICC2, LN, NTC, WBC], 'by means of' [LN, Lns], 'by' [LN; KJV], 'with' [AB; NRSV], 'in' [HNTC; NAB, NIV, REB, TNT], 'into' [NJB], not explicit [CEV, NLT, TEV].

9:13 glorifying^a God through^b the proof^c of this ministry^d
LEXICON—a. pres. act. participle of δοξάζω (LN 87.24) (BAGD 1. p. 204): 'to glorify' [AB, BAGD, HNTC, ICC2, LN, Lns, NTC; CEV, KJV, NAB, NJB, NLT, NRSV], 'to give glory to' [TEV], 'to praise' [BAGD; NIV, TNT], 'to give praise to' [WBC], 'to give honor to' [REB], 'to bring honor and praise to' [CEV]. This participle is translated as a participle: 'glorifying' [Lns]; as a finite verb in the present tense: 'they glorify God' [AB, HNTC; KJV], 'you glorify God' [NRSV], 'they are glorifying God' [NAB], 'they praise God' [TNT], 'they give praise to God' [WBC]; as a finite verb in the future tense: 'they will be glorifying God' [ICC2, NTC], 'will give glory to God' [NJB, TEV], '(they) will give honor to God' [REB], 'men will praise God' [NIV]. See this word also at 3:10.
- b. διά with genitive object (LN 89.76): 'through' [LN, NTC; NRSV], 'by' [LN, WBC; KJV], 'by means of' [LN], 'because of' [AB; NAB, NIV, TEV], 'for' [HNTC, ICC2, Lns; TNT], not explicit [CEV]. This word is translated as indicating a causal relation: 'because of the verification'

[AB], 'because (you have proved)' [NJB], 'for (your generosity will prove)' [NLT], 'for (with the proof this affords)' [REB].
  c. δοκιμή (LN 72.7) (BAGD 1. p. 202): 'proof' [ICC2; REB, TEV, TNT], 'evidence, proof of genuineness' [LN], 'proved' [HNTC; CEV, NAB, NIV], 'will prove' [NLT], '(their) approving' [WBC], 'verification' [AB], 'test' [Lns], 'testing' [NTC; NRSV], 'experiment' [KJV], 'praiseworthy' [NAB]. See this word also at 2:9, 8:2.
  d. διακονία: 'ministry' [Lns; NRSV], 'ministration' [AB; KJV], 'service' [HNTC, NTC, WBC; CEV, NAB, NIV, TEV], 'act of service' [ICC2; TNT], 'help' [NJB], 'generous gifts' [NLT], 'aid' [REB]. See this word also at 3:7, 8; 5:18; 8:4; 9:12.

QUESTION—Who is the implied subject of the participial phrase δοξάζοντες τὸν θεόν 'glorifying God'?
  1. The recipients of the gift in Jerusalem will glorify God [AB, EBC, EGT, He, HNTC, Ho, ICC1, ICC2, Lns, NIC1, NTC, TG, TH, WBC; KJV, NAB, NJB, REB, TNT].
  2. The Corinthians will glorify God [NIC2; CEV, NLT, NRSV].
  3. The subject is generic: people will glorify God [TNTC; NIV, TEV].

QUESTION—What is meant by 'the proof' of the ministry?
  1. The ministry gives evidence or proof of something [AB, EBC, EGT, He, HNTC, Ho, ICC1, ICC2, NAC, NCBC, NIC1, NIC2, NTC, SP, TG, TH]. It demonstrates or proves their character [ICC1] or their love [NCBC, NTC]. God tests the ministry of the Corinthians and proves its genuineness [Lns].
  2. The people of Jerusalem will approve of the offering [WBC].

for[a] the obedience[b] of your confession[c] to the gospel of Christ
LEXICON—a. επί (LN 89.27) (BAGD II.1.b.γ. p. 287): 'for' [AB, HNTC, ICC2, Lns; KJV, NAB, NIV, NJB, NRSV, TEV], 'over' [BAGD], 'because of' [LN, NTC], 'in that they see' [WBC], 'when they see' [REB], not explicit [CEV, NLT, TNT].
  b. ὑποταγή (LN **36.18**) (BAGD p. 847): 'obedience' [AB, HNTC, ICC2, LN, WBC; NIV, NJB, NRSV], 'submission' [LN, NTC], 'submissiveness' [ICC2], 'subjection' [KJV], 'loyalty' [TEV]. This noun is also translated as a verb: 'you obeyed/you obey' [CEV, TNT]; as an adjective: 'obedient' [NAB, NLT]; as an adverb: 'faithfully' [REB].
  c. ὁμολογία (LN 33.274) (BAGD 1. p. 568): 'confession' [AB, BAGD, HNTC, ICC2, LN, Lns, NTC; NIV, NRSV], 'faith' [NAB], 'faith which acknowledges' [WBC]. The phrase 'obedience of your confession' is translated 'you believed the message (about Christ) and you obeyed it' [CEV], 'your professed subjection' [KJV], 'the obedience which you show in professing' [NJB], 'you are obedient to (the good news)' [NLT], 'how faithfully you confess' [REB], 'your loyalty to (the gospel of Christ), which you profess' [TEV], 'not only do you profess (Christ's gospel) but you obey it' [TNT].

QUESTION—How are the nouns related in the genitive construction τῇ ὑποταγῇ τῆς ὁμολογίας ὑμῶν 'the obedience of your confession'?
1. It is an objective genitive: the obedience is to the confession [EBC, Ho, ICC2, NIC1, NTC; CEV, KJV, NAB, NLT, NRSV, TEV, TNT].
2. It is a subjective genitive: the obedience belongs, is associated with, or is created by the confession [LN, NAC, NIC2].
3. 'Confession' is epexegetical of 'obedience': the obedience consists of the confession [AB], accompanies the confession [WBC; NIV], or is shown in the confession [HNTC; NJB].

and (for) the generosity[a] of the contribution[b] for them and for everyone,[c]
LEXICON—a. ἁπλότης : 'generosity' [AB, NTC, WBC; NAB, NIV, NJB, NLT, NRSV, TEV], 'genuineness' [ICC2], 'integrity' [HNTC], 'single-mindedness' [Lns]. This noun is also translated as an adverb: 'generously' [CEV, TNT]; as an adjective: 'liberal' [KJV, REB]. See this word also at 1:12; 8:2; 9:11.
b. κοινωνία (LN 57.98) (BAGD 2. p. 439): 'sharing' [AB, LN; CEV, NAB, NIV, NRSV, TEV, TNT], 'distribution' [KJV], 'fellowship' [HNTC, ICC2, Lns; NJB], 'partnership' [NTC, WBC], 'generosity' [BAGD], 'contribution' [REB], not explicit [NLT]. See this word also at 6:14; 8:4.
c. πᾶς: 'everyone' [NTC, WBC; TNT], 'everyone else' [CEV, NIV, TEV], 'all' [AB, HNTC, ICC2, Lns; NAB, NJB], 'all men' [KJV], 'all others' [NRSV], 'the general good' [REB], not explicit [NLT].
QUESTION—In what way was their generosity 'for everyone'?
It was directed toward all believers [AB, EGT, HNTC, Ho, ICC1, ICC2, Lns, NIC1, NIC2, NTC, TG, TH, TNTC]. It was directed to both Jews and Gentiles [NAC]. 'Everyone' is a general term, indicating they are generous wherever there may be need [WBC].

9:14 and longing-for[a] you (in) their prayer[b] for you because-of[c] the surpassing[d] grace[e] of-God upon[f] you.
LEXICON—a. pres. act. participle of ἐπιποθέω (LN **25.47**) (BAGD p. 297): 'to long for' [AB, BAGD, HNTC, ICC2, Lns, NTC; KJV, NRSV], 'to have a great affection for' [LN], 'to yearn' [WBC], 'to have a yearning love for' [LN]. The phrase ἐπιποθούντων ὑμᾶς 'longing for you' is translated 'with great affection' [**LN**], 'with deep affection' [NLT, TEV, TNT], '(their prayer will express) the affection they feel for you' [NJB], 'longingly' [NAB], 'their hearts will go out to you' [NIV, REB], 'and want to see you' [CEV]. See this word also at 5:2.
b. δέησις (LN 33.171) (BAGD p. 172): 'prayer' [AB, HNTC, ICC2, LN; KJV, NJB, REB], 'prayers' [NTC, WBC; NIV], 'pleading' [Lns]. The phrase 'in their prayer' is translated 'they are praying' [CEV], 'they pray' [NAB, NRSV], 'they will pray' [NLT, TEV, TNT]. See this word also at 1:11.

c. διά with accusative object (LN 89.26): 'because of' [AB, ICC2, LN, Lns, NTC, WBC; NAB, NIV, NJB, NLT, NRSV, REB, TEV], 'on account of' [HNTC, LN], 'for' [KJV], not explicit [CEV, TNT].
d. pres. act. participle of ὑπερβάλλω (LN 78.34) (BAGD p. 840): 'surpassing' [AB, BAGD, HNTC, NTC, WBC; NAB, NIV, NRSV], 'abundant' [ICC2], 'exceeding' [Lns; KJV], 'unbounded' [NJB], 'so very much' [CEV], 'richness of (the grace)' [REB], 'extraordinary' [BAGD; TEV], 'extreme, to a very great degree' [LN], 'wonderful' [NLT], 'wonderfully' [TNT]. See this word also at 3:10.
e. χάρις (LN 88.66) (BAGD 4. p. 878): 'grace' [AB, BAGD, HNTC, ICC2, LN, Lns, NTC, WBC; KJV, NAB, NIV, NJB, NLT, NRSV, REB, TEV], not explicit [CEV]. The phrase 'the surpassing grace of God' is translated 'God used you to bless them so very much' [CEV], 'how wonderfully good God has been to you' [TNT]. See this word also at 1:2, 12; 8:1, 4, 6, 9, 16, 19; 9:8.
f. ἐπί (LN 90.57): 'upon' [HNTC, Lns, NTC], 'on' [BAGD, ICC2], 'in' [KJV], 'to' [BAGD; TNT], 'among' [AB]. The phrase 'upon you' is translated '(God) has given you' [WBC; NAB, NJB, NRSV, REB], '(God) has shown you' [TEV], '(God) has shown through you' [NLT].

QUESTION—In what way would the Christians in Jerusalem 'long' for the Corinthians?
A new bond of love between them now exists [NCBC, TNTC, WBC]. The Christians in Jerusalem now long for a closer relationship with the Corinthians [ICC1], and have a deep gratitude toward them [Lns, TG]. They long to see them [EBC, EGT, HNTC, Lns; CEV], to have fellowship with them [HNTC, ICC2], and are now more open toward them [EBC]. The gift establishes a bond of friendship that will result in prayer for the Corinthians [NAC, NTC].

QUESTION—What does 'the grace of God' refer to?
1. It is that working of God's grace that results in their giving generously [AB, EBC, HNTC, Ho, ICC1, ICC2, NAC, NCBC, NIC2, NTC, TH, WBC; CEV, NLT]. The grace expressed in the gospel stirs up a gracious and free generosity [NIC2]. It refers to God's grace in an all-embracing sense, which prompts the Corinthians to give and unites believers as a result [NTC].
2. It refers to the salvation that is given to the Gentiles [SP].

9:15 Thanks[a] (be) to God for his indescribable[b] gift.[c]

LEXICON—a. χάρις (LN 33.350) (BAGD 5. p. 878): 'thanks' [AB, BAGD, HNTC, ICC2, LN, Lns, NTC, WBC; KJV, NAB, NIV, NJB, NRSV, REB, TNT]. The phrase 'thanks (be) to God' is translated as an imperative 'thank God' [CEV, NLT], 'let us thank God' [TEV]. This word is used in this sense in 8:16. See this word also at 1:2, 12; 8:1, 4, 6, 9, 19; 9:8, 14, 15.

b. ἀνεκδιήγητος (LN **33.202**) (BAGD p. 64): 'indescribable' [AB, BAGD, ICC2, LN, Lns, NTC; NAB, NIV, NRSV], 'beyond words' [LN], 'too wonderful for words' [CEV, NLT], 'unspeakable' [HNTC; KJV], 'beyond all telling' [NJB], 'beyond all praise' [REB], 'beyond measure' [WBC], 'priceless' [TEV]. This adjective is translated 'which cannot be described with words' [LN], 'which no words can describe' [TNT].

c. δωρεά (LN 57.84) (BAGD p. 210): 'gift' [AB, BAGD, HNTC, ICC2, LN, Lns, NTC, WBC; all versions].

QUESTION—What is the gift about which Paul is speaking?

It is Christ [He, Ho, ICC2, NIC1; NLT]. It refers primarily to Christ but also to the grace God gives [EBC, NIC2]. It is Christ, as well as God's love, salvation, and eternal life [NTC]. It is Christ and salvation in him [EGT]. It is that Christ became poor that we might be rich [TNTC]. It is the gospel which Paul proclaims [WBC]. It is the gift of salvation [SP]. It is God's grace, which is the subject of the overall passage [AB]. It is the greatness of God's grace which he has given to the whole church and its members [Lns]. It is God's grace and Christ's sacrifice [NAC]. It is a reference to the grace mentioned in 8:1 and 9:14 [HNTC]. It is Paul's hope for the unity of all Christians through the goodwill between Jew and Gentile Christians [ICC1].

DISCOURSE UNIT: 10–13 [EBC]. The topic is Paul's vindication of his apostolic authority.

DISCOURSE UNIT: 10:1–13:13 [EGT, NIC2, NTC, TNTC]. The topic is the vindication of his apostolic authority [EGT], Corinthians: prepare for Paul's third visit [NIC2], apostolic authority [NTC], Paul responds to a new crisis [TNTC].

DISCOURSE UNIT: 10:1–13:10 [HNTC, ICC1, TG, TH, TNTC, WBC]. The topic is the future threatened [HNTC], Paul's defense of his apostolic authority [TG, TH], vindicating his apostolic authority; the great invective [ICC1], the body of the response [TNTC], fresh troubles in Corinth [WBC].

DISCOURSE UNIT: 10:1–11:33 [NTC]. The topic is Paul's ministry and opponents.

DISCOURSE UNIT: 10:1–11:15 [EBC]. The topic is the exercise of apostolic rights and authority.

DISCOURSE UNIT: 10:1–18 [AB, ICC1, TH; CEV, NAB, NIV, NLT, NRSV, REB, TEV]. The topic is an appeal for obedience [AB], the apostle's authority and the area of his mission [ICC1], Paul defends his work for Christ [CEV], Paul defends his ministry [TH; NAB, NRSV, TEV], Paul's defense of his ministry [NIV], Paul defends his authority [NLT], the challenge to Paul's authority [REB].

DISCOURSE UNIT: 10:1–11 [EBC, NIC2, WBC; NJB]. The topic is the potency of apostolic authority [EBC], Paul's plea not to have to be bold when he comes [NIC2], Paul's reply to accusations of weakness [NJB], Paul's self-vindication [WBC].

DISCOURSE UNIT: 10:1–6 [AB, HNTC, ICC1, TNTC]. The topic is the appeal proper [AB], an appeal for complete obedience [HNTC], reply to the charge of cowardice [ICC1], an earnest entreaty [TNTC].

10:1 I myself,ª Paul, appealᵇ to-you byᶜ the meeknessᵈ and gentlenessᵉ of Christ,

LEXICON—a. αυτός (LN 92.37) (BAGD 1.a.β. p. 122): 'myself' [BAGD, LN]. The phrase αὐτὸς δὲ ἐγὼ Παῦλος is translated 'I myself, Paul' [AB; NRSV], 'I, Paul, myself' [WBC; KJV], 'I, Paul, I myself' [HNTC, ICC2], 'for my own person I, Paul' [Lns], 'I, Paul, personally' [NTC], 'I' [CEV], 'I Paul' [NAB, NIV, NLT, REB, TEV], 'this is Paul now speaking personally – I' [NJB], 'this is the Paul (whom)' [TNT].
  b. pres. act. indic. of παρακαλέω (LN 33.168) (BAGD 2. p. 617): 'to appeal' [AB, BAGD, ICC2, LN, NTC, WBC; NIV, NRSV, REB], 'to make an appeal' [TEV, TNT], 'to urge' [BAGD, HNTC, Lns; NJB], 'to request' [LN], 'to ask' [CEV], 'to beseech' [KJV], 'to exhort' [NAB], 'to plead with' [NLT]. See this word also at 1:4, 6; 2:7, 8; 5:20; 6:1; 7:6; 8:6; 9:5.
  c. διά with genitive object (BAGD A.III.1.f. p. 180): 'by' [AB, BAGD, HNTC, ICC2, Lns, NTC, WBC; all versions except CEV, NLT]. The phrase 'I appeal to you by the meekness and gentleness of Christ' is translated 'I ask you to listen because Christ himself was humble and gentle' [CEV], 'I plead with the gentleness and kindness that Christ himself would use' [NLT].
  d. πραΰτης (LN 88.59) (BAGD p. 699): 'meekness' [BAGD, HNTC, ICC2, LN, Lns, NTC, WBC; KJV, NAB, NIV, NRSV, TNT], 'gentleness' [AB, BAGD, LN; NJB, NLT, REB, TEV], 'Christ was humble' [CEV].
  e. ἐπιείκεια (LN **88.62**) (BAGD p. 292): 'gentleness' [BAGD, HNTC, **LN**, Lns, NTC, WBC; KJV, NIV, NRSV, TNT], 'kindness' [AB; NAB, NLT, TEV], 'graciousness' [BAGD, LN], 'forbearance' [LN; NJB], 'clemency' [BAGD, ICC2], 'magnanimity' [REB], 'Christ was gentle' [CEV].

QUESTION—What is the significance of his use of the phrase αὐτὸς δὲ ἐγὼ Παῦλος 'I myself, Paul'?
  It is emphatic [AB, Lns, NTC, SP, TG] and expresses intensity [Car, HNTC, NTC]. It strongly emphasizes his appeal on a very personal matter that he will now discuss [Car, EGT, ICC1, ICC2, NTC, TH]. He uses it to asserting his authority [AB, ICC2, NAC, NIC1, NIC2, WBC] and express affection [NIC1]. It places considerable emphasis on Paul himself who was the founder of the Corinthian church [TNTC]. It emphasizes that Paul's character and ministry are at issue [NCBC]. It emphasizes that he is present through this letter as he brings up his complaint [NAB]. It distinguishes Paul as an individual apart from any of his associates because this concerns him personally [Car, Ho, Lns, NIC2, SP].

QUESTION—What does it mean for him to appeal 'by the meekness and gentleness of Christ'?

Paul describes his own attitude as he follows the example of Jesus in how he lives and ministers [WBC]. Paul does not want to depart from Christ's character and demeanor by being harsh with them [EGT, HNTC, Ho, ICC2, Lns, NIC2]. For the sake of those who think he is unimpressive and lacks authority because he is not domineering, Paul explains that he patterns his ministry by the virtues of Christ [Car, NAC, NIC2]. Paul is claiming to imitate Christ's virtues and urging the Corinthians to do so as well [NTC, SP]. This functions as an oath formula to assure them of the integrity of his ministry [AB]. The preposition διά 'by' means 'by the model of Christ' [NIC2]. Paul wants to make his appeal in the attitude he says Christ has; because Christ was meek, I beg you [TG, TH]. Paul is saying that because Christ was humble and meek they should accept his appeal [TNTC].

who (when) among you face-to-face[a] (am) lowly[b], but when-absent I-am-bold[c] toward you;

LEXICON—a. πρόσωπον (LN **83.38**) (BAGD 1.c.δ. p. 721). The phrase κατὰ πρόσωπον (literally 'according to face') is translated 'face to face' [BAGD, ICC2, LN, WBC; NIV, NRSV, REB, TNT], 'in person' [AB, BAGD, HNTC, **LN**, NTC; NLT], 'when…facing you' [NJB], 'as far as appearance goes' [Lns], 'in presence' [KJV], 'when present' [NAB], not explicit [CEV, TEV]. See this word also at 1:11; 2:10; 4:6; 5:12; 8:24.

b. ταπεινός (LN **88.64**) (BAGD 2.a. p. 804): 'lowly' [Lns; NAB], 'meek' [**LN**], 'mild' [LN], 'meek and mild' [TEV], 'humble' [NJB, NRSV], 'abject' [BAGD], 'subservient' [BAGD, ICC2, NTC], 'timid' [WBC; NIV, NLT, REB], 'demeaned' [AB], 'base' [KJV], 'a weakling' [TNT], 'go humbly' [HNTC], 'a coward' [CEV].

c. pres. act. indic. of θαρρέω (LN **25.156**) (BAGD p. 352): 'to be bold' [BAGD, HNTC, ICC2, LN, NTC; KJV, NAB, NIV, NLT, NRSV], 'to be full of boldness' [NJB, TNT], 'to make bold' [AB], 'to act brave' [Lns], 'to be brave' [CEV], 'to be courageous' [REB], 'to be full of courage' [**LN**], 'to be haughty' [WBC], 'to be harsh' [TEV]. See this word also at 5:6 and 7:16.

QUESTION—Does Paul literally mean this or is he repeating accusations?

Paul is repeating what his critics have said about him [AB, BAGD, EBC, EGT, He, HNTC, Ho, ICC1, ICC2, Lns, NAC, NCBC, NIC1, NIC2, NTC, SP, TG, TH, TNTC, WBC].

QUESTION—What is the connotation of the word ταπεινός 'lowly'?

Paul's critics meant it in a negative sense, since they interpreted his behavior and demeanor as indicating that he was timid or cowardly [Car, EBC, HNTC, Ho, ICC1, Lns, NAC, NIC1, TH, TNTC, WBC], weak [AB, He, ICC2, NIC2, NTC, TH], servile [EBC, He, NIC2], unimportant [AB, NTC], or unimpressive [ICC2]. On the other hand, Paul understands his lowly behavior and demeanor as being like that of Christ [AB, Car, EBC, HNTC, ICC2, NAC, NIC1, NIC2, NTC, WBC].

10:2 And I-ask[a] not to-(have-to)-be-bold[b] with the confidence[c] (when) being-present, which I-intend[d] to-dare[e] (to-do)

LEXICON—a. pres. mid. or pass. (deponent = act.) indic. of δέομαι (LN 33.170) (BAGD 2. p. 175): 'to ask' [AB, BAGD, HNTC, ICC2, NTC; NRSV], 'to beg' [LN, Lns, WBC; NAB, NIV, REB, TEV, TNT], 'to plead' [LN], 'to beseech' [KJV]. The phrase 'I ask not to have to be' is translated 'my appeal is' [NJB], 'please don't make me' [CEV], 'I hope it won't be necessary' [NLT]. See this word also at 5:20 and 8:4.

b. aorist act. infin. of θαρρέω: 'to be bold' [AB, ICC2, NTC; KJV, NIV, NJB, NLT], 'to show boldness' [HNTC; NRSV], 'to be full of boldness' [TNT], 'to act boldly' [NAB], 'to be brave' [Lns], 'to be harsh' [TEV]. The phrase 'to be bold with confidence' is translated 'to be haughty with a confidence of boldness' [WBC], 'to be firm and forceful' [CEV], 'to be very bold' [NLT], 'to display courage and self-assurance' [REB]. See this word also at 5:6 and 7:16.

c. πεποίθησις (LN 31.82) (BAGD 2. p. 643): 'confidence' [AB, BAGD, ICC2, LN, Lns, NTC, WBC; KJV, TNT], 'assurance' [NAB, REB], 'self-assurance' [NJB], not explicit [CEV, NIV, NLT, NRSV, TEV]. This noun is also translated as an adjective: 'confident' [HNTC]. See this word also at 1:15; 3:4; and 8:22.

d. pres. mid. or pass. (deponent = act.) indic. of λογίζομαι (LN 30.9) (BAGD 2. p. 476): 'to purpose, to propose' [BAGD], 'to have it in mind' [AB], 'to think about' [BAGD, LN], 'to think' [HNTC; KJV, TNT], 'to reckon' [ICC2; NJB, REB], 'to count on' [Lns], 'to expect' [NTC, WBC; CEV, NIV], not explicit [NAB, NLT, NRSV, TEV]. See this word also at 3:5 and 5:19.

e. aorist act. infin. of τολμάω (LN 25.161) (BAGD 2. p. 822): 'to dare' [LN], 'to dare (to use)' [HNTC; NAB], 'to dare to employ' [ICC2], 'to be bold' [KJV], 'to show boldness toward' [LN], 'to be bold enough' [TNT], 'to be courageous' [NTC], 'to summon up courage (against)' [AB], 'to challenge' [Lns], 'to be haughty with (a confidence of) boldness' [WBC]. The phrase τῇ πεποιθήσει ᾗ λογίζομαι τολμῆσαι 'with the confidence...which I intend to dare' is translated 'I expect I will have to be firm and forceful in what I will say to them' [CEV], 'I should have to show the same self-assurance' [NJB], 'that courage and self-assurance which I could confidently display' [REB], 'I may have to be very bold' [NLT], 'I am sure I can deal harshly with' [TEV], not explicit [NIV].

QUESTION—What relationship is indicated by δέ 'and' at the beginning of the clause?

1. It resumes or continues the thought of 10:1 [AB, EGT, HNTC, ICC2, Lns; NJB; and probably CEV, NAB, NIV, NLT, NRSV, REB, TEV, which do not translate it].

2. It is adversative: 'but' [KJV].

against some, the-ones-who-think[a] of-us as conducting-ourselves[b] according-to (the) flesh.[c]

LEXICON—a. pres. mid. or pass. (deponent = act.) participle of λογίζομαι (LN 31.1) (BAGD 1.b. p. 476): 'to think' [HNTC, NTC, WBC; KJV, NIV, NLT, NRSV, TNT], 'to have an opinion' [**LN**], 'to look upon someone as' [BAGD], 'to reason' [AB], 'to reckon' [ICC2; NJB], 'to assume' [REB], 'to count as' [Lns], 'to consider' [BAGD, LN], 'to say' [CEV, TEV], 'to accuse' [NAB]. See this word also at 3:5; 5:19.

b. pres. act. participle of περιπατέω (LN 41.11) (BAGD 2.a.δ. p. 649): 'to conduct oneself' [AB, BAGD, HNTC, NTC], 'to conduct one's life' [ICC2], 'to walk' [BAGD, Lns; KJV], 'to live' [BAGD, LN, WBC; NIV], 'to behave, to go about doing' [LN], 'to act' [CEV, NLT, NRSV, TEV, TNT], 'to be guided by (human motives)' [NJB]. This participle is also translated as a noun: 'behavior' [NAB, REB]. See this word also at 4:2 and 5:7.

c. σάρξ (LN 26.7) (BAGD 7. p. 744): 'flesh' [BAGD, HNTC; KJV], 'fleshly manner' [Lns], 'human nature' [LN], 'human standards' [NRSV], 'the standards of this world' [NIV], 'worldly standards' [AB, WBC], 'worldly manner' [NTC], 'worldly motives' [TEV, TNT], 'human motives' [NJB], 'purely human motives' [NLT], 'a merely human fashion' [ICC2], 'weak human behavior' [NAB], 'dictated by human weakness' [REB], 'like the people of this world' [CEV]. See this word also at 1:17; 4:11; 5:16; 7:1, 5.

QUESTION—Who is Paul talking about?

1. He is referring to certain people who have come into Corinth from outside [AB, Car, HNTC, WBC]. They were false teachers who had infiltrated the church [NTC]. They were imposters and intruders influenced by Judaizing Christianity [Car]. He is talking about Judaizers [Lns], false apostles [NIC1], rival apostles [SP], or false teachers [Ho] as well as those in Corinth who support them [Ho, SP].

2. They were Corinthians who disregarded Paul and persisted in immorality and idolatry [NIC2]. They were a vocal minority in Corinth who supported Judaizing adversaries from Palestine [EBC]

QUESTION—What do Paul's critics mean by saying that he conducts himself 'according to the flesh'?

It means that he is not being governed by the spirit of God [NCBC] or lacks the power of the Spirit in his ministry [NIC2]. He employs worldly standards and motives in his conduct [EBC, NAC], and human powers and methods in his ministry [EBC]. His motives and actions are characterized by self-interest [WBC], he uses means prompted by worldly wisdom [He], he seeks to please himself while dominating others [NTC]. They say that he is weak, cowardly, and servile, and lacks the charismatic power an apostle should have [AB, SP]. They see Paul as ineffective, timid, lacking spiritual and visionary experiences, lacking rhetorical polish and power, and as generally falling short of their standards of spirituality and leadership [Car]. Paul's presumed lack of visions, ecstatic experiences or charismatic spiritual power indicated to them that he was not spiritual but carnal and depended only on fleshly resources for his ministry [Car, HNTC, ICC2, TNTC]. They interpret the fact that Paul did not assert his authority as indicating a lack of spiritual power and the consequent need to depend on flesh [TNTC]. They accuse him of acting lowly and harmless when with the Corinthians but acting bold and powerful when away [Lns]. They are charging that he is fickle [ICC1, NAC], that he is unspiritual, worldly, and domineering [ICC1], that he is self-centered, self-reliant, and governed by his corrupt nature [Ho]. Conducting himself according to the flesh would mean living like people who don't submit to God's will or to Christian principle [TG], but living instead to please themselves [TH].

10:3 For (though) (we-are)-living[a] in (the) flesh,[b] not according-to (the) flesh[c] do-we-wage-war,[d]

LEXICON—a. pres. act. participle of περιπατέω: 'to live' [ICC2, NTC, WBC; CEV, NAB, NIV, NRSV, TEV, TNT], 'to walk' [Lns; KJV], 'to conduct oneself' [AB, HNTC], not explicit [NJB, NLT, REB]. This participle expresses a concessive relationship relative to the clause that follows which contrasts the two conditions 'in the flesh' and 'according to the flesh' [AB, EGT, HNTC, ICC2, NCBC, NIC2, NTC, SP, WBC; all versions]: though in the flesh...not according to the flesh. See this word also at 4:2; 5:7.

b. σάρξ (LN 58.10) (BAGD 5. p. 744): 'flesh' [HNTC; KJV], 'weak, bodily flesh' [Lns], 'the body' [NAB], 'corporeality, physical limitations, life here on earth' [BAGD], 'the world' [AB, NTC; NIV, TEV, TNT], 'this world' [WBC; CEV], 'the human world' [ICC2]. The phrase ἐν σαρκὶ 'for though we are living in the flesh' is translated 'we are human' [NJB, NLT], 'we may be weak and human' [REB], 'we live as human beings' [NRSV]. 1:17; 4:11; 5:16; 7:1, 5.

c. σάρξ (LN 26.7) (BAGD 7. p. 744): 'flesh' [BAGD, HNTC; KJV]. The phrase κατὰ σάρκα 'according to the flesh' is translated 'after the flesh' [KJV], 'after the manner of what is weak, bodily flesh' [Lns], 'according to human standards' [NRSV], 'according to worldly standards' [AB], 'in a worldly manner' [NTC], 'from worldly motives' [TEV], 'as the world does' [WBC; NIV], 'worldly' [TNT], 'in merely human ways' [ICC2], 'like its people' [CEV], 'with human resources' [NAB], 'by human methods' [NJB], 'with human plans and methods' [NLT], not explicit [REB].

d. pres. mid. indic. of στρατεύω (LN 55.4) (BAGD 2. p. 770): 'to wage war' [AB, NTC; NAB, NIV, NLT, NRSV, TNT], 'to make war' [HNTC], 'to carry on a war' [WBC], 'to engage in war' [LN], 'to war' [KJV], 'to campaign' [ICC2, Lns], 'to fight' [LN; TEV], 'to fight battles' [LN; REB], 'to do battle' [NJB].

QUESTION—What is the distinction between ἐν σαρκὶ 'in the flesh' and κατὰ σάρκα 'according to the flesh'?

Paul is saying that it is true that they live in this world [Car, EBC, NTC], are subject to human frailty, physical weakness, and the limitations of life in this world [Ho, NIC2]. They live a normal human existence with all its limitations [NIC1, TNTC], and he has no special powers within himself [NIC2]. Nevertheless they are not conforming to this world's standards [AB, EBC, NAC, NTC, WBC], operating by its motives [HNTC, TG, TH], or using its underhanded tactics [NAC]. They minister not according to human strength [HNTC, NIC2, TNTC], but according to God's power [NIC2]. Paul is saying that living in a mortal body does not mean ministering on a purely mundane level [NCBC]. Even while living within the sphere of earthly life with all its limits they have divine spirit and power for ministry [ICC2]. They are subject to temptations and fears but not governed by them [ICC1]. They are weak as other men and not outwardly impressive, but they don't operate by the weak human skills that only end up in fighting [Lns].

10:4 **for the weapons[a] of our warfare[b] (are) not fleshly,[c] but powerful[d] to God**

LEXICON—a. ὅπλον (LN 6.29) (BAGD 2.b. p. 575): 'weapon' [AB, BAGD, HNTC, ICC2, LN, NTC, WBC; all versions], 'equipment' [Lns].
- b. στρατεία (LN 55.4) (BAGD p. 770): 'warfare' [BAGD, ICC2, LN; KJV, NAB, NRSV], 'campaign' [AB, Lns], not explicit [NLT]. The phrase 'of our warfare' is translated 'with which we go to war' [HNTC], 'we use in our warfare' [NTC], 'we fight with' [WBC; NIV, TNT], 'we use in our fight' [TEV], 'we fight our battles' [CEV], 'with which we do battle' [NJB], 'we wield' [REB].
- c. σαρκικός (LN 26.8) (BAGD 3. p. 743): 'fleshly' [BAGD, HNTC, Lns], 'carnal' [BAGD; KJV], 'human, natural' [LN], 'merely human' [ICC2; NAB, NRSV, REB], 'of human nature' [NJB], 'of the world' [NTC; NIV], 'of this world' [CEV], 'the world's' [TEV], 'worldly' [WBC; NLT], 'ordinary' [AB; TNT]. See this word also at 1:12.
- d. δυνατός (LN 74.2) (BAGD 1.b. p. 208): 'powerful' [BAGD, HNTC, ICC2, Lns; TEV, TNT], 'able' [LN], 'mighty' [KJV, NLT], 'mightily effective' [AB], 'strong enough' [REB]. The phrase δυνατὰ τῷ θεῷ 'powerful to God' is translated 'effective for God' [AB], 'powerful for God' [ICC2, Lns], 'powerful on God's side' [HNTC], 'have divine power' [NTC], 'as God empowers (us)' [WBC], 'we use God's power' [CEV], 'mighty through God' [KJV], 'possess God's power' [NAB], 'have divine power' [NIV], 'have the power in God's cause' [NJB], 'God's mighty (weapons)' [NLT], 'God's powerful (weapons)' [TEV], 'strong enough with God's help' [REB], 'under God they are powerful enough' [TNT].

QUESTION—What are the 'weapons of our warfare' that he is referring to?
1. Paul's weaponry is spiritual. It is the divine power of the gospel [AB, Car, NAC, TNTC]. It is such things as truth, faith, salvation, prayer, and the word of God [Car, NIC1, NTC], evangelism [Car, NIC1], righteousness [Car, NAC, NIC1], the boldness that comes from understanding the gospel of peace [Car], light, love, peace, and God's indwelling spirit [NTC], divine wisdom and the knowledge of God [NAC].
2. Paul is referring to the disciplinary ministry he exercised previously in Corinth as well as his follow-up actions in his severe letter [NIC2].

for the tearing-down^a of strongholds,^b tearing-down^c reasonings^d

TEXT—The phrase λογισμοὺς καθαιροῦντες 'tearing down reasonings' is included in v.5 by NTC, KJV, NIV, NLT, REB, TEV, TNT.

LEXICON—a. καθαίρεσις (LN 20.54) (BAGD 1. p. 386): 'tearing down' [BAGD], 'pulling down' [HNTC; KJV], 'destruction' [BAGD, LN; NAB], 'demolition' [AB], 'wrecking' [Lns]. This noun is also translated as a verb: 'to destroy' [ICC2, NTC; CEV, NRSV, TEV, TNT], 'to demolish' [NIV, NJB, REB], 'to pull down' [WBC], 'to knock down' [NLT].

b. ὀχύρωμα (LN **7.21**) (BAGD p. 601): 'stronghold' [AB, BAGD, HNTC, ICC2, LN, NTC; KJV, NAB, NIV, NRSV, REB, TEV], 'the Devil's strongholds' [NLT], 'fortress' [BAGD, LN, WBC; CEV, NJB, TNT], 'fortification' [Lns].

c. pres. act. participle of καθαιρέω (LN **20.54**) (BAGD 2.b. p. 386): 'to tear down' [BAGD, LN], 'to destroy' [BAGD, ICC2, LN, NTC; CEV, NRSV], 'to demolish' [AB, WBC; NAB, NIV, NJB, REB], 'to pull down' [HNTC], 'to wreck' [Lns], 'to cast down' [KJV], 'to break down' [NLT]. This participle is translated by two finite verbs: 'we destroy...we pull down' [TEV], 'we demolish...and pull down' [TNT].

d. λογισμός (LN 30.11) (BAGD 1. p. 477): 'reasoning' [AB, BAGD, Lns], 'false reasoning' [LN], 'argument' [NTC, WBC; CEV, NIV, NLT, NRSV], 'false argument' [LN; TEV, TNT], 'intellectual argument' [ICC2], 'thought' [BAGD, HNTC], 'idea' [NJB], 'imagination' [KJV], 'sophistry' [BAGD; NAB, REB].

QUESTION—What are the 'strongholds' and how are they to be torn down?

The strongholds are specified in the clauses that follow. They are sophistries [EBC, ICC2, NCBC, SP], arguments [Lns, NCBC, SP], philosophies [Lns], intellectual pretensions [EBC], reasonings [Lns, NIC1], the intellectual culture of the time [He]. These arguments and designs pervert the gospel [NCBC] or undermine Paul's authority as an apostle [AB, NCBC]. They are prejudices and evil practices that hinder the influence of the gospel [ICC1], or arguments and ideas that resist the truth of the gospel [NAC, NIC2, TG, TNTC]. They are Satan's systems, schemes and strategies to obstruct the progress of the gospel [NTC]. They are the opinions of those who set themselves and their reasonings up against God's truth [Ho]. It consists in the sinful thought patterns, pretensions and autonomous reason by which people live in rebellion to God [Car]. It is high-mindedness that does not submit to God [HNTC], the rationalizations of self-centered man [NIC1]. They are the 'reasonings' (λογισμοί) of those who think (λογίζομαι) that Paul is fleshly [NIC2].

10:5 and every high-thing[a] raised-up[b] against the knowledge of God, and taking-captive[c] every thought[d] to obedience[e] to-Christ,

LEXICON—a. ὕψωμα (LN **88.207**) (BAGD 2. p. 851): 'high thing' [KJV], 'height' [BAGD, Lns], 'great height' [AB], 'exalted thing' [HNTC], 'arrogant attitude' [ICC2], 'lofty notion' [WBC], 'presumptuous notion' [NJB], 'pride' [BAGD, LN; CEV], 'proud obstacle' [NRSV, TEV], 'towering obstacle' [TNT], 'proud pretension' [NAB], 'pretension' [NIV], 'arrogance' [**LN**], 'elevated structure' [NTC], 'all that rears its proud head' [REB]. This noun is translated as an adjective modifying λογισμός: 'proud argument' [NLT].

b. pres. mid. participle of ἐπαίρω (LN **39.38**) (BAGD 2.b.α. p. 282): 'to be raised up' [AB, Lns; NRSV, TEV], 'to be reared up' [TNT], 'to lift oneself up' [HNTC], 'to rise up (against)' [BAGD, LN, NTC], 'to raise oneself (against)' [NAB], 'to exalt oneself (against)' [KJV], 'to set oneself up (against)' [NIV], 'to be set up (against)' [NJB], 'to be raised in opposition' [ICC2], 'to be in opposition' [BAGD], 'to oppose' [WBC], not explicit [CEV, NLT]. The phrase 'every high thing raised up (against)' is translated 'all that rears its proud head (against)' [REB]. The phrase 'raised up against the knowledge of God' is translated 'that keeps anyone from knowing God' [CEV, NLT].

c. pres. act. participle of αἰχμαλωτίζω (LN 55.24) (BAGD 2. p. 27): 'to take captive' [AB, BAGD, LN; NIV, NRSV, TEV], 'to make captive' [WBC], 'to lead captive' [NTC], 'to lead into captivity' [HNTC], 'to bring into captivity' [KJV, NAB, NJB], 'to take prisoner' [ICC2; TNT], 'to capture' [Lns; CEV], 'to conquer…and teach' [NLT], 'to compel to surrender' [REB].

d. νόημα (LN **30.15**) (BAGD 2. p. 540): 'thought' [**LN**, NTC, WBC; CEV, KJV, NAB, NIV, NJB, NRSV, TEV, TNT], 'human thought' [REB], 'reasoning' [LN], 'design' [BAGD, HNTC], 'intention' [ICC2], 'device' [Lns], 'mind' [AB], 'rebellious ideas' [NLT]. See this word also at 2:11; 3:14; 4:4.

e. ὑπακοή (LN 36.15) (BAGD 1.b. p. 837): 'obedience' [AB, BAGD, HNTC, ICC2, LN, Lns; KJV, NJB, REB]. This noun is also translated as a verb: 'to obey' [NTC, WBC; CEV, NLT, NRSV, TEV, TNT]; as an adjective: 'obedient' [NAB, NIV]. In the genitive phrase τὴν ὑπακοὴν τοῦ Χριστοῦ the genitive τοῦ Χριστοῦ (literally 'of Christ' [KJV]) is an objective genitive, meaning that Christ is the person to whom the obedience is given [AB, HNTC, ICC2, Lns, NTC, WBC; all versions except KJV]. See this word also at 7:15.

QUESTION—What does it mean to take 'every thought captive to obedience to Christ'?

It means that every scheme for spiritual and intellectual independence from God and every mind is to be drawn to a new allegiance and obedience [Car]. Their thinking must submit to the lordship of Christ [NAC]. Paul intends to expose false patterns of thinking and belief [NTC]. People must submit to the truth of the gospel [AB]. Instead of thinking and planning in a self-centered way, they must think and plan in obedience to Christ [HNTC]. It means a consistent submission of a person's thinking to Christ [NIC2], to think in a way that is obedient to Christ [TG, TH].

10:6 **and being ready[a] to-punish[b] every disobedience,[c] whenever your obedience[d] is-complete.[e]**

LEXICON—a. ἕτοιμος (LN 77.2) (BAGD 2. p. 316): 'ready' [AB, BAGD, HNTC, ICC2, LN, NTC, WBC; NAB, NIV, NRSV], 'in readiness' [Lns; KJV], 'prepared' [BAGD, LN; NJB, REB, TEV, TNT], not explicit [CEV, NLT]. The phrase 'ready to punish' is translated 'we will punish' [CEV, NLT].

b. aorist act. infin. of ἐκδικέω (LN **38.8**) (BAGD 2. p. 238): 'to punish' [AB, BAGD, HNTC, ICC2, LN, NTC; all versions except KJV], 'to bring to justice' [Lns], 'to avenge' [WBC], 'to revenge' [KJV].

c. παρακοή (LN 36.27) (BAGD p. 618): 'disobedience' [AB, BAGD, HNTC, LN, Lns, NTC; KJV, NAB, NJB, NRSV, REB], 'act of disobedience' [ICC2, WBC; NIV, TNT], 'act of disloyalty' [TEV]. The phrase 'every disobedience' is translated 'anyone who refuses to obey' [CEV], 'disobedience in anyone else' [NAB], 'those who remained disobedient' [NLT].

d. ὑπακοή (LN 36.15) (BAGD 1.b. p. 837): 'obedience' [AB, BAGD, HNTC, ICC2, LN, Lns, NTC, WBC; KJV, NAB, NIV, NJB, NRSV, REB], 'loyalty' [TEV]. This noun is translated as a verb: 'to obey' [CEV], 'to surrender' [TNT]; as an adjective 'obedient' [NLT].

e. aorist pass. subj. of πληρόω (LN 59.33) (BAGD 3. p. 671): 'to be complete' [AB, NTC; NIV, NRSV, REB], 'to be made complete' [LN, Lns], 'to become complete' [WBC], 'to be fulfilled' [KJV], 'to be brought to completion' [BAGD], 'to be perfect' [HNTC; NAB]. This verb is translated as an adjective: 'complete' [NJB, TEV]; as an adverb: 'completely' [CEV, TNT]. The idea of complete obedience is translated 'loyal and obedient' [NLT]. The phrase 'whenever your obedience is complete' is translated 'after you became loyal and obedient' [NLT], 'after you have proved your complete loyalty' [TEV].

QUESTION—What does the qualifier 'whenever your obedience is complete' signify?

Paul is saying that once the Corinthian church as a whole becomes obedient, he will punish the outsiders who are causing trouble [AB, Car, Lns, NAC, SP, WBC], along with any who support them [Car]. When the church fully shows its loyalty to him, he will punish the rest who do not [EGT, HNTC, NIC1, TG]. He needs the cooperation of the whole church against the outsiders [ICC2]. He calls upon them to reject the claims and message of the intruders and recognize his authority and his gospel [TNTC]. He is saying that the entire church needs to take action together to eradicate false teaching [NTC]. When the congregation is obedient to the gospel, he will punish those who have brought a false gospel [AB]. They need to disassociate from the intruders, break with idolatry, and submit to Paul, because unless the church as a whole recognizes and supports a spiritual discipline it will be ineffective [EBC]. Paul is saying that when the time comes for the Corinthian church to make their obedience effective and complete (that is, when he comes), he will punish disobedience [He, NCBC]. Paul is saying that he will resort to severity when all else fails, and when it becomes clear who among the Corinthians would be obedient [Ho]. Paul is simply saying that he will punish any in the Corinthian church who revert to a life of disobedience or disloyalty [TH].

QUESTION—What is the obedience of which he speaks?
1. They are to obey Paul [EGT, TG]. They must obey Paul and his gospel [TNTC]. They must obey Paul as a representative of Christ [EBC].
2. They are to obey Christ [CEV, NTC, TH] or God [Ho]. They are to obey Christ through the gospel [AB].
3. They are to obey Christ but also Paul [HNTC, ICC2, WBC].
4. The obedience is the exercise of church discipline [Car]. The obedience means to live in a manner that is consistent with the gospel and to shun immorality, idolatry, and wrong allegiances [NAC].

DISCOURSE UNIT: 10:7–18 [AB, HNTC]. The topic is the appeal supported [AB], a declaration of war on the counter-mission [HNTC].

DISCOURSE UNIT: 10:7–11 [ICC1, TNTC]. The topic is reply to the charge of weakness [ICC1], Paul responds to criticisms [TNTC].

10:7 Look-at^a what (is) before-(your)-face.^b

LEXICON—a. pres. act. impera. or pres. act. indic. of βλέπω (LN 30.120) (BAGD 5. p. 143): 'to look' [HNTC, ICC2, Lns, NTC, WBC; KJV, NIV, NJB, NRSV, REB, TEV], 'to notice' [BAGD], 'to be alert' [AB], 'to consider' [TNT], 'to judge' [CEV], 'to view' [NAB], 'to make decisions' [NLT]. This verb is translated as imperative by AB, BAGD, HNTC, ICC2, Lns, NTC, WBC; NJB, NRSV, REB, TNT]: 'look at the obvious'. The phrase κατὰ πρόσωπον βλέπετε is also considered an idiom for judging on the basis of external appearances and is translated as indicative by CEV, KJV, NAB, NIV, NLT, TEV: 'you are looking at things outwardly'.

b. πρόσωπον (LN **31.31**) (BAGD 1.c.δ. p. 721). The phrase κατὰ πρόσωπον is translated 'outward appearance' [LN; KJV, TEV], 'appearance' [NLT], '(what is) before your eyes' [BAGD, ICC2, Lns;

NRSV], 'before you' [NTC; TNT], '(the evidence) of your eyes' [NJB], 'in front of you' [AB, WBC], 'immediately before you' [HNTC], 'by appearances' [CEV], 'superficially' [NIV], '(look facts) in the face' [REB]. It is understood to refer to what should be obvious by AB, BAGD, HNTC, ICC2, Lns, NTC, WBC; NJB, NRSV, REB, TNT. It is understood to refer to superficial appearances as opposed to what is really true by CEV, KJV, NAB, NIV, NLT, TEV. See this word also at 1:11; 2:10; 4:6; 5:12; 8:24; 10:1.

QUESTION—In the statement τὰ κατὰ πρόσωπον βλέπετε 'look at what is before your face' is he telling them to look at what is obvious or rebuking them for only seeing what is on the surface?

1. He is telling them to look at obvious facts [AB, Car, He, HNTC, Lns, NAC, NCBC, NIC1, NIC2, NTC, SP, TNTC, WBC; NJB, NRSV, REB, TNT]. The fact of the existence of the Corinthian church proves the validity of Paul's apostolic ministry [NAC, NIC2]. They should consider what they know of Paul [Car, NCBC], such as his initial evangelization of Corinth [WBC]. They should look at the fact that Paul is Christ's too [Lns, TNTC]. They should look at the fact that it is Paul who has a claim to apostolic authority [NTC]. They should be alert to the dangers right in front of them [AB].
2. He is telling them that they judge on the basis of appearances [EBC, EGT, ICC1; CEV, NAB, NIV, NLT, TEV].
3. He is asking if they only look on the externals [Ho; KJV].

If anyone[a] is-confident[b] of-himself[c] being Christ's, let-him-consider[d] again[e] in himself this, that just-as he is Christ's, so also (are) we.

LEXICON—a. τις (LN 92.12) (BAGD 1.a.β. p. 820): 'anyone' [HNTC, ICC2, LN, Lns, NTC, WBC; NAB, NIV], 'anybody' [NJB], 'any man' [KJV], 'someone' [AB, LN; REB, TNT], 'a certain man' [BAGD], 'those who' [NLT], 'some' [TEV], 'any of you' [CEV], 'you' [NRSV].

b. perf. act. indic. of πείθω (LN 31.46) (BAGD 2.b. p. 639): 'to be confident' [AB, HNTC, Lns, NTC; NIV, NRSV], 'to be certain' [BAGD, LN], 'to be sure' [BAGD, LN, WBC], 'to be convinced' [BAGD, ICC2, LN; NAB, NJB, REB, TNT], 'to think' [CEV], 'to trust' [KJV], 'to reckon' [TEV], 'to proudly declare' [NLT].

c. ἑαυτοῦ (LN 92.25). This word in the dative case is translated 'with regard to himself' [HNTC], 'to himself' [KJV], 'in his own mind' [ICC2, Lns], not explicit [AB, NTC, WBC; CEV, NAB, NIV, NJB, NLT, NRSV, REB, TNT]. The phrase πέποιθεν ἑαυτῷ 'is confident of himself' is translated 'who reckon themselves' [TEV].

d. pres. mid. or pass. (deponent = act.) impera. of λογίζομαι (LN 30.9, 31.1) (BAGD 2. p. 476): 'to consider' [BAGD, HNTC, LN (31.1), NTC, WBC; NIV], 'to think about' [BAGD, LN (30.9)], 'to think' [CEV, KJV, TEV], 'to ponder' [BAGD, LN (30.9)], 'to reflect' [ICC2, NAC; NJB, NLT], 'to think (again) and reflect' [REB], 'to be aware of' [AB], 'to count on'

[Lns], 'to remind (oneself)' [NRSV], 'to take into one's reckoning' [TNT]. See this word also at 3:5; 5:19; 10:2.
  e. πάλιν (LN **89.129**) (BAGD 4. p. 607): 'again' [HNTC, Lns; CEV, KJV, NIV, REB, TEV], 'on the other hand' [BAGD, LN], not explicit [AB, Lns, WBC; NLT]. The phrase λογιζέσθω πάλιν 'consider again' is translated 'go on to reflect' [NJB], 'to think again and reflect' [REB], 'remind yourself' [NRSV], 'take this also into reckoning' [TNT]. This word may mark contrast: 'on the other hand' [LN], 'conversely' [ICC2].

QUESTION—In what way does ἑαυτοῦ 'of himself' refer to the person in question?
  1. It means 'within himself', where the thinking occurs [ICC1, ICC2, Lns, SP, WBC]. Both the dative ἑαυτοῦ and the verb indicate excessive self-interest [SP].
  2. It means 'of or about himself', as the subject of the thinking [He, HNTC, Ho, NTC].

QUESTION—What is meant by Χριστοῦ εἶναι 'being Christ's'?
  1. It is to represent Christ as his servant or apostle [EBC, HNTC, ICC1, ICC2, NAC, NTC, SP, TG, TNTC, WBC]. It is a special claim to authority [Car, NCBC]. It is a claim to be inspired by Christ and therefore not subject to apostolic authority [He]. To the person in Corinth it means to be a spirit-empowered minister, but to Paul, being in Christ simply means being a Christian [NIC2]. It means being an apostle as well as a genuine Christian [EBC, NTC].
  2. It refers to being a Christian [Lns, TH].
  3. It means that someone makes a special claim to Christ as do those with the Christ party in 1 Cor 1:10 [EGT, Ho].

10:8 For if I-were-to-boast[a] somewhat-more[b] about our authority[c] which the Lord gave

LEXICON—a. aorist mid. (deponent = act.) subj. of καυχάομαι (LN 33.368) (BAGD 2. p. 426): 'to boast' [AB, BAGD, ICC2, LN, Lns, NTC, WBC; KJV, NIV, NLT, NRSV, REB, TEV, TNT], 'to make a boast' [HNTC], 'to brag' [CEV], 'to make a few claims' [NAB], 'to take pride' [NJB], 'to be proud' [BAGD]. See this word also at 7:14.
  b. περισσότερόν τι: from περισσότερος (LN 78.31) (BAGD 2. p. 651), which implies something excessive in extent [LN], and τις (LN 92.12), a reference to something indefinite [LN]. The phrase περισσότερόν τι 'somewhat more' is translated 'a little more' [AB], 'a little too much' [NRSV, TNT], 'too much' [REB], 'further' [HNTC], 'some further respect' [ICC2], 'something beyond that' [Lns], 'somewhat more' [KJV], 'somewhat excessively' [NTC], 'somewhat too much' [TEV], 'somewhat freely' [NIV], 'more than that' [WBC], 'a little too much' [CEV]. The phrase ἐάν [τε] γὰρ περισσότερόν τι καυχήσωμαι is translated 'if I find I must make a few further claims' [NAB], 'maybe I have taken rather too much pride' [NJB], 'I may seem to be boasting too much' [NLT].

c. ἐξουσία (LN 37.35) (BAGD 3. p. 278): 'authority' [AB, BAGD, HNTC, ICC2, LN, Lns, NTC, WBC; all versions except NAB], 'power' [BAGD; NAB]. See this word also at 13:10.

QUESTION—What relationship is indicated by γάρ 'for'?

It introduces what follows in v.8 [AB, ICC1, ICC2, Lns, NTC]. It links v.7, where he mentions their confidence that led them to attack his authority, with v.8 [NTC]. It introduces the validation for his claim to be Christ's servant in v.7b [ICC1, ICC2]. It connects their being recognized as being Christ's (i.e., being Christians) as the basis for statement that follows about their authority [Lns].

QUESTION—What is meant by περισσότερόν τι 'somewhat more'?

1. It is idiomatic [He, NAC, NIC2, NTC, SP, TH]. Paul is making a slight overstatement, boasting somewhat freely or excessively, just a little too much [He, NIC2, NTC, SP, TH]. He is reflecting his opponents' view that he boasted too much [NAC].
2. It is comparative [AB, Car, EGT, HNTC, Ho, ICC1, ICC2, Lns, NCBC, NIC1, WBC]. He is boasting somewhat more than would ordinarily be appropriate [NIC1], more than normal [NCBC], a little more assertively [ICC1], or a little more than in vv.3-6 [EGT]. He will boast about more than being Christ's [AB, Car, HNTC, Lns, WBC]. He will boast more than he already has [Ho, ICC2, NCBC].

QUESTION—Who is 'the Lord'?

1. It is Christ [AB, Ho, ICC1, ICC2, NIC1, NIC2, NTC, TG, TH, TNTC].
2. It is God [NAC].

for (the) building-up[a] and not for (the) tearing-down[b] of-you, I-will- not - be-put-to-shame.[c]

LEXICON—a. οἰκοδομή (LN 74.15) (BAGD 1.b.α. p. 559): 'building up' [BAGD, HNTC, Lns; NIV, NJB, NRSV], 'upbuilding' [AB; NAB], 'to build up' [LN, WBC; NLT, TEV, TNT], 'to build your faith' [REB], 'edification' [BAGD, NTC; KJV], 'to strengthen' [LN], 'for constructive purposes' [ICC2], 'to help (you)' [CEV].

b. καθαίρεσις (LN 74.16) (BAGD 2. p. 386): 'tearing down' [BAGD; NRSV], 'destruction' [AB, ICC2, NTC; KJV, NAB], 'pulling down' [HNTC; NIV], 'to pull down' [WBC; REB], 'knocking down' [NJB], 'wrecking' [Lns], 'to tear down' [LN; NLT, TEV], 'to hurt (you)' [CEV], 'to destroy' [TNT], 'to weaken' [LN]. See this word also at 10:4.

c. fut. pass. (deponent = act.) indic. of αἰσχύνω (LN 25.190) (BAGD 2. p. 25): 'to be put to shame' [BAGD, HNTC, ICC2, Lns; NLT], 'to be ashamed' [AB, LN, NTC; KJV, NIV, NRSV, TEV], 'to be shamed' [NJB], 'to be discredited' [WBC], 'to embarrass' [NAB], 'to be embarrassed' [CEV], 'to make good a boast' [REB], 'to be unrepentant' [TNT].

QUESTION—What does 'building up' mean?

It means to build up their faith [TH], to help them become better Christians [TG], to strengthen their grasp of the gospel [AB], to increase faith and harmony [EBC]. It refers to Paul's demands that they live in accordance with the truth of the gospel, which he expressed in his previous letters [TNTC]. It means to build up the church in holiness and peace [Ho]. It means to build congregations and to nurture them [HNTC, ICC2, NIC2], to strengthen faith and Christian conduct among them [NIC2]. It is to strengthen individuals and churches [NTC].

10:9 So that I-would- not -seem^a so as to-frighten^b you through the letters;

LEXICON—a. aorist act. subj. of δοκέω (LN 31.30) (BAGD 2.a. p. 202): 'to seem' [AB, BAGD, HNTC, ICC2, LN; KJV, NIV, NRSV], 'to appear' [LN, Lns, NTC; TEV], 'to think' [LN, WBC], not explicit [CEV]. The phrase ἵνα μὴ δόξω 'so that I would not seem' is translated 'I am not trying to' [CEV], 'this is not an attempt' [NLT], 'I do not wish' [NAB], 'you must not think' [REB], 'do not think' [TNT], '(shamed) into letting you think' [NJB].

b. pres. act. infin. of ἐκφοβέω (LN **25.257**) (BAGD p. 247): 'to frighten' [BAGD, NTC, WBC; NLT, NRSV, TEV, TNT], 'to frighten to death' [HNTC], 'to terrify' [BAGD, LN; KJV], 'to scare' [AB, Lns; CEV, REB], 'to intimidate' [NAB], 'to effect intimidation' [ICC2], 'to put fear into' [NJB]. The phrase ὡς ἂν ἐκφοβεῖν 'so as to frighten' is translated 'trying to frighten' [NIV, TEV, TNT], '(one who) tries to scare' [REB]. The compounded form of this verb (with the prefix ἐκ) intensifies the meaning of the root verb φοβέω 'to frighten' [ICC1, NIC1, NTC, TG].

QUESTION—What relationship does ἵνα μὴ δόξω 'so that I would not seem' have to its context

1. It introduces a statement of a negative purpose: 'it is not my intent to frighten you' [EGT, ICC2, NIC1, TH; CEV, NAB, NIV, NRSV, TEV], or an imperative statement: 'don't think of me as frightening you' [NIC2, NTC, SP; REB].
2. It introduces a statement of a negative purpose, which is that Paul does not want them to think of him only as trying to frighten them by his letters, since he is willing to enforce them with action as well [AB; NJB, NLT, TNT].
3. It completes an implied thought from v.8: '(I won't boast/boast further) lest I seem…' [Car, EBC, HNTC, Ho, TG].
4. It explains why he said what he did in v. 8; he tells them that his authority is for upbuilding so they won't think he is trying to intimidate them [Lns].
5. It begins a thought that is completed in v.11, with v.10 as a parenthesis: 'lest I appear to be trying to frighten you…let that man consider that what we are in our letters…' [NAC, WBC].

10:10 because,[a] one-says,[b] The letters (are) weighty[c] and powerful,[d]
TEXT—Instead of φησίν 'one-says', some manuscripts have φασίν 'they say'. GNT does not mention this alternative. Only KJV and NAB read 'they say'. CEV, NIV, NLT, and NRSV have 'some say', which is probably for stylistic reasons rather than because of the textual variant.
LEXICON—a. ὅτι (LN 89.33): 'because' [ICC2, LN, NTC], 'for' [AB, HNTC, LN, Lns, WBC; KJV, NIV, NLT, NRSV], not explicit [CEV, NAB, NJB, REB, TEV, TNT].
  b. pres. act. indic. of φημί (LN 33.69) (BAGD p. 856): 'to say' [BAGD, LN]. This verb could be used in an impersonal sense 'it is said' [BAGD (1.c.)]. It is translated impersonally: 'it is said' [AB, NTC; REB]; as referring to an unnamed or unknown subject: 'someone says/said/will say/may say' [ICC2; NJB, TEV, TNT], 'some say/are saying' [WBC; CEV, NIV, NLT], 'they say' [KJV, NAB, NRSV]; as referring to a specific subject: 'he says' [HNTC, Lns].
  c. βαρύς (LN 86.1) (BAGD 2.a. p. 134): 'weighty' [HNTC, ICC2, NTC, WBC; KJV, NIV, NJB, NRSV, REB, TNT], 'heavy' [LN, Lns], 'burdensome' [BAGD, LN], 'demanding' [AB; NLT], 'harsh' [CEV], 'severe' [NAB, TEV].
  d. ἰσχυρός (LN 76.11) (BAGD 2. p. 383): 'powerful' [HNTC, ICC2, LN, NTC; CEV, KJV, REB, TNT], 'strong' [LN, Lns; NRSV, TEV], 'full of strength' [NJB], 'effective' [BAGD], 'impressive' [AB], 'forceful' [WBC; NAB, NIV, NLT].

but the bodily[a] presence[b] (is) weak[c] and the speech[d] contemptible.[e]
LEXICON—a. σῶμα (LN 8.1) (BAGD 1.b. p. 799). This noun in the genitive case (literally 'of the body') is translated 'bodily' [HNTC, Lns; KJV, NRSV], 'physical' [NTC, WBC], 'personal' [ICC2], not explicit [AB; CEV, NAB, NIV, NJB, NLT, TEV, TNT]. See this word also at 4:10 and 5:6.
  b. παρουσία (LN **85.25**) (BAGD 1. p. 629): 'presence' [BAGD, HNTC, ICC2, Lns, WBC; KJV, NRSV], 'appearance' [NTC]. The phrase παρουσία τοῦ σώματος 'bodily presence' is translated 'when he is present' [AB; REB], 'in person' [CEV, NIV, NLT], 'when he is here in person' [NAB], 'when you see him in person' [NJB], 'when he is with us in person' [LN; TEV], 'to look at' [TNT]. See this word also at 7:6.
  c. ἀσθενής (LN **79.69**) (BAGD 1.b. p. 115): 'weak' [AB, BAGD, HNTC, LN, Lns, NTC, WBC; KJV, NLT, NRSV, TEV], '(he is a) weakling' [CEV], 'feeble' [ICC2], 'unimpressive' [NAB, NIV, REB, TNT], 'he makes no impression' [NJB].
  d. λόγος (LN 33.99) (BAGD 1.a.β. p. 477): 'speech' [AB, HNTC, ICC2, LN, NTC; KJV, NRSV], 'speaking' [BAGD, LN; NIV], 'powers of speaking' [NJB], 'speeches' [NLT], 'as a speaker' [REB, TNT], 'rhetoric' [WBC], 'word' [Lns; NAB], 'words' [TEV], not explicit [CEV]. The phrase ὁ λόγος ἐξουθενημένος 'the speech contemptible' is translated

'he has nothing worth saying' [CEV]. See this word also at 1:18; 2:17; 5:19; 6:7; 8:7.

e. perf. pass. participle of ἐξουθενέω (LN 88.195) (BAGD 1. p. 277): 'to be despised' [BAGD, LN], 'to be disdained' [BAGD]. This participle is translated 'contemptible' [AB, ICC2; KJV, NRSV], 'it excites contempt' [HNTC], 'moves us to contempt' [WBC], 'beneath contempt' [REB], 'of no account' [Lns, NTC], 'really bad' [NLT], '(makes) no great impact' [NAB], 'negligible' [NJB], 'nothing' [TEV], 'nothing (worth saying)' [CEV], 'amounts to nothing' [BAGD; NIV], 'insignificant' [TNT].

QUESTION—Does 'speech' refer to the content of what Paul says or his manner of delivery?

It refers to Paul's manner of delivery in public speaking, which did not compare favorably to the rhetoric of Greek orators [AB, EGT, ICC1, ICC2, NAC, NCBC, NIC1, NIC2, NTC, SP, TG, TH, TNTC, WBC]. It is also a reflection of their estimation of Paul's ineffectiveness in exercising authority while in Corinth [ICC2, NIC2], as Paul did not speak boldly in his own defense when he was attacked before [TNTC]. It refers to the impression made by what he says, that he does not assume the same authority when speaking in person as he does in his letters [Ho]. It refers to the content of what he says as well as his manner of delivery [HNTC, Lns].

10:11 Such-a-person[a] let-(him)-recognize[b] this, that such-as[c] we-are in word[d] by letter (when) being-absent, such also (we will be) in-action[e] (when) being-present.

LEXICON—a. τοιοῦτος (LN **64.2**) (BAGD 1., or 3.a.α. p. 821): 'such a person' [BAGD, ICC2, LN, NTC; TEV], 'that sort of person' [NJB], 'such a one' [Lns; KJV], 'the man' [HNTC], 'this person' [WBC], 'those people' [CEV], 'such people' [NAB, NIV, NRSV], 'the ones who say this' [NLT], 'people who talk that way' [REB], 'anyone who thinks like that' [TNT].

b. pres. mid. or pass. (deponent = act.) impera. of λογίζομαι (LN 30.9, 31.1, 29.4) (BAGD 2. p. 476): 'to think about' [BAGD, LN (30.9)], 'to ponder' [BAGD, LN (30.9)], 'to consider' [BAGD, LN (31.1), NTC, WBC], 'to count on' [AB], 'to bear in mind' [HNTC, LN (29.4)], 'to take account of' [ICC2], 'to count on' [Lns]. See this word also at 3:5, 5:19, 10:2 and 10:7.

c. οἷος (LN 58.30, 64.1) (BAGD p. 562): 'such as' [BAGD, ICC2, LN (64.1); KJV], 'of what sort' [BAGD, LN (58.3)], 'the kind' [Lns], 'what kind of' [LN (58.3)], 'what' [AB, WBC; NAB, NIV], 'just the same' [HNTC], not explicit [NJB, NLT, REB, TNT].

d. λόγος (LN 33.98) (BAGD 1.a.α. p. 477): 'word' [BAGD, HNTC, ICC2, LN, Lns; KJV, NAB], 'words' [AB], not explicit [WBC; NIV, NJB, NLT, REB, TNT]. The phrase οἷοί ἐσμεν τῷ λόγῳ 'what we are in word' is translated 'what we say' [NTC; NRSV], 'what I say' [CEV], 'what we write' [TEV]. See this word also at 1:18; 2:17; 5:19; 6:7; 8:7; 10:10.

e. ἔργον (LN 42.11) (BAGD 1.a. p. 307): 'action' [AB, BAGD, HNTC, WBC; NAB], 'actions' [NIV, WBC; REB, TNT], 'act' [LN], 'deed' [BAGD, ICC2, LN, Lns; KJV], 'deeds' [NJB], '(I/we will) do' [NTC; CEV, NRSV, TEV], not explicit [CEV].

QUESTION—What is Paul threatening here?

When he is there in person he will be as decisive and demanding as he is in his letters [TG]. His speech and action will be as drastic as his letters [NCBC]. He will not be timid [EBC]. He will speak plainly and say hard thing face to face [HNTC]. He will assert his authority and stand up to his critics [TNTC]. He will enforce his authority [NIC1]. He will discipline those who continue in immorality [NIC2]. He will confront just as he has in his letters and may excommunicate [WBC]. His action may involve exclusion of the person from the church and possibly the miraculous infliction of suffering [ICC2]. He will be forceful and severe [Car]. His denunciations by letter will not prove to be idle threats [Ho].

DISCOURSE UNIT: 10:12–12:13 [NIC2]. The topic is superlative apostles.

DISCOURSE UNIT: 10:12–18 [EBC, ICC1, TNTC, WBC; NJB]. The topic is legitimate spheres of activity and boasting [EBC], the area of his mission includes Corinth [ICC1], the issue of Paul's ministry [WBC], boasting within proper limits [TNTC], Paul's reply to the accusations of ambition [NJB].

10:12 For we-are- not (so) -bold[a] (as) to-class[b] (ourselves) or to compare[c] ourselves with certain-ones[d] commending[e] themselves,

LEXICON—a. pres. act. indic. of τολμάω (LN 25.161) (BAGD 1.b. p. 822): 'to be bold' [Lns; NAB], 'to dare' [HNTC, ICC2, LN, NTC; CEV, KJV, NIV, NLT, NRSV, REB, TEV, TNT], 'to presume' [BAGD], 'to have (the) audacity' [AB], 'to have (the) effrontery' [WBC], 'to venture' [NJB]. See this word also at 10:2.

b. aorist act. infin. of ἐγκρίνω (LN **58.27**) (BAGD p. 216): 'to class' [AB, BAGD, HNTC, WBC; REB, TNT], 'to classify' [LN, Lns; NAB, NIV, NRSV, TEV], 'to rank' [ICC2; NJB], 'to count (oneself)' [NTC], 'to make (oneself) of the number' [KJV]. The two verbs in the phrase ἐγκρῖναι ἢ συγκρῖναι 'to class or compare' are conflated and translated as one verb 'to compare' [CEV]. This entire clause is translated 'I wouldn't dare say that I am as wonderful as these other men who tell you how important they are' [NLT].

c. aorist act. infin. of συγκρίνω (LN **64.6**) (BAGD 2.a. p. 774): 'to compare' [AB, BAGD, HNTC, ICC2, LN, Lns, NTC, WBC; all versions except NLT], not explicit [NLT].

d. τις (LN 92.12): 'certain persons' [AB], 'certain ones' [Lns], 'certain people' [NAB, NJB], 'some' [KJV, NIV], 'some of those' [HNTC, ICC2, NTC, WBC; NRSV], 'any of those' [REB, TNT], 'those' [CEV, TEV], 'these other men' [NLT].

334   2 CORINTHIANS 10:12

  e. pres. act. participle of συνίστημι (LN 33.344) (BAGD I.1.b. p. 790): 'to
     commend' [BAGD, HNTC, ICC2, NTC; KJV, NIV, NRSV, REB], 'to
     recommend' [AB, BAGD, LN, Lns, WBC; NAB]. The phrase τῶν
     ἑαυτοὺς συνιστανόντων 'certain ones commending themselves' is
     translated 'who think so much of themselves' [CEV], 'who provide their
     own commendation' [NJB] 'who tell you how important they are' [NLT],
     'who rate themselves so highly' [TEV], 'who are now pushing themselves
     forward' [TNT]. See this word also at 3:1; 4:2; 5:12; 6:4; 7:11.
QUESTION—What is Paul's tone in this statement?
  Paul is speaking with irony and sarcasm here [AB, Car, EBC, EGT, He,
  HNTC, ICC1, ICC2, Lns, NAC, NIC1, NIC2, NTC, SP, TG, TH, TNTC,
  WBC; NLT].

but they, measuring^a themselves by themselves and comparing themselves by themselves, do-not understand.^b
LEXICON—a. pres. act. participle of μετρέω (LN 81.2) (BAGD 1.b. p. 514):
     'to measure' [AB, BAGD, HNTC, ICC2, LN, Lns, NTC, WBC; all
     versions except CEV, NAB], not explicit [CEV]. The phrase ἐν ἑαυτοῖς
     ἑαυτοὺς μετροῦντες 'measuring themselves by themselves' is translated
     'people like that are their own appraisers' [NAB].
  b. pres. act. indic. of συνίημι (LN 32.5) (BAGD p. 790): 'to understand'
     [BAGD, LN], 'to comprehend' [BAGD, LN]. The phrase αὐτοὶ οὐ
     συνιᾶσιν 'they do not understand' is translated 'they fail to understand'
     [NTC], 'they have no understanding' [AB], 'they are without
     understanding' [HNTC], 'they appear as without understanding' [WBC],
     'they lack understanding' [ICC2], 'they are not even sensible' [Lns], 'they
     are foolish' [CEV], 'they are not wise' [KJV, NIV], 'they only
     demonstrate their ignorance' [NAB], 'they only show their folly' [NJB],
     'they do not show good sense' [NRSV], 'what foolishness' [NLT], 'what
     fools they are' [REB], 'how stupid they are' [TEV], '(they) are being very
     stupid' [TNT].
QUESTION—What is the connection between the action of measuring and
  comparing in this way and their lack of understanding?
  It is unreasonable, foolish or futile to use oneself as the standard of
  comparison [EBC, ICC1, Lns, NAC, NCBC, SP, TG]. Lack of an objective
  standard is foolish [Car, HNTC, ICC1], and means having no standard at all
  [HNTC]. They fail to understand their own limitations and don't really know
  themselves [AB]. They don't understand the inherent fraud involved in self-
  chosen standards of assessment [ICC2]. They lack understanding of the
  character and qualities of genuine Christian ministry [NIC1]. To use such
  criteria shows that they don't understand what Jesus taught about his
  followers experiencing suffering and persecution [TNTC]. They fail to
  recognize God's working in the spread of the gospel and Paul as Christ's
  representative [NTC]. They were profoundly unable to understand how
  much they were damaging the church [Car].

QUESTION—Is ἑαυτοῖς ἑαυτοὺς 'themselves by themselves' used reflexively or reciprocally?
  1. It is used reflexively; each measures himself relative to himself [Lns, WBC].
  2. It is used reciprocally; they measure themselves by one another or by a standard common to that group [AB, ICC2, NAC, NIC2, SP].
  3. Each measures relative to himself but also by others of the same group [Car, ICC1].

10:13 But[a] we do not boast beyond-limits[b] but according to the measure[c] of the sphere[d] which God apportioned[e] to us as-a-measure,[f] to-reach[g] even as-far-as[h] to-you.

LEXICON—a. δέ (LN 89.124): 'but' [ICC2, LN, Lns; KJV, NLT, TNT], 'yet' [AB], 'however' [HNTC, NTC, WBC; NIV, NRSV], 'by contrast' [NJB], not explicit [CEV, NAB]. The contrast implied by this word is expressed by the phrase 'as for us' [REB], 'as for us, however' [TEV]. The use of the personal pronoun ἡμεῖς 'we' emphasizes the contrast between Paul and those to whom he refers in v.12 [AB, ICC2, Lns, NIC2, NTC, TH, WBC].
  b. ἄμετρος (LN **78.27**) (BAGD p. 45). The phrase εἰς τὰ ἄμετρα is translated 'beyond limits' [BAGD, NTC; NRSV], 'beyond certain limits' [**LN**; TEV] 'beyond measure' [LN; NJB], 'beyond the proper limits' [AB, WBC; NIV, REB], 'outside our proper limits' [TNT], 'over the mark' [NAB], 'without our measure' [KJV], 'in no unmeasured way' [ICC2], 'in regard to things that no one can measure' [Lns]. The phrase εἰς τὰ ἄμετρα 'beyond limits' is translated 'something we don't have a right to brag about' [CEV], 'of authority we don't have' [NLT]. See this word also at 10:15.
  c. μέτρον (LN 81.1) (BAGD 2.b.p. 515): 'measure' [AB, BAGD, HNTC, ICC2, LN, Lns, NTC; KJV], 'standard' [NJB], not explicit [WBC; CEV, NAB, NIV, NLT, NRSV, REB, TEV, TNT].
  d. κανών (LN **80.2**) (BAGD 2.p. 403): 'sphere' [BAGD, LN, NTC; REB], 'sphere of service' [WBC], 'work' [CEV], 'area' [**LN**], 'limits' [BAGD; TNT], 'bounds' [NAB], 'boundaries' [NLT], 'province' [BAGD, HNTC], 'field' [NIV, NRSV], 'territorial schedule' [ICC2], 'jurisdiction' [AB], 'rule' [Lns; KJV], 'standard' [NJB]. The phrase 'according to the measure of the sphere' is translated 'within the bounds/boundaries' [NAB, NLT], 'within the field' [NRSV], 'within the limits of the work' [TEV], 'within the sphere of service' [WBC].
  e. aorist act. indicative of μερίζω (LN **37.100**) (BAGD 2.b. p. 504): 'to apportion' [AB, BAGD, LN], 'to deal out' [HNTC], 'to measure out' [Lns], 'to assign' [ICC2], 'to appoint to (a work)' [**LN**], 'to assign a particular responsibility or give a particular task to' [LN], 'to assign' [BAGD].

f. The genitive noun μέτρου 'as a measure' in the phrase οὗ ἐμέρισεν ἡμῖν ὁ θεὸς μέτρου 'which God apportioned to us as a measure' is not translated by NTC; CEV, NIV, NJB, NLT, NRSV, REB, TEV, TNT. It is translated adverbially as modifying μερίζω: 'as a measure' [HNTC, Lns], 'as our measure' [AB], 'as a measure of interest' [ICC2], 'as our sphere' [WBC], 'a measure (to reach)' [KJV]. It is translated as genitive phrase modifying 'God': 'the God of moderation' [NAB].

g. aorist mid. (deponent = act.) infin. of ἐφικνέομαι (LN 15.84) (BAGD p. 330): 'to reach' [BAGD, HNTC, ICC2, LN, NTC, WBC; KJV, NIV], 'to reach out' [AB; NRSV], 'to come to' [BAGD, **LN**; NJB], 'to get (as far as)' [Lns]. The phrase ἐφικέσθαι ἄχρι καὶ ὑμῶν 'to reach even as far as you' is translated 'leading us to you' [NAB], 'and this plan includes our working there with you' [NLT]; similarly [TEV], 'which permitted us to come as far as Corinth' [REB], 'and (those limits) include you Corinthians' [TNT], 'and you are part of that work' [CEV].

h. ἄχρι (LN 84.19) (BAGD 1.b. p. 128): 'as far as' [AB, BAGD, HNTC, ICC2, LN, Lns, WBC; NRSV, REB], 'to' [LN; NAB, NIV, NJB], 'unto' [KJV], not explicit [NTC; CEV, NLT, TEV, TNT].

QUESTION—What is meant by not boasting εἰς τὰ ἄμετρα 'beyond limits'?

1. Paul will not minister beyond the legitimate limits allotted to him by God [EBC, ICC1, NIC1, NIC2, TG, WBC], nor does he intrude into what has been assigned to others [EGT, NAC, NCBC]. He stays within the limits in that he does not try to assert superiority over others by comparing himself to them [NAC]. He does not boast in the results of the labor of other people [TNTC].

2. Boasting 'in an unmeasured way' refers to the lack of objective standards [Car, HNTC, Lns, NTC], and of boasting in things that cannot be objectively measured [Lns, NTC]. Paul does not decide his own standard of measure [ICC1].

3. It means immoderate or excessive boasting [He, Ho, ICC2, SP], which is inherent in the fact of having no external standard [ICC2].

4. It has a double meaning [AB, ICC1, TH]. Paul will not exceed the limits of how much should be said or the geographical limits of where he has the authority to work [AB, TH]. It refers to the standard of measure as well as the limits of where he is to work [ICC1].

QUESTION—In what sense does Paul use the term κανών 'sphere'?

It is the geographical territory or field which God apportioned to them [Car, EBC, NTC, TG, WBC]. It is the length or extent to which God permitted them to go geographically, hence, their territory [ICC1, Lns]. It is the sphere of ministry God allotted to Paul, which included Corinth [NCBC]. It is the authority for ministry as well as the geographical area in which it is exercised [AB, TH]. It is responsibility for service in a particular area [ICC2, NIC2, TNTC], though not designating a purely geographical category [NIC2]. It is the ministry to which God has commissioned them [HNTC]. It is a course or track in ministry which God marks out and within which God leads [NIC1]. It refers to the competence that God gave them for ministry, which becomes their norm or standard [SP]. God determined Paul's gifts as well as his sphere of labor and activity [Ho]. It is the standard of measure or norm by which claims may be evaluated, which in this case is the fact that Paul was the founder of the church [NAC].

10:14 **For we-are- not -overextending^a ourselves as if not reaching^b (as far as) to you,**

LEXICON—a. pres. act. indic. of ὑπερεκτείνω (LN **68.78**) (BAGD p. 840): 'to overextend' [AB, BAGD, ICC2, LN, NTC], 'to overstretch' [HNTC, Lns], 'to overstretch our commission' [REB], 'to stretch beyond (our) measure' [KJV], 'to overreach' [NAB, NJB], 'to overreach (our) limit' [WBC], 'to overstep a limit' [LN; NRSV], 'to go beyond limits' [**LN**; TEV], 'to go outside (our) limits' [TNT]. The phrase 'for we are not overextending ourselves' is translated 'we are not bragging more than we should' [CEV], 'we are not going too far in our boasting' [NIV], 'we are not going too far when we claim authority over you' [NLT].

b. pres. mid. or pass. (deponent = act.) participle of ἐφικνέομαι (LN **15.84**) (BAGD p. 330): 'to reach' [AB, BAGD, HNTC, ICC2, LN, WBC; KJV, NRSV], 'to reach out' [NTC], 'to come to' [BAGD, **LN**; NIV, NJB, REB], 'to arrive' [LN], 'to get out to' [Lns], not explicit [CEV, NAB, NLT, TEV, TNT].

QUESTION—What does Paul intend by the metaphor of overextension?

He has not extended his ministry beyond his allocated area of service [Ho, NAC, NIC1, NIC2, NTC, TG, TH, WBC] or what he has been commissioned to do [AB, ICC1]. He has not invaded someone else's area of ministry [EGT, HNTC, Lns, NAC, NCBC, NIC1], though his opponents have done so [AB, EBC, Ho, Lns]. Paul is within his rights to minister in Corinth [TNTC]. Although his opponents boast in what someone else has accomplished [Car], Paul's boasting does not extend to anything beyond what he himself has done [ICC2]. Paul is also not overextending his limits by writing this letter [TH].

for we-came^a even^b as-far-as you in^c the gospel^d of Christ.

LEXICON—a. aorist act. indicative of φθάνω (LN **15.84**) (BAGD 2.p. 857): 'to come (to/as far as)' [AB, **LN**, NTC, WBC; KJV, NJB, NRSV, TEV, TNT], 'to get (to/as far as)' [HNTC; NAB, NIV], 'to reach' [LN; REB], 'to arrive' [ICC2, Lns], 'to travel' [NLT]. The phrase 'we came even as far as you in the gospel of Christ' is translated 'we did bring the message about Christ to you' [CEV].

b. καί (LN 89.93): 'even' [AB, ICC2, LN, Lns, NTC], 'also' [KJV], not explicit [HNTC, WBC; CEV, NIV, REB, TEV, TNT]. The phrase γὰρ καί 'for...even' is translated 'indeed' [NAB], 'in fact' [NJB]. The phrase 'even as far as' is translated 'all the way to' [NLT, NRSV].

c. ἐν (LN **89.80**): 'in' [HNTC; KJV, REB], 'with' [AB, ICC2, LN, Lns, NTC, WBC; NAB, NIV, NJB, NLT, NRSV, TNT], not explicit [CEV,

TEV]. The phrase ἐν τῷ εὐαγγελίῳ 'in the gospel' is translated 'in preaching the gospel' [KJV], 'bringing the good news' [LN], 'we did bring the message' [CEV], 'with our preaching' [WBC], 'in the work of the gospel' [REB].

d. εὐαγγέλιον (LN 33.217) (BAGD 2.b.α. p. 318): 'the gospel' [AB, BAGD, HNTC, ICC2, LN, Lns, NTC; KJV, NAB, NIV, REB], 'the good news' [BAGD, LN; NJB, NLT, NRSV, TEV, TNT], 'the message' [CEV], 'our preaching' [WBC].

QUESTION—What is the point of this statement?

1. Paul is reminding them that he came to Corinth first and preached there before his opponents arrived [AB, Car, EBC, HNTC, ICC1, ICC2, Lns, NAC, NCBC, NIC1, NIC2, NTC, SP, TNTC, WBC; NJB, NLT, NRSV, REB, TNT]. Corinth was the farthest point west which Paul had evangelized [NIC1]. They were commissioned to go there and arrived there first, so they have authority [AB]. The limits of labor assigned to Paul included Corinth, and they were they fruit of his ministry [Ho].
2. Paul is saying that they came as far as to Corinth to minister to them [TG], and Corinth is within the limits of their ministry [TEV].

10:15 We do- not -boast beyond limits,^a in (the) labors^b of-others,

LEXICON—a. ἄμετρος (LN 78.27) (BAGD p. 45). The phrase εἰς τὰ ἄμετρα is translated 'beyond limits' [NTC; NRSV], 'beyond our limits' [NIV], 'beyond the proper limits' [AB, WBC], 'outside our proper limits' [TNT], 'beyond our proper sphere' [REB], 'beyond the limits God set for us' [TEV], 'beyond measure' [ICC2; NJB], 'in an unmeasured way' [HNTC], 'without our measure' [KJV], 'more than we should' [CEV], 'immoderately' [NAB], not explicit [Lns; NLT]. See this phrase also at 10:13.

b. κόπος (LN 42.47) (BAGD 2. p. 443): 'labor' [AB, BAGD, HNTC, ICC2, Lns, NTC; KJV, NRSV], 'work' [BAGD, WBC; NAB, NIV, NJB, NLT, REB, TEV], 'hard work' [LN]. The phrase 'the labors of others' is translated 'what others have done' [CEV, TNT].

but^a having hope (as) your faith (is) increasing^b to be-magnified^c among you in abundance^d according-to our sphere,^e

LEXICON—a. δέ (LN 89.124, 89.94): 'but' [HNTC, ICC2, LN (89.124), NTC, WBC; CEV, KJV, NRSV, TNT], 'instead' [NLT, TEV], 'rather' [REB], 'in fact' [NJB], 'and' [AB, LN (89.94)], not explicit [Lns; NAB, NIV].

b. pres. pass. participle of αὐξάνω (LN **78.5**) (BAGD 2.p. 121): 'to increase' [BAGD, HNTC, ICC2, LN, NTC; NJB, NRSV, TNT], 'to be increased' [KJV], 'to grow' [AB, BAGD, **LN**, Lns, WBC; NAB, NIV, NLT, REB, TEV]. The phrase αὐξανομένης τῆς πίστεως ὑμῶν 'as your faith is increasing' is translated 'as you become stronger in your faith' [CEV]. This present tense verb is translated as indicating ongoing action: 'keeps growing' [Lns], 'continues to grow' [WBC; NIV].

c. aorist pass. infin. of μεγαλύνω (LN 79.124) (BAGD 1. p. 497): 'to be enlarged' [LN, NTC], 'to be made large' [BAGD, LN], 'to increase, grow' [BAGD]. The phrase ἐν ὑμῖν μεγαλυνθῆναι '(our sphere) among you will be-increased' is translated 'we may grow in achievement' [ICC2], 'that we may be praised among you' [AB], 'that we may grow in your estimation' [HNTC], 'to be magnified in your midst' [Lns], 'so (our work) may be greatly expanded among you' [WBC], 'we will be able to reach many more of the people around you' [CEV], 'we shall be enlarged by you' [KJV]. 'our influence may also grow among you' [NAB], '(our area of activity) among you will (greatly) expand' [NIV], '(our work) among you will be (greatly) enlarged' [NLT], '(our sphere of action) among you may be (greatly) enlarged' [NRSV], 'we may attain a position among you greater than ever before' [REB], 'that we may be able to do a (much) greater work among you' [TEV], 'our influence among you will be (greatly) increased' [TNT], 'we hope to grow' [NJB].
d. περισσεία (LN 78.31) (BAGD p. 650): The phrase εἰς περισσείαν 'in abundance' is translated 'greatly' [BAGD, NTC, WBC; NIV, NLT, NRSV, TNT], 'greater and greater' [NJB], 'greater than ever before' [REB], 'much greater' [TEV], 'abundantly' [AB, ICC2; KJV], 'in such overflowing measure' [HNTC], '(and) overflow' [NAB], 'for still more' [Lns], 'many more' [CEV]. See this word also at 8:2.
e. κανών: 'sphere' [LN, WBC; REB], 'sphere of action' [NRSV], 'sphere of influence' [NTC], 'influence' [NAB, TNT], 'area' [**LN**], 'area of activity' [NIV], 'work' [NLT], 'jurisdiction' [AB], 'province' [HNTC], 'schedule' [ICC2], 'rule' [Lns; KJV], 'standard' [NJB]. The phrase 'our sphere among you will be increased' is translated 'we will be able to reach many more of the people around you' [CEV], 'we will be able to do a much greater work among you, always within the limits that God has set' [TEV]. See this word also at 10:13.

QUESTION—What is it that Paul hopes will be magnified?
1. Paul hopes that the sphere of his work will be magnified or increased.
  1.1 He wants to expand the range of his preaching beyond Corinth [He, Ho, ICC1, ICC2, NAC, NCBC, NIC1, NTC, WBC; CEV]. When he is no longer distracted by giving attention to the Corinthians he will be free to expand his ministry elsewhere [ICC2, NAC]. As the Corinthians' faith increases it will spread through Paul's ministry [He]. As their faith increases his sphere of influence will spread beyond them [NTC]. Paul wants the track or course of his ministry to enlarge so as to include others farther on [NIC1].
  1.2 He wants to enlarge or strengthen the sphere of his ministry among the Corinthians [Car, NIC2, TG, TNTC; NLT, TEV]. As Paul's ministry is strengthened among them it will spread beyond them [NIC2; NLT].
2. Paul himself hopes to be magnified; that is, that the prestige or influence the apostles have among the Corinthians will increase [AB, EBC, HNTC, Lns, SP, TH; NAB, REB, TNT]. Paul wants his influence among them to

be enlarged and their view of him to improve [EBC]. They should be magnified rather than slandered [Lns]. Their higher view of him will help him to minister elsewhere [HNTC]. As Paul's influence among them grows it will overflow [NAB].

10:16 for[a] the evangelizing[b] (of) the lands-beyond[c] you, not for boasting in what-is-accomplished[d] in (the) sphere of-another.

LEXICON—a. εἰς (LN 89.57, 89.48) (BAGD 1.d.β. p. 228): 'for' [Lns], 'to' [KJV], 'in order to' [LN (89.57)], 'so as to' [ICC2], 'we hope to' [NAB], 'that (we may)' [AB, HNTC], 'so that we may' [NTC; NRSV], 'so that we can' [NIV], 'so that as a result' [LN (89.48)], 'the result is' [WBC], 'then we will be able' [CEV, NLT], 'then we can/may' [REB, TEV, TNT], 'by' [NJB]. This preposition is also seen as being connected to τὰ ὑπερέκεινα 'the lands beyond' instead of the verb εὐαγγελίζω 'to evangelize' [BAGD].

b. aorist mid. infin. of εὐαγγελίζω (LN 33.215) (BAGD 2.a.γ. p. 317): 'to evangelize' [Lns], 'to preach the gospel' [AB, HNTC, ICC2, NTC, WBC; KJV, NAB, NIV, NJB], 'to carry the gospel' [REB], 'to preach the good news' [CEV, NLT, TEV, TNT], 'to proclaim the good news' [NRSV], 'to tell the good news' [LN].

c. ὑπερέκεινα (LN **83.55**) (BAGD p. 840): 'beyond' [LN], 'farther away' [LN]. The phrase τὰ ὑπερέκεινα ὑμῶν 'the lands beyond you' is translated 'countries beyond you' [LN], 'places beyond you' [AB, WBC], 'other places that are far beyond you' [NLT], 'the areas beyond you' [HNTC], 'lands beyond you' [NRSV], 'lands that lie beyond you' [BAGD; REB], 'other countries beyond you' [TEV], 'regions beyond you' [ICC2, NTC; KJV, NIV, NJB, TNT], 'the parts way beyond you' [Lns], 'other lands' [CEV], 'beyond your borders' [NAB]. In the NT this word occurs only here.

d. ἕτοιμος (LN 77.2) (BAGD 1. p. 316): 'ready' [BAGD, LN], 'prepared' [LN]. The adjectival phrase τὰ ἕτοιμα 'what is accomplished' is translated 'what has been accomplished' [BAGD], 'what has been done already' [AB], 'ready-made achievements' [HNTC], 'things already accomplished' [ICC2], 'things already prepared' [Lns], 'things made ready to our hand' [KJV], 'work that is done' [NTC], 'work already done' [CEV, NAB, NIV, NJB, NRSV, REB, TEV, TNT], 'what has already been done' [WBC], not explicit [NLT].

10:17 But the one-boasting, let-him-boast in[a] (the) Lord

LEXICON—a. ἐν (LN 89.26): 'in' [AB, HNTC, Lns, NTC; KJV, NAB, NIV, NRSV], 'about' [WBC; CEV, NLT, TNT], 'of' [ICC2; NJB, REB], 'because of, on account of' [LN]. This is a marker of cause or reason which focuses on instrumentality, either of objects or events [LN], but its use here implies that the boast is actually of events in which God was acting, so that 'in the Lord' becomes 'in/about (what) the Lord (has done)' [NLT, TEV]. That this is a quotation from scripture is shown by quotation marks or italics [AB, NTC, WBC; NAB, NIV, NJB, NRSV], or by a citation formula with quotation marks [CEV, NLT, TEV, TNT].

QUESTION—What is boasting 'in the Lord'?

It is boasting about what the Lord has done [AB, ICC2, TH]. For Paul it is boasting of what God or Christ has done through him [Car, EBC, NAC, NIC1, NIC2, SP] or for him [Car, EBC]. It is to give the Lord the praise he is rightly due [Car]. Paul ascribes glory to the Lord and wants none for himself [NTC]. It is the privilege of knowing the Lord himself [TNTC]. It is to be satisfied with God's approval, not human approval [Ho].

10:18 **For (it is) not the one-commending**[a] **himself that is approved,**[b] **but the-one the Lord commends.**

LEXICON—a. pres. act. participle of συνίστημι (LN 33.344) (BAGD I.1.b. p. 790): 'to commend' [BAGD, HNTC, ICC2, NTC; KJV, NIV, NRSV], 'to recommend' [BAGD, LN, Lns, WBC; NAB, REB]. The phrase ὁ ἑαυτὸν συνιστάνων 'the one commending himself' is translated 'self-commendation' [NJB, TNT], 'the one who engages in self-commendation' [AB], 'you may brag about yourself' [CEV], 'when people boast about themselves' [NLT], 'when we think well of ourselves' [TEV]. See this word also at 3:1; 4:2; 5:12; 6:4; 7:11; 10:12.

b. δόκιμος (LN **30.115**) (BAGD 1. p. 203): 'approved' [AB, BAGD; KJV, NAB, NIV, NRSV], 'really approved' [TEV], 'accepted as approved' [HNTC], 'to be accepted' [REB], 'proved genuine' [ICC2], 'approval' [CEV], 'recognition is won' [NJB], 'considered worthy' [LN], not explicit [NLT, TNT].

QUESTION—Who is 'the Lord' here?

1. It is Christ [AB, Car, EBC, HNTC, ICC2, NCBC, NIC1, NIC2, NTC, TH, WBC]. In v.17 it is Yahweh but here it is Christ [NIC2].
2. It is God [Ho, ICC1, SP, TG].

QUESTION—How might the Lord commend someone?

It is through God's enabling Paul in his ministry [SP]. It is through the consciences of those who have been blessed by Paul's ministry [NIC1]. It is the blessing of God producing fruit in his ministry [ICC1, NIC2]. Paul is commended through the fact of the Corinthian church that exists as a result of his ministry [EGT, NIC2]. It is God's approval during life and after death [EBC]. It will occur when Christ returns [AB], or at the final judgment [Car].

DISCOURSE UNIT: 11:1–12:18 [ICC1; NJB]. The topic is the folly of glorying being forced upon Paul [ICC1], being driven to sound his own praises [NJB].

DISCOURSE UNIT: 11:1–12:13 [AB]. The topic is a fool's speech.

DISCOURSE UNIT: 11:1–12:10 [REB]. The topic is speaking as a fool.

DISCOURSE UNIT: 11:1–21a [AB]. The topic is the prologue to the fool's speech.

DISCOURSE UNIT: 11:1–15 [HNTC, TH, WBC; CEV, NAB, NIV, NLT, NRSV, TEV]. The topic is Paul and the false apostles [TH; CEV, NAB, NIV, NLT, NRSV, TEV], the emissaries identified and opposed [WBC], the church at Corinth endangered by rival apostles [HNTC].

DISCOURSE UNIT: 11:1–6 [EBC, ICC1, TNTC]. The topic is Paul's jealousy for the Corinthians [EBC], the reason for this folly [ICC1], the Corinthians' gullibility [TNTC].

DISCOURSE UNIT: 11:7–15 [ICC1, TNTC]. The topic is glorying about refusing maintenance [ICC1], the matter of financial remuneration [TNTC].

DISCOURSE UNIT: 11:7–12 [EBC]. The topic is financial dependence and independence.

DISCOURSE UNIT: 11:13–15 [EBC]. The topic is false apostles.

11:1 Would-that[a] you-would-put-up-with[b] me (in) a little foolishness.[c] Indeed,[d] do-bear-with me.

LEXICON—a. ὄφελον (LN **71.28**) (BAGD p. 599): 'would that' [BAGD, ICC2, **LN**, Lns]. This verbal particle is translated 'I would that' [WBC], 'would to God' [KJV], 'I wish' [HNTC, LN, NTC; NJB, NRSV, TEV], 'I hope' [NIV, NLT], 'I should like' [REB], 'if only' [AB], 'please (put up with/be patient)' [CEV, TNT], 'you must (endure)' [NAB].

   b. imperf. mid. indic. of ἀνέχω (LN 25.171) (BAGD 1.b. p. 65): 'to put up with' [AB, BAGD, HNTC, NTC, WBC; CEV, NIV, NJB], 'to bear with' [BAGD, Lns; KJV, NRSV, REB], 'to be patient with' [LN; NLT, TNT], 'to endure' [BAGD; NAB], 'to tolerate' [ICC2; TEV].

   c. ἀφροσύνη (LN 32.53) (BAGD p. 127): 'foolishness' [AB, BAGD, HNTC, ICC2, LN, NTC; CEV, NIV, NJB, NRSV, REB], 'folly' [Lns, WBC; KJV, NAB]. The phrase μικρόν τι ἀφροσύνης 'in a little foolishness' is translated 'as I keep on talking like a fool' [NLT], 'when I am a bit foolish' [TEV], 'I am about to be a little foolish' [TNT].

   d. ἀλλὰ καί. This phrase is translated 'indeed' [AB, NTC], 'and indeed' [KJV], 'yes' [HNTC, WBC], 'now' [ICC2], 'but' [NIV], 'but of course' [Lns], 'not that you don't' [NJB], 'I beg you' [NAB], 'please' [NLT, REB, TEV], 'do (bear with me)' [NRSV], not explicit [CEV, TNT].

QUESTION—Is the verb ἀνέχεσθε 'bear with' in the second clause imperative or indicative?

   1. It is imperative: do bear with me [AB, EGT, He, HNTC, ICC2, NAC, NTC, SP, TG, TH, WBC; KJV, NAB, NLT, NRSV, REB, TEV].

   2. It is indicative: you do bear with me [Car, Ho, ICC1, Lns, NIC1; NIV, NJB, TNT]. The statement contains irony [Car, NIC2], either in the sense that some already view him as a fool and are tolerating him like one, or because they are tolerating foolish boasting already on the part of the intruders [Car].

2 CORINTHIANS 11:1

QUESTION—What relationship is indicated by μου 'me'?
1. It is the object of the verb ἀνέχω [AB, EGT, HNTC, Ho, ICC1, Lns, NIC2, SP, TH; NLT, NRSV, REB, TEV, TNT]: bear with me.
2. It is possessive: my foolishness [BAGD, He, NTC, WBC; CEV, NAB, NIV], or foolishness from me [ICC2; NJB].

QUESTION—What is the foolishness of which he is speaking?
It is the foolishness of commending himself or boasting about himself [EBC, EGT, Ho, ICC1, ICC2, Lns, NAC, NCBC, NIC1, NIC2, TG, TNTC]. Paul finds that he must imitate the methods of the intruders [AB, Car], though not their motives [Car]. He must lower himself to the level of his opponents to commend himself [NTC]. To boast in one's own credentials is the opposite of having a sober estimate of oneself [AB]. He must talk about himself in a way that would normally be considered indiscrete [He].

11:2 For[a] I-am-jealous[b] (concerning) you with-a-jealousy[c] of-God,

LEXICON—a. γάρ (LN 89.23): 'for' [HNTC, ICC2, LN, Lns, NTC, WBC; KJV], 'you see' [NJB], not explicit [AB; CEV, NAB, NIV, NLT, NRSV, REB, TEV, TNT].
b. pres. act. indic. of ζηλόω (LN 25.46) (BAGD 1.b. p. 338): 'to be jealous' [HNTC, Lns, NTC, WBC; KJV, NAB, NIV, NLT, REB, TEV, TNT], 'to feel jealousy' [NJB, NRSV], 'to be jealously concerned' [ICC2], 'to be concerned about someone' [BAGD; CEV], 'to have a deep concern for' [LN], 'to care deeply' [AB].
c. ζῆλος (LN 25.46) (BAGD 1. p. 337): 'jealousy' [AB, HNTC, ICC2, Lns, NTC, WBC; all versions except CEV, TEV], not explicit [CEV, TEV]. The phrase θεοῦ ζήλῳ 'a jealousy of God' is translated 'God's jealousy' [Lns], 'God's own jealousy' [AB, HNTC; NJB, TNT], 'the jealousy of God himself' [NAB, NLT], 'the jealousy of God' [REB], 'divine jealousy' [ICC2; NRSV], 'a jealousy that originates in God' [NTC], 'a jealousy God inspires in me' [WBC], 'as concerned about you as God is' [CEV], 'jealous for you, just as God is' [TEV], 'godly jealousy' [KJV, NIV]. See this word also at 7:7, 11; 9:2.

QUESTION—What relationship is indicated by γάρ 'for'?
1. It indicates the reason for his request [AB, Car, EBC, HNTC, Ho, ICC2, Lns, NIC2, NTC]: bear with me in a little foolishness because I am jealous concerning you.
2. It introduces the reason for his foolishness [NIC1]: I am foolishly boasting because I am jealous concerning you.

QUESTION—What area of meaning is intended by ζηλόω 'I am jealous'?
It is a zeal for them and about them prompted by ardent love and personal interest, [NTC]. It is a zealous affection and anxiety about them [AB]. It is a deep and jealous concern [ICC2], a loving, anxious concern [NIC1], an intense concern [TG]. It is an ardent love mixed with personal interest [NTC]. It is a concern to protect the God's honor of another [Ho, ICC2]. It is a passionate concern for their devotion to Christ [EBC]. Paul is zealous to

preserve their purity and devotion to Christ [NAC]. He has an affectionate jealousy about their purity [NCBC]. It is a mixture of outrage at their fickleness, a deep concern for their spiritual well-being, and fear for their future if they don't repent [Car]. Paul fears that they will abandon the faith [HNTC]. (Commentators do not discuss any distinction between 'zeal' and 'jealousy', which in English are distinct and different, though related.)

QUESTION—What is a jealousy that is 'of God'?

It has its source in God [AB, EBC, Ho, NIC2, NTC, TH]. God inspires it in him [WBC]. It is like God's own jealousy [Car, EBC, Ho, ICC1, NIC1, SP, TNTC]. It is divine, not selfish [NCBC]. It is on God's behalf [EGT, Ho]. Paul's jealousy reflects the heart of God [Car]. It is a religious zeal [He]. He has the same concern that God has [Lns, TG], which is for their purity [Lns]. It is a divine jealousy; just as God tolerates no rivals, so also Paul does not tolerate rivals who would corrupt the faith of the Corinthians [NAC]. Paul is jealous for God's interests in the Corinthian church [WBC].

for^a I-betrothed^b you to-one husband^c to present-you^d to Christ (as) a pure^e virgin.^{f}

LEXICON—a. γάρ (LN 89.23): 'for' [AB, HNTC, ICC2, LN, Lns; KJV, NLT, NRSV, REB], 'because' [WBC], 'since' [NAB], not explicit [NTC; CEV, NJB, TEV, TNT].

b. aorist mid. indic. of ἁρμόζω (LN 34.74) (BAGD 3. p. 107): 'to betroth' [AB, BAGD, HNTC, ICC2; REB, TNT], 'to give in marriage' [BAGD, NTC; NAB, NJB], 'to promise in marriage' [LN, WBC; TEV], 'to espouse' [Lns; KJV], 'to promise to' [NIV, NLT], 'to promise in marriage to' [NRSV], 'to choose as a bride for' [CEV].

c. ανήρ (LN 10.53, 9.24): 'husband' [LN (10.53), Lns; KJV, NAB, NIV, NJB, NLT, NRSV, REB, TNT], 'man' [AB, HNTC, ICC2, LN (9.24), NTC; TEV], not explicit [CEV]. The phrase ἑνὶ ἀνδρί 'one husband' is translated 'to one husband' [KJV, NAB, NIV, NLT, NRSV], 'to one as husband' [Lns], 'to a single husband' [WBC; NJB], 'to (her) true and only husband' [REB], 'to him as your one husband' [TNT], 'to one man' [AB, HNTC, ICC2, NTC], 'to one man only' [TEV], 'chosen only for (Christ)' [CEV].

d. aorist act. infin. of παρίστημι (LN **57.81**) (BAGD 1.b.a. p. 627): 'to present to' [AB, BAGD, HNTC, ICC2, LN, Lns, NTC, WBC; KJV, NAB, NIV, NRSV, REB, TNT], not explicit [CEV, NLT, TEV]. This verb is also translated as a phrase: 'for presentation to' [NJB].

e. ἁγνός (LN 88.28) (BAGD 1. p. 12): 'pure' [AB, BAGD, HNTC, ICC2, LN, Lns, NTC; NIV, NJB, NLT, TEV, TNT], 'chaste' [BAGD; KJV, NAB, NRSV, REB], 'undefiled' [WBC], not explicit [CEV, NLT].

g. παρθένος (LN 9.39) (BAGD 1. p. 627): 'virgin' [BAGD, HNTC, ICC2, LN, Lns, NTC, WBC; all versions except NLT]. The phrase 'pure virgin' is translated 'pure bride' [AB; NLT].

QUESTION—Of which verb is ἑνὶ ἀνδρὶ 'to one husband' the indirect object?
1. It is the object of ἁρμόζω 'to betroth' [AB, HNTC, Ho, ICC1, ICC2, Lns, NTC, SP, WBC; KJV, NAB, NIV, NJB, NLT, NRSV, TEV, TNT]: I betrothed you to one husband.
2. It is the object of παρίστημι 'to present' [REB]: to present you to one husband.

11:3 But[a] I-fear[b] lest[c] as the serpent deceived[d] Eve in his cunning,[e]
LEXICON—a. δέ (LN 89.124): 'but' [AB, ICC2, Lns, NTC; CEV, KJV, NIV, NJB, NLT, NRSV, TNT], 'however' [WBC], 'and' [HNTC], 'now' [REB], not explicit [NAB, TEV].
  b. pres. mid. or pass. (deponent = act.) indic. of φοβέομαι (LN 25.252) (BAGD 1.a. p. 863): 'to fear' [AB, ICC2, LN; CEV, KJV, NLT], 'to be afraid' [BAGD, HNTC, LN, Lns, NTC; NIV, NJB, NRSV, REB, TEV, TNT]. The phrase 'I fear' is translated 'my fear is' [WBC; NAB].
  c. μή πως (LN 89.62): 'lest' [HNTC, LN], 'lest perhaps' [ICC2], 'lest in some way' [Lns], 'lest by any means' [KJV], 'that somehow' [NTC; NIV, NLT, TNT], 'that' [AB, WBC; CEV, NAB, NJB, REB, TEV]. The phrase μή πως 'lest' marks negative purpose and often implies apprehension: 'in order that...not, so that...not, lest' [LN].
  d. aorist act. indicative of ἐξαπατάω (LN 31.12) (BAGD p. 273): 'to deceive' [BAGD, HNTC, ICC2, LN, Lns, NTC; NIV, NLT, NRSV, TEV, TNT], 'to quite deceive' [AB], 'to lead astray' [BAGD, WBC], 'to mislead' [LN], 'to trick' [CEV], 'to beguile' [KJV], 'to seduce' [NAB, NJB, REB].
  e. πανουργία (LN **88.270**) (BAGD p. 608): 'cunning' [BAGD; NAB, NIV, NJB, NRSV, REB, TNT], 'craftiness' [AB, BAGD, HNTC, ICC2, LN, Lns, NTC, WBC], 'trickery' [BAGD], 'treachery' [**LN**], 'clever lies' [TEV], 'subtilty' [KJV], not explicit [NLT]. The phrase 'the serpent deceived (Eve) in his craftiness' is translated 'tricked by that lying snake' [CEV]. See this word also at 4:2.
QUESTION—What is Paul's assumption about the identity of the serpent?
The serpent is Satan [AB, EGT, He, Lns, NAC, NIC1, NIC2, NTC, SP, TH, TNTC, WBC].

your minds[a] may-be-corrupted[b] away-from sincerity[c] and purity[d] toward[e] Christ.
TEXT—The phrase καὶ τῆς ἁγνότητος 'and purity' does not occur in some manuscripts. It is included in brackets by GNT with a C rating, indicating difficulty in deciding whether or not to include it in the text. It is omitted by HNTC, WBC; KJV, NJB, REB.
LEXICON—a. νόημα (LN **26.14**, 30.15) (BAGD 1. p. 540): 'mind' [AB, BAGD, HNTC, ICC2, **LN** (26.14), WBC; KJV, NIV, NJB, TEV, TNT], 'thought' [LN (30.15), Lns, NTC; NAB, NRSV, REB], 'you' [NLT]. This noun is also translated as a verb: 'to think' [CEV]. See this word also at 2:11; 3:14; 4:4; 10:5.

b. aorist pass. subj. of φθείρω (LN 20.23, 88.266) (BAGD 2.b. p. 857): 'to be corrupted' [BAGD, HNTC, Lns, NTC, WBC; KJV, NAB, REB, TEV, TNT], 'to be corruptly diverted' [ICC2], 'to be lured away' [AB], 'to be led away' [NLT], 'to be led astray' [NIV, NJB, NRSV] 'to be ruined' [BAGD, LN (20.23, 88.266)]. The phrase 'your minds may be corrupted away from sincerity and purity toward Christ' is translated 'you might stop thinking about Christ in an honest and sincere way' [CEV]. See this word also at 7:2.

c. ἁπλότης (LN 88.44) (BAGD 1. p. 86): 'sincerity' [BAGD, HNTC, LN], 'sincere devotion' [BAGD; NAB, NIV, NRSV, TNT], 'simplicity' [BAGD; KJV], 'simple devotion' [NLT], 'single-mindedness' [Lns], 'single-minded devotion' [NJB], 'single-hearted devotion' [REB], 'full devotion' [TEV], 'total commitment' [AB], 'in an honest way' [CEV]. See this word also at 1:12; 8:2; 9:11, 13.

d. ἁγνότης (LN 88.29) (BAGD p. 12): 'purity' [BAGD, LN, Lns, NTC], 'pure devotion' [AB, ICC2; NIV, NLT, NRSV, TEV, TNT], 'sincerity' [BAGD], 'pure commitment' [AB], 'in a sincere way' [CEV], 'complete devotion' [NAB], omitted [HNTC, WBC; KJV, NJB, REB]. See this word also at 6:6.

e. εἰς (LN 90.59): 'toward' [LN], 'to' [AB, HNTC, ICC2, LN, Lns, WBC; NAB, NIV, NJB, NLT, NRSV, REB, TEV], 'in' [KJV], 'for' [LN], not explicit [CEV, TNT].

11:4 For[a] if the one-coming[b] preaches[c] another[d] Jesus whom we-did- not - preach,

LEXICON—a. γάρ (LN 89.23): 'for' [AB, HNTC, LN, Lns, NTC, WBC; KJV, NIV, NRSV, REB, TEV], 'for, indeed' [ICC2], 'because' [LN; NJB], 'I say this because' [NAB], not explicit [CEV, NLT, TNT].

b. pres. mid. or pass. (deponent = act.) participle of ἔρχομαι (LN 15.81) (BAGD I.1.a.θ. p. 311): 'to come' [BAGD, LN]. The phrase 'the one coming' is translated 'someone comes' [NTC; NAB, NIV, NRSV, TNT], 'a person comes' [AB], 'the person who has come to you' [WBC], 'he who comes to you' [Lns], 'he that cometh' [KJV], 'your visitor' [HNTC, ICC2], 'some newcomer' [REB], 'any chance comer' [NJB], 'anyone who comes to you' [TEV], 'anyone' [NLT], 'some people' [CEV].

c. pres. act. indic. of κηρύσσω (LN 33.256) (BAGD 2.b.β. p. 431): 'to preach' [AB, BAGD, ICC2, LN, Lns; KJV, NAB, NIV, NJB, NLT, TEV], 'to proclaim' [BAGD, HNTC, NTC, WBC; NRSV, REB, TNT], 'tell about' [CEV].

d. ἄλλος (LN 58.36, 58.37) (BAGD 1.e.α. p. 40): 'another' [BAGD, HNTC, ICC2, LN (58.37), Lns; CEV, KJV, NAB, NRSV, REB], 'some other' [AB], 'other than' [LN (58.36), NTC; NIV, NJB], 'different' [BAGD, LN (58.36); NLT, TEV, TNT].

QUESTION—What relationship is indicated by γάρ 'for'?
1. It indicates another reason for the appeal of 11:1, which is that if they can tolerate the intruders, they can tolerate Paul's boasting [AB, Car, EBC, Ho, ICC2].
2. It bridges 11:3–4, introducing an explanation of what he has just said about his fear of them being led astray [ICC1, ICC2, Lns, NIC2, NTC].
3. It gives grounds for the appeal of 11:1 as well as introducing an explanation about his fear of their being led astray [HNTC].

QUESTION—Does ὁ ἐρχόμενος 'the one coming' refer to a specific individual?
1. It refers to a specific person or persons [EBC, HNTC, Lns, NAC, TH, WBC]. It refers to a particular group or its representative [TH]. It refers to the leader of the opposing group [NTC, WBC]. It is a representative singular, referring to specific ones who have already come and generally to any who will come in the future [Lns]. It is an indirect way of referring to his opponents [NAC].
2. It is indefinite or generic, referring generally to a class or type of person [AB, EGT, Ho, ICC1, NIC1, NIC2].

QUESTION—What is meant by 'another Jesus'?
They had an interpretation of the earthly ministry of Jesus that was radically different from Paul's [EBC]. They were preaching a message that was inconsistent with the facts about Jesus [TH]. Paul's statement is simply a condemnation of their wrong teaching about Jesus [AB].
1. They had a triumphalist understanding of Jesus [ICC2, NAC, NTC, TNTC, WBC]. Their interpretation of Jesus was not consistent with the facts of his life and death, and probably gave too little emphasis on his humiliation or suffering [NAC, NTC]. They focused on his power and glory [ICC2, TNTC], but not his weakness and suffering [TNTC]. They proclaimed a lordly, triumphalist Jesus, with themselves as his powerful representatives [WBC].
2. They were Judaizers [Car, Lns, NIC2]. They emphasized the Jewishness of Jesus the Nazarene and the continuation of the Mosaic covenant, but not his lordship as Christ [NIC2]. They presented a different picture of Jesus which stressed his Jewishness in a false way [Lns]. Their Judaizing message diminished their understanding of the sufficiency of Christ, adding supplemental things that are based on human merit and effort as necessary for salvation [Car]. They viewed Jesus from his human side only [He].
3. They were proclaiming some person other than Jesus the son of Mary as deliverer from sin [Ho].

or you-receive^a a different^b spirit which you-did- not -receive, or a different gospel^c which you-did- not -accept,^d you tolerate^e (that) well.^f

LEXICON—a. pres. act. indic. of λαμβάνω (LN 57.125) (BAGD 2. p. 465): 'to receive' [AB, BAGD, HNTC, ICC2, LN, NTC; all versions except TEV], 'to accept' [LN; TEV], 'to get' [Lns], 'to welcome' [WBC].
- b. ἕτερος (LN 58.36, 58.37) (BAGD 1.b.γ. p. 315): 'different' [BAGD, HNTC, ICC2, LN (58.36), Lns, NTC, WBC; NAB, NIV, NJB, NLT, NRSV, REB, TNT], 'completely different' [TEV], 'another' [AB, BAGD, LN (58.37); CEV, KJV], 'other than' [LN (58.36)]. This word is used interchangeably with ἄλλος as its equivalent [BAGD].
- c. εὐαγγέλιον (LN 33.217) (BAGD 2.a. p. 318): 'gospel' [AB, BAGD, HNTC, ICC2, LN, Lns, WBC; all versions except CEV], 'good news' [BAGD, LN], 'message' [CEV]. See this word also at 8:18; 10:14.
- d. aorist mid. indic. of δέχομαι (LN 57.125) (BAGD 1. p. 177): 'to accept' [AB, HNTC, ICC2, LN, WBC; CEV, KJV, NAB, NIV, NJB, NRSV, REB, TNT], 'to receive' [BAGD, LN, Lns, NTC; NLT, TEV]. See this word also at 6:1.
- e. pres. mid. indic. of ἀνέχω (LN 25.171) (BAGD 1.c. p. 66): 'to tolerate' [ICC2; TEV], 'to put up with' [AB, BAGD, HNTC, NTC, WBC; NIV, NJB, REB], 'to be patient' [LN; TNT], 'to bear' [Lns], 'to bear with' [KJV], 'to endure' [NAB], 'to submit to' [NRSV]. The phrase 'you tolerate (that) well' is translated 'you let them (tell you)…you are ready (to receive)' [CEV], 'you seem to believe what anyone tells you' [NLT]. See this word also at 11:1.
- f. καλῶς (LN 65.23) (BAGD 6. p. 401): 'well' [BAGD, LN, Lns; KJV], 'well enough' [AB, BAGD, NTC; REB], 'quite well' [NAB], 'right well' [WBC], 'all right' [HNTC], 'splendidly' [ICC2], 'wonderfully' [TNT], 'easily enough' [NIV], 'readily enough' [NRSV], 'gladly' [TEV], 'only too willingly' [NJB], not explicit [CEV, NLT].

QUESTION—What does it mean to 'receive a different spirit'?
1. It refers to a false spirit, different from the Holy Spirit [He, ICC2, Lns, NAC, NIC2, NTC, SP, TG]: instead of the Holy Spirit, you received a false spirit. The Holy Spirit is a person but the 'different spirit' is a fiction just as a different gospel is no gospel at all [Lns]. It means believing strange ideas about the Holy Spirit [He]. If Jesus is really different from what Paul had taught them, then the nature of the gospel and of the Holy Spirit must also be different [SP]. The different spirit is a misinterpretation of the Holy Spirit, understood primarily in terms of power, ecstasy or visions [NAC]. Acceptance of a different understanding of Jesus implies a different understanding of the Holy Spirit also [ICC2]. Paul is using irony to express the absurdity of receiving another spirit, since believing another gospel does not confer the Spirit [NIC2]. A different spirit would be a Satanic spirit [TG].
2. It refers to a different and wrong attitude [Car, NIC1, TNTC, WBC]. It refers to a kind of experience, such as a spirit of bondage [Car, ICC1] and

a different gospel results in a different religious experience [NIC1]. It refers to certain effects of Christian living expressed in attitude or deportment [WBC]. The attitude in which Paul's opponents operated was authoritarian and overbearing and was inspired by Satan [TNTC].

QUESTION—Is there any difference between the terms λαμβάνω 'receive' and δέχομαι 'accept'?
1. They are used synonymously [AB, HNTC, NIC2, SP, WBC; NLT, REB, TNT].
2. The distinction is that the action of receiving the Spirit is not necessarily voluntary, but accepting the gospel is voluntary [Ho, ICC1, NTC]. Λαμβάνω is more passive, δέχομαι is more active [Lns].

11:5 For[a] I-consider[b] (myself) to-be-inferior[c] (in) nothing[d] to the super[e] apostles.

LEXICON—a. γάρ (LN 89.23, 91.1): 'for' [HNTC, ICC2, LN, NTC, WBC; KJV], 'well' [Lns], 'now' [NJB], 'but' [NIV, NLT], not explicit [AB; CEV, NAB, NRSV, REB, TEV, TNT].
  b. pres. mid. or pass. (deponent = act.) indic. of λογίζομαι (LN 31.1) (BAGD 3. p. 476): 'to consider' [AB, HNTC, LN; NAB, NJB], 'to think' [BAGD, NTC; CEV, NIV, NLT, NRSV, TEV], 'to reckon' [ICC2, Lns; TNT], 'to count' [WBC], 'to suppose' [KJV], 'to be aware of' [REB]. See this word also at 3:5; 5:19; 10:2, 7, 11.
  c. pres. act. infin. of ὑστερέω (LN 87.65) (BAGD 1.c. p. 849): 'to be inferior' [AB, BAGD, ICC2, LN, NTC, WBC; NAB, NIV, NJB, NLT, NRSV, REB, TEV, TNT], 'to be less than' [BAGD], 'to come behind' [HNTC, Lns], 'to be behind' [KJV], 'to lack honor' [LN]. The phrase 'to be inferior in nothing' is translated 'I am as good as' [CEV].
  d. μηδείς (LN 92.23) (BAGD 2.b.β. p. 518): 'in nothing' [BAGD, LN; NAB], 'in regard to nothing' [Lns], 'in no way' [AB, BAGD, HNTC, ICC2, WBC; TNT], 'not in any way' [REB], 'in the least' [NTC; NIV, NJB, NRSV], 'the least bit' [TEV], 'not at all' [BAGD], 'not a whit' [KJV], not explicit [CEV, NLT].
  e. ὑπερλίαν (LN **78.34**) (BAGD p. 841): 'exceedingly, beyond measure' [BAGD]. The phrase ὑπερλίαν ἀποστόλων is translated 'super apostles' [AB, BAGD, HNTC, ICC2, NTC; CEV, NAB, NIV, NJB, NLT, NRSV, REB], 'superfine apostles' [Lns], 'very exceptional apostles' [LN], 'the highest ranking apostle' [WBC], 'the very chiefest apostles' [KJV], 'very superior apostles' [TNT], 'very special apostles' [**LN**], 'those very special so-called apostles of yours' [TEV]. In the New Testament this word is found only here and in 12:11.

QUESTION—What relationship is indicated by γάρ 'for'?
1. It indicates another reason for his appeal in 11:1 [Car, EBC, Ho, ICC2, NIC2]: bear with me because I am not inferior to the super apostles.
2. It gives a somewhat sarcastic rationale for the appeal in 11:1: since you tolerate these others, surely you can tolerate me [ICC1].

3. It refers to and summarizes all of 11:4 [Lns]: 'with regard to that I say...'
QUESTION—Who are the 'super apostles' he is referring to?
  1. They are the intruders in Corinth [AB, Car, EGT, HNTC, ICC1, ICC2, Lns, NAC, NIC1, NIC2, NTC, SP, TNTC]. They are Judaizers [Car, ICC1, NTC], they are false apostles [AB, EGT, TNTC]. Paul is using irony and sarcasm in describing them as this way [AB, ICC1, Lns, NIC1, NIC2, TG, TH].
  2. They are the twelve apostles in Jerusalem [EBC, He, HNTC, Ho, NCBC, WBC]. Paul uses the term 'super apostles' because this reflects the distorted estimation that the intruders have of the Jerusalem apostles [EBC, He, NCBC, WBC].

11:6 But[a] even if[b] (I am) unskilled[c] in-speech,[d] yet[e] (I am) not in knowledge,[f]

LEXICON—a. δέ (LN 89.124): 'but' [ICC2, LN, Lns; KJV], not explicit [AB, HNTC, NTC, WBC; CEV, NAB, NIV, NJB, NLT, NRSV, REB, TEV, TNT].
  b. The phrase εἰ δὲ καί 'but even if (I am)' is translated 'even if there is' [NJB], 'even though I am' [AB], 'but if I am' [ICC2], 'if, indeed, I am' [Lns], 'though I be' [KJV], 'I may be' [HNTC, NTC; NAB, NRSV, TNT], 'I may indeed be' [WBC], 'I may not speak/be' [CEV, NIV, NLT, REB], 'perhaps I am' [TEV].
  c. ἰδιώτης (LN **27.26**) (BAGD 1. p. 370): 'unskilled' [BAGD, HNTC, NTC; NAB], 'layman' [BAGD, ICC2, LN], 'amateur' [AB, BAGD, **LN**; TEV], 'untrained' [WBC; NRSV], 'not trained' [NIV, NLT], 'no (speaker)' [REB], 'a nonprofessional' [Lns], 'inexpert' [TNT], 'something lacking (in)' [NJB], 'rude' [KJV]. The phrase 'unskilled in speech' is translated 'I may not speak as well as they do' [CEV].
  d. λόγος (LN 33.99) (BAGD 1.a.α. p. 477): 'speech' [HNTC, LN, NTC; KJV, NAB, NRSV], 'public speaking' [AB, WBC; NJB], 'oratory' [ICC2], 'speaking' [TEV], 'speaker' [NIV, NLT, REB, TNT]. This noun is also translated as a verb: 'to speak' [CEV]. See this word also at 1:18; 2:17; 5:19; 6:7; 8:7; 10:10, 11.
  e. ἀλλά (LN 91.2) (BAGD p. 38): 'yet' [BAGD, ICC2, LN; KJV], 'but' [HNTC, NTC, WBC; CEV, NAB, NIV, NLT, NRSV, REB, TEV, TNT], 'at least' [BAGD], 'nevertheless' [Lns], not explicit [AB; NJB].
  f. γνῶσις (LN 28.17) (BAGD 2. p. 163): 'knowledge' [AB, BAGD, HNTC, ICC2, LN, Lns, NTC, WBC; KJV, NAB, NIV, NJB, NRSV, REB, TEV]. The phrase 'but not in knowledge' is translated 'I know as much' [CEV], 'I know what I am talking about' [NLT], 'I am as well informed' [TNT]. See this word also at 6:6.
QUESTION—What is Paul saying about his own communication skills?
Paul admits that he lacks professional training in the kind of eloquent oratory so prized by Greeks [EGT, He, Ho, ICC1, NAC, NIC1, NTC], particularly the kind of oratory that the Sophists engage in [AB, HNTC, ICC2, NAC]. He

grants that he is not as rhetorically gifted as his rivals [NIC2, TNTC], or that his skills don't measure up to their standards [WBC]. He says this with irony [NIC1]. Paul only acknowledges that he does not use the artificial techniques of Greek orators and rhetoricians [Car, Lns], not that he had no speaking ability [Ho, Lns]. Paul has consciously rejected such a criterion, but he is not inferior when judged by the right criteria [Car].

but[a] in every-way[b] (and) in everything[c] having-manifested[d] (this) to you.
LEXICON—a. ἀλλά (LN 89.125): 'but' [LN; KJV], 'instead' [LN], 'on the contrary' [HNTC, LN], 'to the contrary' [ICC2], 'rather' [WBC], 'yea' [Lns], 'and' [CEV], 'certainly' [AB, NTC; NRSV], not explicit [NAB, NIV, NJB, NLT, REB, TEV, TNT].
  b. The phrase ἐν παντί (dative singular of πᾶς) is translated 'in every way' [AB, HNTC, ICC2, Lns, WBC; NIV, NRSV], 'in every possible way' [TNT], 'in every conceivable way' [NAB], 'in every respect' [NTC], 'at all times' [NJB, REB, TEV], 'in all circumstances' [TNT], 'thoroughly' [KJV], 'perfectly' [CEV], not explicit [CEV, NAB]. The phrase ἐν παντί...ἐν πᾶσιν 'in every way (and) in everything' is translated 'again and again' [NLT].
  c. The phrase ἐν πᾶσιν (dative plural of πᾶς) is translated 'in all things' [AB, HNTC, NTC; KJV, NRSV], 'all its aspects' [ICC2], 'in all respects' [Lns], 'in all conditions' [TEV], 'in all circumstances' [TNT], not explicit [CEV, NLT]. This is also translated as referring to people: 'to all' [WBC], 'before everyone' [NJB]. The phrase 'in everything having manifested (this) to you' is translated 'we have made known to you the full truth' [REB], 'we have made this perfectly clear to you' [NIV].
  d. aorist act. participle of φανερόω (LN 28.36) (BAGD 2.b.α. p. 853): 'to make known' [BAGD, LN; REB], 'to make clear' [AB; CEV, NIV, TEV], 'to make plain' [TNT], 'to make manifest' [KJV], 'to make evident' [NAB, NRSV], 'to reveal' [HNTC, ICC2], 'to show openly' [NJB], 'to prove' [NLT]. See this word also at 2:14; 3:3; 4:10; 5:10, 11; 7:12.

11:7 Or did-I-commit a sin[a] (by) humbling[b] myself so-that you might-be-lifted-up,[c] because I-preached[d] the gospel[e] of-God to you without-charge?[f]
LEXICON—a. ἁμαρτία (LN 88.289) (BAGD 1. p. 43): 'sin' [AB, BAGD, HNTC, ICC2, LN; NIV, NRSV], 'offense' [KJV, REB]. The phrase ἁμαρτίαν ἐποίησα 'did I commit a sin' is translated 'did I sin' [NTC], 'did I do wrong' [WBC; NLT], 'could I have done wrong' [NAB], 'have I done wrong' [NJB], 'was it wrong for me' [CEV], 'was this my offense' [REB], 'was that wrong of me' [TEV], 'was that sinful' [TNT]. See this word also at 5:21.
  b. pres. act. participle of ταπεινόω (LN 88.56) (BAGD 2.a. p. 804): 'to humble' [BAGD, HNTC, LN, WBC; NAB, NJB, NLT, NRSV, REB, TEV], 'to demean' [AB], 'to lower' [ICC2, Lns, NTC; CEV, NIV], 'to

abase' [KJV]. The phrase ἐμαυτὸν ταπεινῶν 'humbling myself' is translated 'I put myself last' [TNT].
   c. aorist pass. subj. of ὑψόω (LN 87.20) (BAGD 2.p. 851): 'to be lifted up' [BAGD, WBC], 'to be exalted' [AB, BAGD, HNTC, LN, Lns; KJV, NRSV], 'to be raised up' [NJB], 'to be elevated' [ICC2]. This passive form is also translated actively with Paul as the subject: 'to exalt' [NTC; NAB, REB], 'to elevate' [NIV], 'to honor' [CEV, NLT], 'to make important' [TEV], 'to put (you) first' [TNT].
   d. aorist mid. indic. of εὐαγγελίζω (LN 33.215) (BAGD 2.a.α. p. 317): 'to preach' [AB, BAGD, HNTC, ICC2, Lns; all versions except NRSV], 'to proclaim' [BAGD, NTC, WBC; NRSV], 'to tell the good news, to announce the gospel' [LN]. See this word also at 10:16.
   e. εὐαγγέλιον (LN 33.217) (BAGD 1.c., 2.b.β. p. 318): 'the gospel' [AB, BAGD, HNTC, ICC2, LN, Lns, NTC; KJV, NAB, NIV, NJB, REB], 'the good news' [BAGD, LN, WBC; NLT, NRSV, TEV, TNT], 'message' [CEV]. See this word also at 8:18; 10:14; 11:4.
   f. δωρεάν (LN 57.85) (BAGD 1. p. 210): 'free of charge' [AB, NTC; CEV, NAB, NIV, NRSV], 'freely' [KJV], 'as a free gift' [LN], 'without levying a charge' [WBC] 'for nothing' [HNTC; NJB], 'without cost' [LN], 'without payment' [BAGD, LN], 'gratis' [BAGD, Lns], 'without financial reward' [ICC2], 'without expecting anything in return' [NLT], 'I made no charge' [REB], 'I did not charge you' [TEV], 'I charged you nothing' [TNT].
QUESTION—What relationship is indicated by ἤ 'or'?
   It signals a question [WBC], or a rhetorical question [AB, ICC1, NIC2]. [ICC1]. It introduces yet another complaint which he must answer [HNTC, NTC]. It connects this verse with 'unskilled' in the previous verse; he is saying sarcastically that surely someone with something worth saying should charge for it [NIC1]. It connects this verse with the statement in the previous verse; I was clearly manifested as an apostle—or do you think that I am not one just because I did not take the rights of an apostle? [Ho].
QUESTION—What does Paul imply by asking 'did I commit a sin'?
   Paul is using irony and sarcastic exaggeration [EGT, HNTC, NAC, NIC1, NIC2, SP, TG, TH, TNTC, WBC]. This rhetorical question expects a negative answer [AB, ICC1, NIC2, TH]. Paul is asking that if they don't admit the assertions of 11:6, would they then conclude that he sinned in humbling himself to help them and preaching without charge [ICC1].
QUESTION—What is the 'sin' of which Paul is supposedly guilty?
   It is the offense of refusing to participate in the system of donor patronage that was a social norm in the Greco-Roman world because he wanted to avoid the obligations involved in receiving such gifts [ICC2, NAC, NIC2]. The "sin" would be violating the law that a teacher's worth is measure by his fee [NIC1].

QUESTION—In what way did Paul humble himself?
Paul humbled himself by doing manual labor [AB, Car, EBC, ICC1, ICC2, NIC2, SP, TNTC, WBC] and by the deprivation and poverty he experienced [HNTC, ICC2]. He humbled himself by taking no pay, supporting himself instead [Ho, Lns, SP]. Paul experiences humiliation through their treatment of him in recent visits [NIC2]. Paul endures humiliation and shows respect for the Corinthians [TH].

QUESTION—In what way were they being lifted up?
They were spiritually enriched [EGT, HNTC, Ho, ICC2]. They were lifted up to be children of the highest [Lns]. They were lifted to a position of honor in God's presence [NTC]. They were lifted out of their idolatry and their sinful past [Car, EBC]. They were lifted by their conversion [AB]. They were lifted up by the respect Paul showed them even as he endured humiliation [TH]. They were lifted from heathen sins to righteous living [ICC1]. They are exalted by being joined to Christ by the gospel Paul preached [NIC2].

QUESTION—How are the nouns related in the genitive construction 'the gospel of God'?

1. It is subjective: a gospel which came from God [AB, BAGD, ICC1, Lns, NIC2, TG, TH; CEV, NLT, NRSV]. The phrase 'of God' is emphatic: was it a sin to give you something as precious as God's gift for nothing? [Lns, NIC2]. There is a contrast between 'a different gospel' and the one that comes from God [AB, TH]. It is emphatic, emphasizing God's gospel, which is precious, as opposed to what is not a gospel at all [ICC1].
2. It is both subjective and objective [NTC, TG, TH]. It is the gospel that is from God [TG, TH] and is about how God saves [TG]. 'The gospel of God' belongs to God and is proclaimed for God [NTC]. It is the same as 'the gospel of Christ' [NTC].

11:8 I-robbed[a] other churches, taking support[b] for ministry[c] to-you,
LEXICON—a. aorist act. indicative of συλάω (LN **57.234**) (BAGD p. 776): 'to rob' [BAGD, HNTC, LN, Lns, NTC, WBC; CEV, KJV, NAB, NIV, NJB, NLT, NRSV, REB], 'to plunder' [AB, ICC2]. This verb is used in a highly figurative sense [BAGD, LN]. It is translated 'I was robbing them, so to speak' [TEV], 'was that robbery?' [TNT].
b. ὀψώνιον (LN **57.118**) (BAGD 1.b. p. 602): 'support' [BAGD, NTC; NAB, NIV, NRSV, REB], 'money for support' [LN], 'money' [CEV], 'wages' [BAGD; KJV, NJB], 'pay' [AB, HNTC, ICC2], 'sustenance' [Lns], 'expenses' [WBC; TNT], 'contributions' [NLT]. The phrase λαβὼν ὀψώνιον 'taking wages' is translated 'I was paid' [TEV].
c. διακονία (LN 35.21) (BAGD 1. p. 184): 'ministry' [LN, Lns, WBC], 'service' [BAGD]. The phrase πρὸς τὴν ὑμῶν διακονίαν 'for ministry to you' is translated 'to serve you' [NTC; CEV, REB, TNT], 'in order to serve you' [AB; NRSV], 'that I might be able to serve you' [HNTC], 'so as to serve you' [NIV], 'so I could serve you' [NLT], 'to do you service'

[ICC2; KJV], 'in order to minister to you' [NAB], 'in fulfillment of my ministry to you' [WBC], 'in order to work for you' [NJB], 'in order to help you' [TEV]. See this word also at 3:7, 8; 5:18; 8:4; 9:12, 13.

QUESTION—How did Paul 'rob' other churches?

Paul 'robbed' them only in the sense that he took money from them without having giving them any service in return [Car, ICC1, NIC1, TNTC]. In response to a charge that he was living at the expense of the Corinthians he sarcastically says that he robbed other churches in order to serve Corinth [He]. It was robbing in the sense that those who gave could hardly afford what they were giving [HNTC].

11:9 and (while) being with you and having-need[a] I-burdened[b] no-one; for the brothers[c] coming from Macedonia supplied[d] my need,[e]

LEXICON—a. aorist pass. participle of ὑστερέω (LN 57.37) (BAGD 2. p. 849): 'to be in need' [AB, LN; CEV, NRSV, TNT], 'to run into need' [WBC], 'to need something' [NIV], 'to need money' [NTC; NJB, TEV], 'to lack' [BAGD, LN], 'to want' [LN; KJV], 'to fall into want' [HNTC], 'to be in want' [ICC2; NAB], 'to get behind' [Lns], 'to run short' [REB], 'to not have enough to live on' [NLT]. See this word also at 11:5.

b. aorist act. indicative of καταναρκάω (LN **57.224**) (BAGD p. 415): 'to burden' [AB, BAGD, HNTC, **LN**; NRSV], 'to be a burden to someone' [BAGD, LN, NTC; NAB, NIV, NJB], 'to make oneself a burden' [HNTC; TNT], 'to be a dead weight' [Lns], 'to lay a financial burden on' [WBC], 'to become a charge on someone' [REB], 'to be chargeable to' [KJV], 'to bother' [CEV], 'to bother (you) for help' [TEV], 'to ask (you) to help' [NLT].

c. ἀδελφός (LN 11.23): 'brother' [AB, HNTC, ICC2, Lns, NTC, WBC; KJV, NAB, NIV, NJB, NLT, TNT], '(Christian) brother' [LN], 'fellow believer' [LN], 'the Lord's followers' [CEV], 'friend' [NRSV, REB], 'believer' [TEV]. See this word also at 1:1, 8; 2:13; 8:1.

d. aorist act. indicative of προσαναπληρόω (LN 35.34) (BAGD p. 711): 'to supply' [AB, BAGD, HNTC, ICC2, NTC; KJV, NAB, NIV, NRSV, TNT], 'to fill up' [Lns], 'to make good (my deficiency)' [WBC], 'to provide fully' [LN], 'to bring (what is needed/a gift)' [CEV, NJB, NLT, TEV], 'to be fully met' [REB]. The use of the double compound verb could imply the idea of ample provision: 'as much as I needed' [NJB], 'my needs were fully met' [REB], 'brought me everything I needed' [TEV], 'they more than supplied my need' [TNT]. See this word also at 9:12.

e. ὑστέρημα (LN **57.38**) (BAGD 1. p. 849): 'need' [AB, BAGD, HNTC, NTC; NAB, NRSV, REB, TNT], 'what is needed' [LN; CEV, NIV, NJB, TEV], 'what is lacking' [**LN**; KJV], 'want' [BAGD, ICC2], 'shortage' [Lns], 'deficiency' [WBC], not explicit [NLT]. See this word also at 8:14; 9:12.

and in everything I-kept myself not-a-financial-burden[a] to-you and I-will-keep (myself).

LEXICON—a. ἀβαρής (LN 57.225) (BAGD p. 1): 'not being financially burdensome' [LN], 'not burdensome' [BAGD], 'not be a burden' [CEV], 'from being burdensome' [HNTC], 'from burdening' [ICC2], 'from being a burden' [AB, NTC, WBC], 'nonburdensome' [Lns]. The use of this word is a figurative extension from its more literal meaning of 'light in weight' [BAGD, LN], from βάρος 'burden, grief', negated by the alpha-privative (cf. βαρέω 'to burden' in 5:4).

11:10 Christ's truth[a] is in me that this boast[b] will not be silenced[c] to me in the region[d] of Achaia.

LEXICON—a. ἀλήθεια (LN 72.2): 'truth' [AB, BAGD, HNTC, ICC2, LN, Lns, NTC, WBC; all versions]. The phrase ἀλήθεια Χριστοῦ 'Christ's truth' is translated 'the truth about Christ' [CEV]. The phrase ἔστιν ἀλήθεια Χριστοῦ ἐν ἐμοὶ ὅτι 'Christ's truth is in me that' is translated 'as Christ's truth is in me' [AB, HNTC, ICC2; NJB], 'as surely as Christ's truth is in me' [NTC; TNT], 'as surely as the truth of Christ is in me' [NIV, NLT, REB], 'as certain as Christ's truth is in me' [WBC], 'as the truth of Christ is in me' [KJV, NRSV], 'as surely as I speak the truth about Christ' [CEV], 'there is indeed a truth of Christ in my case' [Lns], 'I swear by the Christ that is in me' [NAB], 'by Christ's truth in me I promise' [TEV]. See this word also at 7:14.

b. καύχησις (LN 33.368) (BAGD 1. p. 426): 'boast' [ICC2, NTC; NAB, NJB, NRSV, TEV], 'boasting' [AB, BAGD, HNTC, LN, Lns, WBC; KJV, NIV, NLT, REB, TNT], 'bragging' [CEV]. See this word also at 1:12; 7:4; 8:24.

c. fut. pass. indic. of φράσσω (LN 33.125) (BAGD 1.b., 2. p. 865): 'to be silenced' [AB, BAGD, HNTC, LN; NJB, NRSV, TEV], 'to be barred' [ICC2], 'to be dammed up' [Lns], 'to be stopped' [BAGD, NTC, WBC]. This passive verb is also translated as active: 'to stop' [CEV, KJV, NIV, NLT, TNT], 'to cease' [NAB], 'to bar' [REB].

d. κλίμα (LN 1.79) (BAGD p. 436): 'region' [BAGD, ICC2, LN, Lns, NTC; KJV, NAB, NIV, NJB, NRSV], 'district' [AB, BAGD, WBC], 'territory' [LN], 'province' [HNTC], not explicit [CEV, NLT, REB, TEV, TNT]. The phrase 'in the region of Achaia' is translated 'in Achaia' [CEV], 'throughout Achaia' [REB, TNT], 'anywhere in all Achaia' [TEV], 'all over Greece' [NLT].

QUESTION—How does he use the phrase 'Christ's truth is in me'?

Paul uses this phrase to affirm that he is speaking the truth [AB, Car, EGT, Ho, ICC2, NAC, NCBC, NIC1, NIC2, SP, TG, TH, WBC; all versions]. This is an oath formula [AB, Car, ICC2, NAC, NIC2, SP, TG, TH, WBC] or an asseveration of truth [EGT, NCBC].

1. He means that as surely as Christ spoke the truth, so he also speaks the truth [AB, Ho, ICC2, NIC2, WBC]. Christ, who is truthful, is in Paul and

speaks truthfully in what Paul says [ICC2, NIC2]. Paul's conduct conforms to the example of absolute truthfulness set by Christ [NIC1].
2. He means that as surely as he speaks the truth about Christ, he also speaks the truth in what he says here [EBC, NTC; CEV]. Paul was speaking Christ's truth when he vowed not to give in on this issue [EBC]. Paul is appealing to the truth of the gospel he had preached because that is really what is at stake; the truth of Christ is in him, and he is its vessel [NTC].
3. The 'truth of Christ' in Paul's case is his conversion and call to be an apostle while he was a persecutor; this affected the rest of his life, for Paul had to live by the same grace he had been given [Lns].

QUESTION—What is the boast?
1. It is that Paul preaches the gospel free of charge [EBC, EGT, HNTC, ICC1, ICC2, NAC, NCBC, NIC1, NIC2, TH, TNTC].
2. It is his enthusiasm about the Corinthians themselves [NTC].
3. It is Paul's confidence in his rights as a missionary to that region, as opposed to his opponents who have invaded his territory [WBC].
4. It is the boasting that the Corinthians should be doing about Paul; they should be taking up his case to defend him against the rival apostles who have come to Corinth [Lns].

11:11 **Why?ᵃ Because I do not love you? God knows.ᵇ**

LEXICON—a. διὰ τί (BAGD B.II. 2. p. 181): 'why' [AB, BAGD, HNTC, ICC2; NAB, NIV, NLT, REB, TNT], 'and why' [NTC; NRSV], 'why should it be' [NJB], 'for what reason' [Lns], 'how so' [WBC], 'wherefore' [KJV]. The two questions διὰ τί; ὅτι οὐκ ἀγαπῶ ὑμᾶς; 'Why? Because I do not love you?' are translated as a single question: 'do I say this because I don't love you?' [TEV]; as a statement of fact: 'and it isn't because I don't love you' [CEV].

b. perf. act. indic. of οἶδα (LN 28.1) (BAGD 1.i. p. 556): 'to know' [BAGD, LN]. The phrase ὁ θεὸς οἶδεν 'God knows' is translated with the content of knowing made explicit: 'God knows I do' [AB, Lns, NTC, WBC; NAB, NIV, NJB, NLT, NRSV, REB, TNT], 'God knows the truth about that' [HNTC], 'God knows I love you' [TEV], 'God himself knows how much I do love you' [CEV]. This Greek verb does not have a present tense form, so where a present tense meaning is intended, the form of the perfect tense is used.

11:12 **But what I-do also I-will-do, so-that I-may-cut-offᵃ the opportunityᵇ of those wanting opportunity to-be-foundᶜ also like us in what they-boastᵈ (about).**

LEXICON—a. aorist act. subj. of ἐκκόπτω (LN **13.101**) (BAGD 2. p. 242): 'to cut off' [AB, BAGD, HNTC, ICC2, Lns; KJV], 'to cut the ground from under' [NIV, NJB, NLT, REB], 'to remove' [BAGD], 'to deny' [NRSV, TNT], 'to keep from' [TEV], 'to take away' [NTC], 'to do away with' [**LN**], 'to put an end to' [WBC], 'to eliminate' [LN], 'to deprive at every turn' [NAB], not explicit [CEV].

b. ἀφορμή (LN **89.22**) (BAGD p. 127): 'opportunity' [AB, BAGD, HNTC, ICC2, WBC; NIV, NRSV, TNT], 'occasion' [BAGD, Lns, NTC; KJV], 'chance' [NAB, NJB, REB], 'excuse' [LN], 'reason' [TEV], not explicit [CEV, NLT]. See this word also at 5:12.

c. aorist pass. subj. of εὑρίσκω (BAGD 1.c.γ. p. 325): 'to be found' [BAGD, ICC2, Lns, NTC; KJV], 'to be recognized' [AB; NRSV], 'to be regarded' [WBC], 'to be considered' [NIV], 'to be proved' [NJB], 'to become (in their boasting)' [HNTC], not explicit [CEV]. The phrase 'to be found also like us in what they boast about' is translated 'who boast that their work is just like ours' [NLT], 'to say that in their much-vaunted ministry they work on the same terms as we do' [NAB], 'to put their vaunted apostleship in the same level as ours' [REB], 'for boasting and saying that they work in the same way that we do' [TEV], 'to present themselves as if they had the same office as we' [TNT]. See this word also at 5:3; 12:20.

d. pres. mid. or pass. (deponent = act.) indic. of καυχάομαι (LN 33.368) (BAGD 1. p. 425): 'to boast' [AB, BAGD, ICC2, LN, Lns, NTC, WBC; NIV, NLT, NRSV], 'boasting' [HNTC; NJB, TEV], 'to brag' [CEV], 'to glory' [KJV], 'to claim' [TNT]. The phrase 'in what they boast about' is translated 'in their much vaunted ministry' [NAB], 'their vaunted apostleship' [REB]. See this word also at 7:14; 10:8.

QUESTION—What is it that Paul is doing and will continue to do?

It is his policy of ministering to the Corinthians without accepting any financial payment or gifts [AB, Car, EBC, EGT, HNTC, Ho, ICC1, ICC2, Lns, NAC, NCBC, NIC1, NIC2, NTC, SP, TG, TH, TNTC]. It is his habit of ministering without pay and preaching a crucified Jesus [WBC].

QUESTION—What is the boasting that he opposes?

It is his rivals' claim that they are equal to Paul in ministry [NAC, NIC1, NIC2, NTC], or that they work on the same basis as he does [TG, TH, TNTC]. They boast that they are superior to Paul [Car, Ho]. It is their claim of being apostles [HNTC, ICC1, Lns]. They boast of the support they receive [NCBC]. Their acceptance of support is to them an evidence of their apostleship [EBC, NIC1]. Their boast is that they were owed free maintenance as their due as apostles [EGT] It is their claim to have legitimate authority to minister in Corinth [ICC2]. It is their claim to be sent by Christ and thereby have a legitimate claim to be ministering in what Paul considers his own allotted territory [WBC]. It is their boasting about their social position in Corinth which is based on the fact of their accepting financial gifts, and of their cultivation of friendship with the Corinthians as they honor them for those gifts [SP]. It is boasting in their ministry accomplishments and not in the Lord [AB].

QUESTION—What is Paul's argument?

Although his opponents want to be perceived as ministering on the same basis as Paul, they know that their claim can be seen as false because they take money and he doesn't [Car, EBC, Lns, TG, TNTC]. Paul proves that his ministry is legitimate and based on God's call by the sacrifice he makes to fulfill it, which the opponents cannot claim to do [NIC2]. If they want to prove their equality with Paul, let them serve sacrificially as he does [NAC]. It is too easy to see that they are greedy and Paul is self-sacrificial [Car]. Paul wants to force the intruders to minister as self-sacrificially as he does [Ho]. They want to induce Paul to accept pay so they can claim equality with him by ministering on the same basis [ICC1, NIC1, NTC]. Both Paul and his opponents claim Corinth as their territory, but Paul proves that he is truly their spiritual father by the fact that he does not take pay, since the children don't provide financially for their father [ICC2]. Since his rivals accept pay they can't be Paul's equals or true apostles of Christ, both of whom endure poverty to enrich others [AB].

11:13 For such (men are) false-apostles,[a] deceitful[b] workers, masquerading[c] as apostles of Christ.

LEXICON—a. ψευδαπόστολος (LN **53.75**) (BAGD p. 891): 'false apostle' [AB, BAGD, HNTC, ICC2, LN, NTC; CEV, KJV, NAB, NIV, NLT, NRSV, TEV, TNT], 'pseudo-apostles' [Lns], 'bogus apostles' [WBC], 'counterfeit apostles' [NJB], 'sham apostles' [REB].
  b. δόλιος (LN **88.155**) (BAGD p. 203): 'deceitful' [AB, BAGD, HNTC, LN, Lns, NTC; KJV, NIV, NRSV, TNT], 'dishonest' [BAGD, ICC2; CEV, NJB]. The phrase 'deceitful workers' is translated 'workers of deceit' [WBC], 'confidence tricksters' [REB], 'they practice deceit' [NAB], 'who lie about their work' [TEV], 'they have fooled you' [NLT].
  c. pres. mid. participle of μετασχηματίζω (LN 58.18) (BAGD p. 513): 'to masquerade' [WBC; NIV, REB], 'to disguise oneself' [AB, BAGD, HNTC, ICC2; NJB, NLT, NRSV, TEV, TNT], 'to change' [BAGD, LN], 'to transform oneself' [BAGD, Lns; KJV], 'to pose' [NTC], 'to pretend to be' [CEV]. The phrase 'masquerading as apostles of Christ' is translated 'in their disguise as apostles of Christ' [NAB].

QUESTION—Are these false apostles the same people as the 'super apostles' of 11:5?
  1. The false apostles are the same people referred to in 11:5 as 'super apostles' [AB, Car, EGT, ICC1, ICC2, Lns, NAC, NIC1, NTC, TG, TH, TNTC].
  2. The false apostles are intruders into Corinth whereas the 'super apostles' are the twelve apostles in Jerusalem [EBC, He, HNTC, Ho, NCBC, WBC].

QUESTION—What is meant by 'false apostle'?
  They are not really apostles [EBC, HNTC, ICC1, NAC, NIC1, SP, TG, WBC], so their claim to be apostles is false [Ho, TNTC]. They are false apostles because they were not truly sent to Corinth [AB, ICC2, NTC, TH]. The gospel they preach is a false gospel [AB, EBC, ICC2, Lns, NCBC, NIC2, NTC, WBC]. The Christ they proclaim is not the real one [Car, Lns].

In their message they disguise the truth [He]. They are false apostles by virtue of their pretence [NIC2]; they speak what is false [HNTC] and they are fraudulent [AB, NTC].

QUESTION—Does the description 'deceitful workers' mean that the deception they practice is conscious and deliberate?

It is a conscious and deliberate deception [AB, EBC, HNTC, Ho, Lns, NAC, NIC1, NIC2, NTC, TNTC, WBC].

11:14 **And no wonder;**[a] **for Satan himself masquerades as an angel**[b] **of light.**

LEXICON—a. θαῦμα (LN **25.216**) (BAGD 1.a. p. 352): 'a wonder' [BAGD, LN], 'object of wonder, a marvel' [BAGD], 'something to be wondered at' [**LN**]. The phrase καὶ οὐ θαῦμα is translated 'and no wonder' [AB, HNTC, ICC2, Lns, NTC; NIV, NRSV, REB, TNT], 'and it is no wonder' [CEV], 'well, no wonder' [TEV], 'and little wonder' [NAB], 'and no marvel' [KJV], 'this is nothing to be wondered at' [LN], 'do not be surprised at that' [WBC], 'but I am not surprised' [NLT], 'there is nothing astonishing in this' [NJB].

b. ἄγγελος (LN 12.28) (BAGD 2.a. p. 7): 'angel' [AB, BAGD, HNTC, ICC2, LN, Lns, NTC; all versions], 'messenger' [WBC].

QUESTION—What relationship is indicated by the genitive phrase ἄγγελον φωτός 'angel of light'?

1. 'Light' is used attributively; that is, he appears as a 'shining angel' [AB, EBC, HNTC, ICC2, NAC, NIC2, NTC, SP, TG, TH]. 'Light' means that the angel is bright, pure and happy [Ho].
2. It is a messenger from the world of light [BAGD]. A messenger of light means a messenger of God [EGT].

11:15 **So**[a] **(it is) no great-thing**[b] **if his servants**[c] **also masquerade as ministers**[d] **of righteousness;**[e]

LEXICON—a. οὖν (LN 89.50): 'so' [ICC2, LN; NLT, NRSV, REB, TEV], 'therefore' [AB, HNTC, LN, Lns; KJV], 'then' [WBC; NIV, NJB], not explicit [NTC; CEV, NAB].

b. μέγας (LN **25.207**) (BAGD 2.b.β. p. 498): 'great thing' [BAGD, HNTC; KJV, TEV], 'great wonder' [ICC2], 'wonder' [NLT], 'great surprise' [AB], 'surprise' [AB; TNT], 'surprising' [BAGD, **L N**; NIV], 'astonishing' [NJB], 'strange' [LN; CEV, NRSV]. The phrase οὐ μέγα 'it is no great thing' is translated 'so why does it seem strange' [CEV], 'it is easy enough' [REB].

c. διάκονος (LN 35.20) (BAGD 1.a. p. 184): 'servant' [BAGD, HNTC, LN, NTC, WBC; CEV, NIV, NJB, NLT, TEV, TNT], 'minister' [AB, Lns; KJV, NAB, NLT, NRSV], 'agent' [ICC2; REB]. See this word also at 3:6; 6:4.

d. διάκονος (LN 35.20) (BAGD 1.a. p. 184): 'minister' [AB, Lns; KJV, NAB, NIV, NLT, NRSV], 'servant' [HNTC, NTC, WBC; NJB, TEV, TNT], 'agent' [ICC2; REB], not explicit [CEV].

e. δικαιοσύνη (LN 88.13) (BAGD 2.b. p. 196): 'righteousness' [AB, BAGD, HNTC, ICC2, LN, Lns, NTC, WBC; KJV, NIV, NRSV, TEV, TNT], 'good' [REB], 'uprightness' [BAGD; NJB], 'the justice of God' [NAB]. The phrase μετασχηματίζονται ὡς διάκονοι δικαιοσύνης 'masquerade as ministers of righteousness' is translated 'pretend to do what is right' [CEV], 'pretending to be godly ministers' [NLT].

QUESTION—How are the nouns related in the genitive phrase διάκονοι δικαιοσύνης 'ministers of righteousness'?

1. They pretended to be ministers who taught people to be righteousness [ICC1, ICC2, NAC, NIC1, NIC2, NTC]. The false apostles promoted a righteousness that was based on Mosaic law [ICC1, NIC1, NIC2]. They claimed to be equal with Paul, whose ministry brings righteousness [ICC2, NTC]. Their ministry was to lead to righteousness [NAC]
2. They pretended to be ministers who served the cause of righteousness [Ho, Lns, TH]. They are agents of good, serving good or uprightness [TH] They are ministers who claim to serve the righteousness which comes by faith [Ho, Lns].
3. They pretended to be ministers who served the righteous God [TG] or a righteous cause [He].
4. They pretended to be ministers who were righteousness [EBC, HNTC, WBC]. They were 'righteous servants' [EBC, HNTC, WBC].

whose end[a] shall be according-to[b] their works.[c]

LEXICON—a. τέλος (LN 67.66) (BAGD 1.c. p. 811): 'end' [AB, BAGD, HNTC, ICC2, LN, Lns; KJV, NAB, NIV, NJB, NRSV], 'outcome' [BAGD], 'destiny' [BAGD, NTC], 'fate' [WBC; REB], 'in the end they will get' [NLT, TEV], 'they will get (what they deserve)' [CEV].

b. κατά (LN 89.8): 'according to' [Lns; KJV], 'in accordance with' [LN], 'in accord with' [AB], 'will accord with' [ICC2], 'will match' [NRSV, REB], 'correspond to' [HNTC; NAB], 'appropriate to' [NJB], 'which fits' [TNT], not explicit [WBC; NIV, NLT, TEV]. The phrase κατὰ τὰ ἔργα αὐτῶν 'according to their works' is translated 'what their deeds deserve' [NTC], 'exactly what they deserve' [CEV].

c. ἔργον (LN 42.11) (BAGD 1.c.β. p. 308): 'work' [ICC2; KJV], 'deed' [AB, BAGD, HNTC, LN, Lns, NTC, WBC; NAB, NRSV, REB], 'wicked deed' [NLT], 'act' [LN], 'action' [NIV, TEV], 'what they have done' [NJB], not explicit [CEV].

QUESTION—What is the 'end' of which Paul speaks?

It is the final judgment [AB, Car, HNTC, ICC1, NAC, NIC1, NIC2, NTC, SP, TG, TH, TNTC].

DISCOURSE UNIT: 11:16–12:13 [EBC, TNTC]. The topic is boasting as a fool [EBC], the fool's speech [TNTC].

DISCOURSE UNIT: 11:16–12:10 [WBC]. The topic is Paul's fool's story.

DISCOURSE UNIT: 11:16–21a [EBC]. The topic is justification for foolish boasting.

DISCOURSE UNIT: 11:16–33 [HNTC, ICC1, TH; CEV, NAB, NIV, NLT, NRSV, TEV]. The topic is Paul's suffering for Christ [CEV], Paul boasts about his sufferings [NIV], Paul's sufferings as an apostle [TH; NAB, NRSV, TEV], Paul's many trials [NLT], answering fools according to their folly: qualifications [HNTC], glorying about Paul's service and sufferings [ICC1].

11:16 **Again^a I-say, let no-one think^b me to-be foolish;^c**
LEXICON—a. πάλιν (LN 67.55): 'again' [HNTC, ICC2, LN, WBC; KJV, TNT], 'once more' [Lns], 'once again' [NLT], not explicit [CEV]. The phrase 'again I say' is translated 'I repeat' [AB, NTC; NAB, NIV, NRSV, REB, TEV], 'to repeat' [NJB].
  b. δοκέω (LN 31.29) (BAGD 1.c. p. 202): 'to think' [AB, BAGD, HNTC, LN, Lns; CEV, KJV, NAB, NLT, NRSV, TEV], 'to consider' [BAGD, ICC2], 'to take (me for)' [NTC, WBC; NIV, NJB, REB, TNT].
  c. ἄφρων (LN 32.52) (BAGD p. 127): 'foolish' [BAGD, LN; NAB], 'a fool' [AB, HNTC, ICC2, Lns, NTC, WBC; CEV, KJV, NIV, NJB, NRSV, REB, TEV, TNT]. The phrase 'think me to be foolish' is translated 'think that I have lost my wits' [NLT].
QUESTION—What does 'again' refer to?
  1. It refers to what was said in 11:1 [AB, EBC, EGT, HNTC, Ho, ICC1, ICC2, Lns, NAC, NIC1, NIC2, NTC, SP, TG, TH, TNTC, WBC]. Paul asked them in 11:1 to bear with his foolishness and now does it again [TNTC]. He picks up the 'fool' theme from 11:1 [Lns, NIC2, NTC]. He returns to the subject of foolish boasting [EBC, NAC, NIC1]. He again asks them to listen to him even though he must boast about himself [ICC1]. He says the same kind of thing he did in 11:1, which is that he is not a foolish boaster [Ho]. His appeal for acceptance in 11:16 corresponds to his request to be tolerated in 11:1 [ICC2, SP].
  2. It refers to what has just been said in 11:13–15. Paul views the opponents as fools and does not want to be seen as being like them, though he must boast as they do [Car].

but if not,^a at-least^b accept^c me as a fool, so I too may-boast a little.^d
LEXICON—a. εἰ μή (LN 89.131): 'except that, however' [LN]. The phrase εἰ δὲ μή γε 'but if not' is translated 'but if you will not' [Lns], 'but should it be otherwise' [AB], 'but if you must' [NTC; REB], 'but if you do' [ICC2; CEV, NAB, NIV, NJB, NRSV, TEV, TNT], 'but even if you do' [WBC; NLT], 'and even if you do' [HNTC], 'if otherwise' [KJV], 'however' [LN].
  b. κἄν (BAGD 3. p. 402): 'at least' [AB, BAGD; TEV], 'then' [HNTC, ICC2, NTC; CEV, NAB, NIV, NJB, NRSV, REB, TNT], 'yet' [KJV], not explicit [Lns, NTC, WBC; NLT].

c. aorist mid. (deponent = act.) impera. of δέχομαι (LN 34.53) (BAGD 3.a. p. 177): 'to accept' [AB, HNTC, ICC2, NTC, WBC; NAB, NRSV, TEV, TNT], 'to receive' [KJV, NIV], 'to put up with, tolerate' [BAGD]. The phrase 'accept me as a fool' is translated 'think of me as a fool' [Lns], 'let me be a fool' [CEV], 'treat me as a fool' [NJB], 'listen to me as you would to a foolish person' [NLT], 'give me the privilege of a fool' [REB]. See this word also at 7:15.

d. μικρός (LN 78.9, 67.106) (BAGD 3.a. p. 521): 'a little' [BAGD, ICC2, NTC; CEV, KJV, NLT, NRSV, TEV], 'a little bit' [AB], 'a little (boast)' [WBC; REB, TNT], 'a little (boasting)' [NAB, NIV, NJB], 'little' [LN (78.9)], 'for a little while' [HNTC, LN (67.106)], 'briefly' [LN (67.106)], 'in regard to a little something' [Lns].

11:17 What I-say, I-say not according-to[a] the Lord but as in foolishness,[b] in this matter[c] of boasting.

LEXICON—a. κατά (LN 89.8) (BAGD II.5.a.α. p. 407): 'in accordance with' [BAGD, LN]. The phrase 'according to the Lord' [Lns], is translated 'as one in the Lord' [AB], 'as a servant of the Lord' [HNTC], 'in a Christian way' [ICC2], 'like a Christian' [REB], 'Christian' [TNT], 'on the authority of the Lord' [NTC], 'on/with the Lord's authority' [WBC; NRSV], 'what the Lord would have' [TEV], 'for the Lord' [CEV], 'after the Lord' [KJV], 'as the Lord desires' [NAB], 'something the Lord wants' [NLT], 'as the Lord would' [NIV], 'following the Lord's way' [NJB].

b. ἀφροσύνη (LN **32.53**) (BAGD p. 127): 'foolishness' [AB, BAGD, LN, NTC, WBC; NJB], 'sheer foolishness' [TNT], 'folly' [HNTC, Lns], 'a state of folly' [ICC2], '(as a) fool' [CEV, NIV, NRSV], 'like a fool' [NLT, REB, TEV], 'the manner of a fool' [NAB], 'foolishly' [KJV]. See this word also at 11:1.

c. ὑπόστασις (LN 31.84) (BAGD 2. p. 847): 'matter' [TEV], 'business' [AB], 'situation' [BAGD], '(boasting) project' [ICC2], 'undertaking' [Lns], 'resolve' [NTC], 'frame of mind' [BAGD], 'ground (of making a proud boast)' [WBC], 'confidence' [HNTC, LN; KJV, NRSV, TNT], 'confidently' [REB], 'self-confident' [NIV], 'self-assured' [NAB], 'conviction' [NJB], not explicit [CEV, NLT]. See this word also at 9:4.

QUESTION—What area of meaning is intended by ὑπόστασις 'matter'?

1. It refers to the business or matter at hand, in this case, boasting [AB, BAGD, ICC2, Lns, NAC, SP, TG, TH; TEV]: in this matter of boasting.
2. It refers to confidence as in 9:4 [EGT, HNTC, Ho, ICC1, NIC1, NIC2, NTC; KJV, NAB, NIV, NJB, NRSV, REB, TNT], or to the basis or grounds for confidence [He, WBC]: in this confident boasting. It is his daring or resolve to speak as a fool [NTC].

11:18 Since[a] many boast according-to (the) flesh,[b] I will-boast too.

LEXICON—a. ἐπεί (LN 89.32) (BAGD 2. p. 284): 'since' [AB, BAGD, HNTC, ICC2, LN, Lns, WBC; NAB, NIV, NLT, NRSV, TEV], 'because'

[BAGD, LN, NTC], 'seeing that' [KJV], 'inasmuch' [LN], not explicit [CEV, NJB, REB, TNT].
   b. σάρξ (LN 26.7) (BAGD 6. p. 744): 'flesh' [HNTC, Lns; KJV], 'human nature' [LN]. The phrase 'according to the flesh' is translated 'according to human standards' [BAGD; NRSV], 'on merely human grounds' [NJB], 'for merely human reasons' [TEV], 'about their human achievements' [NLT], 'about their human affairs' [TNT], 'in a worldly way' [AB], 'in the way the world does' [NIV], 'in a worldly manner' [NTC], 'as people of the world' [WBC], 'in an unspiritual fashion' [ICC2], 'about their human distinctions' [NAB], 'of their earthly distinctions' [REB], not explicit [CEV]. See this word also at 1:17; 4:11; 5:16; 7:1; 7:5; 10:3.

11:19 For[a] being (so) wise[b] you gladly[c] put-up-with[d] fools.
LEXICON—a. γάρ (LN 89.23) (BAGD 1.c. p. 152): 'for' [AB, BAGD, HNTC, ICC2, LN, Lns, WBC; KJV, NRSV], 'because' [LN, NTC], 'since' [CEV, NJB], 'after all' [NLT], not explicit [NAB, REB, TEV, TNT].
   b. φρόνιμος (LN 32.31) (BAGD p. 866): 'wise' [AB, BAGD, ICC2, LN, NTC, WBC; all versions except CEV], 'sensible' [BAGD, HNTC], 'intelligent' [Lns], 'smart' [CEV].
   c. ἡδέως (LN **25.129**) (BAGD p. 343): 'gladly' [AB, BAGD, HNTC, ICC2, LN, Lns, NTC, WBC; CEV, KJV, NAB, NIV, NRSV, REB, TEV], 'how glad (you are)' [TNT], 'how happy' [NJB], 'you enjoy' [NLT].
   d. pres. mid. indic. of ἀνέχω (LN 25.171) (BAGD 1.a. p. 65): 'to put up with' [AB, BAGD, HNTC, NTC, WBC; CEV, NAB, NIV, NJB, NRSV, REB], 'to bear with' [BAGD, Lns], 'to be patient with' [LN; TNT], 'to tolerate' [ICC2; TEV], 'to suffer' [KJV], 'to listen to' [NLT]. See this word also at 11:1, 4.

11:20 For[a] you put-up-with (it) if someone enslaves[b] you, if someone devours[c] (you),
LEXICON—a. γάρ (LN 89.23): 'for' [ICC2, LN, NTC; KJV, NRSV], 'because' [LN], 'indeed' [WBC], 'in fact' [CEV, NIV], not explicit [AB, HNTC, Lns; NAB, NJB, NLT, REB, TEV, TNT].
   b. pres. act. indic. of καταδουλόω (LN 37.27) (BAGD p. 410): 'to enslave' [AB, BAGD, HNTC, ICC2, Lns, NTC, WBC; NIV, NJB, TNT], 'to make a slave of' [LN; CEV, NLT, NRSV], 'to gain control over' [LN], 'to bring into bondage' [KJV], 'to tyrannize' [REB], 'to order around' [TEV]. This verb is conflated with the following verb and translated 'to exploit' [NAB].
   c. pres. act. indic. of κατεσθίω (LN **88.145**) (BAGD 2. p. 422): 'to devour' [BAGD, ICC2, Lns; KJV], 'to devour (your) goods' [NTC], 'to eat up' [AB], 'to eat out of house and home' [HNTC], 'to eat all (you) possess' [NJB], 'to take advantage of' [TEV], 'to take complete advantage of' [LN], 'to take everything (you) have' [NLT], 'to exploit' [WBC; NAB, NIV, REB, TNT], 'to cheat' [CEV], 'to prey upon' [NRSV]. Although the Greek text has no direct object for this verb and the one following it, all

versions supply 'you' or some variant of 'your goods' as the implied object.

QUESTION—What is the nature of the 'enslaving'?
1. It refers to the fact that the false apostles treat the Corinthians as their slaves, to serve them [NAC, NCBC, WBC; NLT]. Their leadership is domineering [AB, NIC2, TG, TH], authoritarian [TNTC], tyrannical [EGT, Ho]. The false apostles took over the leadership of the community as tyrants, making the Corinthians slaves to them [Car]. The false apostles have forced their authority on the church [ICC2]. They are slaves in that they have forfeited Christian liberty [NIC1]. They have enslaved them in doctrine, in conduct, and in financial support [NTC].
2. They have brought the Corinthians into slavery to the Mosaic law [EBC, HNTC, ICC1]. They are enslaved to the Judaizers' gospel [HNTC].

QUESTION—What is the nature of the devouring?
It is their consuming the Corinthians' financial resources [Car, EBC, EGT, HNTC, Ho, ICC1, ICC2, NAC, NCBC, NIC1, NIC2, NTC, SP, TG, TH, TNTC, WBC]. The false apostles were like parasites [NIC1], living at the Corinthians' expense [NCBC].

if someone takes-advantage-of[a] (you), if someone exalts-himself,[b] if someone strikes[c] you in the face.

LEXICON—a. pres. act. indic. of λαμβάνω (LN **88.146**) (BAGD 1.c. p. 464): 'to take advantage of' [BAGD, ICC2, NTC; NIV, NLT, NRSV], 'to exploit by deception' [LN], 'to take in' [AB, BAGD], 'to get (you) in his power' [HNTC], 'to capture' [Lns], 'to lay hands on (you)' [WBC], 'to steal from' [CEV], 'to take from' [KJV], 'to impose upon' [NAB], 'to keep under (his) orders' [NJB], 'to get in (his) clutches' [REB], 'to trap' [TEV], 'to prey upon' [TNT].
b. pres. mid. indic. of ἐπαίρω (LN **88.212**) (BAGD 2.b.β. p. 282): 'to exalt oneself' [HNTC; KJV], 'to behave haughtily toward' [**LN**], 'to be arrogant' [LN], 'to act presumptuously' [AB], 'to be presumptuous' [BAGD, ICC2], 'to put on airs' [BAGD; NAB, NLT, NRSV, REB], 'to lift oneself up over' [Lns], 'to set oneself above' [NJB], 'to lord it over' [WBC], 'to think oneself to be better than' [NTC], 'to look down on' [TEV, TNT], 'to strut around' [CEV], 'to push oneself forward' [NIV].
c. pres. act. indic. of δέρω (LN 19.2) (BAGD p. 175): 'to strike' [BAGD, HNTC, ICC2, LN; TNT], 'to slap' [AB, NTC; CEV, NAB, NIV, NJB, NLT, TEV], 'to give a slap' [NRSV], 'to smite' [Lns; KJV], 'to hit' [REB]. The phrase εἰς πρόσωπον ὑμᾶς δέρε 'strikes you in the face' is translated 'he deeply insults you' [WBC].

QUESTION—Is the 'striking' to be understood literally or metaphorically?
1. It is metaphorical, referring to insults [AB, Car, EBC, ICC2, NCBC, SP, TG, TH, WBC].
2. It is literal, meaning that they actually struck the Corinthians physically [EGT, Ho, Lns, NAC, NIC1, NIC2, TNTC].

3. It includes physical striking as well as insults [HNTC].

11:21 **To shame[a] I-say, that we have-been-weak.[b]**
LEXICON—a. ἀτιμία (LN 87.71) (BAGD p. 120): 'shame' [BAGD], 'dishonor' [BAGD, LN]. The phrase κατὰ ἀτιμίαν 'to shame' is translated 'to my shame' [HNTC, ICC2, NTC, WBC; NAB, NIV, NRSV, TNT], 'to your shame' [NJB], 'I am ashamed' [AB; CEV, NLT, TEV], '(I speak) by way of disgrace' [Lns], '(I speak) as concerning reproach' [KJV], '(I admit) the reproach' [REB]. A few take the shame to be the Corinthians' [He; NJB]; all others understand it to be Paul's. See this word also at 6:8.
b. perf. act. indic. of ἀσθενέω (LN 74.26) (BAGD 1.b. p. 115): 'to be weak' [BAGD, HNTC, ICC2, LN, Lns, NTC, WBC; CEV, KJV, NAB, NIV, NJB, NRSV, TNT], 'to be a weakling' [AB], 'to not be strong' [NLT], 'to be timid' [TEV]. The phrase 'we have been weak' is translated 'you call me a weakling' [REB]. Some translate the plural 'we have been weak' as an editorial 'we': 'I have been weak' [REB, TNT].
QUESTION—Why does Paul say he is ashamed?
1. Paul is being sarcastic [AB, Car, EBC, EGT, HNTC, ICC1, ICC2, NAC, NCBC, NIC1, NIC2, NTC, SP, TG, TH, TNTC, WBC].
2. Paul is speaking of his actual humility and lack of self-confidence during past visits with the Corinthians [Ho].
QUESTION—In what way was Paul weak?
Paul and his associates were weak in the sense that they were characterized by gentleness and did not assert their authority [NAC, NCBC]. They were kind and considerate instead of being harsh and aggressive as the opponents [Car, EBC, ICC1]. Paul was gentle where his opponents were forceful [NTC]. His opponents use brute force and call him weak by comparison, to which he agrees [WBC]. He did not assert himself to exercise power [HNTC]. They were weak by contrast with the things listed in 11:20 that the opponents did [EGT, Lns, NIC2, TG, TH]. They were weak in the sense of not being overbearingly authoritarian [TNTC]. He is contrasting his weakness when present with them with the tyranny of his opponents [NIC1]. He is contrasting himself to the status claimed by his opponents [ICC2]. Paul was weak in the sense that he knew he had no power in himself to effect change in people's lives [Ho]. The concept of weakness has a different meaning for Paul than it does for the Corinthians [SP]. Paul accepts for the moment the accusation in 10:10 of weakness in his physical presence [WBC].
QUESTION—What relationship is indicated by ὡς ὅτι 'that'?
Most versions translate ὡς ὅτι as the equivalent of ὅτι 'that', though because of the use of irony and sarcasm it is not clear whether or not more is implied.
1. ὡς ὅτι is the equivalent of ὅτι 'that' [Lns, NTC, SP].

2. The ὡς indicates that what follows is Paul's subjective judgment, which is an ironic admission that he really is weak, as his opponents are saying, but in an entirely different way than they mean, and seen from a totally different viewpoint [AB, BAGD (1.d.β. p. 589)]: by comparison we seem to have been weaklings [AB]. The ὡς indicates that what follows is a statement that Paul does not mean seriously [HNTC]. ὡς ὅτι introduces a quote of what others have been saying about him [ICC2, NIC2]. ὡς indicates that what is stated by ὅτι is what someone else believes, but with which Paul does not agree [Ho, ICC1]. It marks a stance which, with irony, he is adopting for the present, but with which he will give a fuller non-ironical assessment later in 13:3, 4: we have been weak, as it were [WBC]. It introduces a sarcastic statement that he does not actually mean [NJB]: perhaps we have been too weak.

DISCOURSE UNIT: 11:21b–12:10 [AB]. The topic is the speech proper.

DISCOURSE UNIT: 11:21b–29 [EBC]. The topic is Paul's heritage and trials.

But[a] in whatever-way anyone may-be-bold[b] — I-speak in foolishness[c] — I-am-bold also.

LEXICON—a. δέ (LN 89.124): 'but' [ICC2, LN, Lns, NTC; NAB, NLT, NRSV, REB, TEV, TNT], 'yet' [HNTC, WBC], 'howbeit' [KJV], not explicit [AB; CEV, NIV, NJB].

b. pres. act. subj. of τολμάω (LN 25.161) (BAGD 2. p. 822): 'to be bold' [ICC2, Lns; KJV], 'to be audacious' [AB], 'to make a bold claim' [HNTC], 'to dare to boast' [NTC; NIV, NLT, NRSV, TEV], 'to dare to claim' [NAB], 'to presume to make a claim' [WBC], 'to make bold claims' [NJB], 'to want to brag' [TNT], not explicit [REB]. The phrase ἐν ᾧ δ' ἄν τις τολμᾷ 'in whatever way anyone may be bold' is translated 'any bold claim that anyone else can make' [HNTC], 'whatever bold claims anyone makes' [NJB], 'whenever anyone presumes to make a claim' [WBC], 'what anyone else dares to claim/boast about' [NAB, NIV, NRSV], 'whatever they dare to boast about' [NLT], 'if anyone dares to boast about something' [TEV], 'if anyone wants to brag about anything' [TNT], 'if they can brag' [CEV], 'if there is to be bravado' [REB]. See this word also at 10:2, 12.

c. ἀφροσύνη (LN 32.53) (BAGD p. 127): 'foolishness' [BAGD, LN], 'absolute foolishness' [NAB], 'foolishly' [AB, HNTC, ICC2, NTC, WBC; KJV], 'folly' [Lns], 'foolish' [CEV], 'as/like a fool' [NIV, NJB, NLT, NRSV, REB, TEV, TNT]. See this word also at 11:1, 17.

11:22 Are-they Hebrews? I (am) also. Are-they Israelites? I (am) also. Are-they (the) seed[a] of-Abraham? I (am) also.

LEXICON—a. σπέρμα (LN 10.29) (BAGD 2.b. p. 761): 'seed' [HNTC, ICC2, Lns; KJV, NAB], 'descendents' [AB, BAGD, LN, NTC, WBC; NIV, NJB, NLT, NRSV, REB, TEV, TNT], 'from the family of' [CEV].

QUESTION—What is meant by the term 'Hebrew'?
It refers to race or physical descent [HNTC, ICC1, NIC2, SP, TG, TNTC, WBC], to nationality [Ho, ICC1, Lns, NIC1, NTC], to ethnicity [AB, TH, WBC], to the Semitic language [Car, EBC, EGT, He, ICC1, NTC, WBC], to Semitic culture [Car, EBC, EGT, NTC]. It is an archaic title of respect for his nation [NAC]. It means to be Palestinian in origin or family ties [NCBC]. It refers to the language and culture of Palestine [EBC, EGT]. All three designations are essentially the same [Lns, NIC2].

QUESTION—What is meant by the term 'Israelite'?
1. It focuses on the religious meaning of being Jewish [AB, Car, EGT, He, NAC, SP, TG, TH]. It means to be a member of God's people and kingdom [EBC, ICC2, SP], and the religious privilege implied by that [ICC2]. It is to be a member of a social and religious community [TNTC, WBC], one that shares in God's purposes in salvation history [WBC]. It refers to Israel as a theocracy [Ho, ICC1, NIC1], as the people of God [Car, ICC1, TH], the people of the covenant [TG]. It focuses on the people of Israel as the recipients of the covenants, the law, the worship, the promises and the messiah [Car, NAC].
2. It focuses on the social and political meaning of being Jewish [HNTC].
3. It means to be a descendant of Jacob [NIC2, NTC].

QUESTION—What is meant by the phrase 'seed of Abraham'?
1. It refers to being an heir of the covenants [Car, EBC] and of God's promises to Abraham [ICC2]. It is a theological category referring to God's promises and call [SP, TNTC]. It looks at the Jews from a theological point of view [HNTC]. It refers to the history and culture of the nation as being heirs of God's promise [TG]. Of the three titles it is the title with the highest dignity, referring to their being the inheritors of the messianic promises [EGT]. They are the heirs of Abraham and of the promise of the messiah [Ho]. It focuses on the religious meaning of being Jewish but includes ethnicity as well [AB].
2. It refers to their race, as opposed to their language and religion which are covered by the first two terms [He].
3. It is a more general and comprehensive term than the other two [NCBC]. It is a broader category than the other two, both racially and spiritually [NTC].

11:23 Are they servants of Christ? I-speak (as)-being-out-of-my-mind,ª I (am) more;ᵇ

LEXICON—a. pres. act. participle of παραφρονέω (LN **30.24**) (BAGD p. 623): 'to be out of one's mind' [AB, LN; NIV], 'to be out of one's senses' [WBC; TNT], 'to be insane' [LN], 'to be mad' [LN; REB], 'to be beside oneself' [BAGD, Lns], 'to go out of one's wits' [HNTC], 'to be a fool' [CEV], 'as/like a fool' [KJV, NAB], 'to be irrational' [NTC], 'to be irrational' [BAGD], 'like an insane person' [**LN**], 'like a madman' [ICC2; NLT, NRSV, TEV], 'in utter folly' [NJB].

b. ὑπέρ (LN **78.29**) (BAGD 3. p. 839): 'more' [AB, HNTC, WBC; KJV, NAB, NIV], 'even more so' [**LN**; TNT], 'far more' [NLT], 'more than' [LN; NJB], 'to a greater degree than' [LN], 'better than they' [CEV, TEV], 'a better one' [NRSV], 'unequalled' [ICC2], 'way beyond that' [Lns], 'I can surpass them' [NTC], 'I can outdo them' [REB].

QUESTION—Is Paul saying that his opponents are servants of Christ?
1. Paul does not believe that they are servants of Christ [Car, EBC, Ho, ICC1, Lns, NAC, NIC1, NIC2, NTC, SP, TNTC, WBC]. He is saying this for the sake of argument [Ho, ICC1, NIC1, TNTC]. Paul is quoting their claim, not affirming it [Car, EBC, NIC2, NTC].
2. Paul is saying that they are servants of Christ, so they are not the same ones referred to in 11:13ff [HNTC].

in labors^a much-more,^b in prisons^c much-more, in beatings^d more-severe,^e in deaths^f often.^g

LEXICON—a. κόπος (LN 42.47) (BAGD 2. p. 443): 'labor' [AB, BAGD, ICC2, Lns; KJV, NAB, NRSV, TNT], 'work' [BAGD; NJB], 'hard work' [LN], 'toil' [BAGD, LN, NTC, WBC]. This noun is also translated as a verb: 'to work' [CEV, NIV, NLT, TEV], 'to toil' [HNTC], 'to be overworked' [REB]. See this word also at 6:5; 10:15.

b. περισσοτέρως (LN 78.31) (BAGD 1. p. 651): 'more' [AB; NJB], 'far more' [BAGD, WBC], 'more abundant' [KJV], 'many more' [NAB], 'all the more' [LN], 'more often' [REB], 'much greater' [LN], 'far greater' [BAGD; NRSV], 'hard' [TNT], 'harder' [HNTC; CEV, NLT], 'much harder' [NIV, TEV], 'much more diligently' [NTC], 'incomparably abundant' [ICC2], 'excessive' [LN], 'excessively' [Lns]. See this word also at 1:12; 2:4; 7:13, 15.

c. φυλακή (LN 7.24) (BAGD 3. p. 867): 'prison' [BAGD, HNTC, LN, Lns, NTC, WBC; KJV, NIV, NJB, TEV], 'imprisonment' [AB; NAB, NRSV, TNT], 'spells of imprisonment' [ICC2], 'jail' [LN; CEV, NLT]. This noun is also translated as a verb: 'to be imprisoned' [REB].

d. πληγή (LN 19.1) (BAGD 1. p. 668): 'beating' [AB, ICC2, NTC; NAB], 'flogging' [NRSV, TNT], 'blow, stroke' [BAGD], 'stripes' [Lns; KJV]. This noun is also translated as a verb: 'to suffer beating' [WBC], 'to be beaten' [HNTC, LN], 'to be beaten with whips' [CEV], 'to be whipped' [NLT, TEV], 'to be flogged' [NIV, NJB], 'to be scourged' [REB]. This word is translated as referring to blows received in a beating or flogging [BAGD], to the event of a beating or a flogging in which the blows occur [AB, ICC2, NTC; NAB, NRSV, TNT], to the action of being beaten or flogged [HNTC, LN, WBC; CEV, NIV, NJB, NLT, REB, TEV], or to the wounds or stripes which result from the blows [Lns; KJV].

e. ὑπερβαλλόντως (LN **78.34**) (BAGD p. 840): 'more severely' [NTC; NIV, NJB, REB], 'more' [CEV], 'much more' [TEV], 'far worse' [AB; NAB], 'excessively' [**LN**], 'to a very great degree' [LN], 'to a much greater degree, exceedingly' [BAGD], 'above measure' [KJV], 'beyond measure' [HNTC, Lns], 'beyond number' [WBC], 'times without number' [NLT], 'countless' [NRSV]. The phrase 'in beatings more severe' is translated 'whipped excessively' [**LN**], 'exceptionally subject to beatings' [ICC2], 'I have suffered from flogging beyond anything they have known' [TNT]. This adverb is translated as describing the severity of the beatings [NIV, NJB, REB], as well as the frequency of such beatings [AB, ICC2, WBC; NLT, NRSV].

- f. θάνατος (LN **23.117**) (BAGD 1.c. p. 351): 'deaths' [Lns; KJV], 'danger of death' [BAGD, LN; CEV, TNT], 'at the point of death' [AB], 'exposed to death' [HNTC; NIV, NJB], 'mortal danger' [ICC2], 'facing death' [NTC], 'faced death' [NLT], 'face to face with death' [REB], 'at death's door' [WBC], 'near death' [NRSV, TEV], 'brushes with death' [NAB]. See this word also at 1:10.
- g. πολλάκις (LN 67.11) (BAGD p. 686): 'often' [AB, BAGD, HNTC, LN, Lns, NTC; KJV, NRSV], 'more often' [CEV, TEV], 'many times' [BAGD, LN; NJB], 'many a time' [REB], 'frequently' [BAGD, ICC2, WBC], 'frequent' [NAB], 'again and again' [NIV, NLT]. See this word also at 8:22.

QUESTION—Does κόπος 'labor' refer to ministry or to performing manual labor to support himself?

1. It refers to his labor in ministry [HNTC, ICC2, NIC1, SP, WBC]. Paul engaged in arduous evangelistic campaigns [ICC2]. While it refers to ministry here, in 11:27 it refers to self-support [NIC1].
2. It refers to his work as a tent maker [AB, NIC2].
3. It refers to both ministry and to manual labor [NTC].

11:24 Five-times I-received from (the) Jews forty (lashes) minus one,[a]

LEXICON—a. τεσσεράκοντα παρὰ μίαν (see LN 59.76). This numerical phrase is translated as 'forty minus one' [AB, HNTC, ICC2, Lns, NTC; KJV, NAB, NIV, NRSV] and as 'thirty-nine' [WBC; CEV, NJB, NLT, REB, TEV, TNT]. While there is no lexical entry for 'lashes', the implied noun is given as 'lashes' [AB, NTC, WBC; CEV, NAB, NIV, NJB, NLT, NRSV, TEV, TNT], 'stripes' [HNTC, Lns; KJV], 'strokes' [ICC2; REB].

QUESTION—What is the significance of receiving forty lashes less one?

Deut 25:1-3 stipulated that the maximum number of blows in a whipping be limited to forty lashes, and the Jews stopped one short of that to avoid exceeding the limit due to a miscount [AB, EGT, He, Ho, ICC1, ICC2, Lns, NAC, NCBC, NIC1, NIC2, TG, TH, TNTC, WBC]. The whip probably had three lashes, in which case thirteen strokes would mean a total of thirty-nine lashes total [ICC1, NAC, NCBC]. Thirteen lashes were given on the chest and twenty six on the back of the guilty person [He, NAC, NCBC, NTC, TG], thirteen on one shoulder and thirteen on the other [TG]. For an offense serious to merit punishment beyond forty lashes the death penalty would be imposed [Lns].

11:25 three-times I-was-beaten-with-rods,[a] once I-was-stoned, three-times I-was-shipwrecked, I-have-spent a night-and-day in the deep;[b]

LEXICON—a. aorist pass. indic. of ῥαβδίζω (LN 19.8) (BAGD p. 733): 'to be beaten with rods' [AB, BAGD, HNTC, ICC2, LN, Lns, NTC, WBC; KJV, NAB, NIV, NLT, NRSV, REB, TNT], 'to be beaten with sticks' [LN; NJB], 'to be beaten with a big stick' [CEV], 'to be whipped by the Romans' [TEV]. This verb does not indicate how many rods or sticks would be involved (literally meaning 'to-be-rod-beaten'), though all translations except AB and CEV represent the instrument of beating in the plural, 'rods' or 'sticks', which could indicate being beaten by multiple persons at once.

b. βυθός (LN **1.73**) (BAGD p. 148): 'the deep' [LN], 'the open sea' [**LN**]. The phrase ἐν τῷ βυθῷ 'in the deep' [ICC2, Lns; KJV], is translated 'in the sea' [CEV], 'in the open sea' [NIV, NJB, TNT], 'on the sea' [NAB], 'adrift at sea' [BAGD, NTC; NLT, NRSV], 'adrift on the open sea' [WBC; REB], 'in the water' [TEV], 'out in the water' [AB].

11:26 in-journeys[a] often, in-dangers[b] from-rivers, in-dangers from-robbers,[c]

LEXICON—a. ὁδοιπορία (LN 15.20) (BAGD p. 553): 'journey' [AB, BAGD, ICC2, LN, NTC, WBC; NRSV, TNT], 'journeying' [KJV], 'travel' [HNTC, Lns; CEV, TEV], 'to travel' [NAB, NJB, NLT], 'to be on the move' [NIV], 'to be on the road' [REB].

b. κίνδυνος (LN 21.1) (BAGD p. 432): 'danger' [AB, BAGD, HNTC, ICC2, **LN**, NTC, WBC; CEV, NIV, NJB, NLT, NRSV, REB, TEV, TNT], 'peril' [LN, Lns; KJV], 'risk' [BAGD]. This noun is also translated as a verb: 'to be endangered' [NAB].

c. λῃστής (LN) (BAGD 1. p. 473): 'robber' [BAGD, LN, Lns, NTC; CEV, KJV, NAB, NLT, REB, TEV, TNT], 'bandit' [AB, BAGD, HNTC, ICC2; NIV, NRSV], 'brigand' [WBC; NJB], 'highwayman' [BAGD, LN].

in-dangers from (my) countrymen,[a] in-dangers from-Gentiles, dangers in (the) city, dangers in (the) desert,[b] dangers on (the) sea, dangers by false-brothers,[c]

LEXICON—a. γένος (LN 10.1) (BAGD 3. p. 156): 'countrymen' [BAGD, NTC; KJV, NIV, REB, TNT], 'people' [AB, BAGD, WBC; CEV, NJB, NLT, NRSV, TEV], 'race' [ICC2, Lns; NAB]. To clarify that Paul is talking about his own people the modifier 'my' or 'my own' is added by all versions and commentary translations.

b. ἐρημία (LN **1.86**) (BAGD p. 309): 'desert' [BAGD, ICC2, **LN**; CEV, NAB, NLT], 'wilderness' [LN, Lns; KJV, NRSV, REB], 'lonely place' [LN], 'uninhabited region' [BAGD], 'country' [NTC, WBC; NIV], 'open country' [AB; NJB, TNT], 'lonely country' [HNTC], 'the wilds' [TEV].

c. ψευδάδελφος (LN **11.36**) (BAGD p. 891): 'false brother' [BAGD, HNTC, LN, NTC, WBC; KJV, NAB, NIV, TNT], 'pseudo-brother' [Lns], 'pseudo-Christian' [ICC2]. This plural noun is translated 'false brothers and sisters' [AB; NRSV], 'false Christians' [REB], 'people who only pretended to be the Lord's followers' [CEV], 'people masquerading as brothers' [NJB], 'men who claim to be Christians but are not' [NLT], 'false friends' [TEV].

QUESTION—What is the relation of 'false brothers' to the rest of the list of dangers?

Its position at the end gives it emphasis [AB, HNTC, ICC2, NIC2, NTC, SP, WBC]. It was the worst of the dangers [Lns, NIC1], the most startling danger [NAC], and the most to be feared [NIC1]. It is the most insidious danger of all [ICC1].

11:27 with-labor[a] and toil,[b] in sleeplessness[c] often, in hunger and thirst, in fastings[d] often, in cold[e] and nakedness.[f]

LEXICON—a. κόπος (LN 42.47) (BAGD 2. p. 443): 'labor' [AB, BAGD, HNTC, ICC2, Lns; NAB], 'work' [BAGD; TEV], 'hard work' [LN], 'toil' [BAGD, LN, NTC, WBC; NRSV], 'weariness' [KJV], 'to labor' [NIV]. The phrase κόπῳ καὶ μόχθῳ 'with labor and toil' is translated 'I have worked and struggled' [CEV], 'I have worked with unsparing energy' [NJB], 'I have lived with weariness and pain' [NLT], 'I have lived in the midst of labor and toil' [HNTC], 'I have toiled and drudged' [REB], 'I have toiled and suffered hardship' [TNT]. See this word also at 6:5; 10:15; 11:23.

b. μόχθος (LN 42.48) (BAGD p. 528): 'toil' [AB, HNTC, ICC2, LN, Lns; TEV], 'hard labor' [LN], 'hard work' [WBC], 'exertion' [BAGD], 'hardship' [BAGD, NTC; NAB, NRSV], 'painfulness' [KJV], 'pain' [NLT], not explicit [NJB]. This noun is also translated as a verb: 'to toil' [NIV], 'to drudge' [REB], 'to suffer hardship' [TNT].

c. ἀγρυπνία (LN **23.73**) (BAGD 1. p. 14): 'sleeplessness' [LN, Lns], 'without sleep' [NTC, WBC; NIV, NJB, REB, TEV, TNT], 'sleepless nights' [AB, BAGD, ICC2; CEV, NAB, NLT, NRSV], 'wakefulness' [BAGD, HNTC], 'watching' [KJV]. See this word also at 6:5.

d. νηστεία (LN 23.31) (BAGD 1. p. 538): 'hunger' [AB, ICC2, Lns, NTC, WBC; KJV, NAB, NIV], 'hungry' [HNTC; CEV, NJB, NLT, NRSV, REB, TEV, TNT], 'lack of food' [LN], 'without food' [BAGD]. See this word also at 6:5.

e. ψῦχος (LN 79.75) (BAGD p. 894): 'cold' [AB, BAGD, HNTC, ICC2, LN, Lns, NTC, WBC; all versions except TEV], 'without shelter' [TEV].

f. γυμνότης (LN 49.23) (BAGD 2. p. 168): 'nakedness' [HNTC, LN, Lns, NTC; KJV, NAB], 'near nakedness' [ICC2], 'naked' [NIV, NRSV], 'lacked clothing' [NJB], 'lack of sufficient clothing' [BAGD], 'ill-clothed' [AB], 'destitution' [BAGD, WBC], 'cold and exposure' [REB], 'without sufficient clothing' [TNT], 'without enough clothing' [TEV], 'without enough clothing to keep me warm' [NLT], 'not having enough clothes to keep me warm' [CEV].

QUESTION—Was the fasting done for religious purposes?

It was involuntary [AB, Car, EGT, He, Ho, NAC, NIC2, TNTC]. Sometimes Paul did not have time to eat because of his work [TG]. It may have been voluntary or involuntary but it was not done for religious purposes [Lns, NIC1]. Paul's fasting was the result of not having enough food [TNTC]. Paul voluntarily missed meals in order to work or to engage in ministry [ICC1, ICC2, NIC1]. Paul sometimes went hungry because of poverty [NTC]. The fasting may have been due to his refusal to accept financial support from the Corinthians [EBC].

11:28 Apart-from[a] (these) external-things[b] (there is) the daily pressure[c] to-me, the anxiety[d] (about)[e] all the churches.

LEXICON—a. χωρίς (LN 89.120) (BAGD 2.b.ε. p. 891): 'apart from' [HNTC, LN, Lns; REB, TNT], '(other things) apart' [HNTC], 'aside from' [WBC], 'besides' [BAGD, NTC; CEV, KJV, NIV, NJB, NLT, NRSV], 'in addition to' [BAGD], 'not to mention' [AB; TEV], 'leaving unmentioned' [NAB].

b. παρεκτός (LN **58.38**) (BAGD 1. p. 625): 'external things' [NTC; REB], 'all the external things' [NJB], 'what is external' [BAGD], 'other matters' [**LN**], 'other things' [HNTC, ICC2; NRSV, TEV], 'all the other things' [WBC], 'all this' [NLT], 'everything else' [CEV, NIV, TNT], 'besides' [BAGD, LN, Lns], 'the things besides' [Lns], 'the things that are without' [KJV], 'what is unmentioned' [BAGD], 'other sufferings unmentioned' [NAB], 'additional' [LN].

c. επίστασις (LN **25.239, 35.42**) (BAGD p. 300): 'pressure' [AB, BAGD, ICC2, **LN** (25.239), NTC, WBC; NIV, NJB, NRSV, TEV, TNT], 'that which presses upon me' [HNTC], 'the press of a crowd' [Lns], 'that which cometh upon me' [KJV], 'tension pressing on me' [NAB], 'burden' [LN (25.239); NLT], 'I am burdened down' [CEV], 'responsibility' [REB], 'responsibility and concern for' [**LN** (35.42)], 'concern' [LN (25.239)].

d. μέριμνα (LN **25.224**) (BAGD p. 504): 'anxiety' [AB, BAGD, LN; NAB, NJB, NRSV, TNT], 'concern' [NIV, TEV], 'anxious concern' [**LN**; REB], 'anxious care' [ICC2], 'care' [HNTC; KJV], 'worry' [BAGD, LN], 'worrying about' [CEV]. The phrase ἡ μέριμνα πασῶν τῶν ἐκκλησιῶν 'the anxiety about all the churches' is translated 'how the churches are getting along' [NLT].

e. There is no lexical entry for the preposition 'about', the genitive case being used to express the relationship between 'anxiety' and 'all the churches'. This relationship is translated 'about' [CEV], 'for' [AB, HNTC, NTC, WBC; NAB, NIV, NJB, NRSV, REB, TEV, TNT], 'of' [HNTC; KJV], 'over' [Lns], 'how (they) are getting along' [NLT].

11:29 Who is-weak[a] and I-am not weak? Who is-caused-to-stumble[b] and I-do- not -burn?[c]

LEXICON—a. pres. act. indic. of ἀσθενέω (LN 74.26) (BAGD 2. p. 115): 'to be weak' [AB, BAGD, HNTC, ICC2, LN, Lns, NTC, WBC; CEV, KJV, NAB, NIV, NLT, NRSV, REB, TEV, TNT], 'to weaken' [NJB]. The phrase 'who is weak' is translated 'who is the weak person' [WBC], 'when others are weak' [CEV], 'when someone is weak' [TEV], 'if anyone is weak' [TNT], 'is anyone weak' [REB]. See this word also at 11:21.

b. pres. pass. indic. of σκανδαλίζω (LN **88.305**) (BAGD 1.a. p. 752, 2. p. 753): 'to be made to stumble' [AB; NRSV], 'to be caused to stumble into sin' [NTC], 'to be led into sin' [BAGD, ICC2; NIV, TEV], 'to fall into sin' [LN], 'to be tricked into sin' [CEV], 'to be trapped' [Lns], 'to be tripped up' [WBC], 'to be made to fall' [NJB], 'to fall away' [TNT], 'to be led astray' [NLT], 'to be scandalized' [NAB], 'to be offended' [HNTC; KJV], 'to be caused to take offense' [BAGD]. The phrase 'who is caused to stumble' is translated 'if anyone brings about the downfall of another' [REB].

c. pres. pass. indic. of πυρόω (LN **25.229**) (BAGD 1.b. p. 731): 'to burn' [BAGD, HNTC; KJV], 'to inwardly burn' [NIV], 'to be burning' [NTC], 'to be being burned' [Lns], 'to burn with indignation' [AB, ICC2], 'to burn in agony' [NJB], 'to burn with anger' [NLT, REB], 'to get angry' [CEV], 'to be indignant' [NRSV], 'to be aflame with indignation' [NAB], 'to feel indignation' [WBC], 'to be inflamed with sympathy or indignation' [BAGD], 'to burn with distress' [TNT], 'to be filled with distress' [TEV], 'to be worried and distressed' [LN].

QUESTION—In what sense would someone be 'weak'?
1. It refers to vulnerability to temptation [NAC, NIC1, NIC2, TG, TNTC] and immaturity [NAC]. It is spiritual as well as physical infirmity [SP], moral and physical weakness [He]. It refers to those who cannot withstand temptation, doubt, or opposition [Car].
2. It refers to weakness of faith in the sense of undue concern and scruples over minor things [EGT, Ho, ICC1, ICC2, NCBC].
3. It refers generally to being fainthearted and fearful [BAGD].
4. Paul is speaking of the state of having a non-powerful and unimpressive presence, both in terms of physical weakness as well as a non-charismatic personality [WBC].
5. The weakness is the burden of a person's pressures and responsibilities [Lns].

QUESTION—In what corresponding way would Paul be weak?
Paul was patiently sympathetic with the overly scrupulous [EGT, Ho, NCBC]. His weakness was his anxiety over their weakness [ICC1]. He is painfully sympathetic to their physical and moral weaknesses [He]. Paul struggles with the same spiritual weaknesses they must also deal with [NTC]. He feels compassion for their vulnerability to sin, knowing his own

[NIC1]. He is deeply concerned for their vulnerability to temptation [NAC]. Paul can identify with those who have been oppressed and abused by those who have exploited them [NIC2]. Because of his own experience of illness, discouragement and fear he is able to empathize with their weaknesses relative to doubt, temptation and opposition [Car]. In terms of his state of humiliation, his poverty, and unimpressive appearance, Paul is 'weaker' than them all [HNTC]. He identifies with those who are without power to work wonders because he is considered unimpressive physically as well as in his personality [WBC]. Paul's burden of responsibility is as great as or greater than anyone's [Lns].

QUESTION—What area of meaning is intended by σκανδαλίζω 'to cause to stumble'?

1. It refers to causing someone else to fall into sin [EGT, He, Ho, ICC1, ICC2, NAC, NCBC, NIC1, NIC2, NTC, SP, TG, TH, TNTC, WBC; CEV, NIV, NJB, NLT, REB, TEV], to fall into error [ICC1], or to fall away from faith [AB].
2. It refers to offending or upsetting another person [HNTC; KJV].
3. It refers to someone whose work and burden of responsibilities are a crushing load and who is therefore σκανδαλίζεται in the sense of being 'trapped' by that burden [Lns].

QUESTION—In what sense does Paul 'burn'?

He burns with indignation or anger [AB, Car, EGT, HNTC, Ho, ICC2, NAC, NCBC, NIC2, SP, TH, TNTC, WBC]. His anger is directed at those who lead others into sin [Car, Ho, NCBC, NTC, TH, TNTC] or who would harm the faith of others [NAB]. Paul burns with distress over the sinner as well as with anger toward the person causing the sin [NTC]. He burns with shame as well as with indignation [NIC1]. He burns with compassion such that he shares the remorse of the one who sinned [EBC]. Paul experiences the shame and distress over the sin along with the sinner [ICC1]. Paul is saying that if some are 'trapped' by the burden of responsibilities, by comparison he is burning with such burdens, which is to say his are much worse [Lns].

DISCOURSE UNIT: 11:30–33 [EBC]. The topic is escape from Damascus.

11:30 **If it-is-necessary[a] to-boast, I-will-boast (about) the (things) concerning[b] my weakness.[c]**

LEXICON—a. pres. act. indic. of δεῖ (LN 71.34) (BAGD 4. p. 172): 'to be necessary' [AB, BAGD, ICC2, LN], 'to have to' [Lns; CEV, NJB], 'I must' [HNTC, LN, NTC; NAB, NIV, NLT, NRSV, TEV, TNT], 'I must needs' [KJV], 'if there has to be' [WBC], 'if there must be' [REB]. See this word also at 2:3.

b. There is no lexical entry for the preposition 'concerning', the genitive case being used to express the relationship between τά 'the (things)' and τῆς ἀσθενείας μου 'my weakness'. This relation is translated 'of my weakness' [WBC; NAB], 'about my weakness' [AB], 'what belongs to my weakness' [HNTC], 'of the instances of my weakness' [ICC2], 'in

regard to the things pertaining to my weakness' [Lns], 'of the things that show my weakness' [NTC; NIV, NRSV, REB], 'of the things that concern my weakness' [TNT], 'of the things which concern my infirmities' [KJV], 'how weak I am' [CEV], 'about the things that show how weak I am' [NLT, TEV], 'the ways in which I am weak' [NJB].
c. ἀσθένεια (LN 74.23) (BAGD 1.b. p. 115): 'weakness' [AB, BAGD, HNTC, ICC2, LN, Lns, NTC, WBC; NAB, NIV, NRSV, REB, TNT], 'weak' [CEV, NJB, NLT, TEV], 'infirmity' [KJV].

11:31 **The God and father of (the) Lord Jesus, who is blessed[a] to eternity,[b] knows that I-am- not -lying.[c]**

LEXICON—a. εὐλογητός (LN 33.362) (BAGD p. 322): 'blessed' [AB, BAGD, HNTC, ICC2, Lns, WBC; KJV, NAB, NJB, NRSV, REB, TEV], 'praised' [BAGD, NTC; CEV, NIV, NLT, TNT], 'one to be praised' [LN]. See this word also at 1:3.

b. αἰών (LN 67.95) (BAGD 1.b. p. 27): 'eternity' [BAGD], 'always, eternally' [LN]. The phrase εἰς τοὺς αἰῶνας 'to eternity' is translated 'forever' [AB, HNTC, ICC2, LN, NTC; CEV, NAB, NIV, NJB, NLT, NRSV, REB, TEV, TNT], 'forevermore' [KJV], 'ever' [WBC], 'to the eons' [Lns].

c. ψεύδομαι (LN 33.253) (BAGD 1. p.891): 'to lie' [AB, BAGD, HNTC, ICC2, LN, Lns, NTC, WBC; all versions except NLT, REB]. The phrase 'I am not lying' is translated 'I tell the truth' [NLT], 'what I say is true' [REB].

QUESTION—Who is the subject of the phrase ὁ ὢν εὐλογητὸς εἰς τοὺς αἰῶνας 'who is blessed forever'?

The subject of this phrase is 'God' [AB, EGT, He, HNTC, Ho, ICC2, NAC, NCBC, NIC1, NIC2, NTC, SP, TH, TNTC, WBC; CEV, REB].

QUESTION—To what statement or statements does οὐ ψεύδομαι 'I am not lying' refer?
1. It refers to what follows in the immediate context about his escape from Damascus [Car, NAC, NCBC, NTC].
2. It refers to what he has already said [EBC, Ho, ICC2, Lns, NIC2, WBC]. It refers to what he has said in 11:30 about boasting in self-humiliation and weakness [ICC2, Lns, NIC2, WBC]. It refers to the entire preceding narrative about his sufferings [EBC, Ho].
3. It refers to the matters which he is discussing in the immediate context, both before and after this verse [ICC1, NIC1, SP]. It refers to what he has said in 11:30 and to what immediately follows [NIC1].

QUESTION—What is the relation of the phrase ὁ θεός 'the God' to the phrase καὶ πατὴρ τοῦ κυρίου Ἰησοῦ 'and father of our Lord Jesus Christ'?
1. It means 'the God and father of the Lord Jesus Christ' [HNTC, Ho, ICC1, ICC2, Lns, NIC1, NIC2, NTC, SP, TG, TH, WBC; all versions except CEV, NLT]. He is 'God' to Christ's human nature and 'father' to Christ's divine nature [Ho].

2. It means 'God, the father of our Lord Jesus Christ' [AB; CEV, NLT].

11:32 In Damascus the ethnarch^a of Aretas the king guarded^b the city of the Damascenes to arrest^c me,

LEXICON—a. ἐθνάρχης (LN **37.80**) (BAGD p. 218): 'official' [**LN**], 'ethnarch' [AB, BAGD, HNTC, ICC2, LN, Lns, WBC; NAB], 'governor' [BAGD, NTC; CEV, KJV, NIV, NJB, NLT, NRSV, TEV, TNT], 'commissioner' [REB].

b. φρουρέω (LN **37.119**) (BAGD 1.p. 867): 'to guard' [AB, BAGD, HNTC, ICC2, Lns, NTC, WBC; NRSV, TNT], 'to guard against' [LN], 'to have guarded' [CEV, NIV], 'to keep with a garrison' [KJV], 'to put guards around' [NJB], 'to keep/place guards at (the city gates)' [NLT, TEV], 'to keep under watch' [**LN**], 'to keep a close watch' [NAB], 'to keep under observation' [REB].

c. aorist active infinitive of πιάζω (LN 37.110) (BAGD 2.a. p. 657): 'to arrest' [BAGD, HNTC, LN, Lns, NTC; NAB, NIV, TEV], 'to have (me) arrested' [REB], 'to seize' [AB, BAGD, ICC2, LN; NRSV], 'to capture' [WBC; CEV], 'to apprehend' [KJV], 'to catch' [NJB, NLT], 'to lay hold of' [TNT].

11:33 And I-was-let-down^a in a basket^b through a window^c in the wall and escaped^d his hands.^e

LEXICON—a. aorist pass. indic. of χαλάω (LN **15.111**) (BAGD p. 874): 'to be let down' [AB, HNTC, ICC2, **LN**, NTC; CEV, KJV, NJB, NRSV, REB, TEV, TNT], 'to be lowered' [AB, LN, Lns, WBC; NAB, NIV, NLT].

b. σαργάνη (LN **6.148**) (BAGD p. 742): 'basket' [AB, BAGD, HNTC, ICC2, LN, Lns, NTC, WBC; all versions], 'rope basket' [BAGD]. This kind of large basket may have been made of braided rope [LN].

c. θυρίς (LN 7.47) (BAGD p. 366): 'window' [AB, BAGD, HNTC, ICC2, LN, NTC, WBC; all versions except TEV], 'door' [Lns], 'opening' [TEV].

d. aorist act. indicative of ἐκφεύγω (LN 21.14) (BAGD 2.b.β. p. 247): 'to escape' [AB, BAGD, HNTC, ICC2, LN, Lns, NTC, WBC; all versions except NIV, NLT], 'to slip through' [NIV], 'to get away' [NLT].

e. χείρ (LN 76.3) (BAGD 2.b. p. 880): 'hand' [BAGD, LN], 'power' [AB, BAGD, HNTC, ICC2, LN, Lns, NTC; KJV, NAB, NIV, NJB, NRSV, TNT], 'clutches' [WBC; REB], 'him' [TEV], not explicit [CEV, NLT].

QUESTION—What kind of basket was it that Paul escaped in?

The basket was braided [AB, Lns, NCBC, TG, TH] or woven [ICC1, NCBC, NTC, TG]. It was flexible [NIC2]. It was used for fish [Car, ICC1, NIC1, NTC]. It was used for hay or wool [NCBC].

QUESTION—What kind of window did Paul escape through?

It was a window in a house built on the wall of the city [Ho, NTC]. It was a door in the upper story or roof of a house [Lns]. It was an opening or window in the wall itself [He, ICC1].

DISCOURSE UNIT: 12:1–13:10 [NTC]. The topic is Paul's vision and warnings.
DISCOURSE UNIT: 12:1–10 [EBC, HNTC, ICC1, TH; CEV, NAB, NIV, NLT, NRSV, TEV]. The topic is a vision and its aftermath [EBC], visions from the Lord [CEV], Paul's vision and his thorn [NIV], glorying about revelations to Paul's soul and a thorn for his flesh [ICC1], Paul's visions and revelations [TH; NRSV, TEV], visions and revelations [NAB], Paul's vision and his thorn in the flesh [NLT], answering fools according to their folly: revelations [HNTC].

12:1 It-is-necessary[a] to-boast; (it is) not beneficial,[b] but[c] I-will-come[d] to visions[e] and revelations[f] of-the-Lord.

TEXT—Instead of καυχᾶσθαι δεῖ 'it is necessary to boast', some manuscripts have καυχᾶσθαι δή 'indeed, to boast' or καυχᾶσθαι δέ 'but boasting'. GNT selects the reading 'it is necessary to boast' with an A rating, indicating that the text is certain. The reading καυχᾶσθαι δή is taken by KJV which translates the first two phrases together as one clause: 'it is not expedient for me doubtless to glory'.

LEXICON—a. pres. act. indic. of δεῖ (LN 71.34): 'to be necessary' [AB, ICC2, LN, Lns; NRSV]. This verb, along with the present infinitive καυχᾶσθαι, is translated 'I must boast' [HNTC; TNT], 'I must continue to boast' [NTC], 'I must go on boasting' [WBC; NAB, NIV], 'I have to boast' [TEV], 'I have to brag' [CEV], 'I am boasting because I have to' [NJB], 'let me go on boasting' [NLT], 'I must go on with my boasting' [REB]. See this word also at 2:3; 11:30.

b. pres. act. participle of συμφέρω (LN 65.44) (BAGD 2.a., 2.b.β. p. 780): 'to be beneficial' [AB], 'to be helpful, to be profitable' [BAGD], 'to be of advantage' [BAGD, WBC], 'to be expedient' [HNTC, ICC2; KJV]. The phrase οὐ συμφέρον 'it is not beneficial' is translated 'not a furthersome thing' [Lns], 'nothing is to be gained' [NTC; NIV, NRSV], 'it may be useless' [NAB], 'not that it does any good' [NJB], 'it may do no good' [REB], 'it doesn't do any good' [TEV], 'this is foolish' [NLT], 'wrong though it is' [TNT]. See this word also at 8:10.

c. δέ (LN 89.124): 'but' [HNTC, ICC2, LN; CEV, NJB, NLT, NRSV, TEV], 'yet' [Lns], 'so' [TNT], 'and' [NAB], not explicit [KJV, REB]. This is translated as introducing a concessive clause 'although' [AB, NTC; NIV], 'though' [WBC].

d. fut. mid. indic. of ἔρχομαι (LN 15.7) (BAGD I.2.c. p. 311): 'to come to' [BAGD, HNTC, ICC2, LN, Lns, WBC; KJV, REB], 'to deal with' [BAGD], 'to go' [LN], 'to go on to' [NTC; NIV, NRSV], 'to move on to' [AB; NJB]. The next topic is also introduced with a non-metaphorical verb: 'I will now talk of' [TEV], 'I shall now tell of' [TNT], 'let me tell about' [NLT], 'I must speak of' [NAB], 'I must brag about' [CEV].

e. ὀπτασία (LN **33.488**) (BAGD 1. p. 576): 'vision' [AB, BAGD, HNTC, ICC2, LN, Lns, NTC, WBC; all versions].

f. ἀποκάλυψις (LN 28.38) (BAGD 2. p. 92): 'revelation' [AB, BAGD, HNTC, ICC2, LN, Lns, NTC, WBC; all versions except CEV]. The phrase 'revelations of the Lord' is translated 'things that the Lord has shown me' [CEV]. The genitive κυρίου is translated 'of the Lord' [HNTC, ICC2, Lns, NTC, WBC; KJV, NAB, NRSV], 'from the Lord' [NIV, NJB, TNT], 'I received from the Lord' [NLT], 'granted by the Lord' [AB; REB], 'given me by the Lord' [TEV], 'that the Lord has shown me' [CEV].

QUESTION—What is the concessive relationship in this verse?
  1. Paul will talk about visions, even though it does not help [AB, HNTC, ICC2, Lns, NTC, SP, WBC; CEV, NIV, NJB, NRSV].
  2. Paul will boast, even though it does not help [EGT, He, NAC; REB, TEV].
  3. Paul will boast and talk about visions, even though it does not help [NIC2; NAB, NLT, TNT].

QUESTION—How are the nouns related in the genitive construction ὀπτασίας καὶ ἀποκαλύψεις κυρίου 'visions and revelations of the Lord'?
  1. The genitive is subjective; that is, the visions and revelations are from the Lord or granted by the Lord [AB, EGT, He, Ho, ICC1, Lns, NCBC, NIC2, NTC, TG, TH].
  2. The genitive is objective; that is, the visions and revelations are about the Lord [SP].
  3. While the visions and revelations are from the Lord it is also possible that they may be about him as well [ICC2, NIC1, WBC].

QUESTION—Who is 'the Lord'?
  It is Christ [AB, EGT, He, Ho, ICC1, ICC2, NTC, SP, TG].

QUESTION—What distinction is there between visions and revelations?
  A vision involves something that is seen, whereas revelation means that God reveals something about his nature and will [TG]. Revelation is a wider term, encompassing more than just visions [Lns]. Visions are a form of revelation restricted to that which involves apparent sight [Car]. Visions are more specific, but revelation is higher because it communicates the importance of what is seen [Ho]. The revelations make plain what the visions are about [NAC]. In this passage the two terms are used more or less as synonyms and little or no distinction is intended [AB, SP, TG, TH].

12:2 **I-know a-man[a] in Christ (who) fourteen years ago, whether in (the) body[b] I-don't-know, whether out-of[c] the body I don't know, God knows,**

LEXICON—a. ἄνθρωπος (LN 9.24): 'man' [HNTC, ICC2, LN, NTC, WBC; KJV, NAB, NIV, NJB, REB, TEV, TNT], 'person' [AB; NRSV], 'human being' [Lns], not explicit [CEV]. The phrase 'a man in Christ' is translated 'one of Christ's followers' [CEV], 'a Christian man' [REB], 'a certain Christian man' [TEV], 'I' [NLT].

  b. σῶμα (LN 8.1) (BAGD 1.b. p. 799): 'body' [AB, BAGD, HNTC, ICC2, LN, Lns, NTC, WBC; all versions except TEV]. The phrase 'whether in

the body I don't know, whether out of the body I don't know' is translated 'whether my body was there or just my spirit, I don't know' [NLT], 'I don't know whether this actually happened or whether he had a vision' [TEV], 'I don't know if the man was still in his body when it happened' [CEV]. See this word also at 4:6; 5:10; 10:10.
  c. ἐκτός (LN **83.20**) (BAGD 2.a. p. 246): 'out of' [HNTC, ICC2, Lns, WBC; KJV, NIV, NJB, NRSV, REB, TNT], 'outside' [AB, **LN**, NTC; NAB], 'apart from' [LN], not explicit [CEV, NLT, TEV].
QUESTION—Why does Paul speak of his experience in the third person?
  Paul speaks in this manner because of his humility [Lns, NIC1], and because of his desire to avoid or remove boasting [Lns]. He has a sense of awe about it and is hesitant about speaking of special graces [SP]. Paul is embarrassed by boasting and does not want to draw attention to himself [WBC]. He is embarrassed to have to boast [Car, EBC], so he does it in such a way as to show no personal merit on his part and to accent his humiliation [Car]. Paul does not want to imply that he was a special kind of Christian or that the vision gave him a higher status or importance [EBC]. He distances himself from the event so as not to make claims for himself [NIC2]. He wants to avoid the appearance of arrogance [ICC2]. Paul's experience was intensely personal and not something he was eager to discuss openly [EGT, NAC]. Paul wants to avoid being egocentric [He, NAC]. It reflects the fact that Paul has experienced an ecstatic state in which the ego is displaced and transcended or objectified [AB, ICC2, SP]. His experience was so unique and otherworldly he speaks as though it happened to someone else [NIC1]. Paul distinguishes two men in himself; one is the visionary, and the other, which is how he wants to be known, is a weak man [AB, HNTC]. Paul is speaking in a tongue-in-cheek, ironical style, in which a speaker or writer pretends to be less than he really is [TG].
QUESTION—What is the date of Paul's experience?
  Paul's experience was some time in the early to mid 40's AD. It is variously dated in or about 40 AD [HNTC, SP], 42 AD [AB, ICC2, NIC2, NTC], 43 AD [EBC], or 44 AD [NIC1, WBC].

such-a-one was-caught-up[a] to[b] (the) third heaven.[c]
LEXICON—a. aorist pass. participle of ἁρπάζω (LN 18.4) (BAGD 2.b. p. 109): 'to be caught up' [AB, BAGD, HNTC, ICC2, NTC, WBC; KJV, NIV, NJB, NLT, NRSV, REB, TNT], 'to be snatched away' [BAGD, LN], 'to be snatched up' [Lns; NAB, TEV], 'to be taken up' [CEV].
  b. ἕως (LN 84.19) (BAGD II.2.a. p. 335): 'to' [ICC2, LN, Lns, WBC; KJV, NAB, NIV, NRSV, TEV, TNT], 'as far as' [BAGD, HNTC, LN, NTC; REB], 'clear to' [AB], 'into' [CEV, NLT], 'right into' [NJB].
  c. οὐρανός (LN **1.11**) (BAGD 1.e. p. 594): 'heaven' [AB, BAGD, HNTC, ICC2, LN, Lns, NTC, WBC; all versions]. The phrase 'the third heaven' is translated 'the highest heaven' [TEV].

QUESTION—What is the significance of this being called the 'third' heaven?
It is the highest level of heaven [Car, EGT, HNTC, Ho, ICC1, ICC2, Lns, NAC, NIC2, NTC, SP, TG, TH, WBC; TEV]. It is the heaven where God lives [NTC, TH].

12:3 And I-know such a man, whether in (the) body or apart-from^a the body I don't-know, God knows,

LEXICON—a. χωρίς (LN 89.120) (BAGD 2.b.α. p. 890): 'apart from' [AB, HNTC, ICC2, LN, Lns, WBC; NIV, REB, TNT], 'outside of' [BAGD, NTC], 'outside' [NAB, NJB], 'out of' [KJV, NRSV], not explicit [CEV, NLT, TEV].

12:4 that he-was-caught-up into^a paradise^b and heard unspeakable^c words^d which are-not-permitted^e for-man^f to speak.^g

LEXICON—a. εἰς (LN 84.22): 'into' [AB, HNTC, LN, Lns, NTC; CEV, KJV, NJB, NLT, NRSV, REB, TNT], 'to' [ICC2, WBC; NAB, NIV, TEV].
  b. παράδεισος (LN 1.11) (BAGD 2. p. 614): 'paradise' [AB, BAGD, HNTC, ICC2, LN, Lns, NTC, WBC; all versions].
  c. ἄρρητος (LN **33.95**) (BAGD 2. p. 109): 'unspeakable' [Lns, WBC; KJV], 'inexpressible' [BAGD; NIV], 'unutterable' [HNTC, ICC2], 'which cannot be uttered' [NAB], 'not to be spoken' [BAGD], 'that must not be divulged' [AB], 'that cannot be put into words' [LN; TEV], 'that cannot be spoken' [NJB], 'too sacred to utter' [NTC], 'not to be told' [NRSV], 'so secret' [REB, TNT], 'so astounding' [NLT]. The phrase 'unspeakable words which are not permitted for man to speak' is translated 'things that are too wonderful to tell' [CEV], 'words that cannot and may not be spoken by any human being' [NJB], 'so secret that human lips may not repeat them' [REB], 'so secret that no man dare try to put them into words' [TNT].
  d. ῥῆμα (LN 33.9) (BAGD 1. p. 735): 'word' [BAGD, HNTC, ICC2, LN, NTC, WBC; KJV, NAB, NJB, REB], 'utterance' [Lns], 'thing' [AB; CEV, NIV, NLT, NRSV, TEV, TNT].
  e. aorist pass. participle of the impersonal verb ἔξεστι (LN 71.32, 71.1): In the negated form 'must not' [LN (71.32)], 'ought not' [LN (71.32), NTC], 'may not' [NAB, NJB, REB], 'may not dare' [TNT], 'cannot be' [NLT, TEV], 'are not to be' [NRSV], 'to be impossible' [LN (71.1)], 'to be forbidden' [AB], 'to not be permitted' [HNTC; NIV], 'to not be lawful' [ICC2; KJV].
  f. ἄνθρωπος (LN 9.1): 'man' [HNTC, ICC2, NTC; KJV, NAB, NIV, TNT], 'human being' [AB, LN, Lns, WBC; NJB], 'human lips' [REB, TEV], 'mortal' [NRSV], not explicit [CEV, NLT]. The phrase 'not permitted for man to speak' is translated 'that human lips may not repeat' [REB], 'that human lips may not speak' [TEV], 'that no man dare try to put them into words' [TNT], 'too wonderful to tell' [CEV]. This word is used here in the generic sense, 'human being' (LN 9.1), as opposed to how it is used in v.2 to refer to a particular individual (LN 9.24).

g. aorist act. infin. of λαλέω (LN 33.70): 'to speak' [HNTC, ICC2, LN, NTC; NAB, NJB, TEV], 'to tell' [LN; CEV, NIV, NLT], 'to utter' [Lns, WBC; KJV], 'to repeat' [AB; NRSV, REB], 'to put into words' [TNT].

QUESTION—What is the relation of 'paradise' to 'the third heaven'?

They are synonymous terms [Car, HNTC, Ho, Lns, NAC, NIC2, NTC, SP, TG, TH, TNTC, WBC]. Paradise is located in the third heaven [EBC, EGT, He, NCBC].

QUESTION—Does 'unspeakable' mean that they are forbidden to be spoken or that they are so sublime or ineffable that there is no way to speak of them?

1. It is not permitted to speak the kinds of things Paul heard [AB, BAGD, EGT, He, HNTC, Ho, ICC1, ICC2, Lns, NAC, NIC2, TH, TNTC, WBC; REB]. What Paul heard may have been the divine name [ICC2].
2. What Paul heard was indescribable and cannot be communicated in human speech [EBC, NIC1, NTC].
3. What Paul heard was both indescribable as well as prohibited [Car, NCBC, TG].

12:5 About[a] such-a-one I-will-boast, but about myself I-will-not-boast except concerning[b] (my) weaknesses.[c]

LEXICON—a. ὑπέρ with genitive object (LN 90.24): 'about' [LN, NTC; CEV, NAB, NIV, NLT, REB, TEV, TNT], 'on behalf of' [AB, HNTC, ICC2, Lns, WBC; NJB, NRSV], 'concerning' [LN], 'of' [LN; KJV].

b. ἐν (LN 90.23): 'concerning' [LN], 'about' [LN, NTC; NAB, NIV, NLT, TNT], 'with respect to' [LN], 'of' [AB, ICC2; NJB, NRSV, REB], 'in' [HNTC, LN, Lns, WBC; KJV]. The phrase 'in my weaknesses' is translated 'to say how weak I am' [CEV], 'the things that show how weak I am' [TEV].

c. ἀσθένεια (LN 74.23) (BAGD 1.a., 1.b. p. 115): 'weakness' [AB, BAGD, HNTC, ICC2, LN, Lns, NTC, WBC; NAB, NIV, NJB, NLT, NRSV, REB, TNT], 'infirmity' [KJV], 'weak' [CEV, TEV]. See this word also at 11:30.

QUESTION—What are the 'weaknesses' of which he boasts?

They are the sufferings and privations associated with his ministry which are summarized in 11:23–28 [EGT, Lns, NIC2, NTC, WBC]. He is referring to what is described in 12:7ff. [ICC1, ICC2, SP, TNTC], especially the persecutions [ICC1].

12:6 For even-if[a] I-should-want[b] to-boast, I-would-not-be foolish,[c] for I-would-be-speaking[d] (the) truth.

LEXICON—a. ἐάν (LN 89.67): 'even if' [WBC; CEV, NAB, NIV], 'if' [HNTC, ICC2, LN, Lns, NTC; NJB, NRSV, REB, TEV, TNT], 'should (I wish)' [AB], 'though (I would)' [KJV], not explicit [NLT].

b. aorist act. subj. of θέλω (LN 25.1): 'to want' [LN, Lns; TEV, TNT], 'to desire' [LN; KJV], 'to wish' [AB, ICC2, LN, NTC; NRSV], 'to choose' [HNTC, WBC; NIV, NJB, REB], not explicit [CEV, NAB, NLT].

c. ἄφρων (LN 32.52) (BAGD p. 127): 'foolish' [BAGD, ICC2, LN, WBC; CEV, TNT], 'a fool' [AB, HNTC, Lns, NTC; KJV, NIV, NLT, NRSV, TEV], 'talking like a fool' [NJB], 'the boast of a fool' [REB], 'folly in me' [NAB]. See this word also at 11:16.

d. fut. act. indic. of εἶπον (the lexical form of the aorist tense of λέγω) (LN 33.69) (BAGD 1. p. 226): 'to speak' [BAGD, HNTC, ICC2, LN, NTC, WBC; CEV, NIV, NJB, NRSV, REB, TNT], 'to tell' [AB, BAGD, LN, Lns; NAB, NLT, TEV], 'to say' [LN; KJV].

But I-refrain,[a] lest anyone credit[b] to me more-than[c] what he-sees (in)[d] me or hears[e] from[f] me

LEXICON—a. pres. mid. or pass. (deponent = act.) indic. of φείδομαι (LN **13.152**) (BAGD 2. p. 854): 'to refrain' [BAGD, ICC2, LN, NTC, WBC; NAB, NIV, NRSV, REB], 'to decline (to do)' [AB], 'to forbear' [Lns; KJV], 'to avoid' [**LN**], 'to spare (someone)' [HNTC]. The phrase 'but I refrain' is translated 'but I will try not to say too much' [CEV], 'but I will not go on' [NJB], 'but I won't do it' [NLT], 'but I will not (boast)' [TEV, TNT]. See this word also at 1:23.

b. aorist mid. (deponent = act.) subj. of λογίζομαι (LN 31.1) (BAGD 1.a. p. 476): 'to credit (to someone)' [AB, BAGD, ICC2], 'to think' [NTC, WBC; CEV, KJV, NAB, NIV, NLT, NRSV], 'to reckon to' [HNTC, Lns], 'to have an opinion (of)' [TEV], 'to form an opinion of' [TNT], 'to regard, to consider' [LN], 'to form an estimate' [REB], 'to rate (me)' [NJB]. See this word also at 3:5; 5:19; 10:2, 7, 11; 11:5.

c. ὑπέρ (LN 78.29): 'more than' [HNTC, LN, NTC, WBC; NAB, NIV], 'more highly than' [CEV, NLT], 'better than' [NRSV], 'beyond' [AB, LN, Lns], 'which goes beyond' [REB], 'above' [KJV], 'higher' [NJB, TEV], 'too high' [TNT], 'that exceeds' [ICC2].

d. There is no lexical entry for this word. The phrase ὃ βλέπει με 'what he sees (in) me' is translated 'what he sees in me' [HNTC, WBC; NAB], 'what is seen in me' [NRSV], 'what he has seen from me' [NTC], 'what they can actually see in my life' [NLT], 'what he actually sees of me' [TNT], 'the evidence of his own eyes' [REB]. It is also translated as having an implied verb: 'what he sees me to be' [ICC2, Lns; KJV, NJB], 'what he sees me do/doing' [AB; CEV, TEV], 'what I do' [NIV].

e. pres. act. indic. of ἀκούω (LN 24.52) (BAGD 1.b.β. p. 32): 'to hear' [AB, BAGD, HNTC, ICC2, LN, Lns, NTC, WBC; KJV, NAB, NJB, NRSV, TEV, TNT]. The phrase 'what he sees in me or hears from me' is translated 'what you have seen me do and say' [CEV], 'what I do or say' [NIV], 'what they can actually see in my life and message' [NLT], 'the evidence of his own eyes and ears' [REB].

f. ἐκ (ἐξ) (LN 90.16): 'from' [AB, ICC2, LN, Lns, NTC, WBC; NAB, NRSV, TNT], 'of' [HNTC; KJV], not explicit [CEV, NIV, NJB, NLT, REB, TEV].

QUESTION—From what does Paul refrain?
Paul refrains from boasting [ICC1, ICC2, TG, TH, WBC]. He refrains from boasting about his visions [AB, EBC, NIC1, NIC2, TNTC], from boasting about his status and credentials [NTC], or from boasting about his abilities and successes [Ho]. Paul 'spares' the readers from having to hear him speak about himself [He].

12:7 (a) and (because-of)ᵃ the exceeding-greatnessᵇ of-the-revelations. Therefore, so-that I-might-not-exalt-myself,ᶜ
(b) And (because-of)ᵃ the exceeding-greatnessᵇ of-the-revelations, so-that I-might-not-exalt-myself,ᶜ

TEXT—The word διό 'therefore' does not occur in some manuscripts. It is included by GNT with a C rating, indicating difficulty in deciding whether or not to place it in the text. Because there is also considerable syntactic difficulty in this verse it is not clear which versions actually include it. Because of this variant and the syntactic difficulty there is some confusion in how the verse is to be punctuated. The first option listed above, option (a), reflects the punctuation of this verse as shown in the GNT and the inclusion of διό at the beginning of the next sentence, which is where διό would normally occur. This rendering has the disadvantage of making the relation of the clause 'and because of the exceeding greatness of the revelations' to what immediately precedes it less clear. This reading is taken by AB, NTC, WBC; NJB, NLT, NRSV. If the punctuation of GNT is altered, as reflected in option (b) listed above, διό occurs in mid-sentence and its logical function within the sentence is not entirely clear. This reading is taken by HNTC, ICC2, Lns; KJV, NAB, NIV, REB, TEV, TNT.

LEXICON—a. There is no lexical entry for this word, the grammatical relation being indicated in the Greek by the dative case of the noun ὑπερβολή. This relation is translated 'because of' [AB; NIV, NJB, TEV], 'because' [HNTC], 'on account of' [TNT], 'by reason of' [ICC2], 'by' [Lns; REB], 'through' [KJV], 'in the light of' [NTC], 'I am referring to' [CEV], 'as to' [NAB], 'even' [WBC], 'even though' [NLT], 'even considering' [NRSV].
b. ὑπερβολή (LN 78.33) (BAGD p. 840): 'greatness' [Lns], 'exceptional greatness' [NJB], 'extraordinary' [LN], 'extraordinary quality' [BAGD, ICC2], 'extraordinary character' [AB, NTC], 'exceptional character' [NRSV], 'abundance' [KJV], 'magnificence' [REB], 'amazing splendor' [TNT]. This noun is also translated as an adjective: 'extraordinary' [BAGD, WBC; NAB], 'marvelous' [HNTC], 'wonderful' [CEV, NLT, TEV], 'surpassingly great' [NIV]. See this word also at 1:8; 4:7, 17.
c. pres. pass. subj. of ὑπεραίρομαι (LN **88.211**) (BAGD p. 839): 'to exalt oneself' [BAGD], 'to be overly proud' [LN], 'to be overly exalted' [AB], 'to be too exalted' [NTC], 'to be unduly exalted' [HNTC], 'to be exalted above measure' [KJV], 'to be elated' [BAGD], 'to be too elated' [NRSV], 'to be unduly elated' [REB], 'to become elated with pride' [ICC2], 'to be puffed up' [NLT], 'to be puffed up with pride' [**LN**; TEV], 'to feel too

proud' [CEV], 'to lift oneself up unduly' [Lns], 'to become conceited' [WBC; NAB, NIV], 'to get above oneself' [NJB], 'to think too highly of oneself' [TNT].

QUESTION—What is the relation of the phrase τῇ ὑπερβολῇ τῶν ἀποκαλύψεων 'the exceeding greatness of the revelations' to the context?

1. It is related to what immediately follows it in 12:7 [Car, EGT, He, HNTC, ICC1, ICC2, Lns, NAC, NCBC, NIC1, NIC2, SP; KJV, NAB, NIV, REB, TEV, TNT]: Because of the exceeding greatness of the revelations, I was given the thorn in the flesh so that I would not become proud.
2. It goes with what immediately precedes it in 12:6 [AB, EBC, NTC, WBC; NJB, NLT, NRSV]: I refrain, lest anyone credit to me more than what he-sees or hears from me, because of the exceeding greatness of the revelations. I was given the thorn in the flesh so that I would not become proud.

a thorn[a] in[b] the flesh[c] was-given[d] to-me, an angel[e] of-Satan,

LEXICON—a. σκόλοψ (LN **3.54**) (BAGD p. 756): 'thorn' [AB, BAGD, HNTC, ICC2, LN, Lns, NTC, WBC; all versions except CEV, TEV], not explicit [CEV, TEV].
b. There is no lexical entry in the Greek text for the word 'in', the relation of σκόλοψ 'thorn' to σάρξ 'flesh' being indicated by in the dative case of τῇ σαρκί. It is translated 'in (the/my flesh)' [AB, HNTC, NTC, WBC; KJV, NAB, NIV, NJB, NLT, NRSV, REB, TNT], 'for (the flesh)' [ICC2, Lns].
c. σάρξ (LN 8.4, 26.7) (BAGD 1. p. 743): 'flesh' [AB, BAGD, HNTC, ICC2, Lns, NTC, WBC; KJV, NAB, NIV, NJB, NLT, NRSV, REB, TNT], 'body' [LN (8.4)], 'human nature' [LN (26.7)], not explicit [CEV, TEV]. The adjective 'my' is included by HNTC, NTC; NIV, NLT, REB. The phrase 'thorn in the flesh' is translated 'suffer terribly' [CEV], 'a painful physical ailment' [TEV]. 1:17; 4:11; 5:16; 7:1; 7:5; 10:3; 11:18.
d. aorist pass. indic. of δίδωμι (LN 90.90): 'to be given' [AB, HNTC, ICC2, Lns, NTC, WBC; all versions except CEV], 'to be made to experience' [LN], not explicit [CEV].
e. ἄγγελος (LN 12.28) (BAGD 2.c. p. 8): 'angel' [AB, BAGD, HNTC, ICC2, LN; CEV, NAB], 'messenger' [BAGD, Lns, NTC, WBC; KJV, NIV, NJB, NLT, NRSV, REB, TEV, TNT].

QUESTION—Who is the agent of the passive verb 'was given'?
This is a divine passive indicating that God gave the thorn [AB, Car, EBC, He, Ho, ICC1, ICC2, Lns, NAC, SP, TG, WBC]. The Lord gave the 'thorn' [NTC].

QUESTION—Which part of the phrase σκόλοψ τῇ σαρκί 'a thorn to the flesh' is figurative or metaphorical?

1. The word 'thorn' is metaphorical and τῇ σαρκί is concrete, indicating that the metaphorical 'thorn' was something that caused physical pain to his body, his flesh [AB, EGT, Ho, ICC1, ICC2, Lns, NAC, NTC, SP, TG, TH, WBC; TEV].

2. The entire phrase σκόλοψ τῇ σαρκί is metaphorical [Aber NEO, LN]. It is drawn from several similar phrases in the LXX (Num 33:55, Ezek 28:24, Josh 23:13, Judg 2:3) which represent divine discipline through opposition by enemies. The phrase 'thorn in the flesh' metaphorically describes the presence and work of an actual angel of Satan, one which brings opposition and persecution. The cumulative effect of this 'thorn' is summarized by Paul in 12:10 as 'weaknesses, insults, hardships, persecutions and distresses' [Aber NEO]. The thorn in the flesh consists of or includes opposition to Paul and his ministry [LN].

QUESTION—What area of meaning is intended by σάρξ 'flesh'?
 1. It is concrete and refers to Paul's physical body [AB, EGT, Ho, ICC1, ICC2, Lns, NAC, NCBC, NIC1, NTC, SP, TG, WBC; TEV].
 2. It refers to Paul's mortal existence as living life in this world [NIC2].
 3. It refers to Paul's fleshly or sinful nature [Aber NEO].

so-that he-might-beat^a me, so-that I-might-not-be-lifted-up.

TEXT—In some manuscripts the phrase ἵνα μὴ ὑπεραίρωμαι 'so that I may not be lifted up' does not occur this second time here at the end of the verse. It is included by GNT with a B rating, indicating that the text is almost certain. It is omitted only by NIV.

LEXICON—a. pres. act. subj. of κολαφίζω (LN **20.27**) (BAGD 2. p. 441): 'to beat' [BAGD, HNTC, ICC2; NAB, TEV], 'to fisticuff' [Lns], 'to buffet' [NTC; KJV, REB], 'to batter' [WBC; NJB], 'to cause harm to' [LN], 'to abuse' [AB], 'to torment' [NIV, NLT, NRSV], 'to attack' [TNT], not explicit [CEV]. The phrases 'a thorn in the flesh...so that he might beat me' are conflated and translated 'to make me suffer terribly' [CEV]. There is no pronoun 'he' in the Greek text, and all English versions use an infinitive to translate this verb, thus avoiding the pronoun. The 'angel of Satan' is the subject of the action of the verb, and is the one who does the beating or tormenting [AB, Aber NEO, He, HNTC, ICC1, ICC2, Lns, NAC, NIC1, NIC2, NTC, TG, WBC; CEV, NJB, NLT, NRSV, REB, TEV, TNT].

12:8 Three-times concerning^a this I-appealed-to^b the Lord that it/he^c-depart^d from me.

LEXICON—a. ὑπέρ (LN 90.24) (BAGD 1.d. p. 839): 'concerning' [HNTC, LN, Lns, WBC], 'about' [AB, ICC2, LN; NJB, NRSV, TEV], 'for' [KJV], not explicit [NTC; CEV, NAB, NIV, NLT, REB, TNT].
 b. aorist act. indic. of παρακαλέω (LN 33.168) (BAGD 1.c. p. 617): 'to appeal to' [AB, LN; NRSV], 'to plead for/with' [LN, WBC; NIV, NJB], 'to ask' [HNTC], 'to implore' [ICC2], 'to urge' [Lns], 'to beg' [NTC; CEV, NAB, NJB, REB, TNT], 'to beseech' [KJV], 'to pray to' [TEV], 'to call upon for help' [BAGD]. See this word also at 1:4, 6; 2:7, 8; 5:20; 6:1; 7:6; 8:6; 9:5; 10:1; 12:8.
 c. The subject of the verb is not explicit in the Greek text, being implied in the third person singular form of the verb. The pronoun used for the

implied subject is 'it' [AB, ICC2, Lns; KJV, NJB, NRSV]; 'this' [NAB]; 'he' [HNTC]. Versions translating the verb as an infinitive use a pronoun or phrase as the implied object of the infinitive: 'it' [NTC, WBC; NIV, NLT, REB, TEV], 'this suffering' [CEV], 'this' [TNT].
    d. aorist act. subj. of ἀφίστημι (BAGD 2.b. p. 127): 'to depart' [KJV], 'to leave' [ICC2; NAB, NJB, NRSV], 'to go away' [AB, HNTC], 'to stand away' [Lns], 'to keep away' [BAGD]. This subjunctive verb is also translated as an infinitive associated with the verb παρακαλέω 'to appeal to': Paul appealed to the Lord 'to remove it' [NTC], 'to take it away' [WBC; NIV, NLT, TEV, TNT], 'to make it go away' [CEV], 'to rid (me) of it' [REB].
QUESTION—Who is 'the Lord' to whom Paul prays?
    It is Christ [AB, Car, EBC, EGT, He, Ho, ICC1, ICC2, NIC1, NIC2, NTC, SP, TG, TH, WBC].
QUESTION—What is the antecedent to τούτου 'this'?
    1. It is a masculine pronoun and refers to the angel of Satan [Aber NEO, EBC, HNTC, Ho, ICC1, NIC1, NIC2, SP, WBC].
    2. It is a masculine pronoun and refers to the thorn [AB].
    3. It is a neuter pronoun and refers to the situation or problem in general [He, ICC2, Lns, NAC, NTC, TG].

12:9 And he-said[a] to-me "My grace[b] is-enough[c] for-you, for power[d] is-perfected[e] in weakness."[f]
TEXT—Some manuscripts include μου 'my' after δύναμις 'power'. It is omitted by GNT with an A rating, indicating that the text is certain. The reading 'my power' is taken by NTC, WBC; CEV, KJV, NIV, NLT, TEV, though possibly for stylistic reasons only.
LEXICON—a. perf. act. indic. of εἶπον (the lexical form of the aorist tense of λέγω) (LN 33.69): 'to say' [AB, HNTC, ICC2, LN, NTC, WBC; KJV, NAB, NIV, NLT, NRSV, TNT], 'to tell' [LN, Lns], 'to reply' [CEV], 'to answer' [NJB]. The phrase 'he has said to me' is translated 'his answer was' [REB, TEV]. The perfect tense may indicate an act which has ongoing effect, i.e., the answer given continues to be valid. It may also simply be used in place of the aorist form. It is translated as a perfect tense by HNTC, ICC2, Lns; NJB, TNT. It is translated as a simple aorist by AB, NTC, WBC; CEV, KJV, NAB, NIV, NLT, NRSV, REB, TEV.
    b. χάρις (LN 88.66) (BAGD 4. p. 878): 'grace' [AB, BAGD, HNTC, ICC2, LN, Lns, NTC, WBC; all versions except CEV, NLT], 'gracious favor' [NLT], 'kindness' [CEV]. See this word also at 1:2, 12; 8:1, 4, 6, 9, 16, 19; 9:8, 14, 15.
    c. present act. indic. of ἀρκέω (LN 59.46) (BAGD 1. p. 107): 'to be enough' [AB, BAGD, HNTC, LN; NAB, NJB, TNT], 'to be sufficient' [BAGD, ICC2, LN, Lns, NTC, WBC; KJV, NIV, NRSV], 'to be all one needs' [CEV, NLT, REB, TEV].

d. δύναμις (LN 76.1): 'power' [AB, HNTC, ICC2, LN, Lns, NTC, WBC; all versions except KJV], 'strength' [KJV]. See this word also at 1:8; 4:7; 8:3.

e. pres. pass. indic. of τελέω (LN 68.22) (BAGD 1. p. 811): 'to be made perfect' [NTC; KJV, NIV, NRSV, TNT], 'to come to perfection' [HNTC, ICC2], 'to reach perfection' [BAGD; NAB], 'to be completed' [BAGD, LN], 'to be fulfilled' [WBC], 'to be made fully present' [AB], 'to be most fully seen' [REB], 'to be strongest' [CEV], 'to be greatest' [TEV], 'to work best' [NLT], 'to be brought to its finish' [Lns], 'to be at full stretch' [NJB].

f. ἀσθένεια (LN **74.23**) (BAGD 1.b. p. 115): 'weakness' [AB, BAGD, HNTC, ICC2, LN, Lns, NTC, WBC; all versions except CEV, TEV], 'incapacity, limitation' [LN]. This noun is translated as a phrase: 'when you are weak' [CEV, TEV]. See this word also at 11:30; 12:5.

QUESTION—What is the primary meaning of χάρις 'grace' here?

In this context it primarily refers to Christ's power [AB, ICC2], or is closely associated with it [NIC2]. Power and grace are synonyms here [Lns, SP, WBC]. It is Christ's enabling strength [EBC]. His grace is revealed in his power [NTC]. It is the enabling power present in Christ's love that gives strength to endure suffering and hardship [TG]. It is that which enables Christian faith and service and which assures a believer of his standing with God [HNTC]. God's grace is his love that enables faith and endurance [WBC]. It is the force by which God sustains believers throughout their lives [NAC]. It is God's unmerited favor [TH]. It is God's movement in love toward human beings [HNTC, ICC2].

QUESTION—In what way is power 'perfected' in weakness?

God's power is best displayed or manifested when human weakness is most evident [HNTC, Ho, NTC, TNTC]. It becomes more visible as it works through Paul's weakness [NAC]. God's power is more conspicuous and no one is confused about whose power is at work [NIC1]. Paul's weakness is the means by which God's power is revealed [AB]. God's power becomes a reality in weakness [NIC2]. The more a Christian recognizes weakness, the more Christ's enabling strength is evident [EBC]. Because of the problems Paul experienced, the divine power at work in his preaching and ministry is shown to be God's, not Paul's [ICC2, NCBC]. His power is able to work best when Paul is weak [TG]. Christ's power becomes complete in the weak person who depends on him [TH]. God's grace is poured out in greater measure where the weakness and need are greater [Car]. Because of Paul's weaknesses God's power is now the focus of his work [WBC]. God's power finishes its work of humbling Paul when Paul is completely weak [Lns].

most-gladly[a] therefore I-will-boast rather[b] about[c] my weaknesses, so-that the power of-Christ may-rest upon me.[d]

LEXICON—a. ἥδιστα (superlative of ἡδέως) (LN **85.75**) (BAGD p. 344): 'most gladly' [HNTC, WBC; KJV, TNT], 'very gladly' [AB, ICC2, Lns],

'all the more gladly' [NTC; NIV, NRSV], 'gladly' [CEV], 'willingly' [NAB]. This adverb is also translated as a phrase: 'I am glad' [NLT], 'I am happy' [REB], 'I am most happy' [TEV], 'I am happiest of all' [NJB]. See this word in its ordinary form at 11:19.
- b. μᾶλλον (LN 89.126) (BAGD 3.a.β. p. 489): 'rather' [AB, BAGD, HNTC, ICC2; KJV], 'instead' [LN; NAB], 'the more' [Lns], 'all the more' [NTC; NRSV], not explicit [WBC; CEV, NIV, NJB, NLT, REB, TEV, TNT].
- c. ἐν (LN 90.23): 'about' [LN; CEV, NIV, NJB, NLT, TNT], 'in' [HNTC, LN, Lns, WBC; KJV], 'of' [AB, ICC2, NTC; NAB, NRSV, REB, TEV].
- d. ἐπισκηνόω (LN **85.75**) (BAGD p. 298): 'to rest (upon/on)' [HNTC, ICC2, WBC; KJV, NAB, NIV, NJB, REB], 'to dwell (in)' [BAGD, NTC; NRSV], 'to come to dwell' [LN], 'to make its dwelling' [TNT], 'to reside (with)' [AB], 'to spread its tent (over)' [Lns]. The phrase 'so that the power of Christ may rest upon me' is translated 'so that the power of Christ may work through me' [NLT], 'to feel the protection of Christ's power over me' [TEV], 'if Christ keeps giving me his power' [CEV].

QUESTION—What relationship is indicated by οὖν 'therefore'?

It indicates Paul's response to what the Lord has said to him: because Christ's power is made perfect in weakness he will gladly boast about weakness [ICC1, NIC2, NTC, SP]. Paul draws a conclusion about his situation based on the Lord's assurance that his weakness will not hinder his ministry [WBC]. Because of Christ's assurance about the all-sufficiency of God's grace Paul welcomes the weaknesses [NIC1]. Because of the way Christ's power works in weaknesses, he will boast in them [ICC2].

QUESTION—What relationship is indicated by μᾶλλον 'rather'?
1. Paul would rather boast in his weaknesses than to pray for their removal [AB, EBC, Ho, ICC2, NIC1, SP].
2. He would rather boast in his weaknesses than in his visionary experience [ICC2, NIC2, WBC]. Paul would rather boast in his weaknesses than in anything else [HNTC].
3. It intensifies the boasting: I will boast the more [Lns]. It intensifies the adverb ἥδιστα: all the more gladly [NTC; NRSV].

QUESTION—What is implied by Paul's use of the verb ἐπισκηνόω 'to dwell'?
1. Paul employs an image of the *shekinah* glory in the wilderness tabernacle [EGT, He, HNTC, Ho, ICC2, NIC1, NIC2, WBC]. Paul employs vocabulary used of the old covenant tabernacle in which God pitched his tent to dwell among his people [NIC2]. Paul is associating the σκηνή 'tent' or 'tabernacle' and the *shekinah* (with the Hebrew consonantal spelling *s-k-n* being similar to the Greek σκηνή), the glory of God that was present in the tabernacle, with his experience of Christ's power dwelling in him [NIC1]. The power of God, which cannot be separated from his glory, descends upon and dwells in the frail tabernacle of Paul's body [NIC1]. It speaks of the intimate presence of the Lord in Paul's life [NTC]. The concept of the *shekinah* lies in the background and emphasizes the visibility of Christ's power in Paul's life [ICC2]. It

suggests the presence of God that overshadowed Israel in the wilderness [HNTC].
2. This verb is not necessarily intended to connote the *shekinah* or the tabernacle [AB, Lns, SP].

12:10 Therefore I-am-content[a] in weaknesses, in insults,[b] in hardships,[c] in persecutions[d] and distresses[e] for-the-sake-of[f] Christ

LEXICON—a. pres. act. indic. of εὐδοκέω (LN 25.87) (BAGD 2.b. p. 319): 'to be content (with)' [NAB, NRSV, REB, TEV], 'to be quite content (with)' [NLT], 'to be well content (in)' [HNTC], 'to willingly accept' [TNT], 'to be pleased (with)' [AB, LN], 'to take pleasure (in)' [ICC2, LN, Lns; KJV], 'to be glad of' [NJB], 'to be glad to be' [CEV], 'to delight (in)' [BAGD, WBC; NIV], 'to take delight (in)' [NTC]. See this word also at 5:8.

b. ὕβρις (LN **20.19, 33.391, 88.131**) (BAGD 2. p. 832): 'insult' [AB, BAGD, HNTC, ICC2, LN (33.391), NTC, WBC; NIV, NJB, NLT, NRSV, REB, TEV], 'mistreatment' [BAGD, LN (88.131), Lns; NAB], 'ill treatment' [TNT], 'reproach' [KJV], 'injury' [LN (20.19)]. This noun is also translated as a verb: 'to be insulted' [CEV].

c. ἀνάγκη (LN 22.1) (BAGD 2, 3, p. 52): 'hardship' [NTC; NIV, NLT, NRSV, REB, TEV, TNT], 'trouble' [LN], 'distress' [BAGD (2.), LN; NAB], 'occasions of distress' [ICC2], 'calamity' [BAGD (2.)], 'constraint' [NJB], 'catastrophe' [AB], 'anguish' [HNTC, WBC], 'necessity' [Lns; KJV], 'compulsion, torture' [BAGD (3.)]. This noun is also translated as a verb: 'to be mistreated' [CEV]. See this word also at 6:4; 9:7.

d. διωγμός (LN 39.45) (BAGD p. 201): 'persecution' [AB, BAGD, HNTC, ICC2, LN, Lns, NTC, WBC; KJV, NAB, NIV, NJB, NLT, NRSV, REB, TEV, TNT], '(to have) troubles' [CEV].

e. στενοχωρία (LN 22.10) (BAGD p. 766): 'distress' [BAGD, HNTC, LN, Lns, WBC; KJV, NJB, REB], 'difficulty' [BAGD, ICC2, LN, NTC; NAB, NIV, TEV], 'trouble' [BAGD], 'pressure' [AB], 'calamity' [NLT, NRSV], 'frustration' [TNT], '(to have) suffering' [CEV]. See this word also at 6:4.

f. ὑπέρ (LN 90.36): 'for the sake of' [LN, Lns, NTC, WBC; KJV, NAB, NIV, NJB, NRSV, REB, TEV, TNT], 'for the good of' [NLT], 'for' [LN; CEV], 'because of' [AB], 'on behalf of' [HNTC, ICC2, LN].

QUESTION—What relationship is indicated by διό 'therefore'?

Paul draws a conclusion from the spiritual lesson he has learned from Christ [EBC]. Because Christ's power is made perfect in weakness, Paul responds and concludes that he will take pleasure in weakness [NIC1, NIC2]. The Lord's answer provides the reason for Paul's spirituality of the cross [SP]. It is connected to the thought of 12:7; Paul has not fallen into pride and conceit and the thorn has brought its intended benefit to him [WBC]. Because weaknesses give occasion for Christ's power to be displayed, Paul will take pleasure in them [ICC1, ICC2].

QUESTION—What relationship is indicated by the phrase ὑπὲρ Χριστοῦ 'for the sake of Christ'?

1. It is related to the five nouns; Paul's weaknesses, insults, hardships, persecutions, and distresses are suffered for the sake of Christ [Car, EBC, HNTC, Ho, NIC1, NIC2, SP, TG, WBC; CEV].
2. It is related to the verb; for the sake of Christ or because of Christ Paul is pleased with or at least accepts whatever happens [AB, ICC1, ICC2, NCBC; NIV].
3. It goes with the verb as well as with the five nouns; for Christ's sake Paul is content with suffering, since his suffering is for Christ's sake [NTC, TH].

for whenever^a I-am-weak,^b then I-am powerful.^c

LEXICON—a. ὅταν (LN 67.31) (BAGD 1.a. p. 588): 'whenever' [BAGD, ICC2, LN, Lns; NRSV], 'when' [AB, HNTC, NTC, WBC; CEV, KJV, NAB, NIV, NJB, NLT, REB, TEV, TNT].
b. pres. act. subj. of ἀσθενέω (LN 74.26) (BAGD 1.b. p. 115): 'to be weak' [AB, BAGD, HNTC, ICC2, LN, Lns, NTC, WBC; all versions except NAB], 'to be powerless' [NAB]. See this word also at 11:21, 29.
c. δυνατός (LN 74.2) (BAGD 1.a.α. p. 208): 'powerful' [AB, BAGD, Lns, WBC], 'strong' [BAGD, HNTC, ICC2, NTC; CEV, KJV, NAB, NIV, NJB, NLT, NRSV, REB, TEV, TNT], 'able' [BAGD, LN]. See this word also at 10:4.

QUESTION—In what sense is Paul powerful when he is weak?

It is in the context of helplessness and vulnerability that Paul cries out to Christ, who is able through his resurrection power to give grace and power to those who ask [NIC2]. Paul has spiritual strength when he acknowledges how much he needs Christ [TH]. When he loses his own strength he is able to have Christ's strength [NCBC, TG]. God's power working in Paul is most clearly seen when Paul appears weak [Car, NAC]. When Paul is weak it can be seen that the power at work is power in a kingdom and not power in a man [Lns]. God strengthens those who feel and acknowledge their weakness [Ho]. Weaknesses give opportunity for the display of Christ's power [ICC2, NIC1]. When he is weak, Christ's power can become more effective in his apostolic service [AB]. When believers humble themselves and acknowledge their weakness, Christ's power flows through them [WBC]. In his distressing weakness he would never lack grace to be more than a conqueror [EBC].

DISCOURSE UNIT: 12:11–13:13 [REB]. The topic is Paul's final appeal.

DISCOURSE UNIT: 12:11–21 [TH; CEV, NAB, NIV, NLT, NRSV, TEV]. The topic is concern for the Corinthian church [NAB], Paul's concern for the Lord's followers at Corinth [CEV], Paul's concern for the Corinthians [TH; NIV, NLT, TEV], Paul's concern for the Corinthian church [NRSV].

DISCOURSE UNIT: 12:11-18 [HNTC, ICC1, WBC]. The topic is Paul's apostolate justified [WBC], answering objections [HNTC], the credentials of an apostle: exceptional signs and exceptional love [ICC1].

DISCOURSE UNIT: 12:11-13 [AB, EBC]. The topic is the epilogue to the fool's speech [AB], proof of apostleship [EBC].

12:11 I-have-been[a] foolish;[b] you forced[c] me. Indeed,[d] I[e] ought-to[f] have-been-commended[g] by you.

LEXICON—a. pres. act. indic. of γίνομαι (LN 13.3, 13.48): 'to be' [AB, LN (13.3), NTC; NRSV, REB, TNT], 'to become' [HNTC, ICC2, LN (13.48), Lns, WBC; KJV, NAB], 'to turn into (a fool)' [NJB], 'to make (a fool of myself)' [CEV, NIV], 'to act (like a fool)' [NLT, TEV].

b. ἄφρων (LN 32.52) (BAGD p. 127): 'foolish' [BAGD, LN; REB, TNT], 'fool' [AB, HNTC, ICC2, Lns, NTC, WBC; all versions except REB, TNT]. See this word also at 11:16.

c. aorist act. indic. of ἀναγκάζω (LN 37.33): 'to force' [AB, ICC2, LN, NTC; CEV, NJB, NRSV], 'to compel' [HNTC, LN, Lns, WBC; KJV, TNT], 'to drive (me)' [NAB, NIV, REB], 'to make (me)' [NLT, TEV].

d. γάρ (LN 89.23): 'indeed' [NTC; NRSV], 'for' [HNTC, LN, Lns, WBC; KJV], 'since' [AB], not explicit [CEV, NAB, NIV, NJB, NLT, REB, TEV, TNT].

e. The personal pronoun ἐγώ 'I' is used to indicate emphasis in this sentence. This emphasis is expressed in various ways in the versions: 'it was I who ought to have received commendation from you' [ICC2], 'you are the ones who should have been commending me' [NAB], 'indeed you should have commended me' [NTC], 'indeed you should have been the ones commending me' [NRSV], 'it is you that should have been commending me' [NJB], 'you are the ones who ought to show your approval of me' [REB], 'you compelled me, you who ought to have been commending me' [TNT].

f. imperf. act. indic. of ὀφείλω (LN 71.25) (BAGD 2.a.β. p. 599): 'ought' [AB, BAGD, HNTC, ICC2, LN, Lns, WBC; KJV, NIV, NLT, TEV, TNT], 'should' [NTC; CEV, NAB, NJB, NRSV, REB].

g. pres. pass. infin. of συνίστημι (LN 33.344) (BAGD I.1.b. p. 790): 'to be commended' [BAGD, HNTC, Lns, WBC; KJV, NIV], 'to receive commendation' [ICC2], 'to be recommended' [AB, BAGD, LN], 'to commend' [NTC; NAB, NJB, NRSV, TNT], 'to write commendations for' [NLT], 'to speak up for' [CEV], 'to show approval' [TEV]. The phrase 'I ought to have been commended by you' is translated 'my credentials should have come from you' [REB]. See this word also at 3:1, 4:2, 5:12, 6:4, 7:11, 10:12 and 10:18.

QUESTION—How did they 'force' Paul to become foolish?
They forced him into defending himself by the fact that they did not defend him [AB, EBC, EGT, He, HNTC, Ho, ICC1, ICC2, NAC, NCBC, NIC1, NIC2, NTC, TNTC, WBC], by heeding his opponents' boasting [EBC,

NCBC], by being led astray [NAC], and by commending those who attacked Paul [ICC1]. They forced him to show that his rivals do not compare with him at all [Lns].

For[a] (in) nothing[b] have-I-been-inferior[c] to the super[d] apostles, even though[e] I-am nothing.[f]

LEXICON—a. γάρ (LN 89.23): 'for' [AB, HNTC, ICC2, LN, Lns, NTC, WBC; KJV, NIV, NLT, NRSV, TNT], not explicit [CEV, NAB, NJB, REB, TEV].
  b. οὐδέν (LN 92.23) (BAGD 2.b.γ. p. 592): '(in) nothing' [LN, NTC; KJV, REB], '(in) no respect' [BAGD, ICC2, Lns], '(in) no way' [AB, WBC; NAB, TEV, TNT], '(in) no way at all' [HNTC], 'not at all' [NLT, NRSV], 'not in the least' [NIV]. The phrase 'in nothing have I been inferior' is translated 'I am as good' [CEV], '(they) have no advantage' [NJB].
  c. aorist act. indic. of ὑστερέω (LN 87.65) (BAGD 1.c. p. 849): 'to be inferior to' [AB, BAGD, LN, NTC, WBC; NAB, NIV, NLT, NRSV, TEV, TNT], 'to prove inferior to' [ICC2; REB], 'to come behind' [HNTC], 'to be behind' [Lns; KJV], not explicit [CEV, NJB]. See this word also at 11:5, 9.
  d. ὑπερλίαν (LN 78.34) (BAGD p. 841): 'exceedingly, beyond measure' [BAGD]. The phrase ὑπερλίαν ἀποστόλων is translated 'super apostles' [AB, BAGD, HNTC, ICC2, NTC; CEV, NAB, NIV, NJB, NLT, NRSV, REB], 'superfine apostles' [Lns], 'very exceptional apostles' [LN], 'the highest ranking apostles' [WBC], 'the very chiefest apostles' [KJV], 'very superior apostles' [TNT], 'very special apostles' [LN], 'those very special "apostles" of yours' [TEV]. See this word also at 11:5.
  e. εἰ καί: 'even though' [AB, HNTC, ICC2, NTC; NAB, NIV, NLT, NRSV], 'though' [WBC; KJV], 'even if' [Lns; NJB, REB, TEV, TNT], not explicit [CEV].
  f. οὐδέν (LN 92.23) (BAGD 2.b.β. p. 592): 'nothing' [AB, BAGD, HNTC, ICC2, LN, Lns, NTC, WBC; KJV, NAB, NIV, NRSV, TEV, TNT], 'nothing at all' [CEV, NJB, NLT], 'a nobody' [REB].

QUESTION—What is implied in Paul's claim to be 'nothing'?
  It expresses Paul's genuine sense of humility, unworthiness, and weakness [Ho, ICC1, Lns, NAC, NTC, TNTC]. Paul knows that he owes everything to God's grace [AB, Car, Ho, NAC, NIC1, NTC], that he really is nothing apart from God's grace [AB] and the power of Christ [ICC2]. Paul knows that he is nothing in God's eyes and is last among the apostles [EGT]. Paul is nothing in the sense that the signs were performed by God and not by him [NIC2], although in terms of apostolic ministry he is not inferior to his rivals [Car, NIC2, WBC]. Because his claim to apostolic authority is just as good as theirs he does not really see himself as nothing in terms of ministry [ICC2]. Paul is summarizing the Corinthians' low opinion of him [He, Lns]. It is an ironic or sarcastic reference to what his opponents were saying about

him [ICC1, ICC2, TH, TNTC], that is, he may be nothing, but at least he is not inferior to them [ICC1, TG, TH]. If he is nothing, so are they [NAC]. Paul is repeating a charge by his rivals, which in fact really is true but in a different sense than what they meant [HNTC, WBC], and he is glad to acknowledge its truth so that Christ can be seen as everything [WBC].

12:12 **Indeed,[a] the signs[b] of an apostle were-performed[c] among you with all perseverance,[d]**

LEXICON—a. μέν (LN 91.6, **91.3**) (BAGD 2.a. p. 503): 'indeed' [LN (91.6); NAB], 'truly' [KJV], 'at least' [HNTC, Lns], not explicit [AB, ICC2, LN (91.3), NTC, WBC; CEV, NIV, NJB, NLT, NRSV, REB, TEV, TNT].

b. σημεῖον (LN 33.477) (BAGD 1. p. 748): 'sign' [AB, BAGD, HNTC, ICC2, LN, Lns, NTC, WBC; KJV, NAB, NRSV, REB], 'distinguishing mark' [BAGD; NJB], 'things that mark' [NIV], 'that prove' [TEV], 'proof' [NLT, TNT], not explicit [CEV]. The phrase τὰ σημεῖα τοῦ ἀποστόλου 'the signs of an apostle' is translated 'the signs of an apostle' [HNTC, NTC; KJV, REB], 'the signs of a true apostle' [NRSV], 'the signs of the real apostle' [Lns], 'the signs that show the apostle' [NAB], 'the apostolic signs' [AB, ICC2], 'the marks of a true apostle' [WBC], 'the things that mark an apostle' [NIV], 'all the marks characteristic of a true apostle' [NJB], 'every proof that I am truly an apostle' [NLT], 'the proofs of my being an apostle' [TNT]. This phrase is attached to the three nouns in the phrase that follows: 'the powerful miracles and signs and wonders of a true apostle' [CEV], 'the many miracles and wonders that prove that I am an apostle' [TEV].

c. aorist pass. indic. of κατεργάζομαι (LN 42.17) (BAGD 1. p. 421): 'to be performed' [AB, HNTC; NRSV, TEV], 'to be performed successfully' [LN], 'to be accomplished' [BAGD, ICC2, LN], 'to be done' [BAGD; NIV], 'to be wrought' [Lns; KJV], 'to be worked out' [NTC], 'to be at work' [NJB], 'to be displayed' [WBC], 'to be there in the work' [REB]. This verb is also expressed in the active voice with 'I' (i.e., Paul) as the subject: 'to work (miracles, etc)' [CEV], 'to perform' [NAB], 'to do' [TNT], 'to give (proof)' [NLT]. See this word also at 4:17; 5:5; 7:10; 9:11.

d. ὑπομονή (LN 25.174) (BAGD 1. p. 846): 'perseverance' [BAGD, Lns, NTC; NIV, NJB], 'endurance' [AB, BAGD, LN; REB], 'patience' [BAGD; KJV, NAB, NRSV, TEV], 'persistence' [ICC2, WBC]. The phrase πάσῃ ὑπομονῇ 'all perseverance' is translated 'utmost endurance' [AB], 'unfailing endurance' [REB], 'I endured every kind of suffering and abuse' [HNTC], 'all persistence' [ICC2, WBC], 'all perseverance' [Lns], 'great perseverance' [NTC; NIV], 'complete perseverance' [NJB], 'all patience' [KJV], 'great patience' [NAB], 'utmost patience' [NRSV], 'much patience' [TEV], 'I was patient' [CEV], 'I patiently did' [NLT], 'I never failed' [TNT]. See this word also at 1:6; 6:4.

QUESTION—What relationship is indicated by the particle μέν 'indeed'?
1. It is a marker of linkage in discourse that is left untranslated [AB, He, LN (91.3), NTC; CEV, NIV, NJB, NLT, NRSV, REB, TEV, TNT].
2. It introduces the first half of a μέν…δέ concessive statement, of which the contrasting second part that would normally be introduced by δέ is left out but implies a contrast that is not stated.
   2.1 The implied statement is that although the signs were performed, you ignored them [BAGD, Ho, ICC2].
   2.2 The implied statement is that although the signs were performed, that did not take away my weakness [SP].
3. The particle has a restrictive force, 'at least' [HNTC, LN (91.6), Lns; KJV, NAB]; that is, at least the signs of an apostle were performed among you.
4. The particle is used for emphasis: 'truly' or 'indeed' [EGT, ICC1, NIC2].

QUESTION—What is meant by the phrase τὰ σημεῖα τοῦ ἀποστόλου 'the signs of an apostle'?
1. The signs of an apostle are the signs, wonders, and mighty works that prove he is an apostle [ICC2, Lns, NIC2, NTC, TG, TNTC]. Authenticating miracles are recognized signs of apostleship [ICC2]. Although Paul is primarily referring to miracles here, these miracles were also done in a context of enduring suffering, which is an additional sign of his apostleship [NIC2].
2. The signs of an apostle are the various evidences of God's working in his apostolic ministry to validate it [AB, EBC, Ho, NAC, NIC1, WBC]. In addition to the miraculous signs, part of the confirmation of the authenticity of the apostolic ministry is the fact of changed lives among those to whom he ministered [NIC1, WBC], Paul's Christlikeness and morally upright behavior [Ho, NAC, NIC1, WBC], his straightforward dealing with the Corinthians [NAC, WBC], his knowledge of and fidelity to the gospel message [Ho], and of course his perseverance [EBC, NAC].

QUESTION—Who is the agent of the passive verb 'were performed'?
1. Paul uses a passive verb to show that God is the one who performed the works [AB, Car, ICC2, Lns, NAC, NIC2, NTC, SP, TG, WBC]. Paul is not claiming any credit for the signs [AB, EBC, HNTC, ICC1, NIC1, TG, WBC], he is only God's instrument [EGT, ICC1].
2. Paul performed the miracles [TH; CEV, NAB, NLT, REB]. CEV, NAB, NLT, and REB change the passive verb form to active, with Paul claiming to have performed the miracles, though this may be partly for stylistic reasons to avoid using a passive verb.

QUESTION—What does 'perseverance' refer to?
It refers to all the opposition, persecutions, abuse, and suffering he endured for the ministry [Car, EBC, HNTC, NCBC, NIC1, NIC2, NTC, SP, WBC]. It refers to all the hardships he encountered in the context of ministry [AB, NAC, WBC], to the exhaustion, discouragement, and difficulty [ICC1]. It refers to all the afflictions and difficulties that hinder the full realization of

the new creation [ICC2]. The signs were performed under adverse circumstances [Ho]. Paul's endurance in the face of opposition distinguished him from his rivals [EBC]. It means that Paul was persistent and patient in his apostolic work [TG]. It means that Paul exhibited constancy or regularity in performing the signs [He]. Endurance of suffering eliminated the possibility of triumphalism in Paul [SP].

by[a] signs[b] and wonders[c] and works-of-power.[d]

LEXICON—a. There is no lexical entry for the preposition 'by', the grammatical relation being indicated in the Greek by the dative case of the three nouns that follow. This relation is translated 'by' [AB, ICC2, NTC; REB, TNT], 'accompanied by' [HNTC], 'with' [Lns; NRSV], 'along with' [WBC], 'in' [KJV], not explicit [NJB]. This relation is also expressed by a verb phrase: 'I worked' [CEV], 'I performed' [NAB], 'I did' [NLT], 'were performed' [TEV], 'were done' [NIV].

b. σημεῖον (LN 33.477) (BAGD 2. a. p. 748): 'sign' [AB, BAGD, HNTC, ICC2, LN, Lns, NTC, WBC; all versions except TEV], 'miracle' [BAGD], not explicit [TEV].

c. τέρας (LN 33.480): 'wonder' [AB, ICC2, Lns, NTC, WBC; all versions except NJB, REB], 'sign' [LN], 'portent' [HNTC, LN; REB], 'marvels' [NJB].

d. δύναμις (LN 76.7) (BAGD 4. p. 208): 'work of power' [TNT], 'power work' [Lns], 'deed of power' [AB, BAGD, ICC2; NAB], 'demonstration of power' [NJB], 'mighty work' [HNTC, WBC; NRSV], 'mighty deed' [LN; KJV], 'miracle' [BAGD, LN, NTC; NIV, NLT, REB, TEV], 'powerful miracle' [CEV], 'wonder' [BAGD]. See this word also at 1:8; 4:7; 8:3; 12:9.

QUESTION—Is there any difference in meaning between the first and second occurrences of σημεῖον 'sign' in this verse?

1. In the first occurrence it is used in a more general sense [Ho, ICC1, Lns, NAC, NIC1, TH, WBC]. The first occurrence would also include the evidence provided by Paul's life and ministry [ICC1, NAC, NIC1, WBC] as well as his Christ-like character [NAC, NIC1] and his straightforward honesty in his dealings with the Corinthians [NAC]. 'Signs' could include such things as knowledge, effective ministry, the message preached, character, fidelity, as well as miracles [Ho].

2. 'Signs' in the first phrase is equivalent to 'signs and wonders and works of power' in the second phrase [NIC2, SP, TNTC; CEV, TEV].

QUESTION—Is there any significant difference between the three terms used here?

These phrases are traditional phrases with a general meaning and little distinction between them [AB, He]. They are generally equivalent, indicating three aspects of the same reality. That is, a sign is a miracle that points beyond itself to indicate, teach, or confirm something greater; a wonder is a miracle that prompts awe or amazement; and a work of power is an exceptional display of God's power at work [Car, EGT, Ho, ICC1, ICC2, NAC, NIC1, NTC, TH, WBC].

12:13 **What is it in-which^a you-were-treated-worse^b than the other^c churches,**

LEXICON—a. The phrase τί γάρ ἐστιν ὃ 'what is it in which' is translated 'in what respect' [AB, HNTC, ICC2, NTC], 'in what way' [NAB, TNT], 'is there any way in which' [NJB, REB], 'what is it wherein' [KJV], 'what is it then in regard to which' [Lns], 'how' [WBC; NIV, NRSV, TEV], not explicit [CEV, NLT].
  b. aorist pass. indic. of ἑσσόομαι (LN **88.134**) (BAGD p. 313): 'to be treated worse than' [AB, LN, Lns; REB, TEV], 'to be inferior to' [BAGD, NTC, WBC; KJV, NAB, NIV], 'to be worse off than' [BAGD; NRSV, TNT], 'to be put lower than' [HNTC], 'to be devalued (by comparison)' [ICC2], 'to be given less than' [NJB], 'to miss out on a blessing' [CEV]. This clause is translated 'the only thing I didn't do, which I do in the other churches' [NLT].
  c. λοιπός (LN 63.21) (BAGD 2. a. p. 479): 'the other' [AB, BAGD, HNTC, ICC2, LN, NTC, WBC; CEV, NAB, NIV, NLT, NRSV, REB, TEV, TNT], 'other' [KJV], 'the rest' [LN, Lns; NJB].

except that I myself^a did-not-burden^b you? Forgive^c me this wrong.^d

LEXICON—a. αὐτός (LN 92.37) (BAGD 1.c. p. 122): '-self' [LN], '(I) alone' [BAGD]. The phrase αὐτὸς ἐγώ is translated 'I myself' [AB, HNTC, ICC2, Lns, WBC; KJV, NRSV], 'I for my part' [TNT], 'I' [NTC; NAB, NIV, NLT, REB, TEV], 'me' [CEV]. The phrase 'I myself did not burden you' is translated 'I did not make myself a burden' [NJB].
  b. aorist act. indic. of καταναρκάω (LN 57.224) (BAGD p. 415): 'to burden' [AB, BAGD, ICC2, LN; NRSV], 'to be a burden to' [BAGD, WBC; NAB, NIV], 'to become a burden' [NTC; NLT], 'to be a financial burden' [LN], 'to be burdensome' [KJV], 'to make oneself a burden to' [HNTC; NJB], 'to be a dead weight on' [Lns], 'to put pressure on' [TNT], 'to be a charge on' [REB]. The phrase 'I myself did not burden you' is translated 'you didn't have to support me' [CEV], 'I did not bother you for financial help' [TEV]. See this word also at 11:9.
  c. aorist mid. (deponent = act.) impera. of χαρίζομαι (LN **40.10**) (BAGD 2. p. 876): 'to forgive' [BAGD, HNTC, ICC2, LN, Lns, NTC, WBC; all versions except TNT], 'to pardon' [AB, BAGD], 'to deal generously' [TNT]. See this word also at 2:7, 10.
  d. ἀδικία (LN 88.21) (BAGD 1. p. 17): 'wrong' [BAGD, Lns, NTC, WBC; KJV, NIV, NLT, NRSV], 'wrongdoing' [BAGD], 'offense' [AB], 'injury' [HNTC], 'injustice' [ICC2; NAB, TNT], 'unfairness' [NJB], '(for) doing you wrong' [CEV], '(for) being so unfair' [REB, TEV].

QUESTION—What is the tone of Paul's comments here?
  1. Paul is using irony [AB, Car, EBC, EGT, ICC1, ICC2, Lns, NAC, NCBC, NIC2, SP, TNTC, WBC] or sarcasm [He, HNTC, SP, TG, TH]. Paul is

using irony when he talks about their being treated worse than other churches, but when he asks for forgiveness he genuinely means it [NTC].
2. Paul is speaking with tenderness, not sarcasm [Ho]. Although Paul is using an affectionate irony, he is not attacking them sarcastically [NIC1]. His request for forgiveness is genuine because he thinks he truly may have offended them [NTC].

DISCOURSE UNIT: 12:14–13:13 [NIC2]. The topic is preparation for the imminent third visit.

DISCOURSE UNIT: 12:14–13:10 [AB, EBC]. The topic is renewal and conclusion of the appeal [AB], the planned third visit [EBC].

DISCOURSE UNIT: 12:14–21 [AB]. The topic is expressions of concern.

DISCOURSE UNIT: 12:14–18 [EBC, TNTC]. The topic is the promise not to be burdensome [EBC], Paul refuses to burden the Corinthians [TNTC].

12:14 Look,[a] I-am ready[b] to come to you this third-time, and I-will-not-be-a-burden;[c]

LEXICON—a. ἰδού (LN 91.13) (BAGD 1.b.ε. p. 371): 'look' [BAGD, HNTC, ICC2, LN, NTC], 'look here' [AB], 'lo' [Lns], 'behold' [BAGD; KJV], not explicit [WBC; CEV, NAB, NIV, NJB, NLT, REB, TEV, TNT]. See this word also at 5:17; 6:2, 9; 7:11.

b. ἑτοίμως (LN **77.2**) (BAGD p. 316): 'ready' [AB, BAGD, HNTC, ICC2, LN, Lns, NTC, WBC; KJV, NIV, NJB, NRSV, TEV, TNT]. The phrase ἑτοίμως ἔχω ἐλθεῖν 'I am ready to come' is translated 'I am getting ready to pay you a visit' [REB], 'I am planning to visit' [CEV], 'I am about to visit' [NAB], 'now I am coming' [NLT].

c. fut. act. indic. of καταναρκάω (LN 57.224) (BAGD p. 415): 'to be a burden' [AB, BAGD, ICC2, WBC; NIV, NJB, NLT, NRSV, TNT], 'to burden' [BAGD, LN, NTC; NAB], 'to be a financial burden' [LN], 'to be burdensome' [KJV], 'to make oneself a burden' [HNTC; CEV], 'to be a dead weight' [Lns], 'to be a charge' [REB], 'to make demands' [TEV].

QUESTION—What is the function of the particle ἰδού 'look'?
It introduces a change of subject, which is Paul's upcoming trip [NTC, WBC]. It serves to gain the attention of the readers [ICC2] and gives emphasis to what follows [ICC2, TH]. It gives an air of finality and anticipation to the passage that follows [NIC2].

QUESTION—What were the two previous visits?
1. The first visit was the occasion of the founding of the church, during which Paul stayed 18 months. He then paid them a second visit, which was the painful visit referred to in 2:1 and which prompted Paul to cancel a previously planned third visit [AB, Car, EBC, He, HNTC, ICC1, ICC2, NAC, NCBC, NIC1, NIC2, NTC, TG, TNTC, WBC].

2. The first visit was the occasion of the founding of the church, and the second, about which nothing more is known, came after that but before the writing of 1 Corinthians [Lns].

for[a] I-do-not-seek[b] what (is) yours[c] but you. For (it is) not the children[d] (who) ought to-save-up[e] for-the-parents,[f] but the parents for-the-children.

LEXICON—a. γάρ (LN 89.23): 'for' [LN; KJV, NAB, TNT], 'because' [LN; NIV, NRSV], not explicit [CEV, NJB, NLT, REB, TEV].

b. pres. act. indic. of ζητέω (LN 25.9) (BAGD 2.a. p. 339): 'to seek' [HNTC, ICC2, Lns, WBC; KJV], 'to want' [NTC; NAB, NIV, NJB, NLT, NRSV, REB, TEV, TNT], 'to really want' [CEV], 'to desire' [LN], 'to desire to possess' [BAGD], 'to be after' [AB].

c. The phrase τὰ ὑμῶν is translated 'what is yours' [AB; NRSV], 'yours' [Lns; KJV], 'your property' [HNTC], 'your financial assets' [ICC2], 'your money' [NTC; REB, TEV], 'your possessions' [WBC; NIV, NJB, TNT], 'what you have' [CEV, NAB, NLT].

d. τέκνον (LN 10.36) (BAGD 1.a.α. p. 808): 'child' [AB, BAGD, HNTC, ICC2, LN, Lns, NTC, WBC; all versions except NLT], 'little child' [NLT].

e. pres. act. infin. of θησαυρίζω (LN 65.11) (BAGD 1. p. 361): 'to save up' [AB, HNTC, WBC; CEV, NAB, NIV, NJB, TNT], 'to save' [BAGD], 'to store up' [BAGD], 'to store up resources' [ICC2], 'to treasure up' [LN], 'to lay up' [KJV, NRSV], 'to lay up treasure' [Lns], 'to gather treasures' [NTC], 'to pay for food' [NLT], 'to make provision' [REB], 'to provide' [TEV].

f. γονεύς (LN 10.18) (BAGD p. 165): 'parent' [AB, BAGD, HNTC, ICC2, LN, Lns, NTC, WBC; all versions].

QUESTION—In what sense does Paul 'seek' them?

He is interested in their spiritual welfare, to see them prosper spiritually [NTC]. He is seeking the gift of their lives to Christ [AB]. He wants to win their affection for Christ [EBC]. He seeks to gain them for Christ [HNTC], to win them wholly for Christ [NIC1]. He seeks to win them in order to present them as a spouse to Christ [ICC1]. He wants them to continue in allegiance and devotion to Christ, and to show love to Paul as well [Car]. He wants their hearts restored in loyalty to himself [WBC]. He seeks their allegiance to Christ and to himself [NIC2]. He wants their love and cooperation [TG]. He seeks their good, not their goods [He]. He wants to help them, not to get their money [TH]. He wants to win their souls, not their money [Ho].

QUESTION—Is Paul stating an absolute principle concerning the relation of parents and children?

The verb ὀφείλω 'ought' expresses a general truth, not an absolute or universal one [Car, NTC, WBC]. It suggests the superiority of one alternative without ruling out the other. [WBC]. It expresses an accepted norm, but does not mean that it would never be proper for the child to help the parent [ICC1, NIC2]. He is appealing to widely held expectations in Greco-Roman society about parent-child relationships [NAC]. This is not a universal truth from which conclusions should be drawn concerning the financial support of ministry [EBC, HNTC]. It is used as an illustration only [Lns].

12:15 And[a] for-my-part[b] most-gladly I-will-spend[c] and I-will-be-spent[d] for your souls.[e]

LEXICON—a. δέ (LN 89.94): 'and' [HNTC, ICC2, LN; KJV, NJB], 'but' [AB], 'moreover' [Lns], 'so' [CEV, NIV], not explicit [NTC, WBC; NAB, NLT, NRSV, REB, TEV, TNT].
- b. ἐγώ (LN 92.1): 'I' [LN, NTC, WBC; CEV, KJV, NAB, NIV, NJB, NLT, NRSV, REB, TEV], 'I myself' [ICC2], 'for my part' [AB, HNTC], 'I on my part' [Lns], 'as for me, I' [TNT].
- c. fut. act. indic. of δαπανάω (LN **42.27, 57.146**) (BAGD 1. p. 171): 'to spend' [AB, BAGD, HNTC, ICC2, **LN** (57.146), Lns, WBC; KJV, NRSV, TNT], 'to spend myself' [NAB], 'to spend everything' [NTC; REB], 'to spend everything I have' [NIV], 'to spend all I have' [NLT, TEV], 'to spend what I have' [NJB], 'to exert great effort' [**LN** (42.27)], 'to do anything' [**LN** (42.27)], 'spend freely' [BAGD], 'to give all that I have' [CEV].
- d. fut. pass. indic. of ἐκδαπανάω (LN **42.28**) (BAGD p. 238): 'to be spent' [BAGD, ICC2, Lns, WBC; KJV, NAB, NJB, NRSV], 'to be utterly spent' [TNT], 'to be completely spent' [**LN**], 'to be spent up' [HNTC], 'to spend myself' [TEV], 'to be expended' [AB, NTC], 'to expend myself' [NIV], 'to be exhausted' [BAGD], 'to be completely exhausted' [LN], 'to give oneself completely for' [LN]. The phrase δαπανήσω καὶ ἐκδαπανηθήσομαι 'I will spend and I will be spent' is translated 'I will give all that I have and all that I am' [CEV], 'I will spend myself and all I have' [NLT], 'I would spend everything (for you)—yes, and spend myself to the limit' [REB].
- e. ψυχή (LN 9.20) (BAGD 1.c. p. 893, 1.f. p. 894): 'soul' [BAGD, HNTC, Lns; NJB], 'person, people' [LN]. While this word may express Paul's concern for the spiritual condition of the Corinthians, most versions understand the phrase 'your souls' as a Hebraic way of referring to the Corinthians as persons, without reference to their spiritual nature or condition. It is translated 'you' [AB, NTC; KJV, NIV, NRSV, REB, TEV], 'your sakes' [NAB, TNT], 'your behalf' [WBC], 'your spiritual good' [NLT], not explicit [CEV]. See this word also at 1:23.

QUESTION—In what sense does Paul use the term ψυχῶν 'souls'?
1. It is a way of saying 'you'; Paul is concerned for them [Ho, ICC2, Lns, NIC2, WBC; KJV, NIV, NRSV, REB, TEV]. He is speaking of their temporal lives [NTC], the natural life [AB].
2. He is speaking of their souls [NIC1]. He is referring to their spiritual aspect, which is of eternal interest [EGT]. Soul, which means life, is used

to refer to that which is true life [He]. It indicates that he is concerned for their spiritual good [TG]. It speaks of Paul's concern for the whole person [SP, TH], their highest good [EBC], which is their salvation [HNTC].

If (I am) loving you more,ᵃ will-I-be-loved less?ᵇ

TEXT—Instead of εἰ 'if', some manuscripts have εἰ καί 'though', which changes the sentence from a question or rhetorical statement to a concessive clause subordinate to what is stated in the first half of this verse. The resulting sense of the new combined sentence would be 'I will gladly spend myself even though you love me less for doing so'. GNT selects the reading 'if' with a B rating, indicating that the text is almost certain. The reading εἰ καί is taken by KJV, NLT.

TEXT—Instead of ἀγαπῶν 'loving', which is a participle, some manuscripts have ἀγαπῶ 'I love', a finite verb. GNT selects the reading 'loving' with a C rating, indicating difficulty in deciding which variant to place in the text. There is little difference in meaning and for stylistic reasons virtually all versions translate it as a finite verb.

LEXICON—a. περισσοτέρως (LN 78.31) (BAGD 1. p. 651): 'more' [AB, BAGD, ICC2, WBC; NIV, NLT, NRSV], 'more abundantly' [HNTC, Lns; KJV], 'all the more' [LN], 'so much' [TEV], 'so much more' [NJB], 'to a greater degree' [NTC], 'too much' [CEV, NAB, TNT], 'overmuch' [REB]. See this word also at 1:12; 2:4; 7:13, 15; 11:23.

b. ἥσσων (LN **78.38**) (BAGD p. 349): 'less' [AB, BAGD, HNTC, ICC2, LN, Lns, NTC, WBC; all versions], 'to a lesser extent' [**LN**].

QUESTION—What comparison is implied in the words 'more' and 'less'?

1. It indicates a relative change; as Paul's love for them increases theirs is decreased [WBC]. The more Paul loves them sacrificially, the less they respond in kind [NAC]. Paul's love is even greater than before [TNTC, WBC]. Not only is he willing to sacrifice financially, as he has done in the past, but he is even willing to sacrifice his life for them; however, their love is less than before because of allegations they have listened to [TNTC].
2. It means that their love is less than what would normally be expected in the context [LN]. They love him less than they should [AB].
3. It is a mutual comparison; he loves them more than they love him [ICC2, Lns, NIC1], which is not a natural response [ICC2].
4. It compares Paul's love for them with his love for other congregations, as he has paid them more attention by visits and correspondence, but they have loved him less than others did [EGT, NTC].
5. It compares Paul's love for them with a father's love for his children; Paul's love is greater than a father's love for his children, and theirs is less than children's love for a father [Car, EBC].
6. The word περισσοτέρως is used absolutely, not comparatively; his love is so much or so great, and theirs is so much less or so little [TH]. His love is unlimited and theirs is very limited [NCBC].

7. Paul is saying that he is willing to risk losing their affection by doing what love for them prompts him to do. (This is based on acceptance of the variant reading εἰ καί, 'though', which would imply that Paul would give sacrificially even if they loved him less [Ho].)

12:16 So-be-it[a] (then), I did-not-burden[b] you;

LEXICON—a. pres. act. impera. of εἰμί. The phrase ἔστω δέ is translated 'so be it then' [ICC2], 'but be it so' [KJV], 'be that as it may' [NIV], 'now it is agreed' [AB], 'you agree that' [CEV], 'you will agree then' [TEV], 'some of you admit' [NLT], 'let it be assumed that' [NRSV], 'all right' [HNTC], 'all right, then' [NJB], 'all very well, you say' [REB], 'granted' [NAB, TNT], 'but granted' [Lns], 'very well' [NTC], 'though' [WBC].
b. aorist act. indic. of καταβαρέω (LN **22.26**) (BAGD p. 408): 'to burden' [AB, BAGD, Lns; KJV, NAB, NRSV, TNT], 'to be a burden to' [BAGD, NTC, WBC; CEV, NIV, NLT, TEV], 'to make oneself a burden' [NJB], 'to prove a burden' [REB], 'to be a financial burden' [ICC2], 'to lay a burden on' [HNTC], 'to overburden' [**LN**], 'to cause undue hardship' [LN].

QUESTION—What concession is Paul making with the phrase ἔστω δέ 'so be it then'?
1. It refers to the statement that follows, which is that both he and the Corinthians agree that he did not burden them [AB, EGT, Ho, ICC1, ICC2, Lns, NAC, NIC1, NTC, SP, TG, TH, WBC].
2. It refers to what was just said about loving more and being loved less [Car, EBC, HNTC].
    2.1 He is accepting the previous sentence as factual [HNTC].
    2.2 He is saying that even if they don't respond appropriately to his expression of love, he will not change his policy of being a burden [Car].
    2.3 He is saying that whether or not they accept the premise of his loving them more and their loving him less, 'be that as it may, they would at least agree that Paul was not a burden [EBC].

but,[a] being crafty[b] I-took[c] you by-deceit.[d]

LEXICON—a. ἀλλά (LN 89.125): 'but' [HNTC, ICC2, LN, NTC; NAB, NJB, NLT, REB, TEV], 'nevertheless' [AB, Lns; KJV, NRSV], 'yet' [WBC; NIV], not explicit [CEV, TNT].
b. πανοῦργος (LN **88.269**) (BAGD p. 608): 'crafty' [AB, BAGD, ICC2; KJV, NAB, NRSV], 'crafty person' [**LN**], 'crafty fellow' [BAGD, LN, Lns, NTC, WBC; NIV, TNT], 'scoundrel' [LN], 'trickster' [NJB], 'confidence trickster' [HNTC], 'tricky' [TEV], 'sneaky' [NLT], 'sly' [BAGD], not explicit [CEV]. The phrase ὑπάρχων πανοῦργος 'being crafty' is translated 'I was trying to catch you off guard' [CEV], 'I did use a confidence trick' [REB].
c. aorist act. indic. of λαμβάνω (LN 88.146) (BAGD 1.c. p. 464): 'to take in' [AB, BAGD, NTC; NRSV, REB], 'to take advantage of' [BAGD;

NLT], 'to catch (someone)' [HNTC, Lns, WBC; KJV, NAB, NIV, NJB], 'to catch by a trick' [BAGD], 'to take advantage of by trickery' [LN], 'to entrap' [ICC2], 'to trap' [TEV], 'to exploit by deception' [LN]. The phrase δόλῳ ὑμᾶς ἔλαβον 'I took you by deceit' is translated 'I was trying to trick you' [CEV], 'I played a trick on you' [TNT]. See this word also at 11:20.
- d. δόλος (LN 88.154) (BAGD p. 203): 'deceit' [AB, BAGD, NTC; NRSV], 'trickery' [ICC2, WBC; NIV, NJB, NLT], 'confidence trick' [REB], 'guile' [Lns; KJV, NAB], 'craftiness' [HNTC], 'lies' [TEV], 'treachery' [BAGD, LN], 'cunning' [BAGD], not explicit [CEV, TNT].

QUESTION—What relationship is indicated by ἀλλά 'but'?

It is contrastive; even though Paul himself did not burden them, it may be alleged that others whom he had sent have done so [AB, EBC, EGT, He, HNTC, Ho, ICC1, Lns, NCBC, NIC1, NIC2, NTC, SP, TH, TNTC].

QUESTION—What relationship is indicated by the participial phrase ὑπάρχων πανοῦργος 'being crafty'?

It indicates a causal relationship; that is, because I am crafty I did this [AB, EBC, HNTC, ICC2, NIC2, NTC, SP, WBC]. The verb ὑπάρχω is used instead of the more common εἰμί to indicate what someone is by essential character or nature, by habitual condition [EBC, EGT, ICC1, ICC2, NIC1, NIC2, WBC]; that is, Paul is by nature a crafty person.

QUESTION—What is the tone of Paul's comments here?

This statement is an accusation to which Paul is now responding [AB, EBC, EGT, He, HNTC, Ho, ICC1, ICC2, NCBC, NIC1, NIC2, NTC, TH, WBC]. It was either a charge made by his opponents [EGT, Ho, ICC1, WBC] or by some of the Corinthians themselves [NIC2]. He is answering what he suspects they may be thinking [Lns]. He is speaking with irony [Car, WBC]. That this is an accusation or insinuation is indicated in some versions by the addition of 'you say' [NAB, NRSV, REB], 'someone will say' [TEV], 'you think' [TNT], 'they still think' [NLT].

12:17 Anyone of-those-whom I-sent to you, I-did-not[a] take-advantage[b] of-you through him (did-I)?

LEXICON—a. The particle μή (LN 69.15) marks an expected negative response to a question that is posed. This question indicator is translated 'did I' [AB, HNTC, Lns, NTC, WBC; KJV, NIV, NRSV, TEV, TNT], 'did I ever' [NAB], 'have I' [NJB], 'did any (of the men)' [NLT], 'was it (one of the men)' [REB], 'surely it was not' [ICC2], 'were you (cheated)' [CEV].
- b. aorist act. indic. of πλεονεκτέω (LN 88.144) (BAGD 1.a. p. 667): 'to take advantage of' [BAGD, LN, NTC, WBC; NAB, NJB, NLT, NRSV, TEV, TNT], 'to exploit' [ICC2, LN; NIV, REB], 'to make a gain' [KJV], 'to defraud' [AB, BAGD, HNTC], 'to cheat' [BAGD], 'to be cheated by' [CEV], 'to overreach' [Lns]. See this word also at 2:11; 7:2.

2 CORINTHIANS 12:18

12:18 I-urged[a] Titus and I-sent[b] the brother;[c] Titus did- not[d] -take-advantage of you (did he)?

LEXICON—a. aorist act. indic. of παρακαλέω (LN 33.168) (BAGD 3. p. 617): 'to urge' [AB, Lns, WBC; CEV, NAB, NIV, NLT, NRSV], 'to ask' [HNTC; TNT], 'to request' [BAGD, LN], 'to make a request' [ICC2], 'to entreat' [BAGD], 'to appeal to' [BAGD, LN, NTC], 'to beg' [REB, TEV], 'to desire' [KJV], 'at my urging' [NJB]. See this word also at 1:4, 6; 2:7, 8; 5:20; 6:1; 7:6; 8:6; 9:5; 10:1; 12:8.

b. aorist act. indic. of συναποστέλλω (LN **15.69**) (BAGD p. 785): 'to send with' [BAGD, HNTC, LN, NTC, WBC; all versions], 'to send along' [Lns], 'to send along with' [AB].

c. ἀδελφός (LN 11.23): 'brother' [AB, HNTC, ICC2, Lns, NTC, WBC; KJV, NIV, NRSV, TNT], 'the other brother' [NAB], 'our brother' [NIV], 'our other brother' [NLT], '(Christian) brother' [LN], 'fellow believer' [LN], 'the other believer' [TEV], 'another follower' [CEV], 'his companion' [NJB], 'our friend' [REB]. See this word also at 1:1, 8; 2:13; 8:1; 11:9.

d. The particle μήτι (LN 69.16) marks an expected negative response to a question, and is somewhat more emphatic than μή. This question indicator is translated 'Titus did not...did he' [NIV, NRSV], 'did (Titus)' [AB, HNTC, Lns, NTC, WBC; KJV, NAB, NJB, NLT, REB, TNT], 'surely Titus did not' [ICC2], 'would you say that Titus' [TEV]. This question is also presented as a direct statement: 'Titus didn't cheat you' [CEV].

QUESTION—What is the relation between the sending of Titus and this brother and various missions referred to earlier?

1. Paul is referring to the trip mentioned in 8:6a, in which he sent Titus to Corinth to begin the collection [EBC, ICC2, NIC2, NTC, WBC].

    1.1 Titus' first mission was the trip referred to in 2:13 and 7:6, 13, in which he carried the 'sorrowful letter' and dealt with the matter of the sinner who repented. The second was that referred to in 8:6a in which he was to begin the collection, and to which Paul is referring in this passage. The third mission, which has not yet occurred, is that mission anticipated and mentioned in 8:6b and 8:18–22 and which will be for bringing the collection to completion [NTC, TG, TNTC] and to deliver 2 Corinthians [NTC, TNTC] or some portion of it [TG].

    1.2 Titus' first mission was that referred to in 8:6a in which he was to begin the collection, and to which Paul is referring in this passage. The second was the peace-making trip referred to in 2:13 and 7:6, 13, in which he carried the 'sorrowful letter'. The third mission, which has not yet occurred, will be for bringing the collection to completion and to deliver 2 Corinthians, and is that mission anticipated and referred to in 8:6b and 8:18-22 [ICC1, NIC2, WBC].

2. Titus' first mission was when he delivered the 'sorrowful letter' and also began the collection mentioned in 8:6a. This is the mission Paul is referring to here. His second mission, which has not yet occurred, will be

for bringing the collection to completion and to deliver 2 Corinthians, and is that trip referred to in 8:18–22 [EGT, Ho, NAC, NCBC]. The sorrowful letter is canonical 1 Corinthians [EGT, Ho].
   3. Titus' first mission was the trip referred to in 2:13 and 8:6a, in which he delivered the sorrowful letter and began the collection. The mission referred to in 8:18–22 would have been Titus' second, from which he has already returned by the time Paul writes this passage, since chapter 8 is (presumably) part of a different and earlier letter than that which contains chapter 12 [AB, HNTC].
   4. Titus' first mission was prior to the writing of 1 Corinthians, and the second the occasion of delivering 1 Corinthians. During one of those visits he initiated the collection, and it is Titus' conduct during either of those visits of which Paul speaks here in chapter 12. The third mission is the one anticipated and referred to in chapter 8:18–22, which had not yet occurred at the time of writing [NIC1].

QUESTION—What is the relation between this 'brother' and those mentioned in 8:18 and 8:22?
   1. The 'earnest' brother of 8:22 is the same as the brother mentioned here, but is not the same as the brother who is known by all the churches mentioned in 8:18 [AB, HNTC, NCBC, TNTC].
   2. He is referring to the brother mentioned in 8:18, who was well known to the churches and who had been chosen as a delegate in the matter of the collection [NIC1, NIC2, TH].
   3. It is not clear which of the two men he is referring to here [EBC, NAC, NTC, WBC], and it may even be a third man [ICC2, Lns].

Did-we- not^a -conduct-ourselves^b in^c the same spirit?^d Did-we-not (walk)^e in the same steps?^f

LEXICON—a. The particle οὐ (LN 69.11) marks an expected affirmative response to a question. This question indicator is translated 'did we not' [AB, HNTC, Lns, NTC, WBC; NAB, NIV, NRSV, TNT], 'did not he and I' [TEV], 'have we not' [REB], 'was (our conduct) not' [ICC2], 'walked we not' [KJV], 'can you deny that' [NJB]. These two questions are presented as a single direct statement: 'we felt and behaved the same way he did' [CEV], 'we both have the same Spirit and walk in each other's steps, doing things the same way' [NLT].
   b. aorist act. indic. of περιπατέω (LN 41.11) (BAGD 2.a.β. p. 649): 'to conduct oneself' [AB, BAGD, NTC; NRSV], 'to behave' [HNTC, LN], 'to act' [NAB, NIV, TEV], 'to walk' [BAGD, Lns, WBC; KJV, TNT], 'to live' [BAGD, LN], 'to go about doing' [LN], 'to be guided (by the same Spirit)' [REB], 'to follow the guidance (of the same Spirit)' [NJB], 'to have (the same Spirit)' [NLT]. This verb is also translated as a noun: 'our conduct' [ICC2]. The dual propositions 'to conduct oneself in the same spirit' and 'in the same steps' are both governed by this verb, even though it occurs only once in the text. Most versions carry it forward proleptically

to the second question οὐ τοῖς αὐτοῖς ἴχνεσιν 'did we not walk in the same steps' and state it explicitly. It is also translated as two verbs: 'we felt and behaved (the same way)' [CEV]. See this word also at 4:2; 5:7; 10:2-3.

c. There is no lexical entry for this word, the grammatical relation being indicated in the Greek by the dative case of the phrase τῷ αὐτῷ πνεύματι 'in the same spirit'. This relation is translated 'in' [HNTC, ICC2, Lns, NTC, WBC; KJV, NAB, NIV], 'with' [AB; NRSV], 'by' [REB, TNT], 'from (the same motives)' [TEV], not explicit [CEV, NJB, NLT].

d. πνεῦμα (LN 30.6, **41.47**, 12.18) (BAGD 5.d.α. p. 677): 'spirit' [AB, HNTC, ICC2, Lns, NTC, WBC; KJV, NAB, NIV, NRSV], 'Spirit' [BAGD, LN (12.18); NJB, NLT, REB, TNT], 'attitude, disposition' [LN (30.6)], not explicit [CEV]. The phrase 'conduct ourselves in the same spirit' is translated 'to act from the very same motives' [**LN** (41.47); TEV].

e. Implied recurrence of aorist act. indic. of περιπατέω (LN 41.47): 'to behave' [LN]. Although περιπατέω 'walk' is absent from the second clause, it is carried forward proleptically from the first clause by most versions because of the repetition of the particle οὐ and by the use of the dative phrase τοῖς αὐτοῖς ἴχνεσιν 'the same steps'. It is translated 'walk' [HNTC, ICC2, NTC; KJV, NAB, NLT], 'take (the same steps)' [AB; NRSV], 'follow' [WBC; NIV, REB], 'behave' [TEV], 'to be on (the same tracks)' [NJB], not explicit [Lns; CEV]. The two questions 'did we not conduct ourselves in the same spirit? Did we not walk in the same steps' are posed as a single question with the verb 'walk' governing both propositions: 'did we not walk by the same Spirit, and in the same footsteps' [TNT].

f. ἴχνος (LN **41.47**) (BAGD p. 384): 'step' [AB; KJV, NLT, NRSV], 'footstep' [BAGD, HNTC, NTC; NAB, TNT], 'footprint' [BAGD, ICC2], 'track' [Lns; NJB], 'course' [WBC; NIV, REB]. The question οὐ τοῖς αὐτοῖς ἴχνεσιν 'did we not (walk) in the same steps' is translated 'did not he and I behave in the same way' [LN (41.47); TEV], 'we behaved the same way he did' [CEV].

QUESTION—What is meant by the phrase τῷ αὐτῷ πνεύματι 'in the same spirit'?

1. The focus is anthropological; that is, Paul is saying that he and Titus had the same attitudes [AB, HNTC, ICC1, ICC2, Lns, NAC, NIC1, NIC2, NTC, SP, TG, TH, WBC]. The term 'spirit' speaks of internal thoughts and attitudes, and 'steps' describes external actions [Lns, NIC1, NTC]. That is, they were the same in disposition as well as practice [ICC2], in mind as well as conduct [ICC1].

2. The focus is theological; that is, Paul is saying that both he and Titus have the Holy Spirit [NLT] or were guided by the Holy Spirit [NJB, REB, TNT].

2 CORINTHIANS 12:19

DISCOURSE UNIT: 12:19–13:10 [HNTC, ICC1, WBC; NJB]. The topic is warnings and a third visit promised [WBC], Paul's fears and anxieties [NJB], the apostle and the church: the truth [HNTC], final warnings in view of his approaching visit [ICC1].

DISCOURSE UNIT: 12:19–21 [EBC, TNTC]. The topic is fears about the unrepentant [EBC], the real purpose of Paul's fool's speech [TNTC].

12:19 Have-you-been-thinking[a] all-along[b] that we-are-defending[c] (ourselves) to-you?

TEXT—Instead of πάλαι 'all along', some manuscripts have πάλιν 'again'. GNT selects the reading 'all along' with an A rating, indicating that the text is certain. The reading 'again' is taken by KJV.

LEXICON—a. pres. act. indic. of δοκέω (LN 31.29) (BAGD 1.d. p. 202): 'to think' [BAGD, HNTC, ICC2, LN, Lns, NTC, WBC; all versions], 'to suppose' [AB, BAGD, LN]. This verb is translated in a declarative sense, as making a statement [AB, HNTC, Lns, NTC; NJB]; in an interrogative sense, as asking a question [ICC2, WBC; CEV, KJV, NAB, NIV, NRSV, TNT]; with 'perhaps' as suggesting a possibility [NLT, REB, TEV]. See this word also at 11:16.

b. πάλαι (LN **67.141**) (BAGD 2.a. p. 605): 'all along' [AB, BAGD, NTC, WBC; CEV, NIV, NRSV, TEV], 'all this time' [LN, Lns; NJB, REB, TNT], 'for a long time' [BAGD, ICC2], 'for a long time now' [HNTC], 'throughout this recital' [NAB], not explicit [NLT].

c. pres. mid. or pass. (deponent = act.) indic. of ἀπολογέομαι (LN 33.435) (BAGD p. 95): 'to defend oneself' [AB, BAGD, LN, Lns, WBC; CEV, NAB, NIV, NLT, NRSV, TEV, TNT], 'to make a defense' [HNTC], 'to make one's own defense' [NTC], 'to speak in one's own defense' [BAGD], 'to present one's own defense' [ICC2], 'to excuse oneself' [KJV], 'to plead one's own cause' [NJB], 'to address one's own defense' [REB].

QUESTION—Is this sentence a question or a statement of fact?
1. It is a statement of fact [AB, EGT, GNT, HNTC, Lns, NTC; NJB, NLT, REB, TEV]. (GNT punctuates the text as a statement.)
2. It is a question [ICC1, ICC2, NIC1, NIC2, WBC; CEV, KJV, NAB, NIV, NRSV, TNT].
3. The meaning is imperative; that is, don't think we are just defending ourselves [TG].
4. The meaning is relatively unaffected whether it is regarded as a question or as a statement of fact [Car, NAC, NIC2, NTC, SP, TNTC].

QUESTION—To what period does 'all along' refer?
It is referring to his self-defense in this epistle or some portion of this epistle [AB, Car, EBC, ICC1, ICC2, Lns, NAC, NIC1, NIC2, TNTC], especially the last few chapters [ICC1, NIC1]. He refers to what has been said since the beginning of chapter 11 [EGT].

QUESTION—How can Paul truthfully say that he is not defending himself to them?

There is a contrast between 'to you' and 'before God' in the next line; it is to God and not the Corinthians that he must give account, so it is not to them that he is defending himself [Car, EBC, HNTC, Ho, ICC1, ICC2, Lns, NAC, NIC1, NIC2, NTC, TNTC; REB]. His primary concern is their benefit and not his own self-defense [EBC, He, Ho, ICC2, NAC, NIC2]. Paul is not just defending himself since his 'defense' is not primarily self-serving or promoting self-interest [AB, Car, TNTC, WBC]. His real purpose is not to defend himself but to help them be what they should be [TH]. Paul and his associates are not just acting in their own interests and whitewashing themselves [Lns]. Paul does not have to prove his innocence, but he does want to set the record straight [NTC]. It is Paul who is making the accusations, not they, and they are the ones who must defend themselves [NAC].

We-are-speaking before^a God in^b Christ; and everything,^c beloved,^d (is) for^e your edification.^f

LEXICON—a. κατέναντι (LN **90.20**) (BAGD 2.b. p. 421): 'before (God)' [BAGD, HNTC, ICC2, NTC, WBC; KJV, NAB, NRSV, TNT], 'in the presence of (God)' [NJB, TEV], 'in the sight of (God)' [AB, BAGD, **LN**; NIV], 'in (God's) sight' [Lns; REB], 'in the opinion of, in the judgment of' [LN], 'we know that God is listening' [NLT]. The phrase 'we are speaking before God' is translated 'we have been speaking to God' [CEV]. See this word at 2:17 in an identically worded phrase.
b. ἐν (LN 89.119): 'in' [AB, HNTC, ICC2, NTC, WBC; KJV, NAB, NJB, NRSV, TNT], 'with' [Lns], 'one with' [LN], 'in union with, joined closely to' [LN]. The phrase 'in Christ' is translated 'as those in Christ' [NIV], 'as followers of Christ' [CEV], 'as Christ's servants' [NLT], 'as Christians' [REB], 'as Christ would have us speak' [TEV].
c. πᾶς (LN 59.23): 'everything' [AB, Lns; NAB], 'everything we do' [NTC; NIV, NLT, NRSV, TEV], 'all' [LN; NJB], 'all things' [KJV], 'all that we do' [WBC], 'all that we are doing' [HNTC], 'all we want to do' [TNT], '(we did it) all' [CEV], 'all this' [ICC2], 'our whole aim' [REB].
d. ἀγαπητός (LN 25.45) (BAGD 2. p. 6): 'beloved' [AB, BAGD, ICC2, LN, Lns, WBC; NRSV], 'dearly beloved' [KJV], 'dear friends' [NTC; NIV, NJB, NLT, REB, TEV, TNT], 'my dear friends' [HNTC], 'my friends' [CEV], 'my dear ones' [NAB]. See this word also at 7:1.
e. ὑπέρ (LN 90.36) (BAGD 1.b. p. 838): 'for' [AB, ICC2, LN, NTC, WBC; CEV, KJV, NIV, NLT], 'for the purpose of' [HNTC], 'for the benefit of' [Lns], 'for the sake of' [LN; NRSV]. This preposition is also translated by means of an infinitive as indicating purpose [BAGD; NAB, NJB, REB, TEV, TNT]: 'to (build)' [NAB, NJB, REB, TNT], 'to (help)' [TEV].
f. οἰκοδομή (LN 74.15) (BAGD 1.b.α. p. 559): 'edification' [BAGD, ICC2, Lns, NTC, WBC], 'edifying' [KJV], 'upbuilding' [AB], 'building (you)

up' [BAGD, HNTC, LN; NRSV], 'strengthening' [LN; NIV], 'benefit' [NLT], '(your) good' [CEV]. The phrase 'for your edification' is translated as an infinitive phrase: 'to build you up' [NAB, NJB, REB], 'to build up your spiritual life' [TNT], 'to help you' [TEV]. See this word also at 10:8.

QUESTION—What is meant by speaking 'in Christ'?

He speaks as a Christian [Car, NIC2]. He speaks as Christ's servant [TG]. He speaks in union with Christ [ICC1, TH], upon whom his life entirely depends [TH]. His existence and strength depend on union with Christ [HNTC, WBC]. He speaks as representing and depending on Christ [NIC1]. He speaks in a way that is fitting for someone who is aware of his union with Christ [Ho]. He speaks as a selfless Christian [He]. It means that he has stopped speaking in the role of a fool [NAC]. His speaking involves Christ, who commissioned him, and his gospel and his church [Lns]. He is in fellowship with Christ who has sent him [NTC].

QUESTION—What is the 'everything' of which Paul speaks?

It is all of Paul's work [NTC]. It is everything he does [NIV, NLT, NRSV, TEV]. It is anything he has said or done [AB, TG, TNTC], but especially all he has written so far in this letter [AB, TNTC]. It is his relations with the Corinthians as a whole [EBC, HNTC], especially his letters [EBC]. It is all he has said in this letter [EGT, ICC1, ICC2, Lns, NIC2]. It is this part of the letter in which he defends himself [Ho].

QUESTION—What is the edification Paul is talking about?

Paul wants to help them be better Christians [HNTC]. He wants to strengthen their understanding and character in Christ [NIC2]. Through his words he is promoting their vital interests [NIC1], seeking the improvement of their spiritual and moral welfare [ICC2], helping to increase their holiness [ICC1]. The edification is their being brought to spiritual maturity, which can only occur in a context of Christian freedom [NCBC]. He intends to enlarge and enrich their life in their common faith [AB]. Paul is edifying them through his warnings and rebuke [Lns]. Edifying them, which is Paul's purpose, stands in contrast to vindicating himself, which is not Paul's purpose [Car]. Their spiritual life is like a house under construction in which they are able to live, but which is far from complete [NTC].

12:20 For I-fear[a] that-perhaps[b] (when) having-come (to you) I-find[c] you not such-as[d] I-wish[e] and-I-myself be-found by-you not such-as you-wish;

LEXICON—a. pres. mid. or pass. (deponent = act.) indic. of φοβέομαι (LN 25.252) (BAGD 1.a. p. 863): 'to fear' [AB, ICC2, LN, Lns, WBC; KJV, NAB, NRSV, REB, TNT], 'to be afraid' [BAGD, HNTC, LN, NTC; CEV, NIV, NJB, NLT, TEV]. See this word also at 11:3.

b. μή πως (LN 89.62) (BAGD 1.b. p. 519): 'that perhaps' [BAGD], 'that' [AB, NTC, WBC; CEV, NAB, NIV, NLT, NRSV, REB, TEV, TNT], 'that in one way or another' [NJB], 'lest' [HNTC, ICC2, LN, Lns; KJV], 'lest somehow' [BAGD]. See this phrase also at 11:3.

c. aorist act. subj. of εὑρίσκω (LN 27.1) (BAGD 1.c.γ. p. 325): 'to find' [AB, BAGD, HNTC, ICC2, Lns, NTC, WBC; KJV, NAB, NIV, NJB, NLT, NRSV, REB, TEV, TNT], 'to discover, to find out' [LN], not explicit [CEV]. See this word also at 5:3; 11:12.

d. οἷος (LN 64.1) (BAGD p. 562): 'such as' [BAGD, ICC2, LN, Lns; KJV], 'as' [AB, BAGD, NTC, WBC; NIV, NRSV], 'like' [LN], 'what' [NJB, NLT, REB, TEV], 'the sort of man' [HNTC], not explicit [CEV, NAB]. The phrase 'not...such as I wish' is translated 'not to my liking' [NAB], 'different from what I would like' [TNT], 'different from what I should/would like you to be' [NJB, TEV], 'I won't like what (I find)' [NLT]. The phrases 'not...such as I wish...not such as you wish' are conflated and translated 'we won't be pleased with each other' [CEV].

e. pres. act. indic. of θέλω (LN 25.1): 'to wish' [AB, ICC2, LN, NTC, WBC; NRSV, REB], 'to desire' [HNTC, LN], 'to want' [LN, Lns], 'to be pleased with' [CEV], 'to like' [NLT, TNT], 'to like (you) to be' [NJB, TEV], '(to be) to my liking' [NAB]. The phrase 'such as I wish' is translated 'as I would' [KJV]. See this word also at 8:10 and 12:6.

that-perhaps (there would be)[a] strife,[b] jealousy,[c] outbursts-of-anger,[d]
LEXICON—a. There is no lexical entry for the verbal phrase 'there would be'. The implied verbal phrase that connects μή πως 'that perhaps' with the five nouns that follow is translated 'there may be' [AB, NTC; NIV, TNT], 'there may perhaps be' [NRSV], 'there should be' [HNTC], 'there might be' [ICC2], 'there be' [Lns; KJV], 'there will be' [WBC; NJB], 'you may be (arguing...)' [CEV], 'I may find' [NAB, NLT, REB], 'I will find' [NLT, TEV].

b. ἔρις (LN 39.22, 33.447) (BAGD p. 309): 'strife' [BAGD, LN (39.22), Lns, NTC, WBC], 'discord' [AB, BAGD, ICC2, LN (39.22); NAB], 'quarreling' [HNTC; NIV, NLT, NRSV, REB, TEV, TNT], 'quarrel' [LN (33.447)], 'contention' [BAGD], 'arguing' [CEV], 'dispute' [LN (33.447)], 'debate' [KJV], 'rivalry' [NJB].

c. ζῆλος (LN 88.162) (BAGD 2. p. 337): 'jealousy' [AB, BAGD, LN, Lns, NTC, WBC; NAB, NIV, NJB, NLT, NRSV, REB, TEV, TNT], 'envy' [BAGD, ICC2, LN], 'envying' [HNTC; KJV], 'resentment' [LN]. This noun is also translated as an adjective: '(you may be) jealous' [CEV]. See this word also at 7:7, 11; 9:2; 11:2.

d. θυμός (LN 88.178) (BAGD 2. p. 365): 'outburst of anger' [BAGD, HNTC, ICC2; NAB, NIV, NLT], 'outburst of temper' [TNT], 'rage' [BAGD, LN], 'wrath' [BAGD, LN; KJV], 'anger' [Lns; NRSV], 'angry temper' [REB], 'bad temper' [NJB], 'explosive temper' [AB], 'hot temper' [TEV]. This noun is also translated as an adjective: '(you may be) angry' [CEV].

(cases of)[a] selfishness,[b] slander,[c] gossip,[d] arrogance, [e]disorder.[f]
LEXICON—a. There is no lexical entry for the phrase 'cases of', but it is supplied to express the sense implied by the plural of the following four nouns in Greek.
   b. ἐριθεία (LN 88.167) (BAGD p. 309): 'selfishness' [BAGD; NLT, NRSV, TEV], '(outbreaks of) selfishness' [BAGD, NTC], 'selfish ambition' [BAGD, LN, WBC; NAB, TNT], 'self-seeking' [AB], 'self-assertion' [Lns], 'intrigues' [HNTC], 'factiousness' [ICC2], 'factions' [NIV], 'strife' [KJV], 'personal rivalry' [REB], 'rivalry, resentfulness' [LN], 'quarrels' [NJB]. This noun is also translated as an adjective: '(you may be) selfish' [CEV].
   c. καταλαλιά (LN **33.387**) (BAGD p. 412): 'slander' [AB, BAGD, ICC2, LN, NTC, WBC; NAB, NIV, NJB, NRSV], 'evil speech' [BAGD], 'evil speaking' [HNTC], 'backbiting' [Lns; KJV, REB], 'backstabbing' [NLT], 'insulting' [CEV], 'insult' [TEV], 'abusive utterance' [TNT].
   d. ψιθυρισμός (LN **33.404**) (BAGD p. 893): 'gossip' [BAGD, LN, NTC; NAB, NIV, NJB, NLT, NRSV, REB, TEV], 'gossiping' [AB, WBC; CEV], 'whispered gossip' [ICC2], 'whispering' [BAGD, HNTC, Lns; KJV, TNT].
   e. φυσίωσις (LN **88.215**) (BAGD p. 870): 'arrogance' [AB, **LN**, NTC; NIV, NJB, REB], 'arrogant behavior' [TNT], 'pride' [BAGD, LN; TEV], 'inflated opinion' [HNTC], 'conceit' [ICC2, WBC; NLT, NRSV], 'puffing up' [Lns], 'swelling' [KJV], 'self-importance' [NAB]. This noun is also translated as an adjective: '(you may be) proud' [CEV].
   f. ἀκαταστασία (LN 39.34) (BAGD 2. p. 30): 'disorder' [BAGD, HNTC, ICC2, Lns, NTC, WBC; NAB, NIV, NJB, NRSV, TEV, TNT], 'general disorder' [AB; REB], 'rebellion' [LN], 'disorderly behavior' [NLT], 'unruliness' [BAGD], 'tumult' [KJV], 'acting like a mob' [CEV].

12:21 **that when-I-come my God humble[a] me again before you and that-I-would-mourn[b] (over)[c] many (of those) having-sinned-before[d]**
LEXICON—a. aorist act. subj. of ταπεινόω (LN **25.198**) (BAGD 2.a. p. 804): 'to humble' [BAGD, Lns, WBC; KJV, NIV, NLT, NRSV], 'to humiliate' [AB, BAGD, HNTC, ICC2, LN, NTC; NAB, NJB, REB, TEV, TNT], 'to make ashamed' [CEV].
   b. πενθέω (LN **25.142**) (BAGD 2. p. 642): 'to mourn' [AB, BAGD, HNTC, Lns, NTC, WBC; NAB, NRSV, TNT], 'to grieve' [LN; NLT], 'to be grieved' [NIV, NJB], 'to have cause to grieve' [REB], 'to feel like crying' [CEV], 'to bewail' [KJV], 'to weep' [TEV].
   c. There is no lexical entry for this preposition in the Greek text, but it is added for the sake of English style. This preposition is represented in translation as 'over' [AB, ICC2, NTC; NAB, NIV, NRSV, REB, TEV, TNT], 'for' [HNTC, WBC], 'because' [CEV, NLT], '(be grieved) by' [NJB], not explicit [Lns; KJV].

2 CORINTHIANS 12:21

d. προαμαρτάνω (LN **88.293**) (BAGD p. 702): 'to have sinned before' [BAGD; REB, TNT], 'to have sinned beforehand' [BAGD], 'to have sinned previously' [HNTC, ICC2, LN; NRSV], 'to have sinned earlier' [NTC, WBC; NAB, NIV, NLT], 'to be sinning hitherto' [Lns], 'to have sinned in the past' [**LN**; NJB, TEV], 'to have sinned already' [KJV]. This verb is translated by a phrase: 'their former sinning' [AB], 'you have never given up your old sins' [CEV].

QUESTION—With what word or action is πάλιν 'again' to be associated?
1. It is associated with 'humble' [AB, EGT, HNTC, ICC1, ICC2, NCBC, NIC1, NIC2, SP, TG, TH, WBC; NLT, REB, TNT]; God will humble me again.
2. It is associated with 'come' [He, Ho, Lns; CEV, KJV, NAB, NIV, NJB, NRSV, TEV]; when I come again.
3. It is associated with both verbs [EBC, NTC].

QUESTION—In what sense might Paul be 'humbled'?

Paul would be humbled or embarrassed over the poor fruit of his ministry [Car, EGT, TNTC]. He would be humiliated by their disgraceful conduct which would represent a failure of his ministry to them [Car]. He would be humbled by seeing that they had left the way of truth and holiness [Ho]. His humbling would be his public mourning over the unrepentant [NIC2], his sorrow at the sight of their disgraceful condition [Lns]. Their sin would represent a defeat for him, causing him to be sad and discouraged and ashamed of their behavior [TG]. Paul would be morally ashamed of them before God [He]. The humbling would be Paul's mourning and grieving over their shame and guilt [NIC1]. Whatever disgraced his converts was a humiliation to Paul [ICC1]. Paul will be reduced to mourning over them and be forced to discipline them, which he is reluctant to do [AB]. The humbling would be the grief he has over their sin and his great disappointment over their lack of loyalty to him [EBC]. Paul would be humiliated if there were a recurrence of the bad experience he had on his previous trip, and he would feel that he had failed in his mission if he had to discipline them [WBC]. Paul would be humbled if God allowed resistance by opposition and a lack of support by the Corinthians [HNTC]. Paul may have to endure humiliation from the Corinthians again if he has to discipline them [NTC]. Paul would be humbled by having to discipline them, since that would represent a failure of his prior ministry and provide opportunity for his opponents to criticize his teaching about the role of the Holy Spirit in sanctification and Christian living [ICC2].

and not having-repented[a] over the impurity[b] and immorality[c] and licentiousness[d] which they-(have)-practiced.[e]

LEXICON—a. aorist act. participle of μετανοέω (LN 41.52) (BAGD p. 512): 'to repent' [AB, BAGD, HNTC, ICC2, LN, Lns, NTC, WBC; all versions except CEV], 'to give up old sins' [CEV].

b. ἀκαθαρσία (LN 88.261) (BAGD 2. p. 28): 'impurity' [AB, LN, NTC, WBC; NIV, NJB, NLT, NRSV], 'uncleanness' [HNTC, Lns; KJV, NAB, TNT], 'immorality' [BAGD, LN], 'unclean lives' [REB], 'things that are indecent' [CEV], not explicit [TEV].
c. πορνεία (LN 88.271) (BAGD 1. p. 693): 'sexual immorality' [AB, LN, NTC; NJB, NLT, NRSV], 'sexual sin' [NIV], 'sexual vice' [TNT], 'fornication' [BAGD, HNTC, ICC2, LN, Lns, WBC; KJV, NAB, REB], 'prostitution' [BAGD, LN], 'things that are immoral' [CEV], 'immoral things they have done' [TEV].
d. ἀσέλγεια (LN **88.272**) (BAGD p. 114): 'licentiousness' [AB, BAGD, WBC; NRSV, TNT], 'licentious deeds' [**LN**], 'lasciviousness' [HNTC; KJV], 'extreme immorality' [LN], 'sensuality' [BAGD, NTC; NAB, REB], 'debauchery' [BAGD, ICC2; NIV, NJB], 'excess' [Lns], 'things that are shameful' [CEV], 'eagerness for lustful pleasure' [NLT], not explicit [TEV].
e. aorist act. indic. of πράσσω (LN 42.8) (BAGD 1.a. p. 698): 'to practice' [AB, ICC2; NAB, NRSV, TNT], 'to commit' [BAGD, HNTC, Lns, NTC; KJV, NJB], 'to do' [BAGD, LN; CEV, TEV], 'to indulge in' [WBC; NIV], not explicit [NLT, REB].

DISCOURSE UNIT: 13:1-13 [CEV, TEV]. The topic is final warnings and greetings [CEV, TEV].

DISCOURSE UNIT: 13:1-10 [AB, TH, TNTC; NIV, NRSV]. The topic is warning and admonition [AB], further warning [NRSV], final warnings [NIV], final warnings and greetings [TH], Paul threatens strong action on his third visit [TNTC].

DISCOURSE UNIT: 13:1-9 [NAB]. The topic is final warnings.

DISCOURSE UNIT: 13:1-4 [EBC]. The topic is warning of impending discipline.

13:1 This (is the) third-time I-am-coming[a] to you; by[b] (the) mouth[c] of two or three witnesses[d] every word[e] shall-be-established.[f]

LEXICON—a. pres. mid. or pass. (deponent = act.) indic. of ἔρχομαι (LN 15.81) (BAGD I.1.a.β. p. 310): 'to come' [AB, BAGD, HNTC, ICC2, LN, Lns, NTC; KJV, NAB, NRSV, TNT], 'to visit' [CEV], 'to come to visit' [NLT, TEV], 'to confront' [NJB]. This verb is also translated as a noun: 'visit' [WBC; NIV, REB].
b. ἐπί (LN 89.13) (BAGD I.1.b.β. p. 286): 'by' [AB, Lns; CEV, NIV, NLT, NRSV, TEV, TNT], 'on' [ICC2, NTC, WBC; REB], 'only on' [NAB], 'on the basis of' [BAGD, LN], 'at' [HNTC], 'in view of' [LN], 'in' [KJV], not explicit [NJB]. That this word begins a quotation from scripture is shown by quotation marks or italics [AB, HNTC, ICC2, NTC, WBC; NAB, NIV, NJB, NRSV, TEV], or by a citation formula with quotation marks [CEV, NLT, REB, TNT].

c. στόμα (LN 33.74) (BAGD 1.a. p. 770): 'mouth' [BAGD, HNTC, Lns; KJV, TNT], 'testimony' [AB, NTC; NAB, NIV, NLT], 'evidence' [ICC2, WBC; NJB, NRSV, REB, TEV], 'speech' [LN], not explicit [CEV].
d. μάρτυς (LN 33.270) (BAGD 1. p. 494): 'witness' [AB, BAGD, HNTC, ICC2, LN, Lns, NTC, WBC; all versions]. See this word also at 1:23.
e. ῥῆμα (LN 33.98) (BAGD 2. p. 735): 'word' [LN; KJV], 'statement' [LN], 'matter' [BAGD, HNTC, Lns, NTC, WBC; NIV], 'charge' [ICC2; CEV, NJB, NRSV, REB], 'question' [LN], 'point' [AB], 'accusation' [TEV], 'judicial fact' [NAB], 'case' [TNT], 'facts of every case' [NLT].
f. fut. pass. indic. of ἵστημι (LN 76.21) (BAGD II.1.d. p. 382): 'to be established' [HNTC, ICC2, LN, Lns, NTC, WBC; KJV, NAB, NIV, NLT, REB], 'to be upheld' [TEV], 'to be substantiated' [AB], 'to be sustained' [NRSV], 'to sustain' [NJB], 'to be proved true' [CEV], 'to be settled' [TNT], 'to be caused to stand firm' [BAGD]. See this word also at 1:24.

QUESTION—What does Paul imply by mentioning the 'two or three witnesses'?
1. The witnesses are the various occasions in which they have been warned [AB, Car, EBC, HNTC, ICC2, NCBC, NTC, SP, TH, WBC]. Paul is referring to the number of visits he will have paid them [AB, Car, ICC2, NCBC, SP, TH]. The two witnesses may be the sorrowful visit and this letter, and the third will be his next visit [AB].
2. The witnesses are those of a formal judicial hearing. Paul is planning to bring judgment in a congregational hearing on those who have sinned, and will follow proper judicial procedure [EGT, Ho, Lns, NIC1, NIC2]. He will be fair in judging them [TG] and will require adequate testimony [Ho]. Paul is saying that the conflicts between him and the Corinthians must now be settled openly and in public; he can call Timothy and Titus and even God as his witnesses, but they will not be able to call any legitimate witnesses against him [NAC].

13:2 **I-warned**[a] **(when) being-present the second-time and now being-absent I–warn those-having-sinned-before**[b] **and all the-rest,**[c] **that when/if**[d] **I-come again I-will-not-spare,**[e]
TEXT—Some manuscripts include γράφω 'I write' after νῦν 'now'. GNT does not mention this alternative. Only KJV reads 'I write (to them)'.
LEXICON—a. perf. act. indic. of προεῖπον (the lexical form of the aorist tense of προλέγω) (LN 33.423) (BAGD 2.a. p. 704): 'to warn' [HNTC, LN; CEV, NRSV, TNT], 'to give warning' [AB; NIV, REB], 'to give notice' [NJB], 'to forewarn' [NTC], 'to say' [WBC; NAB]. In this tense the verb means 'to have said beforehand/before' [BAGD, ICC2; TEV], 'to have said in advance' [Lns], 'to have told before' [KJV], 'to have already warned' [NLT]. It focuses on having said something prior to the current moment, and not on having foretold something prior to its occurrence.
b. perf. act. participle of προαμαρτάνω (LN 88.293) (BAGD p. 702): 'to have sinned beforehand' [BAGD, HNTC], 'to have sinned previously'

[HNTC, LN; NRSV]. 'to have been sinning hitherto' [Lns], 'to have sinned heretofore' [KJV], 'to have continued in (their) former sinning' [AB], 'to have sinned before' [NAB, NJB, REB], 'to have sinned in the past' [NTC; TEV, TNT], 'to have sinned earlier' [WBC; NIV], 'to have been sinning' [NLT]. The participial phrase τοῖς προημαρτηκόσιν 'those having sinned before' is translated 'the former sinners' [ICC2], 'anyone who doesn't stop sinning' [CEV]. See this word also at 12:21.
  c. λοιπός (LN 63.21) (BAGD 2.b.α. p. 480): 'rest' [AB, HNTC, ICC2, LN, Lns], 'other' [BAGD, LN]. The phrase καὶ τοῖς λοιποῖς πᾶσιν is translated 'all the rest' [AB, HNTC, ICC2, Lns; NAB], 'all the rest of them' [NTC], 'anyone else' [WBC; CEV], 'all other' [KJV], 'all others' [NJB, NLT], 'all the others' [NRSV, TEV], 'any of the others' [NIV], 'everyone else' [REB, TNT]. See this word also at 12:13.
  d. ἐάν (LN 67.32, 89.67): 'when' [ICC2, LN (67.32), NTC, WBC; NJB, REB], 'when and if' [LN (67.32)], 'if' [AB, LN (89.67), Lns; KJV, NAB, NRSV, TNT], not explicit [CEV]. The phrase 'when I come again' is translated 'on my return' [NIV], 'this next time' [NLT], 'the next time I come' [TEV].
  e. future mid. (deponent = act.) indic. of φείδομαι (LN 22.28) (BAGD 1. p. 854): 'to spare' [BAGD, HNTC, ICC2, LN, Lns, NTC, WBC; KJV, NAB, NIV, NLT, TNT], 'to be lenient' [AB; NRSV], 'to show leniency' [REB], 'to have mercy' [NJB]. The phrase 'I will not spare' is translated 'I would punish you' [CEV], 'nobody will escape punishment' [TEV]. See this word also at 1:23 and 12:6.

QUESTION—Does ἐάν imply that Paul is not sure whether he will come again?
  Here it means 'when', because Paul's plans to come again are definite [AB, ICC1, ICC2, Lns, NCBC, NIC1, NIC2, NTC, SP, TH, WBC]. Only the timing is indefinite [NIC2]. However, the conjunction ὅτι can introduce a quotation of direct speech, which would make this Paul's statement during his prior visit [AB, He, ICC1, ICC2, NIC1, TH, WBC] and at the time could have meant 'if', implying uncertainty about his future travels [AB, NIC1, WBC].

QUESTION—What does 'I will not spare' mean that Paul will do?
  He will not be lenient [ICC1] and will certainly discipline the wrongdoer [TH]. It is implied that he will not punish any wrongdoer who repents [WBC]. He will impose a discipline similar to that in 1 Corinthians 5 [Car, EBC, Ho, NAC]. He will excommunicate offenders [AB, Ho, ICC1, NAC, NTC] and inflict a supernatural physical punishment [Ho, ICC1, ICC2, NAC]. Paul will hand them over to Satan only in the sense of declaring to those who denied the gospel that they had alienated themselves from God and had fallen back into the realm of Satan [HNTC].

13:3 since[a] you-seek[b] proof[c] of Christ speaking in[d] me,
LEXICON—a. ἐπεί (LN 89.32) (BAGD 2. p. 284): 'since' [AB, BAGD, HNTC, ICC2, LN, Lns, WBC; KJV, NIV, NJB, NRSV], 'because' [BAGD, LN,

NTC], not explicit [CEV, NAB, NLT, REB, TEV, TNT]. See this word also at 11:18.
b. pres. act. indic. of ζητέω (LN 33.167) (BAGD 2.c. p. 339): 'to seek' [HNTC, Lns, WBC; KJV, REB], 'to demand' [AB, BAGD, ICC2, LN, NTC; NIV], 'to look for' [NAB], 'to ask for' [BAGD; NJB], 'to want' [NLT, TEV, TNT], 'to desire' [NRSV], not explicit [CEV]. See this word also at 12:14.
c. δοκιμή (LN **72.7**) (BAGD 2. p. 202): 'proof' [AB, BAGD, HNTC, ICC2, LN, Lns, NTC, WBC; all versions except CEV]. This noun is also translated as a verb: 'to prove' [CEV]. See this word also at 2:9; 8:2; 9:13.
d. ἐν (LN 90.6): 'in' [HNTC, ICC2, Lns; KJV, NAB, NJB, NRSV], 'by' [LN], 'through' [AB, NTC, WBC; NIV, NLT, REB, TEV, TNT]. The phrase 'Christ speaking in me' is translated 'I am speaking for Christ' [CEV].

QUESTION—What relationship is indicated by ἐπεί 'since'?
It introduces the reason he will not spare them [AB, Car, EGT, HNTC, Ho, ICC1, ICC2, Lns, NCBC, NIC1, NIC2, NTC, TG, TH, TNTC, WBC]: Since you want proof that Christ is speaking powerfully through me I will give you the proof you want by exercising his powerful discipline among you, and I will not spare you. The Corinthians have made it impossible for Paul to spare them because they were demanding that Paul act like Christ who deals powerfully with them [ICC1]. They expected Paul to express his authority more forcefully [EBC, ICC2, NAC, NTC] and discipline offenders more effectively [ICC2, NIC2]. Because of this expectation, they misinterpreted Paul's gentleness [Car, EBC, NTC]. They expected manifestations of supernatural power [AB, Car], especially to punish sinners [ICC2], or charismatic signs of inspiration [WBC]. They expected a more impressive presence and powerful speaking [TNTC].

QUESTION—What relationship is indicated by ἐν 'in'?
It is instrumental; Christ is speaking through Paul [AB, He, HNTC, ICC2, Lns, NCBC, NIC1, NIC2, NTC, SP, TH, WBC]. Paul speaks for Christ [EGT, Ho].

who toward[a] you is-not-weak[b] but is-powerful[c] among[d] you.
LEXICON—a. εἰς (LN 90.41) (BAGD 5. p. 230): 'toward' [AB, BAGD, HNTC, Lns, NTC, WBC; KJV], 'with' [NJB, REB], 'for' [LN], 'on behalf of' [LN]. The phrase εἰς ὑμᾶς 'toward you' is translated 'in your experience' [ICC2], 'when he corrects you' [CEV], 'in dealing with you' [NAB, NIV, NRSV], 'in his dealings with you' [NLT, TNT], 'when he deals with you' [TEV].
b. pres. act. indic. of ἀσθενέω (LN 74.26) (BAGD 1.b. p. 115): 'to be weak' [AB, BAGD, HNTC, ICC2, LN, Lns, NTC, WBC; all versions]. See this word also at 11:21, 29; 12:10.
c. pres. act. indic. of δυνατέω (LN 74.5) (BAGD 1. p. 208): 'to be powerful' [AB, ICC2, Lns, WBC; CEV, NAB, NIV, NRSV], 'to be

mighty' [HNTC; KJV], 'to be a mighty power' [NLT], 'to be strong' [BAGD, NTC], 'to be able to, can' [LN]. The phrase '(he) is powerful among you' is translated 'his power is at work among you' [NJB], 'his power works among you' [TNT], 'he makes his power felt among you' [REB], 'he shows his power among you' [TEV]. It means that someone has the capacity to do something [LN]. See this word also at 9:8.

    d. ἐν (LN 90.56): 'among' [AB, Lns, WBC; NIV, NJB, NLT, REB, TEV, TNT], 'in your midst' [HNTC, ICC2], 'in' [KJV, NAB, NRSV], 'within' [NTC], 'in relation to, with respect to' [LN], not explicit [CEV].

QUESTION—In what sense is Christ powerful toward and among them?

  1. Christ's power is able to be expressed toward them in a negative sense, for their discipline [AB, EBC, NIC2, NTC, TG].

  2. Christ's power has been expressed toward them in a positive sense, in previous ministry to them [HNTC]. It recalls the miracle of their conversion [NAC].

  3. It is used in both senses, and both aspects are in view [Ho, ICC1, ICC2, Lns, NIC1, TNTC, WBC]. Christ, who has shown his power to bless them in the past is equally powerful to discipline them in the present [Ho, ICC1, TNTC]. Paul is quoting a phrase that the Corinthians are saying, but whereas they would interpret Christ's being powerful among them in terms of his supernatural work of ministry among them in the past, what Paul has in mind is Christ's power expressed in discipline in the near future [ICC2, WBC].

13:4 **For indeed**[a] **he-was-crucified**[b] **because-of**[c] **weakness, but he-lives because-of**[d] **(the) power**[e] **of-God.**

LEXICON—a. καί γάρ: 'for indeed' [HNTC, ICC2, NTC], 'indeed' [AB], 'for' [NRSV], 'for in fact' [WBC], 'yes' [Lns], 'true' [REB], 'it is true' [NAB], 'for to be sure' [NIV], 'for though' [KJV, NJB], 'for even though' [TEV], 'although' [NLT], not explicit [CEV, TNT].

  b. aorist pass. indic. of σταυρόω (LN 20.76) (BAGD 1. p. 765): 'to be crucified' [AB, BAGD, HNTC, ICC2, LN, Lns, NTC, WBC; KJV, NAB, NIV, NJB, NRSV, TNT], 'to be nailed to the cross' [CEV], 'to die on the cross' [NLT, REB], 'to be put to death on the cross' [TEV].

  c. ἐκ (ἐξ) (LN 89.25) (BAGD 3.f. p. 235): 'because of' [BAGD, HNTC, LN], 'due to' [Lns], 'in' [AB, NTC, WBC; NIV, NLT, NRSV, REB, TEV], 'through' [ICC2; KJV], 'out of' [NAB, NJB]. The phrase ἐξ ἀσθενείας 'because of weakness' is translated 'he was weak when' [CEV, TNT].

  d. ἐκ (LN 89.25): 'because of' [HNTC, LN], 'by' [AB, NTC, WBC; CEV, KJV, NAB, NIV, NLT, NRSV, REB, TEV], 'through' [ICC2], 'due to' [Lns], 'with' [NJB], not explicit [TNT]. The phrase 'he lives by the power of God' is translated 'the power of God gave him life' [TNT].

e. δύναμις (LN 76.1): 'power' [AB, HNTC, ICC2, LN, Lns, NTC, WBC; all versions except NLT], 'mighty power' [NLT]. See this word also at 1:8; 4:7; 8:3; 12:9, 12.

QUESTION—What relationship is indicated by the phrase καί γάρ 'for indeed'?

It introduces an explanation for the statement made in v.3 [AB, ICC1, ICC2, NIC2, NTC, SP]. It introduces the protasis of a concessive statement; although he was crucified, yet he lives [Ho, ICC1, ICC2, Lns, SP, TG].

QUESTION—What relationship is indicated by the preposition ἐξ (ἐκ) in the phrase ἐξ ἀσθενείας 'because of weakness'?

It indicates reason [BAGD, Car, EBC, EGT, HNTC, Ho, ICC2, Lns, NTC, WBC]: he was crucified because he was weak and could not prevent it. It indicates source; Christ was crucified through weakness [ICC1, Lns, NIC1; NAB, NJB], or out of a condition of weakness [NIC1]. He was crucified in accordance with what appeared to be God's weakness [AB].

QUESTION—What was the weakness?

The weakness was the inherent weakness of mortal human nature [ICC2, NTC, TG, TH]. His weakness was his humbling of himself [HNTC]. His weakness was in adopting vulnerability and accepting suffering and death [Car]. The weakness he assumed made the crucifixion possible [EGT]. His weakness was his non-retaliation and his obedience to God in the crucifixion [EBC].

QUESTION—What relationship is indicated by the preposition ἐκ in the phrase ἐκ δυνάμεως 'because of the power of God'?

1. It indicates reason [AB, EBC, EGT, HNTC, Ho, ICC2, NTC, TG]: Christ lives because of the power of God.
2. It indicates source; his living is through the power of God [ICC1, Lns, NIC1, WBC].

For indeed[a] we are-weak in[b] him, but toward[c] you we-will-live with[d] him because-of[e] (the) power of-God.

TEXT—The words εἰς ὑμᾶς 'toward you' do not occur in some manuscripts. It is included by GNT with an A rating, indicating that the text is certain. It is omitted by NAB.

LEXICON—a. καί γάρ: 'for indeed' [HNTC, ICC2, NTC, WBC], 'indeed' [AB], 'for' [KJV, NRSV], 'yes' [Lns], 'likewise' [NIV], 'also' [TEV], '(we) too' [NAB, NJB, NLT, TNT], 'so' [REB], not explicit [CEV].

b. ἐν (LN 89.119): 'in' [AB, HNTC, LN, Lns, NTC, WBC; KJV, NAB, NIV, NJB, NRSV], 'in union with' [LN; TEV], 'in unity with him' [ICC2]. The phrase ἐν αὐτῷ 'in him' is translated 'just as Christ was' [CEV]. The phrase 'we are weak in him' is translated 'we, too, are weak' [NLT], 'we share his weakness' [REB, TNT].

c. εἰς (LN 90.59): 'toward' [AB, LN, Lns; KJV], 'in relation to' [HNTC], 'with regard to' [NJB]. The phrase 'toward you' is translated 'in our dealings with you' [ICC2], 'in dealing with you' [NLT, NRSV], 'so that

we may deal with you' [TNT], 'in our relations with you' [TEV], 'to serve you' [NTC; NIV], 'when serving you' [WBC], 'you will see' [CEV], 'you will find' [REB].
   d. σύν (LN 89.107) (BAGD 2.b. p. 781): 'with' [AB, BAGD, HNTC, ICC2, LN, Lns, NTC, WBC; KJV, NAB, NIV, NJB, NRSV, REB], 'together with' [LN], 'in' [NLT], not explicit [TEV, TNT]. The phrase 'with him' is translated 'just as Christ does' [CEV].
   e. ἐκ (LN 89.25) (BAGD 3.f. p. 235): 'because of' [BAGD, HNTC, LN], 'by' [AB, NTC, WBC; CEV, KJV, NAB, NIV], 'through' [ICC2], 'due to' [Lns], 'with' [NJB], 'by' [NRSV, REB]. The phrase 'we will live with him because of the power of God' is translated 'we live in him and have God's power' [NLT], 'we shall share God's power in his life' [TEV], 'the power of God will give us his life' [TNT].

QUESTION—What relationship is indicated by the phrase καὶ γάρ 'for indeed'?
   1. It introduces a concessive statement [Ho, ICC1, ICC2, Lns, SP, WBC]; although we are weak we will live with him.
   2. It introduces a second statement which supports what is said in 13:3 [AB, NIC2, NTC, SP].

QUESTION—What is to be understood by the phrase 'weak in him'?
   In union with Christ Paul shares in Christ's sufferings and weakness [EBC, Ho, ICC1, ICC2, Lns, NCBC, NIC1, TG]. He shares the vulnerability that Christ adopted [HNTC]. Because of his close fellowship with the Lord, Paul imitates Christ's meekness and humility and shares in his sufferings [NAC]. Paul's weaknesses are an extension of Christ's own sufferings [NIC2]. By ministering the message of Christ Paul is subject to suffering [NTC]. Through union with him Paul has been crucified with Christ and therefore is subject to persecution just as Christ was [AB]. They are weak just as Christ was, at least as the world counts weakness [EGT]. Just as Christ was, Paul is weak in the sense that he is forbearing and not overbearing [Ho, WBC].

QUESTION—What relationship is indicated by the phrase εἰς ὑμᾶς 'toward you'?
   It refers to their dealings with the Corinthians [AB, Car, EBC, EGT, HNTC, Ho, ICC1, ICC2, Lns, NAC, NCBC, NIC1, NIC2, NTC, SP, TG, TH, TNTC; NLT, NRSV, TEV, TNT]. That is, even though they share the weakness of Christ, who submitted to crucifixion, nevertheless when they deal with the Corinthians they will not be weak but will have the power of his resurrection life [AB, EGT, HNTC, Ho, ICC2, Lns, NCBC, NIC1, NTC].
   It refers to their serving the Corinthians in ministry [NIV, WBC].

QUESTION—What is implied by the future tense of the verb in the phrase ζήσομεν σὺν αὐτῷ 'we shall live with him'?
   The focus is not on eternal life with Christ in the eschatological future but on sharing the living power of the resurrected Christ in the near future when Paul deals with the Corinthians [AB, Car, EGT, HNTC, Ho, ICC1, ICC2, Lns, NIC1, NIC2, NTC, SP].

2 CORINTHIANS 13:5 419

DISCOURSE UNIT: 13:5–10 [EBC]. The topic is a plea for self-examination.

13:5 Examine[a] yourselves (to see) if you-are in the faith,[b] test[c] yourselves.
LEXICON—a. pres. act. impera. of πειράζω (LN **27.46**) (BAGD 2.a. p. 640): 'to examine' [HNTC, LN], 'to test' [AB, LN], 'to put to the test' [BAGD, ICC2, **LN**].
  b. πίστις (LN 31.104) (BAGD 2.d.α. p. 663): 'the faith' [AB, BAGD, HNTC, LN, Lns, NTC, WBC; KJV, NJB, NRSV, TNT], 'faith' [ICC2; NAB]. The phrase 'in the faith' is translated 'in faith' [ICC2; NAB], 'true to your faith' [CEV], 'your faith is really genuine' [NLT], 'living in the faith' [NRSV, TEV], 'living the life of faith' [REB]. See this word also at 1:24.
  c. pres. act. impera. of δοκιμάζω (LN 27.45) (BAGD 1. p. 202): 'to test' [HNTC, LN, NTC, WBC; NIV, NLT, NRSV], 'to put to the test' [AB; REB], 'to put to the proof' [Lns], 'to examine' [ICC2, LN; NAB, NJB, TNT], 'to judge' [TEV], 'to prove' [KJV], 'to prove by testing' [BAGD], 'to try to determine the genuineness of' [LN], not explicit [CEV]. See this word also at 8:8, 22.
QUESTION—What is the emphasis in this sentence?
  The position of ἑαυτούς 'yourselves' at the beginning of the sentence shows emphasis; Paul is saying that it is yourselves that you should be testing, not me, and if you find that you are really Christians then that proves that I am really an apostle [AB, Car, EBC, Ho, ICC1, ICC2, Lns, NAC, NCBC, NIC1, NIC2, NTC, SP, TH, TNTC, WBC].
QUESTION—What does ἡ πίστις 'the faith' refer to here?
  1. It refers to Christian living [AB, He, ICC1, ICC2, NAC, TH, WBC; CEV, NRSV, REB, TEV]. It is comprehensive, focusing on the content of what Paul has preached, the gospel, and how they are living their lives in accordance with the way of Christ [WBC]. It is used comprehensively, indicating the principles of the new spiritual life [ICC1]. It is the whole Christian way and Christian truth [NAC]. It is to live the Christian life as opposed to the life of an unbeliever [ICC2]. It focuses on obedience to what people profess to believe [AB], on living as Christians should [TH]. It is the new existence as a Christian, with Christ living in them [He].
  2. It refers to objective faith [Car, EGT, Lns, NIC2, SP, TNTC]. It is the Christian religion [Car], the content of the gospel [TNTC], with its prepositional and theological content [NIC2]. It is the objective faith and its doctrine, but also includes subjective faith because one is in the objective faith by believing personally with a whole heart [Lns].
  3. It refers to subjective faith, the act of personal trust and belief [HNTC, Ho, NTC].

Or do-you-not-recognize[a] about-yourselves[b] that Jesus Christ (is) in[c] you? Unless-perhaps[d] you-are those-who-have-failed-the-test.[e]
LEXICON—a. pres. act. indic. of ἐπιγινώσκω (LN 27.61) (BAGD 2.a. p. 291): 'to recognize' [AB, BAGD, HNTC, ICC2, LN; NJB, REB], 'to know'

[NTC, WBC; KJV, TEV], 'to fully know' [Lns], 'to discover' [CEV], 'to realize' [NAB, NIV, NRSV, TNT], 'to tell' [NLT].
   b. ἑαυτοῦ (LN 92.25): (in the plural) 'yourselves' [AB, ICC2, LN, Lns; KJV, NAB, NIV, NJB, NLT, NRSV, REB, TEV, TNT], not explicit [HNTC, NTC, WBC; CEV].
   c. ἐν (LN 89.119) (BAGD I.5.a. p. 259): 'in' [AB, BAGD, HNTC, LN, Lns, WBC; all versions except NLT, REB], 'within' [NTC], 'among' [NLT, REB], 'one with, in union with' [LN]. The phrase 'in you' is translated 'in your midst and within you' [ICC2], 'living in you' [CEV], 'in whom (Jesus Christ) is present' [NJB].
   d. εἰ μήτι (BAGD V.2.a. p. 219, VI.9. p. 220): 'unless perhaps' [BAGD (VI..), ICC2, NTC], 'unless indeed' [BAGD (VI.9.), HNTC, Lns; NRSV, TNT], 'unless, of course' [AB; NAB, NIV], 'unless, that is' [NJB], 'unless' [WBC; TEV], 'except' [KJV], 'if not' [REB], not explicit [CEV, NLT]. The particle μήτι in the phrase εἰ μήτι 'unless perhaps' is a somewhat emphatic marker of an expected negative response to a question [LN (69.16)].
   e. ἀδόκιμος (LN 65.13) (BAGD p. 18): 'not standing the test' [BAGD], 'not authentic' [ICC2], 'unproved' [AB], 'disproved' [Lns]. The phrase ἀδόκιμοί ἐστε 'you are those who have failed the test' is translated 'you fail the test' [NTC, WBC; NIV, NJB], 'you fail to stand the test' [HNTC], 'you fail to meet the test' [NRSV], 'you have failed the test' [NLT, REB], 'you have failed' [CEV], 'you have completely failed' [TEV], 'you have failed the challenge' [NAB], 'you are failures' [TNT], 'ye be reprobates' [KJV].
QUESTION—What is the expected answer to this question?
   1. The expected answer to this question, introduced as it is by οὐκ 'not', would be positive, that they do in fact recognize that Christ is in them [AB, EBC, EGT, HNTC, Ho, ICC1, ICC2, Lns, NCBC, NIC1, NIC2, NTC, TG, TH, TNTC, WBC]. Paul uses the possibility of a negative result to challenge and exhort them pastorally [NIC2]. It is an exhortation to them to correct their course before he arrives so he won't have to discipline them [NAC].
   2. The question raises the real possibility that in fact they might not really be Christians after all [Car].
QUESTION—Does ἐν ὑμῖν mean that Christ is among them as a group of believers or dwelling in them as individual believers?
   1. It means that Christ is in them as individual believers [EBC, HNTC, Ho, ICC1, ICC2, NAC, NIC1, NIC2, NTC, TH]. He is in them and they are in him [HNTC].
   2. It means that Christ is among them [NLT, REB]. This would presumably refer to his presence among them as a group.
   3. It means both, that Christ is in them as individuals and among them as a church [AB].

QUESTION—What is the focus of the term ἀδόκιμος 'those who have failed the test'?

It refers to being disproved, unworthy of approval [Ho, NIC2]. It means being found to be false or spurious [Lns, NIC1], to be found to be counterfeit [AB, EBC, NCBC], unauthentic and therefore not really Christian [ICC2]. It speaks of the hardening of heart that leads to spiritual death [NTC].

13:6 But[a] I-hope[b] that you-will-know[c] that we are not those-who-have-failed-the-test.[d]

LEXICON—a. δέ (LN 89.124, 89.94): 'but' [HNTC, LN (89.124); KJV, NJB], 'and' [ICC2, LN (89.94); NIV], 'moreover' [Lns], not explicit [AB, NTC, WBC; CEV, NAB, NLT, NRSV, REB, TEV, TNT].

b. pres. act. indic. of ἐλπίζω (LN 30.54) (BAGD 2. p. 252): 'to hope' [AB, BAGD, HNTC, ICC2, LN, Lns, NTC, WBC; CEV, NAB, NJB, NLT, NRSV, REB, TNT], 'to trust' [KJV, NIV, TEV], 'to expect' [LN]. See this word also at 8:5.

c. future mid. (deponent = act.) indic. of γινώσκω (LN 27.2) (BAGD 3.c. p. 161): 'to know' [Lns; KJV, TEV, TNT], 'to come to know' [AB, ICC2], 'to come to see' [REB], 'to learn' [LN], 'to find out' [LN; NRSV], 'to recognize' [HNTC; NLT], 'to come to recognize' [NJB], 'to understand' [BAGD; NAB], 'to realize' [NTC, WBC], 'to discover' [CEV, NIV].

d. ἀδόκιμος : 'unproved' [AB], 'failures' [TEV, TNT], 'unauthentic' [ICC2], 'disproved' [Lns], 'reprobates' [KJV]. This adjective is translated as a verb phrase: 'to fail to stand the test' [HNTC], 'to fail the test' [WBC; NIV, NJB], 'to fail' [NTC; CEV, NAB, NRSV, REB]. The phrase ἡμεῖς οὐκ ἐσμὲν ἀδόκιμοι 'we are not those who have failed the test' is translated 'we have passed the test and are approved by God' [NLT].

QUESTION—Does ἐλπίζω 'I hope' convey a wish that is uncertain of fulfillment or an expectation that is confident of fulfillment?

Paul is confident of what he is saying [ICC1, ICC2, Lns, NIC1, NIC2, NTC]. He says this as a way of getting them to correct their thinking [TH], to mend their ways [AB].

13:7 And[a] we-pray[b] to God that you not do any wrong,[c] not so-that we appear[d] to-have-passed-the-test,[e]

LEXICON—a. δέ (LN 89.124, 89.94): 'and' [ICC2, LN (89.94)], 'but' [HNTC, LN (89.124), NTC; NRSV, REB, TEV, TNT], 'yet' [AB], 'now' [Lns; KJV, NIV], not explicit [WBC; CEV, NAB, NJB, NLT].

b. pres. mid. or pass. (deponent = act.) indic. of εὔχομαι (LN **33.178**) (BAGD 1. p. 329): 'to pray' [AB, BAGD, HNTC, ICC2, LN, Lns, NTC, WBC; all versions except NJB, REB]. The phrase 'we pray' is translated 'it is our prayer' [NJB, REB].

c. κακός (LN 88.106) (BAGD 1.c. p. 397): 'wrong' [ICC2, NTC, WBC; NIV, NJB, NLT, NRSV, REB, TEV, TNT], 'evil' [AB, BAGD, LN, Lns; KJV, NAB], 'evil thing/s' [HNTC; CEV], 'bad' [LN]. The two negating particles μή and μηδέν in the phrase μὴ ποιῆσαι ὑμᾶς κακὸν μηδέν 'that you not do anything wrong' gives additional emphasis: no evil at all [NTC].

d. aorist pass. subj. of φαίνω (LN 28.55) (BAGD 2.d. p. 852): 'to appear' [AB, BAGD, HNTC, ICC2, LN, Lns, WBC; KJV, NAB, NRSV, TNT], 'to seem' [NTC], 'to have the credit' [NJB]. The phrase ἵνα ἡμεῖς δόκιμοι φανῶμεν 'so that we appear to have passed the test' is translated 'to make ourselves look good' [CEV], 'that people will see that we have stood the test' [NIV], 'to show that our ministry has been successful' [NLT], 'to show that we are a success' [TEV], 'to win approval' [REB].

e. δόκιμος (LN 30.115) (BAGD 1. p. 203): 'approved' [BAGD, Lns; KJV, NAB], 'considered good' [LN], 'to be proved' [AB], 'to be in the right when tested' [HNTC], 'to have stood the test' [NIV], 'to have met the test' [NRSV], 'to have passed the test' [NTC], 'as having passed the test' [WBC], 'to have the credit of passing a test' [NJB], 'visibly authentic' [ICC2], 'good' [CEV], 'successful' [NLT, TNT], '(to be a) success' [TEV], '(to win) approval' [REB]. See this word also at 10:18.

but that you would-be-doing what-is-good,[a] **even-though**[b] **we seem-to-be**[c] **as those-who-have-failed-the-test.**[d]

LEXICON—a. καλός (LN 88.4) (BAGD 2.b. p. 400): '(what is) good' [AB, ICC2, LN, NTC; NAB, TNT], 'morally good' [BAGD], '(the) morally excellent (thing)' [Lns], 'right' [WBC; CEV, NLT], '(that which is) right' [NTC], '(what is) right' [NIV, NJB, NRSV, REB, TEV], '(that which is) honest' [KJV], 'fine' [LN], 'praiseworthy' [BAGD, LN]. See this word also at 8:21. The present subjunctive verb ποιῆτε in the phrase ὑμεῖς τὸ καλὸν ποιῆτε 'that you would be doing what is good' expresses a desire for ongoing action [NTC].

b. δέ (LN 89.124): 'even though' [AB; NAB, NIV, TEV], 'though' [HNTC; KJV, NRSV, TNT], 'even if' [WBC; CEV, NJB, NLT, REB], 'even as if' [NTC], 'while' [Lns], 'whilst' [ICC2], 'but, on the other hand' [LN], [AB],

c. pres. act. subj. of εἰμί (LN 13.1): 'to be' [LN; CEV, KJV], 'to seem to be' [AB; TEV, TNT], 'to seem as though' [ICC2], 'to seem to (have failed)' [NTC; NAB, NIV, NLT, NRSV], 'to seem' [REB], 'to appear to be' [HNTC], 'to appear to (have failed)' [WBC], 'to be as if' [Lns], not explicit [NJB]. It is the subjunctive mood of this verb that gives it the meaning of 'seem' or 'appear'.

d. ἀδόκιμος: 'unproved' [AB], 'in the wrong' [HNTC], 'lacking authentication' [ICC2], 'disproved' [Lns], 'to have failed' [NTC, WBC; NAB, NIV, NLT, NRSV], 'failures' [CEV, REB, TEV, TNT], 'not pass the test' [NJB], 'reprobates' [KJV].

13:8 For we-canᵃ not (do) anything againstᵇ the truthᶜ but (only) forᵈ the truth.
LEXICON—a. pres. mid. or pass. (deponent = act.) indic. of δύναμαι (LN 74.5) (BAGD 3. p. 207): 'can' [AB, BAGD, HNTC, ICC2, LN, WBC; CEV, KJV, NAB, NIV, NRSV, TEV, TNT], 'to be able to' [BAGD, LN, Lns, NTC]. The phrase 'we cannot do anything against the truth' is translated 'our responsibility is never to oppose the truth' [NLT], 'we have no power to resist the truth' [NJB], 'we have no power to act against the truth' [REB], 'we can not fight against it' [CEV]. See this word also at 1:4.
  b. κατά (LN 90.31) (BAGD I.2.b.γ. p. 406): 'against' [AB, BAGD, HNTC, ICC2, LN, Lns, NTC, WBC; all versions except NJB, NLT], 'in opposition to, in conflict with' [LN]. This preposition is also translated as a verb: 'to resist' [NJB], 'to oppose' [NLT].
  c. ἀλήθεια (LN 72.2): 'truth' [AB, BAGD, HNTC, ICC2, LN, Lns, NTC, WBC; all versions]. See this word also at 7:14; 11:10.
  d. ὑπέρ (LN 90.36): 'for' [AB, LN, NTC, WBC; KJV, NIV, NRSV, REB, TEV, TNT], 'stand for (the truth)' [NLT], 'in support of' [AB], 'on behalf of' [ICC2, LN], 'in the interest of' [Lns], 'for the sake of' [LN; NAB], 'to further (the truth)' [NJB], not explicit [CEV].
QUESTION—What relationship is indicated by γάρ 'for'?
  It introduces an argument for what was stated in the preceding verse [NTC]. It introduces an explanation of what he says in the previous verse [HNTC, Ho, ICC2, Lns, WBC]. That is, Paul would be willing for his apostolic authority to remain unproved so long the Corinthians are what they should be [Ho]. Paul is not saying that they actually have failed, just that he is more concerned that the truth prevail than that his reputation be upheld [HNTC, TNTC].
QUESTION—Who is the 'we'?
  It is Paul and his associates [AB, Car, EGT, HNTC, Ho, ICC1, ICC2, Lns, NAC, NIC1, NIC2, NTC, SP, TG, TH, TNTC, WBC]. While this appears to be a general maxim, he applies it to himself and his associates [AB, EBC, He, NCBC, WBC].
QUESTION—In what sense are they not able to do anything against the truth?
  1. They are unable in a personal or moral sense [Car, HNTC, ICC1, ICC2, Lns, NIC2, NTC, TG, TNTC, WBC]. That is, they are constrained in the sense that it would be totally against all that they believe, work for and stand for [NTC, TNTC]. Their zeal for the gospel and the well-being of the Corinthians prevents them from subverting the truth [NTC]. He would not be able to change the gospel without becoming a different person [HNTC]. It would be a perversion of authority for him to use disciplinary power inappropriately [NIC1].
  2. They are actually unable to act against the truth [AB, EGT, Ho, NAC]. They would not be effectively able to misuse apostolic authority even if they wanted to [EGT, Ho]. They are unable to change the reality that the power of Christ's resurrection life works through weakness [NAC]. God

would not act or work supernaturally through Paul's apostolic authority if it were exercised illegitimately [Ho].

QUESTION—What would it mean to do things against the truth?

It would be to exercise apostolic authority in a way that is autocratic [Ho] or contrary to the facts of the case [EGT]. It would be to exercise disciplinary apostolic authority where the truth already has free course in the lives of the people [Car]. It would be to act harshly even if the Corinthians are already living in line with the truth [NIC1, WBC]. It would be to act primarily in order to gain human approval [Lns, NIC2], as opposed to acting based on the truth [NIC2] or devotion to the gospel [Lns]. It would be to subvert the truth by dissimulating or by changing the gospel [NTC], to preach a different gospel [HNTC]. It would be to hinder the progress of the gospel [ICC1, TG] or act in a way that is contrary to the gospel [TNTC]. It would be to overlook or act in a way contrary to the reality that the power of Christ's resurrection life works through weakness [NAC].

QUESTION—What would it mean to do things for the truth?

It would be to promote the gospel [AB, ICC1, Lns, NIC1, NTC, TG] as well as to be truthful [NTC]. It is to be controlled by the truth as opposed to self-interest [NAC]. He can employ apostolic disciplinary authority where the truth of the gospel is not adhered to [Car, Ho, NIC1], to vindicate the cause of truth [NIC1]. It is his engaging in ministry to the Corinthians and his concern for their moral goodness [ICC2]. Paul's life gives expression to the truth [NIC2].

QUESTION—What is 'the truth'?

It is the gospel [AB, HNTC, ICC1, ICC2, Lns, NIC2, TG, TNTC, WBC]. It is the gospel and all that it entails in the life of a Christian [Car]. It is the gospel as well as moral truth generally [NIC2]. It is God's revelation [Ho]. It is truth and righteousness, which are established by God [He]. It is reality as opposed to appearance, which is the way of those who present a different gospel [NTC]. It is true doctrine versus a different gospel [HNTC]. It is truth as opposed to mere appearance [SP]. It is the fact stated in 13:4 that living in the power of God occurs in the context of weakness [NAC].

13:9 For we-rejoice[a] whenever we-are-weak but[b] you are strong. And we-pray-(for) this, your restoration.[c]

LEXICON—a. pres. act. indic. of χαίρω (LN 25.125) (BAGD 1. p. 873): 'to rejoice' [AB, BAGD, HNTC, ICC2, LN, Lns, NTC, WBC;, NAB, NRSV], 'to be glad' [BAGD, LN; CEV, KJV, NIV, NLT, TEV, TNT], 'to be delighted' [NJB], 'to be happy' [REB]. See this word also at 2:3.

b. δέ (LN 89.124, 89.94): 'but' [HNTC, ICC2, LN (89.124); NIV, TEV], 'and' [AB, LN (89.94); KJV, NAB, NRSV, TNT], 'while' [Lns], 'though' [WBC; CEV], 'if only' [NJB, REB], 'if (you are) really' [NLT]. The personal pronouns 'we' and 'you', which are the subjects of the respective subjunctive verbs in the subordinate clauses joined by this conjunction, indicate emphasis in the Greek [AB, ICC2, NTC].

c. κατάρτισις (LN **75.5**) (BAGD p. 418): 'restoration' [AB, HNTC, ICC2, WBC], 'restoration to maturity' [NLT], 'amendment' [REB], 'completion' [BAGD], 'being made complete' [BAGD], 'complete outfitting' [Lns], 'perfection' [KJV, NIV], 'becoming fully qualified, adequacy' [LN]. The phrase τὴν ὑμῶν κατάρτισιν 'your restoration' is translated 'that you may be made perfect' [NTC], 'that you should be made perfect' [NJB], 'that you may become perfect' [NRSV, TNT], 'that you will become perfect' [TEV], 'that you may be built up to completion' [NAB], 'that you will do even better' [CEV]. This word does not occur anywhere else in the New Testament.

QUESTION—What relationship is indicated by γάρ 'for'?

It introduces an amplification of what is said in the second half of 13:7 [AB], and introduces the reason for what was stated [NTC]. It further elaborates 13:7 [NIC2], it introduces a restatement of the thought of v.7 in more general terms [TNTC]. It introduces a restatement of what was said in 13:8 [ICC1]. It introduces a restatement of the thought of 13:7–8 [WBC]. It amplifies his claim in 13:7 that he was concerned for the Corinthians and not himself [ICC2]. It is coordinate with 13:8 and subordinate to 13:7; they want the Corinthians to do what is good, even if they lack opportunity to show evidence of their apostolic authority [Ho]. It sums up the thoughts of 10:1-8 about being bold in exercising authority when he comes [He].

QUESTION—What is the connection between their strength and Paul's weakness?

1. There is a causal relationship.
    1.1. Because the Corinthians are strong Paul appears to be weak. That is, if the Corinthians are sufficiently strong morally and spiritually Paul would not need to exercise disciplinary power and authority and he can be meek toward them, which might appear weak [Car, EGT, He, Ho, ICC1, NAC, NCBC, NIC1, NIC2, WBC].
    1.2. Because Paul is weak the Corinthians are strong. That is, God works through the weak to minister strength to others [AB, Lns, NTC, TNTC]. Through Paul's weakness they experience the power of Christ [AB]. God's power is at work despite Paul's weakness, and Paul's weakness demonstrates that it was the power of the gospel, not his own power [NTC].
2. They not causally related. That is, if you are strong we rejoice, even if we happen to be weak, whether by being wrong or suffering defeat [TG, TH].

QUESTION—What is the κατάρτισις 'restoration' for which he prays?

It is restoring to spiritual strength and wholeness [EBC, NCBC]. It is a restoring and mending [NAC, WBC], reinstating [TH], being restored morally and spiritually [NIC2]. It means to be put into complete order and restored from confusion, evil and contention [Ho], putting into proper condition and unity [WBC]. It is perfecting and restoring to harmonious functioning [NIC1]. It means being restored to good moral conduct [SP] and in their relationship with Paul [NAC, SP, WBC] and with God [SP, WBC]. It means amendment as individuals and corporate upbuilding [AB]. It means to be completely outfitted, being as they should be [Lns]. It is putting right all that was amiss in Corinth to a proper Christian life [HNTC]. It is being restored to living by Christian values, character, maturity, and rejecting the false apostles and the false gospel [Car]. It is spiritual restoration and perfection by turning away from evil, obeying God, and living in conformity with the gospel message from then on [NTC]. It is to become upright again [He]. It is spiritual and moral completion or perfection [TG, WBC], spiritual and moral rectifying and being restored to a proper Christian life [ICC2]. It is the perfecting of their character [ICC1].

DISCOURSE UNIT: 13:10-13 [NAB]. The topic is farewell.

13:10 **This-is-why**[a] **I-write these things (while) being-absent, so-that when-I-am-present I need- not -use**[b] **harshly**[c] **the authority**[d] **which the Lord gave me for edification**[e] **and not for tearing-down.**[f]

LEXICON—a. διά with accusative object (LN 89.26): 'because of, on account of, by reason of' [LN]. The phrase διὰ τοῦτο is translated 'this is why' [AB, WBC; NIV], 'that is why' [NJB, TEV], 'the reason why' [HNTC; TNT], 'on this account' [ICC2], 'for this reason' [Lns], 'so' [NRSV], 'therefore' [NTC; KJV], not explicit [CEV, NAB, NLT, REB]. See this phrase also at 4:1, 7:13.

b. aorist mid. (deponent = act.) subj. of χράομαι (LN 42.23, 41.4) (BAGD 2. p. 884): 'to use' [LN (42.23); CEV, KJV, NLT, TEV, TNT], 'to make use of' [LN (42.23)], 'to act' [BAGD, WBC], 'to proceed' [BAGD], 'to take action' [ICC2], 'to exercise' [HNTC; NAB], 'to treat, to behave toward' [LN (41.4)], 'to deal' [AB, Lns], not explicit [NIV, NJB, NRSV, REB]. See this word also at 1:17; 3:12.

c. ἀποτόμως (LN **88.74**) (BAGD p. 101): 'harshly' [AB, LN, NTC, WBC; NLT, TEV], 'severely' [BAGD; TNT], 'sharply' [BAGD, Lns]. The phrase 'need to use harshly' is translated 'to be harsh' [NIV, NJB], 'to be severe' [NRSV], 'to exercise severity' [HNTC], 'to exercise with severity' [NAB], 'to take severe action' [ICC2], 'to use sharpness' [KJV], 'sharp exercise (of authority)' [REB], 'to be hard on you' [CEV].

d. ἐξουσία (LN 37.35) (BAGD 3. p. 278): 'authority' [AB, BAGD, HNTC, ICC2, Lns, NTC, WBC; CEV, NIV, NJB, NLT, NRSV, REB, TEV, TNT], 'authority to rule, right to control' [LN], 'power' [KJV]. See this word also at 10:8.

e. οἰκοδομή (LN **74.15**) (BAGD 1.b.α. p. 559): 'edification' [BAGD, NTC; KJV], 'upbuilding' [AB, Lns], 'building up' [BAGD, HNTC, LN, WBC; NIV, NJB, NRSV, REB], 'strengthening' [LN], 'constructive work' [ICC2]. The phrase εἰς οἰκοδομὴν 'for edification' is translated as an infinitive phrase 'to build up' [**LN;** NAB, NLT, TEV, TNT], 'to strengthen' [**LN**]. The phrase εἰς οἰκοδομήν 'for edification' is translated 'so that I could help you' [CEV]. See this word also at 10:8; 12:19.

f. καθαίρεσις (LN **74.16**) (BAGD 2. p. 386): 'tearing down' [BAGD, LN, WBC; NIV, NRSV], 'breaking down' [NJB], 'pulling down' [REB], 'destruction' [AB, ICC2, NTC; KJV], 'pulling down' [HNTC], 'wrecking' [Lns]. The phrase εἰς καθαίρεσιν 'for tearing down' is translated 'to tear you down' [**LN**; NLT, TEV], 'to weaken' [**LN**], 'to destroy' [CEV, NAB], 'to demolish' [TNT]. See this word also at 10:4, 8. (This clause is repeated verbatim from 10:8.)

QUESTION—What relationship is indicated by διὰ τοῦτο 'this is why'?
It indicates the purpose for what Paul is writing. Paul has written these things so they would put things into good order, and so that he won't have to assert disciplinary authority when he comes [AB, Car, Ho, ICC1, ICC2, Lns, NIC2, WBC].

QUESTION—What does 'these things' refer to?
It refers to the content of what he has written in chapters 10–13 [AB, HNTC, NIC1, TG, TNTC, WBC]. It refers to the entire letter [Car, EGT, ICC2, NIC2, SP, TH], but especially chapters 10-13 [Car]. (Some commentators see chapters 10–13 as possibly being a separate letter, and the one he would be referring to [AB, TG].) It refers to what he has just said about restoring and perfecting [ICC1]. It refers to his fears and warnings about sin and disorder in Corinth expressed in 12:20-21 [NTC]. It refers generally to his exhortations and warnings [Ho].

QUESTION—Who is 'the Lord'?
1. It is Christ [Ho, NTC]. (In 10:8, where Paul makes the identical statement, AB, Ho, ICC1, ICC2, NIC1, NIC2, NTC, TG, TH, and TNTC identify 'the Lord' as being Christ.)
2. It is God [He]. (In 10:8 NAC identifies 'the Lord' as being God.)

DISCOURSE UNIT: 13:11–13 [AB, EBC, HNTC, ICC1, NTC, TG, TH, TNTC, WBC; NIV, NJB, NLT, NRSV, TEV]. The topic is letter closing [AB], last words and greeting [HNTC], concluding exhortation, salutation, and benediction [ICC1], final exhortation and greetings [TNTC], final greetings [NIV], recommendations, greetings, final good wishes [NJB], Paul's final greetings [NLT], final greetings and benediction [NRSV], final warnings and greetings [TEV], conclusion [EBC, NTC, TG, TH, WBC].

13:11 Finally,[a] **brothers,**[b] rejoice/farewell,[c]

LEXICON—a. λοιπόν (LN **61.14**) (BAGD 3.b. p. 480): 'finally' [AB, BAGD, HNTC, ICC2, LN, Lns, NTC, WBC; KJV, NIV, NRSV], 'and now' [NAB, REB, TEV, TNT], 'to end then' [NJB], 'in summary' [LN], 'I close my letter with these last words' [NLT], not explicit [CEV].

b. ἀδελφός (LN 11.23): 'brother' [HNTC, ICC2, Lns, WBC; KJV, NAB, NIV, NJB, TNT], 'friend' [CEV, REB, TEV], 'dear friend' [NLT], 'fellow believer, Christian brother' [LN]. This plural noun is translated 'brothers and sisters' [AB, NTC, WBC; NRSV]. The term is meant to include both male and female, 'brothers' as well as 'sisters' in Christ [AB, NIC2, NTC]. See this word also at 1:1, 8; 2:13; 8:1; 11:9; 12:18.

c. pres. act. impera. of χαίρω (LN 25.125) (BAGD 1. p. 874): 'to rejoice' [AB, BAGD, HNTC, LN, WBC; NLT], 'goodbye' [HNTC, NTC; CEV, NAB, NIV, TEV], 'farewell' [Lns; KJV, NRSV, REB, TNT]. This imperative is translated 'we wish you joy' [NJB]. See this word (used in the sense of 'rejoice') also at 2:3; 13:9.

QUESTION—What area of meaning is intended for χαίρετε 'rejoice/farewell'?
1. It is an imperative: rejoice [AB, EGT, He, Ho, ICC2, NAC, NIC1, NIC2, SP, TH, WBC; NJB, NLT].
2. It is a farewell salutation [HNTC, Lns, TG, TNTC; CEV, KJV, NAB, NIV, NRSV, REB, TEV, TNT].
3. Both meanings are present, although the farewell is dominant [ICC1, NTC].

be-put-in-order,[a] **be-exhorted,**[b] **be-of- the same –mind,**[c] **be-at-peace,**[d]

LEXICON—a. pres. pass. impera. of καταρτίζω (LN 75.5) (BAGD 1.a. p. 417): 'to be put in order' [BAGD], 'to put things in order' [NRSV], 'to mend one's ways' [BAGD, NTC; NAB, REB], 'to change one's ways' [NLT], 'to be restored' [AB, BAGD], 'to cooperate in one's own restoration' [ICC2], 'to aim for restoration' [WBC], 'to aim for perfection' [NIV], 'to be perfect' [KJV], 'to try to grow perfect' [NJB], 'to strive for perfection' [TEV], 'to go on to perfection' [TNT], 'to pull oneself together' [HNTC], 'to be completely fitted out' [Lns], 'to do better' [CEV], 'to be made adequate, to be completely furnished' [LN]. This imperative could also be middle in form. Because a passive imperative required cooperation on the part of the hearer [ICC2], it is difficult to tell which versions treat it as a middle imperative. HNTC, ICC2, NTC, WBC; NAB, NIV, NJB, NLT, NRSV, REB, TEV, TNT appear to do so or at least to translated the passive imperative with a component of participation and action on the part of the Corinthians. This verb is a cognate of the noun κατάρτισις 'restoration' found in 13:9.

b. pres. pass. impera. of παρακαλέω (LN 25.150) (BAGD 4. p. 617): 'to be encouraged' [BAGD, LN], 'to be comforted' [BAGD], 'to be of good comfort' [KJV]. In this context this passive imperative is translated 'listen to my appeal/appeals' [NIV, NRSV, TEV], 'take our appeal to heart' [REB], 'pay attention to my appeals' [AB], 'pay attention to what I have said' [CEV], 'accept admonition' [ICC2], 'accept encouragement' [NTC], 'let yourselves be admonished' [Lns], 'take my advice' [TNT]. It is also translated as a middle imperative: 'exhort one another' [HNTC], 'encourage one another' [WBC; NAB, NJB, NLT]. See this word also at 1:4, 6; 2:7, 8; 5:20; 6:1; 7:6; 8:6; 9:5; 10:1; 12:8, 18.

c. pres. act. impera. of φρονέω (LN 26.16) (BAGD 1. p. 866): 'to have an attitude, to think in a particular manner' [LN]. The phrase τὸ αὐτὸ φρονεῖτε is translated 'be of the same mind' [HNTC, ICC2, WBC; TNT], 'be of one mind' [AB, NTC; KJV, NIV], 'to have a common mind' [NJB], 'think the same thing' [BAGD], 'keep minding the same things'

[Lns], 'be in agreement' [BAGD], 'live in harmony' [BAGD; NAB, NLT], 'try to get along' [CEV], 'agree with one another' [NRSV, REB, TEV].

d. pres. act. impera. of εἰρηνεύω (LN 88.12) (BAGD 2.b. p. 227): 'to be at peace' [AB, ICC2], 'to live in peace' [LN, Lns, NTC, WBC; KJV, NAB, NIV, NJB, NLT, NRSV, REB, TEV], 'to live at peace' [HNTC], 'to be at peace' [TNT], 'to behave peacefully' [LN], 'to keep the peace' [BAGD]. This imperative is translated 'try to live peacefully with each other' [CEV].

QUESTION—Is the imperative καταρτίζεσθε 'be put in order' middle or passive?

1. It is a middle imperative, soliciting their active involvement [HNTC, Ho, ICC1, ICC2, NTC, SP, TH, TNTC, WBC] or their taking action relative to one another [He]. It is an exhortation for them to fulfill his prayer for their restoration through mending their relationships with God and with each other and by regaining unity in Christ theologically, spiritually and practically [NIC2]. They must cooperate in their restoration [ICC2]. Restoration is to be their aim [WBC]. They are to strive for perfection and restore everything in their lives that needs it [NTC]. They need to reform themselves [Ho], to move to maturity and perfection [Car], to amend their ways [SP, TNTC], to set each other right [He].
2. It is passive; they are to allow this to happen [AB, Lns, NAC, NIC1]. They must be restored [AB] or perfected [NIC1]. The passives are permissive passives [Lns].

QUESTION—What is intended by τὸ αὐτὸ φρονεῖτε 'be of the same mind'?

Paul intends that they live in harmony [He, HNTC], united in faith and feeling [Ho], harmonious in thought and intent [ICC1]. They need to be united in their understanding of the essentials of the faith [NIC1, NIC2, NTC]. He wants them to avoid the quarreling and strife which he warns against in 12:20 [AB, ICC2, NAC]; here he urges the positive of which 12:20 is the negative [AB, ICC2]. This does not mean that they have to agree on everything [NAC, NIC1, NIC2, NTC], but that they have a common intent and purpose [NAC]. They must work through their differences of opinion so their faith will be consistent with the gospel Paul preaches and hence not be divided [Car]. It does not mean giving up individuality [WBC], but requires a harmony of attitude and living [WBC]. They need to pay attention to or mind the same things, which is what Paul has written here [Lns].

and the God of love[a] and peace[b] will-be with you.

LEXICON—a. ἀγάπη (LN 25.43) (BAGD I.2.a. p. 6): 'love' [AB, BAGD, HNTC, ICC2, LN, Lns, NTC, WBC; all versions]. The phrase 'the God of love' is translated 'the God who gives love' [CEV]. See this word also at 2:8.

b. εἰρήνη (LN 22.42) (BAGD 3. p. 227): 'peace' [AB, BAGD, HNTC, ICC2, LN, Lns, NTC, WBC; all versions]. The phrase 'the God of peace' is translated 'the God who gives peace' [CEV]. In early Christian thought this peace was a characteristic of the messianic kingdom and was viewed as more or less synonymous with messianic salvation [BAGD].

QUESTION—What relationship is there between the imperatives and the promise in this verse?

1. The promise is conditional; if they obey the imperatives in the verse, then God will be with them [Car, EGT, He, NIC1, NIC2, NTC, WBC]. Jealousy and strife will block the realization of the presence of God [NIC1]. God bestows these characteristics to them as they actively seek to do what God wants them to do [NIC2]. While God does freely grant these blessings, they can be withdrawn from those who fail to cultivate them [He].
2. The imperatives and the promise are related, but not in a conditional statement. They ought to fulfill the imperatives, and the God who gives love and peace will be with them to help them do it [AB, HNTC, Ho, ICC2, Lns, TNTC]. The promise of God's presence is like the blessing in Luke 10:5-6 where the blessing of peace is available for people of peace. Likewise, love and peace are blessings available for those whose character is not at odds with them [NAC]. He is always present, but the more we are faithful they more his richly and fully his promises are experienced [Lns].

QUESTION—How are the nouns related in the genitive phrase ὁ θεὸς τῆς ἀγάπης καὶ εἰρήνης 'the God of love and peace'?

1. God is the source of love and peace [Ho, Lns, NAC; CEV]. He shows love and makes peace [NAC].
2. God is characterized by love and peace [Car].
3. Both are true; God, who is characterized by love and peace bestows love and peace [AB, HNTC, ICC2, NIC2, NTC, TH, WBC].

13:12 **Greet[a] each-other with a holy kiss.[b] All the saints[c] greet you.**

TEXT—In some versions the second sentence 'all the saints greet you' is v.13. The blessing that follows that, and which is shown here as v.13, becomes v.14 [KJV, NIV, REB]. GNT does not have a v.14.

LEXICON—a. aorist mid. (deponent = act.) impera. of ἀσπάζομαι (LN 33.20) (BAGD 1.a. p. 116): 'to greet' [AB, BAGD, HNTC, ICC2, LN, NTC, WBC; all versions except CEV], 'to salute' [Lns], 'to send greetings' [LN]. The phrase 'greet each other with a holy kiss' is translated 'give each other a warm greeting' [CEV].

b. φίλημα (LN 34.62) (BAGD p. 859): 'kiss' [AB, BAGD, HNTC, ICC2, LN, Lns, NTC, WBC; KJV, NAB, NIV, NJB, NRSV, TNT], 'warm greeting' [CEV]. The phrase 'with a holy kiss' is translated 'with the kiss of peace' [REB, TEV], 'in Christian love' [NLT].

c. ἅγιος (LN 11.27): This plural form is translated 'saints' [AB, HNTC, Lns, NTC, WBC; KJV, NIV, NRSV], 'God's people' [LN; CEV, REB,

TEV, TNT], 'God's holy people' [NJB], 'holy ones' [NAB], 'members of the holy people' [ICC2], 'Christians' [NLT]. See this word also at 1:1; 8:4.

QUESTION—What did the 'holy kiss' signify?

It expresses fellowship [EBC, EGT, Ho, ICC2, NAC, NIC2], unity [Car, EBC, ICC2, NIC1, WBC], mutual confidence [NIC1], and love [Car, Ho, NIC2]. It is a sign of reconciliation [He, NIC1, WBC]. It means they are members of the family of God [EGT, NAC, NTC]. It affirms that they are the body of Christ [AB].

QUESTION—Who are 'all the saints'?

They are the believers of Macedonia [NIC1, NIC2], the churches of Macedonia [NTC], or the believers in the particular location in Macedonia where Paul is writing [AB, Car, EBC, EGT, HNTC, Ho, Lns, NCBC, TG, TH, TNTC]. They are those Macedonian Christians who know he is writing this letter [ICC1, SP]. This reminds the Corinthians that they are accountable to the wider church and not just to themselves [ICC2]. It implies that Paul is part of a growing network of Christians [NAC].

DISCOURSE UNIT: 13:13 [TNTC]. The topic is the benediction.

13:13 **The grace^a of the Lord Jesus Christ and the love of God and the fellowship^b of the Holy Spirit (be) with you all.**

TEXT—Some manuscripts include ἀμήν 'amen' at the end of this verse. GNT does not mention this variant. Only KJV includes it.

LEXICON—a. χάρις (LN 88.66) (BAGD 2.c. p. 877): 'grace' [AB, BAGD, HNTC, ICC2, LN, Lns, NTC, WBC; all versions except CEV], 'favor' [BAGD], 'kindness' [LN]. The phrase 'the grace of the Lord Jesus Christ…be with you all' is translated 'I pray that the Lord Jesus Christ will bless you and be kind to you' [CEV]. See this word also at 1:2, 12; 8:1, 4, 6, 9, 16, 19; 9:8, 14, 15; 12:9.

b. κοινωνία (LN 34.5) (BAGD 1., 4. p. 439): 'fellowship' [BAGD (1.), LN, NTC, WBC; NAB, NIV, NJB, NRSV, REB, TEV, TNT], 'communion' [BAGD (1.), ICC2, Lns; KJV, NRSV], 'close association' [LN], 'participation (in the Holy Spirit)' [AB, BAGD (4.), HNTC]. The phrase ἡ κοινωνία τοῦ ἁγίου πνεύματος μετὰ πάντων ὑμῶν 'the fellowship of the Holy Spirit (be) with you all' is translated 'may the Holy Spirit join all your hearts together' [CEV]. See this word also at 6:14; 8:4; 9:13.

QUESTION—How are the nouns related in the genitive construction ἡ κοινωνία τοῦ ἁγίου πνεύματος 'the fellowship of the Holy Spirit'?

1. The genitive is subjective: the Holy Spirit produces or grants the sense of fellowship that Christians have [Car, EBC, He, ICC1, NCBC, NIC1, NIC2, SP, TH].
2. The genitive is objective: the fellowship or communion believers have is with the Holy Spirit [ICC2, Lns], or is a participation in the Holy Spirit [AB, HNTC, Ho].

3. One sense does not exclude the other; we share in the Holy Spirit because he makes it possible [NTC, TNTC]. While it is primarily subjective both are involved [NIC2].

KEY TERMS IN 2 CORINTHIANS

This is a listing of some of the key terms in this epistle, which are important either because of their frequency of use or because they are central to what Paul is trying to convey. The references indicate all the occurrences in the epistle, though not all of these occurrences are treated in the lexicon in this exegetical summary.

Boast/boasting, confidence
- καύχησις (boast) 1:12; 7:4, 14; 8:24; 11:10, 17
- καύχημα (ground for boasting, object of boasting; boasting, pride) 1:14; 5:12; 9:3
- καυχάομαι (to boast) 5:12; 7:14; 9:2; 10:8, 13, 15, 16–17; 11:12, 16, 18, 30; 12:1, 5-6, 9
- πεποίθησις (confidence) 1:15; 3:4; 8:22
- ἱκανός (competence) 2:6, 16; 3:5
- παρρησία (boldness, free speech; confidence) 3:12; 7:4
- θαρρέω (to be confident, to be bold) 5:6, 8; 7:16
- ὑπόστασις (boastful confidence; undertaking) 9:4; 11:17

Commend, recommend
συνίστημι 3:1; 4:2; 5:12; 6:4; 7:11; 10:12, 18; 12:11

Exhort
παρακαλέω 1:4, 6; 2:7–8; 5:20; 6:1; 7:6-7, 13; 8:6; 9:5; 10:1; 12:8, 18; 13:11
1. to comfort 1:4, 6, 2:7; 7:6, 7, 13.
2. to beseech or entreat 2:8; 5:20; 6:1; 8:6; 9:5; 10:1, 12:8, 18.

Fade away; be annulled, set aside or rendered ineffective
καταργέω
1. To be annulled, set aside, rendered ineffective 3:11, 14
2. To fade away 3:7, 13

The middle and passive forms of this verb are identical. In the middle voice it means to fade away or disappear, and in the passive it means to be set aside, annulled, or rendered ineffective. In chapter three, Paul compares the old covenant, which was being set aside in favor of the new, to the fading glory of Moses' face. In doing so he capitalizes on the fact that the middle and passive forms are identical, though at times it is not clear which way to take the verb, whether as passive or middle.

Flesh
- σάρξ 1:17; 4:11; 5:16; 7:1, 5; 10:2-3; 11:18; 12:7
- σαρκικός (fleshly) 1:12
- 11:18 'according to the flesh' is contrasted with 'according to the Lord' in v.17 and parallels 'according to folly' in v.17.

In this epistle σάρξ normally refers to what is human, carnal, unregenerate or unaided or untransformed by the Spirit of God. In some instances it seems to refer to life as lived in the body, but there is also an intimation of frailty and mortality. In 4:11 the body is 'mortal flesh'. In 7:1 he uses flesh to refer to the body, but because he pairs 'body' and 'spirit' he probably is simply referring to the entire person. In 7:5 he says that their bodies had no rest, but compare to 2:13, where he discusses the exact same situation and says that their 'mind' could not rest. There seems to be a play on meanings in 10:3: we live in the flesh but not according to the flesh. In 12:7 σάρξ could be either the physical body (which is how most people take it), or it could be referring to Paul's carnal inclination to be 'puffed up' with fleshly pride, for which he needed the thorn to puncture it.

Foolishness, foolish
- ἀφροσύνη (foolishness) 11:1, 17, 21; 12:6, 11
- ἄφρων (foolish) 11:16, 19; 12:6, 11

Generosity/Simplicity
- ἁπλότης 1:12; 8:2; 9:11, 13; 11:3

Grace/benefit/privilege
- χάρις 1:2, 12, 15; 2:14; 4:15; 6:1; 8:1, 4, 6-7, 9, 16, 19; 9:8, 14–15; 12:9; 13:13. Examples of different nuances of meaning:
    1. a benefit or blessing 1:15
    2. the privilege of sharing in ministry 8:4
    3. God's dynamic power, governing and inspiring ministry 1:12; 8:1
    4. God's dynamic power and loving presence enabling Paul to endure 12:9
    5. God's loving provision and enabling 9:8
    6. a generous gift or offering from other Christians 8:6 7, 19
    7. the willingness to give generously because of having experienced the love of God 9:14
    8. the experience of God's love that comes through a generous gift 4:15
    9. thankfulness to God 8:16; 9:15
    10. the experience of God's love in the gospel of salvation 6:15
    11. a characteristic or attribute of Christ 8:9
    12. the expression of that characteristic or attribute of Christ toward the Corinthians 13:14
- χαρίζομαι (to pardon) 2:7

Judge, think, evaluate, decide
λογίζομαι
1. to judge or to claim 3:5
2. to account, impute, or judge 5:19
3. to think, think about, understand, judge 10:2, 7, 11; 11:5; 12:6

KEY TERMS

Message
λόγος
1. message 1:18; 5:19
2. word (of God) 2:17; 4:2;
3. speech or letter 6:7; 8:7; 10:10-11; 11:6

Power, powerful
- δύναμις 1:8; 4:7; 6:7; 8:3; 12:9, 12; 13:4
- δύναμαι (to be able) 1:4
- δυνατέω (to be powerful) 9:8, 13:3
- δυνατός (strong, powerful, capable) 10:4; 12:10; 13:9
- ἰσχυρός (strong) 10:10
- ἱκανός (competence) 2:6, 16; 3:5

Prove, approve/disapprove, evidence, test, proof
- δοκιμάζω (to test, approve) 8:8, 22; 13:5
- δοκιμή (proof, evidence) 2:9; 8:2; 9:13; 13:3
- δόκιμος (approved) 10:18, 13:7.
- ἀδόκιμος (unapproved, failing the test) 13:5–7
- πειράζω (to test, evaluate) 13:5
- ἔνδειξις (proof, evidence) 8:24 (see also the verbal form ἐνδεικνυμι also in 8:24)

Service, ministry
- διακονία (service, administration) 3:7-9; 4:1; 5:18; 6:3; 8:4; 9:1, 12–13; 11:8
- διάκονος (servant, minister) 3:6; 6:4; 11:15, 23
- διακονέω (to serve, administer, administrate) 3:3; 8:19-20

Superlatives:
- ἐν παντὶ (in everything) 2:14; 4:8; 6:4; 7:5, 11, 16; 8:7; 9:8, 11; 11:6, 9
- ἐν παντὶ...ἐν πᾶσιν (in every way, in all things) 11:6
- περισσοτέρως (excessively) 1:12; 2:4; 7:13, 15; 11:23; 12:15
- περισσότερος (comparative or superlative of περισσός) (excessive) 2:7; 9:1; 10:8
- περισσεύω (to abound) 1:5; 3:9; 4:15; 8:2, 7; 9:8, 12
- ὑπερπερισσεύω (to overflow) 7:4
- περισσεία (abundance) 8:2; 10:15
- περίσσευμα (abundance) 8:14
- ὑπερβάλλω (surpassing) 3:10
- καθ' ὑπερβολὴν
  1. utterly 1:8
  2. extraordinary 4:7
  3. beyond all measure 4:17
  4. exceptional 12:7

Tribulation, trial, persecution
- θλίψις 1:4, 8; 2:4; 4:17; 6:4; 7:4; 8:2, 13
- ἀνάγκη (distress, trouble; necessity) 6:4; 9:7; 12:10
- στενοχωρία (distress, difficulty, trouble, calamity) 6:4; 12:10

Weakness
- ἀσθενεῖν (to be weak) 11:21; 11:29; 12:10; 13:3, 4, 9
- ἀνθενεία (weakness) 11:30; 12:5, 9, 10; 13:4
- ἀσθενής (weak) 10:10
- ἐξουθενέω (to be contemptible) 10:10

Weighty, grievous, burdensome
- βαρέω (to be weighed down, burdened, crushed) 1:8, 5:4
- ἐπιβαρῶ (to say too much, to press a point too far) 2:5
- βάρος (weight, burden) 4:17
- βαρύς (weighty, hard, severe) 10:10
- καταβαρέω (to be a burden to, to burden financially) 12:16
- καταναρκάω (to be a burden to, to burden financially) 11:9
- λύπη (grief, pain, sorrow) 2:1, 3, 7; 7:10; 9:7
- λυπέω (to grieve, to sorrow; to grieve someone, to cause pain) 2:2, 4–5; 6:10; 7:8-9, 11

Zeal/jealousy
ζῆλος
   1. zeal 7:7, 11, 12, 9:2,
   2. jealousy 11:2, 12:20

www.ingramcontent.com/pod-product-compliance
Lightning Source LLC
Chambersburg PA
CBHW070006010526
44117CB00011B/1448